WASHINGTON FISHING

Little Aru 447

WASHINGTON FISHING

FOURTH EDITION

Terry Rudnick

AVALON
TRAVEL

FOGHORN OUTDOORS:
WASHINGTON FISHING
Fourth Edition

Terry Rudnick

Published by
Avalon Travel Publishing, Inc.
5855 Beaudry Street
Emeryville, CA 94608, USA

Please send all comments, corrections,
additions, amendments, and critiques to:

Ⓕ **OGHORN OUTDOORS®**
WASHINGTON FISHING
AVALON TRAVEL PUBLISHING
5855 BEAUDRY ST.
EMERYVILLE, CA 94608, USA
email: atpfeedback@avalonpub.com
website: www.foghorn.com

Printing History
First edition—1996
Fourth edition—May 2002
5 4 3 2 1

ISBN: 1-56691-400-0
ISSN: 1086-783X

Editor: Jeff Lupo
Series Manager: Marisa Solís
Copy Editor: Valerie Sellers Blanton
Proofreader: Donna Leverenz
Researcher: Christy Thatcher
Graphics: Susan Snyder
Cover Design: Jacob Goolkasian
Production: Jacob Goolkasian, Carey Wilson
Map Editor: Naomi Adler Dancis
Cartography: Mike Morgenfeld, Suzanne Service
Indexer: Laura Welcome

Front cover photo: © Randy Wells

Distributed by Publishers Group West

Printed in the USA by Bertelsmann Services

To the memory of Betty Rudnick,
the best mom any young angler could hope to have.
I miss you.

Contents

SPECIAL TOPICS

SPECIAL TOPICS

Maps

Washington Overview

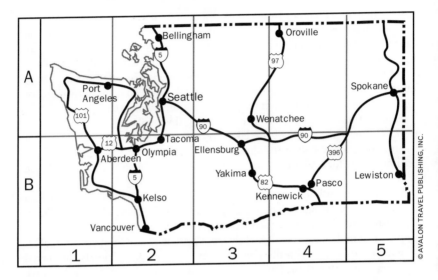

Our Commitment

We are committed to making *Foghorn Outdoors: Washington Fishing* the most accurate, thorough, and enjoyable fishing guide to the state. With this fourth edition, you can rest assured that every fishing spot in this book has been carefully reviewed. When possible, we were able to squeeze in nearby hotels and eateries. However, with the change of seasons, you can bet that some of the fees listed herein have gone up and that some angling destinations may have opened, closed, or changed hands. If you would like to comment on the book, whether it's to suggest a fishing hole we overlooked or to let us know about any noteworthy experience— good or bad—that occurred while using *Foghorn Outdoors: Washington Fishing* as your guide, we would appreciate hearing from you. Reader contribution is what makes this book the Angler's Bible. Please address correspondence to:

> *Foghorn Outdoors: Washington Fishing,* fourth edition
> Avalon Travel Publishing
> 5855 Beaudry Street
> Emeryville, CA 94608
> U.S.A
>
> email: atpfeedback@avalonpub.com

How to Use This Book

One challenge that comes from creating a comprehensive guide to the state's 1,000+ fishing spots is the task of how best to present all the information. We started by dividing Washington into 10 sections using a standard grid format. Each of the 10 sections represents a chapter, which is composed of all fishing spots found in that area. Maps showing the 10 divisions of Washington State can be found on page ix and on the last page of this book. Detailed maps of each section appear at the beginning of each chapter, beginning on page 84.

Here are three different approaches to using this book:

1. If you know the name of the lake, creek, reservoir, pond, river, or coastal area you want to fish or the corresponding geographical area (a town or national park, for example), turn to the index beginning on page 555 to locate it.
2. If you want to fish in a particular part of the state, turn to the Washington State map on the previous page or at the back of the book. Locate the area you're interested in and turn to the corresponding chapter. Since all 10 map sections are provided in detail at the back of the book, you may also locate individual angling destinations with these maps; every fishing spot is clearly numbered. Then you match the number of the site with the description in the corresponding chapter.
3. If you're interested in a particular type of fish and/or want to find out which areas offer the best angling opportunities for that species, turn to the Washington Sport Fish section beginning on page 5 or consult the Species by Location index on page 528.

Acknowledgments

Many people provided valuable assistance as I researched and wrote this book. Especially helpful were Mike O'Malley, Jim Byrd, Mark Kimball, Bob Pfeifer, Larry Peck, Jack Tipping, Bill Freymond, Bill Jordan, and Carol Turcotte of the Washington Department of Fish and Wildlife. Special thanks also to Tom Pollack, Joe Wallman, Warren Cowell, Al Long, and Kelley Hawley. Fellow outdoors writer and bass-fishing fanatic Bob Johansen was especially helpful.

To Roberta, Adam, and Evan, thanks for your support and patience, even when I kept us from being out on the water.

Preface

When Judith Pynn, Acquisitions Editor for Foghorn Press, called me in January 1994 to ask if I was interested in writing a complete guide to fishing in Washington, I was surprised, flattered, and, to tell the truth, not too sure about the idea. I was very impressed by the detail in *Foghorn Outdoors: California Fishing*, written by fellow outdoor writer and good friend Tom Stienstra, but I wasn't sure that I wanted to take on a project of that magnitude. What's more, Northwest fishery managers at that time were warning that the prospects for a coastal salmon season were dim and that other areas of the state would also see severe salmon-fishing restrictions. With morale at an all-time low among Washington anglers, was this really a good time to be thinking about a fishing guide?

Then it occurred to me that perhaps this was the perfect time to be thinking about a guide to Washington fishing. A coastal salmon closure might cause some people to sit at home and complain, but it would prompt the majority to go looking for new places to fish and other species to catch. Washington anglers, I decided, needed a book that would tell them everything they had to know. I think *Foghorn Outdoors: Washington Fishing* does that.

This book contains information on more than 1,000 lakes, reservoirs, streams, rivers, and saltwater fishing areas, including precise driving directions and contacts to call for every body of water. It took six months of nearly constant writing to get it all into book form, and I've been doing the research virtually all of my life.

If you have read any other Foghorn Outdoors guides, such as Tom Stienstra's *Foghorn Outdoors: Pacific Northwest Camping* or *Foghorn Outdoors: Pacific Northwest Hiking* by Ron C. Judd and Dan A. Nelson, you may notice that something is missing from *Foghorn Outdoors: Washington Fishing*. Unlike the other authors, I have declined to give the lakes, reservoirs, rivers, creeks, and marine fishing areas of Washington a numerical rating. I feel that rating these places from 1 to 10 might cause too many anglers to visit the waters with a high rating and put undue fishing pressure on those spots. Some of Washington's best fishing holes are so great because they get light fishing pressure, and sending crowds of anglers to their shores might turn them into not-so-good fishing holes. Some waters that I might give a low rating, on the other hand, could provide excellent fishing on any given day, so why dissuade anglers from fishing them? Another reason I opted to abandon the rating system is that my idea of a "10" might differ greatly from everyone else's.

With that, I encourage you to sit down and spend a little time with this fourth edition of *Foghorn Outdoors: Washington Fishing*. I think you'll discover some things you didn't know about the vast angling opportunities available to us here in the Evergreen State, and I hope that you are able to take advantage of as many of those opportunities as time allows.

As for me, I'm off to revisit some of these places myself, to savor more of the challenge and adventure that is Washington fishing. I'll see you there.

—*Terry Rudnick*

INTRODUCTION

HUSKY SURF PERCH CAN BE CAUGHT FROM THE BEACHES ALONG OCEAN SHORES.

Washington's Top 10 Fishing Lists

Washington's Top 10 Counties for Fishing

1. **Grant County:** This county on the "dry" side of the state has over 170,000 acres of water, including massive Potholes Reservoir, Moses Lake, and more than a dozen of the best trout lakes in Washington.
2. **Grays Harbor County:** The coastal fishery out of Westport, along with all the salmon and steelhead fishing in the Grays Harbor system, make it a mecca for anglers.
3. **Spokane County:** Surprised by this one? You shouldn't be. It has some of the Northwest's best rainbow and cutthroat trout lakes, and angling variety that includes everything from burbot and lake trout to smallmouth bass and tiger muskies.
4. **Clallam County:** Bordered by the Pacific Ocean on one side, the Strait of Juan de Fuca on another, and with some of the state's best steelhead streams at its southwest corner, it has something for every cold-water angler.
5. **Pacific County:** Maybe my prejudices are showing, but the Columbia River estuary, Willapa Bay, and the southern coast are among my favorite fishing spots. The Buoy 10 salmon season and outstanding sturgeon fishing would be enough, but there's much more.
6. **Chelan County:** Lake Chelan's angling variety and the trophy brown trout possibilities at Fish Lake are enough to make Chalan County one of Washington's best-kept fishing secrets, but the secret is getting out!
7. **King County:** How can the state's most populated county offer some of the best fishing? How about Lake Washington; Lake Sammamish; Elliott Bay; the Green, Snoqualmie, and Skykomish Rivers; and a trout lake every couple of miles?
8. **San Juan County:** Any county totally surrounded by water has to be on a top 10 fishing list. The salmon and bottom fish possibilities are almost enough to take your mind off the gorgeous scenery.
9. **Okanogan County:** The trophy trout fisheries in Rufus Woods and Omak lakes would be enough to put Washington's largest county on the top 10 list, but it also has Spectacle, Wannacut, Palmer, Bonaparte, and the Conconullys (lake and reservoir), not to mention the Okanogan River.
10. **Mason County:** The resurgence of salmon fishing on Hood Canal has put Mason County back on the fishing map. Fishing in its many productive trout lakes is a bonus for anglers.

Top 10 State Park Fishing Destinations

1. **Steamboat Rock:** Fishing variety, great weather, excellent camping, and plenty of other activities make it the best of the best.

2. **Fort Canby:** Sturgeon and Buoy 10 salmon are only minutes away via Canby's boat ramp.
3. **Sun Lakes:** Park and Blue Lakes offer excellent rainbow trout fishing.
4. **Potholes:** Bass, walleyes, panfish, and lunker rainbows are within casting distance of the park.
5. **Lake Chelan/25-Mile Creek:** These two parks are at the edge of eastern Washington's top lake for trophy salmon and lake trout.
6. **Anderson Lake:** No camping, but the trout fishing makes up for the drive.
7. **Sequim Bay:** It's an easy run to salmon, halibut, shrimp, crab, and more.
8. **Maryhill:** Columbia River walleyes, sturgeon, salmon, steelhead, and smallmouth bass are all a short run from the park's excellent boat ramp.
9. **Ike Kinswa:** Mayfield Lake has trophy tiger muskies and constantly improving rainbow trout fishing.
10. **Wenberg:** The park is on Lake Goodwin, and several other productive trout lakes are only a few minutes away.

Washington's 10 Largest Natural Lakes

Any angler who subscribes to the belief that size really does matter would assume that the state's biggest lakes offer some of the biggest fish, and to some degree that's a correct assumption here in Washington. Check the listing for each of these lakes in the regional chapters of this book to be sure, though, because bigger isn't always better!

1. **Lake Chelan** (33,100 acres)
2. **Lake Washington** (22,100 acres)
3. **Lake Ozette** (7,800 acres)
4. **Moses Lake** (6,800 acres)
5. **Lake Crescent** (5,100 acres)
6. **Lake Whatcom** (5,000 acres)
7. **Lake Sammamish** (4,900 acres)
8. **Lake Cle Elum** (4,800 acres)
9. **Lake Kachess** (4,500 acres)
10. **Lake Quinault** (3,700 acres)

10 Artificial Reefs of Puget Sound

Natural bottom-fish habitat is in short supply throughout Puget Sound, so in the early 1980s Washington's Department of Fisheries set out to construct a series of underwater rock piles that could provide good cover for lingcod, rockfish, and other bottom-fish species. Those artificial reefs have been providing some of the area's best bottom-fish action ever since. Here's a listing of those reefs and their locations:

1. **Onamac Point:** 1,000 feet north of the Onamac Point navigational light, Camano Island
2. **Gedney Island:** 3,000 feet south of Gedney Island's southern tip
3. **Possession Point:** 600 feet west of the Possession Point navigational buoy

4. **The Trees:** 2.1 miles south of Point Wells, near Edmonds
5. **Alki Point:** 1,000 feet southwest of Alki Point, near West Seattle
6. **Blake Island** 800 feet south of the southern tip of Blake Island
7. **Point Heyer:** 1,000 feet southeast of the KVI radio tower on Point Heyer, Vashon Island
8. **Toliva Shoal:** 1,300 feet northwest of the Toliva Shoal navigational buoy, south of Tacoma
9. **Itsami Ledge:** 1,100 feet northwest of the South Bay navigational light, north of Olympia
10. **Misery Point:** 600 feet north of the Misery Point navigational light

Washington's Top 10 Steelhead Fishing Rivers
1. Lower Columbia
2. Cowlitz
3. Bogachiel
4. Skykomish
5. Quinault
6. Little White Salmon
7. Hoh
8. Grande Ronde
9. Skagit
10. Calawah

Washington Sport Fish

A quick look at a Washington map will help to explain why fishing is such a big deal around here. There's water everywhere, and, although you can't tell it from a map, most of that water has fish in it. The fact that both freshwater and saltwater fishing are available here puts the Evergreen State on a fairly small list among these United States, and we also have some angling opportunities that are one-of-a-kind.

Take, for example, the Strait of Juan de Fuca and Puget Sound. Look at a U.S. map and you'll see nothing like these two inland waterways anywhere else in the country. They comprise millions of acres where small-boat anglers can fish for marine and anadromous fish species in relative protection from stormy seas.

Safe Boating Tips

No fish is worth dying for, but many anglers risk their lives by taking unnecessary chances on the water. Statistics from the Washington State Parks Boating Program show that about half of the people who die in boating accidents every year are anglers. Because we do much of our fishing from the kinds of smaller boats that are most often involved in accidents, we have to be more careful. State Parks suggests that we "know our limits" when it comes to boating safely. Here are five boating rules to live by:

• **Limit the load you carry in your boat.** Overloaded boats are much more likely to capsize, and we fishermen are notorious for carrying along all the tackle boxes, coolers, and fishing partners we can squeeze between the gunwales. Somewhere on your boat there should be a small plate stating maximum capacity in people and pounds, and if you exceed those maximums you're asking for trouble.

• **Limit boating to safe weather and water conditions.** Sure, we like to brag that the best fishing occurs when it's rainy and nasty, but are you and your boat really suited to rough water conditions? If you push your luck on rough water or in bad weather, you may never go fishing again!

• **Limit alcohol consumption.** Alcohol quickly affects your judgment and reactions when you're in a boat. It can also affect your balance, and having one too many in a boat is very dangerous.

• **Limit your movement.** Many an angler has drowned as a result of leaning too far to net a fish, falling overboard while cranking on the starting rope of an outboard motor, or simply shifting their weight too quickly. Keep your weight low and move around as little as possible, especially in a small boat.

• **Limit the time that you aren't wearing a life jacket.** Your chances of surviving a boating accident are simply much better if you're wearing your life vest or float-coat. There's seldom any advance warning when you're about to fall overboard or hit a submerged log and capsize, so simply having life vests or cushions stored under a seat somewhere on board offers little help when they're needed most. Wear a personal flotation device and live to fish again!

Speaking of stormy seas, Washington also has coastal ports unique in their size and the access they provide to saltwater fishing. Grays Harbor, Willapa Bay, and the mouth of the Columbia River offer safe haven to tens of thousands of salmon, halibut, lingcod, and rockfish anglers each year. Neah Bay, at the extreme northwest corner of the state, is a jump-off point for anglers headed not only into the open Pacific but also the productive waters at the western end of the Strait of Juan de Fuca.

And then there's the Columbia-Snake River system and the limitless angling possibilities it provides. The two huge rivers are now mostly a series of still-water reservoirs, but they provide excellent fishing for everything from perch and crappies to huge trout and trophy-size walleyes. Despite the dams and the damage they've done to anadromous fish runs, countless numbers of salmon and steelhead continue to enter the Columbia system each year, often providing fantastic fishing.

The Evergreen State has lakes, streams, and ponds too numerous to count, and most of them offer some kind of angling opportunity. Whether you like catching mountain whitefish from an ice-cold river, bullhead catfish from a roadside pond, or brightly colored brook trout from an alpine lake, you have hundreds of options here in Washington.

So, finding a place to fish is no problem around here, and the regional chapters that make up most of this book list about 1,000 worthwhile places to wet a line, with information about how to get there, what you can expect to find, and who to contact for current conditions.

Take a look at the Species entries for those 1,000 or so locations and you'll realize that there are plenty of options. Some of our lakes, reservoirs, rivers, creeks, ponds, and marine waters offer only one or two species, while others provide a wide range of possibilities. Deciding what to fish for and how to fish for it can be a tough decision. To help make the job a little easier, this front section of the book is dedicated to describing the state's many and varied sport species. Use this species-by-species rundown as a reference when reading about specific waters in other parts of the book. If you see a reference to a particular species mentioned under a fishing spot, turn to this section to find out more about it.

A few fish species are more popular or command more interest from anglers than others, so I've first listed what I consider the top 10 sport fish Washington has to offer and provided a little more detail about them. This top 10 list is made up of fish that are the most exciting and challenging, the most popular with a majority of anglers, the most widely available, or some combination of these qualities.

If you don't find the fish you're looking for in the top 10, it's described farther back, in the "Honorable Mention" listing, which is broken down into freshwater, saltwater, and anadromous (sea-run) categories.

Armed with this how-to information for each of Washington's fish species, you're ready to hit the road for some of the world's best fishing—*Washington Fishing*.

Chinook:
Outsmarting the King

There can be only one king, and here in the Pacific Northwest the title belongs to the chinook salmon, which anglers also rightfully call the king salmon. When it comes to size, strength, speed, streamlined beauty, and table quality, the crown goes to the adult chinook every time.

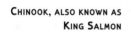

CHINOOK, ALSO KNOWN AS
KING SALMON

PAUL B. JOHNSON

The success of most Washington saltwater fishing trips is measured by the number of kings in the fish box. But, despite its immense popularity, the king's secrets are known and understood by relatively few. It seems that most Washington anglers are content to settle for less, so they limit out on seven-pound cohos or dredge up a couple of sweet-eating bottomfish and call it a day, hoping that maybe their luck will change next time and they'll get a shot at a king.

But to loosely paraphrase Tina Turner, what's luck got to do with it? If you want to catch kings, you fish for kings, and there are really only a few simple rules to remember. Fish the right way, at the right time, in the right places, and you'll catch them consistently.

Tackle, Tactics, and Tips
Fishing Chinooks in Saltwater

Serious saltwater king salmon anglers have a saying that sums up the best time of day to fish: "If you can see the bait, it's too late." In other words, don't plan to pull away from the docks at daybreak; be fishing at daybreak. The hottest chinook bite of the day usually occurs at first light; in July or early August that means sometime between 4 and 4:30 A.M.

If you do sleep in until 5 A.M. and miss the day's best fishing, don't lose hope. Usually there will be a period of feeding activity on the tide change, especially a flood tide. When a tide bite comes on, fish hard while it lasts, since it might be only 10 minutes long. A day in king country often ends the way it starts, with an evening bite during the last few minutes of daylight.

Unlike most other Pacific salmon species, the chinook tends to be a creature of the bottom, found within a few feet of the sand and rocks and sometimes with its nose right down in the dirt. Successful king anglers keep their baits and lures within a foot or

Many Northwesterners are familiar with the common nicknames of some or all Pacific salmon but couldn't tell you the real names of all five on a bet. For the record, "king" salmon is the common name for a chinook, while the nickname "silver" is a reference to the coho. "Dog" salmon are really chum salmon, while "humpies" are pink salmon. And then there's the "red" salmon, common nickname for the sockeye.

two of the bottom, always aware of the depth and yo-yoing their offerings along the bottom contours to stay down in the strike zone.

Fishing bottom doesn't necessarily mean fishing extremely deep. Many of the Northwest's top king spots are in 125 feet of water or less. The key is to find certain kinds of structure that draw bait fish, which in turn draw hungry kings.

Break lines, for example, are places where a flat or gently sloping bottom suddenly breaks off into much deeper water. Kings often patrol the edge of a break line in search of bait fish and sometimes use such lines as migration routes. A trolling path or tidal drift that carries you along such break lines will often put you right in the thick of things.

Plateaus are flat or gently sloping tabletops where the water is shallower than surrounding areas. Bait fish such as herring or candlefish sometimes congregate on these plateaus, and the kings come looking for them.

Bait fish also collect in the current breaks formed by points of land, creating a natural attraction for hungry kings. The edges, where fast and slow water meet on the downstream side of these points, are often best.

Sometimes the best king structure of all, though, is the shoreline itself. Mature chinooks headed for freshwater are like wolves on the prowl, often patrolling coves, small bays, and kelp beds in search of the oil-rich bait fish that will sustain them through the rigors of spawning. Pocket fishing for these near-shore kings provides some of salmon fishing's most spectacular action.

Mooching

Mooching—the salmon-fishing version of stillfishing—with herring bait is one of three angling techniques that take chinook, and it is perhaps the most deadly of the three when done right. Most serious king anglers like their whole or plug-cut herring to make wide, slow barrel rolls as they go through the water, but some like a faster, tighter roll more commonly associated with coho fishing.

Fresh herring make the best bait, and it's often possible to catch a day's supply in the area you're fishing. Strings of small, beaded herring jigs are available at most tackle shops, and when you locate schools of herring it doesn't take long to jig enough for the day's fishing. Besides being fresh and firm, locally caught bait happens to be what local kings are used to eating, so you're "matching the hatch" and not offering some odd-sized bait that the fish aren't used to seeing. Using the right-sized bait for the occasion often makes an important difference.

Many king anglers match their hook size to the size of their bait, using something as small as a size 1 or 1/0 with three-inch baits and going as large as 4/0 or 5/0 with a seven-inch herring. With small baits, some anglers abandon the tandem-hook rigs altogether and thread a single hook twice through the front end of the bait, at the top, then push it into the body cavity, back out the side, and seat it into the side of the bait just in front of the tail.

Proper sinker size is a key to successful mooching for kings. The mooching sinker has to be heavy enough to take the bait down to within a few inches of the bottom and keep it working there, but not so heavy that it hangs straight down and holds the bait motionless.

Most king anglers want a 45- to 60-degree line angle with the water's surface. You may get by with a two- or three-ounce sinker if you're fishing light line (10- or 12-pound monofilament) during a slack tide with no wind, but as line diameter, current, and wind increase, so will the size of the sinker you'll need to keep the bait down.

Unlike cohos, which often hit a bait with the finesse of a demolition driver, chinooks take it slowly and deliberately, so don't get overly anxious. Pay out line when you feel those first two or three tap-tap-taps; then as the fish moves steadily down or away with the bait, drop the rod tip until the line tightens and make sure there's steady pressure before hitting them.

Trolling

There was a time when trolling for big kings meant dragging a bait or lure around behind a sinker weighing up to several pounds, fished on a rod that was better suited to playing pool than to fishing. Fortunately, downriggers have changed all that, and it's now possible to get down to where the kings are while still enjoying the thrill of catching them on light tackle.

A troller willing to work his downriggers can follow the contours of those break lines and rocky points within a few inches of the bottom, keeping a bait or lure right down where it belongs. Some anglers fish whole or plug-cut herring (just like those used for mooching) behind their downrigger balls, while others prefer spoons, wobbling plugs, large streamer flies, or plastic squid (often referred to as "hoochies"). Flies and hoochies have little action of their own, so they're usually trolled behind a flasher, a metal or plastic attractor that rotates in a wide arc that gives the trailing lure an erratic, darting action.

Jigging

Vertical jigging is the Northwest's newest king-fishing technique, growing steadily more popular the past 10 years or so. At least two dozen different jig styles, all of them simulating or approximating the size, shape, color, and wiggle of an injured herring, anchovy, or candlefish, will take kings consistently when fished by a good jigger.

The standard technique is to free-spool the lure to the bottom, then jig it up and down in two- to six-foot sweeps of the rod, dropping the rod tip quickly on the downward stroke to allow the lure to flatten out into a horizontal position. A horizontal jig is a jig that's most active—wiggling, spinning, wobbling, and darting from side to side as it falls through the water.

The Downrigger: A Salmon Troller's Best Friend

It's safe to say that salmon angling in the Northwest isn't the sure thing it once was. Savvy anglers, though, continue to enjoy very good fishing, and some of the most successful are those who have mastered the art of fishing with downriggers.

The principle of the downrigger is simple: fill a large spool with wire, run that wire out a short boom and through a roller, and attach a heavy weight to the end of the wire. Then, attach the fishing line to the wire by means of a release mechanism and you can troll as deep as necessary and still get a great fight from your fish without the drag of any additional weight. Downriggers make life much easier for any kind of salmon fishing, at virtually any depth.

Here are a half-dozen tips for catching more salmon with downriggers:

- **Keep it moving.** Successful downrigger fishermen raise and lower their rigs constantly, all day, to keep their baits and lures where the fish are. That's hard work with a manual machine, explaining why electric models are so popular.

- **Experiment with line releases.** Most manufacturers offer their own styles of release, but they're interchangeable. Play around until you find one you like for your fishing needs. Choose one that releases smoothly and doesn't cause line damage.

- **Use small-diameter, low-stretch line.** Monofilament has a lot of stretch, and when trolling for kings at 50 to 150 feet or deeper, that line stretch translates to missed strikes and lost fish. Today's phenomenal new braided lines, such as Spiderwire and Berkley's Whiplash, are perfect for downrigger fishing.

- **Learn to use "stacking" releases.** It's possible to fish more than one line per downrigger, which offers obvious advantages when the salmon are scattered throughout the water column. Double your downrigger's usefulness and catch more salmon by learning to use the so-called stacking releases.

- **Leave the graphite rods home.** Yes, graphite is great for most fishing, but a glass rod gives better performance with downriggers.

- **Use the right reel for the job.** A good levelwind with a smooth, easily adjustable drag is an absolute necessity for downrigger fishing.

Salmon strikes on a jig are subtle, often nothing more than a slight slackening of the line as the fall of the jig is interrupted, so the jigger has to stay on his toes and react to anything that doesn't feel quite right. Keeping those hooks needle sharp is more important in jigging than in any other kind of salmon fishing, to give the lure that extra split second of hang time in a salmon's jaw between the strike and the instant the jigger reacts and gets the hook set in earnest.

As with other king-fishing methods, it's important to keep the jig working near the bottom, but don't use any heavier jig than you need to reach the desired depth. If you're reaching bottom just fine with a four-ounce jig, try going to a three-ouncer and see if you can still hit bottom OK. A smaller, lighter jig is a more active jig, and an active jig is more likely to catch the eye of a prowling king.

What about rods, reels, and lines for king fishing? Most veterans prefer a 7.5- to 9-foot rod with a sensitive tip, lots of backbone at the lower end, and a long butt for leverage. Such a rod will wear down even the most stubborn 50-pounder if you give it enough time to do its damage. A good jigging rod is lighter and stiffer than the rod preferred for mooching or trolling. Anglers who mooch or jig prefer the sensitivity and strength of graphite, while many downrigger trollers like the more limber fiberglass for its durability and resistance to the abuses of all-day trolling. The reels are revolving-spool jobs, usually levelwinds with enough capacity for at least 150 to 200 yards of line. Jiggers and moochers generally go with smaller, lighter, faster reels than those used by trollers. The monofilament main line ranges from 8- to 40-pound test, with 15- to 25-pound monofilament favored by the majority of anglers. Fishing in deeper water (about 125 feet or more) may call for low-stretch ultrabraid line rather than monofilament. These high-tech lines allow for positive hook-sets at greater depths and, because of their small diameter, allow the use of smaller lures and lighter weights.

Fishing Chinooks in Freshwater

The king's popularity among anglers doesn't diminish much when it moves from saltwater into the freshwater stream where it will eventually spawn and die (or be killed and spawned in a salmon hatchery facility). Freshwater fishing opportunities for chinooks, in fact, are as far-ranging and abundant as the saltwater possibilities. If you're willing to do a little traveling throughout western Washington, you may be able to hook hefty chinook salmon in various rivers from as early as March to as late as November.

Some of the standard rules of king fishing in the marine environment also apply to freshwater fishing. The action is usually best during the first half hour and last half hour of the day, you want your bait or lure hugging the rocky bottom most of the time, and you have to be patient enough to feed 'em line for a few seconds before attempting to set the hook into their tough jaw.

Chinooks that return to their home streams several months before spawning provide the most popular freshwater fishery. Arriving as early as March or April, they've earned the appropriate name "spring chinooks" or "springers," and they can best be described as pure piscatorial energy.

How long they stay in the food-rich Pacific Ocean determines how large those salmon will be when they return to freshwater. Fish that come back after only three years at sea are the little guys of the spring chinook world, if you can call a fish of 10 to 12 pounds a small one. Four-year returnees will weigh in at 14 to 20 pounds, while five-year-olds are the trophies that may run to 30 pounds and larger. Whatever its size, a spring chinook will almost always fight bigger than it really is.

"These fish enter a river with enough energy reserves to get them through until the late summer or fall, and they use their abundant energy to fight back when they feel a hook," says Buzz Ramsey, promotions director for Oregon-based tackle manufacturer Luhr Jensen and Sons and a longtime springer enthusiast.

Blazing runs, rolling jumps, and deep-fighting, slug-it-out tactics are all part of the spring chinook's repertoire when it's at the business end of a fishing line.

Springers tend to move right along on their upstream journey, spending less time holding in resting water and more time chugging upstream than, say, steelhead or fall runs of salmon. The fact that you're often fishing for moving fish may dictate certain angling techniques for these fish.

Spinners account for a good number of moving chinook. Spinner anglers don't cast and retrieve for their fish; they use a two- to six-ounce sinker on a dropper leader to hold the lure in place, and the keys are to fish the right slots and to match the blade size to the amount of current.

Back-trolling wobbling plugs also takes springers and will often work on both moving fish and those holding deeper, slower water. Large Kwikfish and Flatfish are the plugs most commonly used, and they work best when adorned with a sardine wrap—a fillet of fresh sardine lashed to the underside of the plug with several dozen wraps of thread.

Back-bouncing may sound like some kind of Swedish massage technique, but it's another method of taking river chinook, and it works better on holding fish than on movers. As its name implies, back-bouncing is a matter of backing your boat downstream, bouncing a sinker-and-bait rig through fishy-looking water ahead of you. Lifting, dropping, and paying out line as needed, the back-bouncer keeps his sinker slipping along the rocky bottom, always alert for a change in rhythm that could mean he has a customer.

Baits for back-bouncing include large clusters of salmon roe, live ghost shrimp, roe/shrimp combinations, plug-cut herring, and fresh prawns, which are usually dyed pink, purple, or deep red. Picking a best bait may depend on personal preference or local trends, but there are certainly times when one of the aforementioned works better than the others. Veteran springer anglers carry a variety and know the secrets of rigging and fishing them.

Not all spring chinook salmon are caught by boat anglers. Bank fishing with shrimp, roe, herring, prawns, wobbling plugs, and spinners also accounts for good numbers of these fish every season. As with boat fishing, though, the key is often not so much what bait or lure you have tied to the end of your line, but exactly where you place it in the river. You can fish the right lure in the wrong place all your life without ever getting a strike, so do your fishing where other anglers are catching fish and watch closely to learn the springers' travel routes and resting spots in any given stream.

Summer and fall runs of chinook also enter many Washington rivers, and the techniques already discussed will work just as well in September as in April. Patience, however, may become more important to the angler as spring turns to summer and summer turns to fall. Fish that arrive in the rivers later—and thereby closer to spawning time—are often less eager and less cooperative when it comes to taking a bait or lure. Stick with them, however, and you can eventually coax them into hitting.

And when they decide to respond, hang on!

Washington's Top Chinook Waters

Hanford Reach of the Columbia River, Washington coast off Ilwaco, Columbia River from Megler-Astoria Bridge to Buoy 10, Columbia River at Wind River mouth, Lake Chelan, Neah Bay, Port Angeles, San Juan Islands, Strait of Juan de Fuca at Sekiu, Washington coast at Westport, Grays Harbor, and Willapa Bay.

Steelhead: Well Worth a Little Hardship

Snow was falling horizontally, thanks to a 20-mph wind, and the man on the radio had just announced that high temperatures for the Puget Sound area weren't expected to top 25 degrees that day. But it was Saturday, so fishing partner Dave Borden and I were on the road just after daylight, heading for one of our favorite winter steelhead spots on the Puyallup River. Confident that we were the only ones stupid enough to go fishing in that kind of weather, we weren't in any particular hurry.

PAUL B. JOHNSON

STEELHEAD

When we arrived at our usual parking spot, though, another pickup was already there, a pickup that neither of us had seen along the river before.

"Must be somebody who got a new steelhead rod for Christmas," I chuckled. "He won't be here long."

But there were two sets of boot tracks in the snow as we made our way down the winding trail that led to the river, and by the amount of snow that had already fallen on them, they had been made some time before we arrived.

Still, we were confident in our knowledge of the river and in our ability to catch steelhead from it, so we plodded on toward a long stretch of river that had always treated us generously in the past.

Our first little secret spot behind a submerged boulder on the far side of the river had already been worked over, as evidenced by all the tracks at river's edge, so we didn't spend much time there. Things were even worse at our next stop. Near the lower end of a slow-moving pocket that had produced steelhead for us in the past, we found a big patch of crimson in the muddy snow. Our worst fears were being realized—the guys ahead of us seemed to know what they were doing.

Now hoping to catch up with our adversaries and pass them before they reached the best steelhead hole on this entire stretch of river, we quit fishing all the "maybe" spots and took off downriver at a fast walk.

Too late! As we rounded a bend and peered through the blowing snow toward

State Record for Steelhead

Winter-run: 32 lb., 12 oz... . . . . East Fork Lewis River. 1980
Summer-run: 35 lb., 1 oz. . . . . Snake River. 1973

the piscatorial promised land, we could easily make out two vertical forms on the otherwise horizontal landscape. They were fishing our spot, all right, and to make matters even worse, one of them was playing a fish. By the time we strolled up to make a little light conversation with the two strangers, they were beaching their third steelhead of the morning, a sleek, chrome-bright specimen of perhaps 12 pounds.

The fact that two out-of-towners had rolled in and caught three steelhead from one of our favorite haunts was bad enough, but then they had the nerve to rub our noses in it.

"You guys shouldn't have slept in so late this morning," the first one offered. And then the second one really made our day.

"You can't let a little bad weather keep you off the river," he advised.

Rather than saying what we actually thought of their free advice, Dave and I trudged on down the river to find places that hadn't yet been fished.

The big, sea-run rainbow of the Northwest is a wary, streetwise sort of fish that isn't easily fooled or outsmarted, and its strength and stamina are enough to test the skills of any angler. Every time you land one you've accomplished something that the vast majority of anglers never accomplish. Winter steelhead anglers have what normal people might consider an unusual way of looking at things. Members of the steelheading fraternity actually spend lots of money for the privilege of getting up long before daylight, braving icy roads, wading around a partially frozen river in leaky boots, and getting skunked more often than not.

Did you ever wonder how fast fish can swim? The general rule is about 6 to 8 mph for every foot of body length, but those are only sustainable speeds. In a pinch, most fish can achieve bursts of about 50 percent higher than sustainable speeds. While fish like bass and salmon can swim maybe 12 to 15 mph, some saltwater species can really blast off. Barracuda have been clocked at 30 mph, marlin at over 40, and some tuna species at 50 mph!

Most years, about half of Washington's steelhead anglers go through the season without catching a single steelhead, and even when you figure in the experts who catch lots of fish, the average isn't much over half a steelhead per licensed angler for the entire season. I know a guy who started fishing for them in the 1950s and tried for 13 years before actually catching one.

There's obviously something about the steelhead that keeps these anglers going, helping them to put up with the miserable weather and the endless weeks of fruitless casting. The sea-run rainbow trout that we call a steelhead is a thing of beauty and an angling trophy without equal, at least to those who pursue it, and if a winter of fishing provides a single opportunity to hook one, most steelheaders would consider it a winter well spent.

Steelhead are available throughout the year in Washington. Many streams have a winter run that starts as early as November and may last into April. Other rivers are best known for their summer-run steelhead, which migrate from the Pacific Ocean April through October. Many Washington rivers have both winter- and summer-run steelhead, providing at least some chance for anglers to hook one of these trophies 12 months out of the year.

A typical steelhead weighs 5 to 10 pounds, and any fish over 20 pounds is considered a trophy. They occasionally grow as large as 30 pounds or more, and the state-record winter steelie for Washington is a 32-pound, 12-ouncer caught from the East Fork of the Lewis River back in 1980.

Whatever their size, you can depend on them to show amazing strength and stamina when they're at the end of a line, making long, powerful runs and high, twisting leaps from the time they feel the sting of a hook until they're finally landed—or escape to fight again.

Tackle, Tactics, and Tips

For their size and power, steelhead often take a bait or lure with unbelievable subtlety. One of the most difficult things for a beginning angler to learn is how to detect the steelhead's soft strike, to somehow distinguish it from the rhythmic bouncing of the sinker along the rocky river bottom.

Reading the Water

Before worrying about whether or not you'll feel the strike, you first have to locate the fish and put the right bait or lure in front of their noses, neither of which is particularly easy, especially for the novice steelheader.

Steelhead moving through a river toward upstream spawning grounds or hatcheries seldom make the entire trip in one prolonged sprint. They stop to rest along the way, and it's these resting or holding spots where most savvy steelheaders concentrate their efforts. Veteran anglers call it "reading the water," and if you never learn how to do it, you'll never catch many steelhead.

Most of the places steelhead choose to stop and rest along their upstream journey have two things in common. They provide adequate cover, so the fish feel safe and somewhat hidden, and they provide a break from the fastest and heaviest currents. Put another way, holding water is a place where steelhead can hide and rest at the same time. Any place offering that combination of qualities is probably worth fishing for steelhead.

Examples of good holding water might include a slow, deep run immediately downstream from a major rapids or stretch of heavy current. Midstream logs, stumps, or boulders that break the flow of the current are also attractive to migrating steelhead, as are undercut banks and the converging currents where a small stream or side channel meets the main river.

Other kinds of potential holding water may not be so obvious to the angler who sees the river only from the outside. A raging Northwest river may gouge out deep-water channels and small pockets in the river bottom that can't be seen from above, or there may be midsize rocks on the bottom that break the current of a deep-water run without showing any signs on the stream's surface. These are spots where knowledgeable veteran steelhead anglers catch fish while less-experienced steelheaders whip the water to a froth in frustration. It takes a trained hand, sensitive steelhead rod, and thorough knowledge of the river to feel these changes in the bottom that can spell the difference between catching a two-fish limit and just another day on the stream.

If you really want to learn how to catch winter steelhead, study those who are catching fish, and pay special attention not only to how they do things but exactly where they place their casts.

Drift Fishing for Steelhead

Steelhead anglers employ several different fishing techniques, but the most common is referred to as drift fishing. As the name implies, it's a matter of casting across the river or slightly upstream and allowing the bait or lure to drift downstream with the current. The key to successful drift fishing is using the right sinker for the job. You want to keep it near bottom without constantly hanging in the rocks and snags, and you have to adjust sinker size to the depth and speed of the water.

Too large and heavy a sinker will result in constant hang-ups and lost tackle, while too light a sinker won't keep your bait or lure down where it belongs, within a few inches of the river bottom. If you fish all day without bouncing bottom, you have almost no chance of hooking a steelhead.

Drift anglers have plenty of choices about what goes on the end of their lines. A cluster of fresh salmon or steelhead roe is a longtime favorite, and most steelheaders use a special loop knot on their hooks to hold the clusters in place. A live ghost shrimp is another good steelhead bait, and you can dig your own along a muddy beach or buy them from area bait and tackle shops.

As for artificial lures, steelhead will hit metallic-finish spinners and wobbling spoons, leadhead jigs fished below a float, deep-diving plugs, or any of the wide range of steelhead bobbers—brightly colored little pieces of wood, plastic, or foam that come in all sizes and shades.

If you're wondering what rod to use for steelhead, make it an 8.5- or 9-footer with a sensitive tip and a long butt handle. Graphite provides the kind of sensitivity that most steelheaders prefer. A spinning or bait-casting reel with enough capacity to hold at least 125 yards of premium-grade monofilament line in the 10- to 17-pound range rounds out the list of basic tackle requirements.

While drift fishing is the most popular technique for winter steelhead, there are other methods of catching this most challenging of Northwest game fish.

Other Steelheading Techniques

Plunking might be described as the lazy person's steelheading technique. Rather than going to the fish as the drift angler does, the plunker sits on the bank and waits for the fish to come to him. Plunkers use much the same baits and lures that drift anglers use, but instead of letting them move through the water with the current, plunkers anchor the offerings in deep water with a heavy sinker. The key to plunking success is to place that sinker and bait in exactly the right spot, so that a passing steelhead virtually runs into it.

A technique called back-trolling, or plugging, was developed by boaters and has since become a favorite of some bank anglers as well. The idea is to work a diving plug downstream through the river, with tension from upstream, so that it dives to the bottom, wiggling and wobbling enticingly as it's worked through potential holding water.

Leadhead jigs were mentioned earlier, but they deserve special attention since an entire steelheading technique has developed around them over the past decade or so. While leadheads would no doubt catch steelhead if they were simply bounced along the river bottom in conventional jigging style, most steelheaders use them suspended beneath a float or bobber. The float helps to impart action on the jig as it's bounced along on the water's surface, tipping the jig up and down as it moves along. The key to fishing a jig beneath a float lies in adjusting the distance between the float and the jig so the lure is just off the bottom. Too long a line between the two allows the jig to drag and hang on the rocks, but if the distance is too short, the jig will be too high in the water column to attract much interest from the bottom-hugging fish.

Timing can make a big difference in whether you catch winter steelhead or not. Fish move upstream throughout the winter, but a day of heavy rain that causes river levels to rise may draw a large number of fish into the river all at once. That's why the best time to go steelheading is right after the rains stop and a river begins to recede. Some streams rise and fall faster than others, with smaller rivers and creeks usually responding to weather changes more quickly than larger rivers. Getting to know how fast your favorite steelhead river drops after a minor flood and being there when it happens can greatly improve your steelhead catch.

There's another timing factor that can play a big part in your success or lack thereof. Steelhead tend to return to some rivers earlier in the season, some later, and you should learn to fish a few of each kind to help extend your winter steelheading opportunities. Catch statistics compiled by the Washington Department of Fish and Wildlife, which are available to the public, can be valuable in helping you determine which months might be most productive on a particular steelhead river.

You should also know that many—in fact, most—Washington winter steelhead streams are stocked with hatchery steelhead to help supplement runs of wild fish that are not as large as they used to be. Hatchery winter steelhead, for example, tend to come home earlier in the winter than their wild counterparts, so streams with large hatchery plants may be best in December and January, while wild-run rivers and creeks often provide their best fishing during February, March, or even April.

Washington's Top Steelhead Spots

Bogachiel River, Cowlitz River, Drano Lake, East Fork Lewis River, Hoh River, Kalama River, Lower Columbia River, Quinault River, Skagit River, Skykomish River, Snake River, and Snoqualmie River.

Coho: Expect the Unexpected

The coho is a fish for all anglers, one that can be as susceptible to the efforts of the first-time charter boat customer as it is to the skills and equipment of the 30-year veteran of the saltchuck. From the southern Oregon coast to the Bering Sea, the coho, or silver, has long been the bread-and-butter fish of the salmon fishery, caught by the hundreds of thousands every summer.

Its wide distribution and availability, however, doesn't make it a pushover, and for every story about a coho limit, there's a story about someone being totally baf-fled by the fish's unpredictable nature or blistered by its wild,

Coho Salmon

BOB RACE

hook-shaking antics. While there are no guarantees for coho-fishing success, there are some things you can do to catch them more consistently. Cohos large enough to be worth catching—two-and-a-half-year-old fish that have spent a year in saltwater—show up along the Northwest coast as three- to five-pound catches in June. By the end of July, coastal anglers are catching six- to eight-pound fish, and by the end of August the first hook-nosed adult fish start to show. These are the prizes of the coho fishery, and their numbers build as they approach freshwater throughout September. That's when anglers are most likely to catch cohos of 10 to 15 pounds.

Migrations into Washington's inside waters may vary by as much as several weeks during unusual water conditions, but the sport catch records show that you can almost assure good coho catches if you spend time on the water from the last week of August to the third week in September. That's when the largest number of fish are moving in from the Pacific, and it's a time when the average size of those fish goes up almost daily. The farther north you are in the cohos' range, the earlier in this four-week time period you can expect to find peak fishing.

Tackle, Tactics, and Tips
Fishing Coho in Saltwater

Tide rips are the best places to look for coho. These spots where marine currents collide are marked by long, meandering lines of swirling water and floating debris, and they provide a smorgasbord for the coho. Krill—the planktonic crustaceans and larvae that make up the bulk of a young coho's diet—are abundant in tide rips, and even adult salmon will gorge on these suspended little snacks. All those tiny tidbits also attract candlefish, herring, and other bait fish, more major draws for hungry coho. Fish a tide rip thoroughly, because conditions may be different from one side of a rip to the other. All the fish-attracting bait may be on one side, and you might troll along the other side for hours without capitalizing on the bonanza only a few yards away.

State Record for Coho

Saltwater: 22.5 lb. . . . . Strait of Juan de Fuca 2001
Freshwater: 23.5 lb. . . . . Satsop River 1986

Feeding birds are another sign that hungry silvers may be nearby. The Bonaparte gull is called a coho bird by many salmon anglers, and for good reason. Often misidentified as a tern, this small gull with the distinctive black head feeds primarily on krill, and when you see several of them dancing and dipping along the surface, it means they've found food. Since krill is also coho food, well, you get the picture. Herring gulls, murres, and other fish-eating birds may also be an indication that there are cohos below.

When tide rips and birds aren't present, or when there aren't cohos below these obvious signs, it certainly doesn't mean all is lost.

At times like this, savvy silver anglers start paying close attention to their depthsounders to locate the coho or the bait fish that may attract them.

And there are many times when it isn't important to find bait at all. During the height of the inshore migrations in late summer and early fall, thick concentrations of adult cohos may be found in places where krill and bait fish are nonexistent. It's not that they aren't feeding, but just that following certain marine routes is much more important to them than actively searching for food. Find where they're traveling and you'll find action. Cohos headed for Hood Canal and Puget Sound, for example, will often follow narrow pathways through the 12-mile-wide Strait of Juan de Fuca, and when you get on one of these ribbons of silver, you may be in for some of the hottest fishing you've ever had. These coho freeways are often well out in open water, with no obvious reason for their existence.

Cohos are most often caught well up in the water column, usually within 50 feet of the surface and often within 20 feet. But like the bait fish on which they feed, cohos are very light sensitive, and they usually drop deeper as the sun gets higher. On clear, sunny days, near-surface coho action is hottest from sunrise to about 9 or 10 A.M.; then it drops off quickly and stays slow until shortly before sunset. On cloudy days, however, you may find fish within 20 or 30 feet of the top all day.

When they quit biting around midmorning, it's usually because anglers continue fishing for them at the depth they started, while the cohos have dropped into deeper water, beyond where people are fishing. A depthsounder will tell you this if you pay attention to it and react to what it shows you.

Trolling

When silvers are in their usual near-surface haunts, most people troll for them, and it doesn't require any special technique or fancy equipment. A simple spin sinker-and-herring rig will do it, but you can use a diving plane in place of the sinker or add a herring dodger attractor ahead of the bait. If you don't want to use bait at all, troll

Trolling Tips

Trolling is one of the most effective trout-fishing techniques of all, and it's also one of the easiest to master. I like the trolling advice offered by Luhr Jensen & Sons, manufacturer of many Northwest favorite trout-fishing products. Here are some of their suggestions:

- **Troll slowly.** Big fish will seldom expend any more energy than necessary to catch a meal.

- **Vary trolling speed.** Slow, yes, but try a little burst of speed now and then to change the action and vibration pattern of your bait or lure.

- **Work in S curves.** Again, a change in direction causes changes in lure action and depth, triggering strikes. Your offering will slow down and sink a foot or two on the "inside" of the turns while speeding and rising on the "outside," allowing you to cover more of the water column without changing boat speed.

- **Use trolling blades.** Using a string of trolling blades ahead of your bait or lure will increase fishing success. Trolls appeal to several fish-feeding instincts. In addition to producing flash and other visual attraction, a rotating blade gives off vibrations underwater, which spells F-O-O-D to nearby fish. When trolled, strings of blades act as attractors; fish follow the flash and sound to the source, spot the trailing bait or lure, and go after it.

- **Know water depth and visibility.** As a general rule, larger and more blades should be used for deep trolling or for working murky water. Nickel trolling blades work best on bright days and in clear water, while brass and copper finishes are better for murky, deep, or dark water.

- **Use correct leader length.** Baits and lures should be at the end of a leader at least 12 inches behind the blade string, and most anglers prefer leaders of 14 to 18 inches. Bigger blades and longer strings of them generally require longer leaders.

a plastic squid or a large streamer known locally as a "coho fly" 16 or 18 inches behind another type of attractor called a "flasher." A flasher revolves and jerks the squid or fly from side to side, giving it a darting action.

Coho will sometimes feed right on top, and you can catch them by trolling with little or no weight. That's when the coho fly really becomes a killer. When you see surface swirls, a sure sign of top-feeding coho, remove your sinker, tie on a fly, and troll it fast, about seven knots, so that it creates a steady wake without breaking the surface. Serious fly rodders even catch near-surface cohos by casting to them with streamer flies fished on floating or sink-tip fly lines. This technique works both on adult fish returning from the Pacific and immature cohos that you might find in estuaries and inshore waterways throughout the summer. Such a fly fishery has gained popularity in recent years among anglers around Puget Sound, where so-called resident silvers may provide excellent shallow-water fishing throughout the spring, summer, and early fall.

Mooching

Trolling is the preferred coho fishing method, but mooching accounts for thousands of cohos every year. Just ask anyone who spends much time fishing from a charter boat at Westport, and he or she will testify to the effectiveness of mooching for silvers. A coho angler mooching within 40 or 50 feet of the surface with 10- to 14-pound monofilament can fish effectively with a two- or two-and-a-half-ounce sinker, while the troller using the same line may prefer a three- or four-ounce sinker.

Silvers in a biting mood won't hesitate to chase down a fast-moving bait or lure, and lots of them are caught at trolling speeds of three to five knots. But don't troll at a steady speed. Changes in lure speed prompt silvers to strike. You'll improve your coho catch greatly if you do a lot of turning, zigzagging, and throttling up and down.

The speed at which a herring is spinning is just as important as how fast it's moving through the water. Serious coho anglers plug-cut their herring at a sharp angle so that the bait spins in tight, quick circles. Salmon anglers using the standard tandem-hook rig can enhance the bait's spinning action by impaling the herring only on the top hook and allowing the bottom hook to hang free.

As adult cohos near and enter the estuary, they move into range of shore-bound anglers, and that's when Northwest docks, piers, bridges, and beaches become crowded with coho anglers, most of them casting wobbling spoons or such metal jigs as the Buzz Bomb. Although they have usually stopped feeding actively by the time they reach the estuaries, mature cohos remain aggressive, and they'll attack an artificial lure fiercely.

Cohos are more likely than any other Pacific salmon species to hook themselves on the strike. While a Chinook may make pass after pass, tapping a bait softly, sucking it in and spitting it out perhaps a half dozen times before inhaling it for keeps, the coho usually isn't so subtle. The typical response of a salmon angler who has just been blasted by a streaking silver goes something like: "Jeez, whoa, damn!" And it's over.

And they fight about the same way they strike—with reckless abandon and no particular battle plan. They'll race 50 yards one way, turn tail, and charge off 50 yards in the opposite direction, capping the second run with two or three wild, somersaulting leaps, and then the whole sequence may be repeated. Losing a fish for every one you manage to put in the boat is a typical story.

Needle-sharp hooks are a must for the coho angler who wants to put more than an occasional fish in the box. Because of the fish's quick, often surprising strike,

If you don't carry and use a hook file on every fishing trip, you're missing and losing fish that could be caught. Even needle-sharp hooks grow dull quickly once they hit the water, so check hooks often and use that file to keep a sticky-sharp point on the business end. A three-sided point is generally considered the sharpest of all.

you need every advantage you can get, and a hook that will pierce a patch of flesh on incidental contact may hang there just long enough for you to do the rest with an upward sweep of the rod.

Let's face it: the silver salmon's antics will make you look silly often enough even if you keep your hooks sharp and do everything else right. Luckily, there are so many of these hard-hitting, sweet-eating streaks of silver out there that you can be pretty sure of getting another chance.

Fishing Coho in Freshwater

The coho fishery doesn't end when the runs reach freshwater. In rivers where adequate numbers of fish are available, cohos provide excellent stream-fishing opportunities. However, because these adult cohos getting ready to spawn are no longer actively feeding, the angling techniques change from those used in salt water.

Artificial lures account for many of the silvers caught from Washington rivers, with spoons, spinners, and diving plugs heading the list of coho catchers. There's something about the wiggle and flash of these lures that triggers aggressive strikes from fish that have long since stopped taking food. They might still be instinctively attempting to eat, or perhaps the response is a territorial one against what might look like a competing aquatic creature. It might even be a combination of these two or maybe something totally unrelated that we haven't even considered. Whatever the reason, river cohos that ignore a big cluster of fresh roe or some other delectable bait may slam into a flashy plug or spinner with reckless abandon.

While river chinook often stop to rest in the deepest, slowest pools, cohos show a preference for the shallower flats where current flow is moderate. Fish for them in the same kinds of spots where you might find winter steelhead, and chances are you'll find action. Such places as edges of currents, the mouths of tributary streams and side channels, around boulders and other current obstructions, and the flat water immediately above and below white-water riffles are all good places to toss a spinner or back-troll a plug for river cohos.

Washington's Top Coho Waters

Washington coast at Ilwaco, Strait of Juan de Fuca at Neah Bay, Puyallup River, Strait of Juan de Fuca at Sekiu, Snohomish River System, Washington coast at Westport, Grays Harbor, and Willapa Bay.

Pacific Halibut: Heavyweight Champ of the Northwest

Talk about the biggest, baddest, roughest, toughest denizen of the deep you can hope to find in the marine waters of the Northwest, and you can be talking about only one fish, the Pacific halibut. It's a fish that grows to 200, 300, even 400 pounds or more, and it may battle with an angler for several hours before being boated or breaking loose to regain its freedom.

BOB RACE

PACIFIC HALIBUT

What's more, unlike some fish species that were much more abundant 20, 50, or 100 years ago than they are now, Pacific halibut populations boomed a few years back and have more or less held their own since, providing anglers with more chance than ever of doing battle with this monster of the deep. Halibut fishing appears to be here to stay, and that's great news for saltwater anglers from southern Oregon to central Alaska.

Fishery managers offer several explanations for the halibut explosion that began in the early 1980s, but much of the credit apparently goes to the Fishery Conservation and Management Act of 1976, which gave the United States a 200-mile fishing boundary. The 200-mile limit has cut down substantially on the number of Pacific halibut caught by foreign trawlers. Strict prohibitions against the foreign harvest of halibut have provided better escapement and reproduction and more fish available to U.S. anglers.

Washington anglers don't spend much time contemplating the reasons for this halibut comeback. They just know what they like, and they like a fish that grows bigger than a human, fights like a bulldog, and is about as good on the dinner table as any fish that swims. That's why halibut is ranked near the top of my list of top sport fish. If it were more widely available and the halibut season were longer, it would be even higher on that list.

The halibut starts life looking pretty much like any other species of saltwater fish, with one eye on each side of its head and pigmentation giving it color over its entire body. But as the fish grows, some strange things happen, the sorts of things you might expect to see in a Stephen King movie. The left eye moves over to join the other one on the right side of the head, while the body grows flatter and one side turns completely white. By this time it's pretty obvious that this fish is destined for a life on the ocean bottom, and there's little doubt about which side is up.

Tackle, Tactics, and Tips

The halibut spends most of its life on or near the bottom, and that's where you have to fish if you hope to catch halibut consistently. Luckily, halibut prefer a fairly smooth bottom of sand, gravel, and cobble-sized rocks, so dragging your baits and lures around down where they live isn't as costly or as frustrating as it might be with such rock-loving bottomfish species as the lingcod.

When searching out halibut, look for underwater plateaus and gently sloping drop-offs rather than the hard, rough structure you might fish for lings. Finding these underwater humps and side hills is more important than fishing any particular water depth. Depending on the area you fish, you may find halibut as deep as 700 feet or as shallow as 15 feet. Some of the most productive halibut spots along the Washington coast are in 300 to 500 feet of water, but the protected waters of the Strait of Juan de Fuca boast a few halibut humps only 100 feet beneath the surface.

Bait Fishing for Halibut

Halibut can be caught on both bait and artificial lures, and you'll find about an equal number of successful anglers using each. Whole herring are perhaps the most popular Northwest halibut baits, and the bigger the herring, the better. These fish aren't particularly dainty when it comes to taking a meal, and they can inhale a foot-long herring with absolutely no trouble.

While herring are readily available from Northwest bait shops, marinas, even grocery stores, they do have one major shortcoming as halibut bait: they're not all that tough and durable. That's why some halibut anglers prefer other kinds of bait, such as whole squid, pieces of octopus, live greenling or tomcod, and even whole rock crab. All of these stay on a hook better than herring, but they are also much harder to find.

Whatever bait you choose for halibut, you'll probably want to fish it on a wire spreader rig. This L-shaped piece of heavy wire, often homemade from a coat hanger or length of stainless steel, has a swivel at each end and one at the bend. The bait is attached with a short, stout leader to one arm of the spreader and a sinker to the other, while the main line is tied to the middle swivel. Many halibut anglers use a cheap, brass snap-swivel to attach the sinker, so that it tears away on a hang-up and the rest of the rig can be retrieved. A good spreader is balanced so that the arm to which the bait is attached stays horizontal as the rig is dropped through the water. If it tips up too much, the bait will swing up and wrap around the line, a problem that the spreader is supposed to eliminate. To achieve a balanced spreader, be sure the arm that's connected to the sinker is about half the length of the arm connected to the bait.

There's no such thing as a right sinker weight for use with a spreader. A six-ounce sinker may take your bait to the bottom in shallow water with little or no current, but deep-water halibut fishing on a windy day or when the tide is running hard may dictate the use of sinkers as heavy as 24, 32, even 48 ounces or more. Halibut fishing under those conditions tends to be more work than fun.

Since many of the top Northwest halibut spots are in deep water, fishing with bait poses certain problems. The spiny dogfish is one of those problems. Often found in the same places as halibut, this pesky nuisance isn't the least bit shy about attacking anything that smells like an easy meal, and many a bait-fishing halibut angler has spent the better part of a day fooling with dogfish instead of fishing productively for halibut.

Another problem with using bait—especially herring—in deep water is that you have some hard decisions to make if you miss a strike. A missed strike often means a lost bait, but not always, so when you reel back on the rod to set the hook into a halibut and the halibut isn't there, what do you do? Murphy's Law dictates that if you spend the next 20 minutes cranking your spreader bar and heavy sinker to the surface, your bait will be just fine and you'll have just wasted a lot of valuable fishing time and energy for nothing. If, on the other hand, you decide to take your chances and leave your rig down there, you'll probably discover upon finally retrieving your line that you've been fishing with bare hooks ever since the missed strike.

Jigging for Halibut

Using artificial lures will help solve both of these problems, and they're highly effective halibut-getters to boot. Halibut will happily take homemade pipe jigs, manufactured metal jigs, leadheads with plastic grubs or pork rind attached—almost any artificial offering that's heavy enough to reach bottom in the area you happen to be fishing. Dogfish, on the other hand, pretty much ignore these phony imitations of free-swimming protein. What's more, when you miss a halibut strike with an artificial, you simply keep jigging. There's no need to reel the lure up through 450 feet of water to check your bait, because there wasn't any bait to begin with.

As with the sinkers you tie to your wire spreaders, there's no magic-sized metal jig or leadhead that works for halibut. The right size is the one that will reach bottom, but don't overdo it. If you can reach bottom with a 10-ounce lure, don't wear your arm out jigging a 20-ouncer. Use a lure that's just heavy enough to get down to where the fish are, and no heavier.

Charters are available in many of Washington's most productive halibut-fishing areas, and fishing with a pro is certainly recommended to anyone thinking about trying halibut fishing for the first time. Not only do these folks know where the halibut are and how to catch them, but they also know how to deal with a barn-door fish once it's coaxed to the surface, not always an easy task when the fish in question weighs in at 75 pounds or more. They aren't all that big, of course, but if they are, you have to know what to do.

Tackle is included on most halibut charter trips, but serious halibut anglers have their own rods and reels. Typically the rod is a stiff-action five-and-a-half- to seven-footer, usually with a roller tip and often a roller stripper guide, both of which are a very good idea if you use braided Dacron line, as many halibut anglers do.

Braided line has little or no stretch, which can be especially advantageous when you're trying to set the hook into a halibut in several hundred feet of water. Braided Dacron, which is about the same diameter as monofilament of equal breaking strength, offers a real advantage, but the new super braids, made of space-age materials such as Spectra, seem to have been made with halibut fishing in mind. Not only are they low-stretch lines, but their extremely small diameter makes it possible to fish lighter jigs and lighter sinkers in deeper water, which makes a day of deep-water halibut fishing all that much easier. With these smaller-diameter lines, you can also get by using lighter rods and smaller reels.

As mentioned earlier, there are a few places in Washington where halibut may be found in less than 150 feet of water, and in these places you can get by using standard salmon tackle or even the rods and reels you might use for some freshwater species. Since the average halibut caught from our waters is a fish of 15 to 40 pounds, you don't necessarily have to use backbreaking rods, reels, and lines to land them. The heavy tackle often used in deep-water halibut fishing is meant to handle the needed terminal tackle, not the fish you might hook.

Landing Halibut

The battle with a halibut isn't over when you get the fish to the surface. In fact, depending on the size of the fish, your problems may just be starting when that big brown form materializes a few feet below the boat. These are strong fish that can inflict damage on you and your boat if you aren't careful about landing them. Even smaller fish should be dispatched quickly and handled carefully. Rap them several times sharply between the eyes, then cut a couple of gill arches to bleed them as quickly as possible, which takes some wind out of their sails and makes for better eating later. Halibut can also be controlled by looping a rope around their tail and (carefully) through the gills and mouth, then pulling the rope tight and drawing the halibut into a U.

More and more halibut anglers are using harpoons to deal with larger halibut at boatside, and it's a technique worth considering by anyone who fishes seriously for these big strong fish. The harpoon has a detachable head, and that pointed head has a line attached to it. When the harpoon is plunged through the middle of the halibut, the head pivots 90 degrees against the pressure of the line, so that it opens up on the far side of the fish and won't pull back through the hole. The halibut is now tethered on the harpoon line, and the opposite end of the line is tied to a large buoy, which goes overboard when the halibut is harpooned. A minute or two of fighting the buoy usually saps the last of the halibut's strength, and you can control and dispatch it. It's not quite as easy as it sounds, but you get the idea.

Many anglers shoot and/or sever the gill arches of big halibut (over 100 pounds) before attempting to boat them, or, better yet, kill them outside the boat, lash them securely alongside, and never bring them aboard.

Smaller halibut may be gaffed and brought aboard, depending on the size of your boat and the size of your fish box. Remember, though, that even a little 15-pounder can get downright nasty if left to flop around the deck out of control. Get 'em clubbed, cut, and controlled quickly or they'll make a mess and perhaps do some damage. It's important to give these big strong fish the respect they deserve.

Washington's Top Halibut Spots
Freshwater Bay, Hein Bank, La Push, Neah Bay, Northern Washington coast, Port Angeles, and Twin Rivers.

Rainbow Trout: Old Reliable

The first fish I ever caught was a rainbow trout. How about you? Ask any 10 Washington anglers about their earliest angling efforts, and chances are that eight or nine of them will describe some experience involving the ever-present rainbow. A survey of this state's anglers a few years ago showed that 80 percent of them fished for rainbows on a regular basis. They're stocked in and caught from more lakes and streams around here than any other fish, and their adaptability has made them a favorite not only here in their historic range in the Pacific Northwest, but throughout much of the world.

PAUL B. JOHNSON

RAINBOW TROUT

Native populations of rainbow trout in many parts of Washington were long ago depleted by eager trout enthusiasts, so much of the angling action they provide now is the result of stocking efforts by the state's Department of Fish and Wildlife. Millions of rainbows are stocked each year to keep the trout fisheries alive in several hundred Northwest lakes, reservoirs, rivers, and creeks.

Tackle, Tactics, and Tips
Judging by the wide variety of baits and lures used by successful anglers, one might think that the rainbow is some kind of omnivorous scavenger, but in its natural setting it feeds primarily on plankton and small aquatic and terrestrial insects. Given the opportunity, it might gladly gulp a white marshmallow, a small ball of cheese, a plump night crawler, a kernel of corn, a salmon

Sinkers add weight for casting and help to take baits and lures down to where the fish are, but even with sinkers it's possible to have too much of a good thing. Use only as much weight on your line as necessary; too heavy a sinker will take you down into the bottom rocks and snags, so you'll spend more time cussing and re-tying than smiling and catching fish.

State Record for Rainbow Trout

25.71 lb. . . . . Rufus Woods Lake 2002

If you're a photographer and an angler, be sure to always have a few of those empty 35 mm film canisters on hand. They're great for carrying small hooks, swivels, snaps, splitshot, flies, and other little tackle items. They're also airtight, so they'll keep matches dry. In a pinch, you can even snap off the lid, lay your line across the top of the canister, snap the lid back on and have yourself an emergency bobber!

egg, a wad of bread dough, a flashy spinner, a wobbling spoon, a plastic bass plug, a leadhead jig, an artificial fly, or any of dozens of other baits and lures an angler might throw its way, but these are only treats in the rainbow's varied diet. I once saw a kid catch a rainbow of nearly four pounds on a half-inch-thick piece of wiener that he bit off the end of the hot dog he was chomping on while he fished.

Rainbows are so widely available in Washington that it's possible to fish for—and catch—them 365 days a year. Where and when you fish, of course, may determine the angling technique that's most likely to pay off.

Fishing Rainbows in Lakes

In early spring, when the region's lakes and reservoirs are still cold, many anglers stillfish for their rainbows. On a sunny day, when the trout may be drawn to the warmer water near the surface, try suspending a garden worm, a salmon egg or two, a couple kernels of yellow corn, or some combination of these three baits beneath a small bobber. Attach the bobber four to seven feet up the line and fish the rig with little or no additional weight. Even dumb hatchery trout may be light, deliberate biters when the water is still cool and their metabolism is low, so you have to offer them a small meal and be on your toes for subtle strikes.

When even the surface temperatures are low, you may have to reverse your strategy and fish a bait on or near bottom. Lethargic, cold-water rainbows may lie near bottom and take little or no food but may bite if you make them an offer they can't refuse. That means floating a bait just off bottom rather than sus-

Trout anglers who use spinning tackle should always carry a few dry flies and a small bobber with them. When trout are rising for surface insects, you may not get them to bite on the spinners, spoons, or worms you're fishing with, but tie on a fly, add a bobber for casting weight, and you're ready for dry-fly fishing action that usually only fly rodders can enjoy.

pending it from the surface. Small marshmallows are a good bait for this kind of fishing because of their buoyancy, and some anglers will combine that little 'mallow with a salmon egg, kernel of corn, piece of worm, or small piece of cheese. Manufactured floating baits such as Berkley's Power Nuggets work the same way. To make doubly sure that a slow-moving rainbow takes your bait and doesn't get suspicious, use some kind of hollow slip-sinker to anchor it. By running your line through this slip-sinker and either keeping the bail open on your spinning reel or peeling two or three feet of line off your casting reel to provide slack, you decrease the chances of a fish feeling line tension and dropping the bait.

Slow-trolling may also pay off for early-season rainbows. A trout that refuses to chase down a fast-moving lure may be tempted by one that's just barely drifting by, but not all trolling lures are designed for this kind of slow-motion fishing. The blades of many spinners simply won't revolve at slow speed, and heavier wobbling spoons will just hang there and do nothing. Paper-thin spoons, flasher-and-worm combinations, even wet fly or streamer patterns pulled behind the boat may be your best options for this cool-water trolling.

As the water warms and the trout become more active, anglers in search of rainbows have more options available to them. The usual trolled goodies provide consistent catches, and energetic 'bows willingly gobble a wide range of natural and not-so-natural baits.

When spring turns to summer and the water temperature continues to climb beyond the rainbow's comfort level, it may be time to go deep once again. Find a spot well out of reach of the sun's blistering effects, and that's where you're likely to find the rainbow. If you know the whereabouts of cool-water springs or tributary streams, they're good places to fish during the warm months. Where legal, night fishing may be the ticket to success, or you may have to get on the water at sunrise and give up hope by 7 or 8 A.M.

Rainbows come to life again in the fall, as water temperatures drop and the fish go on a feeding spree that will help them put on a little fat for the upcoming winter. Many fly rodders think this is the best time of year to apply their techniques, especially during the first few hours and last few hours of the day, or whenever some kind of aquatic or terrestrial insect hatch takes place to spark trout activity.

If you think you have to give up on the rainbow trout during winter, guess again. Plenty of Washington lakes are open to year-round fishing, and patient anglers can do as well on the cooperative rainbow in January as they can in May. Many of the popular ice-fishing lakes of eastern Washington provide excellent rainbow trout fishing. Again, the key is to fish small baits, usually near bottom. Be alert for light strikes. When fishing artificials in open water during the winter, keep them small and keep them moving slowly. Although fair-weather anglers may not believe it, winter is a good time to fish wet flies and nymph imitations with that fly rod.

Fishing Rainbows in Streams

As for stream fishing, spring starts out with most Northwest rivers and creeks on the cool side, so you may have to work hard to coax rainbows into hitting. Since the streams may also be high and off-color from spring snowmelt, it's often a good time to fish worms and other natural baits that can be rolled slowly along the bottom.

As the streams warm in early summer, anglers enjoy some of their best fishing of the year for rainbows. This is also the time of year when hatchery plants are made in some rivers and creeks, greatly increasing angler success on many waters. The full range of baits, lures, and flies works during this time of year. Washington has special regulations on some streams that may not allow the use of bait, so be sure about the rules that apply to any streams you plan to fish for rainbows or other trout species.

Fishing gets tougher as stream levels drop and the water gets warmer and clearer. Mid-summer to mid-fall is a challenging time for trout anglers in many parts of the state, but those who are knowledgeable and patient manage to find productive fishing. The first rains of fall often spark a flurry of good stream trout fishing that frequently holds up until the season closes for winter or until the weather and water conditions simply become too brutal for most anglers.

For those who may not know, the average Northwest rainbow trout is a fish of perhaps 8 to 11 inches that weighs between half a pound and one pound. Rainbows of 15 to 20 inches, though, are caught throughout the year, and larger fish are certainly within the realm of possibility.

When talking about trophy-class trout, a rainbow subspecies called the Beardslee trout deserves some special mention. It's found only one place in the world: the clear, cold waters of the Olympic Peninsula's Lake Crescent. This unique trout grows to impressive size, often topping 10 pounds, and is usually caught by anglers who deep troll large spoons or plugs.

If you haven't yet gotten to know the rainbow trout, you haven't savored the true essence of freshwater fishing in the Northwest, so do it at your earliest convenience. Whenever and wherever you happen to read this, there are probably rainbows biting nearby.

Washington's Top Rainbow Trout Spots
Fishtrap Lake, Jameson Lake, Lake Scanewa, Mineral Lake, Silver Lake (Whatcom County), Spectacle Lake, Wenas Lake, West Medical Lake, Blue Lake (Grant County), Park Lake, and Rufus Woods Lake (trophy fish).

Largemouth Bass: America's Fish

Jay Wilcox had a pretty good reputation for knowing his way around eastern Washington's best bass fishing, so when he invited me to join him for a half-day trip to one of his favorite spots north of Spokane, I jumped at the chance. Early the next morning I found myself in the back of his high-powered bass boat, casting spinnerbaits around the edge of a big slough off the Pend Oreille River.

Nosing the bow of the big boat to within a few feet of a high bank, Wilcox pitched a black plastic salamander toward the wide

PAUL B. JOHNSON

LARGEMOUTH BASS

mouth of a dilapidated culvert. The little lizard imitation sank only about a foot before the line twitched sharply and Wilcox reared back on his light casting rod to set the hook. Within a minute he was displaying a hefty largemouth bass and a broad smile for my camera.

A second cast with a second plastic salamander drew a second bass strike for Wilcox. At perhaps four pounds, it was a little larger than the first, so another short photo session was in order.

"You give it a try," he said as I put my camera back in its case. "Just cast over there by that culvert."

He failed to tell me about the tangle of wire and rebar that lay hidden off to the left of the culvert, and my spinnerbait didn't travel a foot before becoming hopelessly ensnarled in the mess.

"We'd better just leave it there," my mentor suggested. "The water's only about two feet deep there, so we can get it later. Let's stay back and cast to the culvert a little more before getting too close." So I gave a sharp tug and snapped the line.

As I rummaged through a tackle box in search of anything resembling a plastic salamander, Wilcox made another cast to the culvert and within seconds was involved in another tug-of-war with a scrappy largemouth, this one even larger than the first two. By now I was too intent on retying my tackle to even bother dragging the camera out of its case.

My fishing companion was playing bass number four by the time I was ready to give it another try. My first cast hit the water right above the culvert entrance, and as it sank into the darkness, I felt a tap on the line, then another, and I set the hook. Somebody has to catch the smallest one, and it was apparently my day. The two-pounder provided several seconds of excitement before being coaxed away from the culvert and to the side of the boat.

"Want me to take your picture?" Wilcox asked. I didn't even look up as I unhooked what would normally have been a respectable bass.

Jay hooked and lost a big bass on his fifth cast, then coaxed a largemouth of perhaps five pounds to the boat three or four casts later. It was 15 minutes of the hottest bass fishing I've ever seen, as one of us enjoyed a week's worth of good largemouth fishing in maybe 10 casts.

The largemouth bass is perhaps America's most popular game fish, one that millions of anglers spend billions of hours fishing for each year. That popularity extends to Washington, where the largemouth isn't native but was introduced more than 100 years ago. After a slow start in this part of the world where salmon and trout have long been the main attractions, bass fishing is now a big deal in Washington.

It's easy to understand why largemouth bass fishing has a lot of followers. Ol' bucket mouth is just plain fun to fish for and even more fun to catch. It's a fish that will smash into almost any lure that comes within five feet of it when it's in the mood and nearly tear a fishing rod from the hands of an unsuspecting angler. But when it's not in the mood, it can be the most finicky, cagey, frustrating, and challenging fish that swims. The fun lies in never knowing for sure which personality you're going to encounter on a given day, next to a given stump, or with a given bass.

While the Northwest growing season for largemouths is shorter than in some parts of the country that produce lots of lunkers, anglers here do find their share of bragging-sized bass. A day's catch of bass in the half-pound to two-pound range may also include a three- or four-pound fish, and there are enough six-pound bass in Washington lakes, ponds, and reservoirs to make catching one a real possibility. Now and then someone makes news by catching one over eight pounds.

Tackle, Tactics, and Tips

The largemouth's adaptability is demonstrated by the kinds of places you may find it in Northwest lakes. Often caught from weedy, brushy tangles of vegetation, under lily pads, or around stumps and submerged trees or thick stands of cattails, it's also comfortable beneath overhanging trees or under man-made docks and floats. If none of these bass hiding spots is available, the largemouth can eke out a living around rocky points or submerged boulders.

The kind of habitat you find them in may dictate what lures and fishing techniques you use. Most bass anglers use casting rods and levelwind reels filled with 12- to 20-pound monofilament, but heavier or lighter tackle will get you by. While casting tackle is still prevalent, more and more spinning rods are showing up every season in the boats of serious bass anglers.

A good ol' worm is often the best bait of all, but it should look like a worm when it's in the water! A ball of meat wadded onto a hook doesn't look like a worm, so hook your bait no more than once or twice. You want the thing wiggling and looking as natural as possible.

Bass anglers use a wide range of artificial lures for largemouth bass. Spinnerbaits look like safety pins that have been bent open, with a weighted, skirted hook on one end, a spinner blade or two on the other, and the line attached to an eye in the middle. Depending on their size and design, spinnerbaits may work well at fast, moderate, or slow speeds. Because the hook points inward and is lined up directly behind the wire arm that runs to the spinner blade, this lure is relatively snagless, so it can be fished in thick weeds or brush without constantly hanging up.

Bass anglers also use a wide variety of plugs or hard baits, as they're often called. Some, known as crankbaits, may have large metal or plastic lips in front to catch water and make them dive as they're retrieved. Other plugs, with smaller lips or no lips on the front, are designed to be fished nearer the surface, either with a steady retrieve or in short jerks and jumps that draw the attention of any nearby bass.

Plastic lures such as the black salamanders mentioned earlier are also highly effective for largemouths. They come in many shapes and sizes, from one-inch grubs to 10-inch worm imitations. Fake frogs, lively lizards, creepy crawdads, and phony fish are all made of soft plastic these days, and you can buy them in any color you might imagine. Some, like Berkley's Power Baits, are impregnated with special scents and flavors that seem to convince bass they're eating the real thing. Plastics are often fished with a large, single hook and sliding sinker but may also be used with leadhead jigs or be totally unweighted.

Some of the most exciting largemouth bass fishing of all occurs when the fish are taken on surface lures, because the angler not only feels the fight but gets to see the start of it as a hungry bass boils to the top and pounces on the lure. Various plugs, poppers, and buzzbaits are used for this kind of fishing. All are designed to wiggle, dart, sputter, pop, gurgle, splash, or do all of the above to create a surface disturbance that might attract bass. This top-water bass action is most likely to occur early and late in the day.

Bass anglers spend much of their time fishing the shallows, casting as close as they can to fallen trees, brush piles, stumps, lily pads, coves, and pockets in the banks, rocky points, docks, pilings, and other likely looking bass haunts. These are the places where bass lie in wait for unsuspecting creatures to wander by within striking range. Bass aren't made for long pursuits, so they hide and wait, striking quickly when food—or a lure—is within range.

The types of hiding spots mentioned above protect bass from their predators and hide them from their prey, and they usually hug these places tightly. When fishing these spots, it's often necessary to cast accurately, laying your lure right up against the stumps, brush, and weeds without hitting them and snagging the lure.

The largemouth bass in most Washington lakes don't spend all of their time in the shallows along the shoreline. When the shallows get too warm or too cold, or when the midday sun makes it impossible for bass to find suitable cover in the shallows, they may seek out the comfort and safety of deeper water. Even when they move into what looks from the surface like wide-open water, they seek out drop-offs, submerged boulders and rock piles, underwater creek channels, sunken trees and stumps, springs, ledges, and humps that provide a break in what may be an otherwise smooth bottom. All of these variations in the bottom are known as structure, and structure fishing can be every bit as exciting and productive as fishing the shoreline cover. Many of these open-water fishing spots are too far from the shore to be fished by bank anglers, and serious structure anglers use contour maps and depthsounders to locate them.

Veteran bass anglers put a lot of thought, effort, and money into the pursuit of their favorite fish, but the largemouth can be caught and enjoyed just as well by the more budget-minded and casual angler. Chances are there's a lake or pond within easy driving range of your home that has plenty of largemouth bass.

And if you happen to locate a culvert that opens up into shallow water at the edge of that lake or pond, try casting black plastic salamanders toward it. You never know.

Washington's Top Largemouth Bass Spots

Eloika Lake, Lacamas Lake, Lake Sawyer, Lake Terrell, Potholes Reservoir, Silver Lake (Cowlitz County), Tanwax Lake, and Big Lake.

Smallmouth:
Washington's "Other" Bass

The popularity of bass fishing in general has grown in Washington just as it has throughout the rest of the country over the past 15 or 20 years, but the large-mouth has received most of the attention while the smallmouth has lived in relative obscurity. The largemouth grows to greater size, is much more abundant, and therefore gets most of the hype and the bulk of the fishing pressure.

SMALLMOUTH BASS

But an ever-growing group of western anglers is climbing aboard the smallmouth bandwagon, and the fish's popularity will no doubt continue to grow—for good reason. The smallmouth is above all else a fighter. Decades ago bass expert Dr. James A. Henshall wrote that the smallmouth black bass is "inch for inch and pound for pound, the gamest fish that swims," and that sentiment has been repeated, both orally and in print, thousands of times since. It fights with astonishing strength, and even a pan-sized smallmouth will jerk your string until you hoot and holler. When sheer muscle doesn't work, it may turn on the speed in its attempt to gain its freedom, or it may go airborne any number of times to throw the hook. As often as not it will use its strength, speed, and jumping ability, perhaps all at the same time. Quite simply, when it's hooked, a smallmouth will give all it has until the battle ends—one way or another.

While generally smaller than the largemouth, the bronzeback grows to unusually impressive proportions in this part of the country. The smallmouth records for most western states top six pounds, several states' records are over seven pounds, and a couple—California and Washington—boast state-record smallmouths of more than 8.5 pounds. The top smallmouth for California is a whopping nine-pound, one-ounce fish from Clair Engle Lake, while Washington's eight-pound, 12-ounce record fish came from the Hanford Reach section of the Columbia.

By comparison, the all-tackle world's record, as recognized by both the International Game Fish Association and the National Fresh Water Fishing Hall of Fame, is an 11-pound, 15-ounce monster from Kentucky's Dale Hollow Reservoir.

It should come as no surprise that western waters produce healthy small-mouth bass. The bronzeback likes cooler water than its largemouth cousin, does well in moving water, and flourishes in lakes and streams with rock and/or grav-el bottoms. Sound familiar? The fact is that Washington rivers and reservoirs are in many cases ideal habitat for smallmouths, and when stocked in the right spots, they've grown fast and reproduced well.

State Record for Smallmouth Bass

8.75 lb. . . . . Hanford Reach of the Columbia River 1966

By now you probably already know that neither the smallmouth nor the large-mouth bass is native to the western United States, and we won't spend a lot of time detailing exactly when and how they arrived at their various destinations out here, but most smallmouth transplants to this part of the country occurred between about 1875 and 1925. The ancestors of most smallies caught here arrived in metal milk cans after journeys of several days from back east, and the fact that any made it this far alive is a tribute to the fish's toughness.

Anyone interested in the story of just how bass, shad, catfish, and other exotic fish species came to the western states might want to find a copy of a fascinating book entitled *The Coming of the Pond Fishes*. It details how many of those first transplants were made, when, and by whom. And it's fun reading. The author is Ben Hur Lampman, whose name alone should be enough to inspire at least some reader interest.

Tackle, Tactics, and Tips

Although Washington produces its share of trophy-class smallmouths, a large majority of the smallies caught are in the half-pound to one-pound range, and in many places there are large numbers of even smaller fish. These little guys, however, seem every bit as aggressive as larger fish, and they'll usually pounce on virtually anything happening by that looks the least bit like a potential meal.

While providing a great deal of fun for the angler who takes them on ultralight tackle, large numbers of little smallmouths are often a tip-off to go looking elsewhere for large fish. Six-inch and 16-inch smallmouths aren't often found in the same places at the same time.

You may find smallmouth bass in and around a wide range of cover and structure, but areas with lots of rocks and hard bottoms are usually the best places to start looking. Slide areas with jumbles of broken rock provide excellent places for smallmouths to forage for one of their favorite foods, crayfish. Likewise, boulders of all sizes offer both food and cover for smallmouths. And don't overlook gravel or even sand flats where bass often hunt for sculpins and other small fish. Rocky points of any kind are almost sure to hold bronzebacks at one time or another.

Woody structure may not always hold smallmouths, but it's usually worth investigating. Some of Washington's lakes and reservoirs have submerged forests or at least stump fields beneath their surfaces, and such wood may provide excellent cover and forage for smallies.

Smallmouth bass are susceptible to a wide range of lures and fishing techniques, depending at least in part on what kind of structure you find them in, what they're feeding on, water and weather conditions, and your own preferences in bass fishing.

In relatively open water where the rocks aren't too grabby and the water isn't too shallow, crankbaits can be deadly on smallmouths. Many bass anglers prefer smaller offerings than those they might use for largemouths, but scaling down for smallmouths isn't always necessary or even advantageous. What does often seem to help is offering them something in a crawdad finish, since these little crustaceans do make up a good part of the smallmouth's diet. It's also beneficial most of the time to throw a crankbait that will wiggle and wobble along close to the bottom, so you'll have to carry a variety that includes shallow-, medium-, and deep-running lures.

While some anglers stick with crankbaits for most of their smallmouth fishing, others use the plugs only to locate fish, then settle in to fish via more subtle methods. "Subtle" means plastics to a large number of smallmouth anglers. Such offerings as a two- or three-inch grub fished on a one-sixteenth-ounce or one-eighth-ounce leadhead can be deadly when fished carefully around a submerged boulder pile or along the face of a rockslide. Likewise, a small plastic crawdad, fished Texas-style through a jumble of broken rock or over a cobble bottom, can be lethal. And today's smaller, livelier plastic worms, so popular in finesse fishing for largemouths, also work quite well for smallmouths, as do the hollow, tube-type plastic baits.

When smallmouths are acting finicky or simply feeding on minnows and other small fish, you may want to try ultra-finesse or minijigging for them. This is a technique I learned from bass guru Jeff Boyer several years ago, on a morning when standard methods were providing only modest results. Many western waters that hold smallmouths are also home to steelhead and one or more Pacific salmon species, and Boyer long ago reasoned that imitating a little salmon or steelhead fry might be an effective way to coax a hungry smallmouth. The lure that best represents an inch-long salmonid fry is an inch-long plastic mini-jig, the kind of lure long popular with crappie anglers and West Coast shad anglers. Pick a color such as white, gray, light green, or even blue, fish it on light line, and you're well on your way to fooling smallmouths that might have a taste for tiny salmon and steelhead.

When you can find smallmouths near the surface, get ready for some of the most exciting freshwater fishing you can hope to find anywhere. As you might expect, these bronze beauties that fight so hard and so long when hooked in deeper water can really put on a show when they're near the top. A two-and-a-half- or three-inch minnow-type lure, twitched slowly along the surface, will often draw explosive strikes when smallies are feeding shallow, and they'll tear up the water when you stick a hook in their lip.

All the techniques and lures mentioned so far will take smallmouths from both lakes and moving water, but river smallmouths seem especially responsive to yet another type of lure, and that's the spinner. Pitch one alongside a midstream rock, let it sink a second or two, then reel just fast enough to get the blade turning in the current and you're likely to entice a strong strike from any smallmouth that may be on the lookout for a quick meal. Spinner fishing allows the angler to cover a lot of good water quickly and effectively, and on our large Washington rivers that can pay off. Experiment with various spinner sizes and colors, but be sure that your arsenal includes at least a few lures with fur or feather tails. For whatever reason, smallies seem to prefer these to spinners with bare hooks.

Rods, reels, and lines that work for bass and trout fishing will do the job on most smallmouth waters. A good outfit for casting crankbaits or throwing surface plugs might be a medium-action casting rod, about five feet long, with a small-capacity levelwind spooled with about eight-pound monofilament.

If you aren't any good with a bait-caster, a six-foot spinning rod with a fairly stiff action will do the job, but you may have a little more trouble with line twist unless you add an in-line swivel.

A spinning rod and reel will also work fine for fishing leadheads or pitching spinners, and I'd suggest something in graphite, about 6.5 feet long, with a medium-light action. A cork handle on the rod will help in detecting strikes when you're using plastics. Equip the rod with a good spinning reel that has a smooth drag, and spool up with a fairly abrasion-resistant monofilament. You might carry two reels or at least two spools, one with four-pound line for fishing those little mini-jigs and small leadheads, and one with six-pound mono for most other situations.

Fly anglers needn't feel left out when it comes to taking a crack at the smallmouth. A wide range of streamers and bucktails, fished either on a floating line or a sink-tip, will take them, and when they're near the top they'll gulp many of the same poppers and hair flies that work for surface-feeding largemouths. If you've never experienced true angling excitement, hook a smallmouth on the surface. It's wild.

Washington's Top Smallmouth Bass Spots
Banks Lake, Okanogan River, Palmer Lake, Lake Roosevelt, Lake Sammamish, Snake River, Sprague Lake, and Potholes Reservoir.

Sturgeon: The Northwest's Hottest "New" Fishery?

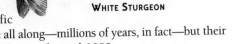

WHITE STURGEON

There's more than a little irony in the fact that sturgeon fishing is one of what you might call the newest, hottest sport fisheries in the Pacific Northwest. Sturgeon have been here all along—millions of years, in fact—but their popularity among anglers has soared since the mid-1980s.

The decline of salmon fishing in many areas and the desire of anglers to find something else to fill the void have no doubt played a part in the growth of the sturgeon's popularity, but there's more to it than that. Sturgeon fishing actually has a heck of a lot going for it.

Take, for example, the size of the fish itself. White sturgeon, the more common of the two species a Washington angler is likely to hook, grows to monstrous

BOB RACE

State Record for Sturgeon

No Record (All large sturgeon must be released)

proportions. Fish measuring six feet long and weighing 100 pounds are fairly common, and there's always the possibility of hooking a really big one, something in the seven-, eight-, even nine-foot class. Fishing just downstream of McNary Dam a couple of years ago, I thought I was pretty hot when I managed to subdue and release an 8.5-foot fish that would have tipped the scales at well over 300 pounds. Before that day was over, however, other members of our group released sturgeon measuring 9.5, 10, and 13.5 feet, reducing my catch to runt-of-the-litter status. If you like the possibility of hooking a freshwater fish that's bigger than you are, sturgeon fishing is your best bet, and the fish's huge size alone qualifies it for any list of Washington's 10 top sport fish as far as I'm concerned.

Although the sturgeon is a bottom-feeder that spends most of its time searching the rocks, sand, and mud for an easy meal, it can be a surprisingly spectacular fighter. When hooked, many of these piscatorial vacuum cleaners will take to the air, coming straight out of the water like a Polaris missile, twisting to one side and crashing back into the river with a resounding splash.

Not every hooked sturgeon will do one of these tarpon-on-steroids impersonations, but it happens often enough to keep it interesting, and it's most likely to happen with a larger fish of six feet or more. On a rainy May morning in 1993, while fishing with Columbia River guide Herb Fenwick, I had the good fortune of watching a white sturgeon over eight feet long jump more than a half dozen times before it was brought to the boat, unhooked, and released to fight again. Three of those jumps brought the big fish almost completely out of the water, and one of those was so close to the boat that we all got wet from the huge splash.

Another time, fishing immediately below Hells Canyon on the Snake River, several of us took turns playing a sturgeon of maybe eight feet. I wanted photos of jumping sturgeon, but as luck would have it, the only time the fish jumped was when I was manning the rod. Some members of the group got their jumping-sturgeon shots, but I didn't.

Besides being big and tough, the sturgeon is one of the Northwest's best eating fish, which certainly hasn't hurt its popularity. Cleaned properly, it's a gourmet's delight whether you bake, barbecue, broil, or smoke it, and a legal-sized sturgeon provides plenty of fresh fish to go around.

Speaking of legal size, there has long been what anglers call a slot limit in effect on sturgeon here in the Evergreen State. That means it's OK to keep fish between 42 inches and 66 inches long, but those under 42 and over 66 have to be released (except on the Upper Columbia River, where the minimum size is 48 inches). Fish under the minimum size are considered babies, while those over 66 inches tend to be mature adults needed for spawning.

While monster-sized sturgeon make for great photos, carrying around a wallet-sized snapshot of a lunker sturgeon to show your fishing buddies can get you into trouble in the Pacific Northwest these days. Not only is it illegal to possess a Columbia River sturgeon over six feet long, but it's also illegal to drag one of the oversized bottom-dwellers into the boat, shoot a few pictures to document the feat, and release the fish. Enforcement personnel with Washington's Department of Fish and Wildlife have publicly announced on more than one occasion that they will show little leniency in dealing with anglers who make big sturgeon say "cheese" before letting them go. Dragging oversized sturgeon onto the beach or into a boat for a short photo session can result in serious injury or even death to the fish, and that's what fisheries officials want to avoid. Sturgeon have no skeletal structure, and when removed from the water, all the fish's weight lies on its internal organs. Since the regulation calling for the release of all big sturgeon is aimed at protecting the large, mature fish needed for spawning, it's necessary that the big ones be released alive and uninjured. Boating or beaching a seven- or eight-footer weighing several hundred pounds could well mean the loss of millions of eggs needed to produce future generations, according to Fish and Wildlife biologists. The older a sturgeon gets, the greater its reproductive potential.

While we've talked only about the sturgeon fishery on the Columbia and Snake Rivers, other big Northwest river systems also have fishable numbers of these prehistoric lunkers. The Chehalis River comes immediately to mind and is probably the best sturgeon fishery outside the Columbia system.

Sturgeon also show up from time to time in other Northwest waterways, sometimes causing great surprise among local residents who at first think they may have a sea monster on their hands. Such a situation arose a few years ago in Seattle, when an 11-foot creature floated up from the depths of Lake Washington, shocking a few boaters and sending young swimmers scurrying for the beach. The monster was eventually identified as a white sturgeon, one that weighed an estimated 600 pounds and may have lived in the lake for upwards of 100 years.

As if to prove the big fish can live almost anywhere, Fish and Wildlife officials treating eastern Washington's Sprague Lake with rotenone to eliminate carp several years ago were surprised to see not one but two big sturgeon come floating to the surface a few hours after the chemical was applied. Since there's no direct link between the lake and any body of water with a known sturgeon population, biologists theorized that the fish were transplanted by humans, probably anglers who had been fishing the Columbia River, two hours away via I-90.

And there are lots more sturgeon legends circulating through the Northwest. I could tell you the one about the guy who hitched his plow horse to a big sturgeon in hopes of dragging it onto the banks of the Columbia, but instead the monster fish dragged the horse into the river, never to be seen again. But if I tell you that one, you might not want to go sturgeon fishing, so forget I even mentioned it.

Tackle, Tactics, and Tips

The Columbia River is the Northwest's top sturgeon producer. Where, when, and how you fish the big river is likely to determine whether you'll catch a lot of sublegal fish, fewer fish but most of them keepers, or even fewer fish but many of them whoppers over the 66-inch maximum legal size.

"It's really a cyclical thing," says Fenwick, who spends several months of the year targeting the big bottom fish. "There are, for example, lots of keepers in the lower river from February through April when the smelt are in the river, and smelt are the preferred bait."

When the smelt disappear in the late spring, however, smaller sturgeon tend to move into the Columbia estuary, where they forage on shrimp, anchovies, and other sources of food. About that same time the vast Columbia River shad runs begin, and that's prime time for hook-and-release fishing on lunker-sized sturgeon of six feet and larger.

I fished with Fenwick during one of those June lunker fests a few years ago and enjoyed a morning on the river I won't soon forget. Starting about 6:15 A.M., we hooked five fish in the seven- to eight-foot range, losing one after a short fight and releasing the other four after lengthy battles—and we were done fishing at noon. Whole shad were used for bait, so we didn't have any problems with little guys getting in the way.

Sometimes, though, especially when you're looking to catch a legal-sized keeper or two, it's best to fish small baits for these hefty fish. Former sturgeon guide Gary Waxbaum of Umatilla, Oregon, once demonstrated that point to me in graphic detail. As we rigged our sturgeon rods for a morning of fishing below McNary Dam, Waxbaum handed me one of his favorite sturgeon rigs, encouraging me to tie it to the end of my line. At first I thought he might be kidding, but his expression was one of absolute seriousness. The rig consisted of a large, brightly colored steelhead bobber on the line above a big single hook, and on the hook was threaded a small strip of belly meat from a salmon he had caught earlier in the summer. The triangular salmon strip was only about two inches long, and the entire bobber-and-bait combination was well under three inches.

"With their fantastic ability to sniff out a meal, sturgeon don't have any problem finding something this small, and I think the bright color of the bobber helps them see it, as well," Waxbaum explained. "And because the whole thing is so small, they can take it right in, and you hook them almost every time."

Later that morning, as we released our fourth sturgeon of the morning on four bites, I was convinced.

Most sturgeon anglers, though, still like bigger baits than the tiny strips of salmon belly favored by Waxbaum. The number one sturgeon bait around here is a whole smelt, usually fished upside down on a braided Dacron leader, so that the hook hangs out the mouth of the bait. A series of half-hitches around the smelt's body secures it to the leader. During late spring, when the shad are running in the Columbia, anglers use a monster-sized version of the same rig, hooking a whole shad upside down and half-hitching it to the leader. In both cases, a swivel is used to connect the braided leader to the main line, and a sliding sinker is threaded onto the main line above the swivel so that it can work its way up and down the line.

Your choice of rods and reels for sturgeon depends on the kind of fishing you do and where you do it. Bank anglers like heavy-action rods as long as 11 feet, which provide added casting leverage. Long casts aren't as vital to boat anglers, so they can get away with rods as short as seven feet. In both cases, though, the reels you use should be large enough to hold at least 200 yards of 30- to 80-pound line. Some bank casters like spinning rods and reels, but revolving-spool levelwinds are preferred by most sturgeon fishermen.

As you might guess, large sinkers are usually required to hold sturgeon baits down near the bottom. In calm water you might get away with a bell or pyramid sinker as light as three or four ounces, but be prepared for deep, heavy water with weights as large as 16 to 24 ounces.

Washington's Top Sturgeon Spots

Columbia River below Bonneville Dam, Columbia River below McNary Dam, Columbia River mouth, Lower Chehalis River, and Snake River.

Yellow Perch: Anytime Is Perch Time

The yellow perch is often overlooked, even scorned, by anglers in search of more glamorous game fish species, seldom getting the respect it deserves. This Rodney Dangerfield of freshwater, however, is a fish for all seasons, and unlike some of those fair-weather species, you can catch a bucketful of perch virtually any month of the year here in Washington. It's so abundant and caught in such great numbers by such a broad range of anglers with a broad range of angling skills that it rates among Washington's top 10 sport fish.

BOB RACE

YELLOW PERCH

The perch's abundance, in fact, is one of the things some anglers don't like about it. It's a highly adaptive and highly productive fish, and when conditions are right, it reproduces too fast for its own good and for the good of the lake or reservoir it inhabits. The result is a lake full of stunted perch too small to interest anglers and too numerous to allow any other fish species to compete. Even patient anglers fishing such a lake give up in frustration after catching 150 perch in two hours, not a one of them longer than five inches.

But show me a lake where the perch population is in balance with its food source and with the populations of other species, and I'll show you some fast fishing for perch big enough to provide worthwhile angling action and some of the best fish fillets you'll find anywhere.

Because of their cooperative nature, wide availability, and willingness to take something as basic as a worm on a hook, perch are perfect starter fish for youngsters or anyone else new to the sport of fishing. Kids like action, and they don't care if the fish they're catching are six inches or 16 inches long; finding a school of perch fits the bill perfectly. Keep that in mind when the fat rainbows aren't cooperating and your six-year-old has eaten the last candy bar. Perch will keep things interesting and help convert that little one into a young angler.

Tackle, Tactics, and Tips

One thing the successful perch angler soon learns is that perch of a certain size tend to hang out with others of the same size, so if you find a school of six-inch perch, it's a good idea to move on until you find larger ones. Most anglers prefer fish of at least eight inches, and 10-inch fish are more like it. Many of Washington's lakes boast populations of perch in the 12-inch class, and there are 15- and 16-inch perch out there to be caught.

Locating small perch is often easy, but finding larger ones more worthy of your angling efforts can be more difficult. Often the key to finding bigger ones lies in fishing deeper water. The little guys spend much of their time feeding in shallow water, and if you fish weed beds and shallow flats of 4 to 10 feet deep, the little guys are all you'll catch. Big perch are often found in 20 feet of water or more, and sometimes much deeper than that. I've caught them at depths of 40 feet while I was fishing bait on the lake bottom for rainbow trout, and my experiences certainly aren't unique.

The major exception to this big-perch/deep-water pattern is in the spring, when adult yellow perch move into the shallows to spawn. Fishing around shoreline weed patches or shallow-water docks and floats can pay big dividends then, and when perch are concentrated to spawn, it's possible to fill a five-gallon bucket with hefty fish from water as shallow as 5 to 10 feet.

But whether the perch are shallow or deep, certain time-proven baits, lures, and techniques always seem to coax them into biting. A plain old garden worm is probably America's all-time top perch-getter, one that's readily available from backyards and bait shops wherever perch are found. If there's any problem with using worms, it's that the juicy morsel often is quickly devoured by a hungry perch, resulting in deeply hooked fish. That's fine if all the biters are big enough to keep and fillet, but not so fine if they happen to be running a skinny five inches apiece. Small perch (or any fish) hooked somewhere south of the tonsils gets to be a messy hassle for an angler and is likely to be killed and wasted. Using large hooks such as size four or six bait holders reduces the problem, as does increasing the size of the worm on that hook, but it doesn't eliminate it completely.

That's why many perch anglers prefer to use artificial lures or bait/lure combinations. The fakes simply aren't as likely to be swallowed, so most of the perch are hooked in the lip, jaw, or roof of the mouth, making it much easier to unhook all fish and release the smaller ones unharmed.

If there's one all-around top artificial lure for yellow perch, it has to be the lead-head jig, adorned with either a plastic skirt, plastic curl-tail grub of some kind, or marabou feathers. One-sixteenth-ounce leadheads usually will do the job for shallow-water fishing on calm days, while one-eighth-ounce and sometimes three-sixteenths-ounce leadheads are better for deeper water and fishing on windy days when it's harder to get a lure down to where the fish are hiding. As for colors, a red-and-white combination is perhaps the all-time favorite among veteran perch enthusiasts, but yellow, chartreuse, black, and combinations of the three can also be effective. Adding a small piece of worm to the hook of any leadhead jig tends to enhance its popularity with yellow perch but isn't an absolute necessity.

When the perch are particularly deep, that's a good time to try vertical jigging for them with any of several styles of metal jigs. Crippled Herring, Hopkins No=EQL, and other so-called jigging spoons in weights of one-sixth to one-half ounce can be deadly on big perch in deep water. Again, adding a little meat to the hook in the form of a small piece of garden worm or strip of perch meat doesn't hurt your odds of drawing strikes. The various scents now available also seem to help.

Vertical jigging with the aforementioned jigs and other small, flashy lures, by the way, is a popular method for taking perch through the ice. Winter ice fishing for perch is a popular pastime December through February during a cold winter in eastern Washington. As in the summer, you're better off fishing near bottom if you want to catch the bigger perch, and if you don't find them in the first hole you chop or drill in the ice, move on to another one. Instead of a worm on the hooks, winter perch anglers often use a small strip of perch meat or the eye of a previously caught perch on the hook of their favorite jigging lure. Those are the most readily available baits, since worms are hard to find in the frozen ground of winter.

Like their big cousin the walleye, yellow perch are not spectacular fighters, so using ultralight rods, reels, and line allows you to get the most from every hooked fish. A four-foot rod weighing only a few ounces and a tiny reel spooled with two- to four-pound monofilament is what many would consider the perfect perch outfit.

Washington's Top Yellow Perch Spots
Lake Sawyer, Lake Washington, Lind Coulee Wasteway, Potholes Reservoir, Scooteney Reservoir, Silver Lake (Pierce County), Soda Lake, and Sprague Lake.

Lingcod: Beauty and the Beast Rolled into One

Some folks might consider the lingcod a homely cuss, but whoever coined the phrase, "Beauty is in the eye of the beholder," may have been a lingcod angler. This fish has a huge head, gaping mouth full of long, pointed teeth, wing-like pectoral fins, and a mottled gray-brown paint job that can't hold a candle to the chrome-sided beauty of a salmon.

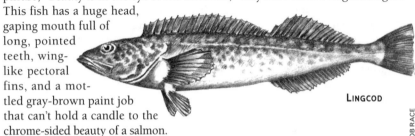

LINGCOD

BOB RACE

But—like your parents said when they were trying to coerce you into going out with the skinny, freckle-faced kid of the opposite sex who lived down the street—looks aren't everything. While the lingcod might have a kisser that would stop a clock, it has plenty to offer anglers. Even though it's not as plentiful as it used to be, the big, tough, nasty lingcod has to rank in the top 10 among Washington's sport fish.

For one thing, lingcod grow to impressive size. Fish of 40 pounds and over are fairly common, especially in the northern half of their range, which extends from Baja California to the Bering Sea. Fish of 50 pounds or better are caught regularly enough to keep things interesting, and now and then they even top 60 pounds; the current International Game Fish Association all-tackle world's record is a 64-pound monster from the Elfin Cove area of Southeast Alaska. Lingcod exceeding 70, even 80 pounds have been reported by anglers but not documented by the IGFA or state fish and game record keepers.

As for fighting ability, a hooked lingcod won't make any blazing, 100-yard runs or come twisting out of the water in a series of spectacular leaps, but it will give you a run for your money. Typically an angler who sets the hooks into a big ling will have little trouble pumping it those first few yards, but just when he thinks he has the battle won, his prize will turn tail, streak for the bottom with amazing speed, and duck into some jumble of broken rocks or deep-sea cavern, where it quickly saws off the line and is free.

Tackle, Tactics, and Tips

The pugnacious lingcod can also be incredibly aggressive and easy to entice. When it decides it's hungry, it will pounce on virtually anything even remotely resembling a free meal, including a wide range of baits and lures. More than one ling has been known to inhale a multihook pipe jig or other metallic phony, fight for a minute or two, come unhooked, and immediately grab the lure again. Any fish that willing to cooperate has to be a favorite of anglers.

But as you might expect with any big, hard-fighting, sweet-eating fish, lots of other anglers are at least as interested in catching lingcod as you might be, and some of them are pretty good at it. There are a few tricks to catching big lingcod, and, if you master them, you'll improve your chances of boating these trophy bottom fish.

Timing

Timing can be everything to the lingcod angler, and we're talking here both about what time of year and what time of day you fish for them.

Lingcod spawn in winter, with the larger females moving up out of the depths to deposit their eggs in the relatively shallow waters of submerged rock piles and rocky pinnacles. The large egg masses are then fertilized by male lings, which hang around to protect them until they hatch. Although the females don't help out with the egg-guarding chores, they don't seem to be in any big hurry to get back to their deep-water haunts, often staying and feeding in the shallower spawning areas for weeks, even months.

The fact that both males and females are to be found somewhat congregated well into spring should be a valuable tip for lingcod anglers. It's a whole lot easier to catch lings when they're fairly well concentrated, and it's certainly easier to fish for them in 75 to 150 feet of water than in 250, 300, or 400 feet of water or more.

Catching the shallow-water lingcod of late winter and early spring requires lighter sinkers and lighter lures, which means you can fish lighter lines, rods, and reels and enjoy their fighting ability that much more. There's also less of a problem with line stretch when you're trying to set the hooks into those toothy lingcod jaws and when you need to feel your way over the rocky bottom with your bait or lure. Quite simply, it's much easier and a great deal more effective to fish for lingcod when they're shallow, as most of them are in the spring.

While springtime fishing for lingcod is some of the year's best, it's important to point out that not all lingcod areas are open to fishing in early spring. Seasonal closures extend into April or May in some places—primarily to protect nest-guarding males and the eggs they're watching over—so be sure to study the fishing regulations before planning that spring ling fling.

The other timing factor involved in lingcod fishing concerns the daily tidal change. Even in shallow water it may be difficult to fish effectively when the tide is snorting along at several knots, so smart lingcod anglers concentrate most of their efforts during high and low slack or on days of moderate tidal flow.

That's when you can best hold directly above those rocky pinnacles and fish them with a minimum of hang-ups and lost lures. Also, lingcod often bite best during minimum tidal flow.

The Search

In order to catch these shallow-water lingcod, of course, you have to find them, and the two most important pieces of equipment in that search are a good chart of the fishing area and a depthsounder. The rocky spires and steep-sided cliffs where lings are most likely to be hanging out will show on a chart as lots of contour lines in close proximity.

Of course, spotting those rocky underwater hillsides that hold lings is easy on a chart, not so easy out on open water. You have to know how to read your compass, line up landmarks, and chart a course accurately to locate them, even though sometimes other boats in the area may make the job much easier. Once you get in the general area, though, you have to watch your depthsounder and concentrate your efforts on the rocky humps and drop-offs where lings are most likely to be.

Tackle and Technique

There's more than one way to catch a trophy ling, and you often have the choice of fishing artificials or bait. Metal jigs, both the real-looking, store-bought slab types and the not-so-perfect pipe jigs you can make at home, are effective lingcod-getters. Like most other big fish, the lingcod's diet consists mostly of smaller fish, and these hunks of metal in various shapes and sizes often look enough like the real thing to coax a lingcod into striking. They're available in weights from under an ounce to over two pounds. Leadheads also account for a lot of Washington lingcod. Most anglers adorn them with large, plastic, curl-tail bodies, but a strip of pork rind is just as effective and usually holds up better to those jagged lingcod teeth. Black, brown, blue, and purple tend to work better than the hot or light colors. Deep-water jigging may require 20- to 32-ounce leadheads, but light-line anglers fishing shallow water in calm tides may get by using jigs as light as a couple of ounces.

There are times when lingcod aren't all that interested in artificials, and that's when you have to go to the real thing to bring them to the dinner table. Dead bait such as whole herring will often do the job, but if you really want to get them interested, you may have to offer them something that's still alive and kicking. It could be a large herring if it's available, or maybe you'll have to first catch a few greenling, rockfish, shiner perch, or other small fish for bait, and then start fishing lingcod. Of all these smaller fish that will do the job as lingcod bait, the greenling is perhaps the best. Averaging about 12 inches long, it's just bite-sized for a husky ling, and it doesn't have all the sharp spines you'll find on rockfish and some other species, so it's easy to handle and easy for a lingcod to swallow. What's more, greenling are easy to find and catch from shallow-water kelp patches and rock piles, and they're hardy enough to stay alive several hours in an aerated live-well or five-gallon pail of water.

Most anglers fish live bait on a wire spreader, snapping on cannonball weights of various sizes to take it to the bottom and using a short, stout leader between the bait and the horizontal arm of the spreader. Some people prefer wire leaders, but 40- to 60-pound monofilament usually works just fine.

Hook size for live-bait lingcod fishing should be at least 6/0, and 8/0 to 10/0 hooks are usually even better. With small baits, such as herring or shiner perch, you can get by with one hook, simply hooking the bait fish through both lips or near the middle of the back. A two-hook rig works better with big baits, such as foot-long greenling or rockfish. Tie the hooks in tandem, at least a foot apart, and run the first one through both lips of the bait fish. The second hook goes under the skin an inch or two in front of the tail. Lingcod may take a bait fish headfirst, tail first, or crossways, and with the two-hook rig you always have at least one point at the right end of the bait. Keep your lingcod hooks razor sharp to get maximum penetration into those hard, toothy jaws.

You want to keep the bait fish swimming just off bottom, which isn't always easy when you're trying to work those jagged rock piles that lingcod seem to love. Watching your depthsounder at all times helps, but you'll also have to drop and retrieve line constantly to follow those rugged bottom contours. Don't simply let the sinker drag bottom all the time; if you do you'll be hung up constantly, either from the sinker lodging in the rocks or because the bait fish will find a little hiding spot and dodge into it.

When jigging artificials, of course, you'll want to set the hooks as soon as you feel anything a bit unusual, but not with live bait. While lings sometimes simply gulp the bait and hook themselves, you'll usually want to give them a couple of seconds to take it down before hitting them. Some anglers don't use the rod to set hooks at all, but simply point the rod toward the water and reel as fast as they can for several seconds. Lingcod often hang onto a bait whether they're hooked or not, and they'll clamp down even harder if they feel it pulling away. This fast-reeling strategy also gets the lingcod away from the bottom faster, giving them less chance to turn back into the rocks and lodge in some crevice from which you'll never remove them.

When playing and trying to boat a bait-hooked lingcod, always remember that it may not be hooked but simply holding onto the bait fish. Pump the fish up to the surface as smoothly as possible, and be ready with a net or gaff when it gets to the top. They'll often let go right at the surface, so stick 'em or scoop 'em an instant before they break water if possible.

If the lingcod is bound for the dining table, smack it once across the eyes with your fish club and quickly slice through a couple of gill arches to bleed it. The table quality of those fillets will be much better that way.

But don't assume for a minute that the only good lingcod is a dead lingcod. All trophy-sized lings are females, and these are also the brood fish that will provide the fisheries in years and decades to come. These fish are tough and have no swim bladder, which means they can be fought, boated, photographed, and released with few ill effects, so if you find good fishing for big lingcod, release a few for next time.

The importance of catch-and-release fishing for lings hasn't become apparent until recent years, and in some Washington waters the ling populations have declined from over fishing. Seasons and limits have become quite restrictive on the inside waters of Puget Sound, the San Juan Islands, and the Strait of Juan de Fuca. Even the once wide-open lingcod fisheries along our coast have had the clamps put on them, so be sure to check the angling regulations before venturing out in search of lings these days.

Selection of rods, reels, and line for lingcod depends a lot on how much fun you want to have with each fish and the kind of fishing you're most likely to do. You may want to go with a fairly stout boat rod, low-geared reel, and 50-pound monofilament or braided Dacron if you plan to fish a lot of live bait/spreader rigs in deeper water. If, on the other hand, you want to really have a good time, maybe set an IGFA line-class record, and fish shallow water, try something like your favorite freshwater flipping rod and a levelwind reel loaded with 10- to 20-pound mono. Such tackle handles small- to medium-weight jigs quite well in water of 75 to 150 feet deep. When fishing lingcod on such light line, however, remember to use a heavy two- or three-foot shock leader between your line and your bait or lure. Running light monofilament directly to the hook is a bad idea, because it simply won't hold up to the rocky bottom and those daggerlike teeth.

Armed with this basic information, you're ready to go lingcod fishing. But remember, I warned you that they're ugly, so if you have nightmares after catching your first one, don't blame me.

Washington's Top Lingcod Spots
La Push, Middle Bank (east end of the Strait of Juan de Fuca), Neah Bay, Port Angeles Rock Pile, beneath the Tacoma Narrows Bridge, and Westport.

Honorable Mention

Freshwater
Cutthroat Trout
Sea-run, coastal, west-slope, and the unique Lake Crescent cutthroat all are available to western Washington anglers, while eastsiders can fish for native cutts or transplanted Lahontan cutthroat. Most are cooperative biters that will take a wide range of baits, artificial lures, and flies. Their willingness to bite and severe losses of suitable habitat have led to declining cutthroat fisheries in some of Washington's formerly hot fishing spots. The sea-run variety of coastal cutthroat has been especially hard hit, so restrictive angling regulations, including wild-cutthroat release and no-bait rules, are in place on some streams.

Fanny packs make great tackle totes for on-the-go anglers. In fact, some tackle companies have realized this and designed fanny-pack-style bags and boxes just for anglers. Keeping your tackle and other equipment on your hip allows hands-free fishing and out-of-the-way tackle storage all in one.

State Record Cutthroat
Sea-run: 6.0 lb., Carr Inlet, 1943
Lake Crescent: 12.0 lb., Lake Crescent, 1961
Lahontan: 18.04 lb., Omak Lake, 1993
West-slope: 1.44 lb., Half Moon Lake, 2000

Cutthroat Tackle, Tactics, and Tips
Resident and sea-run coastal cutts, as well as the west-slope variety, can be whipped quite easily with moderately light tackle, so your six- to seven-foot, medium-light to medium action spinning rod will work just fine. Match it to a spinning reel that will hold 100 to 150 yards of four- to eight-pound monofilament, and you're in business. Coastal and west-slope cutthroat love natural baits, and the best bait of all is a nightcrawler or large garden worm on a size 4, 6, or 8 bait hook. Small wobbling spoons and spinners in silver, gold, brass, red, fluorescent orange, or combinations of these colors also are effective. Fly anglers can take these fish on a variety of wet patterns and nymphs worked around submerged stumps, root wads, sunken trees, and other woody structure with a 4- to 6-weight fly rod and floating or sink-tip line.

To keep your tackle boxes and coolers from sliding all over the boat, use Velcro. A short strip across each end of boxes and coolers, with corresponding strips in the appropriate places on the boat floor, should do the job.

Lahontan and Lake Crescent cutthroat run larger and may require slightly heavier tackle. Both of these larger cutthroat species feed on minnows, sculpins, and crawfish, so trolling with wobbling spoons or diving plugs that resemble these creatures is highly effective. Use a seven- to eight-foot, medium-heavy to heavy action rod for this kind of trolling, and equip it with a levelwind reel large enough to hold at least 150 yards of 8- to 15-pound monofilament or small-diameter braided line.

When the fish are holding at depths of 20 feet or more, you may need a downrigger to take your spoon or plug into the strike zone. In the spring and fall, or when they're found in shallow lakes, Lahontan cutts may be taken on artifical flies. A 6- or 7-weight floating line, five-foot leader, and various wet fly patterns can be deadly for this kind of fishing. My favorite Lahontan fly is a brown Carey Special with peacock body, but maybe you have another favorite pattern that will do the job.

Washington's Top Cutthroat Waters
Omak Lake (Lahontans), Grimes Lake (Lahontans), Lake Lenore (Lahontans), Stillaguamish River system and estuary (sea-runs), Grays Harbor estuary (sea-runs), lower Wynoochee River (sea-runs), lower Hoh River (sea-runs), Amber Lake (west-slope cutts), and Badger Lake (west-slope cutts).

Brown Trout
Although not native to Washington, browns are being stocked in more and more lakes to provide added angling opportunities through the summer and fall. As

they do in their native locales, brown trout stocked in Washington often grow to impressive size. Some eastern Washington lakes and streams have had browns in them for decades, and these waters sometimes give up trophy-class fish of 10 pounds or more. A typical Washington brown trout, though, is a 10- to 16-inch stocked within the past year.

State Record Brown Trout
22.0 lb., Sullivan Lake, 1965

Tackle, Tactics, and Tips
You can catch recently stocked hatchery browns on any of your favorite wobbling spoons, weighted spinners, and small diving plugs, or even on a juicy worm trolled behind a string of gang trolls. Bragging-size browns, however, require lures in bigger bites and heavier, more sophisticated tackle and techniques. Trolling with artificials that imitate the smaller fish on which big browns feed is most effective. I like Rapalas, K12 to K14 Kwikfish, size 3 and 4 J-Plugs, and the 2-ounce or 2.25-ounce Krocodile for this kind of trophy-trout trolling. Use your depthsounder to locate fish, and, if necessary, employ a downrigger to reach them. You'll need a 7.5- to 8.5-foot rod of medium to medium-heavy action to troll this way, and I prefer a levelwind reel that will hold 150 to 200 yards of monofilament or small-diameter braided line. Braided line is better when trolling at substantial depths or trailing a lot of line behind a downrigger in clear water. I prefer glass rods over graphite when using downriggers, and my favorite combination for this type of trolling is Fenwick's Fenglass DR 82C downrigger casting rod and Abu Garcia 5600C4 or 5500C3 casting reel. Those reels are filled with 20-pound Spiderwire, 20-pound Fireline, or 10- to 15-pound Trilene Big Game monofilament.

Washington's Top Brown Trout Waters
Fish Lake (Chelan County), Wenas Lake, Dry Falls Lake, Merrill Lake, Swofford Pond, Crab Creek, and Blue Lake (Okanogan County).

Brook Trout
A char rather than an actual trout, the brookie is abundant in many north-central and far-eastern Washington lakes and streams. Where you find one you'll often find lots of them, although catching one larger than 10 inches may be difficult. Brookies are commonly found in ponds and smaller lakes throughout eastern Washington and in the higher lakes of the Cascades, but a few west-side lakes are also stocked with these brightly spotted salmonids.

State Record Brook Trout
9.0 lb., Wobbly Lake, 1988

Tackle, Tactics, and Tips
Most brookies are easy to catch on small Super Dupers, red-and-white size 0

Mepps spinners, K4 and K5 Kwikfish, bobber-and-worm rigs, and dry flies tied on a size 10 to size 14 hook. Best weapons for casting these brookie-getters are a six-foot, medium-light action spinning rod and four-pound monofilament. If you use a bobber, this outfit will even throw the dry flies far enough to catch fish. Brookies like shallow water, so you can often catch them from the bank, and as often as not you'll see them strike if you're paying attention. Stay low and use shoreline cover to your advantage to keep from spooking them.

Washington's Top Brook Trout Waters
Fish Lake (Spokane County), Fish Lake (Kittitas County), Hyas Lake, Lost Lake (Kittitas County), Okanogan County high-country lakes, Sacheen Lake, Bayley Lake, Deer Lake (Spokane County), and Leech Lake.

Lake Trout
Another char, this big transplant is most commonly called a Mackinaw by western anglers. It grows to more than 30 pounds in Washington and is found in a handful of central and eastern Washington lakes, where it feeds primarily on kokanee, squawfish, suckers, and other small fish. The biggest "trout" caught from Evergreen State lakes on opening day of the spring fishing season usually is a Mackinaw. Lake trout require clean, cold water, so they move deeper as the lakes warm in spring and early summer.

State Record Lake Trout
35.44 lb., Lake Chelan, 2001

Tackle, Tactics, and Tips
A typical Northwest lake trout will run 4 to 10 pounds, so leave the ultralight trout rods at home. Trolling is the best way to catch them early in the spring, when surface water temperatures are still in the 42- to 50-degree range. That's when you can catch them within 20 feet of the top, especially during the first few hours of daylight. Later in spring—or even later in the morning—as the water warms, lake trout move deeper into the water column, and it's time to get the downriggers working. With 'riggers, it's possible to catch these cold-water denizens all summer from some lakes. Plug-cut or whole herring will catch them, but artificials are easier to fish; the old Lucky Louie plugs, Luhr Jensen's J-Plug, and the Ross Swimmer Tail are favorites.

Another effective deep-water tactic for lake trout is vertical jigging. The Crippled Herring, Point Wilson Dart, Mooch-A-Jig, and Krocodile jigging spoon in weights of one to three ounces will drop quickly to whatever depth the lakers are holding, but you have to keep the jig moving up and down for this technique to work. And it's important to keep hook points needle sharp and set the hook at any indication of a strike.

Fenwick's E-Glass Triggerstik FS 85C and Downrigger Casting DR 82C rods are perfect weapons for Mackinaw trolling, but you need something with more backbone for jigging, like Berkley's Air IM7 A92-7-9HB or IM7 A92-8-6H. A good levelwind reel that will hold 150 to 200 yards of line will work with any of these rods. As for line, you can get by with monofilament for shallow-water trolling early in the spring, but for trolling or jigging deep you'll need one of the small-diameter super braids, like Spiderwire or Fireline, in 20- to 30-pound test.

Washington's Top Lake Trout Waters
Lake Chelan, Loon Lake, Deer Lake, Bead Lake, Bonaparte Lake, and Lake Cle Elum.

Bull Trout/Dolly Varden
Populations of these two closely related chars have been drastically reduced by habitat loss and overfishing, so most Washington waters are closed to the taking of either. Check the fishing pamphlet closely, both for exceptions to this closure regulation and for illustrations so you'll know one if you should catch it.

State Record Bull Trout/Dolly Varden
Bull Trout: 22.5 lb., Tieton River, 1961
Dolly Varden: 10 lb., 15 oz., Whitechuck River, 1999

Tackle, Tactics, and Tips
Since bull trout are currently off-limits to Washington anglers, there's no need to talk about how to catch them, except to say that if you do stumble into one, release it unharmed as quickly as possible. Several northern Puget Sound rivers, though, are open to Dolly Varden fishing. Most of these rivers have a 20-inch minimum size limit on Dollies, so you might as well fish them as you would fish for river steelhead, with eight- to nine-foot drift rods and spinning or casting reels large enough to hold at least 150 yards of 8- to 15-pound monofilament. These fish will take half-ounce to three-quarter-ounce wobbling spoons in silver or brass finishes, size 3 or 4 Mepps Aglia or Metric spinners, a cluster of fresh salmon or steelhead roe, or a big nightcrawler rolled along the river bottom.

Washington's Top Bull Trout/Dolly Varden Waters
Skagit River, Skykomish River, Sauk River, Suiattle River, and Whitechuck River.

Kokanee
This landlocked sockeye salmon is a favorite of anglers and fish gourmets alike. Also known as a silver trout, it's found in many Washington lakes, some of which have bonus limits allowing anglers to catch a limit of kokanee in addition to a limit of rainbows or other trout. Washington kokanee average only about 10 or 11 inches, but their excellent table quality makes them a favorite of freshwater anglers.

State Record Kokanee
5.47 lb., Lake Roosevelt, 1993

Tackle, Tactics, and Tips

Trolling, stillfishing, and jigging all are effective fishing methods for kokanee around here. A seven-foot, medium-action rod and small-capacity levelwind reel loaded with six- to eight-pound monofilament for jigging or 10-pound mono for trolling are about right. For stillfishing, use your favorite six- to seven-foot light spinning rod and four- to six-pound line. Most trollers use strings of trolling blades ahead of brightly colored spoons or spinners with plenty of silver, red, and orange somewhere in their finish. Because of the kokanee's soft mouth, it's a good idea to use a short, rubber "snubber" between the trolling blades and the lure to absorb the shock of the strike. Stillfishermen often employ size 8 to 12 "glow" hooks that have a dab of luminescent paint on them for added visibility, and they bait those hooks with maggots, shoe-peg corn, or small pieces of worm. Jigging works well when you locate a large school of kokanee; just drop a quarter-ounce to one-ounce jig (depending on how deep you have to get) and work it up and down through the school. A white or gold half-ounce Crippled Herring is my favorite for this kind of fishing, and it hasn't failed me yet.

Washington's Top Kokanee Waters

Rimrock Lake, Loon Lake, Lake Keechelus, Lake Kachess, Horseshoe Lake (Pend Oreille County), Lake Cle Elum, Lake Chelan, Chapman Lake, Bumping Lake, Clear Lake (Pierce County), Lake Stevens, and Yale Reservoir.

Atlantic Salmon

This immigrant from the far side of the country has been released into Washington waters both by design and by accident. Fish managers from the old State Department of Game stocked Atlantics in several Washington lakes during the 1960s in an attempt to provide something new for Northwest anglers to catch. More recently, commercial fish farmers in several Puget Sound locations have seen large numbers of these same fish escape, sometimes by the hundreds of thousands. These later, accidental "stock-ing" projects, of course, were much more effective at providing angling opportunity than the earlier efforts. For a year or so after the last major Atlantic salmon escape, anglers were finding these fish all over Puget Sound and in several of its major tributaries. This bonus fishing opportunity was exciting for anglers, but it made fish managers more than a little nervous. So far, it looks like Atlantics haven't established themselves in any Washington river systems, but it's still fairly common to catch one of these non-native salmon in Puget Sound and, less frequently, in one of the major river systems that feed the sound. Anglers who catch these accidental tourists of the salmonid world are encouraged to kill and eat them; there are no limits, closed seasons, or other restrictions on the taking of Atlantic salmon in Washington.

State Record Atlantic Salmon

Landlocked: 8.96 lb., Goat Lake (Jefferson County), 1992
Sea-run: 14.38 lb., Green River, 1999

Tackle, Tactics, and Tips
Few, if any, anglers target Atlantic salmon, and those that are caught are usually taken by standard saltwater salmon-fishing or river steelheading methods. I've caught them while I was jigging for chinook salmon, and friends have taken them on spoons, spinners, and roe clusters in the Green, Puyallup, Nisqually, and other Puget Sound steelhead rivers. Don't go out and buy any special Atlantic salmon tackle, at least not unless you hear about another net-pen escape caper.

Washington's Top Atlantic Salmon Waters
Puget Sound, Green and Puyallup Rivers (net-pen escapees), and a handful of high-country lakes that will go unnamed.

Mountain Whitefish
Found in rivers throughout the state, this silvery, foot-long fish is most readily available during the winter, when large numbers of them congregate for spawning. Although they're shaped like a trout, they're easily identifiable by their large, shiny scales, and tiny, pointed mouth.

State Record Mountain Whitefish
5 lb., 2 oz., Columbia River, 1983

Tackle, Tactics, and Tips
Whatever you use to catch these fish, make it small. Their tiny mouth makes it nearly impossible to inhale anything much bigger than a small insect. Standard whitefish baits include maggots and stonefly larvae (most commonly referred to as hellgrammites). These are usually fished on size 10 to 14, short-shanked hooks at the end of a two- or three-pound leader. Some anglers roll the bait along the bottom with the aid of a splitshot or two; others prefer suspending the bait beneath a small bobber. A 6- or 6.5-foot spinning rod with light to medium action works well for both techniques. Fly-fishing 4- to 6-weight rod and sink-tip line is also effective, but remember to keep the flies very small and sparsely tied. Fishing is best in winter, when mountain whitefish congregate in deeper pools, sometimes by the hundreds. If you don't find fish in a likely looking spot, keep moving until you locate a school. If the weather is clear, you'll often see them "flashing" as their scales reflect the sun while they search the bottom for food.

Stream trout and whitefish will almost always take a stone fly nymph rolled along the bottom, but these inch-long insects are difficult to find and catch on the bottom of a chilly stream. To make the job easier, use a three-foot by three-foot piece of fine-wire screen (like from an old screen door). Stand with your back to the current, holding the screen downstream, and kick rocks loose from the bottom with your feet. The hellgrammites will be dislodged and washed into the screen for easy capture.

Washington's Top Mountain Whitefish Waters
Green River upstream from Auburn, Cle Elum River, Columbia River between Vernita and Tri Cities, Kettle River, Methow River, Naches River, Wenatchee River, and Yakima River.

Lake Whitefish

This inhabitant of larger Columbia Basin lakes and reservoirs grows to three or four pounds and may be found in large schools. Try small wobbling spoons for them. Unlike the smaller mountain whitefish, the lake variety was brought to the Northwest from the Midwest several decades ago. Its limited availability here makes it much less popular than in its native range. Big pots of boiled fish and vegetables are a staple in parts of the upper Midwest, and lake whitefish usually are the main ingredient. If you've never eaten boiled fish, take my word for it— we're lucky that tradition didn't come here with the whitefish!

State Record Lake Whitefish
6.63 lb., Lake Roosevelt, 1997

Tackle, Tactics, and Tips
A few hardy anglers catch these fish through the ice, usually working metal jigs or heavy wobbling spoons up and down near the bottom in the depths where whitefish congregate when the water is cold. It's much easier to catch them in the early spring, when they move into the shallows for few weeks. Casting or jigging with a Hopkins NO=EQL, Luhr Jensen Krocodile or Crippled Herring jig in a silver or chrome finish works best and can be accomplished with a 6.5- to 7-foot medium action spinning or casting rod and reel loaded with six- or eight-pound monofilament. Whitefish often come close enough to shore for bank anglers to reach them, but a boat makes it much easier to search out and locate striking fish.

Washington's Top Lake Whitefish Waters
Lake Roosevelt, Banks Lake, Soda Lake, and Potholes Reservoir.

Walleyes

This Midwestern transplant was illegally stocked in the Columbia River system in the 1960s, and now it's a favorite of anglers from the Canadian border to Portland. Walleyes grow to impressive size and provide outstanding table fare. Over the past two decades the waters of the Columbia system have gained a reputation as trophy walleye waters, giving up lunker fish in the 15- to 20-pound range fairly often. A close relative of the yellow perch, the walleye can be identified by its generally green and gold color, its large, reflective eyes, and the white spots at the bottom of the tail and tips of the pelvic fins.

State Record Walleye
18.76 lb., Columbia River, 1990

Tackle, Tactics, and Tips
Trolling and jigging account for most Washington walleyes. Standard trolling gear includes in-line spinner rigs with two hooks tied about three inches apart and

laced with a whole nightcrawler. Hook the crawler so that it hangs perfectly straight and doesn't roll in the water, and use enough weight three to four feet above the spinner so that it stays close to the bottom at all times. An alternative to the spinner-and-worm rig is a deep-diving plug that imitates the small perch, trout, and other fish on which walleyes often feed. Again, the plug must dive deep enough to reach bottom. A medium to medium-heavy casting rod in the seven-foot range, with a long butt, is a good choice for walleye trolling. Fenwick's HMX T70MH Triggerstik and Berkley's LPC701M or LPC701MH Lightning Rods are good examples. Match any of these with an Abu Garcia 5600C4, 5500C3, or similar reel and fill it with 8- to 15-pound monofilament.

Jigging requires lighter tackle; you can get by nicely with a 6.5-foot spinning rod in a medium action and 100 yards of six- to eight-pound monofilament. The standard walleye jig is a one-sixteenth-ounce to quarter-ounce leadhead adorned with a three- to four-inch plastic, curl-tail grub body. Chartreuse, white, smoke, pumpkinseed, and blue are good grub colors. My favorite grub for walleyes is a three-inch Berkley Power Grub in pumpkinseed. Like the trolling rig mentioned earlier, that jig needs to spend most of its time bouncing along the bottom over submerged rock piles, gravel bars, and down the face of shoreline cliffs and broken-rock structure.

Washington's Top Walleye Waters
Lake Roosevelt, Banks Lake, Moses Lake, Potholes Reservoir, and the Columbia River from McNary Dam to Longview.

Crappies
These dark-spotted panfish are fond of submerged limbs, stumps, and other woody cover, and where you find one you'll probably find a school. Like all the rest of Washington's panfish, the crappie is a transplant, but it has established itself in hundreds of lakes throughout the state, as well as much of the Columbia and Snake River systems. It's as good tasting as it is fun to catch, but give yourself plenty of time for filleting if you catch a lot of them.

State Record Crappie
Black Crappie: 4.5 lb., Lake Washington, 1956
White Crappie: 2.8 lb., Burbank Slough, 1988

Tackle, Tactics, and Tips
Two keys to successful crappie fishing are to fish around stumps, trees, brush, and other woody structure and to assume that if you catch one crappie in a spot there are likely others waiting to be caught. My favorite tactic is to hang a one-sixteenth-ounce plastic, skirted jig three to four feet below a bobber and cast it as close as possible on all sides of any woody cover I find, including overhanging branches and brush. I tie the jig directly to the end of my two- or four-pound Trilene XL clear main line and fish it with a light-action spinning rod in the six-foot range.

Washington's Top Crappie Waters

Potholes Reservoir, Lind Coulee Wasteway, Eloika Lake, Scooteney Reservoir, Silver Lake (Cowlitz County), Big Lake, Ohop Lake, and Spanaway Lake.

Bluegill Sunfish

Sometimes growing to 10 inches or more, this husky panfish is becoming increasingly popular among Washington anglers. The best bluegill lakes are east of the Cascades, and late spring usually provides the best bluegill fishing. They aren't only fun to catch, but excellent on the dinner table, comparing favorably to any white-meated freshwater fish that swims.

Grasshoppers make good bait for trout and some panfish, but they're hard to catch. Next time you need a supply, spread an old wool blanket across the ground and walk toward it from different directions. The insects' bristly legs get stuck in the material, making for easy pickings.

State Record Bluegill Sunfish
2 lb., 5.3 oz., Tampico Park Pond, 1984

Tackle, Tactics, and Tips

If there's one all-around top bluegill lure, it has to be the Johnson Beetle-Spin, a simple little rig that's been catching 'gills and other panfish for over half a century. I like the black one with yellow stripes and the yellow one with black stripes, and, yes, I realize the bluegills probably can't tell them apart. I fish the 1-inch, 1/32-ounce size on two-pound monofilament and the 1.5-inch, one-eighth-ounce size on four-pound line. Trilene XL clear is my favorite in both cases, and I fish both on a 5- or 5.5-foot, light-action spinning rod. BeetleSpins sell for only about $1.25 each, so stock up, because you'll lose a few in the thick cover you'll have to fish to catch bluegills consistently. They like tangles of shoreline willows, root wads, beaver lodges, and other spots where there's plenty of wood offering food and cover. These lures bounce over snags pretty well, but you're bound to hang up and lose some. It helps to position yourself directly over such cover and work the lure vertically, but sometimes you simply have to cast and fish it horizontally, resulting in more hang-ups.

Washington's Top Bluegill Sunfish Waters

Sprague Lake, Silver Lake (Cowlitz County), Evergreen Reservoir, Duck Lake, Lake Leland, Swofford Pond, and Lake St. Clair.

Pumpkinseed Sunfish

Considered a nuisance by most anglers, this little panfish is a great first fish for kids and fishing novices. It will take almost any small bait or lure you might throw its way. It's almost always too small to eat, so many anglers who target pumpkinseeds prefer to catch and release. More often than not, they are caught by anglers fishing for perch, crappies, trout, and other species.

State Record Pumpkinseed Sunfish
0.75 lb., Hicks Lake, 1977

Tackle, Tactics, and Tips
The best way to catch pumpkinseed sunfish is to fish for something else; Murphy's Law says they're most likely to grab the bait, lure, or artificial fly you least want them to grab, and then they'll swallow it clear down to their you-know-what, requiring major surgery to get your hook back. But, should you or a boatload of fish-crazy kids with you want to catch pumpkinseeds, try fishing a small worm or piece of worm several feet below a bobber. Have plenty of hooks on hand, because the fish will usually

---

Five Good Reasons to Use a Bobber

A simple plastic or cork bobber is one of the most valuable yet least expensive items in any Washington angler's tackle box. You can buy several of them for a dollar, but they can provide benefits that money can't buy. If you fish lakes and ponds for trout or panfish, the bobber can be your best friend. Here's what a bobber (or float, if you prefer) can do for you:

- **Suspend your bait at the desired depth.** The distance between your bobber and your hook determines how far below the surface you fish. Attach it three feet above the hook to fish near the surface or slide it seven feet up the line to fish seven feet down; it's that simple. A bobber can be especially helpful in floating bait two or three feet above bottom to avoid weeds and snags.

- **Cast farther.** If you're fishing from shore and trying to lob a single salmon egg out to deeper water, you need either a large sinker, which will take the bait strait to the bottom, or a bobber, which adds casting weight but still allows you to fish at some depth other than bottom.

- **Detect strikes more easily.** It often takes a delicate touch and full concentration to tell whether a fish is nibbling your bait, but a bobber makes it a lot easier. It's really quite simple: if the bobber wiggles, there's a fish nibbling. If the bobber disappears, set the hook!

- **See where you're fishing.** Wind and other factors can affect the relationship between where your bait or lure is and where you think it is. When using a bobber, you know the bait is pretty much straight below that little plastic ball you see out there on the water. A bobber is also much more visible than monofilament fishing line, especially at daylight and dusk.

- **Cast flies with your spinning rod.** Tie an artificial fly to the end of your monofilament, attach that little bobber about four feet up the line, and you've turned your spinning rod and reel into an amazingly functional fly-fishing system. The bobber provides the casting weight while allowing you to fish near the surface, the two primary functions of a $50 floating fly line without the expense.

---

swallow the bait, and it's easier to cut the hook off than try to back it out of the sunfish's gut. Small leadheads with plastic skirts or grub bodies won't attract quite as many pumpkinseeds, but more of them will be lip-hooked for easier unhooking. Your favorite ultralight or light action spinning rod and two- to four-pound line will work fine for these panfish that you probably don't really want to catch.

Washington's Top Pumpkinseed Sunfish Waters
Lake Desire, Killarney Lake, Lake Sawyer, Nile Lake, Harts Lake, Kapowsin Lake, Lake Goodwin, Long Lake (Thurston County), and I-82 Ponds 1 and 2.

Rock Bass
This red-eyed panfish is found only in a few south Puget Sound area lakes, where it typically grows to about 10 inches. Because it's found in fewer than a dozen places, most anglers catching their first rock bass wonder what the heck they have at the end of their line; I know I did! Like most panfish, the rock bass is a transplant to the Evergreen State, most likely from the Midwest.

State Record Rock Bass
1 lb., 6 oz., Steilacoom Lake, 1981

Tackle, Tactics, and Tips
I've caught about a dozen of these fat little panfish over the years, no two of them in the same place or on the same bait or lure—so much for tactics! The closest thing to a pattern is that three or four were taken on some kind of small wobbling plug that loosely imitated a little bait fish of some kind. I'd suggest a K3 or K4 Kwikfish in a silver shad, rainbow trout, bronze crawfish, chub, or mayfly finish, and I'd cast or troll it around docks, floats, submerged stumps and logs, and at the edges of thick weed beds. These fish will hit hard and try to escape into thick cover, so go with a fairly stout (medium to medium-heavy) rod, and a good, abrasion-resistant monofilament like six-pound Trilene XT.

Washington's Top Rock Bass Waters
American Lake, Kapowsin Lake, Hicks Lake, Long Lake (Thurston County), and Pattison Lake.

Tiger Muskies
A cross between a northern pike and a muskellunge, this big predator may grow to 30 pounds or larger, and it was first stocked in southwest Washington's Mayfield Lake to provide a trophy fishery and reduce the lake's squawfish population. It was successful on both counts and has subsequently been planted in Spokane County's Newman Lake, Clark County's Merwin Reservoir, Grant County's Evergreen Reservoir, and other big lakes with a rough-fish problem. Lakes stocked with tiger muskies have special regulations, so be sure to check the current fishing pamphlet for specifics before tackling this rough-and-tumble adversary.

State Record Tiger Muskie
28.25 lb., Mayfield Lake, 1995

Tackle, Tactics, and Tips
If you want to catch a tiger muskie, arm yourself with a short, stiff casting or spinning rod, a reel loaded with 12- to 20-pound monofilament, and an assortment of large, minnow-imitating plugs and big bucktail spinners in a variety of colors. Most anglers use a short wire leader between the line and the lure to protect against the fish's long, sharp teeth. Work the lure within about five feet of the surface, especially around submerged logs, stumps, downed trees, and large weedbeds. Important Tip #1: Fishing is best during the last hour or two of daylight, especially after two or three warm summer days. Important Tip #2: Each time you retrieve your lure, make a couple of figure eights with it alongside the boat. Tiger muskies often follow a lure right up to the boat and can't control themselves when it slows and starts spinning around in one spot. Important Tip #3: Leave your expensive graphite casting rod at home. You have only a foot or two of line between the rod tip and the lure when you're making those figure eights, so the muskie's ferocious strike takes the rod straight down, with a sharp smack across the boat's gunwale. A fiberglass rod can take such abuse, but graphite breaks with a resounding pop more often than not.

Washington's Top Tiger Muskie Waters
Mayfield Lake, Newman Lake, Merwin Reservoir, Evergreen Reservoir, and Curlew Lake.

Northern Pike
With long, sharp teeth, a big appetite, and a sullen disposition, the pike is a tough customer, so it's a favorite of many anglers. But its favorite food is smaller fish, including trout and kokanee, so Northwest fishery managers aren't all that fond of this big transplant from the northeastern part of the country. As a result, we have them in only one Washington lake (that we know of), so that's where you have to go if you want an opportunity to catch one.

State Record Northern Pike
32.2 lb., Long Lake (Spokane County), 1995

Tackle, Tactics, and Tips
Like many other big fish, the northern pike feeds mostly on smaller fish, so that's what you want to replicate at the end of your line. Shallow-running Rapalas, Power Minnows, and other wobbling plugs work well, as do three- to four-inch Dardevles, Krocodiles, and other minnow-imitating wobbling spoons. Be sure to use a wire leader between the lure and your line to protect against the pike's nasty teeth. If your plug or spoon doesn't get tangled in the weeds regularly, you

aren't fishing in the right places. A good rod for this kind of fishing is a 6.5- or 7-foot casting stick, medium-heavy to heavy action, with a levelwind reel big enough to hold 150 yards of 14- to 20-pound monofilament.

Washington's Top Northern Pike Waters
Long Lake (Spokane County)

Brown Bullhead Catfish
The state's most abundant member of the catfish family, the brown bullhead is found in lakes and ponds throughout Washington. Although they sometimes grow to five pounds or more, a typical brown bullhead from Washington waters is a fish in the one- to two-pound range. Many Northwesterners won't eat this or any other catfish, but bake or barbecue a couple of these and give them a try, and you'll likely become a brown bullhead enthusiast yourself.

State Record Brown Bullhead
3.9 lb., Ludlow Lake, 1997

Tackle, Tactics, and Tips
All you need to catch brown bullheads is a can of nightcrawlers; a plastic or cork bobber; a medium-action, six- to seven-foot spinning rod and reel full of eight-pound line; and a willingness to go spend a couple of hours in the dark on a nearby lake. As John Fogerty and his Creedence Clearwater boys reminded us more than three decades ago, nighttime is the right time, and it applies to catfishing every bit as much as it does to being with the one you love! Brown bullhead come to life after dark, using their great sense of smell and those funny little barbels on their upper lip to find food in the pitch-black of night. Fishing usually is best in water 3 to 10 feet deep, especially around patches of lily pads, docks, floats, and wood structure above and below the water's surface.

Washington's Top Brown Bullhead Waters
Lacamas Lake, Silver Lake (Cowlitz County), Cottage Lake, Lake Sawyer, Wildcat Lake, Silver Lake (Pierce County), Campbell Lake, Black Lake (Thurston County), Lawrence Lake, and Wiser Lake.

Channel Catfish
They grow to a very impressive size in some of eastern Washington's bigger Columbia River tributaries, and channel cats are now being stocked in more and more Washington lakes as well. Hard fighters that are also excellent on the dinner table, channel catfish are gaining in popularity around here and throughout the country. Heck, there's even a regularly published catfish magazine now, something nobody would have dreamed of writing or reading 20 years ago! In case you wondered, channel catfish are distinguished from other catfish species by their

deeply forked tails and dark spots on their bodies. Both blue and white catfish have forked tails, but neither is spotted.

State Record Channel Catfish
36.2 lb., I-82 Pond 6, 1999

Tackle, Tactics, and Tips
So-called cut baits are a good bet in almost any situation. Depending on where you're fishing and applicable regulations, you may want to try strips of squawfish or sucker meat. Cut the strips about an inch wide and two inches long for your "average" channel cat, but don't be afraid to increase those proportions if you're trying for big ones. Nightcrawlers are also effective, especially in the spring and early summer. They're often easier to find and easier to fish than cut bait and can be just as deadly for hungry cats.

Other possibilities include chicken livers, beef liver, or just about any of the stinkbait concoctions that some anglers like to use in an apparent attempt to demonstrate how strong their stomachs are and how undeveloped their olfactory nerve endings. Western catfish anglers seem to have a pretty wide range of preferences when it comes to hook size, with favorites ranging from as small as size 2 to as large as size 3/0. The choice could depend, of course, on the size of the bait you're using. Perhaps the best advice is to keep the hook just small enough so that it can be completely buried and hidden in the bait. And while we're on the subject of tackle, anglers have many views on the right line, rods, and reels for channel cats. You can, of course, get by with lighter tackle when fishing calm water from a boat than you could ever hope to use when trying to anchor a big bait in the heavy water of a fast-moving river. As a very general rule, you'll probably find that line in the 12- to 17-pound range will usually do the job, as will a seven- to eight-foot rod of medium to medium-heavy action and a reel large enough to hold at least 150 yards of whatever size line you select.

Cleaning or handling of channel cats can be tricky, even moderately dangerous, if you don't respect those sharp spines at the front edges of their pectoral fins and dorsal fin. As with other members of the catfish clan, these spines are sort of a last way to get even with anglers planning a big meal at the expense of the channel cat, and many an angler has felt their painful sting. Some catfish anglers carry pliers or sidecutters at all times, and the first thing they do is break or snip off those spines to avoid an accident. At the very least, respect and avoid the channel catfish's most obvious weaponry.

Washington's Top Channel Catfish Waters
Snake River at the mouth of the Grande Ronde River, Snake River at the mouth of the Palouse River, lower Walla Walla River, Columbia River at McNary Pool, lower Yakima River, Swofford Pond, and Wenas Lake, I-82 Ponds 3, 5, and 6.

Burbot

The so-called freshwater ling, also called a cusk by some fishermen, is found in deeper lakes and reservoirs of central and eastern Washington, where it's especially popular with wintertime ice anglers. Although its head is a lot bigger around than the rest of its eel-like body, a large burbot will provide a thick, white-meat fillet that's excellent on the table. That might explain why burbot populations have been over fished in some Washington lakes.

State Record Burbot
17.01 lb., Palmer Lake, 1993

Tackle, Tactics, and Tips
These long, slim fish like cool water, so they disappear into the depths during the summer and fall months, coming back to life and back into shallower water during the winter, where most are caught through the ice. There is also some early spring jigging for burbot after the ice melts away, but it doesn't last long most years. Belying their slim, trim figures, burbot have big appetites. Some anglers fish for them with huge globs of nightcrawlers or liver on large hooks, and those hooks may be attached to the bottom end of a big, metal flasher. The flasher may pass as another fish to the hungry burbot, since smaller fish make up a major portion of their usual diet. Other anglers fish for them with strips cut from the sides of suckers, squawfish, perch, and other fish, or with whole smelt. These baits are often pinned to the hooks of a large metal jig, such as a chrome Vi-Ke or Krocodile. Jig-and-minnow combinations are also effective. Depending on how deep you're fishing and the weight of your bait and/or lure, you can fish burbot with medium to medium-heavy action rods and 8- to 15-pound monofilament.

Washington's Top Burbot Waters
Lake Chelan, Lake Cle Elum, Lake Kachess, Lake Keechelus, Palmer Lake, Bead Lake, Sullivan Lake, and Lake Roosevelt.

Northern Squawfish

Although long considered a pest, the squawfish's popularity has grown dramatically since it became the target of a Columbia River bounty program early in the early 1990s. The bounty program is aimed at reducing the squawfish population to provide better escapement for salmon and steelhead smolts, but so far there hasn't been much proof that killing squawfish is saving large numbers of smolts. Oh well, catching fish for the money adds excitement for some anglers, and there still seem to be plenty of them, so what's the harm?

State Record Squawfish
7.25 lb., Snake River, 1996

Tackle, Tactics, and Tips
Show me a Bill Lewis Tiny Trap in a silver/blue-back finish, and I'll show you one hell of a squawfish lure. Like everyone else, I've caught my share of squawfish on all manner of baits and lures, but that Tiny Trap is an all-around squawfish slayer. Small Rapalas, Storm Pee Wee Warts, and various crawfish-finish crankbaits are also highly effective. If you'd rather fish bait, try a whole night-crawler or small chunk of beef liver on a fairly large (size 4 or 6) bait hook. Squawfish hit hard but tire quickly, so you don't need heavy tackle, even in big water like the Snake or Columbia River. The same six- to seven-foot, medium-action spinning rod and six- or eight-pound monofilament you use for trout will usually do the job on squawfish. The best fishing is around submerged logs, roots, and boulder piles or riprap along the shoreline, in places where the water is at least four or five feet deep.

Washington's Top Squawfish Waters
Palmer Lake, Bead Lake, Lake Sawyer, Snake River and all its reservoirs, Columbia River and all its reservoirs, and Chehalis River.

Carp
Okay, we'll keep this short, because even carp anglers don't go around bragging about it. But these big, fat fish with scales the size of silver dollars do a have a place on Washington's big menu of angling opportunities. We may not admit it, but most of us have been closet carp anglers at least once in our lives when nobody else was looking. I've coaxed them into taking a tiny mini jig when the smallmouths weren't biting on Banks Lake and even thrown pieces of nightcrawler at them in a shallow slough up in the Potholes Reservoir Dunes. Hey, they fight like crazy on light tackle! I've even tried eating smoked carp and can honestly say it was the worst bite of food I've ever had.

State Record Carp
41.25 lb., Long Lake (Thurston County), 1980

Tackle, Tactics, and Tips
Serious carp anglers, and there are a few of them out there, will tell you that carp are pretty much vegetarians, more likely to gobble a green pea or kernel of yellow corn than a perch-finish crankbait or hammered brass spoon. Small dough balls wadded on a hook also take carp, according to those who pursue this large cousin to the goldfish in your backyard pond. They do grow to impressive proportions, and they're tough fighters as they bulldoze their way around the weedy shallows they so often inhabit, so don't go too light with the tackle unless you just want a good ol' wrestlin' match. A seven-foot spinning rod in medium-heavy action and 8- or 10-pound monofilament will give you a fighting chance of landing any 15-pounders you might stumble across.

Washington's Top Carp Waters
Southern half of Moses Lake, Potholes Reservoir, Banks Lake, and Lower Columbia River sloughs.

Saltwater
Rockfish
Available in shallow-, mid-, and deep-water models, there's a rockfish for virtually every saltwater fishing situation here in Washington. The black rockfish, often found in shallow water and even right on the surface, is perhaps most well known and provides the bread-and-butter action for coastal bottom fish anglers. Other shallow-water species include the blue, yellowtail, copper, and brown rockfish. Mid-depth and deep-water species available to Washington anglers include the China, widow, quillback, canary, tiger, bocaccio, and yelloweye rockfish, the last two of which sometimes top 20 pounds. Many rockfish species are slow growing and susceptible to overfishing. That's exactly what's happened to some of our popular rockfish species and why we now have such restrictive regulations and skimpy limits on rockfish in Puget Sound.

State Record Rockfish
Black Rockfish: 10.25 lb., Tacoma Narrows, 1980
Blue Rockfish: 3.91 lb., Westport, 1996
Bocaccio: 23 lb., 10 oz., Swiftsure Bank, 1987
Canary Rockfish: 10 lb., 9 oz., Neah Bay, 1986
China Rockfish: 4 lb., 3 oz., Duncan Rock, 1989
Copper Rockfish: 10 lb., Point Roberts Reef, 1989
Greenstripe Rockfish: 1 lb., 10 oz., Possession Bar, 1985
Quillback Rockfish: 7 lb., 3 oz., Middle Bank, 1987
Tiger Rockfish: 7.5 lb., Middle Bank, 1989
Vermillion Rockfish: 7.07 lb., Makah Bay, 2000
Yelloweye Rockfish: 27.75 lb., Dallas Bank, 1989
Yellowtail Rockfish: 7 lb., 6 oz., Westport, 1992

Tackle, Tactics, and Tips
It's all in their name: if you want to catch rockfish, you have to find the rocks. These fish thrive in, around, and over hard bottom structure, and if you're bobbing around over mud or sand, you're wasting your time. There are, however, different kinds of rocky structure, at different depths, and that's what determines the kinds of rockfish you're likely to encounter. Whatever species you're after, though, the fishing methods that take them remain fairly constant. From shallow-water coppers and blues to deep-water quillbacks and yelloweyes, they'll all take a leadhead jig adorned with a plastic, curly-tail grub or a bait fish–imitating metal jig bounced along the bottom. Likewise, they'll all take a whole or plug-cut herring spinning past the end of their noses. The main variable is lure size and weight. That copper or blue finning

Get Reel

Most spinning reels, levelwinds, and fly reels are available in both right- and left-hand versions or can be converted for use with either hand. Some anglers aren't aware of this fact, so they go through their fishing life thinking they're stuck with a reel that doesn't work comfortably. Before buying your next reel, experiment with both right- and left-hand models to see which is best for you.

15 or 20 feet beneath the surface can be reached with a half-ounce leadhead or three-quarter-ounce Crippled Herring, but you might need a 12-ounce leadhead or 16-ounce metal jig to get down to where those quillbacks and yelloweyes live. And so it goes with rods, reels, and line for rockfish; your six-foot spinning rod and four-pound monofilament might fish that shallow-water jig very effectively, but you'll need a bigger and stiffer rod, larger reel, and probably ultrabraid line to fish those 200- or 300-foot depths where the bigger lures are required.

The best rockfish action of all? That's easy. Ask anyone who's ever found black, blue, or yellowtail rockfish feeding right on the surface, and they'll tell you about awesome saltwater fishing. Surface rockfish are actively feeding rockfish, and they'll hit virtually anything you throw at them, from bass spinnerbaits to streamer flies to surface poppers. Miss one fish, and it's very likely that two or three others will try to grab the lure before it gets away. And every strike is like a miniature explosion on the water's surface. It could be the hottest fishing you'll find anywhere.

Washington's Top Rockfish Waters
Duncan Rock, Tatoosh Island/Cape Flattery, Waadah Island, Point of the Arches, Flattery Rocks, LaPush "Rockpile," Destruction Island, offshore rock piles northwest of Westport, Sail Rock, Port Angeles "Rock Pile," Middle Bank, Partridge Bank, Lawson Reef, Boundary Reef, Sucia/Patos Island reefs, Alden Bank, and Tacoma Narrows Bridge.

Flounder and Sole
The starry flounder, which sometimes tops 10 pounds, is one of the biggest, best, and most popular of Washington's marine flatfish, but the possibilities also include arrowtooth flounder, Dover sole, petrale sole, English sole, rock sole, sand sole, Pacific sand dab, speckled sand dab, and several others. All but the arrowtooth flounder provide excellent eating. Generally found over sand, gravel, or even mud bottoms, they're easy to fish for and easy to fool with a variety of natural baits and artificial lures. Estuaries and shallow bays often provide excellent flatfish action.

State Record Flounder and Sole
Petrale Sole: 7 lb., 9 oz., Jefferson Head, 1980

Rock Sole: 4 lb., 3 oz., Hein Bank, 1989
Starry Flounder: 8.57 lb., Sekiu Point, 1997

Tackle, Tactics, and Tips

Unlike with rockfish, you're better off fishing for flatfish over soft bottoms of mud, sand, and gravel. That makes for easy fishing, with few hang-ups and hardly any lost tackle. These fish aren't all that choosy, so you can catch them almost as easily on chunks of herring as you can on whole or plug-cut herring. Leadhead jigs with small single-tail or twin-tail plastic grubs will take them, as will metal jigs in appropriate sizes to reach the bottom you're trying to fish. Match your rod, reel, and line to the weight of the lures or sinkers you need and you're in business. A well-prepared flatfish angler would carry a medium-light, 6.5- or 7-foot spinning rod and a reel filled with six- or eight-pound monofilament for shallow water sole and sand dabs; a 7- or 7.5-foot medium-heavy rod with a levelwind full of 10- or 12-pound mono or 20-pound ultrabraid for medium depths and heavier lures; and a deep-water outfit consisting of a 7.5- to 8-foot jigging rod equipped with a beefy levelwind reel filled with 20- to 30-pound ultrabraid.

Washington's Top Flounder and Sole Waters

Clallam Bay, Port Angeles Harbor, Dungeness Bay, Discovery Bay, Hein Bank, north end of Admiralty Bay, Holmes Harbor, Point Jefferson/Port Madison, Oro Bay/Thompson Cove, and Hogum Bay.

Albacore Tuna

This highly migratory fish provides lots of angling excitement when it passes within reach of the Washington charter fleet. In recent years, albacore fishing has been a possibility much more often than not. In fact, we've had strong albacore runs virtually every year for the past 10, and during those El Niño seasons of the mid-1990s it was possible to catch these fast-moving fish within a few miles of the coast. Strong, stubborn, and fast, it's a fantastic sport fish, and its flesh is among the best of all marine fish.

State Record Albacore Tuna

52 lb., Westport, 1997

Tackle, Tactics, and Tips

Most anglers find albacore by trolling four- to six-ounce hex-head jigs with plastic or feather skirts fast enough to skip them along the surface. When the trolling lines draw multiple strikes, the standard response is to spin the boat back over the school, and everyone not playing a fish drops a hook baited with a live anchovy over the side and lets it swim around on a free-spooled line. When a tuna inhales your bait, you count to 10, flip the reel into gear and hang on for all you're worth. Trolling rods are heavy-action 7- to 7.5-footers, and the reels are big and sturdy enough to hold plenty of 40- or 50-pound mono. Stock up on hex-head jigs in a variety of colors. The bait-fishing outfit can be a little lighter than the one used for trolling. I've seen people get away with using medium steelhead drift tackle on a charter boat that wasn't very crowded, but that's pushing your luck if you tie into a longfin of 20 pounds or so. A 7.5-foot rod with a fast taper, equipped with something like an Abu Garcia 7000CL reel or larger and spooled with 30-pound Trilene Big Game line will do the job nicely. Buy a variety of bait hooks in sizes 2 to 1/0 to accommodate live-hooking of anchovies in whatever size are available, and throw in a dozen Rubber Core sinkers of various sizes in case they're needed to take the bait several feet below the surface.

Washington's Top Albacore Tuna Waters
Pacific Ocean offshore from Ilwaco and offshore from Westport.

Saltwater Perch
The redtail surfperch is the most commonly caught prize in the ocean breakers of the Washington coast, while the pile perch and striped seaperch are more likely to turn up around pilings, piers, and jetties in the calmer waters of coastal estuaries, the Strait of Juan de Fuca, and Puget Sound. All three are tough fighters and provide prime, white-meat fillets. One of the most fascinating things about these fish is that they give birth to live young, and pregnant females will hurry up the birthing process when hooked. Most anglers release fish under such circumstances, and you may want to do the same.

State Record Saltwater Perch
Pile Perch: 3 lb., 9 oz., Quartermaster Harbor, 1981
Redtail Surfperch: 4.05 lb., Kalaloch, 1996
Striped Seaperch: 2 lb., 1 oz., Quartermaster Harbor, 1980

Tackle, Tactics, and Tips
Red-tail surfperch require heavier tackle than both pile perch and striped seaperch, because they spend their lives in the pounding breakers of the Pacific coast, where it takes a fairly long cast to reach them and a fairly heavy sinker to hold a bait in position. Use an 8.5- to 9.5-foot casting or spinning rod with plenty of backbone for lobbing one- to four-ounce pyramid sinkers just beyond the first row of breakers. Tie a three-way swivel to your 12- or 15-pound monofilament line, adding a two-foot dropper leader for the sinker to one eye of the swivel and a one-foot leader with a size 4 or 6 bait hook on the end to the swivel's other eye. Bait that hook with the tip of a razor clam neck, half a ghost shrimp, a one-inch section of bloodworm, or some other small morsel of fresh bait. Fish the incoming tide, and if you've scouted the beach at low tide to find lagoons and holes scoured out by the water, you should find action fairly soon.

An incoming tide also provides the best opportunity to catch pile perch and striped seaperch in Washington's more protected bays, harbors, and "inside" waters of Puget Sound. These fish like to feed on newly submerged pilings and jetties as the tide works its way over these structures. The "bite" is often a short one, as the perch move in with the tide, stop to feed briefly in one area, then move on with the tide to greener pastures. As they come to each new structure, though, they'll greedily inhale pieces of mussel, bloodworm, shrimp (either freshly dug or recently purchased cooked varieties), garden worms, and other small baits impaled on a size 8 or 10 hook. You don't need more than about a quarter-ounce sinker to get the bait down to the fish, so there's no need for heavy rods, reels, or lines. Your favorite spinning outfit with four- or six-pound monofilament line will do the job nicely.

Washington's Top Saltwater Perch Waters
Ruby Beach, Kaloloch Beach, Pacific Beach, Copalis Beach, Oyhut Beach, Ocean Shores/Point Brown, Half Moon Bay, Grayland Beach, Long Beach Peninsula from Ocean Park to Leadbetter Point, Port Townsend City Docks, Mukilteo Ferry Landing, Port of Everett, Edmonds Ferry Landing, Port Orchard Docks, and Point Defiance Pier/Vashon Ferry Landing.

Cabezon
It looks like something from a kid's worst nightmare, but this biggest Northwest member of the sculpin family is a prized bottom fish. It grows to 20 pounds and is a tough fighter. Although much of its bulk is composed of head and huge pectoral fins, there's also a substantial amount of prime white meat on the cabezon's thick fillets. The flesh may be a deep, turquoise green when it's sliced off the carcass, but it will turn snowy white after a few seconds in the frying pan or oven.

State Record Cabezon
23 lb., Dungeness Spit, 1990

Tackle, Tactics, and Tips
A stout jigging rod in the seven- to eight-foot range, medium-sized levelwind reel, and plenty of 10- to 15-pound monofilament make up a suitable arsenal for most cabezon fishing in Washington. These fish feed primarily on crabs and other crustaceans, so leadhead jigs adorned with short, plastic grub bodies and various vinyl or rubber skirting make good cabezon strike-getters. Orange, motor oil, yellow, chartreuse, brown, and pumpkinseed are good colors. Given the chance, cabezon will also feed on small sculpins and other fish, so don't be afraid to bounce Crippled Herring, Point Wilson Darts, Nordics, and other metal jigs along the bottom. Like rockfish, cabezon are most likely to be found on hard, rocky, and steep structure, so pay attention to what your depthsounder is telling you as you prospect for this big sculpin.

Washington's Top Cabezon Waters
Tatoosh Island, Waadah Island, Slip Point, Pillar Point, Crescent Bay/Observatory Point, south end of San Juan Island, Waldron Island, White Rock/Danger Rock, and Smith Island.

Greenling

Sometimes called sea trout, kelp greenling, white-spotted greenling, and rock greenling are fun to catch, easy to handle, and very good to eat. The kelp variety is most abundant and most often caught in Washington, both by boat and shore anglers. Commonly used as bait for its bigger cousin the lingcod, the greenling is a worthy sport fish in its own right, putting up a good fight when caught from shallow water on light tackle. Kelp greenling are unusual in that males and females have very different coloration. The female is yellow, tan, or light green with hundreds of rust-colored spots from head to tail, while the male ranges from brown to slate gray with fewer and larger spots that are light blue or blue-green with darker edges.

State Record Greenling
4.42 lb., Sucia Island, 1999

Tackle, Tactics, and Tips
An average Washington greenling weighs well under two pounds, so your freshwater spinning outfit will work just fine, whether you're fishing from piers and jetties or from a boat. There's no need to fish deep with heavy lures or sinkers, either, because greenling may be found as shallow as 10 feet and are most common in 60 feet of water or less. In other words, a half-ounce to one-and-a-half-ounce leadhead with a three-inch plastic grub body or a metal jig in the same weight range is all you'll need to reach them. These lures can be fished effectively with "trout" tackle and four- to eight-pound monofilament. The fish will also take a variety of baits, from pieces of mussel, clam, herring, or bloodworm to whole anchovies and small, plug-cut herring. As their name implies, kelp greening are most abundant in and around kelp beds, but all greenling species may be found near shallow-water rock piles and reefs, around rock jetties, or on steep shoreline drop-offs where the bottom is hard and rocky.

Washington's Top Greenling Waters
Tatoosh Island, Sail Rock, Clallam Bay/Slip Point, Freshwater Bay/Observatory Point, Point Wilson, Skipjack Island, Battleship Island/McCracken Point, O'Neal Island/Rocky Bay, San Juan Island from Deadman Bay to Eagle Cove, and Lopez Island's entire south end.

Pacific Cod

Often called true cod because it's a bona fide member of the codfish family (unlike lingcod and rock cod, which aren't really cod at all), this bottom fish sometimes grows to 15 pounds and is prized for its thick, firm, white fillets. Found both in the ocean and our inside marine waters, cod populations have crashed in many areas where they once provided great angling opportunity. It's now hard to find good cod fishing, and the fishery is completely closed in Puget Sound. The walleyed pollock and tomcod are smaller members of the same family and also provide decent sport and great fish and chips for Washington anglers.

State Record Pacific Cod
19 lb., 10 oz., Ediz Hook, 1984

Tackle, Tactics, and Tips
These fish have a pretty good-sized mouth, and they aren't too picky about what they put in it, so you can catch them on a wide variety of baits and lures. I've done well with four- and six-ounce Metzler Mooch-A-Jigs on many occasions, but chrome Krocodiles, Crippled Herring, and Nordics also work very well. If you're a do-it-yourself type, make up a batch of 4- to 10-ounce pipe jigs with small-diameter tubing, and you can catch cod on them just fine. If you prefer fishing leadheads, rig them with six- or eight-inch plastic worms in purple, gray, black, or blue. Rods, reels, and line for Pacific cod should be only as stout as needed to handle the size jigs and sinkers required to reach bottom. These aren't hard-fighting fish, so they'll come along peacefully on moderately light tackle. Fairly stiff rods of seven to eight feet, of course, work better for jigging than softer, more limber rods, so don't break out the light steelhead drift rod if you'll be bouncing five-ounce jigs along the bottom in 120 feet of water.

Washington's Top Pacific Cod Waters
Eastern Bank, Dungeness Spit, Green Point, Ediz Hook, and Sekiu Point.

Anadromous (Sea-Run)
Chum Salmon
Also called a dog salmon, the chum is no dog when it comes to fighting ability. In fact, this second largest of the five Pacific salmon species is perhaps the toughest and strongest fighter of the bunch. It's also the last to return from the ocean each fall, usually coming back to Washington rivers and creeks in November, December, and January. When they do return, they draw huge crowds of anglers to many of the prime chum-fishing spots. People stand shoulder-to-shoulder in some spots to get a crack at this yellow-and-purple bruiser that was all but ignored by recreational fishermen a decade and a half ago. Huge returns of hatchery chums in recent years have been greatly responsible for this increased interest in the so-called dog salmon.

State Record Chum Salmon
Freshwater: 25.97 lb., Satsop River, 1997
Saltwater: 20.26 lb., Westport, 2001

Tackle, Tactics, and Tips
Catching chums from saltwater is pretty much a mystery to most anglers, although they've made some progress the past few years. Both bank and boat anglers are starting to lace very small "firecracker" herring on a single hook (size 1/0, 1, or 2) and suspend the bait a couple of feet below a bobber.

Chums like their meals in small portions, so they'll generally ignore the four- to six-inch herring baits commonly used for other salmon species. The bobber keeps the small bait near the surface, where migrating chums hang as they head toward freshwater.

Speaking of freshwater, that's where chum salmon angling techniques have been pretty well perfected over the past 10 years or so. Anything will work, as long as it's small and green, so most anglers use tiny chartreuse Corky bobbers, either with or without a small tuft of chartreuse nylon yarn at the head of the hook. On those rare occasions when there are plenty of chums around but no one seems to be hooking them, try changing to another color bobber and/or yarn. I like pale pink, but orange, red, or white may also do the job. Just remember to keep it small, no matter what the color. Fish your bobber rig with just enough weight above the lure to keep it near bottom as it drifts with the current. Remember that these are hard-fighting fish and that there will almost always be lots of other anglers nearby, so use stout tackle. An 8.5-foot, heavy or extra-heavy action drift rod is perfect, and pack your reel with plenty of 14- to 20-pound line. My favorite chum outfit is a Berkley Air IM7 A92-8-6XH casting rod equipped with a 6501C4 (left-handed) levelwind reel filled with 17-pound Trilene XT clear monofilament. Fly fishermen needn't feel left out of the fun when the chums come back to spawn. Most river and estuary anglers like an 8- or 9-weight rod in the nine-foot range, and they cast a floating or sink-tip line with plenty of stout backing behind it. Small, sparsely tied flies of chartreuse, pink, white, and combinations of those colors work best.

Washington's Top Chum Salmon Waters
Hood Canal at Hoodsport, Hood Canal at Potlatch, West Fork Satsop River, Skykomish River, Nisqually River, Mudd Bay/McClane Creek, Oyster Bay/Kennedy Creek, Dosewallips River, Duckabush River, and Skokomish River (catch-and-release).

Pink Salmon
This smallest of the five Pacific salmon returns to Washington streams only on odd-numbered years, but it often returns in very good numbers. The best way to ID a pink is by its extremely small scales—much smaller than those of any other salmon—and by the large, black, oval spots on both the back and the tail. A typical pink salmon—often called a humpback or humpy because of the pronounced hump that forms on the back of the male before spawning—is a fish of two to four pounds, although they sometimes grow to seven or eight pounds. If you catch them for the table, their soft, pink flesh will keep better if you clean them quickly and get them into a cooler filled with ice as soon as possible.

State Record Pink Salmon
Freshwater: 14.49 lb., Skykomish River, 2001
Saltwater: 11.56 lb., Possession Point, 2001

Tackle, Tactics, and Tips

Most of the pinks caught from Washington waters are taken by trolling or casting; they seem to like a moving target. The small, plug-cut herring normally trolled for coho will take pinks, but you'll have better luck on artificials with a pink finish. Luhr Jensen's two- and three-inch Needlefish and three-inch Coyote spoon both come in a pink finish that's perfect for humpies, and both have good wobbling action when trolled near the surface behind a one- to three-ounce crescent sinker. For casting from the beach or docks, many anglers use pink Buzz Bombs in the smaller sizes, but the half-ounce and three-quarter-ounce Crippled Herring is also available in what Luhr Jensen calls "cerise," which is a fancy word for pink. Your favorite steelhead drift rod will work great for humpy trolling, especially if it's on the light side. An eight-footer with a medium action is perfect for trolling up pinks on a six- or eight-pound monofilament line. The same outfit will work for casting, but many anglers prefer spinning equipment of about the same size.

Washington's Top Pink Salmon Waters

Strait of Juan de Fuca at Sekiu, Cornet Bay, Bush Point, Skagit River, and Hood Canal at Hoodsport.

Sockeye Salmon

Although sockeye may be the most highly prized of all Pacific salmon when it comes to table quality, Washington anglers catch very few of them. Sockeye fisheries in Lake Washington and Lake Wenatchee are on-again, off-again affairs, mostly off-again in recent years. Would-be sockeye anglers need to listen for news reports on the subject of possible July season openers or check the Washington Department of Fish and Wildlife's website to be aware of possible openers. There are summertime sockeyes to catch in the Strait of Juan de Fuca every year, but the competition from commercial nets is fierce, and as yet no one has developed an effective means of catching these fish on sporting tackle.

State Record Sockeye Salmon

Freshwater: 10 lb., 10 oz., Lake Washington, 1982
Saltwater: No Record

Tackle, Tactics, and Tips

Get out your favorite salmon trolling rod, fill the reel with 10- to 15-pound monofilament, and get a downrigger installed on your boat if it doesn't already have one. Use your depthsounder to locate the fish, drop your downrigger ball to that depth, and you're in business. And you don't even need bait or a lure! That's right, most sockeye are caught on a bare red hook, fished about 20 inches behind a large, chrome flasher. The flasher draws a closer look from nearby sockeye, and the size 1/0, 1, or 2 red hook passes as food to these plankton-eating salmon. I like monofilament for this kind of fishing because sockeyes have fairly "soft" mouths, and the mono's stretch helps to absorb the shock of hard strikes and head-shaking runs.

Washington's Top Sockeye Salmon Waters
Lake Washington and Lake Wenatchee.

American Shad
This biggest member of the herring family was brought to the West Coast in the 19th century, but it still doesn't get the respect and angling interest it deserves. The best shad fishing around here is in the Columbia, especially the stretch immediately below Bonneville Dam during the month of June, where record shad runs have been the rule in recent years. These fish are very tough fighters, but they're also very bony, so many anglers prefer catch-and-release action to filling a cooler with shad.

State Record Shad
3.44 lb., Columbia River, 1999

Tackle, Tactics, and Tips
Trout-size spinning rods and reels work very well for shad, provided the reel has a smooth drag and is loaded with plenty of fresh six- or eight-pound monofilament. Heavier line is too big for the small, light lures often used for shad, and lighter stuff may not handle some of the big, tough female shad you're likely to hook. Like some other anadromous species, shad don't eat during their freshwater spawning run, but they will instinctively grab a lure, and the best shad lures are small ones. Little, plastic-bodied crappie jigs will do the job in most cases. Long-time shad advocate Al Lasater of Olympia, however, favors a much simpler and more inexpensive lure when he goes shad fishing. He puts a couple of small, plastic beads on the line directly above a size 1 steelhead hook. One bead is usually red, the other either gold or pearl. Sometimes he goes with two red ones. "Let the shad tell you what they like," he says. About 18 inches above the hook, Lasater pinches on two or three large split-shot sinkers. Shad tend to follow fairly specific migration routes as they make their way upstream, so you might waste a lot of time fishing unproductive water if you aren't careful. Current edges are most often the best places to fish. You may also want to fish right along the bank, especially if you're on the deepwater side of a river where there is a lot of current. A shad strike may be as subtle as a runaway truck, but more often the bite is a soft peck that you could miss if you aren't paying attention. Don't be too discouraged, by the way, if you miss a couple of strikes for every one you hook. Besides being thin, the tissue of a shad's mouth is also very smooth, often allowing a hook to slip through without sticking. Keep hooks needle sharp to increase your odds.

Washington's Top Shad Waters
Columbia River from Camas Slough upstream to Bonneville Dam.

Now What? Two Options For After The Catch

Catch-and-Release Tips

Catch-and-release fishing continues to expand throughout Washington and the rest of the country, as anglers and fish managers alike realize its value in providing great sport while helping to ensure future angling opportunity. Releasing fish to fight again, however, takes some effort on an angler's part. Here are five tips for releasing fish unharmed:

- Use artificial lures with single, barbless hooks. Fish caught on artificials are usually hooked in the outer edge of the mouth, where there's less chance of serious injury. A single hook with no barb may be removed quickly with the least possible damage to the fish's head and mouth. Fish caught with bait, on the other hand, often swallow the hook, where it sticks in the tongue, throat, or gills, causing serious injury. Pulling or cutting out the hook usually kills the fish.

- If you do want to release a deeply hooked fish, it's best to cut the leader as short as possible and leave the hook where it is. Chances are it will dissolve in a few days and the fish will have a fairly good chance of surviving.

- Play fish out and release them as quickly as possible. A long fight reduces a fish's chance of survival.

- Release fish without removing them from the water. Netting, handling, and allowing a fish to roll around in the dirt or bottom of a boat leads to scale loss and other injuries that often result in death hours or days later. A quick twist of the hook with forceps or needle-nose pliers while the fish lies on its side at the surface is best.

- After unhooking, don't let an exhausted fish simply sink into the depths. Cradle it gently in the water or move it back and forth a few times to move water over its gills. Allow it to swim away on its own as it regains strength.

Caring for Your Catch

Those of us who enjoy fishing for sport have the opportunity to bring home one of the healthiest foods we can eat, fresh fish. Some anglers, though, don't bother to take the simple steps necessary to ensure that the fish they do kill will come home in the best possible condition for the table. As far as I'm concerned, there are really only five rules of fish care. Here they are, in the order you're most likely to use them after you catch a fish that you plan to take home to dinner.

Kill fish quickly.

It might seem reasonable that fish will "stay fresh" if you keep them alive on a stringer or in one of those submerged baskets after you catch them, and you see a lot of people doing that. But such treatment really doesn't make for good table fare. A fish on a stringer continues to struggle after it's caught, which produces lactic acid

Take a camera on every fishing trip. If you don't have room for a fancy 35 mm with an expensive lens, just drop a pocket camera or one of those disposables in your shirt or coat pocket. Every fish looks its best the moment it's lifted from the water, so that's the time to photograph it, even if you're planning to kill it for the table.

in its flesh. That's the same stuff that makes your muscles ache when you work out, and when it permeates a fish's body it affects the flavor of the flesh. Allowing a trout, perch, or catfish to struggle for several hours after it's caught can only have a negative influence on how it will taste.

What's more, attaching fish to a stringer keeps them up near the surface, where the water is warmer. You'll hear later that keeping fish cool is another of the five rules, and you're breaking that one if you tie fish up near the surface with a short stringer cord. It's much better to remove fish from that warm surface water, kill them with a sharp rap to the head, and keep them on the boat rather than nursing them along in hopes that they'll live through the day.

Allowing fish to suffocate in the bottom of a boat or on the bank is only a little better than dragging them around in warm water, in that it shortens the agony a little, but still it will have a negative effect on the fish's edibility. Not only will fish taste better if you kill them quickly, but it's also more humane than dragging them around on a stringer or letting them flop in the dirt until they suffocate. The bottom line is: carry a fish club of some kind and use it as soon as you land any fish that's destined for the table.

Bleed all fresh-caught fish.

It may sound a little gory to just come out and say you should drain the blood out of the fish you catch, but it's one of the most important things you can do if you like your fish with a light and delicate flavor. The simple fact is that it's usually blood left in the flesh that produces the strong, well, "fishy" taste of fish that many people don't like. More and more anglers are discovering that fish taste much better if they're bled as thoroughly as possible.

Many years ago I started recommending that anglers bleed the halibut they catch, especially if they planned to package large quantities that might spend months in the freezer before it was eaten. Now I bleed virtually every fish I kill for the table, from crappies and perch to salmon, steelhead, and lingcod. They all taste better if they're bled as soon as they're caught.

The easiest way to bleed a fish is to use a sharp knife or scissors to cut through a couple of gill arches or to make a deep cut into the soft tissue immediately behind a gill cover. You'll know if you did it right, because blood should flow freely from the wound. In recent years I've discovered that cutting a couple of gills and also making a deep slice just in front of the tail is even better than the single cut at the gills. The fish bleed out more quickly and thoroughly if cut in those two places. If you forget to take along a knife or scissors, you can use pliers, a hook remover, or your fingers to grab a gill arch and give it a yank.

A fish won't bleed out much if you wait until it's completely dead to make the cut, so most anglers do it immediately before or just after they use their fish clubs. Done properly, this one-two approach will result in a quick death for the fish and much better-tasting table fare.

You may not notice the difference between a fish that's been bled and one that hasn't if you always eat your catch fresh, but store it in the freezer for a month or two and any fish gourmet can tell the difference between fish that's been bled and fish that hasn't.

Keep them cool.
Fish may begin to deteriorate within minutes after they die, but keeping them cool can forestall that deterioration for hours, even days. It's how commercial fishing vessels get away with hauling their catch around for long periods of time before returning to the docks. You may not know it, but the fish you buy at Safeway or Top Foods may have been out of the water for a week or more without freezing. Had it been stored at temperatures of 50 or 60 degrees, it would have been in a landfill in half that time. Although it's nice to think that anglers will take better care of the three or four fish they catch for the table than a commercial fisherman takes with the several tons he may have in the hold of his boat, the same principles apply. The cooler you keep your fish, the longer they'll maintain their just-caught quality.

Which, of course, leads to the question: How cool is cool enough? On a 40-degree afternoon, you're probably okay taking no precautions with your catch. I've caught winter steelhead in February and feeder chinook in March, left the fish lying in the shade for seven or eight hours, and they were in near-perfect condition by the time I got them home. On a 65-degree day, though, you may have to be a lot more careful, and by the time the mercury climbs to 80, you'd better have a cooler full of ice. The standard changes with the conditions, but remember that keeping a freshly caught fish in the shade is better than letting it lie in the sun. Putting a damp cloth or sheet of burlap over that shaded fish is better still, because of the cooling effects of water evaporating off the cloth. Even better than that damp burlap, though, is a layer of shaved ice. Many anglers carry a cooler full of ice on their boat or in their car on every fishing trip, and the catch goes into the cooler as soon as possible. That's not a bad habit to get into.

Clean your fish properly.
Some fish should be gilled and gutted, others filleted and skinned, still others beheaded, gutted, and skinned. Different fish species require different treatment when it comes to separating the good parts from the bad, and it's up to us as anglers to know which treatment is best for which species and how to do it right. Try the gilling and gutting method on some of the more bony species, for example, and you end up with a mess. Have you ever tried gutting a yellow perch or a crappie as you would a rainbow trout? Lots of people have, and they're usually pretty disappointed with the results. The swim bladder doesn't want to come out of the body cavity, and most people have neither the equipment nor the patience to scrape that so-called blood line away from the backbone. And, even if you can accomplish all

that, you still have lots of sharp spines, thick skin, and all those tough scales still attached to the flesh. Here's a hint: perch should be filleted.

If you don't know how to properly separate the bones, kidneys, gills, and other inedible parts from the flesh of a fish, the flesh you do eat may taste stronger than you like it or be otherwise less palatable. With some fish you may even have to trim layers of darker flesh away from layers of lighter meat, because the darker stuff may be so strong you can't eat it. In some cases, the darker flesh can even make you sick. In other words, you have to learn the best techniques for various species and practice until you get it right.

As for when to clean your catch, that may depend on circumstances. As a general rule, the sooner the better, but there might be extenuating circumstances that call for a delay in fish cleaning. For example, filleting and skinning your catch while still on the water is illegal in many places, because it's difficult or impossible to determine the size and/or species of the fish you've caught by looking at a couple of fillets on ice. Other places have rules against discarding fish heads, entrails, and the like into the water. So, know the rules about when and where you can clean your catch, then do it as soon as those rules allow.

Seal in the freshness.

It's just like they say in one of those commercials. If you eat your fish the day you bring them home, you don't have to read this one, but very few of us eat what we catch within a few hours. Those trout, salmon, panfish, bottom fish, or whatever usually have to be packaged for at least some period of time between the moment we land them and the moment we sit down to enjoy them at the table. How you package your catch makes a big difference in table quality, whether it's stored in the refrigerator overnight or kept in the freezer for several months.

For starters, squeeze the air from body cavities of gutted fish and wrap those fillets as tightly as possible in a soft, clinging, plastic wrap. The goal is to keep the fish from being in contact with air as best you can. It's not like you can wrap a little "good air" into the package with the fish and keep the "bad air" out; it's all bad air if it touches your fish for any length of time.

It's okay to refrigerate well-wrapped fish for a few days, but not indefinitely. If you know it's going to be several days before you eat the fish, freezing is the best strategy. If you do freeze it, those zip-seal type plastic bags are okay for short-term storage, but glazing, freezing in water, or vacuum sealing are best for freezing fish more than a couple of weeks. All of these methods keep air away from the fish— and remember that air is the enemy here. You know about freezer burn, which results not from cold temperatures, but from air being in contact with the food. Glazing or freezing fish in water puts a layer of ice between the fish and the air, while vacuum sealing removes the air and presses a thin layer of plastic against the fish. I've frozen well-sealed fish for as long as two years without freezer burn and without any noticeable drop in table quality.

Teaching Kids To Fish: 10 Tips

According to a Chinese proverb, if you give a man a fish, you feed him for a day, but if you teach him to fish, you feed him for life. To take that one step further, if you teach a kid to fish, you have a fishing partner for life. You still have to feed 'em, but that's what McDonald's is for. Here are the 10 most important things to remember when taking kids fishing:

- **Let them help with the planning and preparation.** Finding your destination on a map, hitting the local tackle shop for a few new lures, and loading the car or boat before the trip is part of the adventure, so share it with your young fishing partners.
- **Provide them with good, functional tackle.** Nothing is more frustrating than trying to learn to fish with a brokayen rod, reel that won't work, and rotten line that keeps breaking.
- **Catch fish.** Target a pond or lake that has plenty of hungry hatchery trout or cooperative panfish. Lunkers provide great thrills, but kids will enjoy catching lots of small fish better than few or no big ones.
- **Dress them for all weather possibilities.** Have them dress in layers, and be sure to take along rain gear, rubber boots, and a waterproof hat. They won't mind fishing in the rain as long as they're warm and comfortable. Once they get cold, it's no longer fun.
- **Keep them busy and happy.** Take along lots of snacks, drinks, and even bookays or games in case the fish aren't biting very well. Even waiting is fun if there's something to do between strikes.
- **Don't demand perfection.** Let kids make their own discoveries and their own mistakes. If they want to troll a bass plug for 10-inch trout, who cares? And if they want to do an autopsy on their first fish, that's okay too. Remember, this isn't just a fishing trip for them, it's an adventure.
- **Set a good example.** Practice and teach good fishing manners, tell them the rules, and wear a life jacket to show them it's the thing to do.
- **Quit before it gets boring or miserable.** Sitting in a boat for several hours after the fish stop biting is a drag for anyone, especially kids.
- **Start planning the next fishing trip before you return from the first.** And take the kids fishing as often as possible. They'll grow up faster than you expect, so take advantage of these early opportunities while you can.
- **Don't limit your efforts to your own kids.** The best ones to take fishing are your own, but any kid will do. Ask a friend or neighbor who doesn't fish if you can borrow his or her son or daughter for a few hours on the water. Or, better still, invite both the adults and the children on that fishing trip and help turn the entire gang into a fishing family.

Free Fishing Weekend

Something wonderful happens here in Washington every year during early June. For two days, people can go fishing free! Actually, this fabulous fishing free-for-all isn't unique to the Evergreen State, but here there are a lot more angling options than are available in most of the other states that celebrate Free Fishing Weekend. The event occurs during the weekend at the end of the first full week in June, and it provides a great chance for families to get out on the water together.

License requirements are waived for both freshwater and saltwater fishing on Free Fishing Weekend, whether you're an adult, youngster, state resident, or nonresident. Anglers should note, however, that special catch-record cards are required for some fish species, and those are still required on Free Fishing Weekend. If you want to fish for steelhead, salmon, sturgeon, or halibut, you need the appropriate catch card, even though you wouldn't need a state fishing license. The good news is the catch records are also free; you just have to go to a license dealer or Department of Fish and Wildlife office to get them.

During Free Fishing Weekend you're allowed to fish any lake, reservoir, stream, or body of saltwater open to fishing at the time, but some spots may provide especially good fishing on that particular weekend. Many lakes and streams around the state are selected for special plants of hatchery rainbow trout for the event, and the Department of Fish and Wildlife usually publicizes other "hot spots" that offer particularly good fishing for perch, crappies, and other panfish.

The dates for Free Fishing Weekend in Washington are June 8–9, 2002; June 7–8, 2003; and June 12–13, 2004.

Catch One
For the Record Book

If you thought the days of record-breaking game fish ended long ago in the Evergreen State, guess again. The truth is there are state-record—perhaps even world-record—fish still finning some of this state's lakes, reservoirs, beaver ponds, rivers, creeks, and marine waterways, just waiting for you or someone else to find 'em, hookay 'em, and land 'em. Oh, yes, if you should catch one, you also have to remember to weigh, measure, and report 'em!

For those who think that hookaying potential record-breakers was limited to the "good old days," all you have to do is skim the current record list to discover how wrong you are. The Washington Department of Fish and Wildlife compiles such record information and publishes it every year in its annual *Washington Fishing Guide* pamphlet.

Read through the most current list of state-record catches and you may be surprised to discover that 40 of the current freshwater and saltwater sport-fish records were caught during the decade of the 1990s, and at least five more have been added since the turn of the millennium. Included among those recent record catches were state records for such popular species as walleye, kokayanee, lake trout, Lahontan cutthroat trout, chinookay salmon (freshwater), coho salmon (saltwater), chum salmon (fresh and saltwater), and albacore tuna. Other record-breakers caught in the past few years include state-record Atlantic salmon (both fresh and saltwater), black bullhead, brown bullhead, burbot (freshwater ling), golden trout, lake whitefish, northern pike, northern squawfish, rock bass, tiger musky, yellow bullhead, blue rockfish, cabezon, great sculpin, pink salmon, red-tail surfperch, sablefish, sixgill shark, starry flounder, and yellowtail rockfish.

In fact, only 12 of Washington's state-record fish were caught prior to 1980. So much for all those whoppers we used to catch around here in the good old days.

So, where might someone lookay for the next state-record fish? In many cases, the waters that have already produced record-class specimens are the best places to find another. The conditions that produced Palmer Lake's 17-pound burbot, record chum and coho salmon from the Satsop River, several of the most recent record kokayanee in Lake Roosevelt, and the record 18.75-pound walleye from the Columbia River are pretty much the same as they were when those record fish were caught, and there's a good chance that even bigger ones will be caught from those places in the future. Likewise, if you have your sights set on catching a record blue or channel catfish, the Snake, Columbia, and lower Yakima Rivers have

> If you can measure a fish and do some fairly easy mathematical calculations, you can calculate the fish's weight. Measure around the thickest part of the body to get the girth in inches, and square that number. Multiply that total by the length in inches. Now divide your total by 800 and you get the weight in pounds. So, a fish with a 10-inch girth and a 20-inch length would weigh 2.5 pounds (10x10x20=2000/800=2.5)

produced all our record catfish so far and are the most likely spots to lookay for a new record.

In some cases, there is really only one spot where a particular record might be caught, because the species is limited to only that body of water. Beardslee rainbow trout, for example, are found only in the Olympic Peninsula's Crescent Lake, and only southwest Washington's Mayfield Lake has any tiger muskies big enough to top the current record-holder.

And, if you can believe your fellow fishermen, you might get a tip on where to lookay for a record-breaker from the people who own the current record. When George Weekes brought his state-record Wobbly Lake brookay trout into the Department of Wildlife office in Olympia in 1988, he seemed almost disappointed about it, because the nine-pounder was the smaller of two huge brookayies Weekes had seen in the lake's clear water. When the record fish grabbed his lure, the bigger one spookayed and disappeared.

If you are lucky enough to catch a state-record fish, it's important that you know what to do next. As the Department of Fish and Wildlife advises, the most important first step is to get it weighed as soon as possible on a certified scale (not your bathroom scale or the rusty little scale you've carried around in your boat for the past two decades). Get signatures from the scale operator and at least one other witness to the weighing, then take the fish to a Department of Fish and Wildlife office for verification and positive identification. Record application forms with complete instructions are available at all Department of Fish and Wildlife offices. See the back of the bookay for Washington State fishing records.

CHAPTER A1:
OLYMPIC PENINSULA

©TERRY RUDNICK

WINTER STEELHEADING ON THE QUEETS RIVER

Map A1

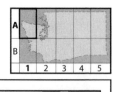

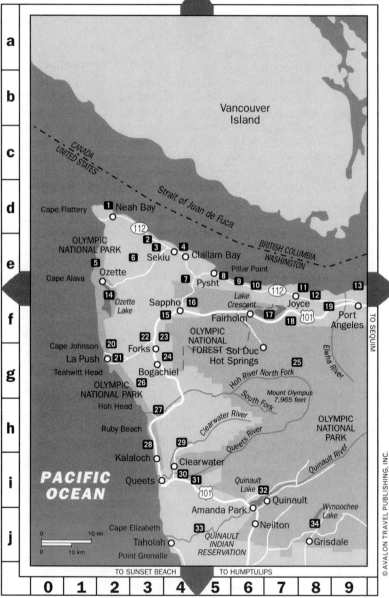

Vancouver Island

CANADA / UNITED STATES

Strait of Juan de Fuca

BRITISH COLUMBIA / WASHINGTON

Cape Flattery

1 Neah Bay

(112)

OLYMPIC NATIONAL PARK

2

3 Sekiu

4 Clallam Bay

6

Pillar Point

5

Cape Alava

O Ozette

7

8

Pysht

9

10

(112)

11

12

13

14

Ozette Lake

Sappho

16

Lake Crescent

Joyce

19

Port Angeles

TO SEQUIM

15

Fairholm

17

18

101

OLYMPIC NATIONAL FOREST

Sol Duc Hot Springs

Cape Johnson

20

22

23

Forks

24

25

Elwha River

La Push

21

Teahwitt Head

26

Bogachiel

Hoh River North Fork

South Fork

Mount Olympus 7,965 feet

OLYMPIC NATIONAL PARK

Hoh Head

27

Clearwater River

Queets River

OLYMPIC NATIONAL PARK

Ruby Beach

28

29

Kalaloch

Clearwater

Quinault River

PACIFIC OCEAN

Queets

30

31

101

Quinault Lake

32

Quinault

Wynoochee Lake

Amanda Park

34

Cape Elizabeth

33

Neilton

Grisdale

Taholah

QUINAULT INDIAN RESERVATION

Point Grenville

0   10 mi
0   10 km

TO SUNSET BEACH

TO HUMPTULIPS

© AVALON TRAVEL PUBLISHING, INC.

Chapter A1: Olympic Peninsula

If Washington still has a last frontier, this is it. Some distance via winding roads from the state's major population centers, "The Peninsula" isn't a place you pass through on your way to somewhere else; it's a destination you reach after a fair amount of planning and preparation. It's steep country, where the Olympic Mountains drop almost vertically into the Pacific Ocean to the west and the Strait of Juan de Fuca to the north. Home to the north coast's famous Olympic Rain Forest, it's a place where raincoats and rubber boots are usually kept within arm's reach. All that precipitation, though, has produced lakes in the flat places and river-making glaciers in the mountains, so there's water to fish wherever you turn. Salmon, steelhead, and trout fishing are the main attractions, and this part of Washington boasts some of the state's best in all three categories. Neah Bay, Sekiu, and LaPush are three of the Northwest's top salmon destinations, and the bottom fishing isn't bad, either. The Sol Duc, Bogachiel, Hoh, Queets, and Quinault Rivers are favorites of steelheaders throughout the Northwest and also give up good catches of salmon and sea-run cutthroat trout. Crescent Lake is the region's biggest body of freshwater and is home to not one but two unique salmonids, the Beardslee rainbow and Crescenti cutthroat trout. Other lakes in the region provide excellent fishing for trout and kokanee, and small-stream cutthroat fishing can be very good in spring and fall. Logging remains a major industry here, though, and many of the Peninsula's rivers and creeks have suffered decades of logging damage that have had an impact on all fish populations. The fishing here isn't as good as it was 30 or 40 years ago, but you could say the same thing about a lot of places. It could be argued that it was sublime here to begin with, so it's still mighty fine by comparison.

STEELHEAD ON THE HOH RIVER

◻ Neah Bay

No one comes to Neah Bay by accident, since it's not on the way to anywhere. Most of the people who brave the narrow, winding, 14-mile stretch of Highway 112 from Sekiu to Neah Bay do so for one reason: to go fishing.

In recent years, with salmon-fishing restrictions greatly affecting Neah Bay, bottom fish have become a huge draw, and this place where the Strait of Juan de Fuca meets the mighty Pacific Ocean offers some of the best bottom fishing to be found anywhere.

Lingcod season on Washington's inside waters (Strait of Juan de Fuca, Puget Sound, San Juan Islands, and Hood Canal) opens in midspring, and that's the traditional start of the season for many Neah Bay regulars. The rocky coastline, scattered islands, and numerous submerged reefs and rock piles provide almost limitless lingcod-fishing opportunities not only in the Strait, but around the corner on the Pacific Ocean side of Cape Flattery.

Duncan Rock, a small island several miles northwest of Neah Bay, is a popular ling fishing spot, but a close look at a nautical chart reveals dozens of other possibilities. The National Oceanic and Atmospheric Administration's (NOAA) Cape Flattery charts 18485 and 18460 are the ones you want if you plan to fish this area. Use them to locate the steep, rocky drop-offs that lings like. Pinpoint those locations with your depthsounder and you'll be in the right neighborhood for Neah Bay lings.

Besides lingcod, near-shore fishing around Neah Bay in the spring and early summer also provides some excellent rockfish action. Black rockfish are the most abundant and most popular. Although commonly lumped in with all the other marine bottom fish, the black is more likely to be found suspended well up in the water column, sometimes right on top. Take along a trout or bass rod to fish for them.

If you're not sure where to look for black rockfish around Neah Bay, Tatoosh Island, at the southern entrance to the Strait, is always a good starting point. So are the shallow reefs to the east of Neah Bay, near Sail Rock. Blacks show a preference for small, light-colored lures, so take along an assortment of leadheads in the quarter-ounce to two-ounce range and plenty of two- to four-inch plastic grubs, worms, and tube skirts in white, clear, smoke, light blue, and other light colors. A selection of metal jigs, such as Darts, Crippled Herring, and Hopkins No=EQLs, weighing from half an ounce to three ounces, will also come in handy for black rockfish. A seven- or eight-weight fly rod and reel equipped with a sinking line also will give you a chance to have some fun with these tough little sea bass.

Blue, yellowtail, copper, brown, and China rockfish, all of which may be caught on light tackle from relatively shallow water, are all found in the Neah Bay area, although they are less abundant than black rockfish. Quillback, canary, bocaccio, yelloweye, and other deep-water rockfish species are also abundant around offshore reefs and underwater ledges. Most of these fish will come from water of 150 feet or deeper.

To many Northwest anglers, Neah Bay's most famous feature is Swiftsure Bank. It's actually more than 20 miles to the north by boat, but this huge reef at the edge of the Pacific Ocean is one of the best places to go in the Neah Bay area for halibut. It's a pretty safe bet that the big reef has given up more halibut to Washington anglers over the past five years than any other spot in the state.

Due to the rather complicated sport halibut seasons of recent years, the best advice I can give to would-be Swiftsure halibut anglers is to plan on fishing in May or early June. Be sure to check on season dates for this year before planning a trip.

The charters operating out of Neah Bay offer the safest, most comfortable way to enjoy Swiftsure halibut action. Contact Big Salmon Fishing Resort directly for details on this year's halibut season or to book a trip (see contact information below).

Swiftsure and Blue Dot aren't the only places where Neah Bay anglers might encounter a hefty halibut. Several areas right around Cape Flattery provide decent halibut fishing, and a number of flatties over 100 pounds have been caught by small-boat anglers within a few minutes' run of port. Perhaps the most productive and certainly one of the closest spots for near-shore halibut fishing is Koitlah Point, more commonly known to anglers as "the Garbage Dump." It provides fair to good spring halibut fishing and is only a five-minute run west from Waadah Island. If you aren't sure where it is, either look for a small cluster of boats or watch for the smoke coming from the hillside on your left as you're running west. That smoke is coming from the dump that gave this halibut hole its name. You'll be fishing here in 175 to 300 feet of water.

Good salmon fishing used to be a sure thing around Neah Bay during the summer and early fall, but there are no longer any sure things where Northwest coastal salmon seasons are concerned. When regulations allow, July is a good month for big chinooks throughout the Neah Bay area. Drift mooching and motor mooching with plug-cut herring accounts for many of the fish, but jigging is also effective. The good news is that the summer king fishery here depends largely on fish bound for the Columbia River, and those runs have been building in recent years. The 2001 run, as most anglers know, was a dandy. Keep your ear tuned to Columbia River fall chinook estimates and plan your July trip to Neah Bay accordingly.

The area south of Tatoosh Island, just off Cape Flattery several miles west of the Neah Bay harbor, is traditionally a good chinook producer. But if you visit when salmon season is open, don't be afraid to ask around when you get there, and be willing to move to where the action is if you don't find good fishing at your primary location. The hot bite may be at any one of a half dozen locations within a 30-minute run of Neah Bay.

Late-summer coho (silver) salmon fishing at Neah Bay is legendary. Trolling a plastic squid or streamer fly behind a flasher or pulling a plug-cut herring within 30 feet of the surface is the standard way to catch these 5- to 20-pound acrobats. Stronger hatchery runs the past few years have made life better for Neah Bay anglers, but the big, late-run fish that used to cause so much commotion were all wild-stock fish, and anglers have had to release all wild coho lately. Planning your salmon-fishing trip to Neah Bay, though, is a year-by-year thing, so pay close attention to the fishing pamphlet and ask around to be sure before locking in your fishing dates.

Location: At Neah Bay on the northwest tip of the Olympic Peninsula; see map A1, grid d2.

Species: Chinook, coho, and pink salmon; Pacific halibut; lingcod; a wide variety of rockfish species.

Facilities: Once home to a half dozen fishing resorts, Neah Bay now has only one, Big Salmon Resort. Charters and boat rentals are available from spring to fall. There's one public boat ramp in town, located immediately west of Big Salmon Resort. There's room to launch two boats at a time if you work at it a little. The launch fee is $7, payable at Big Salmon.

The Makah Marina has moorage, and some of the slips are leased by Big Salmon Resort. Parking can be a problem at the marina, thanks to a lack of trailer-parking spaces and a four-hour parking limit that is sometimes enforced. A grocery/dry goods store carries most necessities, and there's a small café at the east end of town. Tackle and car and boat fuel also are available in Neah Bay.

Directions: Follow U.S. 101 north from Hoquiam or west from Port Angeles to the town of Sappho and turn north on Highway 113, which meets Highway 112 about 11 miles north of Sappho and continues on as Highway 112 about 26 miles to Neah Bay. The road narrows and becomes twisty just past Sekiu.

Contact: Big Salmon Fishing Resort, 360/645-2374 (VHF channel 66) (spring to fall only), website: www.bigsalmonresort.com, email bigsalmon@olypen.com; The Cape Motel and RV Park, 360/645-4450. For nautical charts of the Neah Bay area, contact Captain's Nautical Supply, 206/283-7242.

2 Sekiu River

The stocking of several thousand winter steelhead smolts a year keeps this fishery going through the winter, but it's local anglers who do most of the catching. Let's face it: the Sekiu is a long way from Washington's population centers, and for the three dozen or so steelhead it produces each season, it's hardly worth the drive. Short bursts of fishing action occur throughout the winter once the Makah tribal fishery ends in December.

Cutthroat fishing, on the other hand, can be well worth the trip if you like to do battle with sea-run cutts of 14 to 16 inches. Freshets during the months of October and November offer the best chances of cutthroating success.

Location: Flows into the Strait of Juan de Fuca west of Sekiu; see map A1, grid e3.

Species: Winter steelhead, sea-run cutthroat trout.

Facilities: Food, fuel, and lodging are available in the Sekiu/Clallam Bay area.

Directions: Drive west out of Sekiu on Highway 112. After passing the Hoko-Ozette

Road about two miles west of town, continue for about 2.5 miles to where the highway crosses the Sekiu River. A logging road turning left just before the bridge provides access to the river.

Contact: Washington Department of Fish and Wildlife, Montesano Office, 360/249-4628; Olson's Resort, 360/963-2311, website: www.northolympic.com, email olsons@olypen.com; Curley's Resort and Dive Center, 360/963-2281.

3 Hoko River

December and January are usually the top months to fish this small river for steelhead, especially in its lower reaches from the upper Hoko Bridge downstream to the river mouth. Runs of adult fish from hatchery plants, totaling about 25,000 smolts a year, peak during these months. Check the current fishing regulations pamphlet for special fishing rules during the fall.

On the upper Hoko, which is open to catch-and-release fly-fishing only, anglers take steelhead throughout the winter, but the month of March can be particularly productive. Those fly-fishing regulations apply throughout the summer and winter, so this is a spot to consider if you like to toss feathers and feel like getting away from the worm-dunking folks.

Sea-run cutthroat fishing is best throughout the river in October, but sea-runs can be found in the river from August to December.

Location: Enters the Strait of Juan de Fuca just west of Sekiu; see map A1, grid e3.

Species: Winter steelhead, resident and sea-run cutthroat trout.

Facilities: Food, gas, and lodging are available in Clallam Bay and Sekiu.

Directions: Take Highway 112 about two miles west past Sekiu and turn south (left) on Hoko-Ozette Road, which parallels much of the river.

Contact: Washington Department of Fish

and Wildlife, Montesano Office, 360/249-4628; Olson's Resort, 360/963-2311, website: www. northolympic.com, email olsons@olypen. com; Coho Resort, 360/963-2333; Curley's Resort and Dive Center, 360/963-2281.

4 Sekiu/Clallam Bay

Salmon fishing restrictions have even come to Sekiu in recent years, which is really too bad, because this is one of those places where even the small-boat angler could almost always get out and find a place to catch kings and/or silvers. I'll never forget my first trip to this gem of Northwest salmon-fishing spots. Here on a July evening in the early 1970s, I had the good fortune of catching my first-ever chinook from the Strait of Juan de Fuca. It was one of those third-time's-the-charm events, as the thick-bodied slab of chrome hit the line of one of my companions, stole the bait, hit a second partner's with the same result, and then grabbed my herring-baited hooks and connected solidly. The tails of the two stolen herring still poked out of the 22-pounder's throat as we admired it on the deck of the boat after a 15-minute battle.

Chinooks inhabit the waters in and around Clallam Bay throughout the year, and the area has a long history of providing good catches of 5- to 20-pound blackmouth (immature chinook) during the late winter and early spring. Waters immediately west of Clallam Bay, commonly referred to as the Caves, were for decades considered among the state's top areas for mature chinook (king) salmon during the summer months. Some of those fish topped 40 pounds. In September the waters farther offshore from Sekiu have long been considered among the Northwest's top spots for adult cohos. These big hook-nosed silvers sometimes weigh in at 15 pounds or more. Both the summertime chinook fishery and fall fishery for silvers have been hampered by closures and angling restrictions the past few years, but when the season is open, the action can be excellent. During the past three years, for example, anglers enjoyed fast action on big silvers and lots more fishing elbowroom than they used to have in the good old days of the 1970s and 1980s. Part of the reason was that some of the best fishing occurred while the popular Buoy 10 salmon season was open near the mouth of the Columbia, and people more or less forgot about Sekiu. Those who didn't forget were generously rewarded for their efforts. The addition of pink salmon to the Sekiu catch makes late-summer fishing even hotter during the odd-numbered years when these smallest of Pacific salmon return to Washington.

Bottom fishing remains pretty good here, and with crowds generally smaller than in the past, you may have considerable elbowroom to fish for lingcod and rockfish. You'll find black rockfish in shallow water over submerged rock piles and around kelp beds, and yelloweye, canary, China, quillback, and other rockfish species over submerged rocks in deeper areas.

A special slot limit is in effect on lingcod throughout the Strait of Juan de Fuca, but Sekiu offers a number of rocky areas where you can find keeper lings in the 26- to 40-inch range.

Halibut fishing has gotten very popular throughout this area in recent years, and during the spring-summer season you can usually find someone who knows where the big flatties are biting. Often it's near the mouth of the Hoko River, but other nearby flats may also be worth prospecting. Ask around when you arrive and head for the action. A weekend halibut derby in early July has drawn a lot of attention from anglers here the past couple of years. Halibut fishing around the mouth of the Hoko generally improves as summer progresses, so it's a good place to keep in mind after the spring halibut bite subsides in other areas to the east.

Location: At Sekiu on the north side of the Olympic Peninsula; see map A1, grid e4.

Species: Chinook, coho, and pink salmon; halibut; lingcod; various rockfish.

Facilities: Food, lodging, boat rentals, launch ramps, moorage, bait, tackle, and other needs all are available in Sekiu and Clallam Bay.

Directions: Drive west from Port Angeles on U.S. 101 and either exit to the right onto Highway 112 about four miles from town and continue west, or stay on 101 for about 43 miles to the town of Sappho and turn north on Highway 113. Where Highways 112 and 113 meet about 11 miles north of Sappho, continue northwest for about 15 miles to Clallam Bay and then to nearby Sekiu.

Contact: Washington Department of Fish and Wildlife, Montesano Office, 360/249-4628; Olson's Resort, 360/963-2311, website: www.northolympic.com, email olsons@olypen.com; Curley's Resort and Dive Center, 360/963-2281, 800/542-9680; Van Riper's Resort, 360/963-2334, website: www.vanripersresort.com; Straitside Resort, 360/963-2100, website: www.straitsideresort.com. For nautical charts of the Sekiu/Clallam Bay area, contact Captain's Nautical Supply, 206/283-7242.

5 Northwest Coast

Many of the anglers who fish this hard-to-reach corner of the Pacific Northwest come around the corner from Neah Bay to work their way down the coast to some of the state's traditional salmon and bottom fish hot spots. Others come out of La Push or even run north from the Westport area to these fish-filled waters. Places such as (from north to south) Skagway, Greenbank, Mukkaw Bay, Spike Rock, Father and Son, and the Rock Pile have at various times provided phenomenal fishing for both salmon and bottom fish.

Restrictions on both salmon and halibut have made things tough for anglers here in recent years, but when seasons are open and the Pacific is calm enough to allow small boats to come and go as they please, this stretch of the Washington coast can be an angler's paradise. Likewise, charters from both Neah Bay and Westport sometimes run to this area to capitalize on the good fishing possibilities.

When salmon seasons are open here, big chinooks are often found right in close to the shoreline, where they may corner herring and other bait fish in the shallow water. Early mornings and tide changes often provide the best action, but a hot bite may turn on with little notice and end just as quickly as it begins. The Skagway area is a favorite among Neah Bay anglers for just this kind of fast-action king fishing.

This part of the coast is dotted with underwater humps, hills, and plateaus that act as a magnet for Pacific halibut. Umatilla Reef, west of La Push, is one of the biggest and best known of these halibut spots, and there are dozens of others that are smaller and more difficult to locate but every bit as productive. Some of these humps, which receive light fishing pressure during the short periods when the halibut season is open, are home to barn-door fish averaging 50 pounds or more. A special halibut closure protects some of these humps from anglers, so be sure to check the sport fishing regulations pamphlet for closure boundaries if you aren't sure where they are.

Rockfish and lingcod seasons are more dependable, and there are hundreds of places to catch them between Cape Flattery and La Push. Near-surface black, blue, and yellow-tail rockfish are plentiful for light-tackle anglers, or you can drop a live greenling or other small bottom fish to the bottom over a rocky hump or steep ledge and find lingcod that sometimes top 50 pounds. This is perhaps

Washington's last great stronghold of excellent lingcod fishing. As with salmon fishing, the great bottom fish action is within reach of private-boat anglers when the weather cooperates. But don't forget that this is the wide-open Pacific, and if the ocean is rough, save your adventure for another day when Ma Nature is in a more cooperative mood.

Nautical charts 18485, 18460, and 18480 are extremely valuable to anyone thinking about fishing this corner of the Pacific Northwest.

Location: From Cape Flattery south to La Push on the west side of the Olympic Peninsula; see map A1, grid e1.

Species: Lingcod, rockfish, halibut, and chinook and coho salmon.

Facilities: LaPush has a new marina with nearly 100 slips, fuel, and two new boat ramps. To the north, Neah Bay has cabins, motels, RV parks, and fishing resorts. Charters and boat rentals are available from spring to fall. A grocery/dry goods store carries everything an angler might need. La Push has a small boat ramp and little else, but all amenities are available in Forks, about 18 miles to the east.

Directions: Take U.S. 101 to La Push Road, about two miles north of Forks, and turn west. Follow La Push Road for approximately 14 miles to La Push. Or follow U.S. 101 north from Hoquiam or west from Port Angeles to the town of Sappho and turn north on Highway 113, which meets Highway 112 about 11 miles north of Sappho and becomes Highway 112. Drive west on Highway 112 about 26 miles to Neah Bay.

Contact: Quileute Marina, 360/374-5392 (VHF channel 80); Ocean Park Resort, 800/487-1267, website: www.lapushwa.com; Big Salmon Fishing Resort (Neah Bay), 360/654-2374 (VHF channel 66) (April through September only), website: www.bigsalmonresort.com, email bigsalmon@olypen.com; Olympic Sporting Goods, 360/374-6330. For nautical charts of the Northwest Coast, contact Captain's Nautical Supply, 206/283-7242.

6 Elk Lake

The advice from most folks is "Don't bother," but if you really have the urge to work hard for your trout, this is the only real lake between the Hoko-Ozette Road and Neah Bay. The cutthroats are pan-sized, and if you catch a 14-incher, you've got yourself a trophy. Fish 'em with wet flies or small streamers, your favorite wobbling spoons and weighted spinners, or the time-proven cutthroat getter, a garden worm below a bobber. Give yourself plenty of time to get to and from the lake if you're going for the day.

Location: Northeast of Ozette; see map A1, grid e3.

Species: Cutthroat trout.

Facilities: No facilities are available at the lake. As a local reminded me, "You have to go back to Sekiu or Clallam Bay for a soda pop." The nearest food, gas, lodging, and tackle are available in Sekiu and Clallam Bay.

Directions: Take the Hoko-Ozette Road south off Highway 112 about two miles west of Sekiu and drive about 15 miles to the 7000 Line. The 7000 Line is gated, so you must either walk or ride a bicycle or a horse about five miles to the west side of the lake.

Contact: Olympic Sporting Goods, 360/374-6330.

7 Pysht River

okay, before you can fish it, you have to know how to say it. The "y" is pronounced like a short "i," so it's "Pisht," not "P-eye-sht." To help you remember, just say to yourself: "I fysht the Pysht." (But you might not want to say it when there are lots of people around.) Anyway, the Pysht is a little river that depends on annual steelhead plants of 10,000 to 20,000 fish for its livelihood. During a typical winter, anglers catch 100 to 200 fish.

Since they're hatchery steelies, most of them come back in December or January. In skimming the steelhead catch figures compiled by Washington's Department of Fish and Wildlife, I noticed something a little unusual and at least moderately unnerving about the steelhead fishery here. Those records show that anglers catch a fair number of steelhead from the Pysht in March, which would be cool, except for the fact that the river closes to fishing at the end of February. Hmmm.

Location: Enters the Strait of Juan de Fuca at Pysht east of Clallam Bay; see map A1, grid e4.

Species: Winter steelhead, sea-run cutthroat trout.

Facilities: Clallam Bay, about 10 miles to the north, has food, gas, lodging, tackle, and RV sites.

Directions: Take U.S. 101 to Sappho and turn north on Highway 113, which crosses the river half a mile south of the Highway 112 intersection. Turn left on the gravel road just south of the bridge to follow the river upstream. To follow the river downstream, turn east (right) on Highway 112.

Contact: Washington Department of Fish and Wildlife, Montesano Office, 360/249-4628.

8 Pillar Point

While not the hot salmon-fishing destination it was during its peak years in the 1970s and early 1980s, this somewhat isolated stretch of Juan de Fuca Strait provides pretty good summer king fishing and fair to good action on smaller chinook during the late-winter season that kicks off around the middle of February. What's more, late-summer coho action has returned to Pillar Point after several years of relative inactivity. The rule recently has been one chinook in summer and wild coho release, but that can change from year to year. This is also a good place to fish for pink salmon when they return to Washington waters during odd-numbered years, and the pink fishing was hot during the summer of 2001.

During the spring, the Pillar Point area can be a good base of operations for halibut anglers. Seven or eight miles to the east is the gently sloping beach at the mouth of the Twin Rivers, perhaps the most productive spring halibut spot between Neah Bay and Port Angeles. The halibut season here usually lasts for a couple of months from May to July, but it changes from year to year and may be closed certain days of the week, so bone up on the seasons and regulations before planning your trip.

As far as lingcod and other bottom fish are concerned, there are several steep, rocky drop-offs and submerged rock piles to investigate. You'll need a depthsounder and a good chart to find and fish them effectively, so pick up a copy of NOAA's nautical chart 18460 before heading out.

Location: At Pysht east of Clallam Bay on the Strait of Juan de Fuca; see map A1, grid e5.

Species: Chinook, coho, and pink salmon; Pacific halibut; lingcod; rockfish.

Facilities: With the closure of Silver King Resort in 1996, the nearest motels, RV hookups, fuel, tackle, and boat rentals are now in Sekiu, a half-hour drive to the west. Pillar Point County Park, between the point and the old Silver King site, has a few RV sites and a single-wide boat ramp that's open to the elements. The park is open from May 15 through the end of September.

Directions: Drive west out of Port Angeles on U.S. 101 and either turn right (north) on Highway 112 about four miles from town and follow it 32 miles to the Pillar Point Recreation Area sign, or stay on U.S. 101 about 43 miles to the town of Sappho, turn north (right) on Highway 113, follow it 11 miles to the intersection of Highway 112, turn east

Fishing with Guides and Charters

Booking a trip with a fishing guide or charter is a great way to have lots of fun and learn something in the bargain, provided you ask plenty of questions before laying down your money. Guide and charter operations are found throughout Washington, on both freshwater and saltwater, wherever there's a popular game fish species to be caught and enough people interested in paying to go catch them. I've listed dozens of them on various waters throughout this book.

Paying someone else to do most of the thinking and the work can make a fishing experience more enjoyable. The guide worries about having the boat and equipment ready at first light; the guide deals with the broken tackle, dirty boat, and empty fuel tank at day's end; the guide (usually) has to clean the fish; the guide worries about making the late-evening calls to other anglers to ensure being in the right place at the right time the next day. The customer's main worry is whether he or she brought enough lunch and plenty of film to record the day's achievements.

Although some anglers think fishing with a guide or charter is for novices and part-timers, veteran anglers also can benefit from a guide's vast fishing knowledge, especially his (or her) knowledge of the lake or bay he fishes every day. No two guide or charter services, however, are exactly the same, so do some research before booking a trip. If you're thinking about booking with a company for the first time, here are some of the questions you may want to ask before laying down your money:

- **How long has the guide fished in the area?** Part of what you're buying is experience, and if your guide is a newcomer to the location, he may know little more than you do about fishing the area.

- **Can he provide references?** Happy clients should be willing to recommend people they've fished with, and a good guide will have a long list of satisfied customers. Not every angler is totally happy with the results of every fishing trip, but if the guy (or gal) does things right, the people who have fished with him or her before should have good things to say. No references may mean no happy clients.

(right), and drive about five miles to the Pillar Point sign.

Contact: Olson's Resort, 360/963-2311, website: www.northolympic.com, olsons@olypen.com; Curley's Resort and Dive Center, 360/963-2281, 800/542-9680. For nautical charts of the Pillar Point area, contact Captain's Nautical Supply, 206/283-7242.

9 East and West Twin Rivers

Anglers catch 10 to 20 winter steelhead and about half that number of summer-runs from these two side-by-side rivers during a typical year, so they're hardly worth driving to if you lust in your heart for a steelhead. Most, if not all, of the steelhead caught here are taken by locals who can drop what they're doing and fish these little streams when conditions are right.

The same could be said for sea-run cutthroats, except that there are several times as many cutts in the first place, so your chances of hooking a fish or two are greater overall. The rewards, of course, are smaller with a 14-inch cutthroat than with a 10-pound steelhead, so you decide whether they're worth

- **What is and isn't covered in the cost?** Some trips include a shore lunch, others hot coffee, some may even include a one-day fishing license, but you need to ask long before you get in the boat.

- **Speaking of licenses, does the guide or charter sell them?** Some do, but many don't, and if you show up at daylight without one, you may lose several hours of valuable fishing time waiting for a license dealership to open. Worse yet, you could be left standing on shore as everyone else on the boat goes fishing.

- **Are fish killed or released?** You may want meat but book a trip during a catch-and-release season, for example. Some guides, on the other hand, like to put fish in the box even though you're a catch-and-release angler. Talk about these things on the phone, not after the boat is on the water.

- **What about fish packaging?** Most guides and charters do no more than clean your catch and maybe provide a plastic bag to put it in. If your trip home takes anything more than a few minutes, you'll want it in a cooler full of ice, which you have to provide. Some guides and fishing charters, though, will make arrangements to have your catch frozen, smoked, or canned, then shipped to your home a few days later. That may be something you want to do if you live on the other side of the state or if you're not going straight home after your fishing trip.

- **How long is the fishing day?** Does the day's fishing end at 4 P.M., at dark, or when you catch your limit? Getting your money's worth from a guided trip has more to do with the "quality" of the day than the number of hours you spend on the water, but it's good to know the rules before you begin.

There are no absolutely right and wrong answers; everything depends on what you're comfortable with accepting. If you ask all of these questions and have a problem with any of the answers, you may want to shop around a bit more. In most cases there's more than one company operating on any given body of water, so you always have the option of going elsewhere.

---

the trip. Neither steelhead nor cutthroat smolts are planted, so any fish you hook will be a wild beauty.

Location: Flow into the Strait of Juan de Fuca west of Joyce; see map A1, grid e6.

Species: Sea-run cutthroat trout, a few winter and summer steelhead.

Facilities: The nearest RV park and campground is at Lyre River Park, about eight miles to the east. Food, gas, lodging, and tackle are available in Port Angeles.

Directions: From Port Angeles drive west on U.S. 101 for about four miles and turn right on Highway 112. Drive about 11 miles west to Joyce and continue another 13 miles to bridges that cross both rivers, less than half a mile apart. A gravel road to the south (left) just west of the East Twin and another about 1.5 miles west of the West Twin run upstream to provide access.

Contact: Washington Department of Fish and Wildlife, Montesano Office, 360/249-4628; Lyre River Park, 360/928-3436.

10 Lyre River

This may not be the world's shortest river, but it has to rank right up there near the top of the list. The entire Lyre River, from its headwaters in crystal-clear Lake Crescent to its confluence with the Strait of Juan de Fuca, is a total of five miles long. And the distance that steelhead can travel up the river is even shorter, thanks to an impassable falls about three miles from the river mouth.

For its size, though, the Lyre is a productive steelhead stream, especially in winter. Liberal doses of hatchery smolts provide anglers with the chance to catch about 300 winter steelies here every year, most of them landed during December and January. The best fishing is right after a soaking rain, and I mean right after. The river drops and clears into fishing condition almost immediately after the rain stops.

The summer steelhead fishery here is no big deal, with the annual smolt plants providing maybe 30 to 40 fish during an average summer season. Low, clear water makes for tough fishing until the fall rains stir things up a little. If you do fish the Lyre in summer, you'll have to release anything you catch, including trout.

Location: Enters the Strait of Juan de Fuca west of Joyce; see map A1, grid e6.
Species: Winter and summer steelhead, sea-run cutthroat trout.
Facilities: A campground/RV park near the mouth of the river has a small grocery store, showers, and a laundry facility. All other amenities are available in Port Angeles.
Directions: Take Highway 112 off U.S. 101 about three miles west of Port Angeles and follow it west about 15 miles to the river.
Contact: Lyre River Park, 360/928-3436; Swain's, 360/452-2357.

11 Salt Creek

Although not stocked with hatchery smolts, this tea-colored stream has a self-sustaining wild steelhead run that's healthy enough to provide sport for a few local anglers. They catch about 20 fish from the river during a good season, and only about 10 during a poor year. You probably won't catch any, but feel free to try. Steelheading is allowed only from the mouth of the creek up to the highway bridge.

The 14-inch minimum size limit pretty much eliminates any chance that you might have had to catch a legal resident cutthroat from the creek, but you might find a 14-incher among the sea-run cutts that move in with the first good rains of the fall season. The section of Salt Creek above the highway closes at the end of October and doesn't reopen until June, so be sure to confine your cutthroating to the lower reaches after that.

Location: Enters the Strait of Juan de Fuca at Crescent Bay northeast of Joyce; see map A1, grid e8.
Species: Winter steelhead, resident and sea-run cutthroat trout.
Facilities: Grocery stores are in nearby Joyce, and all other amenities can be found in Port Angeles.
Directions: Take Highway 112 off U.S. 101 about three miles west of Port Angeles and drive west for approximately seven miles to Camp Hayden Road. Turn north (right) on Camp Hayden Road to follow Salt Creek downstream.
Contact: Swain's, 360/452-2357.

12 Freshwater Bay

This is one of my favorite saltwater fishing spots in the entire Pacific Northwest. But before we talk about the fishing, we should talk a little more about the boat ramp and the people who use it. First, if you arrive at the boat ramp and there are only a few boat trailers in the lot, the fishing is probably slow. That doesn't mean you won't catch fish, but you can expect to work for them. Conversely, if the lot is packed when you get there, fishing is hot—or at least it was yesterday. As for the ramp itself, it's not a great place to launch big boats. If the tide is out, you'll have to back down the ramp and perhaps several hundred feet out into the shallow bay. Even when you get to the water, it will only be inches deep, and after backing into it 50 feet more, it will still only be inches deep. It's best to leave this ramp to the smaller, lighter craft or plan your trip so that you're going in and out on the high tide, which makes a long day.

Salmon, especially chinooks, are caught in the Freshwater Bay area throughout much of the year, or at least during any time of the year that salmon season is open. Things are changing in that regard from year to year, so be sure you know what's open and what's not before hitting the water. Summertime chinook and coho fishing has been closed here recently. The prime time to fish for chinooks, of course, is during July and August, and Freshwater Bay has a long history of treating anglers well during this two-month period. Most of the action takes place to the west, from Observatory Point (at the western end of the bay) to the mouth of Salt Creek and Crescent Bay, a distance of about three miles. A few anglers troll this stretch, but most drift-mooch plug-cut herring or fish metal jigs such as the Crippled Herring, Point Wilson Dart, or Metzler Mooch-A-Jig. At times the kings might be right up against the kelp, but be willing to experiment and keep an eye on where other anglers are hooking fish.

Jigging and mooching may also take coho here (regulations permitting), but trolling can sometimes be the most effective way of locating and catching these unpredictable fish. Some are caught along with the chinooks near shore, but most of the time you'll have to move out toward the center of the Strait of Juan de Fuca to locate incoming silvers.

Some of Washington's biggest halibut have been hooked between Freshwater Bay and the mouth of the Lyre River, so serious bottom fishing might be in order if you visit the area in spring or summer. The same metal jigs used for chinook salmon will take halibut, or fish a whole herring on a wire spreader with a big cannonball sinker.

This section of the Strait also has a few underwater rock piles and pinnacles that might produce a lingcod or two. If you can't locate such structure, try for lings right up against the kelp beds and steep rock bluffs at high tide. Lingcod will sometimes move into these areas with the tide, where you can fool them with a whole herring or, better yet, a small, live greenling. You'll have little trouble catching the bait in and around the many kelp beds that line the beach along this entire stretch. These same kelp beds may produce copper, brown, or even black rockfish.

Location: The Strait of Juan de Fuca between Port Angeles and Joyce; see map A1, grid e8.

Species: Chinook, coho, and pink salmon; halibut; lingcod; rockfish; greenling.

Facilities: Freshwater Bay has a concrete boat ramp, lots of parking, and a couple of restrooms, but the ramp is high and dry during low tide. The nearest food, gas, lodging, and tackle are in and around Port Angeles.

Directions: Drive west from Port Angeles on U.S. 101 for about three miles and turn right onto Highway 112, which continues west. After driving just under five miles on Highway 112, turn north (right) onto Freshwater Bay Road and continue 3.5 miles to the bay.

Contact: Swain's, 360/452-2357; Port of Port Angeles, 360/457-8527. For nautical charts of the Freshwater Bay area, contact Captain's Nautical Supply, 206/283-7242.

13 Port Angeles Saltwater

Long a favorite of anglers looking for summertime chinook and coho salmon, Port Angeles no longer offers the wide-open salmon fishery it once had. Coho and chinook season has, in fact, recently been closed here during the summer. But winter and spring fishing remains a good option for resident chinooks, or blackmouth, as they are commonly called. Be sure to check the regulations pamphlet to confirm those "winter" salmon season dates. A series of underwater plateaus just outside Ediz Hook, referred to locally as "the Humps," are good places to start looking for these 5- to 15-pound salmon, but at times the fishing is better to the east, around the Green Point area. Mooching with whole or plug herring accounts for a lot of fish, but this is the birthplace of jigging for salmon in Washington, and such metal jigs as the Mooch-A-Jig, Crippled Herring, and Deep Stinger can be very productive for Port Angeles chinooks.

During odd-numbered years, the waters around Port Angeles are productive for pink salmon that surge through the Strait of Juan de Fuca on their way toward the rivers of Puget Sound. They seem to funnel down into fairly tight schools as they approach the eastern end of the strait, and it isn't unusual for Port Angeles anglers to locate a school of fish and catch a limit in an hour or less.

Green Point, mentioned earlier, can provide very good fishing for springtime halibut. Big fish are rare, but one 20-pounder is enough to provide plenty of good eating for the whole family and a fairly good cross section of your neighbors, as well. Nearby reefs and rock piles, most notably Coyote Bank to the north, also provide fair to good halibut-fishing opportunities when the season is open.

A favorite place to fish for lingcod and deep-water rockfish is referred to simply as the Rock Pile, located several miles offshore to the north of town. Nautical chart 18465, which covers the eastern end of the Strait of Juan de Fuca and Admiralty Inlet, will help you locate it and also provide insights into other worthwhile fishing spots throughout the area.

Location: The Strait of Juan de Fuca from Angeles Point to Dungeness Spit; see map A1, grid e9.

Species: Chinook, coho, and pink salmon; Pacific halibut; lingcod; rockfish; and other bottom fish.

Facilities: Two paved boat ramps are located in the Port of Angeles Boat Haven at the west end of town, and another can be found out on Ediz Hook, the long spit of land that protects the harbor. Of the two Port ramps, the more westerly one is the better of the two. There's a $6 launch fee at both Port-operated ramps, with a $21 annual launch permit available to Clallam County residents. Lodging, restaurants, and all other amenities are available in Port Angeles. Launching is free at the Ediz Hook ramp. The Boat Haven also has a year-round fuel dock, restrooms, showers, bait, and ice. Port Angeles also has plenty of restaurants, grocery stores, motels, bed-and-breakfasts, and other facilities.

Directions: Take U.S. 101 to Port Angeles and continue straight through to the west end of town rather than turning south on U.S. 101 at the end of the main drag. Drive right along the water for one mile to the public boat ramp or continue another mile to Ediz Hook.

Contact: Swain's, 360/452-2357; Port of Port Angeles, 360/457-8527. For nautical charts of the Port Angeles Saltwater area, contact Captain's Nautical Supply, 206/283-7242.

14 Ozette Lake

You might expect a lake this large located this far out in what some might consider the middle of nowhere to offer excellent fishing, but you'd be wrong. The fishing is fair to good at times, but rarely excellent. Part of the problem might be that few serious anglers take the time to thoroughly investigate the lake's potential and unravel its secrets.

Ozette Lake is impressively large, and because of its location so far off the beaten path, it's a place where you can still find angling solitude. Trolling for kokanee might produce some nice fish for the table, and fall cutthroating could pay off with a trophy-class trout, but Ozette doesn't treat everyone to an easy limit, so don't come here for fast action.

You won't find Ozette Lake regulations listed in the Department of Fish and Wildlife's pamphlet, since the lake is in Olympic National Park. Call the park office or find regulations posted at several locations around the lake.

A word of warning: the combination of Ozette Lake's large size, shallow water, and proximity to the open Pacific makes this a bad place to be when the wind starts to pick up. Since most folks who fish here do so in canoes, car-toppers, and other small craft, the five-foot waves that form on Ozette's surface can be deadly. If you boat the lake, be careful and always keep an eye on the weather.

One more word of warning: raccoons are abundant and aggressive around here, so don't leave much lying around where they can get at it, especially at night. If they raid your cooler or steal your fish, you were warned.

Location: South of Ozette on the west side of the Olympic Peninsula; see map A1, grid f2.

Species: Rainbow and cutthroat trout, kokanee, yellow perch, largemouth bass, coho and chinook salmon.

Facilities: Swan Bay has a gravel boat ramp, and a couple more boat ramps are located near the north end of the lake. The campground at the northeast corner of the lake has a single-wide boat ramp, a moorage float, and 18 primitive campsites. A few more campsites are scattered around the lake, most notably at the end of Erickson Bay at the northwest corner of the lake. Lost Resort General Store is located near the campground and has groceries, beverages, and canoe rentals. The nearest gas, food, lodging, and tackle are in Sekiu and Clallam Bay.

Directions: Drive west out of Sekiu on Highway 112 and turn south (left) on Hoko-Ozette Road. Drive 17.4 miles and turn left on Swan Bay Road to reach the east side of the lake, or continue for another four miles to Ozette, at the north end of the lake.

Contact: Olympic National Park, 360/452-4501; Olympic Sporting Goods, 360/374-6330; Lost Resort General Store, 360/963-2899.

15 Lake Pleasant

Lake Pleasant has a somewhat unusual regulation that would hack you off if you were fishing for kokanee and caught a monster, the kokanee of a lifetime that would make you an angling legend in your own time. You see, besides an eight-inch minimum size limit, Lake Pleasant has a 20-inch maximum size limit on kokanee, so if you catch a really big one, you have to throw it back. Now, most of the serious kokanee anglers I know are in it for the meat; they love that firm, red flesh of a mature kokanee better than any other fish that swims. Even though they're law-abiding folks, they might have a very hard time releasing a 21-inch kokanee. I guess they should find a place other than Lake Pleasant to concentrate their kokanee-fishing efforts.

Knowing the reason for the regulation, though, might make it a little easier to swallow. The lake has a small population of sockeye salmon passing through it every year, and it's impossible to tell an ocean-run sockeye from the resident version of the same fish, which we call the kokanee. To protect the larger sockeye while allowing the smaller kokanee to be caught, the Department of

Fish and Wildlife simply imposed a 20-inch maximum size limit. The chances of catching a resident kokanee of 20 inches or more are extremely rare, so any larger fish you might land is almost certainly a protected sockeye. Does that help?

Kokanee and cutthroat fishing can be fairly good here. Trolling is the favorite method of fishing for both. You can get away with fishing fairly shallow in the spring, but as the water warms in summer, you may have to go the leaded-line or downrigger route to stay in the strike zone.

Location: West of Sappho; see map A1, grid f4.
Species: Cutthroat trout and kokanee.
Facilities: There's a single-lane boat ramp at the community beach, with a small moorage float and parking for about eight vehicles in the gravel lot. Lake Pleasant Grocery has the minimum daily requirements. Other amenities are available in Forks.
Directions: Take U.S. 101 north from Forks or west from Port Angeles to Beaver, which is at the west end of the lake. Turn north at Lake Pleasant Grocery onto West Lake Pleasant Road and follow it one-third mile to Lake Pleasant Community Beach.
Contact: Lake Pleasant Grocery (Monday–Saturday 4 A.M. to 8 P.M., Sunday 8 to 8), 360/327-3211.

16 Beaver Lake

Although open year-round and within casting distance of the road, this 40-acre Clallam County lake is fished only by a few local anglers. Most of the people who see it are on their way to or from Neah Bay, Sekiu, and other havens of big-fish opportunity, so Beaver Lake gets little fishing pressure from tourists. The cutthroat here are small but cooperative and will hit a worm dangling beneath a bobber, a Super Duper, Mepps spinner, Rooster Tail, or most any small, flashy offering you might toss their way. Al-

though I've never seen anyone doing it, Beaver Lake would be a good place to go prospecting with a float tube.
Location: North of U.S. 101 at Sappho; see map A1, grid f4.
Species: Cutthroat trout.
Facilities: The lake has a sort of handmade boat ramp that's wide enough to launch small trailer boats or car-toppers, and a big log that serves as a natural fishing pier. Groceries and gas are available in Sappho, but you'll have to go north about 22 miles to Clallam Bay for lodging or camping.
Directions: Take U.S. 101 to Sappho and turn north on Highway 113. Drive about four miles to the lake, which is alongside the road on the right.
Contact: Lake Pleasant Grocery (Monday–Saturday 4 A.M. to 8 P.M., Sunday 8 to 8), 360/327-3211.

17 Lake Crescent

It's rare to find a body of water that boasts a unique species of game fish all its own, so the fact that Lake Crescent has two such species is indeed unusual. This 5,000-acre gem near the north end of the Olympic Peninsula is the only place in the world where you can find the Beardslee rainbow and the Lake Crescent cutthroat trout. Both are native to the lake and sustain themselves without any supplemental help in the form of hatchery plants or artificial propagation, and both grow to impressive size. The record Beardslee trout was a 16-pound, 5-ounce fish, while the Crescent cutthroat record weighed in at 12 pounds. Fish that size need a big meal, and both species feed heavily on the lake's abundant kokanee.

To catch the big guys, troll large plugs and spoons, using downriggers to take your lures into the 90- to 120-foot range where the fish are most commonly found. As in any trophy fishery, though, don't expect to catch fish every time out; you'll get skunked more often than you'll find success. Although it doesn't happen often, every once in a while someone casting from shore around one of the many creek mouths manages to hook a big Beardslee or cutthroat.

Because of their relative rarity and trophy status, both the Beardslee rainbow and Crescent cutthroat are protected by special regulations that include a 20-inch minimum size restriction.

As for the kokanee, they're small but abundant in this cool, clear lake. Trolling accounts for most of them, and when the sun is high on the water, you may have to go nearly as deep for kokanee as you do for the big trout.

Crescent is within Olympic National Park, so you don't need a state fishing license to fish it. Anglers might also be happy to learn that as of late 1998 personal watercraft (Jet Skis, Ski-Doos, etc.) are not allowed on the lake. That could make for more peaceful fishing, especially on a warm summer evening.

Location: Midway between Port Angeles and Sappho; see map A1, grid f7.

Species: Beardslee rainbow trout, Lake Crescent cutthroat trout, kokanee.

Facilities: Log Cabin Resort is on the north end of the lake and has a single-lane boat ramp, rental cabins, a fishing dock, a store, and boat rentals. You can reach it by taking East Beach Road at the east end of the lake. Fairholm Resort is at the west end, just off the highway, and offers similar facilities. In the middle, right along the highway, is Lake Crescent Lodge, which has a paved, single-lane boat ramp with floats and a restaurant with great food. Gas is available along U.S. 101 between the lake and Port Angeles.

Directions: Take U.S. 101 north from Forks or west from Port Angeles, and you can't miss it. Lake Crescent is that deep, clear lake that's right outside your car window for about 12 miles.

Contact: Log Cabin Resort, 360/928-3325 (April through October only), website: www. logcabinresort.net; Lake Crescent Lodge, 360/928-3211; Fairholm General Store and Café, 360/928-3020; National Park Service, 360/452-0330.

18 Lake Sutherland

It doesn't produce as many trophy-class cutthroats as it used to, but Sutherland is still a place where you can expect to find brightly marked cutts along with the hatchery rainbows stocked here for the catching. Anglers occasionally catch a cutthroat to 20 inches, but 8- to 12-inch fish are much more common. Although the lake is open to year-round fishing, most of the 3,000 or so legal-sized rainbows are stocked in March to provide early spring fishing action.

As the trout fishing tapers off in the summer, kokanee fishing improves, and during some years this 370-acre lake provides excellent kokanee catches. Trolling with Wedding Ring spinners and stillfishing with white corn or maggots are good ways to catch them. The lake doesn't have any kind of special bonus limit on kokanee, but it's one of those places where chumming with creamed corn and other attractants is legal. The practice, long popular with lake anglers, is illegal on most Washington lakes but allowed on some of those where kokanee fishing is a big draw.

Location: East of Lake Crescent; see map A1, grid f7.

Species: Cutthroat and rainbow trout, kokanee.

Facilities: Lake Sutherland has a Department of Fish and Wildlife boat ramp and access area with restrooms, located on the south side of the lake 1.5 miles off the highway. Shadow Mountain General Store and RV Park is right across U.S. 101 from the lake. Small stores and gas stations can be found along the highway, and all amenities are available in Port Angeles.

Directions: Take U.S. 101 west from Port Angeles and drive about 12 miles to the lake, which is on the south (left) side of the highway.

Contact: Shadow Mountain General Store and RV Park, 360/928-3043; Swain's, 360/452-2357.

19 Elwha River

Of all the dams built across Northwest rivers and creeks during the past century, few have generated more emotion in recent years than Elwha and Glines Canyon Dams, built on the Elwha in 1912 and 1920, respectively, on a little river that at the time was so far back in the sticks that nobody noticed. It seems that lately everyone has noticed, and "Free the Elwha" has become the battle cry of a broad cross section of folks who would love to see both dams, which were built without any fish-passage facilities or compensation for the fish losses they caused, removed from the river.

Before the dams were built, the Elwha was one of only three rivers used by all eight species of Northwest anadromous fish: chinook, coho, chum, sockeye, and pink salmon; steelhead; sea-run cutthroat trout; and sea-run Dolly Varden. Most impressive of these were the chinooks, since Elwha chinooks sometimes grew to 70, 80, 90, perhaps even 100 pounds. You won't find all eight species here now, at least in numbers large enough to support a fishery. That race of giant king salmon is gone forever, replaced by hatchery chinooks that are lucky to reach 25 pounds. Likewise, the wild coho and steelhead have also been replaced by hatchery runs, while some species simply don't exist in the river at all.

Still, the Elwha provides some good fishing. Anglers catch several hundred winter steelhead here every season, along with a few dozen summer-run fish. The Lower Elwha Indian Tribe gets first crack at these hatchery steelhead and catches a like number in their gill nets before anglers get a crack at the fish. The same goes for coho salmon, which provide some on-again, off-again fishing when conditions are right in October. That's the only month salmon fishing is permitted here, and anglers are allowed to keep only cohos.

Of the two reservoirs, Lake Aldwell has the most to offer anglers. Selective fishery regulations requiring anglers to use only artificial lures and flies with barbless hooks have been in effect here for several years, and the 12-inch minimum size limit ensures that any trout you decide to take home will be well worth keeping. There are a few cutthroat and brook trout in the lake, but wild rainbows provide most of the fishing opportunity. Fishing is best during the summer and fall, after the chilly water has had some time to warm. Time it right during this period and you might get in on some good evening fly-fishing. The special regulations in effect on Lake Aldwell also apply to the stretch of river between the two reservoirs, and it's a place where both spincasters and fly rodders find fair-to-good action on wild rainbows.

Lake Mills may not be worth your fishing time, but when you get above the reservoir and back into the free-flowing river, decent trout fishing is once again available. Trails along the river provide most of the access to this upper stretch of the Elwha, which is well within the boundaries of Olympic National Park.

Location: Flows into the Strait of Juan de Fuca west of Port Angeles; see map A1, grid f8.

Species: Winter and summer steelhead; coho and chinook salmon; rainbow, cutthroat, and brook trout.

Facilities: There's a gravel boat ramp and small parking area at the south end of Lake Aldwell and similar facilities at the north end of Lake Mills. There are U.S. Forest Service campgrounds on Lake Aldwell, and complete amenities are available in Port Angeles.

Directions: Take U.S. 101 west from Port Angeles for about four miles and go right on Highway 112, then right on Elwha River Road after 2.5 miles to reach portions of the lower river. Stay on U.S. 101 for about eight miles from Port Angeles and turn south (left) on Olympic Hot Springs Road to reach upper portions of the river, Lake Aldwell, and Lake Mills.

Contact: Swain's, 360/452-2357.

20 Dickey River

This little river, which runs into the Quillayute about a mile from the Pacific Ocean, is fair for winter steelhead and salmon, and good for sea-run cutthroat in the fall. Although it seldom gives up more than 100 steelhead a season, anglers who fish it in March and April manage to take a fish or two for their efforts. Salmon-fishing regulations have gotten increasingly restrictive, so check the fishing pamphlet carefully before committing to the long drive out to the edge of the state. A good fall rain may bring lots of native cutthroats in from the estuary and provide hot trouting for a day or two.

Location: Northeast of La Push; see map A1, grid g2.

Species: Winter steelhead, sea-run cutthroat trout, chinook and coho salmon.

Facilities: Food, gas, lodging, and tackle are available in Forks.

Directions: Turn west off U.S. 101 onto La Push Road about 1.5 miles north of Forks and turn right on Mora Road to reach the mouth of the river. To fish upper portions of the river, bear right off La Push Road onto Quillayute Road, following it about four miles to Mina Smith Road; turn right and follow it to the river, on the left.

Contact: Olympic Sporting Goods, 360/374-6330.

21 Quillayute River

Though officially only six miles long, the Quillayute is one of the Northwest's busiest salmon and steelhead rivers. That's because every anadromous fish bound for the Bogachiel, Sol Duc, and Calawah Rivers has to pass through the Quillayute to get to its destination. Now, if you're one of those calculating types, you're already thinking that stationing yourself somewhere along the Quillayute will put you in perfect position to ambush tens of thousands of salmon and steelhead that will be funneled right past you as they swim upstream. Unfortunately, most of those fish passing by your ambush point will be going like hell, meaning you won't catch many of them. So much for your logical solution to a sticky problem.

It's true that fish headed for the productive Quillayute tributaries must pass through the lower end of the system to get wherever they're going, but it's the holding fish that provide most of the action for freshwater salmon and steelhead anglers, not moving fish, so the Quillayute isn't the hot spot that it might appear to be at first glance.

But the river is still worth fishing. Anglers here pick off their share of winter steelhead beginning in November and continue catching fish right on through April, not in huge numbers but at a better clip than on lots of other streams. Likewise, it's not a red-hot place for summer-run steelhead, but you can catch 'em here if you work at it.

Spring chinooks bound for the upstream tributaries are also picked off on the Quillayute, although not in particularly large numbers. The springer fishing may be better when the Sol Duc is low and clear, as it often is in the spring. Under those conditions, the salmon may lie in the Quillayute, waiting for a little rain to raise river levels, presenting anglers a good opportunity to pick them off. Although there's the possibility of hooking a fall chinook the size of a compact car, anglers here catch relatively few of them. Most years, in fact, anglers catch more chum salmon than fall chinooks from the Quillayute.

The traditional highlight for fall salmon anglers on the Quillayute has been fishing the annual coho run, but recently the river has been closed to the taking of coho, so for the time being it's best not to count on that possibility.

Location: Enters the Pacific Ocean at La Push on the west side of the Olympic Peninsula; see map A1, grid g2.

Species: Winter and summer steelhead; coho, chum, spring, and fall chinook salmon; sea-run cutthroat trout.

Facilities: A boat ramp and considerable access to the river can be found at Lyendecker Park, where the Bogachiel and Sol Duc Rivers converge to form the Quillayute. Mora Park, farther downstream near the river mouth, also provides access and a rough boat take-out spot. Also nearby is Three Rivers Resort, which offers cabins, RV and tent sites, hot showers, a small store with groceries and tackle, laundry facilities, and a guide service. Food, gas, lodging, tackle, and fishing guides are available in Forks.

Directions: Take U.S. 101 to the town of Forks and turn west on La Push Road about two miles north of town. Drive eight miles and turn right on Mora Road, which parallels the north side of the Quillayute River.

Contact: Olympic Sporting Goods, 360/374-6330; Three Rivers Resort, 360/374-5300, website: www.northolympic.com/threerivers.

22 Sol Duc River

While looking over a salmon-catch report from the Washington Department of Fish and Wildlife one day, I made a discovery about the Sol Duc that I had never picked up on while fishing the river or talking to those who

fish it a lot more often than I do. While most people come to this famous Olympic Peninsula river to fish for steelhead and coho and chinook salmon, the Sol Duc provides anglers with the possibility of catching all five species of Pacific salmon, plus winter and summer steelhead and sea-run cutthroat trout. It's not that you're likely to hook all eight in a single trip or even a single year, but there's that possibility, which makes the Sol Duc a Northwest rarity.

But as I said before, most people come here to fish for steelhead and coho and chinook salmon, and that's where the odds are on the Sol Duc. Winter steelheading is the best bet of all, since anglers catch 1,000 to 2,000 of them here each winter. A slow starter, the river isn't too hot in December, but the months of January through April offer excellent possibilities. January and February offer lots of hatchery fish, but by March the late runs of big Sol Duc natives are on the scene, and you stand a reasonable chance of hooking one in the high teens or even 20 pounds at any time during the month. Big fish remain a possibility through April. Summer-run steelhead aren't stocked here, but the Sol Duc does produce a few dozen per month, beginning in June.

This is the best spring chinook river in the Quillayute system, but low, clear water is more the rule than the exception during the height of the springer runs from April to June. A period of rainy weather during this time may spur some hot chinook fishing, especially if it produces enough water to raise and color the river. Without such conditions, you have to work hard, fish early, and fish late to catch Sol Duc springers. Although difficult to cast and fish with, especially from the bank, herring baits account for a high percentage of the spring chinooks caught here. The normal low water at this time of year not only makes the fish difficult for bank anglers to catch, but makes life miserable for boaters, too, as they bang, clang, and drag their craft through the riffles and rocky stretches of river.

The fall salmon fishery on the river has traditionally been dominated by some good coho fishing that begins as early as August and holds up well into November. Before planning an assault on Sol Duc silvers, though, check the angling regulations, since coho closures have come into play here in recent years.

Location: North and west of Forks, flowing into the Quillayute River; see map A1, grid f3.

Species: Winter and summer steelhead; spring and fall chinook; coho, chum, and sockeye salmon; sea-run cutthroat trout.

Facilities: Three Rivers Resort has cabins, RV and tent sites, a grocery store with tackle and fishing licenses, a restaurant that serves lunch and dinner, hot showers, a laundry, and a guide service. Other guides, motels, bed-and-breakfasts, groceries, gas, restaurants, and more services are available in Forks.

Directions: Drive west from Port Angeles or north from Hoquiam on U.S. 101, which parallels much of the river and crosses it just north of the town of Forks. Whitcomb Dimmel Road, Clark Road, Sol Duc Valley Road, and others to the east and south of U.S. 101 provide access to the upper river. La Push Road and Quillayute Road will take you to the lower river.

Contact: Three Rivers Resort, 360/374-5300, website: www.northolympic.com/threerivers; Olympic Sporting Goods, 360/374-6330; Forks Chamber of Commerce, 360/374-2531.

23 Calawah River

The Calawah isn't a big river, but when it comes to steelhead fishing, it's a reliable one. Thanks to liberal releases of both winter and summer steelie smolts, the Calawah gives up steelhead every month of the year except May. "Why no steelhead in May?" you

might ask. "Because it's closed that month," I might answer.

The salmon fishing isn't as productive and certainly doesn't last as long as the steelheading. There are, however, decent opportunities to catch both coho and chinook salmon here during the summer and fall. Like everywhere else, be sure to check the fishing pamphlet for details on wild-salmon release and other regulations that may apply during your visit.

For those of you who like to do your river fishing from a drift boat, don't just throw your boat in the Calawah without doing a little research first. It has a couple of spots that could eat you alive even if you know what you're doing. Check it out first.

Location: Flows into the Bogachiel River west of Forks; see map A1, grid f3.

Species: Winter and summer steelhead, coho salmon, sea-run cutthroat trout.

Facilities: Three Rivers Resort has cabins, RV and tent sites, a grocery store with tackle and fishing licenses, a restaurant that serves lunch and dinner, hot showers, a laundry, and a guide service. Klahanie Campground is located about six miles upriver from the highway. Food, gas, lodging, and tackle are available in Forks.

Directions: Take U.S. 101 north from Aberdeen or west from Port Angeles to Forks and turn east on Forest Service Road 29 about 1.5 miles north of town to reach the upper Calawah River.

Contact: Olympic Sporting Goods, 360/374-6330; Three Rivers Resort, 360/374-5300, website: www.northolympic.com/threerivers.

24 Bogachiel River

Although there is an open salmon season that provides fair coho and chinook fishing on this major tributary to the Quillayute River, winter steelheading is the main reason virtually everyone comes to the "Bogey." As many as

50,000 winter steelhead smolts are released from the Bogachiel Rearing Ponds every year, and when adult fish from those plants return to the river, things really get busy. The most productive months are December and January, and the most productive and crowded part of the river during this time is the four-mile stretch from the boat launch at the rearing ponds to the boat launch at the Wilson Access, just off La Push Road. Every weekend during December and January, and especially during the year-end holiday period, there's a steady parade of drift boats through this part of the river. And most of them have fish to show for their efforts. Bank anglers also catch their share of hatchery-bound steelhead along this portion of the river. The best access and most productive fishing is from the rearing ponds downstream to the mouth of the Calawah River, but you won't be the only one who knows about it, so don't bother looking for solitude.

Unlike some Northwest rivers that are heavily stocked with hatchery steelhead, the Bogachiel also provides good fishing later in the winter season, and it stays open through April to accommodate anglers and their late-winter fishery. March and April can be nearly as productive as December and January on the Bogachiel, and the average size of the fish is considerably larger. This is the time of year when the Bogey gives up most of its 15- to 25-pound trophy steelhead. It's also the time to concentrate more effort on the upper sections of the river, above the rearing ponds. Boat ramps and bank-fishing spots upstream from the U.S. 101 bridge, including the state park and South Bogachiel Road, get a lot more use in March and April.

Location: Follows the Clallam-Jefferson County line to join the Sol Duc River west of Forks; see map A1, grid g4.

Species: Winter steelhead, chinook salmon, sea-run cutthroat trout.

Facilities: Bogachiel State Park has a few tent and RV sites, plus restrooms, showers, and a boat ramp. Several other boat ramps (some of them not too fancy) are located both upstream and downstream from the highway. Forks has motels, restaurants, grocery stores, gas stations, some rough-and-tumble bars and taverns, and several river-guide businesses.

Directions: Take U.S. 101 north from Hoquiam or west from Port Angeles and drive to Forks. Turn west at the south end of town to reach Bogachiel Road, which goes to the Bogachiel Rearing Ponds. Turn west off U.S. 101 onto La Push Road about two miles north of town to reach the lower end of the river. To reach upper portions of the river, drive east off U.S. 101 on South Bogachiel Road or turn off the highway at Bogachiel State Park, which is well marked.

Contact: Olympic Sporting Goods, 360/374-6330; Bogachiel State Park, 360/374-6356; Three Rivers Resort, 360/374-5300, website: www.northolympic.com/threerivers.

25 Seven Lakes Basin

This cluster of high lakes about 10 miles north of Mount Olympus gets a lot of attention from summertime hikers and anglers, not so much because of its great fishing, but because it's pretty well encircled by a network of trails. Depending on which lake or lakes you fish, you may find a fair-sized rainbow or two, a couple of slim cutthroats, or several smaller brook trout. Because they are fished fairly hard, you won't find very good fishing in any of them, but as long as you're carrying your pack rod or favorite fly rod along on your hike through the Olympics high country, you might as well put it to use.

Sol Duc Lake, the biggest of the bunch at about 30 acres, probably offers the best opportunity to hook a trout or two, but Long, Morganroth, Lunch, Clear, and some of the other lakes might also pay off. Two of the lower (2,800 to 3,000 feet elevation) and westernmost lakes, Mink and Hidden, are within fairly easy reach of the Sol Duc River Trailhead to the west, so you can get to them with a good day hike. Most of the other lakes require a longer hike and more serious climb (to about 4,500 feet).

Location: Southeast of Sol Duc Hot Springs near the Clallam-Jefferson County line; see map A1, grid g7.

Species: Cutthroat, rainbow, and brook trout.

Facilities: Sol Duc Hot Springs Resort has everything from tent sites and RV hookups to cabins with kitchens, a small store, and a restaurant. Just as important to bone-weary hikers and anglers are the tiled hot pools, which may be used for a daily fee even if you aren't staying at the resort. Hot pools are also an attraction if you hike in from Olympic Hot Springs Road. The Olympic Hot Springs aren't fancy, but they're free. All other necessities are available in Port Angeles.

Directions: Drive west from Port Angeles on U.S. 101 for about eight miles to Olympic Hot Springs Road and turn south (left). Continue driving to Boulder Creek Campground at the end of the road and hike several miles to the lakes. Or take U.S. 101 about 25 miles west from Port Angeles to the west end of Lake Crescent and turn south (left) on Sol Duc Hot Springs Road. Follow the road to the end and hike from two to 12 miles to the various lakes, all of which are on the south side of the trail.

Contact: Sol Duc Hot Springs Resort, 360/327-3583; Elwha Resort and Café, 360/457-7011.

26 Goodman Creek

Once a pretty well-kept secret among a few tight-lipped locals, Goodman Creek has become fairly well known in steelhead circles over the past decade or so. The creek produces only a few dozen steelhead each win-

ter, but it's a place for the small-stream enthusiast to get away from at least most other folks.

There's a fair amount of brush and other obstacles in and around it, so a hooked steelhead certainly doesn't always mean a landed steelhead. Although Goodman Creek is now stocked with hatchery smolts, the catch hasn't improved all that much over the time when it was an all-wild steelhead fishery.

Location: Flows into the Pacific Ocean south of La Push; see map A1, grid g3.

Species: Winter steelhead, sea-run cutthroat trout.

Facilities: No facilities are located nearby, but food, gas, lodging, and tackle are available in Forks.

Directions: Take U.S. 101 north from Hoquiam about 95 miles and turn west (left) just north of the Hoh River bridge on Lower Hoh Road (also known as Oil City Road). Drive five miles and turn north (right) on 3000 Road and follow it to the creek.

Contact: Olympic Sporting Goods, 360/374-6330.

27 Hoh River

Liberal plants of winter steelhead smolts and a self-sustaining run of summer steelhead combine to make the Hoh one of the better coastal steelhead rivers, despite a rather intensive tribal net fishery near the mouth of the river. Anglers typically catch between 1,000 and 2,500 winter-run steelies here annually. March is generally a top month to fish the Hoh, but it may also provide excellent catches from December to April. The river produces its share of bragging-sized fish in the 15- to 20-pound range. The catch of summer steelhead is much smaller, usually 300 to 500 fish, but that's not bad at all when you consider the fact that the Hoh is dirty from glacial runoff on and off throughout much of June, July, and August. That higher, dirtier water, in fact, is part of the reason why the Hoh is one of the area's best summer steelheading spots, since most of the rivers to the north and south are low, clear, and hard to fish during much of the summer.

Salmon fishing can be very good here, especially for chinooks. There are some big spring-run fish in the river when it opens to salmon fishing in May, and it's possible to catch chinook salmon here from that point until September or even early October. Check the regulations pamphlet for details on wild chinook release rules that may be in effect while you're there. While adult chinooks—some of them topping 40 pounds—are the star attraction for salmon anglers, the river sometimes hosts large runs of jack (immature) chinooks, and these one- to eight-pound fish are loads of fun to catch. Like their adult counterparts, they'll inhale a large cluster of salmon roe, a fresh ghost shrimp, or a combination of these two popular baits.

Although many of the big-fish anglers in search of salmon and steelhead ignore it, another summertime high point on the Hoh is the sea-run cutthroat fishery. Sea-runs start trickling into the river in July, and by August the fishing can be quite good. These 10- to 18-inch anadromous trout continue to provide fishing opportunity until November. Like cutthroat trout anywhere, they'll take a juicy night crawler rolled slowly along the bottom. The Hoh has a number of small logjams, submerged stumps, and overhanging trees in the water to attract sea-run cutthroats. Fish these woody spots and you'll find trout.

Several good bank-fishing spots are available on both sides of the lower Hoh and off the road along the north side of the upper river. There are also a half dozen decent spots to launch a drift boat, and that's the way many anglers choose to fish this large stream. Several local fishing guides also work the Hoh, most of them out of Forks.

Location: Flows into the Pacific Ocean north of Kalaloch; see map A1, grid h3.

Species: Winter and summer steelhead, chinook and coho salmon, sea-run cutthroat trout.

Facilities: A store and campground are located on the south side of the river just south of the bridge, with another store and campground on the upper river. Both campgrounds have cabins for rent. Motels and other amenities are available in Forks. Several Department of Natural Resources campgrounds are scattered along the river, including Cottonwood Campground on the lower Hoh, and Willoughby, Morgan's Crossing, Spruce Creek, Huelsdonk, and Hoh Rain Forest Campgrounds on the upper river.

Directions: Take U.S. 101 north from Hoquiam or west from Port Angeles. The highway parallels the south side of the river downstream from the Hoh River Bridge, where several gravel roads lead to the north, toward the river. Or turn west on Lower Hoh Road just north of the bridge to drive down the north side of the river. To reach the upper Hoh, turn east on Upper Hoh Road about two miles north of the bridge.

Contact: Westward Hoh Resort, 360/374-6657; Olympic Sporting Goods, 360/374-6330.

28 Kalaloch Surf

This northern stretch of beach doesn't get as much fishing pressure as other parts of Washington's Pacific Coast throughout much of the year, and the perch fishing can be very good. Standard baits that work elsewhere—pieces of razor clam neck, ghost shrimp, limpets, and pieces of blood worm—will do the job. If the perch aren't biting too well, try fishing around the mouth of Kalaloch Creek or Cedar Creek and see if you can find a sea-run cutthroat trout or maybe a school of starry flounder.

Location: Northern Washington coast between the Queets and Hoh Rivers; see map A1, grid h3.

Species: Redtail surfperch, cutthroat trout, sole, flounder.

Facilities: Kalaloch Lodge has cabins, guest rooms, and a restaurant. Kalaloch Campground has RV and tent sites and restrooms with showers. The nearest gas, groceries, and tackle are to the north, at the Hoh River.

Directions: Drive north from Hoquiam for about 65 miles on U.S. 101, cross the Queets River, and start watching for the beach access signs.

Contact: Kalaloch Lodge, 360/962-2271, website: www.visitkalaloch.com.

29 Clearwater River

The Clearwater provides fair steelheading all winter, but to make the most of your trip to this Queets River tributary that lives up to its name, plan your visit for March. That's when the bulk of the Clearwater's wild adult steelhead return from the Pacific (it's not stocked with hatchery smolts). The river gives up maybe 150 winter-runs during a poor season and as many as 300 during a good year. Those numbers are pretty puny when compared to some of the bigger, better-known rivers along this side of the Olympic Peninsula, but it takes only one mint-bright, 15-pounder to make for a good day of March steelheading.

As for salmon, the Clearwater has 'em, but, like winter steelhead, the numbers aren't enough to make many folks drop what they're doing and race to the river. There are a few chinooks to be found, but Clearwater is mostly an October and November coho fishery with spoons and spinners.

Location: Flows into the Queets River east of Queets on the west side of the Olympic Peninsula; see map A1, grid h4.

Species: Winter steelhead, coho and chinook salmon.

Facilities: A rough boat launch is located on the upper river and another is at the confluence of the Clearwater and the Queets, but don't look for much in the way of amenities in this neck of the woods. Food and lodging are available at Kalaloch, 10 miles north on U.S. 101, and all other facilities can be found in Amanda Park, 25 miles south on U.S. 101.

Directions: Take U.S. 101 north from Hoquiam about 62 miles and turn north (right) on Clearwater Road, which roughly parallels the river for more than a dozen miles.

Contact: Olympic Sporting Goods, 360/374-6330; Kalaloch Ranger Station, 360/962-2283 (daytime hours only).

30 Queets River

Winter steelheading is the biggest draw at the Queets River, especially since large numbers of hatchery steelhead smolts started being planted in the Salmon River (see number 31) back in the 1980s. That's why most of the winter fishing pressure, both boat and bank, is concentrated from the mouth of the Salmon downstream. The most popular drift boat trip is from a large gravel bar about a mile above the Salmon down to the Clearwater Road Bridge, a drift of just over five miles. Three other commonly used boat-launching spots are located above Mud Creek, above Matheny Creek, and at Queets River Campground at the end of Queets River Road. These upstream drifts may not produce as many fish, but the chances of hooking a large, wild steelhead are just as good, and you're not as likely to see other anglers. There's also some beautiful fishing water and equally beautiful scenery to be enjoyed. The Queets produces 400 to 1,000 winter steelhead a year, with January and February providing the biggest numbers. If you're willing to fish longer and harder for one crack at a big fish, try it in March or April.

Location: Enters the Pacific Ocean at Queets near the Jefferson-Grays Harbor

County line; see map A1, grid i4.

Species: Winter and summer steelhead, chinook and coho salmon, sea-run cutthroat trout.

Facilities: Queets River Campground is at the end of Queets River Road and has tent spaces with no hookups of any kind. The nearest food and lodging are in Kalaloch, with all amenities available to the south in Amanda Park.

Directions: Take U.S. 101 north from Hoquiam about 60 miles and turn north (right) on Queets River Road, at the Grays Harbor-Jefferson County line. Follow the road, which roughly parallels the river, upstream as far as 14 miles.

Contact: Olympic Sporting Goods, 360/374-6330; Kalaloch Ranger Station, 360/962-2283 (daytime hours only).

31 Salmon River

Generous plants of winter steelhead smolts in recent years have done wonders for the popularity of this little Queets River tributary. As with many other small streams, timing is everything. But if you hit it right, just after a good rain, you can get into some hot small-stream steelheading. If you have just one shot at it, go in January. But, word has gotten out on this steelhead fishery, so don't be too surprised if you have company along the banks of this little river when the fishing is hot. The Salmon is also gaining a reputation for its fall salmon fishing; it produces some hefty kings and big, bright coho during October and early November. Part of this river is within the Quinault Indian Reservation, where a tribal guide may be required. Pay attention to the reservation boundaries.

Location: Flows into the Queets River east of Queets; see map A1, grid i4.

Species: Winter steelhead.

Facilities: The nearest facilities are in Queets, and they're limited. Amanda Park,

several miles to the south, has food, gas, and lodging.

Directions: Drive north from Hoquiam about 60 miles on U.S. 101, turn north (right) on Queets River Road, and drive about 1.5 miles to the bridge over the Salmon River.

Contact: Olympic Sporting Goods, 360/374-6330; Kalaloch Ranger Station, 360/962-2283 (daytime hours only).

32 Lake Quinault

Grays Harbor County's biggest lake is also one of its most lightly fished, probably because of its location nearly 40 miles north of Hoquiam. It receives a fair amount of fishing pressure during the height of the summertime vacation season, mostly from anglers who aren't quite sure how to go about fishing it. But you may have it all to yourself during some of the best fishing times of spring and fall.

Quinault is one of the few Northwest lakes where it's legal to catch and keep Dolly Varden char, and several times a year the lake gives up a Dolly in the four- to eight-pound class. Forget the bobber-and-worm rig or wimpy little spoons and spinners if you want big Dollies. Offer them something better suited to their aggressive nature and hearty appetite, such as a large, minnow-imitating wobbling plug or a two- to three-inch spoon.

The smaller lures will work okay on the lake's cutthroats, some of which run 17 or 18 inches. If your favorite trolling lure fails to entice them, try a Dick Nite or Canadian Wonder spoon in a nickel/brass finish.

Kokanee fishing was once very good in this big, cold lake, but the Quinault Tribe has closed the lake to fishing for all salmon, including kokanee, so these sweet-eating resident sockeyes are no longer available to anglers. If tribal patrol officers even find gang trolls and other potential kokanee tackle in your boat, it could be confiscated, according to the tribal regulation pamphlet.

Lake Quinault is on the Quinault Indian Reservation, so you need a tribal permit to fish it.

Location: At Amanda Park; see map A1, grid i6.

Species: Dolly Varden, cutthroat trout.

Facilities: Lodges and campgrounds are located on both the north and south sides of the lake. There are small boat ramps at Willaby and Falls Creek Campgrounds, both on the south side of the lake. Both the campgrounds and their boat ramps are open only from April through October. Food, gas, and tackle are available in nearby Amanda Park.

Directions: Take U.S. 101 north from Hoquiam about 38 miles and turn east (right) onto well-marked South Shore Road before you cross the river at Amanda Park, or continue on U.S. 101 and turn right on North Shore Road about three miles past Amanda Park.

Contact: Quinault Tribal Office, 360/276-8211; Lake Quinault Resort, 800/650-2362, website: www.lakequinault.com; Lake Quinault Lodge, 800/562-6672, website: www.visitlakequinault.com; Quinault Beach Resort, 360/289-9466.

33 Quinault River

This is a river with three distinct personalities, depending on what part of it you happen to visit. Unfortunately for anglers who may be looking for simplicity in life, the river also has three different management schemes in effect, each with its own governing body and its own set of rules and regulations. For the newcomer, the whole thing may be difficult to sort out, or even to understand. To avoid long explanations, let's just say that you're fishing tribal waters on the lower Quinault from Lake Quinault downstream to the Pacific, state waters from the east end of the lake upstream for about 10 miles, and national park waters the rest of the way up to the river's source.

A substantial majority of the winter steelhead caught from this productive river are taken from the lower section, which is entirely within the Quinault Indian Reservation. The Quinaults release as many as half a million hatchery steelhead smolts a year into the lower river, then harvest 5,000 to 15,000 adult steelhead as they return to the river each winter. Anglers can also get in on the action, but they have to hire and fish with a tribal guide in order to get at any of the lower Quinault. The peak of the hatchery returns are in December and January, so those are the months to fish here if you're looking for quantity. But late winter is better if you want a crack at some of the huge wild steelhead for which the river is still famous. Steelhead of 20 to 25 pounds are caught here every year, and even larger ones are landed now and then.

Those large numbers of hatchery fish never get to the upper Quinault, but anglers still manage to catch a few dozen wild steelhead here each season. Your best shot is in March, but remember that you may fish the upper Quinault's crystal-clear waters for days without a strike, even at that time of year.

Above the park boundary the river is closed during winter steelhead season, opening only for the summer season from late April to the end of October. Anglers catch a few respectable trout from this stretch of the Quinault every year.

There's a small sport salmon fishery on the Quinault, with most fish caught from the lower river. Again, remember that you can't fish here without an Indian guide. Cohos provide most of this fall salmon action, and October is usually the best month.

Location: Flows into the Pacific Ocean at Taholah; see map A1, grid j5.

Species: Winter steelhead, coho salmon.

Facilities: Quinault Indian fishing guides are available out of Taholah, but there isn't much in the way of facilities on the lower river. Amanda Park has food, gas, and other necessities, and there are a couple of major lodges and several campsites on Lake Quinault.

Directions: To get to the upper Quinault, drive north from Hoquiam on U.S. 101 about 36 miles and turn east (right) on South Shore Road before crossing the river at Amanda Park. Drive along the south side of Lake Quinault to the river.

Contact: Quinault Tribal Office, 360/276-8211; Quinault Ranger Station, 360/288-2444; Lake Quinault Resort, 800/650-2362, website: www.lakequinault.com; Lake Quinault Lodge, 800/562-6672, website: www.visitlakequinault.com.

34 Lake Wynoochee

Bring your small boat or even a float tube to this impoundment on the upper Wynoochee River to fish it more effectively. Lake Wynoochee is a big reservoir with lots of possibilities. Fishing isn't great, but there are some nice cutthroat trout that will take spoons, spinners, or small wobbling plugs such as Flatfish, Kwikfish, or Hot Shots.

The lake is open June 1 through October. Not only does it have a late opener like area streams, but it also has a stream-type catch limit of only two trout per day and a 12-inch minimum size limit.

Location: Olympic National Forest north of Grisdale; see map A1, grid j8.

Species: Cutthroat trout.

Facilities: Coho Campground, with its large boat ramp, is located near the dam at the southwest corner of the lake, and two primitive campgrounds (Chetwoot and Tenas) can be reached only by boat or by foot. Fees of $7 to $10 are charged at Coho Campground, but there's no fee for using the primitive campgrounds. There are no stores, gas stations, or lodging facilities near the lake, so bring everything you may need. The nearest food, gas, and tackle are available in Montesano.

Directions: Take Highway 8 and U.S. 12 west from Olympia about 38 miles, turning north (right) on Devonshire Road about a mile west of Montesano. Drive 33.5 miles to the left turn that leads past the base of the dam and to the west side of the lake.

Contact: Olympic National Forest Headquarters, 360/956-2400.

CHAPTER A2:
PUGET SOUND/ HOOD CANAL

MIDDLE BANK CHINOOK

©TERRY RUDNICK

Map A2

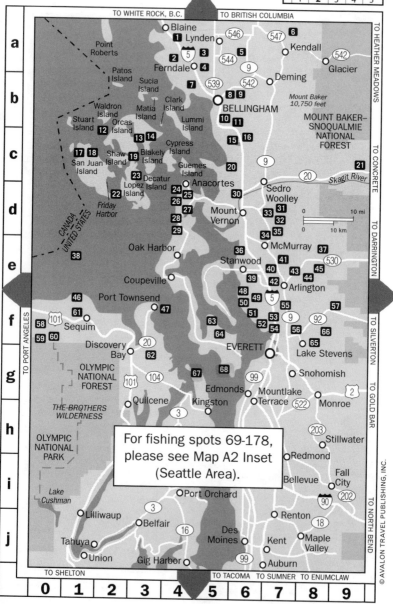

TO WHITE ROCK, B.C.   TO BRITISH COLUMBIA

a

Point
Roberts

Blaine
1 Lynden
546
547 **6**
Kendall
542
Glacier

2 **5** **3**
Ferndale **4**
544
5
9

Patos
Island
Sucia
Island

7
539
542 Deming

b

Waldron
Island
Clark
Island
Matia
Island
8 **9**
BELLINGHAM
Mount Baker
10,750 feet
MOUNT BAKER–
SNOQUALMIE
NATIONAL
FOREST

Stuart
Island
Orcas
12 Island
Lummi
Island
10 **11**

c

17 **18**
13 **14**
Cypress
Island
15 **16**

Shaw
19
Blakely
Island

San Juan
Island
Island
Guemes
Island
20
9
21

23
20 Skagit River

Decatur
Lopez **24** Island
22 Island
Anacortes
Sedro
Woolley

d

Friday
Harbor
25
30

26
Mount
Vernon
33 **31**
32
0   10 mi

27
34 **35**
0   10 km

28

29

e

38

Oak Harbor
36 McMurray
37
Stanwood
41
530
40 **43**
Coupeville
39
42 Arlington
45
44

46
48
50
49
5
55
57

Port Townsend
61
47
51
53 **9** **92**
52 **54** **56**
66
65

f

58 **101**
Sequim
63
64
EVERETT
59 **60**
Lake Stevens

g

Discovery
Bay
20
62
67
68
99
Snohomish

OLYMPIC
NATIONAL
FOREST
104
Edmonds
Mountlake
Terrace
522
Monroe
2

101
Kingston
99

THE-BROTHERS
WILDERNESS
Quilcene
3

h

OLYMPIC
NATIONAL
PARK
203
Stillwater

For fishing spots 69-178,
please see Map A2 Inset
(Seattle Area).
Redmond
i

Bellevue
Fall
City
90
202

Lake
Cushman
Port Orchard

j

Lilliwaup
Renton
18

Belfair
Maple
Valley

Tahuya
16
Des
Moines
Kent

Union
Gig Harbor
99
Auburn

TO SHELTON   TO TACOMA   TO SUMNER   TO ENUMCLAW

CANADA
UNITED STATES

TO PORT ANGELES

TO HEATHER MEADOWS

TO CONCRETE

TO DARRINGTON

TO SILVERTON

TO GOLD BAR

TO NORTH BEND

© AVALON TRAVEL PUBLISHING, INC.

0   1   2   3   4   5   6   7   8   9

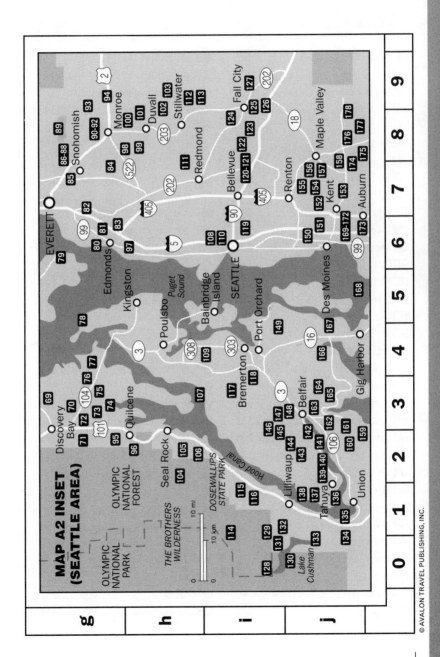

MAP A2 INSET (SEATTLE AREA)

OLYMPIC NATIONAL PARK

OLYMPIC NATIONAL FOREST

THE BROTHERS WILDERNESS

DOSEWALLIPS STATE PARK

Discovery Bay

Quilcene

Seal Rock

Lake Cushman

Hood Canal

Lilliwaup

Tahuya

Union

Belfair

EVERETT

Snohomish

Monroe

Duvall

Stillwater

Fall City

Edmonds

Kingston

Poulsbo

Puget Sound

Bainbridge Island

SEATTLE

Bremerton

Port Orchard

Des Moines

Gig Harbor

Redmond

Bellevue

Renton

Kent

Auburn

Maple Valley

2

94

93

89

86-88

90-92

85

84

98

99

522

82

81

83

80

79

97

78

69

70

104

77

76

75

74

73

72

71

101

95

96

104

105

106

107

114

128

129

130

131

132

133

134

135

136

137

138

139-140

141

142

143

144

145

146

147

148

106

159

160

161

162

163

164

165

166

167

168

169-172

173

174

175

176

177

178

150

151

152

153

154

155

156

157

158

149

117

118

109

108

110

111

119

120-121

122

123

124

125

126

127

102

103

100

112

113

99

3

308

303

16

5

405

202

90

405

18

203

99

10 mi

10 km

g

h

i

j

0   1   2   3   4   5   6   7   8   9

© AVALON TRAVEL PUBLISHING, INC.

Chapter A2: Puget Sound/ Hood Canal

(CONTINUED ON NEXT PAGE)

Home to Seattle, Tacoma, Everett, and Bellevue, this area is where most of the people in Washington live, work, and play. I-5 runs north and south through the center of this mass of humanity, and I-90 heads east from Seattle. When traffic is flowing smoothly, these major freeways provide direct routes to recreational opportunities all over Washington, but smoothly flowing traffic is the exception, not the rule. But even with all its people, all its buildings, all its highways full of parked cars, this population hub of the Evergreen State offers a wealth of angling opportunities. As if the major inland marine waterways of Puget Sound and Hood Canal weren't enough, the region is home to the San Juan Islands, a marine paradise that just happens to provide year-round fishing for salmon and many species of saltwater bottom fish. The region is also laced with streams of all sizes that host impressive runs of chinook, coho, and chum salmon; winter and summer runs of steelhead; and sea-run cutthroat trout that in many cases thrive despite decades of abuse at the hands of farmers, loggers, developers, and polluters. And then there are the lakes, scores of them, that offer everything from pan-size perch and hatchery rainbow trout to hard-fighting smallmouth bass and trophy-class tiger muskies. Some are surrounded by city streets and multifamily housing, others by thick conifer forests; some cover only a few acres, while massive Lake Washington sprawls along the entire eastern flank of Seattle from Renton to Kenmore, some 30 miles away; some are cold, clear, and deep trout lakes, others shallow, weedy, and filed with warm-water species. No, an angler doesn't have to travel far to find good fishing around here, something you can certainly appreciate when the traffic makes it impossible to leave.

CATCHING PILE PERCH ON PUGET SOUND

1 Dakota Creek

Summertime anglers catch a few resident cutthroat at Dakota Creek, and a fall run of sea-run cutthroat also provides some angling action, but the salmon fishery generates the most interest among anglers. As with many small salmon streams, timing is everything, which explains why tourist anglers don't catch many of the salmon.

Location: Flows into Drayton Harbor southeast of Blaine; see map A2, grid a4.

Species: Cutthroat trout, coho salmon.

Facilities: All amenities are available in Blaine and to the south in Bellingham.

Directions: Take I-5 about 1.5 miles south of Blaine and cross over the mouth of Dakota Creek. After passing over it on I-5, continue half a mile and exit to the east (right) on Sweet Road. Go one mile east and turn south (right) on Harvey Road. Drive about a half mile to Hoier Road and turn left; go another half mile and turn right to the creek or continue on to Giles Road, which crosses the creek.

Contact: Wolten's Coast to Coast, 360/332-4077 (ask for Jerry).

2 Lake Terrell

Large, shallow Lake Terrell is ideally suited to warm-water fish, and that's exactly what you'll find here in the greatest abundance. Largemouth bass head the list, and spring and summer bass fishing is excellent, with anglers starting to catch good-sized bass as early as March. The lake has a slot limit to protect fish 12 to 17 inches long.

This 440-acre lake offers some of western Washington's best perch fishing as well, with enough small fish to keep the kids busy and enough large ones to provide a first-rate fish fry. Only about 10 feet deep, Terrell warms fast in the spring and can provide good catfish action as early as April. The brown bullheads continue to bite through spring and summer. If you don't have a boat, try fishing for perch and catfish from the public dock.

Location: West of Ferndale; see map A2, grid a4.

Species: Largemouth bass, yellow perch, brown bullhead catfish, a few cutthroat trout.

Facilities: A Department of Fish and Wildlife access area with a concrete-plank boat ramp and loading float is on the west side of the lake. The boat ramp is closed in conjunction with the boat-fishing closure from October to mid-January. A $10 Washington Department of Fish and Wildlife (WDFW) access decal is required to use the public launch area. Ferndale has restaurants, motels, gas, tackle, and other necessities.

Directions: Take I-5 to the Ferndale exit and turn west to town. Mountain View Road is the main drag out of town to the west. Follow it for four miles to Lake Terrell Road. Turn right and drive about three-quarters of a mile to the lake.

Contact: Lake Terrell Wildlife Area, 360/384-4723.

3 Nooksack River

This vast river system, stretching from northern Skagit County nearly to the Canadian border and from Bellingham Bay to the North Cascades, is a shadow of the once-productive steelhead and salmon river it was a decade or two ago. As recently as 1985, anglers caught more than 1,800 winter-run steelhead from the main Nooksack, but by 1994 the catch had dropped to a dismal 44 fish. The North Fork and South Fork Nooksack contributed only a couple of dozen more winter steelies to that total. And things haven't improved much since then; the 1998–99 catch of winter steelhead from the entire Nooksack system was less than 200 fish. For a river system stocked with 50,000 to 80,000 hatchery steelhead smolts every year, those are mighty poor numbers. The bottom line is whether you choose to plunk the slower waters downstream of Emerson or drift fish the main stem from Emerson up to and including the North and South Forks, steelheading on the Nooksack is a tough proposition. Don't bother.

The same may go for sea-run cutthroat, which once provided excellent angling action. Local anglers do catch a cutthroat here and there throughout the river from September through November, but the harvest-trout fishery certainly isn't worth a long trip from anywhere.

Salmon fishing is a better bet, especially on the main stem of the Nooksack. Boat and bank anglers catch several hundred hatchery coho from the river during September and October each year, a catch that's often made up of about half adult fish and half one- to two-pound jacks. November and December provide some fairly good chum salmon fishing. Regulations over the past several years have required that all chinook salmon be released.

Location: Flows into Bellingham Bay northwest of Bellingham; see map A2, grid a5.

Species: Chinook, coho, and chum salmon; winter steelhead; sea-run cutthroat trout.

Facilities: The best place to launch or take out on the main Nooksack is beneath the Highway 542 bridge over the river at Cedarville. There's a concrete-plank ramp here, but it was in pretty bad condition at last check. Downstream is a public access area off Highway 539 (Meridian Road), a short distance southwest of Lynden where boats can be dragged or carried to the water. There's also a Department of Fish and Wildlife boat ramp and access area south of Ferndale at about river mile six. Located at the north end of Hovander County Park, this ramp sometimes becomes difficult or impossible to use because of silt buildup. A $10 WDFW access decal is required to use the public launch

areas maintained by the Washington Department of Fish and Wildlife. Ferndale RV/Campground, about a mile and a half north of town just off I-5, has tent and RV sites and other camping facilities. Other options include The Cedars RV Resort and Mountain View RV Park. Scottish Lodge Motel, the Best Western Voyagers' Landing, and several bed-and-breakfasts are also available in Ferndale. Dutch Village Inn, Windmill Inn Motel, and Hidden Village RV Park are among the possibilities in Lynden. Sedro Woolley offers the Skagit Motel, Riverfront RV Park, and Wildwood Resort.

Directions: To reach the South Fork Nooksack, exit I-5 onto Highway 20 at Burlington and drive east to Sedro Woolley, then north on Highway 9 to the river. Upper portions of the South Fork may also be reached by driving east from Sedro Woolley on Highway 20 and turning north (left) on Ensley Road. To reach the North Fork and Middle Fork Nooksack, turn east off Highway 9 near Deming onto Highway 542. Turn south (right) onto Mosquito Lake Road to reach the Middle Fork, but stay on Highway 542 to reach several good stretches of the North Fork. Some popular stretches of the main Nooksack are within easy driving range of Highway 9 west of Deming. Turn west off Highway 9 at Everson to drive downstream to Lynden and continue downstream toward Ferndale. Along the way about a dozen roads extend to or near the river. Reach the south side of the main river between Ferndale and Everson by driving east out of Ferndale on Paradise Road and turning north on Northwest Drive. Again, several intersecting roads reach the river.

Contact: Wolten's Coast to Coast, 360/332-4077 (ask for Jerry); Ferndale Campground, 360/384-2622; Scottish Lodge Motel, 360/384-4040; Northwest RV Park, 360/384-5038; website: www.cnw.com.

4 Wiser Lake

This popular bass and panfish lake has been known to give up its share of respectable bass. It has a bass slot limit, explained thoroughly in the regulations pamphlet. Perch and catfish (brown bullhead) fishing is also dependable, but you'll have to work hard to catch a trout. The lake has a year-round season and produces fish from late winter to late fall.

Location: Southwest of Lynden in Whatcom County; see map A2, grid a5.

Species: Largemouth bass, yellow perch, brown bullhead catfish, a few cutthroat trout.

Facilities: There's a concrete-plank Department of Fish and Wildlife boat ramp on the north side of the lake, but like many, it was in sad shape the last time I was there (early 1999). A $10 WDFW access decal is required to use the public launch areas maintained by the Washington Department of Fish and Wildlife.

Hidden Village RV Park is just south of the lake and has both tent and RV spaces, a laundry, a dump station, and other facilities.

Directions: Take I-5 to Ferndale and go east on Axton Road about four miles to Highway 539 (Guide Meridian Road). Turn north (left) on Highway 539 and follow it 10 miles to Wiser Lake Road. Turn right and drive 100 feet to the public access area on the right.

Contact: Hidden Village RV Park, 360/398-1041, email: camp@hiddenvillagerv.com; Washington Department of Fish and Wildlife, Mill Creek Office, 425/775-1311.

5 Fazon Lake

The planting of channel catfish here a few years ago added an interesting twist for Fazon Lake anglers. Bass do well enough to draw anglers from some distance away. The bluegill fishing is pretty good in the spring and summer. And now channel cats. Anglers are just now figuring out how to catch them, mostly on night crawlers. If you get the hang of it, don't get carried away, since a special two-fish catfish limit is in effect. That's more than enough for a good catfish dinner, and it gives you a good reason to come back to Fazon again. Although they aren't anywhere near big enough to keep, tiger muskies were stocked in Fazon for the first time in 2000. Look for them to provide some serious trophy-fish opportunities in the near future.

Location: South of Everson in Whatcom County; see map A2, grid a6.

Species: Largemouth bass, channel catfish, bluegill, tiger musky.

Facilities: A paved access area, boat ramp, and restrooms managed by the Department of Fish and Wildlife are on the south side of the lake. The ramp is a typical concrete-plank type, but it was in tough shape in the spring of 1999, with some of the metal plank fasteners sticking up where they could cause tire damage. Check before launching, just to be safe. A $10 WDFW access decal is required to use the public launch area. Food, gas, and lodging are available in Bellingham.

Directions: Take Highway 542 northeast from Bellingham about four miles to Everson-Goshen Road, turn north (left), and drive four miles to Hemmi Road. Turn right on Hemmi, go a quarter of a mile, and turn left to the lake.

Contact: Yeager's Sporting Goods, 360/773-1080; Washington Department of Fish and Wildlife, Mill Creek Office, 425/775-1311.

6 Silver Lake

Of the many Silver Lakes in the Evergreen State, this is the one that's farthest away from everything. Locate it on a map and you might decide that it's too far away to bother fishing it, but don't be too hasty. This 175-acre lake near the British Columbia border in northern Whatcom County is a jewel of a trout lake, perhaps one of western Washington's best.

It gets a lot of help, in the form of generous hatchery plants that may top 16,000 legal-sized rainbows prior to the season opener in late April. As if that weren't enough, Silver Lake has a self-sustaining population of cutthroat trout, too, and some of those cutts grow to respectable size. If you need more reason to make the long drive to Silver, add brook trout to the menu. They aren't big and they aren't abundant, but they're usually eager, cooperative, and found within casting distance of the bank. Put Silver Lake on your must-do list for spring fishing.

Location: North of Maple Falls in Whatcom County; see map A2, grid a7.

Species: Rainbow, cutthroat, and some brook trout.

Facilities: A single-lane Department of Fish and Wildlife boat ramp is at the north end of the lake with enough room to park about a dozen trailers, and a county park with a ramp is near the south end. A $10 WDFW access decal is required to use the public launch area at the north end of the lake. Silver Lake Park has boat rentals, rental cabins, campsites with and without hookups, play equipment, a bathhouse with showers, a picnic shelter, and barbecue grills. The nearest food and gas are in Deming, 15 miles south. The nearest motels are way back in Bellingham.

Directions: Take I-5 to Bellingham and turn east on Highway 542, following it about 32 miles to Maple Falls. Turn north (left) on Silver Lake Road and drive about four miles to the lake.

Contact: Silver Lake Park, 360/599-2776, website: www.co.whatcom.wa.us/parks/parklist/silver.html; Washington Department of Fish and Wildlife, Mill Creek Office, 425/775-1311.

7 Tennant Lake

Year-round fishing and fair bass action are the main draws at this 43-acre lake. Since there isn't a developed boat ramp, some anglers fish it in float tubes or small rafts and car-top boats. Fishing from any floating device, though, becomes illegal here for a few months beginning in October. Check the fishing pamphlet for the exact dates each year.

Location: Southeast of Ferndale; see map A2, grid b4.

Species: Largemouth bass.

Facilities: The lake has no facilities, but food, gas, lodging, and supplies are available in and around Ferndale.

Directions: Take I-5 to Ferndale and drive south from town on Vista Drive. The lake is directly west of the intersection of Vista Drive and Smith Road.

Contact: Yeager's Sporting Goods, 360/773-1080; Washington Department of Fish and Wildlife, Mill Creek Office, 425/775-1311.

8 Toad Lake

At less than 30 acres, this lake near the north flank of Squalicum Mountain certainly isn't one of Whatcom County's biggest lakes, but when it comes to trout fishing, it's one of the best. Liberal plants of legal-sized rainbows, to the tune of 5,000 fish, are stocked here before the season opens in April, and the early season catch average is often one of the best in the northern Puget Sound region. As the rainbows begin to disappear, kokanee of 8 to 10 inches start to show in the catch.

Location: Northeast of Bellingham; see map A2, grid b5.

Species: Rainbow trout, kokanee.

Facilities: A public access area with a boat ramp and restrooms is located on the lake. All other amenities can be found in Bellingham.

Directions: Take I-5 to Bellingham and then take Highway 542 northeast. Just over two miles off the freeway, Highway 542 crosses over Squalicum Creek and then passes under some power lines. Take the next right, Toad Lake Road, and then bear left off it to the lake.

Contact: Washington Department of Fish and Wildlife, Mill Creek Office, 425/775-1311.

9 Squalicum Lake

You can fish this 30-acre Whatcom County lake year-round, but you can't fish it with your favorite spinning rod. That's because it's a fly-fishing-only lake. Cutthroat trout provide the action, and some of them grow to impressive dimensions. Spring and fall are the best times to fish the lake, but if you're suffering a severe case of wintertime cabin fever, feel free.

Location: Northeast of Bellingham; see map A2, grid b6.

Species: Cutthroat trout.

Facilities: The lake has a public access area and boat ramp, and everything else you'll need is available in Bellingham.

Directions: Take I-5 to Bellingham and follow Highway 542 northeast out of town. About six miles from Bellingham, you'll come to the end of a two-mile straightaway. As the highway turns left, take the gravel road to the right. If you miss it and go straight, you'll quickly come to Squalicum Lake Road, but it doesn't go to Squalicum Lake. Go figure.

Contact: Washington Department of Fish and Wildlife, Mill Creek Office, 425/775-1311.

10 Lake Whatcom

Smallmouth bass fishing has taken off in this big, deep lake on the outskirts of Bellingham. It has lots of smallies over two pounds and now and then gives up a smallmouth over five pounds. Although these scrappy fish are found throughout the lake, the best smallmouth fishing often occurs at the north end, from about Geneva Point northward. Crankbaits, a wide variety of plastic grubs and tubes, and even spinnerbaits account for good smallmouth catches. The lake also provides fair fishing for largemouth bass, some

of which top the five-pound mark.

Kokanee also draw lots of anglers to Whatcom, and it's easy to understand why. Annual kokanee plants here typically total several million, and the lake has long been used as a source of kokanee fry for other lakes throughout Washington. Trolling with Wedding Ring or Jeweled Bead spinners, Needlefish, or small Dick Nite spoons behind a string of gang trolls is effective, but stillfishing with white corn and other small baits also takes kokanee, which come on strong in late May and provide good fishing all summer. A recent development in the kokanee fishery here is that chumming is no longer allowed, due to what you'd have to call misdirected concerns about water quality. Apparently, all the logging that has occurred in the surrounding hills doesn't affect the lake's water quality, but kokanee anglers tossing a handful of creamed corn in the water now and then causes severe pollution.

Kokanee anglers sometimes hook and land one of the lake's hefty cutthroat trout, some of which top 24 inches. A special regulation allowing anglers to keep only one trout over 14 inches is in effect to protect these trophy cutthroats.

Perch fishing has dropped off somewhat in recent years, but the lake still offers some large ones. Most are caught along the north shore and south end of the lake on worms and night crawlers.

If you catch a cutthroat trout here, you now have to release it. Apparently someone is paying attention to the loss of cutthroat spawning at the hands of logging and development, but instead of stopping the damage, the cutthroat fishery is closed.

Location: Southeast of Bellingham; see map A2, grid b5.

Species: Kokanee, cutthroat trout, smallmouth and largemouth bass, yellow perch.

Facilities: There's a three-lane boat ramp with two large floats at Bloedel Donavan Park near the north end of the lake and another at the public access area in South Bay, at the south end. The South Bay facility is a gravel one-lane ramp, with a rock wall along one side to protect it from weather and rough water, so it's usually a good place to launch while avoiding the crowds at the bigger launch to the north. A $10 WDFW access decal is required to use the public launch area maintained by the Washington Department of Fish and Wildlife. Bloedel Donavan Park has a swim beach, picnic area, playground, dressing room, and lots of parking. All amenities are available in Bellingham.

Directions: Take I-5 to Bellingham and then take Exit 254 onto Iowa Street. Drive east on Iowa Street about half a mile to Yew Street and turn north (left). Turn east (right) on Alabama Street and drive about a mile to Electric Avenue. Turn south (right) and go a block to the Bloedel Donavan access area and boat ramp.

Contact: Yeager's Sporting Goods, 360/773-1080; Washington Department of Fish and Wildlife, Mill Creek Office, 425/775-1311.

11 Lake Padden

Anglers pack a lot of fishing activity into a mere six months of open season on this 150-acre lake at the south end of Bellingham. Lake Padden is the mother lode of rainbow trout when the Department of Fish and Wildlife dumps something like 17,000 hatchery trout into the confines of the lake just before the season opens. I wouldn't say that only a bozo can keep from catching rainbows once those hungry hatchery clones hit the water, but I might think it to myself. Anyway, the rainbow fishing is good all spring, and the fish run a hefty 11-inch average and weigh about a half pound apiece.

By June the attention of anglers turns to kokanee fishing, which can be pretty good.

Most of the kokanee are smaller than the average rainbow, and fishing for them can be a little more complicated, but if you locate a school of these fine-eating fish and stay with it, you'll do OK. Cutthroats also begin to come alive in June, and anglers catch a few of them throughout the summer and well into fall.

Part of the joy in fishing Lake Padden is that gas-powered motors aren't allowed, so things are a lot more peaceful than at many of the Northwest's top trout lakes.

Location: South of Bellingham; see map A2, grid b6.

Species: Rainbow and cutthroat trout, kokanee.

Facilities: The lake has a good boat ramp, and a city park provides lots of shoreline access. Food, gas, lodging, tackle, and other facilities are available in Bellingham.

Directions: Take the North Samish Way exit off I-5 at Bellingham and follow the road 2.5 miles to the north end of Lake Padden.

Contact: Yeager's Sporting Goods, 360/773-1080; Washington Department of Fish and Wildlife, Mill Creek Office, 425/775-1311.

12 Northern San Juan Islands

As recently as the mid-1980s, it was still accurate to call the northern San Juans a last frontier of saltwater fishing in the Northwest, but the area was discovered in a big way during the 1990s. Getting to the islands by ferry has become more of a waiting game, especially during the summer and on weekends, and much of the area's once-great bottom fishing has been heavily exploited.

Still, this is an interesting and sometimes productive area to fish. It's one of the few spots where Washington anglers can find places to fish for salmon throughout much of the year, and such places are indeed rare. In fact, the chinook fishing can be downright good if you time your trip right. Winter and spring blackmouth fishing (see the regula-

No Boat? No Problem!

Although saltwater fishing is commonly associated with boats and expensive tackle, it doesn't have to be that way. In the Puget Sound area there are lots of places for anglers without a boat to catch saltwater species of many kinds. The best opportunities for shore-bound anglers are at the more than 50 public fishing piers scattered along the shores from Blaine and Port Angeles all the way down the Sound to Olympia. Most of them have free parking nearby, and many have restrooms, lights for night fishing, fish-cleaning facilities, and easy accessibility for anglers with disabilities. Here's a complete listing:

1. Port Angeles City Pier
2. Blaine Dock (Port of Bellingham)
3. Gooseberry Point Ferry Dock (west of Bellingham)
4. Boulevard Park Pier (Bellingham)
5. Sixth Street Dock (Port of Bellingham)
6. Anacortes Municipal Pier
7. Friday Harbor Marina Docks
8. LaConner Marina Docks
9. Bowman's Bay Pier
10. Cornett Bay Docks
11. Whidbey Naval Seaplane Base Pier
12. Oak Harbor Pier (Flintstone Park)
13. Coupeville Pier
14. Kayak Point County Park Pier (south of Stanwood)
15. Langley City Pier
16. John Wayne Marina (Sequim Bay)
17. Fort Worden (Port Townsend)
18. Port Hudson (Port Townsend)
19. Fort Flagler (Marrowstone Island)
20. Pier 1 (Port of Everett)
21. Mukilteo Pier
22. Meadowdale
23. Edmonds Pier
24. Indianola Pier
25. Suquamish
26. Keyport
27. Bownsville
28. Silverdale
29. Illahee City Pier
30. Point White (southeast corner of Bainbridge Island)
31. Illahee State Park Pier
32. Tracyton Coal Dock
33. Park Avenue Pier (Bremerton)
34. Bremerton Pier (First Street Dock)
35. Waterman Point Pier (Sinclair Inlet)
36. Annapolis Dock (Retsil)
37. Port Orchard Pier
38. Shilshole Marina (A Dock)
39. Elliot Bay (Seattle Fishing Pier)
40. Duwamish Head (west side of Elliot Bay)
41. Spokane Street Bridge (Elliot Bay)
42. Blake Island Pier
43. Harper Pier (Yukon Harbor)
44. Des Moines Marina Pier
45. Redondo Pier
46. Dash Point Pier
47. Tramp Harbor (east side of Vashon Island)
48. Point Defiance Park Pier
49. Les Davis Pier (Tacoma)
50. Old Town Dock (Tacoma)
51. Clyde Davidson Memorial Pier (Steilacoom)
52. Luhr's Beach Pier (north of Olympia)
53. Twanoh State Park Pier (southern Hood Canal)
54. Hoodsport Pier (Hood Canal)
55. Point Whitney Pier (nothern Hood Canal)
56. Hood Canal Bridge Pier
57. Port Townsend City Dock

tions pamphlet for season dates) can be especially productive along the west side of Waldron Island, the west side of Orcas Island, and the Point Lawrence area on the east side of Orcas Island. Pink salmon fishing during odd-numbered years can be good on the north and east sides of Orcas Island, especially for trollers using flasher-and-squid or flasher-and-spoon combinations.

The slow-growing lingcod and rockfish populations have taken a heavy pounding, but there are still lots of submerged reefs and rock piles that might produce a hefty ling or a good catch of quillback rockfish. Some of the same places also offer a chance at a big, colorful yelloweye rockfish, one of the truly impressive bottom-fish species of the Northwest. The rockfish limits have taken a nosedive here as they have throughout most of Washington's "inside" marine waters, and at last word you could keep only one a day in the islands. Open-water reefs north of Waldron Island and around the far-northern islands (Patos, Sucia, and Matia) offer the best bottom fishing, but you might also find a big ling along the edges of the larger islands as well. The rocky shoreline along the west side of Orcas, for example, still gives up a worthwhile lingcod now and then.

To learn more about boating and fishing the northern San Juans, buy a couple of good nautical charts before visiting the area. NOAA nautical chart 18421 provides an overview, but you may also want to get a copy of charts 18430, 18432, 18433, and 18434.

Location: Marine waters immediately surrounding Orcas, Stuart, Waldron, Patos, Sucia, Lummi, and the smaller islands making up the northern half of the San Juan Island group; see map A2, grid c2.

Species: Chinook, coho, and pink salmon; lingcod; various rockfish and other bottom fish species.

Facilities: Marine state parks in the northern San Juans include those at Clark, Doe, Jones, Matia, Patos, Posey, Stuart, and Sucia Islands. Stuart Island has both floats and buoys in two locations, Reid Harbor and Prevost Harbor. Sucia Island marine campers may choose moorage buoys from among those in Echo Bay, Fox Cove, Shallow Bay, Ewing Cove, Snoring Bay, and Fossil Bay.

Fossil Bay also offers nearly 800 feet of moorage float space. Marine park float and dock space costs $8 per night for boats under 26 feet, $11 per night for boats 26 feet and over; moorage buoys cost $5 per night. Annual moorage permits are also available and are valid at all marine parks. They cost $50 for boats under 26 feet, $80 for larger boats. Moorage, fuel, and other boaters' necessities also are available at Bartwood Lodge, Deer Harbor Marina, West Sound Marina, West Beach Resort, and Rosario Resort. There are several good restaurants and places to shop in Eastsound and Orcas, located pretty much at opposite ends of Orcas Island. Marine assistance is available from Tim's Marine/ACA Team, (360)-378-9636 (VHF ch. 16).

Paved launch ramps are available at six locations on Orcas Island:

- **Bartwood Lodge:** The ramp at Bartwood Lodge is near the northernmost tip of the island. It's a concrete one-lane ramp with a summertime loading float. Drive north out of Eastsound on Horseshoe Highway and go right on Mount Baker Road, following it a quarter mile to North Beach Road. Turn left on North Beach Road and drive half a mile to Anderson Road, turning right and driving three-quarters of a mile to the resort sign.
- **Smuggler's Resort:** Follow the above directions out of Eastsound. Smuggler's is immediately east of Bartwood at the northern tip of the island. This is another one-lane concrete ramp.

- **West Beach Resort:** From the Orcas Island ferry landing, drive north on Horseshoe Highway past Eastsound and turn west (left) on Enchanted Forest Road, following it just under three miles to the resort. The single-lane concrete ramp has a loading float. It's available to resort guests and by appointment to nonguests. Round-trip launching and parking costs $10 per day.

- **West Sound Marina:** A portable hoist with a loading float is at the marina, which is located on Deer Harbor Road, about 2.5 miles northwest of the Orcas Island ferry landing. The launch fee increases with the size of your boat.

- **Obstruction Pass:** The fifth ramp on the island, managed by San Juan County Parks, is near the south tip of the island on Obstruction Pass. To reach it, follow Point Lawrence Road east from Olga for three-quarters of a mile and turn south (right) on Obstruction Pass Road, following it a mile and a half to the ramp. This is a one-lane concrete ramp with a loading float that comes out of the water in winter.

- **Rosario Resort:** A sixth ramp, located near Rosario Resort on the east side of East Sound, has parking for registered resort guests only. It's a one-lane concrete ramp. To reach it, drive just over 13 miles east from the Orcas Ferry landing on Horseshoe Highway, then right on Rosario Road to the resort.

Ramps on the mainland that provide the nearest departure points to the northern San Juans include those at Washington Park and Cap Sante Marine in Anacortes, the four-lane Washington State Parks ramp at Cornet Bay, the one-lane ramp at Bowman Bay, the small ramp at Larrabee State Park a few miles south of Bellingham, and ramps at Squalicum Harbor and Fairhaven Marinas in Bellingham. Skyline Marina southwest of Anacortes doesn't have a ramp, but many boaters use its 50-ton sling to launch for their runs to the San Juans.

Directions: Take the ferry from Anacortes to Orcas Island or launch at Anacortes and run west, across Rosario Strait. From the south, run north across the Strait of Juan de Fuca from Sequim or Port Angeles.

Contact: Washington State Parks and Recreation Commission, 360/902-8844; Deer Harbor Marina, 360/376-3037 (VHF ch. 78); Port of Friday Harbor, 360/376-2688 (VHF ch. 66), website: www.portfridayharbor.org; West Sound Marina, 360/376-2314 (VHF ch. 16); Rosario Resort, 360/376-2222 (VHF ch. 78); Bartwood Lodge, 866/666-2242; Tim's Marine/ACATeam, 360/378-9636 (VHF ch. 16); Washington State Ferries, 800/843-3779; Fish Tales Charters, 360/293-5766. For nautical charts of this area (NOAA charts 18421, 18423, 18430, 18431), contact Captain's Nautical Supply, 206/283-7242.

13 Cascade Lake

The combination of hatchery plants and some self-sustaining populations makes fishing a worthwhile proposition in this shallow Orcas Island lake. The Department of Fish and Wildlife stocks rainbows here to provide steady fishing action all spring, but there are also cutthroats in the lake to help prolong the fun and excitement into June. By that time, kokanee are on the bite, giving anglers something to do throughout much of the summer. Things get pretty busy around Cascade Lake in the summer, so if you're thinking about catching fish in July and August, plan on hitting the water early or staying well into the evening.

Location: Just east of Eastsound on Orcas Island; see map A2, grid c3.

Species: Rainbow and cutthroat trout, kokanee.

Facilities: Moran State Park offers bank fishing and a boat ramp, as well as a limited number of tent sites. All other amenities are available in Eastsound, including some interesting shops and restaurants.

Directions: Take the ferry from Anacortes to Orcas Island and drive north to the town of Eastsound. From there drive southeast on Orcas-Olga Road about four miles to the lake, which is on the left.

Contact: Moran State Park, 360/376-2326; Washington State Parks and Recreation Commission, 360/902-8844 (information) or 800/452-5687 (reservations).

14 Mountain Lake

At nearly 200 acres, this is the biggest lake in the San Juans. At more than 100 feet deep, it's also the deepest and coolest, and it provides good fishing throughout the summer. The lake has a year-round fishing season, but fishing sometimes gets off to a slow start, due at least in part to the lake's cool temperatures. Once it gets going, though, it offers good kokanee fishing. All the usual trolling and stillfishing techniques work for these 10- to 12-inch salmon. If you want trout, try trolling or casting small spoons or spinners around the shallows at the edge of the lake. Fly-fishing on a summer evening also pays off here for brookies and cutts, which average about eight inches.

Location: Eastern Orcas Island; see map A2, grid c3.

Species: Kokanee, cutthroat and brook trout.

Facilities: Moran State Park provides public access and a boat ramp, as well as a few tent sites for campers. Other amenities are available in Eastsound.

Directions: Take the ferry from Anacortes to Orcas Island and drive north on Orcas-Olga Road through Eastsound, continuing southeast on Orcas-Olga Road. Drive past Cascade Lake for two miles to Mountain Lake.

Contact: Moran State Park, 360/376-2326;

Washington State Parks and Recreation Commission, 360/902-8844 (information) or 800/452-5687 (reservations).

15 Lake Samish

This 815-acre lake within easy view of freeway drivers is really two distinctly different lakes connected by a narrow neck of shallow water. The main lake, except for its large size and the relatively deep hole near its center, is a lot like hundreds of other western Washington lowland lakes, with a gently sloping bottom that provides shallow water for good bass and crappie fishing. There are also some decent-sized brown bullheads to be found here, but the locals are quick to point out that the catfish action isn't what it was a decade ago.

Farther out, where the water drops off to 50, 60, even 70 feet or more in a couple of places, kokanee anglers do pretty well in June and July. This section of the lake also has some big cutthroats, which bite best in the fall.

The west end of the lake has a totally different personality. The bottom drops off quickly from the 10-foot shoals where the bridge crosses the narrow channel, and the middle of this upper lake has spots nearly 150 feet deep. This deep water stays cool throughout the lake's year-round season, which makes it a worthwhile possibility for kokanee and cutthroats even during the warm days of midsummer. This is one of those relatively rare Washington lakes where chumming is permitted, so stillfishing for kokanee can be a productive bet. Lake Samish has some restrictive regulations on cutthroat fishing, so be sure to check the fishing pamphlet for details before you hit it big and find yourself with more trout than you're supposed to have.

Two words of caution: First, if you launch at the public access area on the east side, take it easy. As mentioned above, the ramp was in tough shape last time I was there, with some of the concrete slabs missing and others broken or out of alignment. You could get stuck or damage your trailer here. The second warning is about the personal watercraft riders who flock to Samish in the summer. Crazy is the only way to describe it.

Location: Southeast of Bellingham; see map A2, grid c5.

Species: Cutthroat trout, kokanee, largemouth bass, crappie, brown bullhead catfish.

Facilities: A public access area and boat ramp are on the east side of the lake, and a Whatcom County Parks launch is at the northwest corner. Both are suitable for launching smaller boats, but check out the public access ramp before using it. At last look it was in pretty rough shape. A $10 WDFW access decal is required to use the public launch areas maintained by the Washington Department of Fish and Wildlife. Samish Park, a part of the Whatcom County Parks system, is open for day use until 9 P.M. in the summer, with a $3 fee to nonresidents of the county. Food, gas, and tackle are readily available in Bellingham, and there are plenty of accommodations nearby, including bed-and-breakfasts and motels.

Directions: Take I-5 to approximately six miles south of Bellingham, where the freeway parallels the east side of the lake for about two miles. Exit 242 takes you to the lake's south end; Exit 246 leads to the north end.

Contact: Yeager's Sporting Goods, 360/773-1080; Washington Department of Fish and Wildlife, Mill Creek Office, 425/775-1311.

16 Cain Lake

Planted rainbows provide good trout fishing at Cain Lake for the first several weeks of the season and again in the fall. Trolling with various lake trolls and worms is the standard plan of attack, but smaller lures and sportier tackle are also effective. Largemouths begin to go on the bite in May, and bass fishing is good throughout the summer. There are a fair number of homes around the lake, and the many docks offer some of the best bass fishing. This isn't, however, a good place to trailer your big bass boat if you're looking to put it through its paces and blow the carbon out of that 200-horse Mercury outboard. The lake has a no-wake speed limit, and gas-powered engines are prohibited. If you like catching and eating perch, Cain is a good choice—it has some big ones.

Location: South of Lake Whatcom on the Whatcom-Skagit County line; see map A2, grid c6.

Species: Rainbow trout, largemouth bass, yellow perch.

Facilities: Cain Lake has a public access area with a single-lane boat ramp and toilets; there's room for only about 10 cars. A $10 WDFW access decal is required to use the public launch areas maintained by the Washington Department of Fish and Wildlife. Bellingham, about 10 miles to the northeast, offers the nearest amenities, including lodging and a choice of restaurants.

Directions: Drive about 11 miles north from Burlington on I-5 and take the Alger exit, driving east about a mile to Alger. From Alger, take Cain Lake Road out of town to the east and follow it 3.5 miles to Camp 2 Road. Turn left and follow Camp 2 Road one-third of a mile to the lake.

Contact: Glenhaven Country Store, 360/595-9114.

17 Egg Lake

The rainbows are planted during the spring, the bass are self-sustaining, and both provide good fishing in this tiny San Juan Island lake. Although covering only seven acres, Egg Lake is a big hit, mainly because it's the island's only consistent trout fishery. There isn't much carryover from the 1,000 or so hatchery trout stocked here each year, so your chances of catching a big rainbow are slim. The bass fishing turns on early, often by April, and remains fairly good until fall. The lake is open year-round, but if you fish it from October to March, you can expect to have it pretty much to yourself.

Location: Immediately west of Sportsman's Lake, northwest of Friday Harbor on San Juan Island; see map A2, grid c1.

Species: Rainbow trout, largemouth bass.

Facilities: A Department of Fish and Wildlife access area and a boat ramp are located on the west side of the lake. Other amenities can be found in Friday Harbor and Roche Harbor.

Directions: Take the Anacortes ferry to Friday Harbor (San Juan Island), turn right at the top of the hill, and drive northwest on Roche Harbor Road. About half a mile past Sportsman's Lake, turn left on Egg Lake Road and follow it for about half a mile to the lake.

Contact: Skagit Anglers, 360/336-3232; Island Bicycles, 360/378-2350.

18 Sportsman's Lake

This is the best bass-fishing lake in the San Juans, and some anglers think it's one of the best in western Washington. The 65-acre lake is only about 10 feet deep at its deepest point, has lots of brushy cover and weeds around its edges, and grows some pretty impressive largemouths.

Sportsman's Lake is open year-round, but May to September offers the best fishing for bass. The only problem is that during the warm months the lake is choked with weeds. You'll still catch fish, but use something that's as weedless as possible or you'll lose a lot of tackle. Most Sportsman's Lake regulars gear up for all the vegetation, using 17- to 25-pound line to help turn hooked bass away from the thick tangles.

You might be disappointed if you fish the lake for trout, but persistent casting with a small wobbling spoon or trolling with a Kwik-fish or Flatfish might eventually turn up a decent-sized cutthroat. Do your trout fishing in the spring before the weeds get too thick.

Location: Northwest of Friday Harbor on San Juan Island; see map A2, grid c1.

Species: Largemouth bass, a few cutthroat trout.

Facilities: Sportsman's Lake has a boat ramp and access area, and all other amenities are available in Friday Harbor and Roche Harbor. You need a $10 Department of Fish and Wildlife access decal to use the lake's boat ramp.

Directions: Take the Anacortes ferry to Friday Harbor (San Juan Island), turn right at the top of the hill, and drive northwest on Roche Harbor Road. The lake is on the left side of the road about five miles from Friday Harbor.

Contact: Skagit Anglers, 360/336-3232; Island Bicycles, 360/378-2350.

19 Killebrew Lake

Either fish this small lake from the bank or wade in with your float tube to explore it more thoroughly. At only 13 acres, Killebrew Lake is usually overlooked and only lightly fished. The bass aren't big, but they're fairly abundant. It's a good place to fish a bobber-and-worm combination for yellow perch.

Location: South end of Orcas Island; see map A2, grid c3.

Species: Largemouth bass, yellow perch.

Facilities: Orcas has food, fuel, lodging, and other amenities.

Directions: Take the ferry from Anacortes to Orcas Island, turn right as you exit the ferry ramp, and drive east on White Beach Road about 2.5 miles to the lake, which is on the left immediately west of the Dolphin Bay Road intersection.

Contact: Skagit Anglers, 360/336-3232; Island Bicycles, 360/378-2350.

20 Samish River

Although it doesn't get a lot of publicity, fall salmon fishing can be worth a trip to the Samish. Both adult and jack chinooks begin to show in August and provide good fishing through September and into early October. Coho fishing can range from fair to good in October—fair when there aren't many 12- to 18-inch jack cohos in the river and good when the jacks show up. By November the focus of the salmon fishery turns from the last of the jack cohos to the small run of chums that provide only marginal fishing action. Salmon fishing is open only on the lower river from the mouth to I-5.

Steelheading is a possibility throughout the Samish River. Be sure to check the regulations pamphlet, though, because wild steelhead-release rules are usually in effect throughout the season. The best steelhead catches here are usually recorded in January, with December and February a toss-up for second-best fishing months.

Location: Flows into Samish Bay west of Sedro Woolley in Skagit County; see map A2, grid c6.

Species: Winter steelhead; chinook, coho, and a few chum salmon; sea-run and resident cutthroat trout.

Facilities: A KOA campground is located on the river about a mile south of the salmon hatchery on Old U.S. 99. The nearest food, gas, lodging, and tackle are in Burlington and Mount Vernon.

Directions: To reach the lower Samish River, exit I-5 to the west just north of Burlington and follow Highway 11 about 2.5 miles to Allen West Road. Turn west (left) and drive 1.5 miles to Thomas Road; then turn north (right) and drive half a mile to the river. To fish the upper river, take the Bow Hill Road exit off I-5 and drive east toward the Samish Salmon Hatchery, following Prairie Road up the river. Prairie Road first hits the river three miles east of I-5.

Contact: Burlington KOA, 360/724-5511; Yeager's Sporting Goods, 360/773-1080.

21 Grandy Lake

Trolling and casting small wobbling spoons or fishing a bobber-and-worm combination will produce trout here for patient anglers. Grandy isn't a big lake, so it's possible to fish it comfortably from a float tube or canoe.

May and September are good months to fish the lake, and if I were to visit in September, I'd take along a lightweight fly rod and a selection of small streamer patterns. The bass here grow to four or five pounds, and if you want one, concentrate your efforts from June through August, especially during those warm, calm evenings.

Location: Northeast of Hamilton in Skagit County; see map A2, grid c9.

Species: Cutthroat trout, largemouth bass.

Facilities: The lake has a rough boat ramp where small boats may be launched. A private campground is located at the intersection of Highway 20 and Baker Lake Road, about four miles from Grandy Lake. The nearest food, gas, tackle, and lodging are in Hamilton.

Directions: Drive 16 miles east on Highway 20 from Sedro Woolley and turn north on Baker Lake Road about five miles east of Hamilton. Follow Baker Lake Road four miles to Grandy Lake.

Contact: Creekside Camping, 360/826-3566; Yeager's Sporting Goods, 360/773-1080.

22 Southern San Juan Islands

The southern San Juans offer more salmon-fishing opportunities than the northern islands, thanks in part to their proximity to the Strait of Juan de Fuca and the many productive banks near the east end of the strait. Anglers out of Friday and Roche Harbors and Shaw and Lopez Islands can easily run south to fish Middle, Hein, Salmon, and Eastern Banks, often finding good blackmouth, halibut, and lingcod fishing for their efforts. These areas are especially good for salmon in late winter and spring. May is often the time to fish them for lingcod and halibut.

During odd-numbered years the strait is also a good place to fish for pink salmon, which pour through these waters by the hundreds of thousands. August and early September mark the peak of the pink salmon runs, and fishing at that time may be simply a matter of trolling a small herring or flasher-and-hoochie rig near the surface for an hour and going home with your limit. Although tens of thousands of sockeye salmon also pass through the strait and through some of the major waterways within the islands, anglers catch very few of them. One of these years some inventive salmon angler is going to unlock the key to catching saltwater sockeyes consistently, and then look out!

Closer to the islands, the west side and south end of San Juan Island is a productive salmon-fishing spot in its own right, especially in the summer when adult kings are passing through the area. Such places as Lime Kiln Point, Pile Point, Eagle Point, and Cattle Point give up some husky fish in July and August, and if you time your trip so that you're around during a series of evening flood tides, try jigging or mooching around tiny Goose Island, just inside San Juan Channel from Cattle Point. Winter blackmouth fishing can also be good within the protected waters of the islands. Several points and bays on either side of San Juan Channel are among the favorite spots for this cold-weather salmon fishing.

As for bottom fish, if you don't want to run to Middle Bank or Hein Bank for halibut or lingcod, you might find a decent ling or two along the west side of San Juan Island. There are several rocky reefs and steep drop-offs to fish, and all of them have something worthwhile living on, in, or around them. Look closely at NOAA nautical chart 18421 or one of the other San Juan charts, and you'll quickly spot other rocky humps that might be worth investigating. And remember, there's now a one-fish limit on rockfish here, so it's not a place you'd want to plan a summer fishing vacation with the intention of filling a cooler with rockfish fillets.

Kelp greenling are readily available along all rocky shorelines and kelp beds, in 10 to 50 feet of water. They'll hit small metal jigs or herring strips.

Location: Marine waters immediately surrounding San Juan, Lopez, Shaw, Decatur, Blakely, Cypress, and the smaller islands that constitute the southern half of the San Juan Island group; see map A2, grid d2.

Species: Chinook, coho, pink, and sockeye salmon; halibut; lingcod; various rockfish; greenling.

Facilities: San Juan Island has five public saltwater boat ramps, located at Roche Harbor Resort (north end of the island), Snug Harbor Resort (northwest corner of the island), San Juan County Park (in Smallpox Bay, halfway down the west side of the island), Shipyard Cove Marina (Friday Harbor), and Jackson Beach (in Griffin Bay southeast of Friday Harbor).

Lopez Island ramps include those at Odlin County Park (north end of the island, a mile from the ferry landing), Islands Marine Center (in Fisherman Bay, west side), Hunter Bay (southeast corner of the island) and MacKaye Harbor (southwest corner). Shaw Island's only boat ramp is in Indian Cove, near South Beach on the southeast side of the island.

Ramps on the mainland that provide the

nearest departure points to the northern San Juans include those at Washington Park and Cap Sante Marine in Anacortes, the four-lane Washington State Park's ramp at Cornet Bay, the one-lane ramp at Bowman Bay, the small ramp at Larrabee State Park a few miles south of Bellingham, and ramps at Squalicum Harbor and Fairhaven Marinas in Bellingham. Skyline Marina southwest of Anacortes doesn't have a ramp, but many boaters use its 50-ton sling to launch for their runs to the San Juans.

The state marine park on James Island (immediately east of Decatur Island) offers 134 feet of float space and five moorage buoys, as well as primitive campsites and pit toilets. Moorage fees are $8 a night for boats under 26 feet, $11 for boats 26 feet and over.

Spencer Spit Marine State Park, at the northeast corner of Lopez Island, has 16 moorage buoys, primitive campsites, restrooms, and picnic tables. There are four moorage buoys and four campsites on Blind Island, another state marine park located near the entrance to Blind Bay on the north side of Shaw Island.

A fourth marine state park is located on Turn Island, just east of Friday Harbor in San Juan Channel. It has three moorage buoys, primitive campsites, and picnic tables. The fee for moorage buoys at all marine state parks is $5 per night.

Odlin County Park on Lopez Island has 30 campsites with a low beach and small dock for loading and unloading only, pit toilets, and water. More plush accommodations, from rustic cabins to comfortable suites and bed-and-breakfast units, are available in Friday Harbor, Roche Harbor, Lopez (Fisherman Bay), and Snug Harbor. Hotel de Haro, more than 100 years old and one of the prettiest places in the islands, is in the heart of Roche Harbor and has more than 50 units of various kinds.

Moorage, fuel, power, showers, pump-outs, groceries, and other amenities for boaters can be found at the Port of Friday Harbor, Roche Harbor Resort, and Snug Harbor Resort, all on San Juan Island; The Lopez Islander and Island Marine Center on Lopez Island; Blakely Island General Store and Marina on Blakely Island; and Little Portion Store (limited guest moorage) on Shaw Island. Marine assistance is available from Tim's Marine/ACATeam in Friday Harbor.

Directions: Ferry from Anacortes to Lopez Island, Shaw Island, or San Juan Island or launch at Anacortes and run west, across Rosario Strait. From the south, run north across the Strait of Juan de Fuca from Sequim or Port Angeles.

Contact: Fish Tales Charters, 360/293-5766; Island Adventure Charters and Tours, 360/293-2428; San Juan Islands Visitor Information Center, 800/468-3701; Port of Friday Harbor, 360/378-4477, website: www.portfridayharbor.org; Roche Harbor Resort, 360/378-2155 (VHF ch. 16, 9); Snug Harbor Resort, 360/378-4762; Lopez Islander, 360/468-2233 (VHF ch. 78); Islands Marine Center, 360/468-3377 (VHF ch. 69); Shipyard Cove Marina, 360/378-5101; Blakely Island General Store and Marina, 360/375-6121; San Juan County Parks, 360/468-4413; Little Portion Store, 360/468-2288; Tim's Marine/ACATeam, 360/378-9636 (VHF ch. 16); Washington State Parks and Recreation Commission, 360/902-8844 (information) or 888/226-7688 (reservations); Washington State Ferries, 800/843-3779. For nautical charts of this area (NOAA charts 18421, 18423, 18429, 18430, 18433, 18434), contact Captain's Nautical Supply, 206/283-7242.

23 Hummel Lake

Although open to year-round fishing, Hummel is most productive during the spring and summer. Legal-sized hatchery rainbows provide much of the angling action in May, but by June the bass and bluegills start providing good fishing. Besides its small size—only 35 acres—Hummel Lake is only about 10 feet deep, which explains why it warms quickly and quits producing trout during the summer.

Location: East of Fisherman Bay near the north end of Lopez Island; see map A2, grid c3.

Species: Rainbow trout, largemouth bass, bluegill.

Facilities: The lake has a public access area and boat ramp, and there are tent sites at Spencer Spit State Park, about three miles away. You'll have to boat or ferry to Orcas or Friday Harbor for other necessities.

Directions: Take the ferry from Anacortes to Lopez Island and drive south from the ferry dock on Ferry Road about two miles to the T, where you should go left. From there it's about two miles to the lake, which is on the left.

Contact: Spencer Spit State Park, 360/468-2551; Washington State Parks and Recreation Commission, 360/902-8844 (information) or 888/226-7688 (reservations).

24 Heart Lake

Fishing is good at Heart Lake for the first several weeks after the April opener, but by summer the action drops off. The hatchery rainbows planted here tend to run a little larger than those stocked in other western Washington lakes, so a May fishing trip to Heart could provide a limit of 10- to 11-inch trout. Trolling with small versions of the Dick Nite, McMahon, Triple Teazer, and other small spoons is effective here. Stillfishing is also productive, especially if you use Berkley Power Bait in pink or any of the other hot colors.

Location: Southwest of Anacortes; see map A2, grid d4.

Species: Rainbow trout.

Facilities: A boat ramp is located at the public access area, and Anacortes has all the needed amenities.

Directions: Take I-5 to Burlington, turn west on Highway 20, and drive 18 miles to Anacortes. Drive west through town to 11th Avenue and turn south (left). Follow 11th Avenue to Heart Lake Road, which continues south to the lake, on the right.

Contact: Skagit Anglers, 360/336-3232; Washington Department of Fish and Wildlife, Mill Creek Office, 425/775-1311.

25 Whistle Lake

You can't drive to the shores of this 30-acre lake south of Anacortes, which is part of its charm. You can, however, carry in a small boat or float tube to help you explore this mixed-species fishery. Cast or troll a small Super Duper or dark-colored Rooster Tail spinner around the edges of the lake for cutthroats, or fish a bobber-and-worm rig to catch both trout and perch. The lake also has a fairly good largemouth bass population, yet another good reason to fish it from a boat, canoe, or float tube. Whistle Lake has a year-round season but produces best from late spring to fall.

Location: South of Anacortes; see map A2, grid d4.

Species: Cutthroat trout, largemouth bass, yellow perch.

Facilities: A small access area is located at the north end of the lake. Food, gas, and lodging are available in nearby Anacortes.

Directions: Take I-5 to Burlington, turn west on Highway 20, and drive to Anacortes. Turn south (left) as soon as you get into Anacortes and follow the only road that continues south. The lake is about 1.5 miles out of town.

Contact: Skagit Anglers, 360/336-3232; Washington Department of Fish and Wildlife, Mill Creek Office, 425/775-1311.

26 Lake Erie

Lake Erie is one of Skagit County's top trout lakes, especially the first month or so following the late-April season opener. Stocked with legal-sized hatchery rainbows, Lake Erie also offers the very real possibility of larger fish in the 12-inch range. Trolling and stillfishing are both productive here, and you might try fly-casting around the edges of the lake late in the day. Most of the bass here are small, but they can provide fast action as the weather warms in June and July.

Location: Southwest of Anacortes on Fidalgo Island; see map A2, grid d4.

Species: Rainbow trout, largemouth bass.

Facilities: The public access area is at the west end of the lake and has a boat ramp and restrooms. Other amenities are available in Anacortes.

Directions: Take Highway 20 west from I-5 and drive about 13 miles to Dean's Corner. Turn south (left) and drive two miles to Campbell Lake Road. Turn right, drive about 1.5 miles to Rosario Road, and turn left to the lake.

Contact: Skagit Anglers, 360/336-3232; Ace in the Hole Tackle, 360/293-1125; Lake Erie Resort, Grocery, and Trailer Park, 360/293-2772.

27 Campbell Lake

Sort of a northern version of Cowlitz County's Silver Lake (number 75 in chapter B2), Campbell has a little something for everyone. It's especially popular with bass anglers, who come here to prospect for largemouths that sometimes top seven pounds. I like working plastics and spinnerbaits around the rocky island in the center of the lake, but there are plenty of other places to cast for bass here. This 400-acre Skagit County lake ranks right up there with the best of western Washington's bass producers. It's no slouch when it comes to perch

fishing, either, providing some of the county's biggest and best catches of these delectable panfish. Night fishing during the spring and summer produces good caches of brown bullhead catfish. The lake also offers rainbow and cutthroat trout, although there are certainly better trout-fishing lakes nearby, such as Heart, Erie, and Pass Lakes.

Location: South of Anacortes on Fidalgo Island; see map A2, grid d4.

Species: Largemouth bass, yellow perch, brown bullhead catfish, rainbow and cutthroat trout.

Facilities: The lake has a public access area with a boat ramp and toilets. Food, gas, lodging, and tackle are available in Anacortes about four miles to the north.

Directions: Take I-5 to Burlington and turn west on Highway 20, driving about 13 miles to Dean's Corner (just past the golf course on the left). Turn south (left) and drive about two miles to the lake. Campbell Lake Road turns west (right) as you approach the north end of the lake.

Contact: Skagit Anglers, 360/336-3232; Lake Campbell Motel, 360/293-5314.

28 Pass Lake

To steal a line from Henry Ford, you can fish Pass Lake any way you want, as long as it's with a fly rod. This pretty 100-acre lake is open year-round to fly-fishing only and produces some beautiful trout. It's also one of western Washington's most popular and productive fly-fishing lakes. In addition to fly-fishing only, the rule here now is also catch-and-release only, although most Pass Lake regulars have been catching and releasing for years. Some of the rainbows taken here look like mature steelhead, weighing in at five pounds or more. Brown trout of 20 to 24 inches are well within the realm of possibility, too.

Planting Atlantic salmon in Washington

was an experiment that failed in most lakes, but there are some of these large-spotted transplants in Pass Lake, adding to the attractive variety. Gas-powered motors aren't allowed here, and the lake is popular with float-tubers.

Location: Southwest corner of Fidalgo Island just north of Deception Pass; see map A2, grid d4.

Species: Rainbow, brown, and cutthroat trout; Atlantic salmon.

Facilities: The lake has a public access area with a boat ramp and restrooms. Nearby Deception Pass State Park has about 60 tent sites that are first-come, first-served. The nearest food, gas, lodging, and tackle are in Anacortes and Oak Harbor.

Directions: Take I-5 to Burlington and turn west on Highway 20, following it about 18 miles toward Deception Pass State Park. Turn right off Highway 20 onto Rosario Road; then take an immediate right into the gravel boat ramp on Pass Lake.

Contact: Deception Pass State Park, 360/675-2417; Washington State Parks and Recreation Commission, 360/902-8844 (information) or 888/226-7688 (reservations); Skagit Anglers, 360/336-3232.

29 Cranberry Lake

Most anglers come here to fish for hatchery rainbows, but patient types willing to work a little harder for bigger fish also like Cranberry Lake. Carryover rainbows to 16 or 18 inches keep people coming back for more, and the possibility of catching a brown trout also adds incentive. At least one Department of Fish and Wildlife biologist says that Cranberry has browns similar in size to those in Pass Lake, which is known for its trophy trout. Fish around the weedy spots near the shallow south end of the lake, and there's a good chance of being rewarded with a couple of decent largemouth bass. Fish a bobber-and-

worm rig during the day for perch or at night for brown bullheads.

Although not listed as such in the fishing regulations pamphlet, Cranberry is one of those lakes where gas-powered engines are not allowed. Should you decide to visit Cranberry Lake in the fall, take along your salmon rod or steelhead tackle, because the fishing can be good for coho and pink salmon right from West Beach, at the western end of the park near the entrance to Deception Pass.

Location: Near the northwest tip of Whidbey Island; see map A2, grid d4.

Species: Rainbow and some brown trout, largemouth bass, yellow perch, brown bullhead catfish.

Facilities: Deception Pass State Park maintains a small, gravel boat ramp on the north end of the lake and a fishing pier on the east side. The state park has about 60 tent sites, which are available on a first-come, first-served basis. The nearest gas, food, lodging, and tackle are in Anacortes and Oak Harbor.

Directions: Take I-5 to Burlington and turn west onto Highway 20, following it west, then south about 20 miles to Deception Pass State Park. Cross the Deception Pass bridge, drive about half a mile, and turn west (right) to the lake.

Contact: Deception Pass State Park, 360/675-2417; Washington State Parks and Recreation Commission, 360/902-8844 (information) or 888/226-7688 (reservations).

30 Lower Skagit River

Once home to western Washington's most glorious run of summer chinook salmon and the state's top winter steelhead producer, the lower Skagit has gone downhill considerably since the mid-1970s. Still, there's enough angling variety available to make a trip to the Skagit worthwhile if your timing is good.

That famed summer chinook fishery is no longer an option, since anglers may now take only pink, coho, and chum salmon from the Skagit; at least that's what the regulations have dictated lately. Pink salmon only show here during odd-numbered years, but when they do, they can provide fast action for about five weeks from the middle of August to late September. Trolling or casting small wobbling spoons and diving plugs in such hot colors as pink, orange, and red is most likely to work on Skagit River pinks, most of which run two to four pounds. Some anglers intercept the pink salmon run when it enters the lower river and work their way upstream with the fish, enjoying hot fishing action several days in a row. Chum salmon enter the Skagit in good numbers every year, providing some hot fishing from about the middle of October through December. November is usually the best month for chums, and anything green or chartreuse is the best lure for these tough fighters.

Despite hatchery plants totaling in the hundreds of thousands, anglers seldom catch as many as 3,000 winter steelhead a year from the Skagit these days. That's not too impressive when compared to the good old days of the '60s, when this big river sometimes gave up as many as 34,000 winter steelies a year and consistently produced sport catches of more than 20,000 steelhead each winter. Still, as they say, on any given day... The best given days often occur in January, February, and March, and during that period fair numbers of fish are caught by plunkers on the lower river, drift anglers from Sedro Woolley upstream, and boat anglers throughout this entire stretch of the Skagit.

If you want to learn how to fish this long, wide river—with lots of secrets, by the way—it's a good idea to hire a guide, at least for the first day. Several fishing guides work out of Mount Vernon, Sedro Woolley, and the smaller towns upriver, and they know more about the Skagit than you could hope to learn

on your own over several weeks of experimenting and exploring.

Sea-run cutthroat fishing can be fairly good at times during September and October, especially downstream of Sedro Woolley, and the lower Skagit remains one of the few places in Washington where it's still legal to keep a Dolly Varden or two as part of your daily bag limit. Any Dolly you keep, however, must be at least 20 inches long.

Location: From Skagit Bay northeast to Concrete; see map A2, grid d6.

Species: Winter and summer steelhead, sea-run cutthroat trout, Dolly Varden, pink and chum salmon.

Facilities: Many boat ramps are located along this stretch of river, including those at Conway (South Fork Skagit), off Moore Road (North Fork Skagit), Edgewater Park (Mount Vernon), Burlington, Sedro Woolley, Lyman Road (between Lyman and Hamilton), at Hamilton, and Birdsview. Riverbend RV Park near Mount Vernon, Riverfront RV Park at Sedro Woolley, and Creekside Camping near Concrete all have tent and RV sites. Mount Vernon, Sedro Woolley, and Concrete all offer motel and bed-and-breakfast accommodations. Food, gas, and other amenities are also available in all three towns.

Directions: Take I-5 to Exit 221 and drive west through Conway on Fir Island Road. Turn north (right) on Dike Road or Mann Road to fish the South Fork Skagit or continue west on Fir Island Road to Moore Road and turn north (right) to fish the North Fork. Exit I-5 at Mount Vernon and drive west on Penn Road or Highway 536 to reach the main stem Skagit from the forks upstream to the I-5 bridge. To reach the river upstream of I-5, drive east on Highway 20 from Burlington and turn south (right) onto various roads in and around Sedro Woolley, Lyman, Hamilton, Birdsview, and Concrete. Most of these ramps are maintained by the

Department of Fish and Wildlife, so a $10 WDFW access decal is required to use these public launch areas.

Contact: Sedro Woolley Chamber of Commerce, 360/855-1841; Creekside Camping, 360/826-3566; Washington Department of Fish and Wildlife, Mill Creek Office, 425/775-1311.

31 Clear Lake

Open year-round, Clear Lake offers at least some angling opportunity during all but the dead of winter. Rainbow and cutthroat trout fishing are fair in the spring and fall, and, if you work at it, you might find some rainbows through the summer in the 40-foot depths near the southwest corner of the lake.

June and July provide some good largemouth bass fishing, especially along the weedy southern shoreline, the north end, and the east side of the lake, all of which are virtually undeveloped and natural. The many pilings and shoreline brush in the big cove at the north end of the lake are also especially inviting to bass anglers. You can find cooperative yellow perch here almost year-round. If you're into night fishing, Clear Lake offers a pretty good shot at one- to two-pound brown bullheads from about mid-May through September.

Location: South of Sedro Woolley; see map A2, grid d7.

Species: Rainbow and cutthroat trout, largemouth bass, yellow perch, brown bullhead catfish.

Facilities: A newly renovated concrete-slab ramp is at the public access area. A $10 WDFW access decal is required to use the public launch areas maintained by the Washington Department of Fish and Wildlife. The county park on the west side of the lake has moorage and offers some bank-fishing access. The nearest food, gas, lodging, and tackle are in Burlington.

Directions: Exit I-5 just north of Mount Ver-

non on College Way, which becomes Highway 538, and drive four miles east to Highway 9. Turn north (left) and drive just over three miles to the lake. To reach the public access area, turn east off Highway 9 onto Old Day Creek Road and drive half a mile to C Street; turn right into the access area.

Contact: Lake McMurray Store, 360/445-3565.

32 Beaver Lake

Many of the locals refer to this 73-acre lake as Mud Lake, which, although it may have some rather unsavory connotations, at least helps to distinguish it from the dozen or more other Beaver Lakes in Washington. This Beaver (or Mud) Lake contains a fair population of pan-sized cutthroat trout that provide some angling action in the spring and fall. Don't bother looking for a deep spot to try for trout, because you won't find one. The depths of Beaver Lake extend to only about 10 feet, and much of it is only five to seven feet deep. During the summer, the lake offers good perch fishing and a fair chance for largemouth bass and brown bullheads.

Location: South of Sedro Woolley; see map A2, grid d7.

Species: Cutthroat trout, largemouth bass, yellow perch, brown bullhead catfish.

Facilities: The Department of Fish and Wildlife maintains a public access area with a two-lane gravel boat ramp and toilets on the lake's west side. A $10 WDFW access decal is required to use this public launch area. The nearest stores and facilities are in Mount Vernon and Sedro Woolley.

Directions: Take I-5 to just north of Mount Vernon and turn east on College Way (Highway 538). Drive four miles to Highway 9, turn north (left), and drive to Walker Valley Road. Turn right and drive about 1.5 miles to the lake.

Contact: Lake McMurray Store, 360/445-3565.

33 Big Lake

Although open year-round, Big Lake is at its best in spring, summer, and early fall. This large (545 acres), shallow lake warms quickly in the spring, and when it does, the bass, perch, catfish, and crappie fishing really turn on. I've visited this lake as early as the middle of March and encountered bass anglers working its shoreline in search of largemouths. Well known for its excellent bass fishing, it is also a great panfish lake, with both perch and crappies growing to worthwhile size. The brown bullheads also get bigger than average here, and they draw lots of anglers to the lake every evening throughout the summer.

Evening and early morning, in fact, are the best times to fish the lake during the warmer months, since it becomes infested with water-skiers and other speed demons during the day. Night fishing is a productive bass-fishing method here throughout the summer. A typical Big Lake bigmouth is a fish of one or two pounds. Except for the weedy, grassy south end, the lake is highly developed, so fishing around the many docks and piers is one of the more productive systems. The four major points of land around the shoreline are also good bets for bass.

Although not often considered a trout lake, Big Lake does produce a few large cutthroats, most of which make their way here through Lake Creek, which flows into the south end of Big Lake from Lake McMurray.

Location: Southeast of Mount Vernon; see map A2, grid d7.

Species: Largemouth bass, yellow perch, crappie, brown bullhead catfish, a few cutthroat trout.

Facilities: A state access area and boat ramp are located on the lake. There's also a well-equipped resort on the west side of the lake that offers RV and tent sites, a boat ramp, boat rentals, a store with tackle, and snacks. The resort is open only from spring to early fall. There's a grocery store with tackle and fishing licenses near the north end of the lake. Additional facilities are available in Mount Vernon.

Directions: Take I-5 to Conway and turn east on Highway 534, following it six miles to Highway 9. Go north on Highway 9 to the lake, or exit I-5 just north of Mount Vernon on College Way (Highway 538), drive four miles, and turn south (right) on Highway 9 to the lake.

Contact: Big Lake Grocery, 360/422-5253.

34 Lake Sixteen

Generous plants of legal-sized rainbows help provide about a month of good fishing here after the lake opens in late April. Summertime fishing is slow, but anglers do manage to catch a few fair-sized cutthroats in June and July. There's usually another short flurry of angling activity on this 40-acre lake in the fall, with both rainbows and cutthroats showing in the catch at that time.

Location: East of Conway in Skagit County; see map A2, grid d6.

Species: Rainbow and cutthroat trout.

Facilities: The west side of the lake has a Department of Fish and Wildlife access area, a boat ramp, and toilets.

Directions: Take the Conway (Highway 534) exit off I-5 and drive east on Highway 534 about two miles to Lake Sixteen Road. Turn north (left) up the steep hill and drive half a mile to the lake.

Contact: Lake McMurray Store, 360/445-3565.

35 Lake McMurray

This is one of Skagit County's most popular trout lakes, as evidenced by the 15,000 or so legal-sized rainbows stocked here before opening day in late April every year. With spots over 50 feet deep, Lake McMurray stays cool enough to provide fairly good trout fishing well into the summer. The trout catch occasionally includes rainbows to five pounds, and anglers also catch a few trophy-sized cutthroats.

As trout-fishing interest begins to wane, various warm-water species draw increased attention. The lake is famous for its big perch, and crappie fishing can also be good throughout the summer. Although a Department of Fish and Wildlife survey here several years ago failed to turn up any bass, the locals will tell you (often in a whisper) that there are both largemouth and smallmouth bass in the lake and that they sometimes grow to hefty proportions. Past seasons have produced at least one largemouth of eight pounds, so McMurray is capable of growing some dandies. Don't get in a hurry while fishing here, by the way, since the lake has a 5 mph speed limit.

Location: Southeast of Conway in Skagit County; see map A2, grid d7.

Species: Rainbow trout, largemouth and some smallmouth bass, black crappie, yellow perch.

Facilities: The southeast corner of the lake has an access area and a boat ramp. Parking space is limited, and the place is a mob scene the first few weekends of the season. On the west side of the lake is Lake McMurray Store, which carries tackle, licenses, food, and beverages.

Directions: Drive to Conway on I-5 and exit east on Highway 534, which meets Highway 9 on the west side of the lake about six miles off I-5. Turn south (right) on Highway 9, drive a mile to Lake McMurray Lane, and turn north (left) into the access area.

Contact: Lake McMurray Store, 360/445-3565; Hook, Line, and Sinker, 360/651-2204.

36 Ketchum Lake

Trout fishing is pretty much a put-and-take proposition in this Snohomish County lake of just under 20 acres. The Department of Fish and Wildlife stocks about 2,000 legal-sized rainbows here each spring, and most of them disappear in fairly short order. Ketchum Lake produces some surprisingly big largemouth bass now and then, and night fishing for 10- to 12-inch brown bullhead catfish is productive in the spring and summer. Perch fishing is also a good bet here, with seven- to eight-inchers coming fast and furious once you locate a school. Crappies also have made an appearance at Ketchum in recent years, so explore the shoreline brush and anyplace you can find submerged wood for a shot at these popular panfish. This is also a good place to take small kids out for an afternoon of bluegill and pumpkinseed sunfish action; all you need is a can of worms and a bobber. The fish are ready and waiting. All you have to do is get out and ketchum. Sorry, I just had to say it.

Location: North of Stanwood; see map A2, grid e6.

Species: Rainbow trout, largemouth bass, bluegill, brown bullhead catfish, crappies, yellow perch.

Facilities: A boat ramp and access area are located near the south end of the lake. Other amenities are available in Stanwood.

Directions: Exit I-5 onto Highway 532 about three miles north of the Stillaguamish River bridge and head west toward Stanwood about five miles to Prestliens Road. Turn north (right) and drive three miles to Ketchum Lake Road, then turn east (right) to the lake.

Contact: Stanwood Coast to Coast, 360/629-3433; Hook, Line, and Sinker, 360/651-2204.

37 Lake Cavanaugh

This big, cool lake is open to year-round fishing, but the angling action often gets off to a slow start. You'll catch some rainbows and brookies in May, but June and July are often better. The kokanee and cutthroat don't often come to life before July, and August is often the best month to fish for both. If you're persistent enough to put in the time and effort, you might catch some large cutthroats here. Bass fishing is best in July, but you might hook a worthwhile largemouth anytime from June through September.

The worst part of fishing Cavanaugh is that the water-skiers and personal-watercraft riders come to life about the same time the trout do, which means you may run into lots of competition for space on the water unless you fish early or late in the day. Avoid fishing on the weekends if you can.

Location: Northwest of Oso just north of the Skagit-Snohomish County line; see map A2, grid e8.

Species: Rainbow, cutthroat, and brook trout; kokanee; largemouth bass.

Facilities: A public access area and boat ramp are located near the east end of the lake, and limited facilities are available in Oso, about four miles away.

Directions: Drive northeast from Arlington on Highway 530 and turn north (left) at Oso on Lake Cavanaugh Road, or take the College Way (Highway 538) exit off I-5 near Mount Vernon and drive east to Highway 9. Turn south, drive past Big Lake, and turn east (left) on Lake Cavanaugh Road, following it about 10 miles to the lake.

Contact: Lake McMurray Store, 360/445-3565; Hook, Line, and Sinker, 360/651-2204.

38 Banks of the Eastern Strait of Juan de Fuca

The first time I ever took my own boat to Hein Bank, one of the two most well-known banks at the east end of the Strait of Juan de Fuca (along with the Middle Bank), the fishing was beyond slow. It was, in fact, as though my fishing partner and I were exploring some sort of biological desert. We gave it about seven hours of our lives and then returned to Sequim, where we soon discovered that other anglers fishing Hein Bank that day absolutely hammered both chinook salmon and Pacific halibut. It was strange, though, because we hadn't seen any of those other boats that were pulling into the ramp with full fish boxes. By now you might already know where this story is going, but it took us a while to discover that we had followed the wrong course and ended up spending the day not on Hein Bank, but on Eastern Bank, several miles away. Get off course just a little around the east end of the Strait of Juan de Fuca and it could happen to you.

The positive side of all this is that these eastern banks offer several possibilities for the visiting saltwater angler, and if one of the banks happens to be less than generous, a little prospecting on the others may well turn up some hot fishing.

The largest of these underwater plateaus is Middle Bank, which is well known for its late-winter chinook, springtime lingcod, and spring/summer halibut fishing that can sometimes be quite good. February usually produces some of the best salmon fishing, and the resident blackmouth that come off Middle Bank run on the hefty side. Ten- to 15-pounders are common, which is a whole lot larger than the average blackmouth being caught from Washington waters that time of year. Tidal conditions make it tough for mooching and jigging, but for downrigger anglers it's foolproof, according to Larry Carpenter, owner of Master Marine in Mount Vernon.

Although it has been hit hard by lingcod anglers over the past decade or so, Middle Bank still is one of the better places to look for a husky spring ling, especially around the shallow, rocky northwest corner of the bank. Halibut are found farther south, over the sand and gravel bottoms that predominate on the bank's central and southern portions. For those who have never been there, Middle

Bank lies south of Pile Point on the south side of San Juan Island and due east of Victoria, British Columbia. A small portion of the bank extends across the United States and Canadian border.

Hein Bank, which juts up to within a few feet of the surface about three miles southeast of Middle Bank, has long been a favorite of springtime blackmouth anglers and also has a pretty good reputation as a halibut producer. Halibut catches used to be higher when the season was open in March, but there are enough of them around in April and May to provide a fair chance of hooking one. Both the salmon and halibut come here to feast on candlefish, which congregate on the bank by the millions. For that reason, jigging with a Deep Stinger, Point Wilson Candlefish Dart, or other metal jig in a candlefish design can be very effective. Mooching with whole or plug-cut herring also works here, though, so if you're not a jigging enthusiast, you can still catch fish off Hein Bank. If you arrive early in the morning and don't catch fish—especially salmon—right off the bat, there's no need to panic. Tide changes usually prompt the best fishing action, so stick with it until the bite comes on. Calm weather is a must for fishing this spot in the middle of the Strait of Juan de Fuca, many miles from the nearest shore. Hein Bank is marked with a navigation buoy near its north end.

A little farther to the southeast is Eastern Bank, a large plateau that has a bit of a reputation for providing on-again, off-again salmon and halibut action. When it's good, it can be very good, but when it's bad, forget it. Take it from someone who's been there when it's bad.

East and a little south of Eastern Bank lies Partridge Bank. Located not far off Whidbey Island a short distance northwest of Partridge Point, this bank is marked with a bell buoy near its south end. It's a sometimes salmon spot, and its rocky areas are also known to give up rockfish and lingcod.

Salmon Bank, aptly named for the blackmouth and summer chinook fishing it sometimes provides, is actually an extension of the southeast tip of San Juan Island. Marked with a buoy, it's easy to spot when you come out of San Juan Channel and round Cattle Point.

Although not as well known among anglers as some of the others, McArthur Bank can be a productive spot for lingcod and rockfish. Long and narrow, it runs north and south between the south end of Lopez Island and the northwest corner of the shoal that extends around Smith Island.

The most southeastern of the banks is Dallas Bank, which lies on the north side of Protection Island, a few miles west of Port Townsend. While overshadowed by Mid Channel Bank and other local salmon spots, it sometimes provides good fishing for late-winter blackmouth. Rockfish, lingcod, and an occasional halibut are other possibilities here.

Location: At the east end of the Strait of Juan de Fuca north of Sequim and south of Victoria and the San Juan Islands; see map A2, grid e1.

Species: Chinook salmon, Pacific halibut, lingcod, various rockfish and other bottom fish species.

Facilities: Public boat ramps are available in Port Angeles, Sequim, Port Townsend, the west side of Whidbey Island, Anacortes, and the San Juans. These areas also have motels, restaurants, fuel, tackle, and other facilities as well.

Directions: Launch at Port Angeles, Sequim, or Port Townsend and run north. Run southwest from Anacortes or south from San Juan Island.

Contact: Fish Tales Charters, 360/293-5766;

John's Sporting Goods, 425/259-3056, website: www.johnssportinggoods.com.

39 Sunday Lake

So you're looking for a good place to go test that new float tube or the 10-foot plywood boat you just bought at a garage sale for only $50 more than you would have paid for a new one? Sunday Lake is just that sort of place. At only 37 acres, it's small enough to investigate thoroughly in a day, and its limited boat-launching facilities keep most of the big, hot-rod bass boats away. The fact that the lake isn't stocked with trout also helps keep the crowds small. Take along your favorite bass rod or ultralight panfish outfit and you'll have a good time, especially from May to July and again in September.

Location: East of Stanwood; see map A2, grid e6.

Species: Largemouth bass, crappie, yellow perch.

Facilities: The lake has a small access area with a rough boat ramp that's suited only to canoes and row boats small enough to be carried to the water. There's also a fishing float and a nearby pit toilet. If you're looking for a nice place to stay within five minutes of the lake, try Sunday Lake Bed-and-Breakfast, 2100 Sunday Lake Road, 360/629-4356. The nearest food, gas, lodging, and tackle are in Stanwood.

Directions: Take I-5 to Highway 532 and drive west to 28th Avenue NW. Turn south (left) and drive less than a mile to the lake.

Contact: John's Sporting Goods, 425/259-3056, website: www.johnssportinggoods.com; Hook, Line, and Sinker, 360/651-2204.

40 Pilchuck Creek

Steelheading is a tough proposition on this little Stillaguamish River tributary. I wouldn't call it a lost cause, but if there's such a thing as one step above the lost cause category, Pilchuck Creek might fit the definition. Despite hatchery plants of winter-run steelies totaling 5,000 to 10,000 fish annually, the creek gives up no more than two dozen fish a year to anglers. January is the top month, but even then it's lousy. Summer steelhead are even harder to catch than winter-runs, and anglers do it only a few times a year. Selective fishery regulations requiring artificial lures with barbless hooks during the summer season don't help matters, but there just aren't that many steelhead available in the first place.

Cutthroat fishing is better, especially when the sea-run cutts move in with the fall rains. Those artificials-only regulations remain in effect, though, during the prime cutthroat-fishing time, so the fishing isn't quite as good as it might be if it were legal to use night crawlers.

Location: Flows into the Stillaguamish River near Sylvana; see map A2, grid e7.

Species: Winter and summer steelhead, resident and sea-run cutthroat trout.

Facilities: Small grocery stores and a few gas stations are in the vicinity of the creek, but little else. The nearest food, gas, tackle, and lodging are in Arlington.

Directions: To reach the lower section of the creek, exit I-5 onto Highway 530 and drive west, through Sylvana to Norman Road, which parallels about two miles of Pilchuck Creek. Some of the middle portion of the creek is accessible by taking the Highway 532 exit off I-5 and driving east toward Highway 9. This road crosses the creek midway between I-5 and Highway 9, two miles from the interstate. To reach upper portions of Pilchuck Creek, take Highway 9 north from Arlington and turn east (right) on Grandstrom Road, which parallels the west side of the creek for several miles.

Contact: John's Sporting Goods, 425/259-3056, website: www.johnssportinggoods.com; Hook, Line, and Sinker, 360/651-2204.

41 Bryant Lake

You can fish much of 20-acre Bryant Lake from the bank, but a float tube might be very helpful. Much of the lake is surrounded by thick vegetation, and you have to be somewhat of a brush buster to get within casting range in many places. Be careful of floating mats of rotting logs and grass that look like solid ground—until you find yourself submerged to your armpits. The lake is open year-round, but June, July, and September are the best fishing months. Some of the cutthroats are fairly large (over 11 inches), and June bassing can be good for one- to two-pound fish. Arrive at daybreak or stay until dusk and try surface plugs for bass.

Location: Northwest of Arlington in Snohomish County; see map A2, grid e7.

Species: Largemouth bass, crappie, cutthroat trout.

Facilities: No facilities are available at the lake, but food, gas, and tackle can be found in Arlington.

Directions: Take the Highway 530 exit off I-5 and drive four miles east to Arlington and the junction with Highway 9. Turn north on Highway 9, drive three miles, and watch for a couple of wide turnouts on the right side of the road. There's no sign, but if you reach the intersection of 268th Street NE, you've gone about a third of a mile past them. Trails of about 100 yards lead from the highway to the lake.

Contact: Lake McMurray Store, 360/445-3565; Hook, Line, and Sinker, 360/651-2204.

42 Stillaguamish River

Can you say "Stillaguamish"? Lots of visitors from other parts of the country can't, but that doesn't keep them from coming here to try their luck on one of western Washington's most famous steelhead streams. The Stilly has long been a favorite of both winter and summer steelheaders, and it also offers fair salmon and trout fishing.

The North Fork Stillaguamish is especially famous, having been among the favorites of Zane Grey and his fly-fishing cronies several decades ago. It's still open only to fly-fishing during the summer months, and feather tossers may catch as many as 500 fish during a good season. July usually produces the best summer-run catches, but you can find summer steelies here throughout the summer and fall. January and February are the top months for winter steelheading on the North Fork Stilly.

The South Fork Stillaguamish also provides both winter and summer steelheading, but on a smaller scale than the North Fork. A year that sees anglers catch 150 summer steelies and 200 winter-runs is a good one on the South Fork. Read the current fishing pamphlet carefully before any steelheading trip to the Stillaguamish, as regulations have altered a little from season to season over the past few years.

Sea-run cutthroat fishing used to be a big draw during the fall, but the harvest trout aren't as abundant as they once were. There are, however, some flurries of activity from August to November that provide good cutthroat action. The main Stilly and North Fork are now catch-and-release only for trout during the summer and fall season.

Only the main river downstream from the confluence of the North and South forks is open to salmon fishing, and then only for pinks (odd-numbered years) and chums. There are also chinooks and cohos in the river, but they've been off-limits to anglers lately. Pink salmon runs peak in early September, and what there is of a chum run happens during November.

Location: Flows into Port Susan west of Arlington in Snohomish County; see map A2, grid e7.

Species: Winter and summer steelhead,

chum and pink salmon, sea-run cutthroat trout, Dolly Varden.

Facilities: Food, gas, tackle, fishing licenses, and one motel (Arlington Motor Inn) are available in Arlington.

Directions: Take I-5 to Highway 530 and turn west toward the lower river or east toward Arlington to reach upstream stretches of the river. Highway 530 parallels the North Fork Stillaguamish. To reach the South Fork, drive east on Highway 530 out of Arlington, turn south (right) on Arlington Heights Road, and south (right) again on Jordan Road.

Contact: Hook, Line, and Sinker, 360/651-2204.

43 Lake Armstrong

Most of the rainbows are legal-sized fish planted in the spring, but there is some carryover and therefore some chance of finding a two-pound rainbow here. The rainbows bite best in April and May, with cutthroat adding a little excitement in May and continuing into the summer. Fall fishing is fair for cutts and a few rainbows. At 30 acres, Armstrong can be fished effectively in a float tube or canoe.

Location: North of Arlington; see map A2, grid e7.

Species: Rainbow and cutthroat trout.

Facilities: A public access area and boat ramp are located on the lake. Food, gas, lodging, and tackle are available in Arlington.

Directions: Take I-5 to Highway 530 and drive east to Arlington. Head north out of town on Highway 9 and turn east (right) on Armstrong Road. Drive about half a mile to the first left and follow the gravel road to the lake.

Contact: Hook, Line, and Sinker, 360/651-2204; Lake McMurray Store, 360/445-3565.

44 Ebey (Little) Lake

The newly gated road up Ebey Hill has turned a 300-yard hike into a two-mile hike, but it will probably make the already good trout fishing even better. Fly-fishing-only regulations have been in effect here for years, and Ebey has long been a favorite among the fly-rod set. The limit is one fish per day, and it must be at least 18 inches long. Although there are certainly a few legal 18- to 22-inch rainbows and cutts to be found here, most anglers are content to hook and release several 10- to 16-inchers for their day's efforts.

Part of the fun of fishing Ebey is that feeling that you're in some other part of the world, like maybe Florida's Everglades. Stumps and snags poke their bony heads through the lake's surface around much of the shoreline, adding an eerie sense of mystery to the place. Although open all year, the lake offers its best fishing from May to September or early October.

Location: Northeast of Arlington; see map A2, grid e8.

Species: Rainbow and cutthroat trout.

Facilities: The lake has no facilities. The nearest food, gas, lodging, and tackle are in Arlington.

Directions: Exit I-5 onto Highway 530 and drive east through Arlington. Just past Trafton, turn south (right) onto Jim Creek Road and drive just over four miles to the gravel road on the left, known locally as Ebey Hill Road. Stay on the main gravel road for about two miles to the new gate, where you have to park and hike the remaining two miles to the short trail that leads to the left off the road. From the start of the trail, it's about 300 yards to the water's edge.

Contact: Hook, Line, and Sinker, 360/651-2204.

45 Riley Lake

Spring plants of about 3,000 rainbows a year supplement a self-sustaining population of pan-sized cutthroats in this 30-acre lake near Arlington. Those hatchery fish keep things hopping through May, when the cutthroat action picks up. Trolling with all the usual small spoons and spinners or gang-troll-and-worm combinations will work here during spring and early summer. In the fall, casting or trolling a fly becomes effective, especially during the evening hours.

Location: South of Oso in northern Snohomish County; see map A2, grid e8.

Species: Rainbow and cutthroat trout.

Facilities: The lake has a public access area with a boat ramp and toilets. The nearest food, gas, tackle, and lodging are in Arlington and Granite Falls.

Directions: Take I-5 to Highway 530 and drive east through Arlington. About four miles east of town, turn right to Trafton and stay on the main road, which winds southward and becomes 242nd Street NE. Lake Riley Road splits off to the left about six miles from the highway and leads to the lake.

Contact: Hook, Line, and Sinker, 360/651-2204.

46 Dungeness Spit

Salmon and bottom-fish action at Dungeness Spit has a reputation for being hot one day and cold the next, so most of the fishing pressure is from local anglers who can afford to check it out on a regular basis and go back to doing something else if it happens to be one of those cold days. Restrictive salmon-fishing regulations have cut into this fishery much the same as in other areas along the Strait of Juan de Fuca, but when the season is open, chinook fishing can be worthwhile just inside the tip of the spit and on the outside near the bend—known locally as the "Knuckle." Jigging can be especially productive in both spots.

Anglers looking for lingcod and rockfish might want to run about two miles northeast from the tip of the spit to fish the rocky humps lying offshore. Yelloweye, canary, and quillback rockfish were historically quite abundant here. Restrictions that have dropped the rockfish limit to one a day have

certainly influenced bottom fish opportunities, but other options still make this fishery worthwhile. There are also several less dramatic humps just to the east of the spit, and these underwater plateaus sometimes produce good catches of halibut.

Location: Strait of Juan de Fuca north of Sequim; see map A2, grid f1.

Species: Chinook, coho, and pink salmon; halibut; lingcod; rockfish and several species of smaller bottom fish.

Facilities: A boat ramp is located on Dungeness Bay about three miles from the tip of the spit. Food, gas, lodging, and tackle are available in Sequim.

Directions: By land, take U.S. 101 to Sequim, turn north (right) on Sequim-Dungeness Way, and follow it about 11 miles to the water and public boat ramp. By boat, launch in Sequim Bay and run north about 10 miles to the end of the spit, or launch at Port Angeles and run about 15 miles east.

Contact: Thunderbird Boathouse, 360/457-4274; Swain's, 360/452-2357; Sequim Bay State Park, 360/683-4235; Washington State Parks and Recreation Commission, 360/902-8844 (information) or 888/226-7688 (reservations).

47 Port Townsend and Admiralty Inlet

Resident chinook salmon provide good fishing in several spots here once the season opens in February, but the most popular and most productive place is certainly the underwater hump known as Mid Channel Bank. This submerged plateau is also good for summertime kings, but recent closures have taken a large bite out of that fishery. A few anglers troll here for chinooks, but mooching plug-cut herring and jigging are the two top fishing methods. The Point Wilson Dart jig, developed right here in Port Townsend, is a favorite salmon-getter. Many of the adult salmon returning to Puget Sound rivers in the

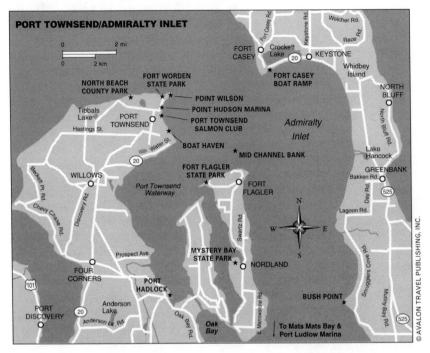

PORT TOWNSEND/ADMIRALTY INLET

© AVALON TRAVEL PUBLISHING, INC.

summer and fall are funneled through the narrow inlet, and they once provided good angling action. There still are times during August and early September when the coho fishing can be very good, especially during the first and last two hours of daylight. Migrating cohos sometimes pass by within reach of anglers casting from the beach around Marrowstone Point and Fort Flagler State Park at the north end of Marrowstone Island. Closures on coho and chinook fishing, though, have become more and more common in recent years and have made planning difficult for salmon anglers. The best recent summer fishing has been for pink salmon that pass through by the tens of thousands in August. Be sure to check the fishing pamphlet and ask around before making long-range plans for a salmon trip to this area.

Several spots offer productive bottom fishing. Some halibut and a few lings are caught from the west end of Mid Channel Bank during their respective spring seasons. The rocky humps and kelp beds just west of the Point Wilson Lighthouse can be worth fishing for small rockfish (one-fish daily limit these days) and an occasional lingcod. Partridge Bank, located to the north a short distance offshore from Partridge Point on Whidbey Island, can be a good bet for spring and summer rockfish and springtime lingcod fishing. **Location:** West side of Whidbey Island; see map A2, grid f3.

Species: Chinook, coho, and pink salmon; lingcod; halibut; various rockfish.

Facilities: On the Port Townsend side of the inlet, boat ramps are located at Fort Worden State Park, Point Hudson, Fort Flagler and Mystery Bay State Parks, the Oak Bay County ramp, and Mats Mats Bay. Whidbey Island ramps include those at Dave Mackie County Park, Bush Point, Fort Casey State Park, and the Hastie Lake ramp. Fort Worden and Fort Flagler State Parks have RV hookups. Fort Casey, Fort Ebey, and Fort Worden State Parks all have tent sites. Port Townsend is a popular tourist town with all amenities and more than enough little shops for you to spend all of your money in a single day.

Directions: Take U.S. 101 to Discovery Bay and turn north on Highway 20, following it 13 miles to Port Townsend, where several boat ramps are available. Or from the east, launch at any of several ramps on the west side of Whidbey Island to reach the area.

Contact: Fort Flagler State Park, 360/385-1259; Fort Ebey State Park, 360/678-4636; Fort Worden State Park, 360/385-4730; Washington State Parks and Recreation Commission, 360/902-8844 (information) or 888/226-7688 (reservations); The Fish In Hole, 360/385-6829. For nautical charts of this area, contact Captain's Nautical Supply, 206/283-7242.

48 Martha Lake

It's one thing for a state to have several Clear, Blue, or Silver Lakes, but this is one of three Martha Lakes within a few miles of each other. (The lake near Alderwood Manor in southwestern Snohomish County is described in number 83; the other, just north of Lake Cassidy, isn't fishable.) Although this Martha Lake is open to year-round fishing, the rainbows bite best in the spring. That's no doubt because most of them are stocked here in the spring, and anglers eagerly awaiting their arrival are on hand to take advantage of the situation. This popular 58-acre lake gets about 6,000 legal-sized rainbows every April, and they provide fast action through May. The cutthroats usually come to life about the time the rainbow fishery tapers off, with fishing for cutts at its best in the fall.

Location: Northwest of Marysville near Warm Beach; see map A2, grid e6.

Species: Rainbow and cutthroat trout.

Facilities: The lake has a public access area and boat ramp, as well as a resort where anyone hardly ever answers the phone. The nearest food, gas, and lodging are at Smokey Point, and the closest tackle is in Marysville.

Directions: Take the Smokey Point exit off I-5 north of Marysville and drive west about seven miles on Highway 531. Bear right to Lakewood Road, which runs along the south side of the lake.

Contact: Martha Lake Resort, 360/652-8412; Lake Goodwin Resort, 360/652-8169; Hook, Line, and Sinker, 360/651-2204.

49 Lake Ki

It's easy to understand why this is one of western Snohomish County's most popular fishing lakes. A major highway runs right by it to provide easy access. But more important, though less than 100 acres in size, Lake Ki is stocked with as many as 6,000 legal-sized rainbow trout just before the late-April opener every spring. Those planters, some of which weigh in at nearly three-quarters of a pound, provide lots of bent rods and plenty of smiles through May and into early June. Whether you like to troll Ford Fenders and worms or soak Power Bait on the bottom, your technique will probably prove effective if you fish Lake Ki during the first several weeks of the season.

The trout fishing tails off during the summer and makes a little comeback in the fall; but during the time trouting is slow, bass fishing can be very productive. Like many other Snohomish County lakes, this one has a slot limit protecting bass between 12 and 17 inches long. Most anglers release their bass, but if you decide to keep a couple for the table, double-check the fishing pamphlet for details on this special regulation.

Location: Northwest of Marysville; see map A2, grid f6.

Species: Rainbow trout, largemouth bass,

yellow perch.

Facilities: Wenberg State Park is at nearby Lake Goodwin, as are Lake Goodwin Resort and Cedar Grove Resort (see number 51). Lake Ki has a public access area with a boat ramp. Smokey Point and Marysville offer food, gas, lodging, and tackle.

Directions: Take I-5 to Smokey Point and turn west on Highway 531, which runs right alongside the north end of the lake.

Contact: Lake Goodwin Resort, 360/652-8169 or 800/452-5687; Wenberg State Park, 360/652-7417; Washington State Parks and Recreation Commission, 360/902-8844 (information) or 888/226-7688 (reservations); Hook, Line, and Sinker, 360/651-2204.

50 Lake Howard

This is another little lake that's well suited to the adventurous angler who wants to get away in a float tube, canoe, or small inflatable and just cast or troll around for the morning. Although Lake Howard does offer a few fairly large cutthroats, they may or may not interrupt your solitude. The lake has a pretty large population of bass, but I don't know of anyone who has ever caught a large one. At least you won't have a lot of water-skiers or big bass boats washing you up into the shoreline weeds. Lake Howard is open year-round, with April, May, June, and September best for bass. April, May, September, and October are the best trout months.

Location: Northwest of Marysville; see map A2, grid f6.

Species: Rainbow and cutthroat trout, largemouth bass.

Facilities: The lake has a public access area and boat ramp, neither of which is too fancy. The nearest amenities are in Smokey Point and Marysville.

Directions: Take I-5 to Smokey Point and turn west on Highway 531. Drive to Lakewood Road, bear right, and then turn south (left)

on 65th Avenue NW, which goes about a quarter of a mile to the lake.

Contact: Lake Goodwin Resort, 360/652-8169 or 800/242-8169; Hook, Line, and Sinker, 360/651-2204.

51 Lake Goodwin

This is one of those western Washington lakes with a year-round season that actually offers pretty good fishing the whole time. Most of the rainbows—about 5,000 of them—are planted in the spring, but you can usually find one or two in a cooperative mood even in the fall or winter. Trout can get lost in the depths of this big lake (nearly 550 acres) and not be found by anglers for some time, so you have a decent chance of finding a carry-over rainbow of 16 inches or better here. The cutthroats are also available throughout much of the year, and some of them grow to impressive size, too.

As for warm-water fish, the one-two combination of largemouth and smallmouth bass makes this a popular lake with spring and summer bass anglers, who catch a few largemouths over five pounds and an occasional smallmouth of three pounds or more. Perch fishing is good throughout the year, with fall often best for big ones.

Location: Northwest of Marysville; see map A2, grid f6.

Species: Rainbow and cutthroat trout, largemouth and smallmouth bass, crappie, yellow perch.

Facilities: Wenberg State Park is on the east side of the lake and has a boat ramp ($3 launch fee), restrooms, showers, and tent and RV spaces. Lake Goodwin Resort, at the north end of the lake, also has tent and RV sites, as well as a small store with tackle and licenses, propane gas, laundry facilities, and an RV dump station. Cedar Grove Resort, on the west side of the lake, has tent and RV spaces and an RV dump station.

Directions: Take the Smokey Point exit off I-5 and drive west five miles on Highway 531, then turn south (left) on Lake Goodwin Road to reach the east side of the lake. Highway 531 becomes Lakewood Road at that point, and if you drive past Lake Goodwin Road on Lakewood, you soon come to the north end of the lake. To reach the west side of Lake Goodwin, continue on to 52nd Avenue and turn south (left).

Contact: Wenberg State Park, 360/652-7417; Washington State Parks and Recreation Commission, 360/902-8844 (information) or 888/226-7688 (reservations); Lake Goodwin Resort, 360/652-8169 or 800/242-8169; Cedar Grove Resort, 360/652-7083; Hook, Line, and Sinker, 360/651-2204.

52 Shoecraft Lake

Although stocked with legal-sized hatchery rainbows every spring, this 135-acre lake with a year-round fishing season is better known for its warm-water fish than for its trout. It offers both largemouth and smallmouth bass, which isn't all that common among western Washington lakes. Spring is good for both, with largemouths continuing to bite through the summer. The perch, catfish, and crappie fishing can be excellent during the spring and summer, too.

Location: Northwest of Marysville; see map A2, grid f6.

Species: Rainbow trout, largemouth and smallmouth bass, crappie, yellow perch, brown bullhead catfish.

Facilities: Shoecraft Lake has a public access area, a boat ramp, and pit toilets near its southwest corner. Cedar Grove Resort is a mile away on the west side of Lake Goodwin. Lake Goodwin Resort and Wenberg State Park are both within two miles, on Lake Goodwin.

Directions: Exit I-5 at Smokey Point and drive west on Highway 531, which becomes Lakewood Road near the north end of Lake Goodwin. Turn south (left) on 52nd Avenue NW and follow it about 1.5 miles to the lake.

Contact: Cedar Grove Resort, 360/652-7083; Lake Goodwin Resort, 360/652-8169 or 800/242-8169; Wenberg State Park, 360/652-7417; Washington State Parks and Recreation Commission, 360/902-8844 (information) or 888/226-7688 (reservations); Hook, Line, and Sinker, 360/651-2204.

53 Crabapple Lake

This 35-acre lake half a mile east of Lake Goodwin may be fun to explore in your canoe, car-topper, or float tube, but don't expect too much in the way of fast fishing. Largemouth bass have made an appearance here in recent years (what a surprise), and they can be caught in all the usual ways. Crabapple is now a good place to go exercise your arm on largemouths of about a pound apiece. Feel free to thin the sunfish population as much as you want, even if it means casting to them with a bobber and half a worm. The strategy might pay off with a trout or two, but the odds are against it.

Location: Northwest of Marysville; see map A2, grid f7.

Species: Rainbow trout, largemouth bass, pumpkinseed sunfish.

Facilities: The lake has a rough boat launch and limited access area. Wenberg State Park, half a mile away, has tent and RV spaces, showers, and other facilities. Lake Goodwin Resort, two miles away, has tent and RV sites, showers, and a store that sells tackle, licenses, and some groceries.

Directions: Exit I-5 at Smokey Point and drive west on Highway 531. Turn south (left) on Lake Goodwin Road and go left at the Y intersection after passing the state park entrance. Continue about one-third mile to the lake, which is on the left.

Contact: Wenberg State Park, 360/652-7417;

Washington State Parks and Recreation Commission, 360/902-8844 (information) or 888/226-7688 (reservations); Lake Goodwin Resort, 360/652-8169 or 800/242-8169; Hook, Line, and Sinker, 360/651-2204.

54 Loma Lake

This 21-acre Snohomish County lake is stocked with hatchery rainbows in the summer, and they provide a few weeks of worthwhile trout action. After that, it's time to go bass fishing. Private docks and floats, submerged trees and brush, large lily pad fields, and stands of cattails provide a wide variety of bass-fishing spots, so you could spend an entire day exploring this little lake if you're a serious bass angler. If panfish are your bag, there's a good deal of submerged wood structure to provide good crappie fishing. Motors of all kinds are prohibited on the lake, so it's a great one to explore in a canoe or float tube.

Location: North of Marysville; see map A2, grid f7.

Species: Rainbow trout, largemouth bass, crappie.

Facilities: The public access area has a gravel boat ramp and parking area, with a pit toilet. Lake Goodwin Resort two miles away has tent and RV sites, showers, and a store that sells tackle, licenses, and some groceries.

Directions: Take the Smokey Point exit (Exit 206) off I-5 and drive west on 172nd Street NE (Lakewood Road) for 3.5 miles to McRea Road NW. Turn south (left) on McRea Road and follow it one mile to 16th Avenue NW, turning right and following it half a mile to 154th Street NW. Turn left and go one-third mile to the Department of Wildlife access sign on the right.

Contact: Wenberg State Park, 360/652-7417; Washington State Parks and Recreation Commission, 360/902-8844 (information) or 888/226-7688 (reservations); Lake Goodwin Resort, 360/652-8169; Hook, Line, and Sinker, 360/651-2204.

55 Gissberg Ponds

You can carry your car-topper, canoe, or float tube from the parking lot to the water, but it's really not necessary on this pair of small ponds just a few yards off the busy interstate. They cover only a total of 15 acres, so you can just about reach the middle with a good cast from the beach.

Indeed, easy bank access and the fact that you don't need a boat to fish effectively are the main reasons these ponds are very popular with Snohomish County anglers. They're heavily stocked with hatchery rainbows, and ample populations of panfish help to make this a great place to take the kids. Channel catfish have also been stocked here, and anglers are now allowed to keep two of them per day. Note that the park is open during daylight hours only, but also remember that the ponds are open to year-round fishing, so any day's a good day to visit this easy-access twosome.

Location: North of Marysville; see map A2, grid f7.

Species: Rainbow trout, largemouth bass, yellow perch, channel catfish, bluegill.

Facilities: There's a county park with restrooms and picnic tables near the southeast corner of the ponds. Food, gas, lodging, tackle, and other facilities are in the ever-growing Smokey Point complex, right across the freeway.

Directions: Take I-5 to exit 206 (Smokey Point) and turn west. Drive one-third mile to 27th Avenue NE and turn south (left). Follow 27th Avenue NE one-quarter mile to 169th Place NE and turn left, following the road until it curves and becomes Twin Lakes Avenue, which leads to a park on the shore of the ponds.

Contact: Hook, Line, and Sinker, 360/651-2204.

56 Lake Cassidy

This 125-acre lake is open to year-round fishing and is popular with both trout and bass anglers. Most of the trout action takes place in April and May, after the Department of Fish and Wildlife has made its annual deposit of about 5,000 legal-sized rainbows. Many of those planters are gone by June, and the trout fishing gets tough after that. Bass fishing, however, takes off in late May or early June, depending on whether there's ample warm weather to raise water temperatures and spur the largemouths to thoughts of love—or whatever it is bass feel at spawning time. The lake produces some good catches of largemouths that time of year, and decent bass catches continue through the summer. Summertime perch and crappie fishing is also productive, and night fishing produces some good catches of 10- to 14-inch brown bullheads from June through August.

Location: East of Marysville; see map A2, grid f7.

Species: Rainbow trout, largemouth bass, crappie, yellow perch, brown bullhead catfish.

Facilities: The Department of Fish and Wildlife has a public access area and boat ramp on the west side of the lake, and all other facilities are available in nearby Lake Stevens and Marysville.

Directions: Take I-5 to Everett and turn east on U.S. 2, then north on Highway 204. Turn north again on Highway 9 and drive just over three miles to the sign pointing right to Lake Cassidy.

Contact: John's Sporting Goods, 425/259-3056, website: www.johnssportinggoods.com; Hook, Line, and Sinker, 360/651-2204.

57 Canyon Creek

Like so many other Northwest streams that have given way to development and devastating logging practices, Canyon Creek isn't the steelhead producer it used to be. Fish it in July or August and you might find a summer steelhead or two, but the fishing isn't hot. Winter steelheading has been better than summer-run fishing lately, but not by much.

A 100-fish winter season is a good one here. That catch is spread out through December, January, and February. Each winter rain brings thick, dirty water through the creek, making for tough fishing.

Location: Flows into the South Fork Stillaguamish River near Granite Falls; see map A2, grid f8.

Species: Winter and summer steelhead, resident cutthroat trout.

Facilities: Mountain View Inn is located on the Mountain View Highway north of Granite Falls and less than a mile from the creek. Food and gas can be found in the town of Granite Falls.

Directions: Drive east from Lake Stevens on Highway 92 for about eight miles to the town of Granite Falls. Take the Mountain Loop Highway north from town and, after crossing the South Fork Stillaguamish at Granite Falls, take any of several roads to the left to reach the lower portion of the creek. To reach upper Canyon Creek, stay on the Mountain Loop Highway for about 6.5 miles to Forest Service Road 41, turn left, and follow the road upstream about six miles.

Contact: Hook, Line, and Sinker, 360/651-2204; Mountain View Inn, 360/691-6668

58 Morse Creek

This little stream that crosses under U.S. 101 just east of Port Angeles may be worth investigating from December through February if you're in the mood for some steelhead fishing and other northern Olympic Peninsula streams are out of shape from too much rain. The Department of Fish and Wildlife plants about 15,000 steelhead smolts here every year, enough to provide at least the possibility of hooking a fish or two for your efforts. Although an occasional summer steelie is taken from the creek or at least marked as such on the steelhead report cards returned to the WDFW, this isn't a place you'd want to spend a lot of time fishing specifically for summer-run fish.

Resident cutthroat provide some action after Morse Creek opens in early June, and by September a fair number of sea-run cutts are usually available. Sea-run fishing may hold up until steelhead enter the river in December.

Location: Enters the Strait of Juan de Fuca just east of Port Angeles; see map A2, grid f0.

Species: Winter steelhead, sea-run and resident cutthroat trout.

Facilities: A KOA campground is located about three miles east of the creek on the south side of U.S. 101. Food, gas, lodging, and tackle can be found in and around Port Angeles.

Directions: Drive west from Sequim on U.S. 101. The highway crosses over the creek a mile west of Deer Park Road, and a gravel road just west of the bridge parallels the creek upstream from the highway.

Contact: Swain's, 360/452-2357; Port Angeles KOA, 360/457-5916.

59 Siebert Creek

Summertime fishing at Siebert Creek is pretty much a matter of catch and release, since few of the creek's resident trout grow to the legal minimum size of 14 inches. Things improve a little in September and October when a few sea-run cutthroats make their way in from the Strait of Juan de Fuca.

Location: Flows into the Strait of Juan de Fuca at Green Point east of Port Angeles; see map A2, grid f0.

Species: Resident and sea-run cutthroat trout.

Facilities: Port Angeles KOA is about a mile west of the creek, on the south side of the highway. All other amenities are available in Sequim and Port Angeles.

Directions: Drive west from Sequim or east from Port Angeles on U.S. 101 and turn north on Lewis Road about midway between the two towns to reach the lower portion of the creek, or turn south on Blue Mountain Road to get to the upper reaches of the creek. Gravel roads to the west (right) at about 3.5 and 4.5 miles provide creek access.

Contact: Port Angeles KOA, 360/457-5916; Swain's, 360/452-2357.

60 McDonald Creek

Summertime fishing for resident cutthroat provides mostly catch-and-release action, but persistent anglers manage to hook an occasional trout over the minimum legal size of 14 inches. Some sea-run cutthroats entering in the fall make it a little easier to catch something for the table.

Location: Flows into the Strait of Juan de Fuca west of Dungeness; see map A2, grid f0.

Species: Resident and sea-run cutthroat trout.

Facilities: Port Angeles KOA is about three miles west of the creek. All other facilities are available about six miles east in Sequim.

Directions: Drive west from Sequim or east from Port Angeles on U.S. 101. Turn south about 5.5 miles west of Sequim on Sherburn Road to fish the upper creek, or bear north on Barr Road to get to the lower section.

Contact: Swain's, 360/452-2357; Port Angeles KOA, 360/457-5916.

61 Dungeness River

Once a very productive salmon, trout, and steelhead stream, the Dungeness has fallen on hard times over the past couple of decades. As a result, it doesn't even have a summer trout and steelhead season any more, at least not on the main river downstream from Gold Creek. Winter steelheading for hatchery fish is a decent possibility, and the river now offers a halfway decent opportunity to catch hatchery coho during a season that starts around the middle of October. Considering the fact that the Dungeness not all that long ago had strong runs of four salmon species, this coho fishery still is only a shadow of what the river once offered.

If you're a trout angler, your only chance on the Dungeness is some distance upstream, from the mouth of Gold Creek up, where you might hook a legal-size resident cutthroat of 14 inches or better.

Location: Enters the Strait of Juan de Fuca north of Sequim; see map A2, grid f1.

Species: Winter and summer steelhead, sea-run cutthroat trout, coho salmon.

Facilities: Rainbow's End RV Park is about 1.5 miles west of the river. Sequim Bay State Park, about six miles east, has about two dozen RV sites. Food, gas, tackle, and lodging are available in Sequim and Port Angeles.

Directions: Take U.S. 101 to Sequim and turn north on Sequim Avenue–Dungeness Way, which crosses the river near its mouth. Roads to the left near the river mouth provide access upstream. To reach the upper portion of the Dungeness, drive west from Sequim about 1.5 miles and turn south (left) on River Road.

Contact: Rainbow's End RV Park, 360/683-3863; Sequim Bay State Park, 360/683-4235; Swain's, 360/452-2357.

62 Anderson Lake

This 70-acre lake ranks right up there with the best trout lakes in Washington. It's one of few western Washington lakes that's planted with fingerling trout rather than legal-sized fish, and by opening day of the following year, these little guys have grown to a respectable 12 inches. A fairly large percentage of those

12-inchers aren't caught and carry over a second winter, which is why Anderson produces above-average numbers of two- to three-pound rainbows every season.

Some rather unusual regulations help get those young fish through their first season. The lake opens in late April with typical trout-fishing regulations, meaning it's OK to use bait and barbed hooks. But on September 1 selective fishery regulations go into effect, so bait and barbed hooks are out. This allows anglers to catch and release all those eager little fingerlings without ripping their entrails out, which means more trout survive until the season closes at the end of October.

Location: Northwest of Chimacum on the Quimper Peninsula; see map A2, grid g3.

Species: Rainbow trout.

Facilities: Anderson Lake State Park is a day-use park with no camping facilities, but it has restrooms and a boat ramp that's suitable for car-toppers and small trailer boats. The nearest food, gas, lodging, and tackle are available in Discovery Bay and Port Townsend.

Directions: Take U.S. 101 to the south end of Discovery Bay, turn east on Highway 20, and drive about four miles to Anderson Lake Road, where you turn east (right). Follow Anderson Lake Road about 1.5 miles to the lake, which is on the left.

Contact: Washington State Parks and Recreation Commission, 360/902-8844 (information) or 888/226-7688 (reservations); Gray Wolf Angler, 360/797-7177.

63 Goss Lake

The Department of Fish and Wildlife stocks about 5,000 legal-sized rainbows here just before the opener every spring, but the lake also has a pretty good population of cutthroats to provide angling variety. Unlike nearby Lone Lake (number 64), Goss is fairly deep, with some holes near the west side reaching down 60 feet or more, which means the trout fishing holds up fairly well during the summer. Trolling is good in spring and fall, but you may have to anchor up and try stillfishing near the middle of the lake or along the west side from June through August.

Location: On Whidbey Island northeast of Freeland; see map A2, grid f5.

Species: Rainbow and cutthroat trout.

Facilities: A small Department of Fish and Wildlife access area with a single-lane boat ramp is on the east side of the lake. A $10 WDFW access decal is required to use the public launch areas maintained by the Washington Department of Fish and Wildlife. The nearest food, gas, and lodging are in Langley, two miles east.

Directions: Take the ferry from Mukilteo to Clinton and drive northwest on Highway 525 about 10 miles to Freeland. Turn north (right) on East Harbor Road and east (right) on Goss Lake Road. Goss Lake is about 1.5 miles away, on the right.

Contact: John's Sporting Goods, 425/259-3056, website: www.johnssportinggoods.com; Ted's Sports Center, 425/743-9505.

64 Lone Lake

Open year-round, this 90-acre Whidbey Island lake is a fair bet for spring and fall trout fishing. It's stocked with legal-sized rainbows in the spring, but the catch in April and May includes a pretty good mix of carryovers that may run as large as 18 inches and weigh more than two pounds. The lake's maximum depth is only about 15 feet, shallow even by western Washington standards, which explains why summertime fishing is a pretty tough proposition.

Location: On Whidbey Island east of Freeland; see map A2, grid f5.

Species: Rainbow trout.

Facilities: The lake has a Washington Department of Fish and Wildlife access area, a boat ramp, and restrooms at its north end. The nearest amenities are in Clinton.

Directions: Take the ferry from Mukilteo to Clinton, and then take Highway 525 about seven miles northwest to Bayview Road, where you should turn north (right). Drive just under two miles to Andreason Road, turn west (left), and drive half a mile to Lone Lake Road, which leads south to the lake's access area.

Contact: John's Sporting Goods, 425/259-3056, website: www.johnssportinggoods.com; Ted's Sports Center, 425/743-9505.

65 Lake Stevens

Even though it covers more than 1,000 acres and offers some kind of fishing action 12 months of the year, Lake Stevens doesn't get the publicity or recognition it deserves. Like many year-round lakes, it plays second fiddle to the area's many prime April-to-October trout lakes. It's really a gold mine of fishing opportunity that most anglers overlook.

Summertime kokanee fishing can be especially good, whether you prefer to catch these little landlocked sockeye salmon with trolling gear or stillfishing rigs. If you stillfish, this is one of relatively few Washington lakes where it's legal to chum with creamed corn or other baits to attract kokanee to your hooks.

Don't be too surprised if your kokanee-fishing efforts draw the attention of an occasional rainbow or cutthroat trout. If you want to fish specifically for trout—and the lake has some big ones—try the time-proven lake trolls with worms or troll a Triple Teazer, Dick Nite, Flatfish, or Kwikfish behind a quarter-ounce trolling sinker that will help take the lure a few feet beneath the surface. Some of the best trout action occurs from March through May and from September to mid-November.

Lake Stevens does have a fairly good reputation for its largemouth bass fishing, and it usually comes through with a few fish in the six- to eight-pound range every summer. Although most serious bass anglers release their catch, it's OK to keep one bass a day, provided it's at least 18 inches long. With eight miles of shoreline, there's no problem finding plenty of docks, floats, and other structures to explore if you're in search of a hefty largemouth. Smallmouth bass are also available in fairly good numbers, and that alone should make this lake more popular with western Washington anglers.

Perch fishing is a decent bet throughout the year, with the lake giving up its share of perch in the foot-long range. Crappie fishing is best in the spring and fall.

Location: At the town of Lake Stevens east of Everett; see map A2, grid f8.

Species: Rainbow and cutthroat trout, kokanee, largemouth and smallmouth bass, crappie, yellow perch.

Facilities: The Department of Fish and Wildlife maintains an access area with a good boat ramp on the east side of the lake, and there's also a county park on the west side with a launch ramp and fishing dock. Food, gas, lodging, and all other amenities are plentiful throughout the area.

Directions: Take I-5 to Everett and turn east on U.S. 2. Turn north on Highway 204 and follow it about three miles to the lake.

Contact: John's Sporting Goods, 425/259-3056, website: www.johnssportinggoods.com; Hook, Line, and Sinker, 360/651-2204; Snohomish County Parks Department, 425/339-1208.

66 Bosworth Lake

Don't fish 95-acre Bosworth Lake the first couple weeks of the season unless you like lots of company. This is one of the most popular of Snohomish County's several dozen productive trout lakes, thanks to heavy plants of hatchery rainbows. Most of those planters are standard-issue eight-inchers, but the Department of Fish and Wildlife includes enough half-pounders to keep it interesting.

Cutthroats are scarce, but you might find one here and there as you catch rainbows in the spring and early summer. Fall fishing is best for cutts, but because they aren't as abundant as rainbows, few anglers target them. A growing bass population in the lake has added some variety to what has traditionally been considered a trout-only fishery, so summer sees somewhat of a change in emphasis from trout to bass fishing.

Location: South of Granite Falls in Snohomish County; see map A2, grid f8.

Species: Rainbow and cutthroat trout, largemouth bass.

Facilities: A Department of Fish and Wildlife access area on the lake has a boat ramp and toilets. Food, gas, and lodging can be found in Granite Falls.

Directions: Take I-5 to Everett and exit east on U.S. 2, then turn north on Highway 204 and cross Highway 9 to Lake Stevens. Drive northwest from Lake Stevens toward Granite Falls on Highway 92. Turn south on Ray Gray Road just west of Granite Falls and south again on Robe-Menzel Road, following it two miles to Utley Road. Turn right and drive about a mile to the lake, which is on the right.

Contact: John's Sporting Goods, 425/259-3056, website: www.johnssportinggoods.com.

67 Point No Point

Salmon seasons have been weird around here the past few years, but this is still one of those spots in Puget Sound where you usually can go out and catch 'em. Depending on open seasons (check the fishing pamphlet constantly to be sure), you can find good blackmouth chinook fishing on and around the point throughout the fall and winter, and fall coho runs also cruise by this spot in fairly good numbers. Late-fall chum salmon fishing can be very good, with the tail end of October and early November usually the best bet. Pink salmon are within range of anglers who troll near the surface or cast from the beach from about Labor Day until the end of September.

Although generally a place where traditional techniques such as trolling flasher-and-hoochie combos and mooching with herring have always been the rule, more and more fly-fishing enthusiasts are turning up around here. Some of them are casting from boats, but casting from the beach is also a possibility. Candlefish and other bait species often crowd the shallows here, especially from mid- to late summer, and when that happens you might hook almost anything here on a small, flashy streamer pattern of some kind. Sea-run cutthroat trout are often the objective of long-rod anglers at No Point, but cohos and even chinooks will sometimes smack these little imposters.

Bottom fishing isn't great in the immediate area around Point No Point, but if you consult a good chart of the area (no. 18477), you'll find a few rocky ledges and humps worth prospecting for lings and rockfish. If you're after rockfish, don't forget that new regulations allow only one per day here and in other parts of Puget Sound. Pacific cod aren't anywhere near as abundant here as they were a dozen years ago, but you may still find one now and then over moderately soft bottoms. To the northwest, there are a couple of drop-offs out from Foulweather Bluff that occasionally produce a decent halibut during the spring season.

Location: Extreme northeastern tip of the Kitsap Peninsula; see map A2, grid g4.

Species: Chinook, coho, chum, and pink salmon; lingcod; Pacific cod; cutthroat trout; various rockfish; flounder; sole; sculpin.

Facilities: Point No Point Resort has a boat sling (no ramp), cabins and RV sites, restrooms with showers, and a small store with fishing tackle.

Directions: Take Highway 104 west from Kingston and turn north (right) on Miller Bay Road, or take Bond Road north from Poulsbo to Miller Bay Road and go left. Drive north on Miller Bay Road just over seven miles. As you approach Hansville, turn right at the bottom of the long hill on Point No Point Road and follow it three-quarters of a mile to Point No Point Resort, on the left.

Contact: Point No Point Resort, 253/638-2233.

68 Possession Point

This is another of those long-time favorite salmon-fishing spots around Puget Sound that continues to provide decent fishing despite salmon seasons that have ranged from sporadic to nonexistent in recent years. Depending on seasons—and be sure to read a current copy of the state fishing regulations pamphlet if you aren't up to speed—Possession offers resident blackmouth chinooks throughout much of the year, with adult coho a possibility from midsummer through fall. Coho fishing was good here in 2000 and 2001. Late summer and early fall offer decent possibilities for pink salmon during odd-numbered years, not only off the Possession Bar area but to the west in the well-known Humpy Hollow area near Mukilteo. The 2001 pink salmon runs brought excellent fishing to this entire area in August and early September.

This isn't one of the Puget Sound area's top bottom-fishing areas, but you need only study a nautical chart for a few minutes to notice that there are a few very likely possibilities for deep-water lings and rockfish (be sure to check the regulations for lingcod seasons and the conservative rules and limits on these bottom fish). I won't spoil your fun by pinpointing any of the rocky drop-offs that typically hold these fish, but I will recommend NOAA chart 18473 to get you started in exploring all the possibilities for this section of the northern Puget Sound.

Location: South tip of Whidbey Island; see map A2, grid g5.

Species: Chinook, coho, and pink salmon; lingcod; various rockfish, including flounder, sole, and sculpin species.

Facilities: There's a new boat ramp at Mukilteo State Park and public ramps at Mukilteo to the south and Everett to the north, with several more around the south end of Whidbey Island. Food, gas, lodging, tackle, and other necessities are widely available in the Everett-Mukilteo-Edmonds area.

Directions: Launch at Mukilteo and run about four miles to the southwest, or launch at Edmonds and run north just under seven miles.

Contact: Ted's Sports Center, 425/743-9505; Mukilteo State Park, 425/353-2923; Washington State Parks and Recreation Commission, 360/902-8844 (information) or 888/226-7688 (reservations).

69 Gibbs Lake

This is another lake that's better suited to getting away from the rat race than it is to catching lots of fish. You'll probably have it to yourself except for the occasional passing car, and you might even catch a decent trout. Night fishing with night crawlers will produce a few 10- to 14-inch catfish.

One word of caution, especially if you decide to fish on a Friday or Saturday evening: Gibbs is somewhat of a party spot for the local kids. If the boom boxes get too loud, the noise could scare the fish. The noise may also make you want to strangle someone, so leave before the urge gets too strong.

Location: Southeast of Discovery Bay in Jefferson County; see map A2 Inset, grid g3.

Species: Cutthroat trout, brown bullhead catfish.

Facilities: The lake has no access area or other facilities. Food, gas, lodging, and tackle are available in Discovery Bay and Quilcene.

Directions: Drive to Quilcene on U.S. 101,

turn onto Chimacum Road, and head northeast. Turn west (left) onto Eaglemont Road about two miles after crossing Highway 104. Drive about a quarter of a mile and turn north (right) on West Valley Road. Continue about 1.5 miles to Gibbs Lake Road and turn west (left). Gibbs Lake Road runs right alongside the lake.

Contact: The Fish In Hole, 360/385-7031; Quilcene Hotel, 360/765-3868.

70 Peterson Lake

The fishing at Peterson Lake is nothing to get excited about, but you can escape the crowds and maybe spend a few relaxing hours in your float tube or small boat. Most of the fish are small, so take light tackle.

Location: South of Discovery Bay in Jefferson County; see map A2 Inset, grid g3.

Species: Cutthroat trout, yellow perch, a few largemouth bass.

Facilities: The lake has no facilities at all, but food, gas, lodging, and tackle are available in Quilcene and Discovery Bay.

Directions: Take U.S. 101 to Highway 20 at the south end of Discovery Bay and turn east toward Port Townsend. Turn south (right) on Eaglemont Road and south (right) again on Peterson Road. Drive two miles and take a hard right onto the unsigned gravel road leading to the lake.

Contact: The Fish In Hole, 360/385-7031; Quilcene Hotel, 360/765-3868.

71 Lake Leland

This 100-acre lake just off U.S. 101 is heavily seeded with hatchery rainbow trout and provides good trout fishing throughout much of its year-round season. The hottest fishing is from April to June, but fall fishing can also be productive and offers a lot more solitude. Try all your favorite trolling and stillfishing techniques during the spring and casting or trolling dry flies early in the fall.

Leland also grows some good-sized large-mouth bass that provide solid fishing opportunities throughout the summer. In fact, the lake has one of the healthiest populations of big bass to be found anywhere in western Washington, making it perhaps the state's best-kept secret as a largemouth lake. Spinnerbaits and other weedless or semiweedless lures should be included in your arsenal because there's a lot of wood, brush, and weedy cover to fish. Leland has a bass slot limit that requires anglers to release all bass between 12 and 17 inches long. Bluegill fishing is only fair, but midsummer nights provide very good catfish action for anglers casting bobber-and-night-crawler rigs around the edge of the lake.

One word of warning if you fish Leland on a warm weekend or holiday: It's kind of the party spot of western Jefferson County. Be prepared for boom boxes, beach blankets, and other distractions.

Location: North of Quilcene in Jefferson County; see map A2 Inset, grid g2.

Species: Rainbow trout, largemouth bass, black bullhead catfish, bluegill.

Facilities: A Department of Fish and Wildlife access area with a double-wide gravel boat ramp and toilets is located at the lake, and it features a fishing float as well as plenty of room for bank fishing. A county park across the road from the access area has tent and RV sites and restrooms. The nearest food, gas, and tackle are in Discovery Bay and Quilcene. The closest lodging is in Quilcene.

Directions: Drive north on U.S. 101 from Quilcene and turn left on Lake Leland Road. If you miss the first sign, just continue on and you'll get a second chance at Lake Leland Road about a mile farther up the road. From the east take Highway 104 west from Hood Canal Floating Bridge and turn south onto U.S. 101; then drive about 3.5 miles to Lake Leland Road, which is on the right.

Contact: The Fish In Hole, 360/385-7031; Quilcene Hotel, 360/765-3868.

72 Crocker Lake

The bass, catfish, and other warm-water species once available here probably are gone, at least for the time being. Crocker was in the news during the spring of 1998, when a northern pike was caught from the lake and created all kinds of excitement. The Department of Fish and Wildlife (in my opinion) overreacted a bit and gave the lake a hefty application of rotenone to snuff out everything that swam in the lake—all the fish, anyway—in case the lake contained more than the one pike that had been caught. They feared that the large, predatory pike might make their way downstream into Snow Creek, where they could feast on small salmon and steelhead. Pike survival in Snow Creek would be unlikely at best, but, just to be sure, Crocker was treated and replanted with rainbow trout. Lately the lake has been closed to fishing completely, although that should be a short-term problem. Be sure to check the current fishing regulations and seasons pamphlet before fishing here, though.

Location: South of Discovery Bay in Jefferson County; see map A2 Inset, grid g3.

Species: Rainbow trout.

Facilities: The lake has a public access area and a single-wide, concrete-slab boat ramp, but look it over before you back your expensive boat trailer into the lake. There have been a couple of nasty chuckholes around the ramp in recent years, and you wouldn't want to drop into one of them and disappear. They may not be quite that bad, but they would do some damage.

Limited facilities are available to the north in Discovery Bay. To the south Quilcene has one hotel and one motel, as well as food, gas, and other supplies.

Directions: Driving north on U.S. 101 from Quilcene, you'll see the lake on the right about three miles north of Lake Leland. From the east take Highway 104 west from the Hood Canal Floating Bridge and turn south onto U.S. 101; drive about a mile to the lake, which is on the left. Be careful when you turn off the highway into the access area; there's a nasty drop-off that will bend a wheel or ruin a tire if you hit it too fast.

Contact: The Fish In Hole, 360/385-7031; Quilcene Hotel, 360/765-3868.

73 Tarboo Lake

Although only 24 acres in size, Tarboo gets a generous supply of hatchery rainbows every spring, so it provides good fishing for several weeks after the late-April opener. Rainbow carry-over is also quite good, so the chances of hooking a large trout of 14 inches or better are pretty decent. While fishing for those planters, don't be too surprised if you hook a 12-inch cutthroat or two. Try trolling a small Flatfish or Kwikfish, and if that doesn't work, a slowly trolled Carey Special fly might do the trick. The lake was stocked with coho salmon for a few years in the late 1990s, but that practice has been discontinued, at least for now. Stay tuned.

Location: Northeast of Quilcene in Jefferson County; see map A2 Inset, grid g3.

Species: Rainbow and cutthroat trout, coho salmon.

Facilities: The only facilities at the lake are a public access area and boat ramp (with a stump at the end of it that gets in the way of boaters who don't pay enough attention), but Quilcene has a hotel, a motel, groceries, tackle, and gas.

Directions: Take U.S. 101 to Quilcene and turn off the highway to the right at the sign pointing to Chimacum, which puts you on Center Road. Follow Center Road north to Tarboo Lake Road, turn west (left), and drive

exactly three miles to the lake.

Contact: The Fish In Hole, 360/385-7031; Quilcene Hotel, 360/765-3868.

74 Tarboo Creek

Nearby road access along much of Tarboo Creek's length makes it difficult to find a legal-sized resident trout here after about the first three days of the season. Fall, however, provides some fair to good fishing for sea-run cutts to about 16 inches. Fish right after a short period of high water anytime during the month of October, and you'll probably do all right.

Location: Flows into Tarboo Bay northeast of Quilcene in Jefferson County; see map A2 Inset, grid g3.

Species: Resident and sea-run cutthroat trout.

Facilities: The nearest food, gas, tackle, and lodging are in Quilcene.

Directions: Take U.S. 101 to Quilcene and turn off the highway onto Chimacum Road toward Chimacum. Turn east (right) on Dabob Road, drive about two miles to the creek, and turn either upstream or down on roads that parallel the stream.

Contact: The Fish In Hole, 360/385-7031; Quilcene Hotel, 360/765-3868.

75 Sandy Shore Lake

The rainbows planted in Sandy Shore Lake average about nine inches and provide pretty good fishing through April and May. By June early morning and evening fishing are best, and by July this is pretty much a bass lake. There are some respectable largemouths here, but you'll likely catch several 8- to 10-inchers for every worthwhile bass.

Location: Southwest of Port Ludlow in Jefferson County; see map A2 Inset, grid g3.

Species: Rainbow trout, largemouth bass.

Facilities: There are no facilities at the lake. The nearest food, gas, tackle, and lodging are in Quilcene and Port Ludlow. An RV park is also located in Port Ludlow.

Directions: Take Highway 104 west from the Hood Canal Bridge or east from Discovery Bay and turn south onto Sandy Shore Road, following it about two miles to the lake.

Contact: The Fish In Hole, 360/385-7031; Port Ludlow RV Park, 360/437-9110; Port Ludlow Resort, 800/732-1239, website: www.portludlowresort.com.

76 Ludlow Lake

The season here runs year-round, but the best fishing occurs immediately after the Department of Fish and Wildlife makes its annual March or April plant of about 500 legal-sized rainbows. The action usually lasts about a month. Although Ludlow Lake covers only about 15 acres, it offers decent bass fishing all summer, especially for anglers who carry in small boats, canoes, or float tubes. Perhaps the lake's biggest claim to fame is the fact that it produced the state-record brown bullhead catfish in 1997. No one has come close to equaling that feat since, but decent catfish catches are made here from time to time during a warm summer night.

Location: West of Port Ludlow in Jefferson County; see map A2 Inset, grid g3.

Species: Rainbow trout, largemouth bass, brown bullhead catfish.

Facilities: The lake has no facilities. The nearest food, gas, tackle, and lodging can be found in Quilcene and Port Ludlow. There's also an RV park in Port Ludlow.

Directions: Take Highway 104 west from the Hood Canal Bridge or east from Discovery Bay and turn north onto Sandy Shore Road. About a quarter mile off the highway Sandy Shore Road makes a sharp left turn, with a gravel road turning to the right. Take that gravel road and drive about 100 yards to the short trail (also about 100 yards) leading toward the lake.

Contact: The Fish In Hole, 360/385-7031; Port Ludlow RV Park, 360/437-9110; Port Ludlow Resort, 800/732-1239, website: www.portludlowresort.com.

77 Teal Lake

Though nothing spectacular, this 15-acre lake by the side of the road is stocked with legal-sized rainbows every spring and provides fair angling opportunities from April to June, plus a little surge of activity again in the fall. Teal Lake is somewhat out of the way if you don't happen to live around the east end of Jefferson County, but it could be worth a visit some Saturday in May when you don't have anything else to do. The mood here is laid-back, as it should be with fishing.

Location: South of Port Ludlow in Jefferson County; see map A2 Inset, grid g4.

Species: Rainbow trout.

Facilities: The lake has no public access area as such, but bank access is allowed, and it's OK to launch small boats along the shore. The nearest food, lodging, and other amenities are in Port Ludlow.

Directions: Take Highway 104 to about three miles west of the Hood Canal Floating Bridge's west end and turn north on Teal Lake Road. Drive two miles to the lake, which is on the west side of the road.

Contact: The Fish In Hole, 360/385-7031; Port Ludlow RV Park, 360/437-9110; Port Ludlow Resort, 800/732-1239, website: www.portludlowresort.com.

78 Buck Lake

Except for the county park and two or three houses set back from the water, Buck Lake looks pretty much as it must have 50 years ago. There aren't any docks, piers, bulkheads, or closely cropped lawns, and a few hours here may give you the feeling that you're well off the beaten path. The brush, trees, and weeds surrounding most of the lake offer plenty of shallow-water trout cover that seems to call out for you to cast an artificial fly in that direction.

At just over 20 acres, Buck Lake is as inviting to the float-tuber or canoe enthusiast as it is the guy with a 16-foot trailer boat. In fact, that canoe would be more practical here, since gas-powered motors can't be used on Buck Lake. Although most anglers come here to fish for planted rainbows and an occasional brookie or cutthroat, the bass population continues to grow, and abundant shoreline cover makes this an exceptional place to try for largemouths.

Location: North end of the Kitsap Peninsula; see map A2 Inset, grid g5.

Species: Rainbow, brook, and a few cutthroat trout; largemouth bass.

Facilities: A small county park on the lake provides bank access and a boat ramp. Food, gas, and tackle are available in Hansville. Lodging and other amenities can be found in Poulsbo.

Directions: Take Highway 104 west from Kingston and turn north (right) on Miller Bay Road, or take Bond Road north from Poulsbo to Miller Bay Road and go left. Drive north on Miller Bay Road just over seven miles. Immediately past the signs pointing right to Point No Point, turn left on Buck Lake Road, following it just over half a mile to the third 90-degree corner. Bear right at that third turn and follow the road down the hill a quarter mile to the lake.

Contact: The Northwest Angler, 360/697-7100, website: www.nwangler.com.

79 Deer Lake

Heavily stocked with hatchery rainbows, this 80-acre Whidbey Island lake is a steady producer early in the season. A regular who said he had fished Deer for over 30 years once told me that if you can't catch a limit of trout here on opening day you should give up fishing completely. I don't think I'd make that recommendation to anyone, but the liberal spring trout plants certainly do offer anglers a great chance of success. Spring plants of legal-sized rainbow trout in recent years have ranged from 3,500 to 7,500 fish, more than enough to keep anglers happy. But perhaps the best thing about Deer is that it's quite deep, so many of those spring planters scatter to the depths after the early season onslaught, where they continue to provide good trout-fishing opportunities throughout much of the summer and again in the fall.

Bottom line: This is a trout lake worth visiting virtually anytime during its April through October season. If you stay into the night, try a bobber-and-worm rig for pan-sized catfish. And yes, you're right, it's not the only Deer Lake in Washington. My unofficial count lists it as one of seven lakes by the same name, but it's the only one on Whidbey Island, if that helps.

Location: West of Clinton near the southeast corner of Whidbey Island; see map A2 Inset, grid g6.

Species: Rainbow and cutthroat trout, brown bullhead catfish.

Facilities: A Department of Fish and Wildlife access area and boat ramp are located at the northeast corner of the lake. Food, gas, and several bed-and-breakfasts are available in Clinton.

Directions: Take the Washington State Ferry from Mukilteo to Clinton, drive up the hill several blocks, and turn left on Holst Road, following it southwesterly from town. The lake is on the right, just over a mile from Clinton.

Contact: John's Sporting Goods, 425/259-3056, website: www.johnssportinggoods.com; Ted's Sports Center, 425/743-9505.

80 Lake Serene

This 42-acre lake close to the King-Snohomish County population centers doesn't always live up to its name, especially after the April plants of hatchery trout. Those plants are usually quite generous—something in the neighborhood of 3,500 fish—so the trout fishing holds up fairly well despite the lake's popularity. The warm weather of summer, however, tends to put an end to the trout fishing, thanks to the fact that the lake is quite shallow throughout. If there's anything resembling a deep spot where you might try for summertime rainbows, it would be the area of 25-foot-deep water near the east end of the lake. Worms, marshmallows, Berkley Power Bait, salmon eggs, and all the usual spoons and spinners seem to work here when the bite is on.

On the bright side, that warm summer weather signals the start of decent bass fishing at Serene. Try top-water offerings early and late in the day, and plastics or spinnerbaits when the sun's a little higher on the water.

Location: Southwest of Everett; see map A2 Inset, grid g6.

Species: Rainbow trout, largemouth bass.

Facilities: A public access area with a boat ramp and toilets is located at the west end of the lake. Food, gas, lodging, and other amenities are available to the south in Lynnwood.

Directions: Drive north from Lynnwood on Highway 99 to Shelby Road and turn west (left). Drive three-quarters of a mile to 43rd Avenue, turn north (right), and drive three blocks to the lake.

Contact: Ted's Sports Center, 425/743-9505.

81 Stickney Lake

At only 26 acres, Stickney is a small lake with quite a lot to offer anglers. It receives an annual plant of about 1,000 legal-sized hatchery rainbows, which provide fair action through the spring, by which time bass fishing is good enough to draw interest from many Snohomish/King County bass enthusiasts. Perch

fishing is good enough from early spring through late fall to make this a worthwhile bet as a place to take the kids for some can't-miss fishing. If the weather is good and the junk food holds out, stay into the night for catfish.

Location: Southwest of Everett; see map A2 Inset, grid g6.

Species: Rainbow trout, largemouth bass, yellow perch, brown bullhead catfish.

Facilities: A Department of Fish and Wildlife boat ramp with an access area and toilets is located on the north end of the lake. Food, gas, tackle, and lodging are available nearby in Lynnwood.

Directions: Take Highway 99 north from Lynnwood or south from Everett, turn east on North Manor Way, drive half a mile to Admiralty Way, turn south (right), and drive about 100 yards to the lake.

Contact: Ted's Sports Center, 425/743-9505.

82 Silver Lake

This 100-acre lake within casting range of I-5 between Everett and Seattle is open to year-round fishing and has something to offer throughout much of that 12-month season. Hatchery rainbows, including a pretty good mix of one-pounders, draw most of the angler interest from March to May. Both boat and bank anglers score some good catches then, using just about all the old stand-by baits and lures that take trout everywhere else.

By May the kokanee action usually turns on, although this isn't known as one of western Washington's top kokanee waters. As summer progresses, kokanee anglers sometimes find themselves gravitating toward the middle of the lake, where the small sockeye salmon may school in the cool depths of the lake that extend down to 50 feet.

As kokanee fishing fades, usually by September, rainbows and some cutthroats become more readily available, providing fair stillfishing and trolling action until the cold winds of November send anglers looking for more comfortable places to spend their days.

Location: South of Everett; see map A2 Inset, grid g7.

Species: Rainbow and cutthroat trout, kokanee.

Facilities: A city park with bank access and restrooms is located on the west side of the lake, and it's possible to fish from the bank or launch a small boat in several spots along the lake's eastern shore. Silver Lake RV Park is on the west side of the lake and has both RV and tent sites, as well as a boat ramp and beach access for park guests. Food, gas, lodging, and tackle are available throughout the Everett area.

Directions: Southbound on I-5, take Exit 189 and drive south on Highway 527 to 112th Street SW. Turn west (right) and drive a quarter of a mile to Silver Lake Road; then turn south (left) and drive 150 yards to the lake. Northbound on I-5, take Exit 186 and drive east to Highway 527. Turn north (left) and drive to 112th Street SW and turn left, then left again on Silver Lake Road.

Contact: Silver Lake RV Park, 425/338-9666; John's Sporting Goods, 425/259-3056, website: www.johnssportinggoods.com.

83 Martha Lake

Yes, there are Martha Lakes all over the place, but this one is in Snohomish County. What's that, you say? There are three Martha Lakes in Snohomish County? Well, this is the one that's just under 60 acres. Huh? There are two Martha Lakes in Snohomish County that are under 60 acres? Well, this is the one near Alderwood Manor. Aha, now you know which Martha Lake I'm talking about. Who's in charge of naming these lakes, anyway?

This Martha Lake is stocked primarily with hatchery rainbows, although a few cutthroats make their way into the mix some years.

Spring fishing produces better trout catches, but the ambience is better in fall, especially if you like more solitude. The lake gives up a few large bass from time to time and is fairly famous for its summertime catfish action.

Location: Northeast of Alderwood Manor; see map A2 Inset, grid g6.

Species: Rainbow and cutthroat trout, largemouth bass, yellow perch, brown bullhead catfish.

Facilities: A Department of Fish and Wildlife access area with a boat ramp and toilets is at the southeast corner of the lake, with food, gas, and tackle available in Mill Creek or to the north in Everett. Lodging is available near the freeway exit.

Directions: Drive north from Seattle or south from Everett on I-5 and turn east on 164th Street SW (Exit 183 off the freeway). The lake is about half a mile off the freeway, on the north (left) side of the street.

Contact: Ted's Sports Center, 425/743-9505.

84 Snohomish River

Two of western Washington's better steelhead and salmon rivers, the Skykomish and the Snoqualmie, join to form the big, slow-moving river known as the Snohomish. Since all the sea-run fish bound for the Sky and the Snoqualmie have to pass through the Snohomish, it stands to reason that it can be a productive fishing spot, and it is.

The reason it isn't an even better producer is that it's so big, slow, and deep, that it's difficult to read. There aren't many distinguishable holding spots for salmon and steelhead, so many anglers come here, scratch their heads, and say to themselves, "Where do I start casting?" Veteran local anglers do all right, but visitors often have a tough time of it. The river's size and the nature of its shoreline give boat anglers a definite advantage, and it's those boat anglers who score the best catches from the Snohomish throughout the year.

The coho run is the backbone of the fall salmon fishery here, and October is the prime month to get in on the action. Backtrolling with various diving plugs or casting flashy spoons and spinners are the techniques that take them best. Catchable numbers of cohos continue to pass through the Snohomish in November, and some large chums are also available by then to add to the intrigue of a morning's fishing. Pink salmon are present in good numbers during odd-numbered years, and September is usually the best month to fish them. September is also perhaps the most productive month for sea-run cutthroat and Dolly Varden, although both are available from midsummer to late fall.

As for steelhead, the Snohomish shines brightest as a winter stream, often ranking among the state's top 10 as a winter steelie producer. Catches of 2,000 or more per season are fairly common on the Snohomish River. December and January, when large numbers of hatchery fish pass through on their way to upstream hatchery facilities at Tokul Creek and the Reiter Ponds, are the top months to fish the Snohomish. Backtrolling plugs or diver-and-bait combinations account for good numbers of winter steelhead, as does plunking with fresh roe clusters, various winged bobbers, or combinations of the two. Summer steelheading is also a possibility here, but the numbers don't compare to the winter catch. The best months for summer-run steelies are June and July.

Location: Enters Puget Sound immediately north of Everett; see map A2 Inset, grid g7.

Species: Winter and summer steelhead; sea-run cutthroat trout; Dolly Varden; coho, chum, and pink salmon.

Facilities: Boat ramps are located on the river in Everett, Snohomish, and off 115th Avenue SE, about midway between Snohomish

and the Highway 522 bridge. Food, gas, lodging, and tackle are readily available in Snohomish and Everett.

Directions: Take I-405 to Highway 522 at Woodinville and turn east. Drive 12 miles to the bridge that crosses the Snohomish just below the confluence of the Snoqualmie and Skykomish Rivers. Turn north (left) on Elliott Road and drive two miles to the first of several roads leading to the east (right) toward the river at various points. An alternative is to take I-5 to Everett and drive east on U.S. 2 to Snohomish, where two highway bridges cross the river. Cross the river and turn west (right) on River Road to fish the south side of the river between Snohomish and Everett.

Contact: John's Sporting Goods, 425/259-3056, website: www.johnssportinggoods.com; Sky Valley Traders, 360/794-8818; Hook, Line, and Sinker, 360/651-2204.

85 Blackman's Lake

Located within the city limits of Snohomish, this 60-acre lake gets plenty of attention from local anglers throughout its year-round fishing season. Hatchery plants include some one-pounders, but most of the 3,000 or so planted rainbows are typical seven- to nine-inchers. April, May, and June are the best months for rainbows here, but cutthroats usually bite better a little later in the year. September and October offer good chances for catching both 'bows and cutts. Perch fishing is good all season, and all you need to catch them is a supply of garden worms.

Location: At Snohomish; see map A2 Inset, grid g7.

Species: Rainbow and cutthroat trout, largemouth bass, yellow perch.

Facilities: A Department of Fish and Wildlife access area and boat ramp are located on the south end of the lake, and a city park provides access as well. A fishing pier located near the north end of the lake is wheelchair accessible. Food, gas, lodging, and other facilities are nearby in Snohomish.

Directions: Take I-5 to U.S. 2 at Everett and head east toward Snohomish. After about five miles, turn south on Highway 9 and follow it about 1.5 miles to the lake, which is on the left.

Contact: Sky Valley Traders, 360/794-8818.

86 Flowing Lake

If there's such a thing as a western Washington lake that's perfectly suited to both trout and bass fishing, it might be Flowing Lake, which is open to fishing year-round. The lake's more than 130 acres can be roughly divided between the shallow east side and the deep west side, offering suitable water for bass and trout.

If you want bass, head for the fast-warming shallows at the northeast or southeast corners of the lake in early spring, before the rest of the lake has even started to warm. Much of the water in these areas is less than 20 feet deep, and the shoreline offers lots of good bass-holding cover. Like many of the more popular Snohomish County lakes, Flowing Lake has a slot limit that allows anglers to kill only bass that are shorter than 12 inches or longer than 17 inches.

If you're after trout, fish virtually anywhere in the lake during the spring, but as the air and water temperature begins to climb in early summer, concentrate more of your effort in the western one-third of the lake. There the depth ranges to more than 60 feet in places, and you can stillfish near bottom or troll deep to continue catching rainbows after other trout lakes have quit producing. The lake is well stocked with hatchery rainbows in the spring, and the plants often include some lunker brood fish in the two-pound range.

Location: North of Monroe; see map A2 Inset, grid g8.

Species: Rainbow trout, largemouth bass.

Facilities: The Department of Fish and Wildlife maintains a public access area with a boat ramp and toilets near the southeast corner of the lake. There's also a good deal of bank-fishing access, and a boat ramp is available at the Snohomish County Park at the north end of the lake. Food, gas, tackle, and lodging are available in Snohomish and Monroe.

Directions: Take U.S. 2 to Snohomish, turn east on Three Lakes Road, and drive about five miles to the lake.

Contact: Sky Valley Traders, 360/794-8818.

87 Panther Lake

This 45-acre lake near Snohomish is very much a typical mixed-species western Washington lake where nothing extraordinary ever seems to happen. It's stocked with legal-sized hatchery rainbows in the spring, but most of them get caught by early summer, at which time many anglers turn their attention toward bass and panfish. The bass fishing is fair for small bass, and if you locate a school of crappies, you can enjoy some worthwhile light-tackle action, too. Night fishing for brown bullheads produces some good catches, most of them from the shallower waters at the north end of the lake. The lake holds a few cutthroat, some of them decent sized, and they offer fair angling opportunity during the spring and fall.

Location: Northeast of Snohomish; see map A2 Inset, grid g8.

Species: Rainbow and cutthroat trout, largemouth bass, crappie, brown bullhead catfish.

Facilities: A Department of Fish and Wildlife access area with a boat ramp and toilets is located on the lake's west side. Food, gas, lodging, and tackle are available in Snohomish and Monroe.

Directions: Take U.S. 2 to Snohomish and drive east on Three Lakes Road. About three miles east of Snohomish, turn north (left) at Jamison

Corner onto Panther Lake Road, which leads less than a mile to the west side of the lake.

Contact: Sky Valley Traders, 360/794-8818.

88 Storm Lake

One of the great things about fishing 78-acre Storm Lake is that if the fishing is bad, you can go try your luck at Flowing Lake (see number 86) about 150 yards away. The good news, though, is that the fishing usually isn't bad at all. Storm Lake is stocked with something like 6,500 legal-sized hatchery rainbows every spring, providing steady angling action well into June. Cutthroats show in the catch from time to time, usually later in the summer and in the fall, but most are caught by accident rather than by design. October can be an excellent month to fish for Storm Lake trout, but few anglers take advantage of the opportunity. Largemouth bass of a pound and up can provide good fishing during the warm days from May through July.

Location: North of Monroe; see map A2 Inset, grid g8.

Species: Rainbow and some cutthroat trout, largemouth bass.

Facilities: A public access area and boat ramp are located near the north end of the lake. Food, gas, lodging, and tackle are available in Snohomish and Monroe.

Directions: Take U.S. 2 to Snohomish and drive east on Three Lakes Road about five miles to the lake.

Contact: Sky Valley Traders, 360/794-8818.

89 Lake Roesiger

When it comes to fishing opportunity, this is one of Snohomish County's most impressive lakes. It's open year-round, and it would probably take you all 365 days to thoroughly probe its more than 350 acres and depths of more than 110 feet.

Lake Roesiger is really more like three lakes in one: the largest and deepest northern section,

where trout and kokanee flourish; the shallow flats of the lake's narrow, wasplike midsection, where bass and panfish thrive; and the south end of the lake, much like the north end but a little smaller and not quite so deep.

One of the best things about Roesiger is that the fishing holds up throughout so much of the year. You stand nearly as good a chance of catching trout in July as you do in May (you just have to fish a little deeper for them). Since the lake is stocked with as many as 10,000 legal-sized rainbows every spring, there are usually plenty of them still around in summer. And if the trout aren't biting in July, maybe the kokanee will be. Use your depthsounder to locate them and be willing to troll deep if necessary. If all else fails on a warm summer morning, hit the lake's middle section and cast for bass, some of which top four pounds. Throw in perch, bluegills, and catfish in case you somehow get bored, and it's easy to understand why Roesiger is so popular with Snohomish County anglers.

Location: Northeast of Monroe; see map A2 Inset, grid g8.

Species: Rainbow trout, kokanee, largemouth bass, yellow perch, bluegill, brown bullhead catfish.

Facilities: Besides a Department of Fish and Wildlife access area and boat ramp near the south end of the lake, a county park offers a fishing pier and bank angling access on the east side. Food, gas, tackle, lodging, and other amenities are available in Monroe.

Directions: Take U.S. 2 to Monroe, turn north (left) on Woods Creek Road, and drive about 12 miles to the lake.

Contact: Sky Valley Traders, 360/794-8818; Lake Roesiger Park, 425/388-6600.

90 Chain Lake

When you consider the variety of species available and the fact that it has a year-round season, this little lake has quite a lot to offer anglers. Its 23-acre size is well suited to fishing from a float tube, small boat, or canoe, whether you happen to be a trout, bass, or panfish angler. Rainbows are planted in March or April. Chain doesn't produce many lunkers of any species, but it's usually good for some kind of angling action anytime from about March to November.

Location: North of Monroe; see map A2 Inset, grid g8.

Species: Rainbow and cutthroat trout, largemouth bass, crappie.

Facilities: A small public access area with a rough boat ramp is located near the east end of the lake. All amenities are available in Monroe.

Directions: Take U.S. 2 to Monroe and turn north (left) at the light on Lewis Street, which becomes 195th Avenue SE. The road turns left after three miles and becomes Chain Lake Road just before you get to the lake. Follow the signs about a mile from there.

Contact: Sky Valley Traders, 360/794-8818.

91 Wagner (Wagner's) Lake

Though covering only about 20 acres, Wagner is a popular trout lake in the spring and a producer of some fairly good bass fishing in the summer. It's usually stocked with about 1,000 legal-sized rainbows before the late-April opener, but there aren't many hiding places for them in this little lake that's only about 20 feet in its deepest spot. In other words, the term "fished out" may well apply here after the first few weekends of the season.

While not really a haven for trout, this shallow lake with a weedy shoreline is perfect for bass—and for bass anglers. It's easy to understand why someone took it upon himself or herself to stock bass here illegally.

Location: Northeast of Monroe; see map A2 Inset, grid g8.

Species: Rainbow trout, largemouth bass.

Facilities: A public access area with a boat ramp and toilets is located on the lake's west side. Food, gas, tackle, and lodging are available in Monroe.

Directions: Take U.S. 2 to Monroe and turn north (left) on Woods Creek Road. Drive about 2.5 miles to Wagner Lake Road, turn left, and drive a mile to the lake, which is on the right.

Contact: Sky Valley Traders, 360/794-8818.

92 Woods Creek

This large tributary to the Skykomish River offers a little bit of something for every kind of trout angler, from those who never leave sight of the road to those who like to get out and do some hiking to find solitude and maybe even a couple of trout that haven't seen a bait or lure for at least a few days. Try casting small spinners, such as a Metric or Panther Martin, from July to September. If you fish it earlier (it opens June 1), bait might work better because of the still-cool water conditions. After Labor Day, when the creek is at its lowest and warmest, try a light-action fly rod and your favorite wet-fly patterns. Your best bet for a keeper trout of 14 inches or larger is probably in June.

Location: Northeast of Monroe; see map A2 Inset, grid g8.

Species: Cutthroat trout.

Facilities: Food, gas, tackle, and lodging are available in Monroe.

Directions: Take U.S. 2 to Monroe and turn north (left) on Woods Creek Road or Florence Acres Road to reach the two forks of Woods Creek. Both roads roughly parallel the stream for about six miles.

Contact: Sky Valley Traders, 360/794-8818.

93 Cochran Lake

This 35-acre lake near Monroe doesn't get much attention from anglers, but it does have limited public access and offers fair spring and fall trout fishing. Carry your small boat, canoe, or float tube to the beach and go for it. After about the end of May, you shouldn't have much company. The trout fishing remains fairly good even into the heat of summer, thanks to a large area around the middle of the lake that is deep and cool, with depths plunging to 50 feet or more in some places.

Location: Northeast of Monroe; see map A2 Inset, grid g9.

Species: Rainbow trout.

Facilities: There's a rough access area where small boats and canoes can be launched, but it's not suitable for trailer boats. Food, gas, lodging, and tackle are available in Monroe.

Directions: Take U.S. 2 to Monroe and turn north (left) on Woods Creek Road, following it about six miles to the lake, which is on the left.

Contact: Sky Valley Traders, 360/794-8818.

94 Skykomish River

Long one of the Puget Sound region's most popular, most publicized, and most productive steelhead rivers, it's probably impossible to say anything about the Sky that hasn't already been said hundreds of times and written at least once. But that's never stopped me before, so here goes.

This big, beautiful river is consistently among the top two or three winter steelhead producers in Washington, giving up at least 1,000 fish per winter season and some years more than doubling that output. Strong hatchery returns in December and January make those two months the best times to fish the Sky, but unlike many other Northwest streams, this one doesn't experience a February lull, so the fishing can be as good then as it is earlier in the winter. March and April see the winter steelie fishery here turn to a catch-and-release affair, one of the best and most popular of its kind in the Northwest. The biggest concentrations of winter steelheaders—and often the biggest catches—are around the Reiter Ponds steelhead facility and from Sultan downstream to Monroe, but you might find a willing fish almost anywhere along the Sky during the height of the winter season. If you fish Reiter Ponds, arrive early—as in long before daylight—and take along a selection of leadhead jigs to fish beneath a float. The area is known for its grabby boulder bottom, and the jig-and-float combination will save you lots of frustration and lost tackle. That combo also catches steelhead.

Summer steelheading can also be extremely good on the Sky. The summertime catch sometimes tops the 2,000-fish mark, making the Skykomish an occasional entry on Washington's list of top 10 summer steelhead producers. June, July, August, and September all provide excellent summer steelheading possibilities. As on many Northwest streams, gearing down to lighter tackle and using a more subtle approach are often the key to summer steelhead fishing success here.

Cohos and chums share the salmon-fishing limelight on the Skykomish during a typical fall salmon season, with pinks playing a big part during odd-numbered years. Salmon angling is allowed up to the confluence of the forks, but it's hard to beat the numerous pools and drifts from Sultan down to Monroe, a stretch of river that's as good as any salmon stream in the country. Pinks show up in September (every other year), cohos in October, and chums are most numerous in November. Fish for all three, and you'll quickly see the improvement in fish strength and stamina as the runs change.

The Skykomish—the entire Snohomish system, for that matter—is one of the few places in Washington where it's legal for anglers to catch and keep Dolly Varden as part of the daily trout limit. Any Dolly you keep must be at least 20 inches long, but fish of legal size are certainly within the realm of possibility. The Sky, in fact, has produced much larger Dolly Varden. The state-record anadromous Dolly, a whopper of exactly 10 pounds, was pulled from the river back in 1982.

Location: Joins the Snoqualmie River southwest of Monroe; see map A2 Inset, grid g9.

Species: Winter and summer steelhead; Dolly Varden; coho, chum, and pink salmon.

Facilities: A boat ramp and access area are just below the Lewis Street bridge in Monroe, another ramp about two miles upstream from the bridge off Ben Howard Road, and two near the Mann Road bridge at Sultan. Food, gas, tackle, and lodging are available right along the highway in Monroe.

Directions: Take U.S. 2 through Monroe and continue east along the north side of the river, or drive south through Monroe, cross the bridge, and turn east (left) on Ben Howard Road to reach fishing spots along the south side of the river.

Contact: Sky Valley Traders, 360/794-8818.

95 Little Quilcene River

Near as I can tell from Department of Fish and Wildlife catch records, anglers caught a grand total of two steelhead from this river from 1991 to 1994, making it perhaps the state's worst winter steelhead stream. Why the Department of Fish and Wildlife bothers to leave the season open all winter is a mystery. You're better off fishing the Little Quilcene for sea-run cutthroat, which show in fair numbers from September to November. It's hard to find a legal-sized resident trout over the 14-inch minimum during the rest of the season.

Location: Flows into Quilcene Bay near Quilcene in Jefferson County; see map A2 Inset, grid g2.

Species: Resident and sea-run cutthroat trout, winter steelhead.

Facilities: The nearest food, gas, tackle, and lodging are in Quilcene.

Directions: Take U.S. 101 north from Quilcene or south from Discovery Bay and turn west on Lords Lake Loop Road about 2.5 miles north of Quilcene. The road parallels the lower river, makes a jog away from it for two miles, then cuts back toward and crosses the river. Just before crossing, you can turn west (right) on Forest Service Road 2909 to reach upper sections of the river.

Contact: The Fish In Hole, 360/385-7031; Quilcene Hotel, 360/765-3868.

96 Quilcene River

The stocking of hatchery rainbow trout has been discontinued here, and the fairly liberal regulations that went with the hatchery plants have been replaced with catch-and-release rules and selective fishery limitations. That means you can't use bait, and only artificial lures with single hooks can be used for all fishing here. The good news is that a catch-and-keep fishery for hatchery coho salmon has become a reality once again on the river, at least on the lower portion of the Quilcene. The salmon season opens in August and runs through October, offering the opportunity to catch as many as four silvers a day, and many anglers took advantage of that opportunity during the fall of 2001. If fishing holds up that well, look for the Quilcene to become one of the Olympic Peninsula's favorite salmon streams.

Location: Flows into Quilcene Bay near Quilcene in Jefferson County; see map A2 Inset, grid h2.

Species: Coho salmon.

Facilities: The U.S. Forest Service's Falls View Campground, located between the highway and the river, has tent and RV sites and restrooms. The Cove RV Park and Grocery north of Brinnon has RV hookups, groceries, tackle, and fishing licenses. The nearest hotel/motel accommodations are in Quilcene.

Directions: Drive south from Quilcene or north from Brinnon on U.S. 101 and turn west onto Big Quilcene River Road about two miles south of Quilcene. The road parallels the river upstream for several miles.

Contact: Olympic National Forest, Quilcene Ranger District, 360/765-3368; The Cove RV Park and Grocery, 360/796-4723; Mount Jupiter Recreation (for reservations at Falls View), 360/796-4886.

97 Lake Ballinger

A spring stocking of about 5,000 hatchery rainbows provides most of the trout fishing here, but the warm-water species are self-sustaining and doing just fine. Troll or stillfish with any of your favorite trout offerings in April or May and you should catch your share of planted rainbows.

Ballinger can be an especially productive bass lake, coming on with some husky largemouths by the end of April and continuing to provide good fishing through the summer. If you're looking for bass and all else fails, spend some time casting around the small island on the west side of the lake; it may not produce, but it looks as if it should. The standard bass slot limit is in effect here, making it illegal to keep any bass between 12 and 17 inches long.

The perch and crappies tend to be on the small side but big and abundant enough to provide some good light-tackle possibilities. The bullhead catfish also run small, but late spring and summer fishing for them can be quite productive. Again, start around the island if you don't have a better idea.

Location: West of Mountlake Terrace just north of the Snohomish-King County line; see map A2 Inset, grid h6.

Species: Rainbow trout, largemouth bass, yellow perch, crappie, brown bullhead catfish.

Facilities: A city park with a boat ramp and fishing pier is near the north end of the lake. Food, gas, lodging, and tackle are all available within a few minutes' drive in Mountlake Terrace.

Directions: Take I-5 to the north end of Seattle and go west at Exit 177 on Highway 104 (also known as 205th Street at this point). The road runs along the south shore of the lake about half a mile off I-5.

Contact: Ted's Sports Center, 425/743-9505.

98 Devil's Lake

You may have a hell of a time trying to catch a limit of lunkers here, but Devil's Lake does offer some potential in the spring and fall. At under 15 acres, it's certainly small enough to afford some good float-tubing opportunity, but light plants of hatchery trout keep Devil's from being much more than a nice place to spend a little time on the water. Perch are almost too abundant here, to the point of sometimes becoming pests for trout anglers. If you want perch, just cast a bobber-and-worm rig.

Location: Southwest of Monroe; see map A2 Inset, grid h8.

Species: Rainbow and cutthroat trout, yellow perch.

Facilities: A public access area and boat ramp are located on the lake. Food, gas, lodging, and tackle are available in Woodinville and Monroe.

Directions: Take I-405 to Highway 522 and turn east. About 1.5 miles east of Maltby, turn south (right) on Echo Lake Road. Drive just under two miles to Devil's Lake Road, turn left, and drive a mile to the lake.

Contact: Sky Valley Traders, 360/794-8818.

99 Echo Lake

You wouldn't think that a lake covering only 17 acres would offer much in the way of season-long angling opportunities, but Echo

Lake might surprise you. Hatchery plants include a few rainbows and a few cutthroats, and, as you might expect, the majority of them are caught during the spring invasion of eager anglers. But this year-round lake can also be productive in the summer and fall, which is something you can't say about many small western Washington trout lakes.

Echo Lake's prolonged productivity each year is probably due to the lake's unusual depth. Some places in the middle of the lake are over 50 feet deep, and that's no doubt where some of the spring plants wind up. That's also where you should concentrate your angling efforts if you want to hook a decent trout or two during the summer or early fall.

Location: Southwest of Monroe; see map A2 Inset, grid h8.

Species: Rainbow and cutthroat trout.

Facilities: A public access area with a boat ramp and toilets is located on the east side of the lake. Monroe has food, gas, tackle, and lodging.

Directions: Take I-405 to Highway 522 and turn east. Pass through Maltby (watch closely or you'll miss it), continue about 1.5 miles to Echo Lake Road, turn right, and follow the road south to the lake.

Contact: Sky Valley Traders, 360/794-8818.

100 Fontal Lake

Thanks to the rough logging road, poor boat ramp, and lack of easy bank access, you had to be somewhat of a pioneer to fish this 35-acre lake even in the good old days when the rough road extended all the way to the lake. Now, since the last two miles of the road are closed to vehicles, you have to be even more of a Lewis and Clark type to taste the pleasures of this tree-lined lake near the King-Snohomish County line.

Your trailblazing efforts, however, could pay off with a Fontal Lake grand slam—at least one rainbow, one cutthroat, and one brook trout in your daily five-fish trout limit. Some local anglers are more than a little ticked off about the road closure, but some of them may have been part of the reason for the gate. Littering and other slobbish behavior were part of the reason for Weyerhaeuser's decision to gate the road.

Energetic anglers who don't mind working harder to get away from the crowds are happy with the current situation, however, and if solitude is a factor in your decision to go trout fishing, Fontal may be worth investigating. One look at this jewel of a lowland lake will make you glad you put forth the effort.

Location: Southeast of Monroe; see map A2 Inset, grid h8.

Species: Rainbow, cutthroat, and brook trout.

Facilities: A rough boat ramp is located near the south end of the lake, but there are no other facilities. The nearest food, gas, and tackle are in Duvall, and the nearest lodging is in Monroe.

Directions: Take U.S. 2 to Monroe and turn south on Highway 203. Drive 2.5 miles to High Rock Road and turn east (left). Turn east (left) again on Lake Fontal Road and follow it about six miles to the locked gate about two miles from the lake. The last leg of the trip must be completed on foot, bicycle, or horseback. The road belongs to a private timber company.

Contact: Sky Valley Traders, 360/794-8818.

101 Lake Hannan

Often overlooked by anglers scrambling to nearby Fontal Lake, this south Snohomish County lake is a worthwhile angling destination in its own right. It isn't a great place for large trailer boats, but you can easily shoulder a small car-topper or canoe and launch on the west side of the lake. Lake Hannan is open year-round, and there's hardly ever a crowd, so fish it whenever the urge strikes. Although you couldn't prove it by me,

Hannan is reputed to hold some large carryover rainbows.

May is the best time to visit if you like to troll or stillfish, with fly-fishing a good option in June, September, and October.

Location: Southeast of Monroe; see map A2 Inset, grid h8.

Species: Rainbow and cutthroat trout.

Facilities: There are no facilities on the lake. Food, gas, tackle, and lodging are available in Monroe.

Directions: Take U.S. 2 to Monroe and turn south on Highway 203. Drive about 2.5 miles to High Rock Road and turn east (left). Turn east (left) on Lake Fontal Road and drive seven miles to the west side of the lake, which is on the right.

Contact: Sky Valley Traders, 360/794-8818.

102 Lake Margaret

A heavy dose of hatchery trout every spring before the April opener draws a lot of anglers for the first month of the season to small, 44-acre Lake Margaret. Rainbows provide the bulk of the angling action, but spring plants usually include a few cutthroats, some of which survive the early season onslaught and are available to take baits and lures during the last few weeks of the season in October. If you want solitude and a chance to use your float tube here, fish Margaret in the fall. Your best chance for a decent-sized bass is May through July, when the water warms considerably and the largemouths come to life.

Location: Northeast of Duvall near the King-Snohomish County line; see map A2 Inset, grid h9.

Species: Rainbow and cutthroat trout, largemouth bass.

Facilities: The west side of the lake has a Department of Fish and Wildlife public access area with a boat ramp and toilets. A $10 WDFW access decal is required to use the public launch areas maintained by the Washington Department of Fish and Wildlife. The nearest food and gas are in Duvall. Lodging and tackle are available to the north in Monroe.

Directions: Take Highway 203 to Duvall and just north of town turn east on Cherry Valley Road and follow it out of town. Turn north (left) on Kelly Road and drive about three miles to the lake.

Contact: Sky Valley Traders, 360/794-8818.

103 Lake Joy

Covering more than 100 acres and reaching depths of 50 feet, this is a lake with lots of trout-producing potential that has never been realized. There's no public access area, and fish-planting efforts over the years have been sporadic. Some large trout may be lurking in the lake's chilly depths, but few anglers come to search for them. Deep trolling or even vertical jigging are logical options. Fishing worms, night crawlers, or maggots around the edge of the lake will take some respectable yellow perch.

Location: Northeast of Stillwater; see map A2 Inset, grid h9.

Species: Rainbow and cutthroat trout, yellow perch.

Facilities: The lake has no formal access area, but boats may be carried to the water near its north end. The nearest food and gas are in Duvall and Carnation. Lodging and tackle are in Monroe.

Directions: Take Highway 203 south from Duvall or north from Carnation to Stillwater. Turn east on Kelly Road, drive about three miles to Lake Joy Road, and turn right. The road circles the lake.

Contact: Sky Valley Traders, 360/794-8818.

104 Lake Constance

You'll love this high-country trout lake once you reach it. But getting to it isn't a particularly easy task. The two-mile trail is steep, almost vertical in spots, and certainly not for anglers with too much stomach hanging over their belts or two-pack-a-day habits. (The pan-sized trout in Lake Constance aren't worth risking a heart attack.) If you're fit and energetic, though, the beauty of this place is worth a little huffing and puffing—actually, a lot of huffing and puffing.

Take your fly rod and a good selection of dry and wet patterns to fish the edges of the lake, or pack a light spinning rod to cast quarter-ounce spoons and spinners toward the middle of the lake. If you plan to stay overnight, you'll need a permit in advance, and there's a limit of 20 campers per night. To reserve a permit, call Staircase Ranger Station at the number below.

Location: Near the forks of the Dosewallips River in Jefferson County; see map A2 Inset, grid h2.

Species: Rainbow and brook trout.

Facilities: Dosewallips Campground, about two miles west of the Lake Constance Trailhead, has campsites and water, but other necessities are back at Brinnon, on U.S. 101.

Directions: Take U.S. 101 north to Brinnon and turn west (left) on Dosewallips Road, following it some 14 miles to the Olympic National Park boundary. Just inside the park boundary on the right is the trailhead for the Lake Constance Trail. From there it's a steep two-mile hike to the south end of the lake.

Contact: Olympic National Forest, Staircase Ranger District, 360/877-5569; Olympic National Park, 360/452-0330.

105 Dosewallips River

I have fond memories of the first time I ever fished this small, clear stream on the eastern flank of the Olympics, and those positive thoughts remain even though the fishing isn't that good here anymore. I caught a chrome-bright winter steelhead just above the U.S. 101 bridge that January morning in 1975, and I relive that moment every time I pass the Dosey.

I haven't caught a steelhead from the river since that first one, nor have most other steelhead anglers who have fished the Dosewallips in the past 10 years or so. This was once a stream that gave up 250 to 300 winter-runs every season, but a good year now sees about 25 steelhead caught from the Dosewallips, most of them by local anglers who can run out and fish it when conditions are right. The lower river near the state park has some good steelhead holes and drifts, and the steep canyon farther upstream is also an intriguing and beautiful place to fish, even if you go fishless.

The Dosey has a good run of chum salmon in November and December, and there's usually a short (six weeks or so) chum season during that time. Chum fishing is usually open only from the U.S. 101 bridge downstream, though. Be sure to check out the regulations pamphlet for complete details on this short chum salmon fishery. Although I didn't list pink salmon as one of the species in the river, there's a more or less unofficial catch-and-release fishery on them here during odd-numbered years, mostly among a small group of fly casters.

Sea-run cutthroats are lightly fished here but can provide good action after a fall rainstorm. This is strictly a catch-and-release fishery, since only hatchery steelhead and chums are fair game for catch-and-keep anglers on the Dosewallips.

Location: Enters Hood Canal at Brinnon; see map A2 Inset, grid h2.

Species: Winter steelhead, chum salmon, sea-run cutthroat trout.

Facilities: Dosewallips State Park is one of the newer, more modern facilities in the Washington State Parks system and offers 40 RV sites with complete hookups, as well as restrooms and showers. It also offers several hundred yards of river access for anglers. Nearby Brinnon General Store has groceries, tackle, and fishing licenses. The Bayshore Motel is right on the highway at the intersection of Dosewallips Road for folks who want a permanent roof over their heads.

Directions: Drive north from Shelton on U.S. 101 to Dosewallips State Park or continue past the park and turn west (left) on Dosewallips Road to parallel the north side of the river for several miles.

Contact: Dosewallips State Park, 360/796-4415; Washington State Parks and Recreation Commission, 360/902-8844 (information) or 800/452-5687 (reservations); Brinnon General Store, 360/796-4400; Bayshore Motel, 800/488-4230.

106 Duckabush River

A quick look at the menu might lead you to think that the Duckabush is a pretty hot river, but the fishing is fair at best. Although both summer and winter steelhead do enter the river, they arrive in drips and trickles, not floods. Anglers catch half a dozen summer-runs and a dozen and a half winter-runs in a typical year. Fall chum salmon fishing is considerably better, but the season is short, lasting only about six weeks in November and December. Sea-run cutthroat fishing can also be productive, with September and October the best months. It used to be legal to keep hatchery cutthroats from the Duckabush, but since there are no hatchery cutthroats to catch, the Department of Fish and Wildlife finally got realistic and made the Duckabush a catch-and-release-only river for everything but hatchery steelhead and chums during the fall season.

The lower river has a lot of private land, greatly limiting angler access. If you're the adventurous and energetic type, drive up the road to about a mile past Collins Campground and hit the trail upriver to fish some

beautiful trout water. You won't find many trout over the minimum size limit of 12 inches, but you'll enjoy yourself.

Location: Enters Hood Canal near Pleasant Harbor; see map A2 Inset, grid h2.

Species: Chum salmon, winter and summer steelhead, sea-run cutthroat trout.

Facilities: A U.S. Forest Service campground is located about six miles upstream on Duckabush Road. There's also a ranger cabin that can be rented ($25 per night), located about four miles up Duckabush Road. Dosewallips State Park, about five miles north, has 40 RV sites with complete hookups, restrooms, and showers. Brinnon General Store on U.S. 101 at Brinnon has groceries, tackle, and fishing licenses. The Bayshore Motel, six miles away, offers the nearest lodging.

Directions: Drive north from Shelton on U.S. 101, cross the river, and turn west on Duckabush Road.

Contact: Olympic National Forest, Hood Canal Ranger Station, 360/765-2200; Dosewallips State Park, 360/796-4415; Bayshore Motel, 800/488-4230.

107 Upper Hood Canal

Salmon fishing prospects have improved considerably throughout Hood Canal since we produced the first edition of this book back in 1996. There are still problems, most notably with wild coho and summer chum runs that were once poured into Hood Canal tributaries by the tens of thousands, but other fisheries have come on strong in recent years, thanks mostly to heavy doses of hatchery salmon stocked to supplement the wild runs.

Anglers on this northern half of the canal don't benefit from the big hatchery salmon plants as much as those who fish waters to the south, but even here the fishing outlook is brighter than it was five or 10 years ago. There is, for example, a worthwhile coho fishery in Quilcene Bay and Dabob Bay that opens in mid-August and offers anglers the chance to catch up to four silvers a day. This productive fishery with the extra-large daily limit results in larger returns of hatchery coho bound for the Quilcene River. To the north, anglers often make good catches of salmon, especially chums, on the public fishing pontoon that runs alongside the Hood Canal Floating Bridge. Again, hatchery salmon bound for facilities near the southern end of the canal provide most of the action.

Fishing for immature blackmouth chinooks is fair in March, with much of the action coming from a few time-proven spots scattered along the east and west sides of the canal. Sprawling Dabob Bay is perhaps the best possibility. The west side of the bay, including Red Bluff, Point Whitney, and Jackson Cove, offers fair numbers of winter chinooks and is fairly well protected from the wind. Nearby access is available at Quilcene and Wawa Point. Mooching with plug-cut herring is most popular here, but both jigging and trolling will also take winter blackmouth. Other spots likely to produce a chinook or two from late fall to early spring include Hazel Point and Oak Head (both at the south end of the Toandos Peninsula) and Misery Point (near Seabeck).

Dabob Bay also offers some decent fishing opportunities for sea-run cutthroat trout, especially in the shallows around the edges of Quilcene and Tarboo Bays and Jackson Cove. The Dosewallips and Duckabush River estuaries also have sea-runs for anglers on the west side of the canal. On the east side, there's fair cutthroat fishing available from Seabeck Bay up to and including Big Beef Harbor. Chances are you could find sea-run cutts in many other places along both sides of the canal. If you feel a little adventurous, I recommend that you simply take off trolling along the beach anywhere, staying in 5 to 10 feet of water and paying special attention

wherever a small stream flows into the canal. Remember, though, that throughout Hood Canal you must release wild cutthroats and may kill only hatchery fish that sport at least one clipped fin.

Smaller rockfish, particularly coppers, are available almost wherever you can find shallow, rocky humps along the bottom. Many are caught accidentally by anglers fishing for salmon and cutthroats, but you can improve your chances of putting a couple of sweet, white-meat fillets in the deep fryer if you concentrate your efforts around rocky points and submerged reefs that offer the kinds of solid bottom structure these fish like. Do the same kind of prospecting in deeper water and you might find a yelloweye, canary, or other, larger, deep-water rockfish. Remember, though, that the one-fish limit on rockfish in effect throughout Puget Sound also applies here.

The steeper, deeper, more jagged rock bottoms will also produce lingcod, but remember that these big, toothy bottom dwellers are available only for about six weeks in May and June, and they're protected by very specific minimum and maximum size limits and other regulations. Lingcod habitat is limited in northern Hood Canal, but if you use your nautical chart and your depthsounder, you'll find a few. NOAA chart 18441 is a must for this kind of prospecting. If natural bottom-fish habitat fails to produce, you might try the man-made structure placed in Hood Canal specifically for that purpose. I'm talking about the artificial reef constructed near Misery Point by the Department of Fisheries. Its exact location is 600 feet north of the Misery Point navigational light, and it's marked by a buoy. Lingcod, greenling, cabezon, and several species of rockfish call it home.

While the salmon, lingcod, and other large glamour fish may be somewhat hard to find, it's accurate to say that the north end of Hood Canal has its share of overlooked angling possibilities. Smallish flounder and sole can be found over sand and gravel bottoms in virtually every bay and estuary along either side of the canal, and they'll hit anything from garden worms, pieces of herring, and salad shrimp to small metal jigs and leadheads with plastic grubs. Those worms and shrimp will also take pile perch and striped seaperch from around the many docks, wharves, and pilings that line much of the canal. Fish them on the incoming tide, especially where the rising waters are just beginning to reach the exposed woody structure.

Location: Foulweather Bluff south to Triton Head on the west side of the Kitsap Peninsula; see map A2 Inset, grid h3.

Species: Chinook and chum salmon, sea-run cutthroat trout, various rockfish, Pacific cod, pile perch and striped seaperch, various sole and flounder, a few lingcod.

Facilities: Boat ramps on both sides of the canal provide access to the north end of Hood Canal. They include:

- **Termination Point Ramp:** Starting at the north end of the canal, there's a two-lane concrete ramp near Shine Tidelands State Park, just north of the west end of the Hood Canal Floating Bridge. The ramp is tucked away in Bywater Bay at the end of Termination Point Road. Wood and other debris sometimes collect on and around this ramp, which has a $3 launch fee.

- **Hicks County Park Ramp:** This Jefferson County Parks ramp is near the entrance to Squamish Harbor, a mile and a half west of the Hood Canal Floating Bridge's west end off Shine Road. It's a single-lane concrete ramp with a gravel parking area for about a dozen cars and trailers. Driftwood and sand also pile up in front of this ramp, sometimes making it difficult to launch.

- **Salsbury Point Ramp:** Across the canal and immediately north of the floating bridge's east end is the three-lane concrete ramp at Salsbury Point County Park. This Kitsap County Parks and Recreation facility has loading floats, a large paved parking area, and restrooms.

- **Quilcene Marina:** The marina is on the west side of Quilcene Bay. This Port of Port Townsend facility has a one-lane concrete ramp with a loading float and a large gravel parking area. It's well protected from rough water and provides easy access to Dabob Bay. Quilcene Marina has limited open moorage, power to the docks, fuel, boat repairs, restrooms with showers, and boat-sewage pump-out facilities.

- **Point Whitney Ramp:** South of the entrance to Quilcene Bay is Point Whitney, where there's a single-lane ramp near the Department of Fish and Wildlife's shellfish research facility. Although there's a concrete ramp down there somewhere, it was buried under sand and gravel in 1998 and 1999, making it usable only for car-toppers and small trailer boats towed by four-wheel-drive vehicles. The parking area is also gravel. A sign near this ramp reminds boaters that the U.S. Navy sometimes tests torpedoes and "other underwater weapons" in Dabob Bay; when the red beacons light up, go elsewhere to launch.

- **Misery Point Ramp:** This Department of Fish and Wildlife ramp is a one-laner with a concrete surface and large, gravel parking area. This is another ramp where sand and gravel often get in the way of launching, but nearby Scenic Beach State Park makes this a handy ramp for camper-boaters visiting the north end of the canal. A $10 WDFW access decal is required to use this public launch area.

- **Triton Cove:** Formerly a private resort, Triton Cove is now a Washington State

Parks facility. This single-lane, concrete ramp has a loading float and dock, with room to park about two dozen cars and trailers. Watch for the large rock just out from the ramp, slightly to the south. There's a $3 launch fee, with an annual permit available for $40.

Seabeck Marina offers open moorage, fuel docks (gas only), restrooms, and restaurants. At Pleasant Harbor Marina you'll find guest and permanent moorage, power and water to the docks, fuel docks, a convenience store and deli, restrooms with showers, and other facilities. Camping facilities on and around the northern half of the canal include Dosewallips State Park (off U.S. 101 near the mouth of the Dosewallips River), Scenic Beach State Park (near Seabeck), and Kitsap Memorial State Park (at Lofall, south of the Hood Canal Floating Bridge).

Directions: Take U.S. 101 north about 11 miles from Shelton or south 10 miles from Discovery Bay to reach much of the west side of the canal. To reach Dabob Bay and the west side of the canal along the Toandos Peninsula, take Highway 104 to the west side of the Hood Canal Floating Bridge and turn south on South Point Road. To get to the east side of the canal, take Highway 3 or Highway 16 to Bremerton and drive north on Highway 3 to Seabeck Highway, which runs west to Warrenville and Seabeck. Another route is to continue north from Bremerton on Highway 3, which parallels the east shore of the canal from Kitsap Memorial State Park north to Port Gamble. Other roads off Highway 3 and Highway 104 provide further access to the canal's east side.

Contact: Quilcene Marina, 360/765-3131; Seabeck Marina, 360/830-5179; Dosewallips State Park, 360/796-4415; Cove Park, 360/796-4723; Scenic Beach State Park, 360/830-5079; Kitsap Memorial State Park, 360/779-3205;

Washington State Parks and Recreation Commission, 360/902-8844 (information) or 800/452-5687 (reservations). For nautical charts of this area, contact Captain's Nautical Supply, 206/283-7242.

108 Haller Lake

This 15-acre urban lake is open to year-round fishing, but your best chance to catch a couple of trout occurs in the spring, after the Department of Fish and Wildlife has stocked it with its annual plant of several hundred pan-sized rainbows. The bass fishing isn't worth a long trip from anywhere, but you might be able to catch enough decent-sized perch to keep you satisfied.

Location: North of Northgate; see map A2 Inset, grid i6.

Species: Rainbow trout, largemouth bass, yellow perch.

Facilities: The lake doesn't have a public access area as such, but it's possible to carry a boat to the water off North 125th Avenue or Meridian Street. Food, gas, tackle, and lodging are available at Northgate, a few blocks to the east.

Directions: Take I-5 to North 130th Street (Exit 174) and drive west half a mile to North 125th Avenue. Turn south (left), drive two blocks, and the lake will be on the left.

Contact: Wilderness Sports, 425/746-0500.

109 Island Lake

This is a very popular spot among Kitsap Peninsula trout anglers every spring, and you need only glance at a map to understand why. It's one of only two decent lakes on the entire peninsula north of Bremerton. The other is Buck Lake (see number 78), more than 20 miles away from the Bremerton population centers. Weekends and evenings get fairly busy here, but healthy plants of hatchery rainbows seem to provide enough trout to go around.

Despite the sometimes large crowds of anglers and the development along part of the shoreline, the lake still manages to maintain a natural feeling. That's due in part to the tree-covered island near its west side and no-gas-engines regulation that keeps boat noise down and the speeders away. Although Island is not a big lake, there's room here for anglers to try stillfishing, trolling, and fly-casting, and all three groups manage to catch their share of pan-sized rainbows.

Location: Northeast of Silverdale, map A2 inset, grid i4.

Species: Rainbow trout.

Facilities: There's a large Kitsap County park near the northwest corner of the lake, with restrooms, picnic tables, and a gravel beach. Farther down the west side of the lake is an extension of the park, with a boat ramp for car-toppers only. Between the two park sections is a walkway with a fishing pier that was completed in 1996.

Directions: Take Silverdale Way north from Silverdale to Bennington Drive northwest and turn east (right). Go down the hill a mile to the lake.

Contact: The Northwest Angler, 360/779-7100; Kitsap Sport Shop, Silverdale, 360/698-4808, website: www.kitsapsports.com.

110 Green Lake

A year-round season, generous plants of hatchery trout, and hundreds of thousands of people living within walking distance combine to make Green Lake one of the Northwest's most heavily fished bodies of water. Fishing spots don't get much more urban than this 255-acre lake almost in the heart of Seattle, but it provides surprisingly good angling opportunity throughout much of the year.

Annual plants of brown and rainbow trout sometimes top 20,000 fish, most of them in spring and early summer. Angling crowds are smaller and the trout fishing is often better in the fall than in the spring. Thousands of browns and rainbows are caught here on worms, salmon eggs, marshmallows, and other standard fare, but a surprising number of anglers stroll to the shores of Green Lake with fly rods in hand and spend the early morning or evening casting wet, dry, and nymph patterns.

Trout fishermen should benefit from the addition of triploid rainbow plants that were first made here in 2001. These fast-growing heavyweights should do well in the nutrient-rich waters of a lake that has a limitless supply of duck and goose crap. That reality may not do much for their reputation as table fare, but it's a sure thing the newly stocked triploids will be a hit with anglers who like to catch hefty trout.

According to local mythology, Green Lake is home to some lunker largemouth bass, but like the sophisticated urbanites who inhabit the dry land around them, the bass here have seen it all and aren't particularly agreeable to chomping down on just any old spinnerbait, plastic worm, or crankbait within striking distance. If you want to catch big bass here, finesse is the key.

Among the more recent additions to the Green Lake angling menu are two species you might not expect to find in a place like the middle of Seattle. Channel catfish are stocked from time to time in an apparent effort to keep things from getting too predictable, and even the big, toothy tiger muskie is a recent addition to the Green Lake ecosystem. It will be a few years before anyone catches a bragging-size tiger from the lake, but when it happens, watch out—the local television stations will turn out in droves!

Location: Within the city of Seattle; see map A2 Inset, grid i6.

Species: Rainbow and brown trout, largemouth bass, yellow perch, rock bass, channel catfish, brown bullhead catfish.

Facilities: Green Lake doesn't have a boat

ramp, but car-toppers and other small craft may be carried to the edge of the lake and launched. A concessionaire at the north end of the lake has boats for rent. There are several public fishing docks and piers around the lake, and bank fishing is a possibility in numerous locations. Downtown Seattle is only a few miles away, and all amenities are also found along Aurora Avenue (Highway 99).

Directions: Take Highway 99 north from Lake Union in Seattle, and at N.W. 65th Street watch for the lake on the east (right) side of the road.

Contact: Wilderness Sports, 425/746-0500; Patrick's Fly Shop, 206/325-8988.

111 Cottage Lake

Although stocked with hatchery rainbows, Cottage has a long history of being among western Washington's best possibilities for lunker largemouth bass. This big-bass potential went unrealized for nearly 15 years, when Cottage was locked up in private ownership without any public access. The lake reopened to public fishing again in 1992, and the lunker bass are once more within reach of most anglers. Bass fishing is best May throuh July, also the best months for crappies and catfish. Perch and trout bite well in the spring and fall.

Location: East of Woodinville; see map A2 Inset, grid h7.

Species: Rainbow trout, largemouth bass, yellow perch, crappie, brown bullhead catfish.

Facilities: The new King County park on the lake has fishing piers and a launch site for small boats (hand carry only). Food, gas, and tackle are available in Woodinville, and there are numerous motels along I-405.

Directions: Take I-405 to Highway 522 and head east to Woodinville. Turn east (right) on Woodinville-Duvall Road about a mile north of Woodinville and follow it three miles, watching for signs pointing south (right) to

the lake. If you come to Avondale Road, you've gone about a quarter of a mile too far.

Contact: Washington Department of Fish and Wildlife, Mill Creek Office, 425/775-1311; King County Parks and Recreation Department, 206/684-7050.

112 Tolt River

December, January, and February are the top months to fish this little Snoqualmie River tributary if you're looking for anything that resembles consistent fishing action. The Tolt is far short of a sure thing even then, but at least that's when the bulk of the adult steelhead from hatchery smolt plants usually return to the river.

Those plants, by the way, may vary considerably from year to year, which can have a drastic effect on steelheading success two years later. Plants in recent years have ranged from a low of 7,000 fish to a high of 25,000 fish. As for summer steelhead smolts, the river gets a few thousand some years, none at all other years. That might explain why the summer steelhead catch on the Tolt is barely worth talking about.

Special selective fishery regulations are in effect here during the general summer season, and parts of the river are open to catch-and-release fishing during this time. Be sure to read the regulations pamphlet before embarking on a summer trout or steelhead fishing trip to the Tolt.

Location: Flows into the Snoqualmie River near Carnation; see map A2 Inset, grid h9.

Species: Winter and summer steelhead, cutthroat trout.

Facilities: Those who want to fish from a drift boat or raft can launch at the upper end of Tolt River Road and take out at the mouth of the river near Carnation. Food and gas are available in Carnation, and tackle and lodging can be found in Monroe.

Directions: Take Highway 203 to Carnation

and turn east on Tolt River Road, which parallels the north side of the river.

Contact: Sky Valley Traders, 360/794-8818.

113 Langlois Lake

Stocked with 4,000 to 5,000 legal-sized rainbows each spring, Langlois is a favorite of east King County anglers for the first several weeks of the season, from late April to late May. Large crowds are on hand through May, especially on weekends, but by June the mobs thin out and it's time for serious anglers to give this trout factory a try. June, September, and October offer excellent opportunities for patient anglers to do battle with some real trophy-class trout. The fish missed or lost by early season anglers wise up quickly in this extremely clear lake, where visibility in the water may exceed 20 feet, and once they realize the dangers, they get extremely wary. They also tend to go deep, and in Langlois, "deep" means some spots of nearly 100 feet.

To catch lunker trout from the clear depths, try trolling or stillfishing with as light a leader as you dare, and plan on spending some time playing any hooked fish as long it takes. The rewards for doing everything right could well be a rainbow of four pounds or larger. If you're up to giving Langlois' trophy rainbows a try, you'll need a boat. The entire shoreline, except for the public access area, is privately owned, so bank fishing is a virtual impossibility.

Although generally overlooked, bass fishing is also a decent bet at Langlois. It occasionally gives up a largemouth in the two- or three-pound class, mostly to anglers fishing top-water offerings in the evening or to patient types working plastics or spinnerbaits around shoreline cover. Most of the Langlois bass, though, are fish of one pound or smaller.

Some years, but not all, Langlois receives a fairly generous planting of summer-run steelhead from a local hatchery. Needless to say,

those plants provide some genuine excitement for anglers who happen to be on hand afterwards.

Location: Southeast of Carnation; see map A2 Inset, grid h9.

Species: Rainbow trout, largemouth bass, steelhead.

Facilities: The lake has a public access area and boat ramp. Food, gas, and tackle are available in Carnation. Lodging can be found to the north in Monroe or to the south in Snoqualmie.

Directions: Take Highway 203 to Carnation and drive south through town. About a mile south of town, turn east (left) on Lake Langlois Road, also known as N.E. 24th Street, which runs about two miles to the east side of the lake.

Contact: Sky Valley Traders, 360/794-8818.

114 Lena Lakes

Lena Lake, the larger, lower one of the two, has lots of visitors during the summer hiking season, but most are not anglers or are casual anglers, so the serious trout enthusiast has a chance of taking a respectable trout or two for a few hours' effort. Brookies are more abundant, but if you catch a cutthroat or rainbow, it's likely to be a little larger. Evening fishing with a fly rod or fly-and-bubble combination on a spinning rod might be your best bet.

You'll break a sweat and do some huffing and puffing to reach Upper Lena, but the fishing might be worth the effort. Even if you don't catch trout, the scenery (especially the early summer wildflowers) will make the trip worthwhile. July, August, and September are prime fishing and viewing months.

Location: Near the Jefferson-Mason county line north of the Hamma Hamma River; see map A2 Inset, grid i1.

Species: Rainbow, cutthroat, and brook trout.

Facilities: Lena Creek Campground has 14

tent and RV sites, water, and vault toilets. The camping fee is $7 per night. Lena Lake has about 30 tent sites, plus vault toilets. There's no camping fee for this hike-in campground. There are also a few campsites at Upper Lena Lake. The nearest food, gas, and tackle are in Eldon, back on U.S. 101. Hoodsport and Shelton to the south have all amenities.

Directions: Drive north from Shelton on U.S. 101 and turn west (left) onto Forest Service Road 25 about 2.5 miles north of the Hamma Hamma River bridge. Follow Forest Service Road 25 about eight miles to Lena Creek Campground. From there it's a 2.5-mile hike to Lena Lake and more than four more steep miles to Upper Lena Lake.

Contact: Olympic National Forest, Hood Canal Ranger District, 360/877-5254.

115 Armstrong Lake

Though there's nothing to get excited about as far as hot fishing is concerned, Armstrong is a nice little lake for escaping from the crowds. At less than five acres—and far enough off the road to avoid detection by casual passers-by—Armstrong is fished primarily by a few regulars from Mason and Jefferson Counties. Pack your float tube to the edge of the lake, and you can easily reach all the spots with lots of fish. Try it with a fly rod and selection of small, dry patterns during a late-spring evening, and you'll have some fun with smallish trout. Be sure to take along your insect repellent—the mosquitoes here are the size of bats.

Location: West of U.S. 101 and north of Eldon in Mason County; see map A2 Inset, grid i1.

Species: Cutthroat and brook trout.

Facilities: There's nothing at the lake except bank-fishing access. The nearest food, gas, tackle, and lodging are back on U.S. 101.

Directions: Drive north from Shelton on U.S. 101 and turn west on Forest Service Road 25

about two miles north of Eldon. Take the first gravel road to the right (about two miles up Forest Service Road 25) and follow it just under two miles to the lake, which is on the right after you've passed under a big power line and just before the road goes under the line a second time.

Contact: Eldon Store, 360/877-5374.

116 Hamma Hamma River

This has become a catch-and-release-only stream, almost not worth mentioning in a fishing book anymore. It does have pretty strong runs of chum salmon, but the Hamma Hamma is closed to all salmon fishing, so forget the chums if you're looking for fishing action. Fair numbers of sea-run cutthroats offer decent catch-and-release possibilities beginning in August, but the river closes to fishing for awhile on August 31, so cutthroat fishing is virtually eliminated. During past years, the Hamma Hamma received small plants of hatchery rainbows, but in 1997 those plants were discontinued, so catching a rainbow now would be a rare accomplishment. The river isn't stocked with hatchery steelhead smolts, and it shows; anglers catch only a handful of winter steelies each season.

Location: Flows into west side of Hood Canal at Eldon; see map A2 Inset, grid i1.

Species: Sea-run and resident cutthroat trout, rainbow trout, a few winter steelhead.

Facilities: The U.S. Forest Service's Hamma Hamma Campground on the north bank of the river has 15 tent and RV sites, vault toilets, and drinking water. There's also a Forest Service cabin six miles upriver, available for $25 a night (up to six people). Food, gas, and tackle are available at the tiny town of Eldon, with lodging in Hoodsport and Shelton.

Directions: Drive north from Shelton on U.S. 101 and turn left on Forest Service Road 24 (Jorsted Creek Road) or Forest Service Road

25 to reach upper sections of the river from the south or north side. If you take Forest Service Road 24, turn right on Forest Service Road 2480 to reach the river. A short section of the lower river is accessible from U.S. 101, near the highway bridges.

Contact: Olympic National Forest, Hood Canal Ranger District, 360/877-5254; Eldon Store, 360/877-5374.

117 Wildcat Lake

Heavy plants of hatchery rainbows and the possibility of mixed-bag catches help to make this 110-acre lake near Bremerton one of Kitsap County's most popular. It's stocked with more than 8,000 legal-sized rainbows every spring before the opener, and occasional plants of sea-run cutthroats and pan-sized coho salmon keep the trout catch from becoming too predictable. Trout anglers are most likely to catch fish in the 8- to 10-inch range in the spring, but fall fish run about a foot apiece, and there's always the chance for a carryover rainbow of 15 inches or larger.

If you prefer warm-water fish to salmonids, work your way slowly and carefully around Wildcat's many docks and floats for a crack at largemouth bass. Although not common, bass to four pounds and better can sometimes be found here. Summertime fishing during the evening and dead of night provides fair fishing for brown bullheads.

Location: Northwest of Bremerton; see map A2 Inset, grid i3.

Species: Rainbow and cutthroat trout, coho salmon, largemouth bass, brown bullhead catfish.

Facilities: The lake has a large public access area with a concrete boat ramp and a gravel ramp alongside it, plus pit toilets and plenty of room for bank anglers. Scenic Beach State Park is about 10 miles to the northwest. Food, gas, tackle, and lodging are available in Bremerton.

Directions: Drive north out of Bremerton on Highway 3 and turn west on the Seabeck Highway. Go about six miles and turn west (left) on Holly Road. Drive half a mile to Lakeview Road, turn south (left), and drive to the north side of the lake.

Contact: Washington Department of Fish and Wildlife, Montesano Office, 360/249-4628.

118 Kitsap Lake

Although the largest crowds of trout anglers turn out here in the spring, some folks will tell you that fall is the best time of year to fish for Kitsap Lake's rainbows and cutthroats. This large, 240-acre lake is open to year-round fishing and isn't heavily stocked with trout, so many people try it once or twice in the spring, find only fair fishing, and give up. The result is a light spring harvest and plenty of trout still around when the water begins to cool in the fall. You might find a two-pound rainbow here in September or October, and some of the cutthroats grow even larger.

As for bass, Kitsap has a pretty good reputation as a largemouth producer. There are lots of docks and floats to investigate around most of the lake's shoreline, but I hardly ever get past the fishy-looking water along the brushy, grassy south end of the lake. It has "The bass are right here!" written all over it, and I just can't resist. It's a great place to cast top-water plugs early in the morning and during the last hour of the evening. Those hours are the best times to fish Kitsap Lake during the summer months, when water-skiers, personal watercraft riders, and other hot-rodders are not all over the lake.

The lake has some large bluegills, which will hit jigs or Beetlespins best in May and June. Those are also good months to fish night crawlers or worms at night for brown bullheads.

Location: Immediately west of Bremerton; see map A2 Inset, grid i4.

Species: Rainbow and cutthroat trout, largemouth bass, brown bullhead catfish, bluegill.

Facilities: There's a blacktop public access area with restrooms and a two-lane boat ramp at the southwest corner of the lake. Kitsap Lake Park on the west side of the lake has a boat ramp, lots of bank fishing, and restrooms. Bremerton has food, gas, tackle, and lodging.

Directions: Take the Seabeck Highway west out of Bremerton and turn south (left) on East Kitsap Lake Road a mile from town or West Kitsap Lake Road two miles from town.

Contact: Washington Department of Fish and Wildlife, Montesano Office, 360/249-4628.

119 Lake Washington

It's too bad salmon fishing isn't as good here as it used to be, because with all the other things this lake has to offer, summertime salmon action would make it one of western Washington's best all-around angling spots. Depending on the year, there are still times when salmon fishing is a possibility, but it's no longer something anglers can depend on. We saw, for example, a good sockeye fishery here in 2000, but in 2001 the numbers didn't materialize so there was no season. Chinook and coho seasons have been nonexistent here since 1997. Most everyone knows that the best way to catch sockeye is with a bare red hook trolled behind a large flasher, but not everyone is aware that coho and chinook (when either is legal game) can be caught quite readily on a metal jig twitched vertically wherever you can locate a small school of fish with your depthsounder.

That said, let's talk about the more dependable fishing on Lake Washington. Trout fishing can pay big rewards, especially in the spring and fall, since there are some hefty rainbows and cutthroats inhabiting the lake. Both sometimes grow to 20 inches or larger. Unfortunately, rainbows over 20 inches have to be released. That's right, released, because steelhead fishing is closed here, and rainbows over 20 inches are considered steelhead. To catch a lunker cutthroat or rainbow, try trolling on the north side of the Highway 520 bridge or the I-90 bridge, but don't get too close; regulations require anglers to stay at least 100 yards from either structure. The shallow flats near the north end of the lake at Kenmore can also be productive trolling grounds for big trout. Other good trolling possibilities include the East Channel near the mouth of Kelsey Creek, the Mercer Slough, Rainier Beach, and virtually all the way around Mercer Island. If stillfishing is your preference, try fishing worms, red salmon eggs, marshmallows, or Power Bait at Waverly Park in Kirkland. Of all the fishing docks on the lake, it seems to provide the best trout action. Other possibilities include Logboom Park in Kenmore, Houghton Beach Park in Kirkland, and Chism Park in Bellevue.

Not much is left in the way of largemouth bass cover in the lake, except for the many docks and floats around its shoreline and the network of sloughs and shallow bays in and around the Washington Park Arboretum on the south side of Union Bay. This area offers lots of lily pads, submerged logs and stumps, old pilings, and other prime largemouth cover.

Smallmouth bass also inhabit the lake, but you probably won't find a lot of them in any one place. Try casting in spring and summer around docks and pilings and any of the many gravel beaches and rocky areas that dot the shoreline. All the shoreline development and the creation of smooth gravel beaches that eliminated largemouth habitat around this lake was better suited to the needs of the smallmouth, and they flourish in all those man-made gravel beds, concrete bulkheads, and other rocky structures.

Yellow perch may not be considered an angling highlight on most Northwest lakes, but

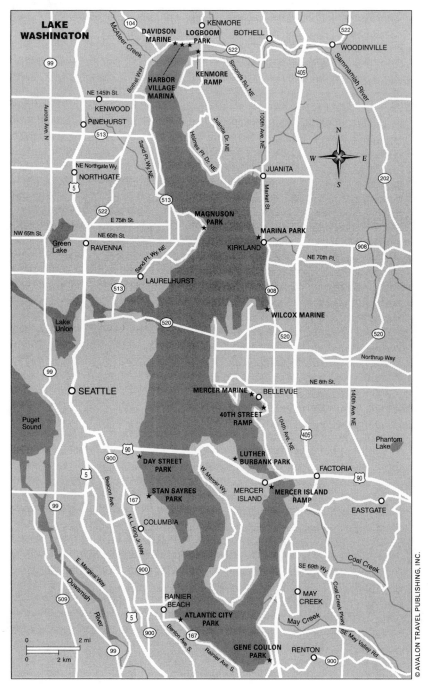

LAKE WASHINGTON

© AVALON TRAVEL PUBLISHING, INC.

they are here, because they grow to extremely impressive size. It isn't at all unusual to catch 12-inch perch from Lake Washington, and fish of 15 inches or larger are within the realm of possibility. Since perch of similar age and size often school together, you may be in big-fish perch business if you can locate the right spots. The best big-perch action is in the fall, from October to December, and some of the best fishing is in the northern part of the lake. Try a small leadhead jig with a piece of worm on the hook, or if the perch are quite deep, put a piece of worm on the hook of a Crippled Herring, Hopkins No=EQL, or similar jigging spoon and work it vertically through the depths.

Location: Immediately east of Seattle; see map A2 Inset, grid i6.

Species: Rainbow and cutthroat trout; largemouth and smallmouth bass; yellow perch; chinook, coho, and sockeye salmon.

Facilities: Boat ramps are located at Kenmore, Juanita Creek, Holmes Point, Moss Bay, Sweyolocken Park, Newport Shores, Gene Coulon Park, Cedar River Trail, Atlantic City Park, South Ferdinand Street Park, Stan Sayres Park, the west end of the I-90 bridge, Sunnyside Avenue, and Magnuson Park. More than two dozen parks and fishing docks provide access for shore-bound anglers. Food, gas, tackle, and lodging are available in Kirkland, Bellevue, Renton, and Seattle.

Directions: There are so many ways to get to so many access points on this huge lake that it's impossible to list them all here. One is to take I-405 north to Kirkland and turn west (left) on Central Way. Turn north on Market Street to reach some of the more northerly parts of the lake or turn south on Lake Washington Boulevard (which eventually becomes Bellevue Way) to reach fishing docks, parks, and boat ramps along the rest of the lake's east side.

Contact: Washington Department of Fish and Wildlife, Mill Creek Office, 425/775-1311.

120 Phantom Lake

Though overshadowed by nearby Lake Sammamish (see number 121), this 63-acre lake is a good bass lake in its own right. Open throughout the year, it's at its best from April to June, when it commonly gives up largemouths in the two- to three-pound range. A slot limit protects 12- to 17-inch bass from harvest.

Just in case you can't get the bass to hit, bring along a light spinning rod so you can spend a little time catching some of the lake's chunky crappies and yellow perch. Both can be caught on small leadheads with red-and-white plastic skirts. Add a small piece of worm to the jig and the perch will hit even faster. Night fishing is fair for foot-long catfish from May to September.

Location: Immediately west of Lake Sammamish; see map A2 Inset, grid i7.

Species: Largemouth bass, crappie, yellow perch, brown bullhead catfish.

Facilities: A Bellevue city park on the west side of the lake has a small fishing dock, and boats can be launched there. Before launching, you must get a launch permit from the Bellevue Parks Department. Food, gas, tackle, and lodging are available in Bellevue.

Directions: Take I-405 to Bellevue and turn east (right) on N.E. Eighth Street. Drive about 2.5 miles to 156th Avenue and turn south (right). Follow 156th Avenue just under two miles to the lake, which is on the left.

Contact: Bellevue City Parks, 425/455-6881; Washington Department of Fish and Wildlife, Mill Creek Office, 425/775-1311.

121 Lake Sammamish

The most important thing you need to know about Lake Sammamish is that the boat ramp at the state park isn't open 24 hours, so if you want to launch before daylight or fish until after dark, you should use one of the private parks instead. The second thing you should know is that Sammamish is western

Washington's premier smallmouth bass lake. Although these bronzeback fighters have been in the lake many years and there's absolutely no secret about it, Sammamish continues to provide good smallmouth fishing for those willing to work at it a little. The many old pilings and submerged trees around the south end of the lake are especially productive places to search for smallies. But fish may also be found around any of the dozens of docks and floats on the lake or over many of the gravel-bottom beaches where homeowners and Washington State Parks have dumped tons of sand and gravel to turn the once-muddy lake bottom into an environment more pleasing to human water lovers. While all this development has eliminated a lot of the largemouth habitat the lake once had, it's almost perfect for smallmouths. As for what to use, try small leadheads with green, gray, or clear plastic skirts to imitate the salmon fry on which Sammamish smallmouths have grown accustomed to feeding. The clean, generally snag-free bottom is also conducive to casting crankbaits, and be sure to take along at least a couple with crawfish finishes.

Many of the big lily pad beds and other vegetation that used to make Sammamish a topnotch largemouth lake are gone, but it's still possible to catch one here and there. Some of the bass caught are big ones, weighing in at three pounds or larger.

Sammamish is home to some big, beautiful cutthroat trout, some of them topping 20 inches and weighing well over two pounds. Casting or trolling Needlefish, Canadian Wonders, Dick Nites, and other minnow-imitating wobblers will take them, as will trolling night crawlers behind a string of trolling blades or stillfishing with night crawlers.

Location: Northwest of Issaquah; see map A2 Inset, grid i7.

Species: Cutthroat trout, smallmouth and largemouth bass, yellow perch, brown bullhead catfish.

Facilities: A 10-lane boat ramp, floats, and bank-fishing access are all at the state park, which encompasses the lake's entire south end. There's room to launch about 10 boats at a time at this expansive ramp. Vasa Park, a private operation near the southwest corner of the lake, also has a boat ramp, docks, and bank fishing. Food, gas, tackle, and lodging are available in Bellevue and Issaquah.

Directions: Take Exit 15 off I-90 and turn north (over the freeway if you're eastbound). Follow S.E. 56th Street one mile to East Lake Sammamish Parkway, turn north (left), and drive one mile to the boat launch sign on the left.

Contact: Washington Department of Fish and Wildlife, Mill Creek Office, 425/775-1311; Lake Sammamish State Park, 425/455-7010; Washington State Parks and Recreation Commission, 360/902-8844; Sammamish Guide Service, 425/392-6827; Vasa Park, 425/746-3260.

122 Pine Lake

With sprawling Lake Sammamish less than two miles away, you might expect Pine Lake to be overlooked by King County anglers, but it gets at least its share of fishing pressure during its April through October season. For Issaquah anglers, Pine is the nearest lake with spring plants of legal-sized hatchery trout, a big draw in and of itself. Although the plants usually total only about 1,000 fish, they include both rainbows and cutthroats for variety. A few trout somehow manage to survive the early season festivities and hang around long enough to provide fair fall fishing. That's perhaps the best time to fish specifically for cutts, and good places to find them are around the lake's three inlet streams, located at the southwest, southeast, and northeast corners of the lake.

Although brown trout aren't common, Pine does offer anglers the possibility of catching a hefty brown of three pounds or better. Perhaps of greater interest to anglers was the introduction in 2001 of several hundred fast-growing triploid rainbows, fish that entered the lake at over a pound and which will grow to several pounds if not caught during the first year or so they're in the lake.

Pine offers pretty good bass fishing in the spring and fall, especially in and around the shallow bays at the lake's southeast and southwest corners. Water in both is well under 10 feet, so it warms fast in the spring and tends to draw a bulk of the spawning bass during May and early June.

Location: North of Issaquah; see map A2 Inset, grid i8.

Species: Rainbow and cutthroat trout, a few brown trout, largemouth bass.

Facilities: A King County park on the east side of the lake provides beach access, restrooms, picnic tables, a partly covered fishing pier, and a place to launch car-top boats. Park hours are 8 A.M. to 8:30 P.M. Food, gas, tackle, and lodging are available in Issaquah, three miles south of the lake.

Directions: Take Exit 15 off I-90 and turn north (over the freeway if you're eastbound). Follow S.E. 56th Street one mile to East Lake Sammamish Parkway, turn north (left), and drive just over a mile to 43rd Way. Turn right on 43rd Way and follow it up the hill 2.5 miles to the Pine Lake County Park entrance on the left.

Contact: Washington Department of Fish and Wildlife, Mill Creek Office, 425/775-1311.

123 Beaver Lake

Long a favorite of King County trout anglers and stocked with liberal doses of hatchery rainbows every spring, Beaver has also gained a well-deserved reputation for its fine largemouth bass fishing. This is actually a small chain of connected lakes, with the largest of the bunch getting the bulk of the attention from anglers. The smaller lakes at either end of the big lake are also worth investigating, especially for bass and panfish. The best trout fishing is in May and September, while top months for bass, perch, and bullheads are June, July, and August.

Location: Northwest of Fall City; see map A2 Inset, grid i8.

Species: Rainbow trout, largemouth bass, yellow perch, brown bullhead catfish.

Facilities: The east side of the lake has a public access area with a boat ramp and toilets. Food, gas, tackle, and lodging are readily available in and around Issaquah.

Directions: Take I-90 to Issaquah and drive north out of town on Issaquah–Fall City Road. Signs pointing north about three miles out of town lead the way to the lake, which is 1.5 miles north of Issaquah–Fall City Road.

Contact: Sky Valley Traders, 360/794-8818.

124 Snoqualmie River

Hatchery winter steelhead bound for the steelhead facility on Tokul Creek are the biggest draw to the Snoqualmie, and much of the fishing pressure occurs from Fall City upstream. The short stretch of river from the mouth of Tokul Creek to Fall City often produces hundreds of winter-runs from December to March, with both bank and boat anglers sharing in the fun. Many of the boaters backtroll Hot Shots, Wiggle Warts, and other diving plugs, but drift fishing with roe, shrimp, and various drift bobbers also produces winter steelies. The bulk of the hatchery run returns early in the winter, and December and January provide the best fishing. The Snoqualmie receives about 150,000 winter steelhead smolts a year to keep things hopping.

Hatchery plants of summer steelhead aren't so liberal, totaling only about 30,000 smolts a year, but that's enough to provide anglers with the chance to catch 400 to 500 of these sunburn steelies every summer. Unlike many Northwest summer steelhead streams, the

Snoqualmie provides fairly consistent action June to October, giving anglers plenty of time to get their summer-run fix.

Although anglers in search of bigger game don't think much about it, there's a fairly productive trout fishery on the upper reaches of the Snoqualmie above the famous Snoqualmie Falls. Salmon and steelhead don't get past the falls, and the fisheries on the Upper and Lower Snoqualmie are as different as night and day. I-90 crosses the South Fork Snoqualmie near North Bend and parallels it much of the way to the Snoqualmie Pass summit. The North Fork Snoqualmie is accessible via Weyerhaeuser Company roads out of Snoqualmie, while the Middle Fork is reached by logging roads running east from North Bend.

As in many western Washington rivers, mountain whitefish are fairly abundant but generally overlooked. There's a special winter season (no trout allowed) December through March for them on the upper river and all forks.

Location: Joins the Skykomish River southwest of Monroe; see map A2 Inset, grid i8.

Species: Winter and summer steelhead, cutthroat trout, mountain whitefish.

Facilities: There are access points of various quality in several places along the river, including Duval, the mouth of the Tolt River, midway between Carnation and Fall City off Highway 202, the mouth of the Raging River, and just below the mouth of Tokul Creek, all on the main Snoqualmie. On the South Fork there are rough put-in spots for kayaks and other small boats at the 436th Avenue bridge in North Bend and at Olallie/Twin Falls State Park. Similar rough launches are available on the Middle Fork Snoqualmie at the concrete bridge on Middle Fork Road, at the end of Tanner Road SE, and at the bridge in North Bend where Ballarat Road crosses the river. Food and gas are available in Fall City. Lodging and tackle can be found in Snoqualmie

and North Bend.

Directions: Take I-90 to Preston and drive north four miles to Fall City, or take Highway 202 from Redmond east 14 miles to Fall City, cross the river, and either turn right and continue on Highway 202 upstream or turn left and take Highway 203 downstream.

Contact: Sky Valley Traders, 360/794-8818.

125 Raging River

This small, fast-moving river that flows under I-90 gets almost as little notice from Washington's anglers as it does from the thousands of travelers who race east or west along the busy freeway above it. That's not difficult to understand, since access to the river is limited, good fishing water is relatively scarce, and returning steelhead runs are only a fraction of what they are in some of the area's bigger and more popular rivers.

Still, thanks primarily to hatchery plants ranging from 5,000 to 10,000 smolts per year, the Raging does give up a few dozen winter-run steelhead and a handful of summer steelies every year. The most readily accessible part of the river is the several-hundred-foot stretch immediately above where the Raging enters the Snoqualmie. Fish it with eggs, shrimp, small bobbers, bobber-and-yarn, or eggs-and-yarn combinations. And remember that in some places, especially if there's been a day or two of rain, the Raging lives up to its name. If you hook a hefty steelhead at the tail end of a small pole and it takes off downstream, you'd better have on your running shoes.

Location: Joins the Snoqualmie River at Fall City; see map A2 Inset, grid i9.

Species: Winter and summer steelhead.

Facilities: Food, gas, tackle, and lodging are available in Fall City and Snoqualmie.

Directions: Take I-90 to Preston and turn north onto Preston–Fall City Road, which parallels the river.

Contact: Sky Valley Traders, 360/794-8818.

126 Lake Alice

Variety and fairly generous plants from Department of Fish and Wildlife hatcheries help to make this small lake just north of I-90 very popular among King County anglers. It's possible to catch rainbows, cutts, and brookies all in the same day, especially if you confine your fishing efforts to the fairly shallow water around the lake's shoreline during spring and early summer. As is usually the case in Northwest lakes, the brook trout are small here, but planted cutthroats run close to a pound apiece, and carryover rainbows of a pound and a half or larger are more common than you might expect from a lake of only about 25 acres.

And, as if all that trout-fishing variety weren't enough, there are also largemouth bass to about three pounds here to be hooked. They'll take all the usual bass stuff, so throw a few spinnerbaits, top-water plugs, or plastic worms into your tackle box before heading this way.

Location: South of Fall City; see map A2 Inset, grid i9.

Species: Rainbow, cutthroat, and brook trout; largemouth bass.

Facilities: The east side of the lake has a Department of Fish and Wildlife public access area with a boat ramp and pit toilets. Food, gas, tackle, and lodging are available in Fall City, Snoqualmie, and North Bend.

Directions: Take Highway 202 or Preston–Fall City Road from I-90 to Fall City. Drive south from Fall City on Lake Alice Road SE about three miles to the lake.

Contact: Sky Valley Traders, 360/794-8818.

127 Tokul Creek

This is one of the few places I know of where anglers are not only allowed but invited to fish for anadromous fish within a few yards of their destination at a state-operated hatchery facility. As you might guess, there's nothing particularly charming or aesthetically pleasing about this fishery, with anglers crowding the shores of the rushing creek, trying to head off adult steelhead as they fight their way upstream toward the hatchery. This steelhead fishery has some of the earmarks of shooting fish in a barrel, but it's more challenging.

Tokul Creek goes like hell between the fishing boundary and the stream's confluence with the Snoqualmie River, with nothing that looks like the holding water familiar to most steelheaders. The fast water also makes for tricky fish-fighting conditions; it's often a matter of setting the hook and then sprinting downstream in an attempt to keep up with the racing steelhead. Several hundred fish are caught this way each winter from Tokul Creek. December and January are usually the top months to fish it. In fact, they're two of only four months when you *can* fish the creek; it's open to fishing only during the December to March winter steelhead season.

Location: Enters the Snoqualmie River southeast of Fall City; see map A2 Inset, grid i9.

Species: Winter steelhead.

Facilities: Food and gas are available in Fall City. The nearest lodging is in Snoqualmie and North Bend, and the closest tackle is in North Bend.

Directions: Take I-90 to Preston and drive north to Fall City or take Highway 202 from Redmond to Fall City, cross the river, and turn right to continue on Highway 202 upstream to Tokul Creek.

Contact: Sky Valley Traders, 360/794-8818.

128 Mildred Lakes

You'll earn your fish here, not because they're wise ol' trophies that know every trick in the book, but because the hike into these lakes is a real expedition. You can lose the trail if you aren't paying attention, especially after reaching the first lake and forging on to find the other two. The westernmost lake is the largest and most productive, but it also requires the longest hike. Since the round-trip to these high-country lakes is about 10 miles, you'll need at least a weekend to fish them and still enjoy the scenery, which is as good as it gets anywhere. I recommend giving yourself three days and two nights just so you have plenty of fishing time.

Take along a selection of Panther Martin or Bang Tail spinners, a few plastic floats, and several fly patterns, and you should catch trout. Casting bubble-and-fly combos should work best in the evening.

Location: Headwaters of the Hamma Hamma River in the Mount Skokomish Wilderness; see map A2 Inset, grid i0.

Species: Cutthroat and brook trout.

Facilities: These are hike-in lakes with no developed facilities. Several good primitive camping spots can be found around the lakes. The nearest food, gas, tackle, and lodging are in Hoodsport back on U.S. 101.

Directions: Drive north from Shelton on U.S. 101 and turn west (left) on Forest Service Road 25, which runs along the north side of the Hamma Hamma River. Stay on Forest Service Road 25 all the way to its end at the concrete bridge over the Hamma Hamma; hit the trail, hiking the last four-plus miles to the first of the three lakes.

Contact: Olympic National Forest Headquarters, 360/956-2400.

129 Elk and Jefferson Lakes

You have to do quite a lot of driving but very little walking to reach these high lakes on the east side of the Olympic National Forest. They hold a mix of smallish trout that will, on a good day in June and July, take bait, hardware, or artificial flies. A small boat or float tube is very helpful in fishing these waters. The lakes are far enough off the highway that many anglers like to double their fishing opportunities by visiting both on the same trip. I always do.

Location: West of Eldon in Mason County; see map A2 Inset, grid i1.

Species: Brook, cutthroat, and rainbow trout.

Facilities: The nearest tent and RV sites are at Hamma Hamma Campground, about five miles north on Forest Service Road 25. The closest food, tackle, and gas are in Eldon on U.S. 101. Hoodsport has lodging.

Directions: Drive north on U.S. 101 from Shelton and turn west (left) on Jorsted Creed Road (Forest Service Road 24). Drive 1.5 miles on Forest Service Road 2480 and follow it several miles to Forest Service Road 2441. Turn south (left) and drive 2.6 miles to a short spur road on the right. Elk Lake is less than 100 yards down a well-used trail. Drive another four miles past Elk Lake to Jefferson Lake on the left.

Contact: Olympic National Forest, Hood Canal Ranger District, 360/877-5254.

130 Lake Cushman

The most exciting thing about Lake Cushman may be that its bull trout population, which spawns above the lake in the Upper North Fork Skokomish River, has been making a slow but steady recovery in recent years, offering the possibility of a bull trout fishery once again occurring in this 4,000-acre impoundment. Overfishing and illegal snagging almost wiped out this run of huge char—some of which top 10 pounds—but they're responding well to fishing closures and other measures that have been in place for several years to protect them. The Department of Fish and Wildlife hasn't made any promises yet, but if and when it decides to open the fishery again, these trophy-class fish with a taste for smaller fish will be susceptible to large wobbling spoons and plugs trolled through the depths. They would never provide hot fishing action, but it would only take one 10-pounder to make your day.

In the meantime, kokanee salmon and cutthroat trout continue to provide most of the angling action on Lake Cushman. Both fisheries have been up and down in recent years. Most kokanee here are caught by trollers, with worms, maggots, or white corn usually added to the hooks of a Wedding Ring or similar spinner, which in turn is pulled behind a string of larger trolling blades. As in most kokanee fishing, locating a school and keeping your bait at the proper depth are the keys to success.

Cutthroats are often caught on the same rigs used by kokanee anglers throughout the spring and summer. But in fall, after the kokanee fishery has come to an end, cutthroat fishing remains a productive possibility, especially for anglers trolling Dick Nites, Triple Teazers, and similar wobbling spoons.

Location: Northwest of Hoodsport in Mason County; see map A2 Inset, grid j0.

Species: Cutthroat trout, a few brook and rainbow trout, kokanee and chinook salmon, largemouth bass.

Facilities: There are three boat ramps on the east side of the lake, one a Department of Fish and Wildlife ramp near the south end, one at Lake Cushman Resort a little farther north, and a third at Lake Cushman State Park. Lake Cushman Resort has cabins, RV and tent sites, a grocery store, and moorage floats. Lake Cushman State Park offers about 60 tent sites and 30 RV sites with full hookups, as well as restrooms, showers, and an RV pump-out facility. Lake Cushman Grocery just west of the lake has food and some tackle. Other amenities are in Hoodsport.

Directions: Take U.S. 101 to Hoodsport, turn west on Highway 119 (Lake Cushman Road), and follow it about five miles to the lake, which is on the left.

Contact: Lake Cushman Resort, 360/877-9630, website: www.lakecushman.com; Lake Cushman State Park, 360/877-5491.

▊131▊ Price (Price's) Lake

Big, shallow Price Lake is full of brush, weeds, stumps, and some of Mason County's largest trout. Don't bother bringing your bobber-and-worm rigs along, though, because the lake has selective-fishery regulations requiring anglers to use artificial lures and flies with barbless hooks only. And you don't even need to bring your creel or your cooler, because this is strictly a catch-and-release fishery. That helps to explain why there are a few 20- to 24-inch trout available to Price Lake anglers. But even if you get skunked, this is one of those places where you won't really mind. The peace, quiet, and lack of shoreline development are enough to make the trip well worth the effort. Bank access is tough, so bring along your float tube or a small boat that's light enough to be carried to the water's edge. Fishing can be excellent in spring and fall.

Location: West of Lilliwaup in Mason County; see map A2 Inset, grid i0.

Species: Rainbow, cutthroat, and brook trout.

Facilities: No facilities are available at the lake, but Lake Cushman State Park has tent and RV sites, showers, and restrooms. Lake Cushman Resort and Lake Cushman Grocery are near the south end of the lake, and food, gas, tackle, and lodging are available in Hoodsport.

Directions: Take U.S. 101 to Hoodsport, turn west onto Highway 119 (Lake Cushman Road), and drive exactly 7.7 miles, passing Lake Cushman State Park. About half a mile past the park, turn right onto a gravel logging road. The road splits, and you'll want to stay to the left, following it about two miles to a wide spot in the road that serves as a parking area. Take the trail from the parking area about one-eighth of a mile to the lake.

Contact: Lake Cushman State Park, 360/877-5491; Lake Cushman Resort, 360/877-9630, website: www.lakecushman.com; Nelson's Tru Value Hardware, 360/877-9834.

132 Melbourne Lake

Visit Melbourne Lake in the spring to see the wild rhododendrons in bloom, but not for the great fishing. As with most cutthroat fisheries, Melbourne starts off slowly, and many early-season anglers give up on it before it comes to life. Those who fish it in late April and May find only fair fishing, but those who wait until summer or fall often make good catches of 10- to 14-inch cutts. With no boat ramp and limited shoreline access, this shallow, 35-acre lake is well suited to fishing from a float tube, canoe, or small inflatable.

Although pristine and well off the beaten path, the lake does draw some slobs, especially on holiday weekends. The boom-box and beer-bust crowd rolls in to shatter the solitude now and then. After Labor Day, though, you should find peace and quiet.

Location: Northwest of Lilliwaup in Mason County; see map A2 Inset, grid i1.

Species: Cutthroat trout.

Facilities: There's absolutely nothing at the lake except a few spots along the shore where you can carry or drag a small boat to the water and a couple of rough tent sites around the edge of the lake. The nearest food, gas, tackle, and lodging are in Hoodsport.

Directions: Drive north from Shelton on U.S. 101 and turn west (left) on Jorsted Creek Road (Forest Service Road 24). Drive 5.8 miles and turn left onto the rough road leading down the hill toward the lake. Stay on this road two miles and watch for the lake on your right, just past the second road to the right.

Contact: Olympic National Forest, Hood Canal Ranger District, 360/877-5254.

133 Kokanee Lake

Also known as Lower Cushman, this 150-acre reservoir is in some ways a miniature version of the real Lake Cushman (number 130) immediately upstream. Narrow and fairly deep, it holds a few large trout that anglers seldom hook. Planted rainbows—some 4,000 of them in a typical year—provide most of the catch. All the usual baits and lures come into play here, but most of the locals prefer to troll gang-troll-and-worm rigs for their fish. May, June, and October are best for trout, with kokanee biting best in July and August. Don't use your big outboard on this lake; it has a 7.5-horsepower maximum for boat motors.

Location: West of Hoodsport in Mason County; see map A2 Inset, grid j0.

Species: Rainbow and cutthroat trout, kokanee.

Facilities: There's a small Department of Fish and Wildlife boat ramp with limited bank access near the dam at the south end of the lake. You'll need that WDFW $10 access decal to use the ramp/access area. Lake Cushman Resort is less than three miles to the north, and Lake Cushman State Park is about six miles north. Lake Cushman Grocery is right across Highway 119 a mile from the lake. Food, gas, tackle, and lodging are available in Hoodsport.

Directions: Take U.S. 101 to Hoodsport and turn west onto Highway 119 (Lake Cushman Road). Drive just under three miles to Cushman-Potlatch Road and turn left. Go just under a mile to Lower Lake Road, turn right, and drive down the hill to the boat ramp near the south end of the lake.

Contact: Lake Cushman Resort, 360/877-9630, website: www.lakecushman.com; Lake Cushman State Park, 360/877-5491.

134 Skokomish River

The first time I ever fished the Skoke I was impressed, but not as impressed as steelheading companion Dave Borden, who hooked and landed a pair of bright January steelhead within an hour of parking alongside the river and starting to cast. We were returning from a fishless trip to the Dosewallips and Duckabush Rivers, and we decided to test the Skokomish simply because we had a couple of hours to kill before either of us had to be home. For Dave, at least, it was a successful test, and I got a few good photos for my efforts.

As it turned out, though, our first try at Skokomish River steelheading—more than 20 years ago—would be our most successful, and any angler who catches two winter steelies from this badly abused Hood Canal tributary in a single outing these days has pulled off a minor miracle. Although stocked with 20,000 to 30,000 winter steelhead smolts each year, the annual sport catch seldom tops 20 fish for the entire season. The North Fork Skokomish, dammed (or is that damned?) in two places to form Cushman and Kokanee Lakes, provides virtually no steelheading opportunity. The only catch-and-keep fishery on the forks of the Skokomish is on the South Fork, where anglers may keep two trout of 12 inches or more per day during the summer and early fall. Like the rest of the river, selective regulations are in effect on the South Fork, so you have to use artificial lures with single, barbless hooks.

The bright spot on the Skokomish in recent years has been the salmon fishing. Thanks at least in part to angling restrictions on Hood Canal and increases in returns of hatchery fish, the fall salmon action has improved substantially on the Skokomish since the mid-1990s. The main river below Highway 101 has had a catch-and-keep salmon season that has been quite good lately, especially for late-summer chinooks and fall chums. Limits and season lengths seem to be getting more liberal by the year, but with the improved fishing have come larger crowds, and some of the better fishing holes are very crowded during the best fishing times.

Location: Flows into the south end of Hood Canal in Mason County; see map A2 Inset, grid j0.

Species: Winter steelhead; resident and sea-run cutthroat trout; chinook, coho, chum, and pink salmon.

Facilities: A Forest Service campground is located on the upper South Fork Skokomish, at the mouth of Brown Creek. Potlatch State Park, about five miles north of the river on U.S. 101, has two dozen camping sites, some with RV hookups. Food, gas, tackle, and lodging are available in Shelton to the south and Hoodsport to the north.

Directions: Take U.S. 101 north from Shelton and turn west (left) on Skokomish Valley Road to drive upstream. To reach lower portions of the river, turn east off U.S. 101 onto Purdy Cutoff Road and follow the river downstream. The South Fork Skoke is paralleled by Skokomish Valley Road (Forest Service Road 23) and other Forest Service roads cutting off the main road to the right.

Contact: Verle's Sport Center, 360/426-0933; Potlatch State Park, 360/877-5361; Olympic National Forest, Hood Canal Ranger District, 360/877-5254.

135 Lower Hood Canal

The most well-known and popular sport fishery in southern Hood Canal the past several years has been the chum salmon fishery in front of the Hoodsport Salmon Hatchery. Running for about two months from the middle of October to the middle of December, it gives hundreds of anglers the opportunity to do battle with perhaps the toughest salmon that swims, the chum or dog salmon.

Hooking a tough chum on drift tackle or a favorite fly rod is always great sport, but this fishery has taken somewhat of an ugly turn in recent years. Since fishing space is limited, anglers sometimes get into turf squabbles or resort to name-calling when someone's hooked fish tangles with the lines of other anglers. There's something of a grudge between anglers who fly-fish and those using casting or spinning tackle. Some fish are killed and then thrown in the bushes or left to rot on the beach by anglers who decide they don't want to take them home. There are even conflicts between anglers and Indian gill-netters who sometimes crowd in to fish the only place where anglers are allowed. To help alleviate some of the problems, the main channel of Finch Creek—through which the chums pass on their way to the hatchery—has been closed to fishing as of the 1999 season, spreading anglers out more and reducing the problem of snagging. If you're going to give this fishery a try, wear your chest waders, take along a good selection of small green flies or small steelhead bobbers and green yarn, and fish during the week if you can to avoid some of the crowds. Better yet, branch out and fish some of the other places nearby that offer good fishing. Some people even line up along the beach in downtown Hoodsport and catch their share of these hard-fighting salmon.

Pink salmon are now also being reared at the Hoodsport Hatchery, and during odd-numbered years the late-summer crowds of "humpy" anglers almost rival the numbers who turn out later in the year for chums. Many of the same restrictions and fishing boundaries are in effect, so check the fishing pamphlet to be sure where and how you're allowed to fish.

There's some blackmouth-fishing opportunity during the winter, but it's a hit-and-miss proposition at best. Spots near the beach at Lilliwaup, Hoodsport, Ayres Point, and east of Union offer a few fish, but even fewer anglers are enthusiastic enough to give them much of a try.

The south end of the canal offers a good deal of sea-run cutthroat fishing, but most of the fish are from wild stocks and must be released. All the major estuaries have sea-runs, but those at Lilliwaup, Dewatto, and the mouth of the Tahuya River can be especially worthwhile.

Sole, flounder, and perch are abundant and underfished throughout the southern half of the canal. Look for sole and flounder in areas of fairly flat, soft bottom. Pile and striped perch may be found in the same areas but are best caught around docks and pilings. All these species will take small baits of any kind.

If you're thinking about fishing southern Hood Canal, by the way, check the regulations pamphlet concerning crab season before you set out. Except from mid-April to mid-July, crab pots are usually legal, and it often pays to put out a couple of them as you set out for the day's fishing. Even if the fish aren't biting, a couple of big Dungeness crabs could make the day a success. Areas around Union, Tahuya, Potlatch, and the mouth of the Skokomish River can offer especially good crabbing. Check the regulation pamphlet closely for details about the legalities.

Location: In Mason County; see map A2 Inset, grid j1.

Species: Chinook, chum, and (sometimes) pink salmon; sea-run cutthroat trout; a few rockfish and lingcod; sole and flounder; pile perch; striped seaperch.

Facilities: There are ramps on both sides of southern Hood Canal:

- **Triton Cove State Park:** The northernmost ramp in this part of the canal (also mentioned in the Upper Hood Canal section) is on the west side of the canal, at Triton Cove, where there's a Washington State Parks ramp. This single-lane concrete ramp has a loading float and dock, with room to park about two dozen cars and trailers. Watch for the large rock just out from the ramp, slightly to the south. There's a $3 launch fee, with an annual permit available for $40.

- **Mike's Beach Resort:** Located near Lilliwaup, this facility has a launch that will handle boats up to about 22 feet. It's a one-lane concrete ramp with a loading float and limited parking. There's a launch fee, depending on the size of the boat. Mike's Beach Resort has boat rentals, RV/tent sites, cabins, dormitory-style rooms, and divers' air. Hoodsport & Dive, in Hoodsport, has kayak and scuba equipment rentals, air fills, and dive charters.

- **Menard's Landing:** There's a one-lane gravel ramp at Tahuya on the north side of the canal's Great Bend. This Port of Tahuya ramp is best suited to small trailer boats and craft that can be carried to the water. Like the ramp's use, its gravel parking area is limited.

- **Hood Canal Park (Potlatch) Ramp:** Just south of Potlatch on the west side of the canal is a Tacoma Public Utilities ramp, a two-lane concrete launch with a large gravel parking lot. Launching is free here, but be very careful of fast-moving traffic from the north when you're turning south out of the lot.

- **Union Ramp:** There's a free ramp with limited parking in the town of Union and an excellent ramp ($4 fee) at Twanoh State Park.

- **Port of Allyn Ramp:** Located a mile west of Belfair State Park, off Highway 300, this single-lane ramp has a gravel parking area with room for about half a dozen cars and trailers. Launching here is free.

- **Summertide Resort:** This private resort and marina 16 miles west from Belfair on Highway 300 is open only from spring to fall. The ramp is adequate for most trailer boats. Summertide Resort and Marina has over 550 feet of moorage docks, restrooms with showers, RV/tent sites, rental cabins, and a small store.

Rest-a-While Resort between Hoodsport and Lilliwaup has RV sites, a dry-storage boat yard, and a small store. Hoodsport Marina and Cafe has limited guest moorage and a waterfront restaurant. A short distance south, on the north edge of Hoodsport, is Sunrise Motel and Restaurant, with nearby moorage facilities. South of Hoodsport is Potlatch State Park, which has RV/tent sites, five mooring buoys, restrooms, and showers. Hood Canal Marina in Union has guest moorage, power to the docks, gasoline, and marine repairs. To the east is Alderbrook Inn, where there's over 2,000 feet of dock space, power to the docks, restrooms with showers, boat-sewage facilities, boat rentals, a restaurant, swim beach, and other amenities. Farther east is Twanoh State Park, where there are over 190 feet of moorage float space, seven moorage buoys, RV and tent sites, restrooms with showers, a large gravel swim beach, picnic tables and cooking shelters, and a small stream with large runs of chum salmon in it during the late fall. Belfair State Park, about three miles west of Belfair on Highway 300, has over 180 tent and RV sites, but access by boat is limited by the shallow mud flats.

Directions: Take U.S. 101 north from Shelton to reach the entire west side of the canal. To reach the south side from the Great Bend to the tip, take Highway 106 east from U.S. 101 or west from Belfair. To reach the north side of the canal from the tip to the Great Bend, take Highway 3 to Belfair and turn west on Highway 300.

Contact: Mike's Beach Resort, 360/877-5324, website: www.mikesbeachresort.com (Mike's offers a 5 percent discount on all services if you bring this book in with you); Rest-A-While Resort, 360/877-9474; Summertide Resort, 360/275-2268; Potlatch State Park, 360/877-5361; Twanoh State Park, 360/275-2222; Belfair State Park, 360/275-0668; Washington State Parks and Recreation Commission,

360/902-8844 (information) or 888/226-7688 (reservations); Cushman Marine, 360/877-5244, website: www.cushmanboats.com, email: cushman@hctc.com. For nautical charts of this area, contact Captain's Nautical Supply, 206/283-7242.

136 Wood and Wildberry Lakes

Spring plants of legal-sized rainbows provide most of the action at Wood and Wildberry Lakes, and since the Department of Fish and Wildlife stocks only a few hundred of them, the action usually ends by June. These small lakes are fished primarily by local anglers, because out-of-towners are often unable to find them and end up at nearby Maggie Lake or one of the more well-known lakes to the north. I know, because it's happened to me. Their small size and lack of developed boat-launching facilities make Wood and Wildberry good candidates for float-tube fishing. Wildberry Lake may show as Buck Lake on some older maps. The season here is a standard late-April through October run.

Location: Northwest of Tahuya and north of Hood Canal's Great Bend; see map A2 Inset, grid j1.

Species: Rainbow trout.

Facilities: Both lakes have bank-fishing spots but little else. The nearest food and gas are back on Highway 300, and the closest tackle and lodging are in Belfair. Belfair State Park, which you'll pass as you make your way west on Highway 300, offers tent and RV sites, showers, and restrooms. Cady Lake Manor, on nearby Cady Lake, is a classy, comfortable bed-and-breakfast with a great view.

Directions: Take Highway 3 to Belfair and turn west on Highway 300, following it toward Tahuya. Go north near Tahuya on Belfair-Tahuya Road for about 1.5 miles to Jiggs Lake, which is on the right. Continue north half a mile past the lake and turn left at the next intersection. From there it's two miles to Wood Lake and just under three miles to Wildberry Lake, with small signs along the road pointing the way.

Contact: Belfair State Park, 360/275-0668; Washington State Parks and Recreation Commission, 360/902-8844 (information) or 888/226-7688 (reservations); Cady Lake Manor, 360/372-2673, website: www.cadylake.com, email: inquiries@cadylake.com.

137 Dewatto Area Lakes

Aldrich, Cady, Don (also called Clara), Robbins, and U Lakes, all 10 to 17 acres in size and within just over a mile of each other, are havens for small-boat anglers and float-tubers who like to get away from the hustle and bustle of big waters with lots of high-speed boating activity. Their small size and limited boat-launch facilities help to keep the high-speed thrill-seekers away and provide a quality experience for anglers. Tee Lake, which covers 38 acres and has a fair amount of development around it, is the exception, so don't be surprised if the water-skiers and personal watercraft jockeys try to buzz you. A large bass plug equipped with two or three treble hooks cast in the direction of the culprits may help to keep them at bay.

Of the six lakes, Cady may be the gem of the bunch. Development around its shores is all but nonexistent, and fly-fishing-only regulations help to keep the crowds small. The other lakes are productive in May and June, but Cady provides fair to good fishing from spring through fall. Cady became a catch-and-release lake in 2000, which suited most of its regular visitors just fine. All these lakes open in late April and close at the end of October.

Location: Southwest of Belfair on the east side of Hood Canal; see map A2 Inset, grid j1.

Species: Rainbow trout in all six lakes, cutthroat trout in Cady Lake, largemouth bass and yellow perch in Tee Lake.

Facilities: Except for U Lake, all have small Department of Fish and Wildlife access areas with boat ramps suitable for car-toppers and other small boats. Small stores in the area have groceries and gas, and complete facilities are available in Belfair. Belfair State Park, between Belfair and the lakes on Highway 300, has 33 tent sites and 47 RV sites with water, electricity, and sewer hookups. Cady Lake Manor is a spiffy bed-and-breakfast, located right on the shores of Cady Lake.

Directions: Take Highway 3 to Belfair and turn west on Highway 300 (North Shore Road). Turn north (right) on Belfair-Tahuya Road at the town of Tahuya and drive about four miles to Dewatto Road. Turn west (left) and watch for Tee Lake Road on the right. West of Tee Lake, roads to the left lead to Cady, Don, U, Robbins, and Aldrich Lakes. Watch closely for signs pointing to each.

Contact: Belfair State Park, 360/275-0668; Washington State Parks and Recreation Commission, 360/902-8844 (information) or 888/226-7688 (reservations); Cady Lake Manor, 360/372-2673, website: www.cadylake.com, email: inquiries@cadylake.com.

138 Dewatto River

Like the nearby Tahuya (see number 140), this small Hood Canal tributary is hardly worth a long trip just for the fishing. Regulations have changed from hatchery-only fish to total catch-and-release on trout and steelhead, so things are tough. The only catch-and-keep fishery on the river now is the six-week salmon season that allows anglers to take up to two cohos per day. Check the regulations pamphlet for dates on that one.

Location: Flows into Hood Canal east of Lilliwaup; see map A2 Inset, grid j1.

Species: Sea-run cutthroat trout, coho salmon, a few winter steelhead.

Facilities: Tent and RV sites, restrooms, and showers are available at Belfair State Park,

on Highway 300. The town of Belfair has food, gas, lodging, and other amenities.

Directions: Take Highway 9 to Belfair and turn west on Highway 300. Turn north (right) at Tahuya onto Belfair-Tahuya Road, then west (left) on Dewatto Road to Dewatto, which is located at the river mouth. From there, follow Dewatto-Holly Road upstream.

Contact: Belfair State Park, 360/275-0668; Washington State Parks and Recreation Commission, 360/902-8844 (information) or 888/226-7688 (reservations); Cady Lake Manor, 360/372-2673, website: www.cadylake.com, email: inquiries@cadylake.com.

139 Maggie Lake

Some 2,000 legal-sized rainbow trout from Department of Fish and Wildlife hatcheries are on hand to greet anglers when this 25-acre lake opens to fishing in late April every year. Most of those trout are gone by the end of May, and as soon as the fishing slows, most early season anglers go looking for greener pastures. But if you like warm-weather trout fishing, don't be afraid to stick with this one all summer long. Maggie Lake sits in a deep basin and has spots more than 70 feet deep, making it one of Mason County's deepest lakes and one of the most likely to provide decent trout fishing even during the warm spells of summer. Things may get a little busy with swimmers and the like June through August, but if you get on the water early in the day, they won't be a problem.

Location: Southwest of Belfair in Mason County; see map A2 Inset, grid j2.

Species: Rainbow trout.

Facilities: A public access area with a boat ramp is located near the south end of the lake. Belfair State Park, about 12 miles away on Highway 300, has tent and RV sites, restrooms, and showers. Other accommodations, along with food, gas, tackle, and lodging, are available in Belfair.

Directions: Take Highway 3 to Belfair and turn west onto Highway 300 (North Shore Road), following it to Tahuya. Turn north (right) at Tahuya onto Belfair-Tahuya Road and drive about 2.5 miles to the lake, which is on the right.

Contact: Belfair State Park, 360/275-0668; Washington State Parks and Recreation Commission, 360/902-8844 (information) or 888/226-7688 (reservations); Cady Lake Manor, 360/372-2673, website: www.cadylake.com, email: inquiries@cadylake.com.

140 Tahuya River

Though it's called a river, the Tahuya becomes little more than a small creek during the summer months, providing decent trout-fishing opportunity, except that all the fish you catch must be released. Sea-run cutthroating becomes a good possibility when fall rains raise the river level, but again it's a catch-and-release proposition, and you have to use artificial lures and flies with single, barbless hooks. Catch-and-release rules are also in effect during the winter steelhead season. But if you like small-stream steelheading, Tahuya River is a pretty good place to get away from the crowds. If you're lucky, you might even hook a fish.

The good news is the coho salmon runs here have improved enough to allow for a catch-and-keep fall season. Silvers are fair game here for about six weeks, beginning in mid-September, and anglers are allowed to keep two fish per day. Be sure to check the fishing pamphlet for dates and any changes on those rules from year to year.

Location: Flows into the south end of Hood Canal at the Great Bend; see map A2 Inset, grid j2.

Species: Resident and sea-run cutthroat trout, some winter steelhead.

Facilities: Belfair State Park is the nearest place with tent and RV sites. Food, gas, lodg-

ing, and tackle are available in Belfair.

Directions: Take Highway 9 to Belfair and turn west onto Highway 300, following it to Tahuya. Turn north (right) on Belfair-Tahuya Road, then east (right) on Tahuya River Road, which parallels the west side of the river.

Contact: Belfair State Park, 360/275-0668; Washington State Parks and Recreation Commission, 360/902-8844 (information) or 888/226-7688 (reservations); Cady Lake Manor, 360/372-2673, website: www.cadylake.com, inquiries@cadylake.com.

141 Howell Lake

Pan-sized rainbows from Department of Fish and Wildlife plants provide some pretty good action here for a few weeks in the spring. Then things drop off and most anglers forget about Howell for another year. Some of the old-timers who fish here say the lake contains a few brook trout, but I have yet to see anybody catch one.

Location: West of Belfair in Mason County; see map A2 Inset, grid j2.

Species: Rainbow trout.

Facilities: A rough boat ramp is located at the northwest corner of the lake. Food, gas, lodging, and tackle can be found back toward Belfair. Belfair State Park is on the south side of Highway 300, just west of Belfair, and has tent and RV sites, showers, and restrooms.

Directions: Take Highway 3 to Belfair and turn west on Highway 300. Drive about half a mile past Belfair State Park and turn north (right) at the sign pointing the way to nearly a dozen area lakes. About half a mile after crossing the Tahuya River bridge, turn left on the road with signs pointing to Howell, Tee, and other area lakes. Drive two miles to Howell Lake Road, turn left, and drive about half a mile to the lake.

Contact: Belfair State Park, 360/275-0668; Washington State Parks and Recreation Commission, 360/902-8844 (information) or

888/226-7688 (reservations); Cady Lake Manor, 360/372-2673, website: www.cadylake.com, email: inquiries@cadylake.com.

142 Haven Lake

Often one of Mason County's better early-season trout producers, Haven is stocked with enough hatchery rainbows and cutthroats to keep everyone happy, at least for a while. This 70-acre lake with lots of homes and development around its shores usually produces a good per-rod catch average during the first few weeks of the April through October season, but like any good thing, it doesn't last. The trout fishing is tough by June and stays slow all summer, picking up somewhat in September.

Location: Northwest of Belfair in Mason County; see map A2 Inset, grid j2.

Species: Rainbow and cutthroat trout.

Facilities: The lake has a public access area with a boat ramp and toilets. The nearest gas, food, lodging, and tackle are in Belfair and the vicinity. Belfair State Park has tent and RV sites, restrooms, and showers.

Directions: Take Highway 3 to Belfair and turn west on Highway 300. Drive about half a mile past Belfair State Park and turn north (right) at the sign pointing the way to Haven and other area lakes. Continue about seven miles to the lake.

Contact: Belfair State Park, 360/275-0668; Washington State Parks and Recreation Commission, 360/902-8844 (information) or 888/226-7688 (reservations); Cady Lake Manor, 360/372-2673, website: www.cadylake.com, email: inquiries@cadylake.com.

143 Lake Wooten

Both spring and fall fishing can be good here, but the lake gets pretty busy with swimmers, skiers, and other sun seekers throughout the summer, so fishing opportunities drop off at that time of year. If you do decide to fish it

in July or August, get on the water early in the morning and try stillfishing the 35-foot-deep hole about 200 feet offshore near the east end of the lake. Rainbows, including some hefty carryovers, provide most of the action, but Wooten is also planted with some large cutthroats for variety.

Location: Northwest of Belfair in Mason County; see map A2 Inset, grid j2.

Species: Rainbow and cutthroat trout.

Facilities: The lake has a boat ramp and access area. Belfair State Park, about a mile to the southeast, has 33 tent sites and 47 RV sites that are complete with water, electrical, and sewer hookups. Belfair offers the nearest food, gas, tackle, and lodging.

Directions: Take Highway 3 to Belfair and turn west on Highway 300. Drive about half a mile past Belfair State Park and turn north (right) at the sign pointing the way to Wooten and other area lakes. Drive about seven miles to Haven Lake and continue along its east side another mile to Lake Wooten. The road runs completely around the lake.

Contact: Belfair State Park, 360/275-0668; Washington State Parks and Recreation Commission, 360/902-8844 (information) or 888/226-7688 (reservations); Cady Lake Manor, 360/372-2673, website: www.cadylake.com, email: inquiries@cadylake.com.

144 Twin Lakes

Although they total only about 20 acres, Twin Lakes are heavily stocked with legal-sized rainbows by the Department of Fish and Wildlife. Would you believe about 8,000 7- to 10-inch rainbows each spring? All those hungry hatchery trout provide good fishing throughout the spring, and it doesn't matter much whether you like to dunk worms, troll spinners, or cast flies, although fly casters seem to be in the minority around here most of the time. The lakes are virtually connected, so you can fish either or both in one trip. The best trout action is from the opener in late April until about mid-June.

Location: Northwest of Belfair in Mason County; see map A2 Inset, grid j2.

Species: Rainbow trout.

Facilities: A primitive campground and small boat ramp are located on Big Twin, the eastern of the two lakes. Belfair State Park, about 20 minutes away, has tent and RV sites, restrooms, and showers. Food, gas, tackle, and lodging are available in Belfair.

Directions: Take Highway 3 to Belfair and turn west on Highway 300. About half a mile past Belfair State Park, turn right at the sign pointing to Twin and other area lakes. Drive just under three miles to Elfendahl Pass Road, turn north (right), drive three miles, and turn west (left) on the gravel road leading past Camp Spillman to Twin Lakes. A sign marks the right turn to the lakes.

Contact: Belfair State Park, 360/275-0668; Washington State Parks and Recreation Commission, 360/902-8844 (information) or 888/226-7688 (reservations).

145 Panther Lake

Most of the trout-catching activity on this 100-acre lake just west of Tiger Lake (number 147) occurs from late April through early June, during the first six weeks or so of the season. By the start of summer, anglers have caught most of the 5,000 or so legal-sized rainbows stocked here, but a few may still be around to provide fair fishing in the fall. The lake also has enough brown bullheads to provide fair catfish opportunities during the spring and summer.

Location: Kitsap-Mason County line north of Belfair; see map A2 Inset, grid i3.

Species: Rainbow trout, brown bullhead catfish.

Facilities: A gravel boat ramp is located on the south side of the lake, and the parking area and restrooms are across the road.

Belfair offers the nearest grocery stores, gas stations, and other facilities. Belfair State Park, with tent and RV sites, is about eight miles south of the lake.

Directions: Take Highway 3 to Belfair and turn west on Highway 300. About a mile west of Belfair, turn north (right) on Sand Hill Road and drive about seven miles to Gold Creek Road. Turn left and almost instantly you're on Panther Lake Road, which encircles the lake.

Contact: Washington Department of Fish and Wildlife, Montesano Office, 360/249-4628; Belfair State Park, 360/275-0668; Washington State Parks and Recreation Commission, 360/902-8844 (information) or 888/226-7688 (reservations).

146 Mission Lake

Pretty little Mission Lake and its small access area get lots of fishing pressure early in the season, but the crowds disappear by June and forget to come back for the good fall angling opportunities. Fishing closes at the end of October, but the last month of the season offers a good chance for rainbows averaging a foot long and sometimes pushing a foot and a half. Making autumn even more attractive is the occasional stocking of large cutthroats in the lake. Cutts often come on strong in the fall, and Mission Lake cutthroats are no exception. Take a fly rod and a good selection of wet flies and nymph patterns to get the most from your trip.

Location: West of Gorst on the Kitsap Peninsula; see map A2 Inset, grid i3.

Species: Rainbow and cutthroat trout, brown bullhead catfish.

Facilities: A small gravel access area and boat ramp for car-toppers and small trailer boats is located at the southeast corner of the lake. Belfair, about seven miles to the south, has the nearest food, gas, tackle, and lodging.

Directions: Drive to Belfair on Highway 3, turn west on Highway 300, and drive about a mile to Sand Hill Road. Turn north (right) and drive about seven miles to Tiger Lake. Turn right to Tiger-Mission Road and drive 1.5 miles to the south end of Mission Lake.

Contact: Washington Department of Fish and Wildlife, Montesano Office, 360/249-4628.

147 Tiger Lake

Thanks to one of those wonderful quirks of geography, you have to launch in Kitsap County to fish this Mason County trout lake. The public access area and boat ramp at the north end of Tiger lies just across the Mason-Kitsap County line, while most of the lake's 100 acres are in Mason County. OK, so that may have been a big deal back in the old days of county fishing licenses, but it isn't now.

What's important is that Tiger is heavily stocked with about 8,000 legal-sized rainbows every spring just before the April opener, and early season fishing here is often some of the best in Mason (and Kitsap) County. The Department of Fish and Wildlife often throws a few large cutthroats into the spring mix, adding variety and a fair chance for a bragging-sized trout. Come back in the fall; you'll find good fishing and small crowds.

Location: North of Belfair on the Kitsap Peninsula; see map A2 Inset, grid i3.

Species: Rainbow and cutthroat trout.

Facilities: The large, gravel access area at the north end of the lake offers room to launch at least three boats at a time, with plenty of space for casting from the bank. Belfair offers the nearest food, gas, tackle, and lodging. Belfair State Park is about seven miles south of the lake.

Directions: Drive to Belfair on Highway 3, turn west on Highway 300, and drive about a mile to Sand Hill Road. Turn north (right) and drive about seven miles to the lake, which has roads all the way around it.

Contact: Washington Department of Fish and Wildlife, Montesano Office, 360/249-4628; Belfair State Park, 360/275-0668; Washington State Parks and Recreation Commission, 360/902-8844 (information) or 888/226-7688 (reservations).

148 Union River

Although in past decades it has been worth visiting for decent steelhead and trout fishing, the Union probably isn't worth a trip of more than maybe two blocks if you're looking for a fishing spot. Seasons here have become catch-and-release only, which is fine, except you're not likely to find anything to catch and release.

Location: Flows into the tip of Hood Canal near Belfair in Mason County; see map A2 Inset, grid j3.

Species: Winter and summer steelhead, sea-run and resident cutthroat trout.

Facilities: Restaurants, grocery stores, tackle, gas stations, and motels are abundant in Belfair. RV and tent sites, restrooms, showers, and other amenities are available at Belfair State Park, just west of Belfair.

Directions: Take Highway 3 to Belfair and turn north on Old Belfair Highway, which parallels much of the river for about four miles.

Contact: Belfair State Park, 360/275-0668; Washington State Parks and Recreation Commission, 360/902-8844 (information) or 888/226-7688 (reservations).

149 Long Lake

This 315-acre lake south of Port Orchard is most productive after it has warmed in the spring. Good-sized largemouths can be caught during spring and summer, but be sure to check the fishing pamphlet for details about the slot limit that requires you to throw back bass in the 12- to 17-inch size range.

Summertime crappie fishing can be quite

good. Be prepared for an encounter with a school of cooperative crappies by taking along your favorite ultralight spinning outfit or light-action fly rod. Your best shot at hooking a big cutthroat here is in the fall, especially in October and November.

Location: South of Port Orchard in Kitsap County; see map A2 Inset, grid i4.

Species: Largemouth bass, crappie, bluegill, some cutthroat trout.

Facilities: The lake has a public access area with boat ramps and toilets. Food, gas, tackle, and lodging are available in Port Orchard and a little farther north in Bremerton.

Directions: Take Highway 16 south from Port Orchard, turn east (left) on Sedgewick Road, and then south (right) on Long Lake Road, which parallels the east side of the lake.

Contact: Washington Department of Fish and Wildlife, Montesano Office, 360/249-4628.

150 Angle Lake

This popular lake within sight of Seattle-Tacoma International Airport is open to year-round fishing. The annual spring plant of about 6,000 rainbow trout doesn't last too long, with your best shot at catching them being March through May.

But the bass and panfish action holds up all summer. Anglers catch some good-sized bass around the lake's many docks and floats beginning in May. Nice summer days bring out the crowds, so consider doing your summertime bass fishing early in the morning, late in the evening, or, as some anglers prefer, during the night. Perch fishing is good throughout most of the year, and the lake has some whoppers.

The lake has an 8 mph speed limit, which keeps the speed demons away and helps to ensure calm water for anglers even when the lake is fairly crowded.

Location: Southeast of the Seattle-Tacoma International Airport; see map A2 Inset, grid j6.

Species: Rainbow trout, largemouth bass, yellow perch, crappie.

Facilities: A King County park on the west side of the lake has a boat ramp; food, gas, lodging, and other amenities are available within casting distance along Pacific Highway South.

Directions: Take the 200th Street exit off I-5 near Des Moines and drive west on 200th Street to Pacific Highway South. Turn north (right) and drive about four blocks to the lake, which is visible on the right.

Contact: Auburn Sports and Marine, 253/833-1440.

151 Green River

Once one of Washington's top winter steelhead rivers, the Green has been a tough nut for anglers to crack in recent years. It has barely made the top 10 among the state's winter steelhead streams lately, even though it used to consistently rank near the head of that list. Although it's planted with nearly 200,000 winter steelhead smolts annually, the winter catch in recent years has hovered down around the 1,000 mark. The Green just isn't the steelhead river it used to be.

When winter steelhead are in the Green, the stretch of river from Kent upstream to Flaming Geyser State Park is one of the most popular among anglers. Several good bank-fishing spots are found along Green River Road, which runs along the east side of the river between Kent and Auburn. Green Valley Road, which runs upriver several miles east of Auburn, is also a good bet for access to lots of potentially productive steelhead water. One of the favorite fishing spots along this stretch is immediately upstream and downstream from the Highway 18 bridge. To reach it, take the Green Valley Road exit off Highway 18 and turn left almost immediately into the gravel parking area between the road and the river. A trail leads downriver under the bridge.

There's nothing special you need to know about fishing the Green for winter steelhead. When it's low and clear, you can take fish on small spoons and metal-finish spinners, and during normal flows you can fish roe, shrimp, bobbers, and all the other offerings you might throw at winter fish on your favorite stream. One thing you can't do here during the winter is fish from a boat. You can use a drift boat or other craft for transportation, but if you want to fish you have to get out and cast from the bank.

The boat-fishing regulation doesn't apply during the summer, and many anglers launch near the Whitney Bridge or farther upstream at Flaming Geyser State Park and make the day-long float down to the Highway 18 bridge. Fishing for steelhead holds up pretty well on the Green throughout the summer, with decent catches June through August. While the Green Valley Road area is a favorite with many summer steelheaders, the waters farther upstream, near the rearing ponds at Palmer, are also productive for summer-runs.

Fall salmon fishing can also be productive on the Green, especially around the Kent area and along Green River Road between Kent and Auburn. Once a good chinook producer, the river is now closed for chinooks, but coho fishing can be good in October. The usual metallic spoons and spinners that work elsewhere will do the job here. Early in the fall, when the silvers first move into the river, you might also get them to take a cluster of fresh roe or a ghost shrimp, especially if it's enhanced with a small tuft of nylon yarn or a brightly colored steelhead bobber. Fall is also the time for sea-run cutthroat fishing, and the entire lower river (from Kent downstream) holds trout in September and October. Try rolling night crawlers along the bottom to tempt them.

Oh yes, we can't talk about the Green without mentioning the Atlantic salmon fishery that has developed since 1997. The result of a mass escape from net-pen facilities in Puget Sound, it provided some hot fishing for a while that year, and anglers have caught more and more of these inadvertent transplants ever since. Some of them are quite large. Even though the Washington Department of Fish and Wildlife isn't very happy about the fish entering the state's streams, they do keep track of records for the species, and in September 1999 the Green produced a whopping Atlantic of over 14 pounds, the current state record. The previous record was over 13 pounds, also from the Green, so they do reach impressive proportions.

Location: Flows into Elliott Bay and Puget Sound at Seattle; see map A2 Inset, grid j6.

Species: Winter and summer steelhead, coho and chum salmon, cutthroat trout.

Facilities: Food, gas, lodging, tackle, and all other facilities are available in Auburn and Kent.

Directions: Take Highway 167 to Highway 18 and drive east through Auburn to Green Valley Road. Turn east (right) and follow Green Valley Road east along the river. To fish lower portions of the Green, follow Highway 167 between Auburn and Kent and take any of several crossroads off the freeway to reach the river. The Meeker Street exit, for example, will take you to some deep pools right along the freeway.

Contact: Auburn Sports and Marine, 253/833-1440.

152 Panther Lake

Although stocked with a few hatchery rainbows in the spring, this small lake between Kent and Renton is better known for its bass fishing. If you like fishing weeds, brush, and other vegetation, this is the place for you. Panther Lake is no more than seven or eight feet deep and filled with all sorts of greenery in which bass can hide. Bring an assortment of spinnerbaits, buzzbaits, Texas-rigged plastic worms, and other weedless or at least moderately weedless bass baits. The thick tangles produce some good-sized largemouths.

The lake covers only about 33 acres, small enough to fish effectively from a float tube. You can also get small car-toppers into the lake, but the primitive launch isn't adequate for larger trailer boats. Because of all those weeds, catfishing is best accomplished with a night crawler suspended from a bobber so that it hangs just over the tops of the weeds.
Location: Northeast of Kent; see map A2 Inset, grid j7.
Species: Largemouth bass, rainbow trout, brown bullhead catfish.
Facilities: A rather rough boat ramp is located on the east side of the lake. Other amenities are available in Kent and Renton.
Directions: Take the Benson Highway (Highway 515) north from Kent and go through the intersection at South 208th Street. Turn right on the next street north of South 208th Street, drive less than half a mile to a Y in the road, and go right to the lake.
Contact: Auburn Sports and Marine, 253/ 833-1440.

153 Lake Wilderness

This one can be a little unpredictable when it comes to trout fishing. Some years it provides excellent early season catches of 8- to 10-inch hatchery rainbows and a few 15-inch carryovers, while other years it starts off slow and then tapers off quickly. Although the lake is fairly shallow, its clean waters support a kokanee population, and trolling for these tasty little sockeye salmon can be fairly pro-

ductive in June and July.

If you fish the lake, take a boat or float tube because the water is quite shallow around the public beach-fishing spots, and it takes an impressive cast to get your bait or lure out into water more than about 10 feet deep.
Location: East of Kent; see map A2 Inset, grid j7.
Species: Rainbow trout, some kokanee.
Facilities: A Washington Department of Fish and Wildlife access area and boat ramp and a King County park provide lots of bank access. The nearest food, gas, tackle, and lodging are in Kent.
Directions: Take Highway 18 north from Auburn and turn east (right) on Highway 516 (Kent-Kangley Road). Drive about 3.6 miles and turn north (left) at the signs pointing the way to Lake Wilderness Park and Lake Wilderness Golf Course. Drive about 1.5 miles to the lake, which is on the right.
Contact: Auburn Sports and Marine, 253/ 833-1440.

154 Shady Lake

This south King County lake has an unusually short season, opening to fishing on June 1 and closing at the end of October. It covers only about 21 acres and is a favorite with float-tubers and small-boat anglers. The planting of various-sized trout and some carryover from year to year mean you never know whether the next fish you catch will be an eight-incher or a three-pounder.

Because of the lake's small size, short season, and relatively light plant of legal-sized trout, Shady gets less fishing pressure than many other lakes in this part of King County. You probably won't catch a limit here, but you will enjoy some peace, quiet, and solitude, certainly part of what fishing is all about.
Location: Northeast of Kent; see map A2 Inset, grid j7.

Species: Rainbow and cutthroat trout.

Facilities: The south end of the lake has a public access area with a boat ramp. Other amenities are in Renton, Kent, and Maple Valley.

Directions: Drive east from Renton on Petrovitsky Road and turn north (left) on 196th Drive, which leads to the lake.

Contact: Auburn Sports and Marine, 253/833-1440.

155 Lake Desire

This popular south King County lake is now open year-round, and spring plants of legal-sized rainbows and a few larger cutthroats provide consistent angling action. Spring and fall are the best times to fish it for trout. Anglers catch rainbows and cutthroats by trolling most of the standard offerings or stillfishing with worms, marshmallows, salmon eggs, Power Bait, or cheese. Bass fishing can be good during the spring and summer, and the lake produces a few hefty largemouths.

The entire lake is quite shallow, and that goes for the boat ramp. Be careful when launching, especially if you have a larger boat that requires a trailer.

Location: Southeast of Renton; see map A2 Inset, grid j7.

Species: Rainbow and cutthroat trout, largemouth bass, yellow perch.

Facilities: The lake has a public access area with a new fishing dock and boat ramp at its north end. Other facilities are available in Renton.

Directions: Drive east from Renton on Petrovitsky Road, turn north (left) on 184th Avenue SE, and follow it half a mile to Lake Desire Drive. Turn left and drive just under a mile to the lake.

Contact: Auburn Sports and Marine, 253/833-1440.

156 Otter (Spring) Lake

Some folks call it Otter Lake, some call it Spring Lake, and others don't care one way or the other. What's important here is that this 67-acre lake between Renton and Maple Valley offers a wide range of fishing possibilities throughout much of the year. It sometimes gives up rainbows to four pounds, although liberal spring plants of hatchery trout make nine-inchers a more likely possibility. The trout fishing can be quite good in April and May.

While the rainbow fishery here is well known, the lake's fair-sized cutthroats are a better-kept secret, according to Tom Pollack at Auburn Sports and Marine, who happens to live fairly close to the lake. Anglers who latch onto a large cutthroat just don't make too big a deal of it, he says.

The gently sloping flats near the south end of the lake warm quickly in the spring and stay warm all summer, providing some good fishing opportunities for bass, perch, and catfish. Try top-water plugs early and late in the day for bass, and dark-colored spinnerbaits or plastic worms while the sun is high. A bobber-and-worm rig will take the perch and catfish.

Location: Southeast of Renton; see map A2 Inset, grid j7.

Species: Rainbow and cutthroat trout, largemouth bass, yellow perch, brown bullhead catfish.

Facilities: A public access area and boat ramp are located near the northeast corner of the lake. The nearest amenities are in Kent, Renton, and Maple Valley.

Directions: Drive east from Renton on Petrovitsky Road and turn north (left) on 196th Avenue SE. Turn left again on S.E. 183rd Street and drive to Spring Lake Drive. The lake is on the left.

Contact: Auburn Sports and Marine, 253/833-1440.

157 Shadow Lake

One of many King County lakes that have gone from an April through October season to year-round in recent years, Shadow offers good spring trout fishing and fair action again in the fall. Planted rainbows of 8 to 10 inches are standard fare, but the spring plants often include a few brood-stock trout that run a pound and a half to three pounds each. Trolling is more popular here than still-fishing, but if you have your heart set on staying in one place and waiting for the trout to come to you, try anchoring at the north end of the lake just west of the entrance to the canal that leads to the boat ramp.

That 1,200-foot canal that connects the boat ramp to the main lake, by the way, is a pretty good place to fish for Shadow Lake bass. Tom Pollack, who works at Auburn Sports and Marine, says he always makes his way slowly through the narrow canal when boating in and out of the lake, casting to both sides as he goes. The strategy pays off with a largemouth or two more often than not, he says.

Perch are found throughout the lake and will hit worms or small jigs all spring and summer. Crappies also like little leadheads, fished around submerged wood or weedy cover.

Location: Northeast of Kent; see map A2 Inset, grid j7.

Species: Rainbow trout, largemouth bass, yellow perch, crappie.

Facilities: A boat ramp is located at the north end of the lake. All other facilities are available in Renton.

Directions: Drive east from Renton on Petrovitsky Road and turn south (right) on 196th Avenue SE, then east (left) on 213th Street. Drive half a mile to the lake, on the left.

Contact: Auburn Sports and Marine, 253/833-1440.

158 Lake Meridian

Spring hatchery plants of 8,000 to 9,000 legal-sized rainbows draw most of the angling attention on this 150-acre lake near Kent, but fishing for bass and other warm-water fish can be good during the late spring and summer. Largemouth bass are fairly abundant, and the lake has a few smallmouths as well. Try surface plugs around the docks first thing in the morning and during the last few minutes of light in the evening, or work spinnerbaits and crankbaits around the many docks and floats during the day for largemouths. Smallmouths may also be caught on the surface early and late, or fish small plastic grubs on one-sixteenth- or one-eighth-ounce leadheads during the day. The bass fishery here often holds up into and through the night. If you need incentive to give bassing a try, how about a 5.5-pound smallmouth caught here during the spring of 1995? I thought that might work.

Location: Southeast of Kent; see map A2 Inset, grid j7.

Species: Rainbow trout, largemouth and smallmouth bass, yellow perch, brown bullhead catfish.

Facilities: The county park has bank access and a boat ramp that closes at sunset, while the WDFW ramp is open 24 hours. The nearest food, gas, lodging, and tackle are in Kent.

Directions: Take Kent-Kangley Road (Highway 516) east from Kent about three miles until you see the lake right alongside the road on your left. Turn left into the county park at the lake's southeast corner or go a block past it to the light and turn left to reach the Department of Fish and Wildlife boat ramp on the east end of the lake.

Contact: Auburn Sports and Marine, 253/833-1440.

159 Benson Lake

This 80-acre lake just east of Mason Lake (number 160) drops off steeply from the bank on both its east and west side, providing bank anglers a good opportunity to catch trout. That helps to explain why the public access area on the east side of the lake is often crowded with shore anglers—they catch fish there. But sometimes there are so many bank anglers at the access area that boaters have a tough time getting in and out of the water. It's a minor problem because both boat and bank anglers catch their share of Benson Lake rainbows and cutthroats. The lake, open late April through October, gets a generous plant of 6,000 legal-sized rainbows and a few large cutts every spring, providing good trout-fishing opportunities well into summer.

As you might guess just by the look of the place, Benson also has a lot of bass in it. Most of them are fairly small, but after a couple days of warm weather you might be surprised at how abundant they are. The bottom is clean enough to allow you to fish crankbaits or work more slowly around the docks and natural cover with spinnerbaits or plastics.

Location: Southwest of Allyn in Mason County; see map A2 Inset, grid j2.

Species: Rainbow and cutthroat trout, largemouth bass.

Facilities: The gravel access area on the east side of the lake has a gravel boat ramp and room for several cars and boat trailers. When boating activity isn't too heavy at the ramp, there's room for about half a dozen bank anglers to try their luck. Twanoh State Park to the north on Hood Canal offers tent and RV sites, restrooms, and showers. The nearest food, gas, tackle, and lodging are available in Belfair and Shelton.

Directions: Take Highway 3 north from Shelton or south from Belfair and turn west on Mason Lake County Park Road. Turn left on East Ben-son Road and almost immediately turn right into the public access area at the lake.

Contact: Verle's Sport Center, 360/426-0933; Twanoh State Park, 360/275-2222; Washington State Parks and Recreation Commission, 360/902-8844 (information) or 888/226-7688 (reservations).

160 Mason Lake

Kokanee fishing can be quite good here, but in July and August when this fishery is at its peak, you had better plan on arriving early in the morning or fishing late in the evening. Mason Lake gets very busy during the rest of the day. At nearly 1,000 acres, it's one of the area's biggest lakes, and it's very popular with water-skiers, swimmers, and other non-angling water enthusiasts. Anglers don't have much chance against all that competition on a warm summer day.

If you do go kokanee fishing, try trolling a Wedding Ring spinner or other small, flashy offering behind a string of trolling blades. Add a maggot, a kernel of white corn, or a small piece of worm to the lure's hooks and you're in business. As in all kokanee fishing, use your depthsounder to pinpoint the depth at which the fish are concentrated or keep varying your trolling depth until you find the first fish, and then stay with that depth to locate others. And speaking of depth, this lake has plenty, with some spots plunging 80 to 90 feet.

You may also catch a few rainbow trout as you troll for kokanee. Trolling small wobblers and spinners near the shoreline also produces rainbows, as does stillfishing near the bottom with various baits or suspending a worm, salmon egg, or combination of the two beneath a bobber.

Shoreline areas of the lake also offer largemouth bass, some of them growing to impressive size. Most of the perch are small, but if you find a pocket of large ones, stick with it for a while and see if you can come out with enough of them for a fish fry. The same goes for the bullheads, which are available around the edge of the lake throughout the summer.

Small perch are abundant here and bite throughout the year-round season. Catfish action is best at night from June through August.

Location: Southwest of Allyn in Mason County; see map A2 Inset, grid j2.

Species: Kokanee, rainbow trout, largemouth bass, yellow perch, brown bullhead catfish.

Facilities: There's a Department of Fish and Wildlife access area and boat ramp on the lake, as well as a county park with a boat ramp and room for bank fishing. Twanoh State Park is only a few miles to the north and has more than 60 tent and RV sites. The nearest food, gas, tackle, and lodging are in Belfair and Shelton.

Directions: Take U.S. 101 to Shelton and exit east onto Highway 3 through Shelton; continue northeasterly on Highway 3 to Mason-Benson Road about 11 miles out of Shelton. Turn left and drive about three miles to the lake.

Contact: Verle's Sport Center, 360/426-0933; Twanoh State Park, 360/275-2222; Washington State Parks and Recreation Commission, 360/902-8844 (information) or 888/226-7688 (reservations).

161 Prickett (Trails End) Lake

Stocked with about 4,000 legal-sized rainbows every spring, this 75-acre lake with a year-round season provides its best fishing in April and May. Since most of the lake is less than 20 feet deep, it warms quickly in the summer, but the 30-foot hole about 300 yards off the boat ramp might be worth investigating if you need a trout fix during the warmer months. Trout fishing picks up again in September and October.

For catfish, try the shallow north end of the lake from May through July.

Location: West of Allyn in Mason County;

see map A2 Inset, grid j3.

Species: Rainbow trout, black bullhead catfish.

Facilities: The access area has a small gravel parking lot and gravel boat ramp. Both have very limited room, and the boat ramp tends to clog with dollar pads and other vegetation late in the summer. Twanoh State Park, about six miles to the west on Highway 106, has 47 tent sites and 18 RV spaces with hookups, restrooms, and showers. Restaurants, fast food, lodging, tackle, and other facilities are available in Belfair.

Directions: Drive south from Belfair or north from U.S. 101 near Shelton on Highway 106 and turn east on Trails Road (a sign at the start of the road points the way toward Mason Lake Road). Go 1.5 miles on Trails End Road, turn left on Trails End Road (rather than going straight on what at that point becomes Mason Lake Road), and proceed half a mile to the lake's access area, which is on the left.

Contact: Twanoh State Park, 360/275-2222; Washington State Parks and Recreation Commission, 360/902-8844 (information) or 888/226-7688 (reservations).

162 Devereaux Lake

Except for a boat ramp and a Girl Scout camp, you might think you're on a wilderness lake out in the middle of nowhere when you're in the middle of this large Mason County lake surrounded by trees and with no residential development. You have to like that in a lake, even on days when the fishing is lousy.

But the fishing at Devereaux is usually several cuts above the lousy category. Spring plants of 4,000 rainbows help to provide decent trout fishing well into June, and by that time the kokanee action is starting to pick up. Then just as the kokanee fishing falls off, fall rainbows go on the bite. While pan-sized fish account for most of the catch, Devereaux has a pretty good reputation for its lunker carryovers, and Department of Fish and Wildlife personnel like to talk about the possibility of hooking rainbows to five pounds here. It's never happened to me, but my excuse is that I don't fish the lake very often.

Location: North of Allyn in Mason County; see map A2 Inset, grid j3.

Species: Rainbow trout, kokanee.

Facilities: The Department of Fish and Wildlife has a large access area with a concrete boat ramp near the north end of the lake, and the big fir log next to the boat ramp is a perfect spot to sit and fish from the access area. Both Belfair and Twanoh State Parks are within reasonable driving range, six and 10 miles, respectively, and both have tent and RV sites, restrooms, and showers. Food, gas, and lodging are available both to the north and south on Highway 3. Tackle is available in Belfair.

Directions: Take Highway 3 south from Belfair or north from Allyn and turn west onto Devereaux Road, then drive about one-quarter mile to the lake, which is on the left.

Contact: Washington Department of Fish and Wildlife, Montesano Office, 360/249-4628; Belfair State Park, 360/275-0668; Twanoh State Park, 360/275-2222; Washington State Parks and Recreation Commission, 360/902-8844 (information) or 888/226-7688 (reservations).

163 Coulter Creek

Forested and green, this is a pretty little stream in one of the prettiest parts of the entire Northwest, especially in the fall, when fishing is at its best. Coulter Creek has a fairly good population of resident trout, but few ever achieve the 14-inch minimum size required of a keeper. Fall runs of sea-run trout, however, often contain fish of 14 to 16 inches. Since the creek is small, it usually takes a good rain to draw sea-run fish in, so fish it in foul weather if you can.

Location: Flows into North Bay at the extreme north end of Case Inlet near Allyn; see map A2 Inset, grid j3.

Species: Sea-run and resident cutthroat trout.

Facilities: Food and gas are available in Allyn, with the nearest lodging and tackle in Belfair. Belfair State Park is about nine miles from the creek via Highway 3 and Highway 300.

Directions: Take Highway 3 south from Belfair or north from Shelton and turn east onto Highway 302 at the town of Allyn. Drive about three miles to the Coulter Creek fish hatchery and turn north (left) to follow the east side of the creek.

Contact: Washington Department of Fish and Wildlife, Montesano Office, 360/249-4628; Belfair State Park, 360/275-0668; Washington State Parks and Recreation Commission, 360/902-8844 (information) or 888/226-7688 (reservations).

164 Wye Lake

Some fishing memories have little to do with fishing, and I can't think about Wye Lake without remembering what I saw there one Sunday morning in the summer of 1995. It was cool and rainy, and even at 8 A.M. I couldn't hear or see any sign of human activity on or around the lake. But as I stepped out of my car in the lake's small, gravel public access area, I discovered I wasn't alone. I was sharing the boat ramp with thousands—that's right, thousands—of little brown frogs. I don't know where they were coming from or where they were going, but they obviously had spent the night camping out in the Wye Lake access area, and I couldn't take a step for fear of crushing about a half dozen of them beneath my size 13s. Luckily I had parked well away from the water where most of the major toad frenzy was taking place, so I backtracked carefully toward the car and went somewhere else to fish, leaving the Wye Lake boat ramp to the great hordes of minifrogs (or maybe they were toads) that had claimed it.

Although the idea of launching into some Stephen King–esque tale about little amphibious creatures invading Kitsap County is mighty tempting, it's time to get back to the subject at hand, which happens to be fishing. The shores of this alphabetically shaped lake, originally called Y Lake for obvious reasons, are lined with homes, cabins, docks, and floats, which might lead you to suspect that this is one of those raucous, busy places where no self-respecting angler would be caught dead. But despite all the development, care has been taken to leave the lake as natural as possible. You feel as if you're fishing somewhere wild and natural, even though the signs of humanity are everywhere.

The lake is stocked with legal-sized rainbows in the spring, and some midnight biologist has started a pretty good culture of largemouths, too. What this means is that you can find good trout fishing through May and fair bass fishing from May until early fall.

Gas motors are prohibited on the lake, and it's an excellent place to prospect for either trout or bass from a float tube. Just watch out for the little toads in the access area.

Location: Southwest corner of Kitsap County southeast of Belfair; see map A2 Inset, grid j3.

Species: Rainbow trout, largemouth bass, brown bullhead catfish.

Facilities: A gravel access area and concrete boat ramp are at the south end of the lake, with pit toilets and enough room to park maybe a dozen cars. The nearest food and gas are about four miles south in Vaughn. Food, gas, tackle, and lodging are available in Belfair.

Directions: From the east, take Highway 16 to Bethel and turn west (left) on Lider Road, drive about two miles to Lake Flora Road,

and turn left. Drive about four miles to Dickenson Road and turn south (left), following it about three miles to where it makes a hard right and becomes Carney Lake Road. Another hard right in the road quickly follows, and at that point, turn right onto Wye Lake Boulevard. Take the first left and drive down the hill about 200 yards to the boat ramp, on the right. From the west, take Highway 3 south from Bremerton or north from Belfair and turn east onto Lake Flora Road. Turn south (right) onto Dickenson Road and follow it to Wye Lake Boulevard.

Contact: Washington Department of Fish and Wildlife, Montesano Office, 360/249-4628.

165 Carney Lake

Except for opening day of the season in late April, this is a quiet and peaceful place to fish, thanks in part to its location well off the beaten path and some distance away from most western Washington population centers. The boat ramp is small, the lake is in a rural setting with only a handful of homes around its shores, and there's lots of wildlife. Canada geese are more or less full-time residents here. Throw in the fact that the lake has a prohibition against internal combustion engines and you have yourself a mighty fine place to fish.

The 2,000 or so legal-sized rainbows stocked in the spring get anglers through the first segment of Carney's split season, which closes at the end of June. Fishing reopens September 1, and until the season closes on October 31, there's a pretty good chance of finding a bragging-sized rainbow or two. Fall fly-fishing can be especially good, but bait and hardware enthusiasts also catch their share.

Location: Kitsap-Pierce County line southeast of Belfair; see map A2 Inset, grid j3.

Species: Rainbow trout.

Facilities: A rather rough, gravel access area and boat ramp are located on the west side of the lake, but there are no other facilities in the immediate area. The nearest gas and groceries are at the BP station where you turn onto Wright-Bliss Road. Tackle and lodging are available in Belfair and Purdy.

Directions: Take Highway 16 to Purdy and turn west on Highway 302. Less than a mile after passing the sign pointing to the Minter Creek Salmon Hatchery, turn west (right) at the intersection where the sign points toward Shelton. Drive about three miles to Wright-Bliss Road and turn north (right). Drive just over two miles to the lake, which is on the right.

Contact: Washington Department of Fish and Wildlife, Montesano Office, 360/249-4628.

166 Horseshoe Lake

Moderate plants of legal-sized hatchery rainbows provide fair fishing here in the spring, and there are enough small bullheads available for you to catch a pail of them for a catfish fry.

One of the highlights of a visit to Horseshoe Lake is the big bed of lily pads near the boat ramp at the public access area. The pink and white lilies are gorgeous in early summer, so take your camera and lots of color film along even if you forget the bait and potato chips. Those pad fields, by the way, are good places to start looking for bass and catfish.

With a late April through October season, Horseshoe offers good trout fishing in May and early June. Catfish action is best May through July.

Location: At the Kitsap-Pierce County line northwest of Purdy; see map A2 Inset, grid j4.

Species: Rainbow trout, largemouth bass, brown bullhead catfish.

Facilities: A large gravel access area and boat ramp are located at the southwest corner of the lake, and nearby Horseshoe Lake County Park offers bank fishing and restrooms. Food and gas are available on Highway 302, near

the junction with 94th Avenue. Tackle and lodging are a few miles away in Purdy.

Directions: Take Highway 16 to Purdy and turn west on Highway 302. Cross the tip of Henderson Bay at Wauna and continue approximately two miles to 94th Avenue NW. Turn north (right) and drive 1.4 miles to the boat ramp, which is located immediately past the county park on the right side of the road.

Contact: Washington Department of Fish and Wildlife, Montesano Office, 360/249-4628.

167 Crescent Lake

This 47-acre lake is open to year-round fishing, but your best chance of success is during the spring, following the visit by the Department of Fish and Wildlife's fish-stocking truck. Fish it in May and you'll do all right on 8- to 10-inch rainbows, but fishing can be lackluster the rest of the year.

Location: East of Purdy near the Pierce-Kitsap County line; see map A2 Inset, grid j4.

Species: Rainbow trout.

Facilities: The west side of the lake has a public access area with a boat ramp. Food and gas are available in Purdy, and food, gas, tackle, and lodging can be found a few miles to the south in Gig Harbor.

Directions: Take Highway 16 to Purdy, turn right on Crescent Lake Road, and drive east about two miles to the west shore of the lake.

Contact: Gig Harbor Chamber of Commerce, 360/851-6865.

168 Central Puget Sound

Some of the Northwest's most famous saltwater fishing spots are located here—places such as Tacoma's Point Defiance, Seattle's Elliott Bay, and the Kitsap Peninsula's Point Jefferson, affectionately known by generations of anglers as Jeff Head. Although these and other traditional central Puget Sound salmon-fishing spots may not always be as productive as they were in past decades, there are times when they provide action that's as good as anything the region has to offer. Season restrictions in some areas have taken large bites from what used to be year-round salmon fishing, but others parts of the central sound remain open throughout much of the year, providing realistic opportunities for anglers to catch chinooks, cohos, pinks, or chums about seven months out of 12.

The waters from the Tacoma Narrows bridge to the northern tip of Vashon Island have (so far) escaped most of the serious season-cutting measures and serve as a good example of the salmon fishing still available in central Puget Sound. Point Defiance and the waters immediately to the east—known locally as the Clay Banks—at times provide excellent fishing for resident chinooks, or blackmouth, in November and again when the late-winter season opens in mid-February. These same places once were hot spots for summertime kings of 20 to 40 pounds, but such piscatorial brutes are much rarer these days. Farther east, Commencement Bay—more famous for its toxic bottom sediments than for its fishing—still provides some solid summer and fall salmon as silvers bound for the Puyallup River stage in the bay before moving into the river. During odd-numbered years, pink salmon congregate off the mouth of the Puyallup, often providing even hotter angling action than that offered by the annual coho extravaganza. Other decent salmon spots open much of the year include Point Dalco (at the south end of Vashon Island), Quartermaster Harbor (between the south end of Vashon and Maury Islands), and the waters around Redondo, where anglers casting from the Redondo Pier catch almost as many salmon as nearby boat anglers catch.

And while we're on the subject of piers, there are lots of them available to anglers throughout central Puget Sound, providing angling access to a range of fish species that includes everything from rock crab and pile perch to coho and chinook salmon. They include the Point Defiance, Les Davis, and Old Town Dock Piers along the south side of Tacoma's Commencement Bay; the Dash Point Pier between Tacoma and Federal Way; south King County's Des Moines and Redondo Piers; Blake Island Pier at the island's north end; the First Street Dock, Park Avenue, Waterman, Annapolis, and Port Orchard Piers on Sinclair Inlet; the Silverdale Pier and the Coal Dock on Dyes Inlet; the Keyport, Brownsville, and Illahee Piers along the west side of Port Orchard; Indianola and Suquamish Piers on the shores of Port Madison; Elliott Bay's Pier 86; the Duwamish Head Pier; Shilshole Bay's A Dock; and the Edmonds Pier.

Back to the topic of salmon fishing, the waters of Puget Sound around Seattle and Bremerton are in a different management area than those to the south, and salmon-fishing regulations here have been more restrictive. Summertime closures have come into play in some areas, at times keeping anglers from getting a crack at mature kings and silvers in some spots and keeping them guessing about season openings and closings in others. In a nutshell, it's gotten complicated. Elliott Bay, for example, until a few years ago offered excellent chinook fishing right at Seattle's front door, but in recent years it's been illegal for anglers to keep chinooks in the bay, even while gill-net fisheries continued to take their toll. Jefferson Head, by the same token, is a year-round chinook producer, but since 1995 a limit restriction has prevented anglers from keeping any chinooks from July through October, and a one-chinook limit is in effect during the winter and spring months.

Winter fishing, however, is another story, and there are still places out of Seattle and

Bremerton where feeder blackmouth are plentiful in November and again when the season opens in February. Allen Bank, between Blake Island and the northern tip of Vashon Island, often provides excellent winter blackmouth fishing, as does the Manchester area in the entrance to Rich Passage. The Port Orchard area is another spot that's sometimes red-hot for five- to 10-pound chinooks during the late fall and winter. Various spots along the east side of Bainbridge Island can also be good for winter chinooks, most notably Skiff Point and Point Monroe. Point Jefferson (Jefferson Head) can be an excellent blackmouth spot all fall and winter, especially on an incoming and high tide.

Rockfish and lingcod aren't as abundant here as they were before anglers discovered them when the salmon fishing began to drop off, but there are still places in the central sound where fair bottom fishing can be found. Rock breakwaters, such as those found at Shilshole Bay and Edmonds, are home to both and are often overlooked as anglers head for deeper, more distant bottom-fishing spots. These rock jetties also have greenling and the occasional cabezon, both worthy light-tackle adversaries and welcomed additions on the dinner table.

Natural rock piles and rocky drop-offs, such as the fairly well-known spots around the south end of Bainbridge Island and offshore from Jefferson Head, show on any Puget Sound nautical chart. In addition, this part of the sound has several artificial reefs constructed by the Department of Fisheries during the 1970s and 1980s. They include underwater rock piles near Point Heyer (east side of Vashon Island), just off the south end of Blake Island, south of Seattle's Alki Point, and near Edmonds (two miles south of Point Wells). All are marked with buoys to make them easy to locate.

Small-boat anglers and those without a boat may be overlooking some of the best saltwater angling action the central sound has to offer if they aren't spending lots of time around the area's thousands of docks and bulkheads. These structures, which serve as homes to barnacles and mussels, draw large schools of striped seaperch and pile perch during the spring and summer, and these hard-fighting, sweet-eating fish will take almost any small bait you put in front of them. The waterfront areas of Tacoma, Seattle, and Bremerton are teeming with these cooperative fish—sometimes topping three pounds—and they're just waiting for anglers to come along with light enough tackle and a soft enough touch to catch them.

Location: Marine waters from the King-Snohomish county line south to the Tacoma Narrows; see map A2 Inset, grid j5.

Species: Chinook, coho, pink, and chum salmon; lingcod; various rockfish; saltwater perch; sole; flounder.

Facilities: The launch fee is $4 at Shilshole, where there are restrooms, restaurants, and other facilities nearby. Food is within walking range of the Armeni launch, which also has a $4 fee. Moorage, picnic areas, and plenty of parking are available at the free Dockton Park ramp. The launch sling at Des Moines Marina has fuel, restrooms, restaurants, and stores within walking distance, with launch fees starting at about $6 round-trip. The $4 launch ramp at Redondo has restrooms and a restaurant nearby but is open only during limited hours. The sling at Ole and Charlie's also has limited hours of operation, and launch fees vary with boat length. Boat and motor repairs are available at the site. The launch ramp at the old Asarco plant doesn't have any facilities, but it's free and offers ample parking. There's room to launch three boats at a time at the Point Defiance ramp, with fuel, bait, and groceries available at the nearby boathouse. The launch fee here is $3 round-trip. The free Gig Harbor ramp has no facilities on site, but all are available nearby. The same is true at Manchester. Brownsville Marina has a two-lane ramp with a $2 launch fee, as well as moorage, fuel, showers, and a deli/store. The free, double-wide ramp at Port Orchard has fuel and restrooms close by. The Evergreen Park ramp in Bremerton is also free, with ample parking, picnic areas, and clean restrooms. The ramp at Lion's Field Park is free and has plenty of parking.

Directions: Launch at Shilshole Bay (off Seaview Avenue, Ballard), Don Armeni ramp (off Harbor Avenue, West Seattle), Dockton Park (off Dockton Road, Vashon Island), Des Moines Marina (off Highway 509), Redondo (off Redondo Beach Drive), Ole and Charlie's Marina (off Marine View Drive, Tacoma), Asarco ramp (off Ruston Way, Tacoma), Point Defiance (off Pearl Street, Tacoma), Gig Harbor (at the foot of Randall Street), Manchester (off Main Street), Brownsville (off Highway 303), Port Orchard (off Bay Street), Poulsbo (behind the marine science center), Evergreen Park (off 14th Street, Bremerton), or Lion's Field Park (off Ledo Street, Bremerton) to fish any of several potentially productive spots in these areas.

Contact: Shilshole Bay Marina (Seattle), 206/728-3385; Seacrest Marina (Seattle), 206/932-1050; Breakwater Marine, 253/752-6663; Point Defiance Boat House (Tacoma), 253/591-5325; Auburn Sports and Marine, 253/833-1440. For nautical charts of this area, contact Captain's Nautical Supply, 206/283-7242.

169 Lake Fenwick

Okay, it's time for another quiz. In 10 words or less, what's this lake's biggest claim to fame? I'll give you a big hint: it has something to do with fishing tackle. No, the lake isn't perfectly round like a spool of monofilament, but nice try. If you guessed that this lake is named after the famous tackle company, you're very close. In fact, the famous tackle company is named after this lake. Yes, one of the founders of Fenwick Tackle lived near here and named his fledgling rod company after this little King County lake. Isn't some of the information in this book absolutely fascinating?

But what you really want to know about is the fishing, right? Well, I can help you out there, too. This 18-acre lake is open to year-round fishing and is stocked with hatchery rainbows of about 7 to 10 inches each spring. Carryovers to the next spring, or even through the summer, were pretty much an impossibility until recently, when an aeration system was installed to keep Fenwick oxygenated. If it works as expected, look for better opportunities to catch some bigger rainbows from the lake. Fenwick has lots of natural cover in the form of brush, submerged trees, and weeds, offering bass anglers plenty of chances to do their thing.

Good perch and catfish populations provide added angling variety. Along with the trout, these warm-water species may be caught from the fishing dock at the City of Kent's park near the north end of the lake. The boat ramp is on the lake's west side, and if you're going to use your boat here, remember that gasoline motors aren't allowed.

Location: Southwest of Kent; see map A2 Inset, grid j6.

Species: Rainbow trout, largemouth bass, yellow perch, brown bullhead catfish.

Facilities: The city of Kent has a boat ramp and fishing dock on the lake, with other amenities available to the east in Kent and to the southwest in Federal Way.

Directions: Take I-5 to the South 272nd Street exit north of Federal Way and drive east on 272nd Street. As you start down the hill, look for Lake Fenwick Road, turn north (left), and watch for the lake on the right.

Contact: Auburn Sports and Marine, 253/833-1440.

170 Steel (or Steele) Lake

As with the other lakes around Federal Way, leave the big gas-burner home if you fish Steel. Internal combustion motors aren't allowed here. You don't need one to get around here anyway, since the lake covers only about 47 acres. But for its size it offers lots of fishing variety.

Planted rainbows of 7 to 10 inches draw much of the angler interest when Steel first opens in late April, but it isn't long before the lake's largemouth bass, perch, and other warm-water fish are commanding most of the attention. The shallow west end of the lake warms first and is the first to start providing good bass fishing, but by June anglers are usually catching bass from the many docks and floats that line much of the lake's shoreline. This lake is capable of producing some hefty bass, with fish of seven and eight pounds being caught more often than most people might expect. Perch fishing can be very good from spring to fall, and during the heat of the summer Steel Lake offers good fishing for brown bullheads.

Location: In Federal Way, west of I-5; see map A2 Inset, grid j6.

Species: Rainbow trout, largemouth bass, crappie, yellow perch, brown bullhead catfish.

Facilities: A City of Federal Way park has a boat ramp and roomy fishing dock. All other facilities are available in the area.

Directions: Take I-5 to Federal Way and take the South 320th Street exit. Exit to the west on 320th Street and drive several blocks to Pacific Highway South, turn north (right), and go eight blocks to South 312th Street. Turn east (right) on 312th Street and follow it to the lake, on the left.

Contact: Auburn Sports and Marine, 253/833-1440.

171 Star Lake

Now open to year-round fishing, Star is one of the deeper lakes in the south King County area, so the trout fishing here holds up well into the summer. You'll have to switch from near-surface trolling or fishing a worm beneath a bobber to anchoring a marshmallow or Berkley Power Nugget to the bottom with a sliding sinker, but you can catch rainbows here into July if you want.

You can also catch warm-water fish in July. The 34-acre lake has a few largemouth bass, which can be caught around any of the many docks and floats, and it also has a fair population of brown bullheads to provide summertime night-fishing possibilities.

Location: Northeast of Federal Way; see map A2 Inset, grid j6.

Species: Rainbow trout, largemouth bass.

Facilities: The lake has a rough boat ramp and limited beach access. All amenities are available in Federal Way.

Directions: Take I-5 to the South 272nd Street exit, go east on 272nd Street to Military Road and turn south (right). Drive several blocks to Star Lake Road, turn left, and follow it to 37th Avenue South, which dead-ends at the lake.

Contact: Auburn Sports and Marine, 253/833-1440.

172 Lake Dolloff

Although visible from I-5, this 21-acre lake is just hard enough to reach to keep fishing pressure down compared to the other lakes in the area. Maybe that's why the legal-sized rainbows—along with a few big brood-stock trout thrown in for excitement—tend to provide decent fishing action a little more into the summer than some other King County lakes. Whatever the reason, you can usually find fairly good trout fishing here through June and again in September and October. This lake, by the way, is open year-round.

Something else that seems to be a fairly well-kept secret (at least until now) is that Dolloff produces some big largemouth bass during the course of a typical summer.

The shallow pothole area at the west end of the lake provides not only good bank-fishing access but is also a good place to fish for the lake's abundant yellow perch and to try your luck at night fishing for brown bullheads. If all else fails, try worms for both.

Few anglers go anywhere specifically to fish for crappies, but Dolloff might be a place to do just that. It boasts some of the largest crappies you'll find anywhere in the Puget Sound area, with 12-inchers well within the realm of possibility.

Location: In Federal Way just east of I-5; see map A2 Inset, grid j6.

Species: Rainbow trout, largemouth bass, yellow perch, crappie, brown bullhead catfish.

Facilities: The south side of the lake has a Department of Fish and Wildlife boat ramp and access area, and other amenities are nearby in Federal Way.

Directions: Take I-5 to Federal Way and exit onto South 320th Street. Turn east on 320th Street and drive to Military Road. Go north (left) on Military Road and drive about a mile to where the road passes under the freeway. Turn right just before you drive under the freeway on South 310th Street and follow it completely around the lake to the south side.

Contact: Auburn Sports and Marine, 253/833-1440.

173 North Lake

North Lake is often crowded during the first few weekends of the season, but the trout fishing often gets better after those crowds taper off. Be patient and start fishing it in mid-May and you might do all right on 10- to 12-inch rainbows. Springtime plants of legal-sized rainbows usually include a few brood-stock trout, some of which may top three pounds. If you don't have a boat to get out and troll all the usual things, try casting from the bank along the trail that extends south

from the boat ramp. A bobber-and-worm or bobber-and-jig might work best when the water is still cool, but as the lake warms, you might try casting a bobber-and-fly combination with your spinning rod.

Bass and perch populations have grown considerably here in recent years, and the lake produces some fairly hefty largemouths. The numerous docks dotting the edge of the lake provide plenty of places for bass anglers to try their luck. As for perch, you may not have to go looking for them; they may find you, especially while you're prospecting for trout with that bobber-and-worm rig around the edge of the lake.

Location: West of Auburn; see map A2 Inset, grid j6.

Species: Rainbow trout, largemouth bass, yellow perch.

Facilities: The lake has a boat ramp with beach access for fishing. Food, gas, lodging, and other amenities are nearby in Federal Way.

Directions: Take I-5 to the South 320th Street exit in Federal Way and turn east on 320th Street. Drive half a mile, turn south (right) on Weyerhaeuser Way, and go another half mile to the lake's access area on the left.

Contact: Auburn Sports and Marine, 253/833-1440.

174 Lake Morton

The Department of Fish and Wildlife stocks this popular southeastern King County lake with about 4,000 rainbow trout each year to keep anglers happy, and the fishery holds up fairly well until about June. Now and then the department throws in a few larger cutthroat for variety, and these fish may average 14 inches and weigh a pound each. Summertime trolling may also turn up a kokanee or two, although these small landlocked salmon are not planted in the lake.

There are enough two- to three-pound bass here to make it well worthwhile bringing your bass gear along. As for perch, try fishing a garden worm or leadhead jig-and-worm combination under a bobber at the north end or narrow south end of the lake. Morton produces some hefty perch that are well worth pursuing. Remember that gas motors are not allowed on this 66-acre lake, so confine your means of locomotion to oars or electric motors.

Location: East of Auburn; see map A2 Inset, grid j7.

Species: Rainbow and cutthroat trout, kokanee, largemouth bass, yellow perch.

Facilities: The northwest corner of the lake has a good boat ramp with beach fishing.

Directions: Drive east from Covington on Covington-Sawyer Road and take the second road to the south (right) to the lake.

Contact: Auburn Sports and Marine, 253/833-1440.

175 Lake Sawyer

At first glance, Lake Sawyer is an average-sized, average-looking suburban western Washington lake, complete with nice homes, beach cabins, and diving boards, but don't let first impressions fool you. Beneath all those trappings of suburbia is a lake that offers year-round fishing for a wide range of cold-water and warm-water species.

Perhaps best known among Sawyer's many possibilities is its bass fishery. It isn't the kind of place where you can hang a plastic worm or spinnerbait from your line and start hooking bass one after the other, but if you're patient enough to fish all morning or all evening to hook a couple of bass, those fish might be three to five pounds. Odds are that most of the bass you'll hook will be largemouths, but don't be surprised if your efforts produce a smallmouth from time to time. Smallies to four pounds are occasionally caught.

Although much of the lake is developed, there are plenty of docks, floats, and other forms of man-made cover to prospect for bass. If you like fishing weeds and heavier cover, try the southeast corner of the lake, which is the only part that is still pretty much undeveloped. If you're looking for your best crack at hooking (and hopefully releasing) a really large bass, you might do your fishing during the spawn, which usually takes place here from late May through June.

The lake has some fairly large perch and crappies, and if you can locate a school of either, you can expect some hot fishing and sweet eating. Small leadhead jigs will take both of these popular panfish, but if you want perch, you might try tipping the jigs' hooks with a small piece of worm.

Trolling the middle portions of the lake during the spring or fall may produce rainbow or cutthroat trout as well as kokanee. During the summer months, anglers who want to avoid the water-skiers and speed-boaters might want to fish early or late in the day. That's when the speed limit on the lake is a mere 8 mph. During the middle of the day, that limit goes up to 30 mph, so the water may get churned up pretty well. Those faster boats, however, aren't allowed inside the string of marker buoys that line the shallows about 100 feet offshore, so you can get away from some of the craziness by staying close to the beach while fishing.

Location: Northwest of Black Diamond; see map A2 Inset, grid j8.

Species: Largemouth and smallmouth bass, rainbow and cutthroat trout, kokanee, yellow perch, crappie, brown bullhead catfish.

Facilities: A paved boat ramp is at the northwest corner of the lake, plus a resort that has rental cabins and trailers, RV sites, boat and canoe rentals, and a country store. Lake Sawyer Store, a short distance away, has tackle and sells fishing licenses.

Directions: Drive east from Kent on Kent-Kangley Road (Highway 516) and turn south (right) on 216th Avenue, which is about three miles east of Highway 18. Just over a mile down 216th Avenue, turn east (left) on Covington-Sawyer Road to the lake.

Contact: Sunrise Resort, 253/630-4890; Auburn Sports and Marine, 253/833-1440.

176 Ravensdale Lake

Without a road running right to its shores, this 18-acre lake offers float-tubers and anglers willing to carry small boats to the water a chance to escape the crowds. There is some bank-fishing opportunity, but a small craft of some kind certainly offers an advantage.

A more or less self-sustaining population of cutthroats provides decent spring and fall fishing, and every now and then someone hooks a trout of 15 or 16 inches. This is a no-bait lake, so take along only your favorite spoons, spinners, nymph patterns, and other artificials, and if you want to keep a trout for the table, it has to be at least 12 inches long.

Location: North of Black Diamond; see map A2 Inset, grid j8.

Species: Cutthroat trout.

Facilities: The lake has no facilities. Kanaskat-Palmer State Park, about seven miles east via Lake Retreat-Kanaskat Road, has limited tent and RV sites. The nearest food, gas, lodging, and tackle are in Kent and Enumclaw.

Directions: Drive east out of Kent on Kent-Kangley Road to Georgetown. Turn south on Black Diamond Road and drive about half a mile to Ravensdale. The lake is a 50-yard hike off Black Diamond Road immediately west of Ravensdale.

Contact: Kanaskat-Palmer State Park, 360/886-0148.

177 Lake Twelve

It's a fairly long drive for most folks—except, of course, those who happen to live in Black Diamond—but the angling variety available in this 45-acre lake can make the trip worthwhile. Open year-round, Lake Twelve offers its best trout fishing in May and June, after the Department of Fish and Wildlife has made its annual plant of 2,000 8- to 10-inch rainbows and a sprinkling of cutthroats pushing a pound apiece. Fall trout fishing can also be fairly productive.

In the summer, bass fishing draws some interest, and there are good numbers of perch to catch if the largemouths have lockjaw. Bring along a can of night crawlers and stay until dark to catch a string of brown bullheads, most of which run 10 to 13 inches.

Location: Northeast of Black Diamond; see map A2 Inset, grid j8.

Species: Rainbow and cutthroat trout, largemouth bass, yellow perch, brown bullhead catfish.

Facilities: The lake has a boat ramp and toilets at its public access area. Food and gas are available in and around Black Diamond. Kanaskat-Palmer State Park, about four miles to the east, has limited tent and RV sites, restrooms, and showers. The nearest lodging and tackle are found in Enumclaw.

Directions: Take Highway 169 north from Enumclaw to Black Diamond and turn east (right) on Green River Gorge Road. Turn north (left) on Lake Twelve Road (270th Street SE) about 1.5 miles out of Black Diamond and drive half a mile to the lake.

Contact: Kanaskat-Palmer State Park, 360/886-0148.

178 Retreat Lake

Although it covers more than 50 acres, this King County lake with a year-round season near the base of Sugarloaf Mountain isn't anything to get excited about. Public access is limited since there's no boat ramp or Department of Fish and Wildlife access area, and the lake doesn't receive any hatchery plants. Still, a small population of trout survives here, and panfish action can at times provide worthwhile results during the summer.

Location: Northeast of Black Diamond; see map A2 Inset, grid j8.

Species: Rainbow and cutthroat trout, largemouth bass, yellow perch.

Facilities: The lake has no facilities, but Kanaskat-Palmer State Park, with a few tent and RV sites, restrooms, and showers, is about six miles away, to the east. Enumclaw and Kent offer the nearest food, gas, tackle, and lodging.

Directions: Take Kent-Kangley Road east from Kent to Georgetown. About 1.5 miles east of Georgetown, turn south (right) on Lake Retreat–Kanaskat Road and drive half a mile to the lake, which is on the left.

Contact: Kanaskat-Palmer State Park, 360/886-0148.

CHAPTER A3:
NORTH CASCADES

©TERRY RUDNICK

TROLLING LAKE CHELAN

Map A3

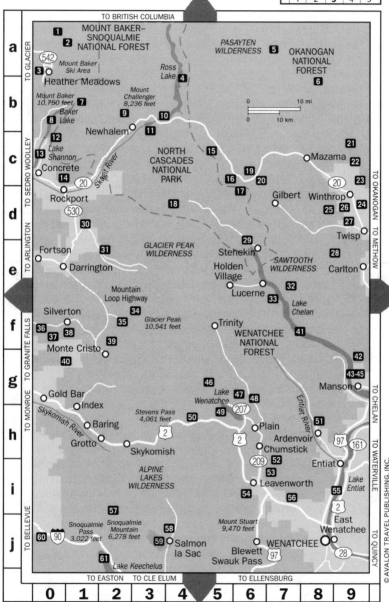

TO BRITISH COLUMBIA

a
TO GLACIER

1
2
MOUNT BAKER–
SNOQUALMIE
NATIONAL FOREST

PASAYTEN
WILDERNESS **5**

OKANOGAN
NATIONAL
FOREST
6

542
Mount Baker
Ski Area
3
Heather Meadows

Ross
Lake
4

b
TO SEDRO WOOLLEY

Mount Baker
10,750 feet **7**
8
Baker
Lake

Mount
Challenger
8,236 feet
9
10

Newhalem
11

0   10 mi
0   10 km

12
Lake
Shannon
13
Concrete
14
20

c

NORTH
CASCADES
NATIONAL
PARK

15

19
16 **20**
17

Mazama
21
22

d
TO ARLINGTON

Rockport
530

18

Gilbert

20 **23**
Winthrop
25 **26** **24**
27
Twisp
28
Carlton

TO OKANOGAN / TO METHOW

30

e

Fortson
31
Darrington

GLACIER PEAK
WILDERNESS

29
Stehekin
Holden
Village
Lucerne
33

SAWTOOTH
WILDERNESS

32
Lake
Chelan

f
TO GRANITE FALLS

Silverton
36
37 **38**
Monte Cristo
40

Mountain
Loop Highway
34
35
39

Glacier Peak
10,541 feet

Trinity

WENATCHEE
NATIONAL
FOREST

41

42

g

Gold Bar
Index

46
Lake
Wenatchee
47 **48**
49 207

43-45
Manson

Entiat River

h
TO MONROE

Baring
Grotto
Skykomish

Skykomish River

Stevens Pass
4,061 feet
2

50

2

Plain
Ardenvoir
Chumstick
209 **52**
53
Leavenworth

51
97 161

TO CHELAN / TO WATERVILLE

i

ALPINE
LAKES
WILDERNESS

54

55
Lake
Entiat
2

56

j
TO BELLEVUE

57
Snoqualmie
Pass
3,022 feet
60 90

Snoqualmie
Mountain
6,278 feet
58
59 Salmon
la Sac
61
Lake Keechelus

Mount Stuart
9,470 feet

Blewett
Swauk Pass

WENATCHEE
97

East
Wenatchee
28

TO QUINCY

TO EASTON   TO CLE ELUM   TO ELLENSBURG

0   1   2   3   4   5   6   7   8   9

© AVALON TRAVEL PUBLISHING, INC.

Chapter A3: North Cascades

This is where people go to find mountains, woods, and wilderness. The wild lands to explore here include Mount Baker–Snoqualmie National Forest, Okanogan National Forest, Glacier Peak Wilderness, Sawtooth Wilderness, Wenatchee National Forest, and Alpine Lakes Wilderness. The region's only major city is Wenatchee, and for every one person living in the region there are dozens of Douglas fir and lodgepole pine trees. If one of the reasons you go fishing is to find solitude, the North Cascades region probably has what you're looking for. There are lots of high-country lakes and miles of mountain streams where you can fish all day without running into anyone else. But there's also a lot of big water that holds trophy-class trout and salmon, and you can't keep that kind of fishing a secret. Lake Chelan promises the best lake trout (Mackinaw) fishing in Washington, a chance to catch 20-pound chinook salmon, lots of foot-long rainbow trout, limits of fine-eating kokanee, and some of central Washington's best smallmouth bass fishing. Fish Lake gives up more trophy brown trout than any other lake in the state. At Lake Wenatchee you can catch and release a 10-pound bull trout and, some years, find the only open season on sockeye salmon anywhere east of the Cascades. If there were a little more room here, I'd tell you about the big Dolly Varden in the upper Skagit River, the fat trout of Baker Lake, the big walleyes that inhabit the Columbia below Wenatchee …

©TERRY RUDNICK

LAKE CHELAN

1 Tomyhoi Lake

If you're expecting to hike four miles one-way to a little alpine lake where you can cast from one end to the other, you'll be surprised at what you find. Tomyhoi is better than three-quarters of a mile long and covers nearly 100 acres. What's more, it's pretty deep, so your favorite spoon, spinner, or artificial fly will, quite literally, only scratch the surface. But that may be enough to catch a couple of pan-sized brookies from around the edge of the lake. Catching two or three rainbows may require a little more effort and some longer casts, but it can certainly be done. It wouldn't be a bad idea to take along a jar of salmon eggs, Power Bait, or even a few dozen worms, and if the weather is warm and sunny, don't be shy about fishing bait on the bottom for a chance at a large rainbow. Snow and ice are usually gone from the lake by late June, with July and August offering the best weather and fishing conditions.

Location: Northeast of Shuksan in the Mount Baker Wilderness; see map A3, grid a0.

Species: Rainbow and brook trout.

Facilities: There's nothing at the lake but bank access and primitive campsites. Silver Fir Campground (U.S. Forest Service) is located at the junction of Highway 542 and Forest Service Road 3065. The nearest food, gas, tackle, and lodging are in Deming.

Directions: Take I-5 to Bellingham and exit east on Highway 542. Follow Highway 542 about 52 miles up the North Fork Nooksack River beyond Glacier to Forest Service Road 3065. Turn north (left) and follow Forest Service Road 3065 four miles to the trail on the left, which leads to the lake. From there it's a four-mile hike to the water.

Contact: Mount Baker–Snoqualmie National Forest, Mount Baker Ranger District, 360/856-5700; Mount Baker–Snoqualmie National Forest, Glacier Public Service Center, 360/599-2714.

2 Twin Lakes

This pair of 20-acre lakes nestled between Goat and Winchester Mountains has lots of visitors during an average summer season, and the fishing pressure keeps trout populations in check. Since the lakes are quite deep, someone occasionally hauls a bragging-sized fish onto the beach. I would suggest fishing a marshmallow-and-salmon-egg combination or adding a lively worm to a marshmallow or Power Nugget and fishing the combination near bottom to have a crack at one of these Twin Lakes trophies. Use a quarter-ounce slip-sinker, and when it's time to cast, don't be afraid to let it fly. These high-country lakes are open and fishable from late June to about mid-September.

Location: Northeast of Shuksan in the Mount Baker Wilderness; see map A3, grid a1.

Species: Rainbow trout.

Facilities: The U.S. Forest Service's Silver Fir Campground is about five miles to the south of the lakes and has tent and trailer sites, restrooms, picnic tables, and drinking water. Other amenities are available in Deming, 32 miles west on Highway 542.

Directions: Take I-5 to Bellingham and exit east on Highway 542, following it 52 miles up the North Fork Nooksack River beyond Glacier to Forest Service Road 3065. Turn north (left) and follow Forest Service Road 3065 about five miles to its end, where the lakes are on the left.

Contact: Mount Baker–Snoqualmie National Forest, Mount Baker Ranger District, 360/856-5700; Mount Baker–Snoqualmie National Forest, Glacier Public Service Center, 360/599-2714.

3 Galena Chain Lakes

You might find a large brookie or two in Iceberg Lake, the largest of the five major lakes in this system, but trout of 7 to 10 inches provide the bulk of the angling action on these small and relatively easy-to-reach high lakes on the northeastern flank of Mount Baker. Upper and Lower Bagley Lakes, the easternmost lakes in the chain and the closest to the Mount Baker Ski Area, get quite a lot of fishing pressure, but you're a little more likely to beat the crowds if you hike west to Iceberg, Hayes, or Galena Lakes.

No matter which of the lakes you fish, you'll be treated to some of the most fantastic scenery in the North Cascades, including bird's-eye views of Mount Baker. All of these lakes are best fished late in the summer, after the deep snows have had time to melt away.

Location: Southwest of the Mount Baker Ski Area; see map A3, grid a0.

Species: Brook trout.

Facilities: The lakes have no facilities, but Silver Fir Campground, managed by the U.S. Forest Service, is about eight miles away. Food, tackle, gas, and lodging are available at Deming, to the west on Highway 542.

Directions: Take I-5 to Bellingham and exit east on Highway 542, following it up the North Fork Nooksack River to the Mount Baker Ski Area. Continue on to the end of the road and the parking area, where a six-mile loop trail will take you to the five lakes.

Contact: Mount Baker–Snoqualmie National Forest, Mount Baker Ranger District, 360/856-5700; Mount Baker–Snoqualmie National Forest, Glacier Public Service Center, 360/599-2714.

◪ Ross Lake

It's one of western Washington's biggest lakes, but only a tiny segment of the angling population has fished it. This may sound like a *Jeopardy* answer, but it's really Ross Lake, the 21-mile-long Skagit River impoundment behind Ross Dam that backs up from near the North Cascades Highway to the British Columbia border and beyond. You really have to want to fish Ross Lake, since there aren't

any perfectly simple ways to go about it. Invest the time and effort, though, and you might be rewarded with good summertime trout fishing.

Ross is managed as a quality fishery with special regulations, which means you can't use bait, and all lures and flies must have single, barbless hooks. The daily limit is three trout, and the minimum size is 13 inches. Unlike most of the state's smaller lakes with selective fishery regulations, it's OK to use boats equipped with gas motors when you're fishing this long lake where the wind sometimes comes booming down the canyon. Besides having special regulations, Ross Lake has a special season, opening July 1 and closing at the end of October.

Rainbows provide most of the fishing action, and trolling with small spoons or spinners takes many of them. Trolling with a variety of fly patterns is also effective. You'll catch a few cutthroats for your efforts and an occasional brook trout. Although they must be released, the lake also has some large Dolly Varden, and from time to time someone brings a huge one to the boat.

Location: In the east end of Whatcom County; see map A3, grid b4.

Species: Rainbow, cutthroat, and brook trout; Dolly Varden.

Facilities: The only boat ramp on the lake is at the north end, but Ross Lake Resort near the dam at the south end has cabins and bunkhouse units for more than 80 guests, plus boat rentals (14-footers with 9.9 horsepower outboards) and other amenities. There are also U.S. Forest Service campsites at Green Point, Cougar Island, Big Beaver Creek, Little Beaver Creek, and Silver Creek, all on the west side of the lake. Campsites on the east side include those at Roland Point, McMillan Creek, May Creek, Rainbow Point, Devil's Junction, Ten-Mile Island, Ponderosa, Lightning Creek, Cat Island, and

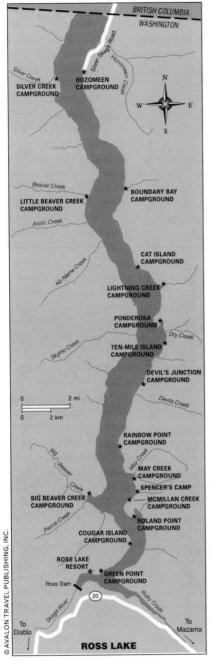

BRITISH COLUMBIA
WASHINGTON

Silver Creek
SILVER CREEK
CAMPGROUND

HOZOMEEN
CAMPGROUND

Silver-Skagit Road

Hozomeen Creek

N
W E
S

Beaver Creek
LITTLE BEAVER CREEK
CAMPGROUND

BOUNDARY BAY
CAMPGROUND

Arctic Creek

No Name Creek

CAT ISLAND
CAMPGROUND

LIGHTNING CREEK
CAMPGROUND

PONDEROSA
CAMPGROUND

Dry Creek

TEN-MILE ISLAND
CAMPGROUND

Skymo Creek

DEVIL'S JUNCTION
CAMPGROUND

0   2 mi

0   2 km

Devils Creek

RAINBOW POINT
CAMPGROUND

Big Beaver

May Creek

MAY CREEK
CAMPGROUND

SPENCER'S CAMP

BIG BEAVER CREEK
CAMPGROUND

MCMILLAN CREEK
CAMPGROUND

Pierce Creek

ROLAND POINT
CAMPGROUND

COUGAR ISLAND
CAMPGROUND

ROSS LAKE
RESORT

Ross Dam

GREEN POINT
CAMPGROUND

Skagit River

20

Ruby Creek

To
Diablo

To
Mazama

ROSS LAKE

© AVALON TRAVEL PUBLISHING, INC.

Boundary Bay. Ross Lake Resort offers food, gas, tackle, and lodging.

Directions: Take Exit 230 off I-5 at Burlington and drive 68 miles east on Highway 20 to Diablo. Catch the Seattle City Light tugboat at 8:30 A.M. or 3:00 P.M. to the base of the dam, where you'll be picked up and ferried to Ross Lake Resort. Hikers may continue east on Highway 20, past Diablo to the trailhead east of the lake. Some 10 campsites are scattered along the trail to about two-thirds of the way up the lake. (A water taxi service from the resort is also available to take you to any of these campsites.) If trailering a boat to the north end, take I-5 to Bellingham and turn east on Highway 539 to Sumas. From there continue east on Canada Highway 401 to the Silver Creek cutoff, two miles west of Hope, then drive south to Hozomeen, on the east side of the lake.

Contact: Ross Lake Resort, Rockport, WA 98283, 206/386-4437 (Seattle phone number), website: www.rosslakereorts.com; Ross Lake Ranger Station, North Cascades National Park, 360/873-4590.

5 Hidden Lakes Chain

This is one of the most interesting places I've never fished. That's right, I said never fished, and since I'm not getting any younger, I may never make it. Of course, if I do try, the 12-mile trek to these wilderness lakes could do me in before my time, so I may have to pass. If you plan to hike to these four productive trout lakes, you'd better be tough or have plenty of time to make the trip. Although not a steep hike, it's a long one. May I recommend saddling up ol' Scout or booking a trip with an outfitter who spends considerable time in these hills? That way, your backside will be sore, but you'll reduce wear and tear on your legs and feet. Plan your trip for sometime between early July and mid-September, when you're least likely to encounter snow.

Once you make it to the general area, you'll have four lakes to choose from, each with its own distinctive personality. Cougar Lake is the southernmost of the bunch and the first you'll reach as you hike or ride in from the south. Next in line is First Hidden, then Middle Hidden, and finally Big Hidden Lake. Those who've been there say that each is a wonderful place to cast a small, red-and-white Dardevle spoon or Panther Martin spinner into the depths, let it sink several feet, and then retrieve it just fast enough to keep it working enticingly through the clear water. Early and late in the day find a shoreline log or boulder to cast from and try your hand with the dry fly of your choice on a lightweight fly rod. Or cast with your favorite spinning outfit about five feet down the line from a clear plastic casting bubble.

Most of the rainbows you'll catch from any of these lakes will run 9 to 12 inches, the cutts a little smaller. Brook trout will average about eight inches.

Location: In the Pasayten Wilderness in northwest Okanogan County; see map A3, grid a7.

Species: Rainbow, cutthroat, and brook trout.

Facilities: This is wilderness, so take everything you need. The last chance for food, gas, and other necessities is in Winthrop.

Directions: Take Highway 20 to Winthrop and drive 10 miles north up the Chewack River on Forest Service Road 51. Turn west (left) on Forest Service Road 5130 and follow it 17 miles to the trailhead at the end of the road. From there it's a 12-mile hike to the first lake.

Contact: Okanogan National Forest, 509/826-3275.

6 Black Lake

If you get an early start, you can hike in, fish the lake several hours, and make it out the same day—but why hurry? This deep, 66-acre lake has plenty to offer, both in terms of decent fishing and above-average scenery.

Black Lake produces some large rainbows late in the summer, after the water has had ample time to warm. Take a fly rod to get the most from your stay, but if all you take is a spinning outfit, you'll probably score a couple of nice trout to fry over the campfire. Although the lake is open year-round, the best fishing and weather conditions are from mid-May to early October.

Location: North of Winthrop in Okanogan National Forest; see map A3, grid b8.

Species: Rainbow and cutthroat trout.

Facilities: Several primitive campsites can be found around the lake. The nearest formal U.S. Forest Service campground is Camp 4, 10 miles back down the road. The closest food, gas, lodging, and tackle are in Winthrop.

Directions: Take Highway 20 to Winthrop and drive north on Chewack River Road (Forest Service Road 51). Stay on the main road past Camp 4 and turn west (left) on Forest Service Road 100. Follow Forest Service Road 100 to the end and hit the trail for nearly four miles to the lake.

Contact: Okanogan National Forest, 509/997-2131; Methow Valley Visitor Center, 509/996-4000.

7 Baker River

The trout season here is a short one, running only from July 1 to 31 and September 1 to October 31. During that time you'll find a few rainbows and cutthroats in this Skagit River tributary, and maybe have a chance to catch a big Dolly Varden. This is one of only a few Washington rivers where it's legal to keep a Dolly, but it has to be at least 22 inches long to be fair game. The Baker also has a salmon season, but it's even shorter than the trout season, lasting only during the month of July. During that time anglers catch a few sockeye salmon. Be sure to check the regulations pamphlet for details on both of these fisheries, which change quite regularly. It's a long drive for only fair fishing, but the clear water and steep-sided canyons of the Baker River Valley help to make it a worthwhile trip. If you lace up your hiking boots and work your way upriver to boldly go where you think no one has ever gone before, the scenery will get better, but you may not notice much improvement in the fishing.

Location: Flows into the north end of Baker Lake near the center of Whatcom County; see map A3, grid b1.

Species: Rainbow and a few cutthroat trout, Dolly Varden, sockeye salmon.

Facilities: Three U.S. Forest Service campgrounds are located near the north end of Baker Lake, along the west side, providing good take-off points for anglers heading up the river. All other facilities are back down on Highway 20 in Hamilton and Concrete.

Directions: Take Highway 20 east from I-5. About five miles east of Hamilton, turn north (left) on Baker Lake Road and follow it about 28 miles to the upper end of the lake and the Forest Service road that follows the river a short distance upstream. From there you can hike up the east side of the river.

Contact: Mount Baker–Snoqualmie National Forest, Mount Baker Ranger District, 360/856-5700.

8 Baker Lake

Kokanee draw most of the attention at this 3,600-acre Baker River impoundment, where koke anglers can be rewarded generously. The waters around the south end of the lake near the two dams often produce the best kokanee catches, but if you pay close attention to your depthsounder as you explore the lake, you may find a school of these little salmon almost anywhere. All the usual trolling and stillfishing strategies take Baker Lake kokes, but check the fishing regulations pamphlet closely before going after them. Among other unusual rules here, there's an 18-inch maximum size limit, established to help protect a depleted population of ocean-run sockeye salmon that still trickles into the lake.

As with kokanee, you might find a respectable rainbow trout almost anywhere on this big reservoir, but I recommend fishing around the mouths of the many streams that flow into the lake. Maybe I just have a prejudice for such spots and spend more time around the creek mouths than anywhere else, but I've found that the fresh, moving water, like that near the mouths of Sandy, Little Sandy, Boulder, Park, Shannon, Noisy, Anderson, and the other creeks entering Baker, are hard to beat when you're searching for a trout on the prowl. Try trolling a Triple Teazer, Dick Nite, Canadian Wonder, or similar wobbling spoon in silver/red head, and don't be afraid to troll it at the middle depths or deeper if you're looking for a bragging-sized rainbow. Even if you don't catch one, you'll enjoy the grand view of Mount Baker (if you can ignore all the clear-cuts in the foreground).

Location: North of Concrete in the Mount Baker National Forest; see map A3, grid b0.

Species: Kokanee, rainbow trout.

Facilities: U.S. Forest Service campgrounds and boat ramps are located at Horseshoe Cove, Panorama Point, Park Creek, and Shannon Creek, all on the west side of the lake, and Maple Grove, on the east side. The nearest food, gas, tackle, and lodging are back on Highway 20 in Hamilton and Concrete.

Directions: Take Highway 20 east from I-5. About five miles east of Hamilton, turn north (left) on Baker Lake Road and follow it about 17 miles to the first of several roads leading right toward the lake.

Contact: Mount Baker–Snoqualmie National Forest, Mount Baker Ranger District, 360/856-5700.

9 Thornton Lakes

Lower Thornton is the biggest and easiest to reach of the three lakes and therefore the most heavily fished. I'm not particularly proud to admit that I've never caught a trout there, but it's true. I'm sure that other, more skilled anglers have more positive stories to relate. Middle Thornton is the smallest lake in the chain, and it's not particularly productive either, but the upper lake does give up some fairly good catches now and then. If you're thinking about going to the trouble of hiking to any of these waters, I recommend you go for broke and hike all the way to the uppermost of the three and concentrate your angling efforts there. Spend at least one morning or evening casting flies around the shoreline, where hungry cutthroats and an occasional brook trout are likely possibilities. Although open to year-round fishing, these lakes are best fished May through October.

Location: Northwest of Newhalem in southern Whatcom County; see map A3, grid b2.

Species: Cutthroat and brook trout.

Facilities: Lots of primitive campsites can be found around the shores of all three lakes. The nearest food, gas, and lodging are back on Highway 20 and in the Marblemount area.

Directions: Take I-5 to Burlington and drive east on Highway 20. Go about 10 miles past Marblemount and turn north (left) on Thornton Creek Road, which ends at the trailhead to Thornton Lakes. From there it's about a three-mile hike to the first lake.

Contact: North Cascades National Park, 360/856-5700.

10 Diablo Lake

The first time I ever stopped to try my luck at Diablo was in late summer, and it made sense to me when one of the anglers I talked to at the boat ramp suggested that I should "fish deep." Stopping near one of the spots he recommended, I tied a half-ounce Krocodile spoon to my line and dropped it over the side of the boat. This was back in the early 1970s, and I didn't even own a depth-sounder, so I didn't know what I was getting myself into. My plan was to pay out line until the heavy wobbler found bottom, reel up a couple of feet, and put the motor in gear to begin some serious deep trolling. But three minutes later the Krocodile was still dropping and the spool of my old Mitchell 300 spinning reel had only four or five wraps of line left on it. Undaunted, I reeled the lure back to the surface, replaced the reel's low-capacity spool for the one that held more than 200 yards of 10-pound monofilament, and started the whole process over again. I don't know if that half-ounce Krocodile ever hit bottom, but when I estimated that I'd let out 250 feet of line, I decided that was deep enough. When I engaged the motor, of course, the lure began to climb toward the surface, and I never did really "fish deep" in Diablo Lake. Nor did I catch any trout that September afternoon. I did, however, make one very important discovery: Diablo is one damned deep lake. This reservoir, resulting from a dam in one of the Skagit River's steepest canyons, reportedly has places more than 300 feet deep.

The moral of this story is that if you plan to fish deep at Diablo, you'd better take along your downrigger. The good news is that during most of Diablo's year-round season, it isn't necessary to ply the deep, dark depths in order to catch rainbows and cutthroats. Shallower shoreline areas, such as the two large bays along the north side of the reservoir, can be adequately productive. The ever-popular gang-troll-and-worm combination works as well here as anything for trout that range 8 to 18 inches.

Location: On the Skagit River immediately south of Ross Lake in the southeast corner of Whatcom County; see map A3, grid b3.

Species: Rainbow and cutthroat trout.

Facilities: Diablo Lake Resort has a boat ramp (for resort guests only), tackle, tent and RV sites, restrooms, and showers. There's a two-lane, concrete ramp with a loading float at Colonial Creek Campground, near the south end of the lake. Colonial Creek also has more than 150 campsites, restrooms, showers, and other amenities. Marblemount and Concrete are the nearest places offering lodging, food, and gas.

Directions: Exit I-5 at Burlington and drive east about 68 miles on Highway 20 to the lake.
Contact: Diablo Lake Resort, 206/386-4429 (Seattle).

11 Gorge Lake

This lowermost and smallest of three back-to-back reservoirs on the upper Skagit River is stocked with hatchery trout and also offers the very real possibility of hooking a lunker carryover from its green depths. Those cool depths are certainly worth fishing for trout throughout the summer, when many western Washington lakes are too warm for productive trout action. Much of Gorge Lake's bottom is more than 100 feet beneath the surface, and the water is plenty cool to keep rainbows and cutthroats actively feeding through the hottest days of July and August. Drop a couple of salmon eggs down there, use a downrigger to take your favorite trout lure into the depths, or try vertical jigging with a three-quarter-ounce Crippled Herring or Krocodile spoon.
Location: On the Skagit River immediately downstream from Diablo Lake in southeastern Whatcom County; see map A3, grid b3.
Species: Rainbow and cutthroat trout.
Facilities: A U.S. Forest Service campground and a boat ramp are both near the upper end of the lake. Diablo Lake Resort, three miles east, has tent and RV sites, showers, restrooms, and tackle. Marblemount and Concrete offer complete facilities.
Directions: Take I-5 to Burlington and turn east on Highway 20, following it 65 miles to the lake.

Contact: Mount Baker–Snoqualmie National Forest, Mount Baker Ranger District, 360/856-5700.

12 Watson Lakes

OK, so you have to hike a few miles, but for your efforts you can fish any of six lakes in fairly close proximity. Big and Little Watson are the largest of the bunch and the main attractions for anglers, but the smaller Anderson Lakes a half-mile hike to the south may also strike your fancy. There are four Anderson Lakes, named 1, 2, 3, and 4 by some highly creative hiker.

A dry fly fished along the shoreline at daylight or dusk will take trout from all these lakes. When the sun is higher in the sky, cast a small spoon, spinner, fish salmon eggs, or egg-and-marshmallow combo on the bottom.
Location: East of Baker Lake in southern Whatcom County; see map A3, grid c0.
Species: Rainbow trout.
Facilities: The lake has no facilities. The nearest food, gas, tackle, and lodging are in and around Concrete.
Directions: Drive east from I-5 on Highway 20. At the town of Concrete, turn north (left) on Baker River Road and drive up the east side of Lake Shannon about 11 miles to the south end of Baker Lake and Forest Service Road 1107. Turn right, drive to spur road 1107-022, and turn left, driving to the end of the road and the beginning of the 2.5-mile trail to the lakes.
Contact: Mount Baker–Snoqualmie National Forest, Mount Baker Ranger District, 360/856-5700.

13 Lake Shannon

Get out your leaded line, downriggers, Wedding Ring spinners, Glo-Hooks, or whatever it is you like to use for kokanee and be sure to take them along if you plan on fishing this 2,100-acre reservoir. Kokanee fishing is the name of the game for anglers on this lower of two impoundments on the Baker River. The kokes aren't particularly big here, but they are usually plentiful (especially June throuh August), so a little searching with your depthsounder or taking some time to watch where and how other anglers are catching them should put you into some action.

If you happen to hook a lunker over 18 inches, it's probably a sea-run sockeye rather than a kokanee, and it must be released unharmed.

Location: Immediately north of Concrete in Skagit County; see map A3, grid c0.

Species: Kokanee.

Facilities: A boat ramp is located on the southeast corner of the lake, at the end of a gravel road to the left off Baker River Road. Unless some repair work has been done on it lately, it's a rather steep and rough launch, so think twice about bringing your 20-footer. There's a motel in Concrete and an RV park just off Highway 20 on Baker Lake Road. Food, gas, and tackle are also available in Concrete.

Directions: Drive east from I-5 on Highway 20. At the town of Concrete, turn north (left) on Baker River Road, which parallels the east side of Lake Shannon.

Contact: North Cascade Inn, 800/251-3054, website: www.north-cascade-inn.com; Creekside Camping, 360/826-3566.

14 Upper Skagit River

It's still possible to catch steelhead from the upper Skagit, but you'll have to work a lot harder at it than in the good old days. Back then, some Skagit fishing guides ran two trips a day, getting steelhead limits for their clients in the morning and taking a second group in the afternoon, often finding limits for them, too. Catching a two-fish steelhead limit is no longer a sure thing here, and even catching one fish isn't guaranteed, whether you're fishing during the summer or the winter. The best months for winter-runs are January, February, and March, and there's a fair possibility of finding a summer-run steelhead if you fish June through August.

Casting fresh shrimp, back-trolling plugs, or pitching weighted spinners into the deep green pools and drifts of the upper Skagit may also draw strikes from the river's big Dolly Varden, some of which exceed the river's 20-inch minimum size limit.

Location: From Concrete upstream to Diablo; see map A2, grid c1.

Species: Winter and summer steelhead, Dolly Varden.

Facilities: There are several boat ramps along this upper stretch of the Skagit:

- **Fabor's Ferry Ramp:** The Washington Department of Fish and Wildlife's Fabor's Ferry ramp is a one-lane concrete launch located about five miles east of Concrete off Highway 20.

- **Howard Miller Steelhead Park:** Farther upstream near Rockport is the Howard Miller Steelhead County Park, managed by Skagit County Parks and Recreation. Accumulations of sand sometimes clog this ramp.

- **Skagit River Bald Eagle Natural Area Ramp:** This access area and ramp, which were all but washed out as of spring 1999, are located off Highway 20.

- **Marblemount Ramp:** Washington Department of Fish and Wildlife–maintained, this ramp lies beneath the Cascade River bridge across from Marblemount. It's another one where large amounts of sand sometimes pile up and make launching difficult.

- **Copper Creek Ramp:** This ramp is located at the mouth of Copper Creek, about five miles east of Marblemount.

- **Goodell Creek Campground:** Although there's no formal ramp at Goodell Creek Campground, paddlers and steelhead anglers sometimes carry or drag their boats to the water here.

Remember that a $10 WDFW access decal is required to use the public launch areas maintained by the Washington Department of Fish and Wildlife.

Directions: Take I-5 to Burlington and turn east on Highway 20. The highway follows the Skagit upriver nearly 60 miles to Diablo Dam.

Contact: Rockport Country Store, 360/853-8531; Rockport State Park, 360/853-8461; Washington State Parks and Recreation Commission, 360/902-8844 (information) or 800/452-5687 (reservations).

15 Granite Creek

Thousands of people drive right by Granite Creek on any given summer's day, but only a handful ever stop to fish it. Those who keep going may be doing the right thing, since the aesthetics aren't all that great and the trout aren't all that big or all that abundant. It's not that the North Cascades aren't beautiful, but on Granite Creek you can't quite get far enough away from the highway traffic to escape the sound of cars and RVs racing by.

Location: Parallels the North Cascades Highway through eastern Skagit County; see map A3, grid c5.

Species: Rainbow and brook trout.

Facilities: There's nothing in the immediate area. Food, gas, tackle, and lodging can be found in Concrete and Hamilton.

Directions: Take Highway 20 east from Marblemount or west from Winthrop. The highway parallels and crisscrosses the creek for about 15 miles between Rainy Pass and the south end of Ross Lake.

Contact: North Cascades National Park, 360/856-5700.

16 Lake Ann

Although a relatively short hike away from one of Washington's busy summertime highways, the trail to Lake Ann doesn't host nearly as many anglers as it does casual hikers, photographers, and other outdoor enthusiasts. It's worth the half-hour walk to try for 7- to 10-inch cutthroats in the gin-clear water. Arm yourself with a few of your favorite weighted spoons and spinners and plenty of insect repellent.

Western Washingtonians on their way to or from the popular trout lakes of the Okanogan country might consider stopping here for two or three hours to break up the long drive over the North Cascades. Open year-round, Lake Ann is best fished June through September.

Location: West of Highway 20 at Rainy Pass, just south of the Okanogan-Skagit county line; see map A3, grid c5.

Species: Cutthroat trout.

Facilities: The nearest camping area is the Forest Service's Lone Fir Campground, about 11 miles east on Highway 20, which has tent sites and a few RV sites, water, and restrooms.

Directions: Take Highway 20 east from Ross Lake or west from Winthrop to Rainy Pass, drive to the southern end of the parking areas, and hit the trail heading west about 1.5 miles to the lake.

Contact: Okanogan National Forest, Winthrop Ranger District, 509/996-2266; North Cascades National Park, 360/856-5700.

17 Rainy Lake

Although not a place where you can escape humanity, Rainy Lake has all the other qualities of a high-country lake, including crystal-clear water and magnificent scenery. What's more, you can stop near the highway to straighten out after several hours behind the wheel, walk to the lake for two hours of exercising your arms with a fly rod, and still get to where you're going on schedule. You might even hook a couple of sassy cutthroat trout for your efforts. You'll probably encounter other anglers, but at 54 acres, this lake is big enough to give you plenty of elbowroom throughout the June through September period when most folks visit.

Location: West of the North Cascades Highway at Rainy Pass in northern Chelan County; see map A3, grid d6.

Species: Cutthroat trout.

Facilities: The U.S. Forest Service campground at Lone Fir has 21 tent sites and six RV sites, as well as water and restrooms. The nearest amenities are in Winthrop.

Directions: Drive east from Ross Lake or west from Winthrop on Highway 20 to the large parking area on the south side of the highway at Rainy Pass. It's an easy stroll of about half a mile to the lake from the south end of the parking lot.

Contact: Okanogan National Forest, Winthrop Ranger District, 509/996-2266; North Cascades National Park, 360/856-5700.

18 Trapper Lake

You really have to want to fish this 145-acre, high-elevation lake, since it's not the kind of place you stumble on by accident. Although Trapper is a beautiful lake in an even more beautiful setting, it offers only fair fishing for small rainbows and an occasional cutthroat. As in the case of many Washington lakes, overuse has taken its toll on the impressive cutthroat fishing Trapper Lake used to offer. But if you use fishing as your excuse to lace on the hiking boots and don a day pack, this one is worth visiting. Just stay on the trails, pack out everything you take in, and enjoy the experience. This is a summertime fishery in a place that's snow-covered and iced up from October to May.

Location: Three miles southeast of Cascade Pass; see map A3, grid d4.

Species: Rainbow and cutthroat trout.

Facilities: Cottonwood is the nearest campground, but there are several others along

the road from Stehekin. The closest stores, food, lodging, and tackle are in Stehekin.

Directions: Take Highway 20 to Rockport and turn south on Highway 530 (Sauk Valley Road). After crossing the Skagit River, drive about 1.5 miles to Rockport-Cascade Road and turn east (left). Cross the Cascade River near the Skagit Fish Hatchery, turn right at the T on Cascade Road, and continue east to Cascade Pass. From there it's about a four-mile hike by trail to the north side of the lake. From the east take the passenger-only ferry up Lake Chelan to Stehekin and head north on the only road out of town. Go to Cottonwood Campground and hike up the hill to the south about three-quarters of a mile to the lake.

Contact: North Cascades National Park, 360/856-5700; North Cascades Stehekin Lodge, 509/682-4494, website: www.stehekin.com; Stehekin Valley Ranch, 509/682-4677, website: www.courtneycountry.com.

19 Cutthroat Lake

True to its name, you'll find cutthroat trout here, lots of them. In fact, according to the Department of Fish and Wildlife, you'll find too many of them. This is one of those places where on a good day you'll hook smallish cutts cast after cast, and you may even get tired of casting before they get tired of biting. Though they won't be large fish, feel free to catch a limit for the frying pan. If you're a less-than-adequate fly caster and want to do something to bolster your self-esteem, Cutthroat Lake could be the place for you. Although the fish season here is year-round, the best action is in the spring and again in the fall.

Location: Northwest of Washington Pass near the Okanogan-Chelan-Skagit County line; see map A3, grid c6.

Species: Cutthroat trout.

Facilities: The U.S. Forest Service's Lone Fir Campground has 21 tent sites and six RV sites, but the nearest concentration of food, gas, lodging, and other amenities is in Winthrop.

Directions: Take Highway 20 east from Ross Lake or west from Winthrop to Forest Service Road 400 (also known as Cutthroat Creek Road), which is about midway between Lone Fir and Washington Pass. Turn west on Forest Service Road 400 and drive about 1.5 miles to its end, where a one-mile trail leads southwesterly to the lake.

Contact: Okanogan National Forest, Winthrop Ranger District, 509/996-2266.

20 Early Winters Creek

This fast-moving stream right along the highway is tough to fish and produces only fair catches at best. Try it in late June or early July with worms and you might catch a keeper or two, but don't expect too much.

Location: Parallels the North Cascades Highway from Washington Pass to the Methow River; see map A3, grid c7.

Species: Rainbow and cutthroat trout.

Facilities: Early Winters, Klipchuck, and Lone Fir Campgrounds (all U.S. Forest Service) are scattered along the highway within casting distance of the creek. They offer tent sites, toilets, and drinking water. Winthrop has food, gas, tackle, and lodging.

Directions: Take Highway 20 west from Winthrop. The highway parallels the creek for about 15 miles.

Contact: Okanogan National Forest, 509/826-3275.

21 Chewack (Chewuch) River

Special regulations on this Methow River tributary mean you have to leave the worms and salmon eggs home during the general summer season. Although you can find success by fishing a small nymph pattern on a sink-tip line, many anglers prefer to work a small spinner through the deeper pools and medium-

depth runs. Whether you go with flies, spinners, or some other form of artificial, be sure it has a single, barbless hook. These selective fishery rules, along with strict catch-and-release regulations, are now in effect through the summer season in order to protect endangered steelhead on the upper Columbia River system. There is a catch-and-keep winter whitefish season here, but it also has special rules on hook size, aimed at protecting against the accidental hooking (or landing) of any steelhead.

Location: Flows into the Methow River at Winthrop; see map A3, grid c9.

Species: Rainbow and cutthroat trout, mountain whitefish.

Facilities: Five U.S. Forest Service campgrounds are scattered along the river between Winthrop and Thirtymile Campground. Winthrop has several motels and a couple of RV parks, as well as food, gas, and tackle.

Directions: Take Highway 20 to Winthrop and drive north up Chewack Road (Forest Service Road 51) or Eastside Chewack Road (Forest Service Road 5010), both of which closely parallel the river.

Contact: Okanogan National Forest, 509/826-3275; Pine-Near Trailer Park, 509/996-2391; Methow Valley KOA Campground, 509/996-2258, website: www.methownet.com/koa; Chewuch Inn, 509/996-3107, website: www.chewuchinn.com.

22 Buck Lake

Although well off the heavily traveled highways, this forest lake is easily accessible, so it can get busy during the summer, especially on long holiday weekends. The fishing is just fair for pan-sized trout from intermittent hatchery plants. They'll take small spinners, salmon eggs, marshmallows, and an assortment of artificial flies.

Location: North of Winthrop in Okanogan National Forest; see map A3, grid c9.

Species: Rainbow trout.

Facilities: The U.S. Forest Service's Buck Lake Campground has four tent sites and five sites suitable for small RVs. Other amenities can be found in Winthrop.

Directions: Take Highway 20 to Winthrop and drive north on Chewack River Road (Forest Service Road 51), then turn west (left) on Forest Service Road 100 and drive about 2.5 miles to the lake.

Contact: Okanogan National Forest, Winthrop Ranger District, 509/996-2266.

23 Pearrygin Lake

Generous loads of hatchery rainbow fingerlings that grow to good size in a hurry help to make this one of eastern Washington's favorite trout lakes. Most of the rainbows run 9 to 10 inches when the lake opens to fishing in late April, but Pearrygin also offers a better-than-average shot at carryovers that may range 14 to 20 inches. These bonus trout are beautiful, red-meated fish that are as good in the frying pan or oven as they are in front of a camera lens.

The usual trout-fishing goodies are all popular here, with anglers who stillfish favoring Berkley Power Bait, worms, salmon eggs, and marshmallows, not necessarily in that order. Trollers like Rooster Tail and Bang Tail spinners, small Hot Shot plugs, Flatfish, Kwikfish, Triple Teazers, Dick Nites, and Canadian Wonders.

Location: Northeast of Winthrop; see map A3, grid c9.

Species: Rainbow trout.

Facilities:

- **Pearrygin Lake State Park:** The state park ramp has one lane with a loading float and parking for about 30 cars with trailers. There's a $4 launch fee (and a $40 annual permit available) if you're not camping at the park.

- **Derry's Resort:** The ramp at Derry's Resort also is one lane, but it has no loading float. A fee is charged to launch. This resort, run by the Department of Wildlife, has RV sites with full hookups, tent sites, rental cabins, motor boats and paddleboats for rent, playground equipment, a large swimming area, convenience store, RV dump station, and a large lawn area near the water.

- **Jeffrey's Silverline Resort:** The ramp at Jeffrey's Resort is unpaved and has a couple of loading floats. A fee is charged to launch. Jeffrey's has RV and tent sites, restrooms with showers, a swim beach, and a small store. Other amenities are available in Winthrop.

- **Department of Fish and Wildlife's Ramp:** Located at the Washington Department of Fish and Wildlife's public access area, this ramp is gravel and has room for about two dozen cars and boat trailers. A $10 WDFW access decal is required to use the public launch area.

Directions: Take Highway 20 to Winthrop and turn north on County Road 9137, following it 1.5 miles to County Road 1631. Turn east (right) on County Road 1631 and drive half a mile to the lake.

Contact: Pearrygin Lake State Park, 509/996-2370 (April to November); Derry's Pearrygin Lake Resort, 509/996-2322 (April to November only).

24 Davis Lake

Like Cougar and Campbell Lakes to the east and north (see numbers 25 and 26 in chapter A4), Davis Lake has for many years had a fishing season that opens in September and runs through March. More recently, a catch-and-release season has been added during what used to be the "closed" period from April 1 through August 31. This 40-acre lake southeast of Winthrop is sometimes a little too warm for great fishing when it first opens, but by October the rainbows usually come alive, offering good open-water fishing until early December and then sometimes decent ice fishing for a few weeks in January and February. Late-season trout action may be good when the ice opens up.

Stillfishing with red salmon eggs has long been a favorite method of taking Davis Lake rainbows, but in recent years more and more anglers have been finding success with Berkley's various Power Bait offerings.

Location: Southeast of Winthrop; see map A3, grid d9.

Species: Rainbow trout.

Facilities: The lake has a public access area with a boat ramp. Motels, RV parks, restaurants, grocery stores, and other facilities are nearby in Winthrop.

Directions: Take Highway 20 to Winthrop and drive southeast out of town on County Road 9129 to Bear Creek Road. Turn east (left) on Bear Creek Road and continue to Davis Lake Road, where you should turn south (right). Drive about a mile on Davis Lake Road to the lake, which is on the right.

Contact: Pine-Near Trailer Park, 509/996-2391; Methow Valley KOA Campground, 509/996-2258, website: www.methownet.com/koa; Chewuch Inn, 509/996-3107, website: www.chewuchinn.com.

25 Patterson Lake

This 130-acre lake usually stays cool well into the spring, which sometimes translates into slow early season fishing and better action as May turns to June. (The season runs late April throuh October.) Most of Patterson's rainbows (the result of fingerling plants the previous year) average about 10 inches on opening day, growing to 11 or 12 inches by the end of the summer.

Trolling with Wedding Rings or worms behind a string of trolling blades is popular here, and if you prefer lighter gear, try a green Rooster Tail, which has long been a Patterson Lake producer. Berkley's Power Bait in a variety of colors has taken this area by storm in recent years, but you'll also find anglers taking trout on salmon eggs, marshmallows, and combinations of the two. I know from personal experience that stillfishing with a couple kernels of yellow corn on a small egg hook is also effective. Add one small split shot so it sinks to the bottom, leave the bail open on your reel, and give the fish plenty of time to take it. I spent several days catching limits of fat rainbows with this technique when I was a kid fishing Patterson for the first time, and it still works today.

Artificial flies are also effective at Patterson, both cast with standard fly rods and trolled on monofilament with spinning tackle. Productive fly patterns here are nymphs and wet flies in olive green, brown, and black color schemes. Those tied on size 8 or 10 hooks seem to work best.

One of the pleasant things about fishing here is that water-skiers and speedboaters are kept at bay by a 10 mph speed limit. That means you can stay on the water to enjoy the fishing and the view of the nearby pine-covered hills all day long, even during those warm days of summer.

Location: Southwest of Winthrop; see map A3, grid d8.

Species: Rainbow trout, some brook trout.

Facilities: The lake has a public access area with restrooms and a boat ramp, as well as a long-established private resort. Winthrop, three miles to the east, has all the other amenities.

Directions: Take Twin Lakes Road (County Road 9120) southwest from Winthrop, turn west on Patterson Lake Road (County Road 1117), and drive four miles to the lake.

Contact: Patterson Lake Resort, 509/996-2226.

26 Twin Lakes

These popular lakes receive substantial plants of hatchery rainbow trout, which are known to put on ounces and inches quickly. Both Big Twin (80 acres) and Little Twin (23 acres) have special regulations or seasons. Big Twin Lake has what the Department of Fish and Wildlife calls "selective fishery regulations," which means that you have to use artificial lures or flies only, and the daily catch limit is just one fish. That's OK, of course, if the one trout you keep happens to be a plump 17 inches, which is well within the realm of possibility here. I like to fish a green Carey Special fly on Big Twin during May or early June, but you can catch rainbows using a wide variety of artificial lures.

Little Twin is one of several Okanogan County lakes to have a winter-only fishing season, which usually runs from December 1 through the end of March. Like its bigger neighbor, Little Twin Lake offers up some impressive trout throughout the winter months, with 11-inchers quite common and carryovers to 16 inches or larger a good possibility. Try fishing a single red salmon egg or Berkley Power Bait near the bottom of the lake for the best results at Little Twin. In what has become something of a trend on lakes that once had winter-only fishing seasons, this one is also open to catch-and-release-only fishing April through November.

Location: South of Winthrop; see map A3, grid d9.

Species: Rainbow trout.

Facilities: Both lakes have public access areas and boat ramps, with a resort on Big Twin that offers limited groceries, tackle, boats, tent and RV sites, showers, and restrooms. Lodging and other amenities are available in Winthrop.

Directions: Take Highway 20 south from Winthrop, drive about two miles to Twin Lakes Road, and turn west (right). Follow Twin Lakes Road approximately 1.5 miles to Big Twin Lake. Little Twin is reached by following a road that runs along the east side of Big Twin.

Contact: Big Twin Lake Resort and Campground, 509/996-2650, website: www.methownet.com/bigtwin.

27 Twisp River

Like other Okanogan County rivers, this one now has selective-fishery regulations and catch-and-release rules in effect to protect wild steelhead. The season runs June through September, but it's hardly worth the effort now that hatchery plants have ceased.

Location: Joins the Methow River at the town of Twisp; see map A3, grid d9.

Species: Rainbow trout.

Facilities: U.S. Forest Service campgrounds at War Creek, Mystery, Poplar Flat, and South Creek offer a total of about three dozen tent and trailer sites, with the largest number available at War Creek and Poplar Flat. These two larger campgrounds also have drinking water, which isn't available at South Creek or Mystery. Food, gas, lodging, RV parks, and other amenities are available in and around Twisp, including Riverbend RV Park, just north of town.

Directions: Take Highway 20 to Twisp and turn east on Twisp River Road, which follows the river upstream for miles.

Contact: Okanogan National Forest, Twisp Ranger District, 509/997-2131; Riverbend RV Park, 509/997-3500, website: www.riverbendrv.com.

28 Black Pine Lake

Neither the lake nor its brook trout are particularly large, but together they draw a fair amount of attention from both local and visiting anglers. Black Pine is a pretty lake in a beautiful setting, which makes the experience good whether the brookies are biting or not.

The lake is a favorite of float-tube anglers who work the shoreline casting flies or hardware into the weed beds around the perimeter of this crystal-clear lake. If you pay attention, you can sometimes see the fish before they strike. Small Canadian Wonders, Triple Teazers, and other little wobbling spoons in silver, bronze, or half-and-half color combinations are effective lures here. May, June, September, and October tend to produce the largest numbers of trout.

To hook larger fish, try trolling these offerings as deep as possible in some of the lake's deeper water. Trolling flies can also be an effective method of catching the big guys. A favorite technique is to troll as deeply and as slowly as possible using a fly pattern appropriately called a Stick. It's nothing more than a number 10 hook wrapped with green chenille, no tail, no hackle, but the Black Pine brookies seem to respond to it, and that's all that counts around these parts.

Location: Southwest of Twisp; see map A3, grid e9.

Species: Brook trout.

Facilities: The lake has a U.S. Forest Service campground, a boat ramp, and a fishing dock. All other necessities can be found in Twisp.

Directions: Take Highway 20 to Twisp and drive west on Poorman Creek Road about 3.5 miles to Forest Service Road 300. Turn south (left) here and drive approximately six miles to the lake. Rough, bumpy Forest Service Road 300 is best suited for pickups and four-wheel-drive rigs, so take it slow and easy.

Contact: Okanogan National Forest, Twisp Ranger District, 509/997-2131; Riverbend RV Park, 509/997-3500; website: www.riverbendrv.com.

29 Stehekin River

Like Domke Lake to the south (see number 33), the Stehekin is a popular spot during the summertime tourist season. It has lots of special regulations, so be sure to check the fishing pamphlet very carefully before even making a cast. The river now is a catch-and-release fishery only (it's been close to that for several years, so most anglers won't notice). This out-of-the-way end of Lake Chelan does offer some decent-sized trout for the persistent angler, and there are a lot of touristy things to do, such as shopping and touring historic Stehekin. The fishing may keep you occupied for only a day, but plan on spending at least a couple more exploring the Stehekin Valley.

Location: Flows into the north end of Lake Chelan; see map A3, grid d6.

Species: Rainbow and cutthroat trout.

Facilities: Lodging is available at North Cascades Stehekin Lodge and Stehekin Valley Ranch. Half a dozen National Park Service campgrounds are scattered along the river as far upstream as Bridge Creek. Food, some tackle, and lodging are available in Stehekin.

Directions: Take U.S. 97 to the south end of Lake Chelan and the town of the same name and then take the $21 passenger ferry ride to Stehekin at the north end of the lake. Work your way upstream on foot or catch the shuttle bus at Stehekin, ride it 12 miles to the mouth of Agnes Creek, and work your way downstream from there. The river is closed above Agnes Creek.

Contact: North Cascades National Park, 360/856-5700; North Cascades Stehekin Lodge, 509/682-4494, website: www.stehekin.com; Stehekin Valley Ranch, 509/682-4677, website: www.courtneycountry.com.

30 Sauk River

There was a time, about two decades ago, when the Sauk was one of Washington's top two or three big-fish steelhead streams. Winter-run steelies in the 20-pound class were a distinct possibility, and every once in a while someone boated or beached a monster of 25 pounds or better. I remember a newspaper item that told of an angler's first trip to the Sauk, during which he landed not one but two steelhead over 20 pounds in a single day. Such catches might be a virtual impossibility these days, but the Sauk still has a trophy-fish mystique that makes it special to those old-timers (like me) who remember it at its best.

If you caught a trophy-class steelhead from the Sauk now, chances are pretty good that you'd have to release it, since those big, wild fish tend to return in March and April, a time when steelhead regulations here now allow catch-and-release angling only. During the regular (catch-and-keep) winter season, anglers catch several dozen steelhead, most of them during January and February. Both boat and bank fishing are effective, and Sauk River anglers use pretty much all the usual steelhead baits and lures to take fish.

The river also has a small run of summer steelhead, and anglers find them scattered throughout the river from the summer season opener in June through the end of August. They catch a few summer-runs in September and October also, but during those months all steelhead caught from the Sauk have to be released.

It's OK to keep a Dolly Varden from the Sauk if it's over 20 inches long, and the river gives up a fair number of these big predator fish. Try night crawlers or large spoons to fool them. Luhr Jensen's Krocodile in virtually any of the metallic finishes is a good Dolly Varden getter.

Location: Flows northward to join the Skagit River near Rockport; see map A3, grid d1.

Species: Winter and summer steelhead, Dolly Varden, cutthroat trout.

Facilities: Rockport State Park, located near the mouth of the Sauk on the north bank of the Skagit River, has 50 RV sites with hookups and a limited number of tent sites,

as well as restrooms with showers. U.S. Forest Service campgrounds located at Clear Creek and Bedal also have tent and RV sites. Food, gas, tackle, and fishing licenses are available in Darrington.

Directions: Take I-5 to Burlington and turn east on Highway 20, following it 32 miles to Rockport. Turn south (right) on Highway 530 at Rockport and follow it 19 miles up the Sauk River Valley to Darrington. An alternate route is to turn east off I-5 on Highway 530 near Arlington and follow it to Darrington. The Mountain Loop Highway and Darrington–Clear Creek Road parallel the east and west sides of the Sauk, respectively, upstream from Darrington.

Contact: Sauk River Trading Post, 360/436-1500, website: www.saukrivertradingpost.com; Mount Baker–Snoqualmie National Forest, Darrington Ranger District, 360/436-1155; Rockport State Park, 360/853-8461; Washington State Parks and Recreation Commission, 360/902-8844 (information) or 800/452-5687 (reservations).

31 Suiattle River

The good news is that the Suiattle is one of several streams on the Skagit River system where it's still OK to keep a Dolly Varden should you happen to hook one, and there still are some to hook. The better news is that regulations have changed in recent years to allow anglers an opportunity to take summer steelhead here in September and October. Add it all up and the Suiattle is worth a summertime visit. You will encounter a few paddlers along the river, some of whom don't understand how to be considerate of anglers, but they shouldn't bother you much. To cover all the bases, fish night crawlers; they're effective for Dolly Varden and will attract the larger cutthroats, and the occasional summer steelhead you might encounter may also show an interest.

Avoid some of the summertime angling pressure and improve your chances of hooking fish by getting away from the road, which is easier to do downstream from Buck Creek than it is farther upstream.

Location: Joins the Sauk River north of Darrington; see map A3, grid e2.

Species: Summer steelhead, cutthroat trout, Dolly Varden.

Facilities: A U.S. Forest Service campground with tent and RV sites, restrooms, and picnic tables is located at Buck Creek, about 16 miles upriver. Food, gas, lodging, and tackle are available in Darrington.

Directions: Take Highway 530 east from I-5, through Arlington, then through Darrington. Right after the highway crosses the Sauk River about seven miles north of Darrington, take the first right onto Forest Service Road 26, which follows the Suiattle River upstream.

Contact: Sauk River Trading Post, 360/436-1500, website: www.saukrivertradingpost.com; Mount Baker–Snoqualmie National Forest, Darrington Ranger District, 360/436-1155.

32 Lake Chelan–Sawtooth Wilderness Lakes

If you're the kind of hiker/angler who likes to get your money's worth out of a trip, you could easily spend two weeks on the trail and/or on the water here. There are about a dozen and a half named lakes along Sawtooth Ridge, including (north to south) West, Middle, East Oval, Star, Bernice, Libby, Upper and Lower Crater, Surprise, Upper and Lower Eagle, Boiling, Cub, the two Martin Lakes, Cooney, and Sunrise. A particular lake's productivity and even what species of trout the lake produces might well depend on how recently (or if) the lake has been planted by Department of Fish and Wildlife personnel or by volunteers who have packed fish in on their backs. But no matter what, you'll soon find a lake that offers trout willing to take your bait or lure.

Although individual lakes or even two or three lakes may be within reach of a one-day hike, you'll greatly increase your odds of finding good fishing if you plan on spending at least a couple of days sampling what this spectacular part of Washington has to offer. The best time to visit this area is in June and July or after Labor Day weekend in September.

Location: East of Lake Chelan; see map A3, grid e7.

Species: Rainbow and brook trout.

Facilities: The U.S. Forest Service campground at the junction of Foggy Dew Creek and North Fork Gold Creek is the nearest roadside camping area. It has a dozen tent sites and pit toilets but no drinking water. The nearest food, gas, tackle, and lodging are in Twisp and Pateros.

Directions: To reach the northern lakes, drive west from Twisp on Twisp River Road to Buttermilk Creek Road and turn south (left). Drive about 4.5 miles to Forest Service Road 4300-500 and turn west (right), driving about three miles to the end of the road and a trail continuing west about eight miles to the first lake. To reach the central lakes in the long chain, drive north from Pateros or south from Twisp on Highway 153 and turn west on Gold Creek Road (Forest Service Road 4340). Stay to the right on Forest Service Road 4340 for about seven miles and turn left on Forest Service Road 300, which is a dirt road. Follow the road just under five miles to its end and hit the trail at the Crater Creek Trailhead. From there it's a 3.5-mile hike to Crater Lake. An alternate route to the southernmost lakes in the chain is to turn left off Gold Creek Road onto Forest Service Road 200 (at Foggy Dew Campground) and follow it about four miles to the end, where the trail up Foggy Dew Creek begins.

Contact: Okanogan National Forest, Twisp Ranger District, 509/997-2131.

33 Domke Lake

A popular side trip for summertime visitors to Lake Chelan, Domke sees lots of camping and angling activity from about mid-June to Labor Day. It holds some large trout, but you may have to fish long and hard to catch one. Pan-sized rainbows will hit dry flies during the first and last two hours of daylight, but you may have to break out the spinning rod to find success during the rest of the day. I would recommend hiking in one day, spending the night, and coming out the next afternoon. That should give you enough time to fish and explore this beautiful corner of Wenatchee National Forest.

Location: South of Lucerne on the west side of Lake Chelan; see map A3, grid f7.

Species: Rainbow and some cutthroat trout.

Facilities: There are six U.S. Forest Service campsites at Domke Lake, two at Lucerne, and four at nearby Refrigerator Harbor. Food, lodging, tackle, and other necessities are available in Chelan.

Directions: Take U.S. 97 to the town of Chelan and catch the ferry up Lake Chelan to Lucerne ($21 round-trip). From there it's less than a two-mile hike on the clearly marked trail to the north end of the lake.

Contact: Wenatchee National Forest, Chelan Ranger District, 509/682-2576.

34 Glacier Peak Lakes

Anglers who visit any of 18 or so lakes above the headwaters of the Suiattle and White Chuck Rivers near Glacier Peak get a chance to fish some beautiful little lakes and take in fabulous alpine scenery at the same time. What's more, these lakes are stocked regularly (but not annually) with tiny rainbow trout fingerlings, most of which are packed in on the backs of Department of Fish and Wildlife personnel and volunteer hiker/anglers. If you ever meet any of these folks along the trail, be sure to thank them, because if it weren't for their efforts, most of Washington's high-country lakes would be barren of fish.

Although there isn't much of a trail system to them, the cluster of lakes near Lime Mountain (south of Sulphur Creek Campground on the upper Suiattle) are close enough together that they can all be fished in a single day. This chain of nine lakes includes the three Box Mountain lakes, Rivord Lake, Twin Lakes, and the two Milk Lakes. A few miles to the southeast and accessible from trails off Forest Service Roads 2550, 2710, and 2710-011 are Indigo, Crystal, Meadow, Emerald, and Diamond Lakes, all of which offer good summertime fishing. Farther south are Round Lake, Camp Lake, and Lake Byrne. These three can be reached from the south by a trail off Forest Service Road 49 or from the north by a trail starting at the end of Forest Service Road 23.

Lake Byrne is not only the biggest lake of the entire bunch at 50 acres, but it's also the closest to Kennedy Hot Springs, a popular muscle-soothing stop for hikers near the west flank of Glacier Peak. Depending on your priorities, you can either stay an extra hour to cast for trout at the end of your soak or you can stay an extra hour to soak at the end of your fishing trip. Either way, you win.

The fishing season here is determined by the snow pack and ice cover, which usually recede by late June. July and August are the closest to being sure-thing months, but during the extremely heavy snowfall year of 1999, some of these lakes didn't open until the end of September. Take along a selection of small Flatfish, Daredevil spoons, and Metric Spinners, as well as several dry flies, which can be cast with the addition of a small plastic bobber about four feet up the line.

Location: Immediately north and west of Glacier Peak in Mount Baker–Snoqualmie National Forest near the Snohomish-Chelan county line; see map A3, grid f3.

Species: Rainbow trout.

Facilities: U.S. Forest Service campgrounds are located throughout the area, including Buck Creek and Sulphur Creek Campgrounds on the Suiattle River, White Chuck Campground at the confluence of the White Chuck and Sauk Rivers, and Bedal Campground at the confluence of the North Fork and South Fork Sauk River. All have campsites, toilets, and drinking water. The nearest food, gas, tackle, and lodging are in Darrington.

Directions: To reach the Lime Mountain lakes, drive north from Granite Falls on Highway 530 about seven miles and turn east (right) on Forest Service Road 26. Follow it 25 miles to the end and hike up Milk Creek Trail. After two miles, secondary trails to the right lead one to three miles to the lakes. Meadow Mountain area lakes are reached by driving south from Granite Falls on Mountain Loop Highway and turning east (left) on Forest Service Road 23. Turn left onto Forest Service Road 27 and right onto Forest Service Road 2710, drive to the end, and hike five to eight miles to the various lakes. To reach Lake Byrne, stay on Forest Service Road 23 to the end and hike five miles to the lake.

Contact: Mount Baker–Snoqualmie National Forest, Darrington Ranger District, 360/436-1155.

35 White Chuck River

Fish it during most of the summer months and you'll understand how the White Chuck (or Whitechuck, depending on where you see it written) got its name. It's often a milky white or grayish color, making for pretty tough fishing if you aren't the patient type. But if you fish it with small salmon egg clusters or lively night crawlers and let the bait soak a few seconds in every likely spot you can find, you'll eventually find success. You can keep Dolly Varden from the White Chuck, provided they're at least 20 inches long, and some of them grow a whole lot larger than 20 inches. Just ask Leroy Thompson of Darrington, who in August 1999 caught a whopping 10-pound, 15-ounce Dolly from the White Chuck that earned him a new state record for the species. Thompson's lunker broke the previous record, which stood for 19 years, by nearly a full pound. Despite a road that provides easy access to most of the river, the colored water helps to keep angling pressure on the White Chuck fairly light.

Location: Flows into the Sauk River southeast of Darrington; see map A3, grid f2.

Species: Cutthroat trout and Dolly Varden.

Facilities: U.S. Forest Service campgrounds with tent and trailer sites are located to the north at Clear Creek and to the south at Bedal, both on the Sauk River. The nearest food, gas, tackle, and lodging are in Darrington.

Directions: Take Highway 530 east from I-5 to Darrington, cross the Sauk River just east of town, and turn south (right) on the Mountain Loop Highway (Forest Service Road 22). Cross the White Chuck River at its confluence with the Sauk River and turn east (left) upstream.

Contact: Sauk River Trading Post, 360/436-1500, website: www.saukrivertradingpost.com; Mount Baker–Snoqualmie National Forest, Darrington Ranger District, 360/436-1155.

36 Heather Lake

This is one of those high-country lakes you can fish without devoting four days of your life to it and without crawling on hands and knees over 10 miles of broken rock with a 60-pound pack on your back. You will gain about 800 feet in elevation over the one-mile trail, so it's no stroll through the park. But you can hike in, fish several hours, and hike out in a single day if you stay on the move.

The shallow 15-acre lake doesn't produce many lunkers, but the steep, rugged cliffs surrounding it and the snow banks that linger well into summer make Heather Lake a nice place to spend the day casting small spinners or dry flies to the pan-sized rainbows. Snow and ice have usually melted by late May, and the fishing can be worthwhile anytime from then until late September.

Location: East of Granite Falls in Snohomish County; see map A3, grid f0.

Species: Rainbow trout.

Facilities: U.S. Forest Service campgrounds at Turlo and Verlot have both tent and RV sites, while a third campground at Gold Basin has tent sites only. The Forest Service's Verlot Public Service Center has maps of the area and other useful information. Food, gas, tackle, and lodging are available in Granite Falls and along the Mountain Loop Highway.

Directions: Take Highway 9 to Lake Stevens and turn east on Highway 92, following it to Granite Falls. Continue east out of Granite Falls on the Mountain Loop Highway to Verlot, and after crossing the South Fork Stillaguamish River, turn south (right) on 102nd Street NE (Forest Service Road 42). Drive about 1.5 miles to the trailhead on the left. It's a steep, one-mile hike to the lake. If you reach the Heather Creek Bridge on 102nd Street NE, you've gone about 0.3 mile past the trail.

Contact: Mount Baker–Snoqualmie National Forest, Darrington Ranger District, 360/436-1155; Mount Baker–Snoqualmie National Forest, Verlot Public Service Center, 360/691-7791.

37 Lake Twentytwo (or Twenty-Two, or even 22)

This is a high-country lake that's definitely worth the effort it takes to reach it. Although the trail is fairly steep, it's only about two miles each way, and you should be able to make it in two hours even if you stop to wet a line in the creek along the way. But don't spend too much time fishing for the finger-length stream trout, because there's bigger game up ahead in Lake Twentytwo.

At 45 acres and more than 50 feet deep in places, this little jewel nestled in a steep basin has its share of bragging-sized trout. And though the size and depth help the lake grow good-sized trout, they also make it more difficult to fish than most other high lakes. Take along some bait and some fairly large egg sinkers, which will allow you to ply the depths for bigger fish. Stillfishing with bait also allows you more time to sit back and take in the scenery. Be sure to take your camera as well as your favorite spinning or fly rod.

Location: East of Granite Falls in Snohomish County; see map A3, grid f0.

Species: Rainbow trout.

Facilities: U.S. Forest Service campgrounds at Turlo and Verlot have both tent and RV sites, while a third campground at Gold Basin has tent sites only. The Forest Service's Verlot Public Service Center has maps of the area and other useful information. Food, gas, tackle, and lodging are available in Granite Falls and along the Mountain Loop Highway.

Directions: Take Highway 9 to Lake Stevens and turn east on Highway 92 to Granite Falls. Continue east from Granite Falls on the Mountain Loop Highway. After crossing the South Fork Stillaguamish River about a mile east of the Verlot Campground, continue just under another mile to the parking lot and trailhead, on the right. From there it's a hike of just less than two miles up Twentytwo Creek to the lake.

Contact: Mount Baker–Snoqualmie National Forest, Darrington Ranger District, 360/436-1155; Mount Baker–Snoqualmie National Forest, Verlot Public Service Center, 360/691-7791.

38 Boardman Lake, Upper Boardman (Island) Lake, and Lake Evan

Since the road runs right to its shores, Lake Evan is the best bet if you're looking for easy access and a place to take the kids for an afternoon getaway. Expect to catch an occasional cutthroat and small brook trout. But larger and more out-of-the-way Boardman is more likely to produce a couple of keepers. At 50 acres and with depths as great as 25 feet, it holds some fair-sized rainbows.

You'll probably break a sweat getting farther up the hill to Upper Boardman (also called Island Lake), but the fishing and scenery make it worth the effort. The 10-acre lake features a small island, and it has fair numbers of pan-sized cutthroats and brookies to keep you casting. The snow and ice are gone from these lakes from about Memorial Day to the end of September, so visit during that period, unless you want to work harder than necessary.

Location: East of Granite Falls in Snohomish County; see map A3, grid f1.

Species: Rainbow, brook, and cutthroat trout.

Facilities: The U.S. Forest Service campgrounds at Terlo, Verlot, and Gold Creek all have tent sites, and all but Gold Creek have trailer sites. The nearest food, gas, tackle, and lodging are in Granite Falls.

Directions: Take Highway 9 to Lake Stevens and turn east on Highway 92 to Granite Falls. Take the Mountain Loop Highway east from Granite Falls and turn south (right) on Forest Service Road 4020 (about 4.5 miles after crossing the South Fork Stillaguamish River near Verlot Campground). Stay on Forest Service Road 4020 for about four miles to where it more or less ends at Lake Evan. Boardman Lake is about three-quarters of a mile south of Lake Evan, via a trail. Follow the creek uphill from the southeast corner of Boardman to reach Upper Boardman, also called Island Lake.

Contact: Mount Baker–Snoqualmie National Forest, Darrington Ranger District, 360/436-1155; Mount Baker–Snoqualmie National Forest, Verlot Public Service Center, 360/691-7791.

39 Goat Lake

Fairly easy to reach by way of a trail that isn't all that steep, this high-country lake gets substantial fishing pressure during the summer and early fall. Still, it provides decent fishing for mostly pan-sized brookies that are within easy reach around the lake's shoreline. Since the main trail peters out near the lake's north end, the fishing often improves as you work your way around to the south end and southeast corner of the lake.

While brookies are the main attraction, Goat Lake reportedly holds some large rainbows as well, and such stories are easy to believe. The lake is large (64 acres) and one of the deepest in Washington's high country (100 feet in spots), providing plenty of places for a shy old lunker rainbow to hide. Take along some deep-running lures or even a supply of bait for fishing the depths if you want to try for one. Fish Goat Lake June through September, when the ice and snow are gone.

Location: In Henry M. Jackson Wilderness in Snohomish County; see map A3, grid f2.

Species: Brook and a few rainbow trout.

Facilities: The U.S. Forest Service's Bedal Campground, located on the Mountain Loop Highway about three miles past the turnoff to Forest Service Road 4080, has both tent and RV sites, plus restrooms and drinking water. The nearest food, gas, tackle, and lodging are in Granite Falls.

Directions: Take Highway 9 to Lake Stevens and turn east on Highway 92 to Granite Falls. Take the Mountain Loop Highway east from Granite Falls, and about three miles east of Monte Cristo Road, turn south (right) on Forest Service Road 4080. Follow Forest Service Road 4080 for five miles to the end, where a

trail heads uphill just over a mile to the lake.
Contact: Mount Baker–Snoqualmie National Forest, Darrington Ranger District, 360/436-1155; Mount Baker–Snoqualmie National Forest, Verlot Public Service Center, 360/691-7791.

40 Spada Lake (Sultan Reservoir)

This big, deep, cool reservoir has a lot to offer the patient angler in search of quality trout fishing.

Under "selective fishery" management by the Department of Fish and Wildlife, Spada Lake has no-bait regulations and all lures must have single, barbless hooks to accommodate safe catch-and-release until an angler kills his or her limit and has to quit for the day. Another noteworthy regulation is that the maximum size limit is 12 inches, which is unusual for a Washington lake.

You can have a motor on your boat, but it must be electric and not gas powered.

Because of Spada's restrictive regulations and its distance from a major highway, fishing pressure is light compared to other western Washington lakes. Many anglers come here simply to practice catch-and-release, so Spada doesn't become fished out by early summer. June and July, in fact, are very good months to fish it. Don't be too surprised if you have the good fortune of hooking a husky rainbow of 18 inches or better. The fishing season here runs from late April through October.
Location: Northeast of Startup in Snohomish County; see map A3, grid g1.
Species: Rainbow and cutthroat trout.
Facilities: A boat ramp is located near the east end of the lake. The nearest food, gas, lodging, and tackle are back on U.S. 2 in the towns of Sultan and Monroe.
Directions: Take U.S. 2 to Sultan; about a mile east of town turn north on Sultan Basin Road, following it about 15 miles to the lake.
Contact: Sky Valley Traders, 360/794-8818;

Mount Baker–Snoqualmie National Forest, Skykomish Ranger District, 360/677-2414.

41 Lake Chelan

Talk about summertime at Lake Chelan and most people think of hot boats, cold drinks, and cool sunglasses. It's a place to zip around on water skis and lounge about coated in suntan lotion. Yes, Chelan is all these things, but it's also one of north-central Washington's most popular fishing spots.

The chinook salmon fishing has been so good in recent years that it's beginning to draw anglers away from the traditional fisheries over on Puget Sound. Chelan was first stocked with chinook in 1974, and for the past several years, the Washington Department of Fish and Wildlife has planted 100,000 chinooks annually.

Unlike most of the chinook salmon that saltwater anglers are used to chasing, Lake Chelan salmon are seldom concentrated around schools of bait fish. In fact, smaller fish make up only a slight part of their diet, according to Rick Graybill, one of the area's premier fishing guides.

"They feed primarily on freshwater shrimp," Graybill told me the first time I fished the lake with him. "That makes for the sweetest, reddest salmon flesh you'll ever put on a barbecue, but it also means you have to cover a lot of water in search of scattered fish that only have to cruise around with their mouths open whenever they want a meal."

Covering a lot of water in search of fish means trolling, and that's the technique that accounts for most Lake Chelan chinooks. Early and late in the day when the light-sensitive shrimp are nearer the surface, trolling in the top 60 feet of water will pay off. But as the sun gets higher in the sky, the shrimp and the salmon that feed on them get deeper in the water, and anglers have to take their baits or lures deeper and deeper to find fish. In a lake that plunges to 1,500 feet in places, you'd better be equipped with downriggers or forget about catching salmon throughout most of the day. You may have to fish 200 to 250 feet down to catch them.

Downrigger trolling at depths of 200 feet or more is challenging, to say the least, and Lake Chelan salmon anglers have to be on their toes at all times. Line stretch is a problem when there's that much monofilament between the rod tip and the downrigger weight; and these salmon are notoriously light biters, so many strikes go unnoticed. To help improve the odds, watch the tip of your trolling rod constantly, and when you notice the slightest signs of a bump on the rod tip, take the rod from its holder and jerk the heck out of it to release the line and set the hook. Whole and plug-cut herring account for many Lake Chelan chinooks, as do herring strips fished behind flashers. A variety of plugs and wobbling spoons are also effective.

The same trolling methods that catch salmon also account for good numbers of lake trout, or Mackinaw. Chelan is one of only a handful of Washington lakes where this largest member of the char family can be found. Anyone who read the first two editions of this book may recall that Rick Graybill predicted several years ago that Chelan would produce the next state-record Mackinaw, and his prediction came true in May 1999. Phillip Rettstatt of Twisp was trolling a Silver Horde plug when he fooled the record breaker, which weighed in at 31 pounds, 2.75 ounces. That's nearly a pound larger than the previous state-record lake trout, which was caught from Loon Lake way back in 1966. But Rettstatt's record lasted only two years before it was topped by more than two pounds! In August 2001, Lyle Smith caught a 33-pound, 6.5-ounce Mackinaw to shatter the record once again. Lake trout were first stocked here around 1980, and tens of thousands of them have been planted since that time. Most of the lakers caught here range from 10 to 16 pounds, but some have topped the 20-pound mark, and they continue to add inches and pounds. The best fishing for salmon and lake trout is March through July, but you might catch one virtually any month of the year.

The lake is open to year-round fishing, and if you're not into trolling for lunkers, you can always find other fisheries to keep you occupied. Chelan, for example, is stocked with as many as 100,000 rainbow trout each year, and both bank and boat anglers make good catches of them all around the south end of the lake. Bank anglers catch some good-sized rainbows at Riverfront Park at the extreme south end, as do guests at the nearby Caravel Resort.

Kokanee are among Washington's most popular freshwater fish, and Lake Chelan has 'em. The freshwater shrimp have had a negative impact on kokanee, but anglers still make some good catches of these sweet-eating little sockeye salmon. Trolling produces most of them, and like the salmon and lake trout, you often have to troll quite deep to catch Lake Chelan kokanee. Your best shot at a kokanee here is June through August.

Although it's a fairly well-kept secret, Lake Chelan also offers good smallmouth bass fishing. The warmer waters at the south end of the lake provide some of the best action. There's no shortage of rocky points, submerged boulder piles, and gravel beaches for smallmouth anglers to try their luck. May, June, and July are the best bass months.

If you want to try something completely different, ask the locals about burbot, commonly known as freshwater lings. These prehistoric-looking denizens of deep water provide year-round action at Chelan, although the best fishing is during the winter and early spring. They're long, slim, and ugly, but the white-meated burbot is always a hit at the dinner table. There used to be no limit on them here, and some anglers filled buckets with burbot as recently as the early 1990s. A conservative five-fish burbot limit is now in effect, and if you find a good spot, it won't take long to catch your limit.

Location: Stretches from the town of Chelan to Stehekin in Chelan County; see map A3, grid f7.

Species: Chinook salmon, lake and rainbow trout, kokanee, smallmouth bass, burbot.

Facilities: The Caravel Resort is right on the lake and within walking distance of the Riverfront Park boat ramp and all the shops and restaurants in downtown Chelan. Many of the units have fully equipped kitchens and all are a few steps from the lake. If you want to soak away sore muscles after playing all those fish, try one of its hot tub suites. Reservations are recommended for the summer months. Write or call Caravel Resort, P.O. Box 1509, Chelan, WA 98816, 509/682-2582 or 800/962-8723. RV and tent spaces are available at Lake Chelan State Park, but in the summer most spaces are reserved far in advance. There are also private RV parks and campgrounds in and around Chelan.

As for boat ramps, there are five on the lake:

- **Riverwalk Ramp:** This free two-lane ramp with a loading float and room for 14 cars with trailers is reached by turning on Farnham Street next to Chelan High School and following it about 200 yards to Emerson Street, which leads down a short hill to the ramp.
- **Lakeshore Marina Ramp:** On the left side of Highway 150 as you drive north out of town is another two-lane ramp with floats. It has a $3 launch fee and $2 parking fee.
- **Manson Parks and Recreation District Ramp:** This is the lake's biggest and best ramp, a spiffy, four-lane concrete job with three loading floats and room for well over

100 vehicles. It's located just off Highway 150 at Wapato Lake Road across the road from Mill Bay Casino. There's no use fee.
- **Lake Chelan State Park:** This is a single-laner with loading floats. The launch fee is $4 round-trip, with a $40 annual permit available that lets the user launch at any Washington State Parks ramp. Launching is free at the state parks if you're camping there.
- **25-Mile Creek State Park:** This single-lane ramp with loading floats has a $4 round-trip launch fee. A $40 annual permit that lets the user launch at any Washington State Parks ramp is available. Launching is free at the state parks if you're camping there.

Directions: Take I-97 north from Wenatchee about 31 miles to the south end of the lake, or turn north (left) on Navarre Canyon Road at about the 24-mile mark and follow it to Lake Chelan State Park, about a quarter of the way up the lake.

Contact: Chelan Chamber of Commerce, 800/4-CHELAN (800/424-3526). To book a salmon/lake trout trip, write or call Rick Graybill at Graybill's Guide Service, P.O. Box 2621, Chelan, WA 98816; 509/667-9203, website: www.rgraybill.com; Darrell & Dad's Family Guide Service, 509/966-8678, email: antonj@aol.com; Washington State Parks and Recreation Commission, 360/902-8844 (information) or 800/452-5687 (reservations); Stehekin Lodge, 509/682-4494, website: www.stehekin.com.

42 Antilon Lake

Once a natural lake, the lower end of Antilon was dammed many years ago and the water level now fluctuates with the seasons. Spring and early summer fishing offers the possibility of hooking a brown trout of two or three pounds. Although most of the locals stillfish with eggs, worms, marshmallows, and all the usual stuff, if you really want a big brown, you might try offering it something a little more in line with its big-fish appetite. A small Rapala or similar minnow-imitating plug might do the trick.

The same minnow-imitating plugs, if twitched along the surface early and late in the day or retrieved in a series of short jerks and stops, might also turn up a largemouth bass. Antilon reportedly has some fair-sized largemouths in it, according to local angler Dave Graybill, although I've never seen anyone catch one. But then, I've never fished here specifically for bass, so my expertise on the subject is limited at best. Try it for yourself to be sure.

Several small streams enter the upper portion of the lake, and they offer fair to good fishing for wild cutthroats and some brook trout. This would be a good place to take that lightweight fly rod you've been longing to use.

Antilon's location in a narrow, pine-covered valley well off the beaten path makes it a good place to do some wildlife watching while you fish. Ospreys nest near the lake, and there are mule deer throughout the area. But be careful, especially if you wander too far away from other anglers. While you're watching wildlife, some of the wildlife may be watching you, especially the big cats. The area has a healthy cougar population, and they get hungry, too. Rattlesnakes can also be a problem here.

Location: North of Manson on the east side of Lake Chelan; see map A3, grid g9.

Species: Brown and cutthroat trout, largemouth bass, crappie, bluegill.

Facilities: There's a large, flat area on a knoll overlooking the upper end of the lake that can be and has been used as a camping spot, but many of the people who came before have been real slobs, so there's a lot of broken glass and other garbage on the ground. Food, RV sites, gas, and tackle are available in Manson. Lodging is available in Chelan.

Directions: Drive northwest out of Chelan on Highway 150 toward Manson. Turn right five miles from Chelan on Wapato Lake Road, then right on Grade Creek Road, where there's a sign reading Antilon Lake. From there it's 4.2 miles to the east side of the lake, the last mile on a rough, rutted, dirt and gravel road.

Contact: Kamei Resort, 509/687-3690 (April through October only).

43 Dry Lake

Contrary to its name, Dry Lake isn't dry at all. It has enough water to support a thriving population of bass and panfish, and the bassing is good enough to draw the attention of serious anglers from throughout central Washington. If all the stories are true, Dry Lake has produced a few largemouths in the seven- to nine-pound range.

The abundance of small panfish not only provides easy pickin's for hungry bass but makes this lake a good one for kids and other not-too-patient anglers. A bobber and worm will provide all the action any youngster could want, or suspend a Mini Jig or similar leadhead below the bobber for variety.

The lake also has brown bullheads, according to surveys conducted by the Department of Fish and Wildlife, so those bobber-and-worm rigs might also come in handy for a little night fishing.

A word of warning is in order if you're planning to fish Dry Lake or any of those nearby (including Antilon, number 42, and Wapato, number 44) from the bank. This is rattlesnake country, so pay attention to what you're doing and where you're walking. One wrong move could ruin your day. Be especially careful if you have youngsters in tow.

Location: North of Manson on the east side of Lake Chelan; see map A3, grid g9.

Species: Largemouth bass, crappie, yellow perch, bluegill, brown bullhead catfish.

Facilities: Food, camping, and gas are available in and around Manson, while lodging and other amenities can be found in Chelan.

Directions: Drive northwest out of Chelan on Highway 150 toward Manson, turn north (right) on Totem Pole Road as you're entering town, and follow it northwesterly about 3.5 miles to the south end of the lake.

Contact: Kamei Resort, 509/687-3690 (April though October only).

44 Wapato Lake

Wapato provides some of central Washington's best spring trout fishing, with limits and near-limits of plump rainbows more the rule than the exception. The trout sometimes run to 20 inches or more, but 10- to 16-inchers make up the bulk of the catch. The best fishing occurs during the first two months of the season, from late April to late June, but the lake also offers good fall fishing. If you do decide to visit Wapato after August 1, be advised that the trout-fishing regulations change on that date to selective fishery regulations, which means you can fish only with artificial lures and flies with single, barbless hooks. Those regulations remain in effect until the end of the season on October 31.

Both trolling and stillfishing work here for trout, so do some experimenting until you find the hot combination. One effective technique is to drift a Carey Special fly well behind the boat in 10 to 15 feet of water. Use the oars as little as possible to keep the surface disturbance to a minimum. The Carey Special is tied in many variations, and those with either red or chartreuse bodies seem to work best here.

Wapato has long been home to a thriving population of warm-water fish, including some lunker largemouth bass. Over the past few years, the lake has produced some bass in the nine-pound range, so we're talking trophy bass. Here's a tip that may help warn you when it's time to pick up your bass rod and make a cast or two: The lake is full of small panfish, and you can see them milling around in the shallows. If they suddenly disappear, it means a big predator is nearby. The primary big predator in this lake is the largemouth bass, so take the hint. Cast a crankbait or plastic worm out and see what happens.

The little bass, crappies, and sunfish have grown somewhat out of control here in recent years, so you're more likely to find small, stunted panfish than fish big enough to eat, and they're beginning to make inroads into the trout population by out-competing the trout for food. If you fish Wapato, take home a bucket of little panfish if you get the chance. Your cat or rosebushes will love you for it.

Although not something you'd want to hook, Wapato Lake is full of turtles, and for someone who isn't used to seeing a lot of these armored reptiles in the wild, it can be a hoot.

Location: North of Manson on the east side of Lake Chelan; see map A3, grid g9.

Species: Rainbow trout, largemouth bass, bluegill, crappie.

Facilities: The lake has a public access area and a boat ramp, plus three private campgrounds, one at each end, which have RV hookups, tent sites, boat ramps, restrooms, and showers. Food, gas, and tackle are available in Manson. More amenities can be found in Chelan.

Directions: Take Highway 150 from Chelan toward Manson for about five miles and turn right on Swartout Road. Go two miles and turn right on Wapato Lake Road, which parallels the entire southwest side of the lake. To reach the boat ramp and Paradise Resort, turn north on East Wapato Lake Road and drive 0.1 mile to both facilities, on the left.

Contact: Kamei Resort, 509/687-3690 (April through October); Wapato Lake Campground, 509/687-6037.

45 Roses Lake

For many years a winter-only fishery with a December through March season, Roses is now open to year-round fishing, and it's still one of Chelan County's better bets for chunky rainbows. Red salmon eggs, used alone or in combination with corn, marsh-mallows, or other baits, account for many of the fish. Now that anglers can fish it during the spring and summer, trolling is also a good possibility, and virtually all the usual wob-blers, spinners, and gang-troll-and-bait com-binations will produce. Don't be surprised if your efforts pay off to the tune of a rainbow in the two-pound range. As if the fat rainbows weren't enough, Roses has also been stocked with brown trout to help make things a lot more interesting. Channel catfish also have been stocked here to fatten up the pos-sibilities for warm-water anglers.

And while you're at Roses, take a few min-utes to ponder the large sign posted at the boat ramp. If you can understand it, you're smarter than I am. It reads: "Maximum Speed 3 mph, except 6 A.M. to 7 P.M., November 1 through April 1." I don't know anyone who would want to drive a boat faster than three miles an hour on Roses Lake during the winter. All that ice would have to be tough on the prop.

Location: North of Manson on the east side of Lake Chelan; see map A3, grid g9.

Species: Rainbow trout, brown trout, channel catfish, largemouth bass, crappies.

Facilities: The southeast end of the lake has a single-lane boat ramp and a large dirt access area. Nearby facilities in Manson include food, tackle, camping, and gas. Everything else you may need is available in Chelan.

Directions: Take Highway 150 from Chelan toward Manson. Turn right on Wapato Lake Road and drive three miles to Roses Avenue. Turn left on Roses Avenue and drive three-quarters of a mile to Green Avenue, following it 0.4 mile to the boat ramp on the right.

Contact: Kamei Resort, 509/687-3690 (April through October only).

46 White River

This glacial stream is often milky from sum-mer runoff, but you can still catch trout if you stick with salmon eggs, worms, and Berkley Power Bait. The part of the river above the mouth of the Napeequa River, however, has selective regulations where bait isn't allowed, adding considerable challenge to the game.

Once stocked with generous loads of hatchery trout, the White is pretty much self-sustaining now, so the action isn't as fast and furious as it used to be. You might still hook an occasional Dolly Varden here, but if you do, you have to release it. In fact, you have to release any trout or trout like critter over 20 inches long. June and July are the best months to fish the White River.

Location: Flows into the west end of Lake Wenatchee; see map A3, grid g5.

Species: Rainbow and cutthroat trout, Dolly Varden.

Facilities: A state park with about 200 tent sites is located near the east end of Lake We-natchee, and two U.S. Forest Service camp-grounds can be found near the west end, each with a few tent sites, restrooms, and drink-ing water. U.S. Forest Service campgrounds at White River Falls and Napeequa Crossing have five tent sites each. Food, gas, tackle, and lodging are available in Leavenworth.

Directions: Drive east from Monroe or west from Leavenworth on U.S. 2 and turn north onto Highway 207, following it 12 miles along the north side of Lake Wenatchee and eight more miles up the White River.

Contact: Wenatchee National Forest, Lake Wenatchee Ranger District, 509/763-3103; Lake Wenatchee State Park, 509/763-3101; Washington State Parks and Recreation Commission, 360/902-8844 (information) or 800/452-5687 (reservations); Washington

Department of Fish and Wildlife, Wenatchee Office, 509/662-0452.

47 Fish Lake

This 500-acre lake has a reputation for its trophy-class browns, some of which top five pounds. Now and then someone lands a really big one in the 8- to 10-pound range. As with any trophy fishery, it's more complicated than going out, catching a couple of monsters, and going home. Trollers usually drag Rapalas and other minnow-imitating plugs around for hours at a time between strikes, and the fly anglers who work the west end and north and south sides of the lake with various streamers and wet flies typically go even longer between one fish and the next. Of course, if the next fish turns out to be a five-pounder, it's always worth the wait and the extra effort.

The rainbows are more cooperative and dependable than the browns. Spring trolling or drifting with the wind, using a small string of gang trolls ahead of a Wedding Ring spinner, Triple Teazer, or worm, may catch you a quick limit of fat 10- to 12-inchers. The rainbow fishery can be good almost all year, even during the winter, when anglers commonly catch some nice ones through the ice.

Most anglers come to Fish Lake for the trout fishing, but if you stay more than a day and don't try to catch a mess of perch, you're missing out on some fine eating. The perch are also in a biting mood throughout the year, and some anglers brave winter storms and icy roads just to fish them through the ice of January. Although always good eating, a yellow perch caught in winter is the best of all, and when they run nine to 12 inches, as they do here, they're almost worth risking your neck on treacherous highways.

The lake also offers largemouth and smallmouth bass, although the numbers aren't as good as they were a few years ago. But you still stand a chance of hooking a big fish of either species.

Location: Northeast of Lake Wenatchee; see map A3, grid g6.

Species: Rainbow and brown trout, largemouth and smallmouth bass, yellow perch.

Facilities: The lake has no public boat ramp, but for a small fee, you can launch at the Cove Resort, which also has rental boats and motors, a couple of cabins, and tent and RV sites. There's a small café with good food on U.S. 2, just west of the Highway 207 intersection. Food, gas, lodging, and tackle are available in Leavenworth, to the east.

Directions: Take U.S. 2 over Stevens Pass or east from Wenatchee and turn north on Highway 207 about 14 miles northwest of Wenatchee. Stay on 207 past the intersection of Highway 209 and over the river on the steel bridge, and then bear right at the Y. From there it's a short distance to the lake, which is on the left.

Contact: The Cove Resort, 509/763-3130; Wenatchee National Forest, Lake Wenatchee Ranger District, 509/763-3103; Washington Department of Fish and Wildlife, Wenatchee Office, 509/662-0452.

48 Chiwawa River

No, it's not Chihuahua, as in the Mexican dog, but Chiwawa, as in the small tributary stream to the Wenatchee River. This is another stream where hatchery plants once provided the fishery but have dried up in recent years. In fact, for now at least, it's closed to all fishing. That may change in the near future, so stay posted, and we'll keep this rather scenic stream listed until we here long-term bad news.

Location: Flows into the Wenatchee River southeast of Lake Wenatchee; see map A3, grid g6.

Species: Rainbow and cutthroat trout.

Facilities: Lake Wenatchee State Park about five miles west of the river is the closest thing to a full-service campground in the area, with about 200 tent sites but no hookups. The Forest Service's Nason Creek Campground offers an additional 75 tent sites, plus water and restrooms. The nearest food, gas, lodging, and other facilities are in Leavenworth.

Directions: Drive east from Stevens Pass or west from Leavenworth on U.S. 2 and turn north on Highway 207 near Lake Wenatchee. At Nason Creek Campground turn east (right) onto Highway 206 and follow it about four miles southeast to Plain. Turn north (left) on Chiwawa River Road (Forest Service Road 62) and follow it for about 20 miles up the river.

Contact: Wenatchee National Forest, Lake Wenatchee Ranger District, 509/763-3103; Lake Wenatchee State Park, 509/763-3101; Washington State Parks and Recreation Commission, 360/902-8844 (information) or 800/452-5687 (reservations); Washington Department of Fish and Wildlife, Wenatchee Office, 509/662-0452.

49 Lake Wenatchee

It would be nice to be able to say that Lake Wenatchee offers huge bull trout and sockeye salmon along with its abundant kokanee, but both have had their ups and downs in recent years and are currently down. I vividly remember stories coming from the old Telma Resort over 20 years ago, stories of big, dumb bull trout that sometimes topped 10 pounds and would readily inhale a slowly trolled plug-cut herring or large, minnow-imitating plug. Back then, very few anglers bothered to spend time fishing for these big but somewhat lethargic trophies. Now bull trout populations throughout the Northwest are in trouble, and you can't keep one even if you're lucky enough to hook and land it.

Anadromous sockeye salmon may show up in good numbers one year but not the next, so you can't count on getting a chance at them most of the time. There was a good (but short) sockeye season in 2001, when large numbers of fish had to be "helped" upriver to reach the lake during a period of extremely low river flow. When there is a season, anglers troll bare hooks in black or red finishes behind a slowly revolving flasher, the same technique that works on Seattle's Lake Washington when the sockeye runs are good over there.

That leaves the kokanee, and in recent years Lake Wenatchee has risen to the top as a kokanee producer. The fish aren't particularly large, but they've been abundant enough lately to allow for a 16-fish daily limit, a limit that many veteran anglers may achieve in a couple of hours. Trolling a Wedding Ring, Needlefish, or other small, flashy spinner or spoon behind a string of trolling blades is one way to catch them, and don't forget to add that kernel of white corn to the lure's hooks for even more appeal. Summertime is kokanee time, with July usually the top fishing month. When the sockeye season is closed, any kokanee/sockeye over 16 inches must be released, since it's considered a migratory sockeye.

Location: North of Leavenworth; see map A3, grid h5.

Species: Kokanee, sockeye salmon, bull trout.

Facilities: There are about 30 tent sites (no hookups) at Lake Wenatchee State Park, located just off Highway 207 near the west end of the lake. The state park also has a boat ramp. Glacier View Campground, on the south side of the lake via Forest Service Road 6607, has 20 campsites and a boat ramp. Dirty Face Campground (U.S. Forest Service) is at the northwest corner of the lake and has three campsites. The nearest restaurant is on U.S. 2, just west of the intersection of U.S. 2 and Highway 207. Other food, gas, lodging, RV parks, and supplies are located in Leavenworth.

Directions: Drive east from Monroe or west from Leavenworth on U.S. 2 and turn north on Highway 207, which parallels the north side of the lake.

Contact: Wenatchee National Forest, Lake Wenatchee Ranger District, 509/763-3103; Lake Wenatchee State Park, 509/763-3101; Washington State Parks and Recreation Commission, 360/902-8844 (information) or 800/452-5687 (reservations); Leavenworth Chamber of Commerce, 509/548-5807; Washington Department of Fish and Wildlife, Wenatchee Office, 509/662-0452.

50 Nason Creek

No longer stocked with hatchery trout by the Department of Fish and Wildlife, Nason has ceased to be the put-and-take trough it used to be every summer. Now you have to work at it if you want to find success in this easy-access stream. In fact, you have to work at it even harder than you do on most Washington trout streams, since this is a no-bait fishery where you have to use artificial flies and lures with single, barbless hooks.

The creek opens to fishing June 1 of every year, but fishing conditions are often tough at that time, thanks to spring runoff and cool water. Wait until late June or July and you'll probably enjoy the experience a lot more. By September the creek is quite low, but the first precipitation of fall may provide some decent angling action. The season closes at the end of October.

Location: Parallels U.S. 2 east of Stevens Pass; see map A3, grid h4.

Species: Rainbow and cutthroat trout.

Facilities: White Pine Campground (U.S. Forest Service) has nine tent sites, plus restrooms and drinking water. Food, gas, tackle, and lodging are available in Leavenworth, and there's a good restaurant at the intersection of U.S. 2 and Highway 207.

Directions: Take U.S. 2 about 60 miles east from Monroe or 26 miles west from Leavenworth and use various turnouts and side roads to stop and fish the creek.

Contact: Wenatchee National Forest, Lake Wenatchee Ranger District, 509/763-3103; Washington Department of Fish and Wildlife, Wenatchee Office, 509/662-0452.

51 Entiat River

Like other Columbia River tributaries in this neck of the woods, the Entiat has little to offer summertime anglers these days. Restrictions aimed at protecting upper Columbia steelhead have the Entiat shut down completely during the time of year when it used to provide pretty good fishing for both steelhead and hatchery rainbow trout. Decent whitefish action is available December through March, but be sure to check the fishing pamphlet for regulations on hook size that are aimed at keeping whitefish anglers from "accidentally" becoming steelhead anglers.

Location: Enters the Columbia River at Entiat; see map A3, grid h8.

Species: Rainbow trout, mountain whitefish, summer-run steelhead.

Facilities: Cottonwood, North Fork, Silver Falls, Lake Creek, and Fox Creek Campgrounds (all U.S. Forest Service facilities) are scattered along the upper half of the Entiat and offer nearly 100 campsites among them. For anglers visiting the lower Entiat, there's a city park in town with 31 RV sites, showers, and a trailer dump. Food, tackle, and gas are also available in Entiat.

Directions: Take U.S. 97 to the town of Entiat and turn west on Entiat River Road, which follows the river upstream for well over 30 miles.

Contact: Wenatchee National Forest, Entiat Ranger District, 509/784-1511; Washington Department of Fish and Wildlife, Wenatchee Office, 509/662-0452.

52 Eagle Creek

Like the Chumstick it flows into (see number 53), Eagle Creek is readily accessible from the road that runs much of its length. It provides a few pan-sized trout early in the season and then dries up as a worthwhile angling possibility. The season runs June 1 through October 31.

Location: Joins Chumstick Creek north of Leavenworth; see map A3, grid i7.

Species: Rainbow and cutthroat trout.

Facilities: Food, gas, lodging, tackle, and other facilities are available in Leavenworth.

Directions: Take U.S. 2 to Leavenworth and turn north on Highway 209. Drive about two miles to Eagle Creek Road (Forest Service Road 7520) and turn east (right) to follow the creek upstream.

Contact: Wenatchee National Forest, Leavenworth Ranger District, 509/782-1413; Washington Department of Fish and Wildlife, Wenatchee Office, 509/662-0452.

53 Chumstick Creek

The good news is that a state highway provides plenty of easy access to this bubbling stream just north of Leavenworth. The bad news is that a state highway provides plenty of easy access to this bubbling stream just north of Leavenworth. Chumstick gets quite a lot of fishing pressure and seldom produces a trout of noteworthy (or even worthwhile) size. It's a nice, cool little creek, but not worth too much of your time if you're a serious angler.

Location: Joins the Wenatchee River near Leavenworth; see map A3, grid i7.

Species: Rainbow and cutthroat trout.

Facilities: Everything you need, including a wide range of motels, hotels, and bed-and-breakfasts, all with a Bavarian theme, are available in Leavenworth. Food, gas, and tackle are also available.

Directions: Take U.S. 2 to Leavenworth and turn north on Highway 209, which parallels

the creek for several miles.

Contact: Wenatchee National Forest, Leavenworth Ranger District, 509/782-1413; Washington Department of Fish and Wildlife, Wenatchee Office, 509/662-0452.

54 Icicle Creek (Icicle River)

Impressive returns of hatchery-run spring chinook salmon put the Icicle on Washington's angling map in the early 1990s, but it also drew crowds of anglers to this pretty, small stream on the eastern flank of the Cascades. All of those anglers were crowded into the two miles of stream from the fish hatchery down to the mouth. When fishing was hot, the river gave up more than its share of 10- to 25-pound salmon, the vast majority of them during the month of May. June catches ran a distant second. When the season is open, all the usual spring chinook rigs work here, including salmon egg clusters, fresh ghost shrimp, egg-shrimp combinations, and diving plugs.

Lately, though, the season hasn't been open. Low salmon returns have failed to even meet hatchery needs, so there hasn't been a surplus for anglers to catch. In fact, the lower river has been closed to fishing completely in recent years, putting the skids not only on salmon fishing, but steelheading as well. That leaves trout fishing above the hatchery, which is fair, but selective regulations disallow the use of bait, so it's not a good place to take the kids for their stream-fishing introductory lesson.

Location: Southwest of Leavenworth; see map A3, grid i6.

Species: Rainbow trout, summer steelhead, chinook salmon.

Facilities: Seven U.S. Forest Service campgrounds are scattered along the creek, all with at least some campsites. Working upstream, Eightmile Campground has 45 sites, Bridge Creek Campground has six, Johnny Creek Campground has 56, Ida Creek Campground has 10, Chatter Creek Campground has 12, Rock Island Campground has 22, and Blackpine Creek Horse Camp has eight. There's also a large private RV park and campground about three miles up Icicle Road. Motels, bed-and-breakfasts, gas, food, and other facilities are available nearby in Leavenworth.

Directions: Take U.S. 2 to Leavenworth and turn south on East Leavenworth Road or Icicle Road to parallel the lower end of Icicle Creek. Icicle Road (Forest Service Road 7600) continues upstream some 15 miles past the national fish hatchery on the lower end of the creek.

Contact: Wenatchee National Forest, Leavenworth Ranger District, 509/782-1413; Icicle River RV Park and Campground, 509/548-5420, website: www.icicleriverrv.com; Washington Department of Fish and Wildlife, Wenatchee Office, 509/662-0452.

55 Columbia River

Steelhead and trout fishing, once a big deal on this stretch of the Columbia, are pretty much a bust until further notice. The decision to protect upper Columbia steelhead resulted in no-fishing rules for salmonids in these parts, and that isn't likely to change anytime soon. There are, however, still some other angling possibilities.

This portion of the big river may not be one of the most well-known walleye spots on the vast Columbia River system, but it does give up some trophy-class fish. Trolling with some of the same diving plugs that work for steelhead will also take walleyes, or you can troll spinner-and-worm rigs near bottom to find fish.

If your interests run toward smaller game, this stretch of the Columbia has a number of warm bays and rocky shoreline areas where you can find fair numbers of smallmouth bass. The east side of Turtle Rock, just

upstream from Lincoln Rock State Park, is one good place to look. This part of the river also has fair numbers of rainbow trout, and campers often catch them from the fishing docks at the state park. Those same docks also provide good summertime fishing for pan-sized catfish.

Location: North and south of Wenatchee; see map A3, grid i9.

Species: Summer steelhead, walleye, rainbow trout, brown bullhead catfish, smallmouth bass.

Facilities: Three boat ramps are located in and around Wenatchee, plus one at Lincoln Rock State Park and another at the town of Entiat. There's also a Douglas County park with a nice boat ramp and floats at Orondo, on the east side of the river. Lincoln Rock State Park has about 70 RV sites with hookups and a limited number of tent sites without hookups. It also has several fishing docks where people catch fish day and night. Wenatchee has a wide range of motels, bed-and-breakfasts, restaurants, and other facilities.

Directions: Drive east on U.S. 2 or west on Highway 28 to Wenatchee and turn north on U.S. 97 to follow the river upstream.

Contact: Lincoln Rock State Park, 509/884-8702; Washington State Parks and Recreation Commission, 360/902-8844 (information) or 800/452-5687 (reservations); Washington Department of Fish and Wildlife, Wenatchee Office, 509/662-0452.

56 Wenatchee River

Once among the very best summer steelhead streams in the Northwest, the Wenatchee has fallen victim to its own success, and for the immediate future, at least, steelhead and trout fishing here are no more. Measures to protect dismally small wild steelhead stocks throughout the upper Columbia system have included blanket closures on steelhead and trout fishing, and the Wenatchee was included on the no-fishing hit list. During years of strong salmon runs, spring chinook fishing remains a decent possibility on the lower Wenatchee, but that's about it for any salmonid angling action these days.

Although few visiting anglers come here to fish for whitefish, locals know that the Wenatchee is one of eastern Washington's best bets for mountain whitefish, especially during the winter months. That's when these silver-sided fish congregate in the river's deeper pools—sometimes by the thousands—and anglers fishing small baits or tiny wet-fly patterns can enjoy the kind of hot angling action that can bring joy to an otherwise frigid central Washington afternoon. Now that it's pretty much the only game in town, maybe whitefish angling will really catch on around here. Naaahhh.

Location: Joins the Columbia River at Wenatchee; see map A3, grid i7.

Species: Rainbow trout, mountain whitefish, steelhead, chinook salmon.

Facilities: Four U.S. Forest Service campgrounds along the river above the lake provide a total of 23 campsites. Tumwater Campground, on the lower river just off U.S. 2, has 80 campsites, including some that are large enough for trailers and other RVs. Lake Wenatchee State Park, with its 30 tent sites, restrooms, and picnic area, is another good possibility. Additional RV sites, motels, restaurants, grocery stores, gas stations, and other facilities are available in Leavenworth, Cashmere, and Wenatchee.

Directions: Take U.S. 2 east from Wenatchee and you'll parallel more than 25 miles of the lower Wenatchee River. To reach the middle stretch of the river, turn east off U.S. 2 onto River Road near Tumwater Campground and drive upriver. To fish the Little Wenatchee above Lake Wenatchee, turn north off U.S. 2 onto Highway 207 and drive up the north side of the lake. About a mile west of the lake's

west end, turn south (left) onto Forest Service Road 6500, which runs along the river's north side for about 15 miles.

Contact: Wenatchee National Forest, Lake Wenatchee Ranger District, 509/763-3103; Wenatchee National Forest, Leavenworth Ranger District, 509/782-1413; Lake Wenatchee State Park, 509/763-3101; Washington State Parks and Recreation Commission, 360/902-8844 (information) or 800/452-5687 (reservations); Wenatchee Chamber of Commerce, 800/572-7753; Washington Department of Fish and Wildlife, Wenatchee Office, 509/662-0452.

57 Alpine Lakes Wilderness

Would you believe this area has something in the neighborhood of 200 lakes, ranging in size from a couple of acres to nearly 300 acres, most of them holding at least one species of trout, and all located within some of the most spectacular alpine country anywhere in the world? If you don't mind getting out and working up a sweat to get to your little piece of heaven, this is the place for you. Of course, other people want a piece of heaven too, so don't plan on having it all to yourself during the narrow window of opportunity when these lakes are ice free and the snow has melted out of the trails enough to allow passage. In fact, something like 100,000 people visit this wilderness area during a typical summer. Fishing season on most of the lakes opens when Mother Nature says it does and can close in a hurry any time after Labor Day, so everyone has to get what they can out of the wilderness area during only a few weeks in June, July, August, and September.

Some of the lakes are within relatively short hiking distances of Forest Service roads and even major freeway systems. Olallie, Talapus, Rainbow, Island, and Blazer Lakes, for example, all lie within a mile and a half of each other at the southwest corner of the wilderness and are within a three- to five-mile hike off I-90 near the Bandera Airstrip. If you continue on past Olallie, you'll soon come to Pratt Lake, then Lower Tuscohatchie and tiny Melakwa Lakes. I fished several of these in a mere two days back when I was about 13 years old (shortly after lakes were first invented). Immediately north of these are My Lake (love that name), Kaleetan, Snow, Upper and Lower Wildcat, Caroline, Big and Little Derrick, Hatchet, Horseshoe, Shamrock, and Emerald Lakes, even the smallest of which is stocked periodically.

Lake Dorothy, one of the wilderness area's biggest lakes, can be reached and fished in a morning's time via Forest Service Road 6412 (Miller River Road) near the northwest corner of the wilderness. A short distance beyond Dorothy are Bear, Deer, and Snoqualmie Lakes. South of this popular group lie a number of smaller but productive lakes, including Nordrum, Judy, Carole, Charlie Brown, Upper and Lower Garfield Mountain, Rock, Lunker, Green Ridge, Hi-Low, Pumpkinseed, Le Fay, Myrtle and Little Myrtle, Merlin, Nimme, Goat, Horseshoe (another one), Hester, Little Hester, and Big Snow Lakes. A couple of miles east are several of the area's biggest lakes, including Copper, Big Heart, Angeline, Chetwoot, Otter, Locket, and Iswoot Lakes.

Many of the lakes in the Alpine Lakes Wilderness are only for the accomplished, experienced hiker/angler. Grace, Charles, Margaret, Cup, Larch, and some of the other lakes in the northeastern portion of the wilderness are far from the nearest road, and you have to know where you're going in order to find them. Waptus, Spade, Shovel, Venus, Rowena, and other lakes in the Chelan County portion of the wilderness are also well back from any roads, as are many of the King County lakes in the system. Not only are many of the lakes a long way from the nearest road, but many don't even have particularly good trails leading to them. Some of these off-the-trail lakes may offer better trout fishing, but you'd better be a pro with map and compass if you plan to visit any of them.

Lakes or streams located more than a mile or two off the road require a little special planning on the part of any angler headed that way. Traveling light is, of course, one of the keys, whether you're going in only for the day or for an extended stay of several days or even weeks. I'll assume that anyone planning an extended trip already knows the dos and don'ts of high-country hiking. For the rest of you, though, think seriously about what you'll need and what you won't, and take only the necessities.

Unless you're a fly-fishing fanatic, take along only one rod for all-purpose fishing, and make it a lightweight spinning rod. With a six-foot rod and small spinning reel spooled with four- or six-pound monofilament, you can fish flies as well as baits and lures; just take along a couple of plastic floats (bobbers) for additional casting weight. By the same token, if you like fishing with salmon eggs and think you may need several different shades to cover all the possibilities, dump part of the contents of several jars into one or two jars, rather than packing a jar of each color. Each jar you eliminate is that much less weight you'll have to carry. Remember, too, that even a two-piece spinning rod is three feet long when it's broken down, long enough to catch on overhanging limbs and other obstacles if it's carried vertically on your backpack. Seriously consider a four- or five-piece pack rod or buy a lightweight rod tube for any pack trip you might take. There's nothing worse than hiking five miles to a trout-filled lake and discovering that you've broken six inches off your only fishing rod on the trip in.

Location: South of Skykomish in eastern King County; see map A3, grid i2.

Species: Rainbow, brook, golden, and cutthroat trout.

Facilities: This is a wilderness area, so don't even bother asking about restaurants or motels. Stay on the trails and make camp where others have gone before you. Note: Day-use and camping permits are required for everyone entering the Alpine Lakes Wilderness. They're free and are available from local ranger district offices and information centers and at most trailheads. Food, gas, lodging, and tackle are available at several locations along U.S. 2 and I-90, including Monroe, Sultan, North Bend, and Cle Elum.

Directions: There are nearly as many trails and potential travel routes into this area as there are lakes within its vast boundaries, so I won't take up several pages of this book describing the many possibilities. I will say that you can get to some of the various lake trails off U.S. 2 via Forest Service Roads 6412, 68, and 6830, Icicle Road, and several trails off the south side of the highway; off I-90 via Taylor River Road, Lake Dorothy Road, Forest Service Road 9030, and several major trail systems beginning near the highway and Kachess and Salmon la Sac Roads; and even off back roads leading north and west from U.S. 97 (Blewett Pass Highway). To nail down details on various trails into this wilderness area, buy a map of the Mount Baker–Snoqualmie National Forest and another of the Wenatchee National Forest ($3 each) from any U.S. Forest Service office and most ranger district offices. You would also be smart to invest in a copy of Foghorn's *Pacific Northwest Hiking* by Ron C. Judd and Dan A. Nelson, which provides complete details on hikes to many lakes in the Alpine Lakes Wilderness, as well as other high-country lakes and streams throughout Washington and Oregon.

Contact: Alpine Lakes Wilderness Hot Line, 800/627-0067; Mount Baker–Snoqualmie National Forest, Skykomish Ranger District, 360/677-2414; Mount Baker–Snoqualmie National Forest, North Bend Ranger District, 206/888-1421; Wenatchee National Forest, Cle Elum Ranger District, 509/674-4411; Wenatchee National Forest, Leavenworth Ranger District, 509/782-1413.

58 Upper Cle Elum River

Once well stocked with hatchery trout throughout the summer, the upper Cle Elum no longer receives hatchery plants, which means pretty tough fishing these days. You'll find a respectable rainbow here and there from late spring to mid-fall, but the angling action certainly isn't anything to get worked up about. The pine-covered hills around Salmon la Sac, however, are mighty pretty, and the scenery is good enough to keep your mind off the slow fishing at least for a few hours.

Location: Flows into the north end of Lake Cle Elum south of Salmon la Sac; see map A3, grid j4.

Species: Rainbow trout.

Facilities: The U.S. Forest Service campground at Salmon la Sac has more than 100 campsites for tents and RVs. The Forest Service's Red Mountain and Cle Elum River Campgrounds also have campsites, water, and restrooms. The town of Cle Elum has food, gas, tackle, and lodging.

Directions: Take I-90 to Cle Elum and turn north on Highway 903, staying on it all the way up the east side of Lake Cle Elum and paralleling the river upstream.

Contact: Wenatchee National Forest, Cle Elum Ranger District, 509/674-4411.

59 Cooper Lake

Sometimes a slow starter, this high-country lake above Kachess Lake (see number 1 in chapter B3) often provides good brook trout fishing beginning around the end of May or early June. Most of the brookies here run seven to nine inches, but occasionally the measuring tape is stretched to double digits. Casting wet or dry flies, small Super Dupers, and other bite-sized artificials will take them, but you can also use salmon eggs or worms successfully.

Now and then rainbows are caught from the shoreline areas that produce brookies. If you want to improve your chances for a fat 'bow, however, troll farther out toward the middle of the lake. That's also where you'll find the kokanee, which come on strong from about the middle of June to the middle of August. Like the trout, Cooper Lake kokanee are on the small side.

Gas-powered motors aren't allowed on the lake, so pack your electric motor along or plan on rowing.

Location: Northwest of Salmon la Sac; see map A3, grid j3.

Species: Rainbow, brown, and brook trout; kokanee.

Facilities: A launch ramp and nearly 30 tent sites are available at the U.S. Forest Service's Owhi Campground, on the lake's north shore. Food, gas, tackle, and lodging are available in and around Cle Elum.

Directions: Take I-90 to Cle Elum and turn north on Highway 903. Drive three miles past the north end of Lake Cle Elum and turn west (left) on Forest Service Road 46. Follow it about five miles to Forest Service Road 4616, turn north (right), and follow the road along the north side of Cooper Lake.

Contact: Wenatchee National Forest, Cle Elum Ranger District, 509/674-4411.

60 Rattlesnake Lake

Leave the salmon eggs and Power Bait behind when you head for Rattlesnake; it's had special no-bait angling regulations for years. Something else it's had for a long time is a reputation for fluctuating greatly in size depending on winter and spring weather condi-

tions, and we're not talking subtle differences. Rattlesnake may be as large as 110 acres in April and as small as 10 or 15 acres in September. The size (and depth) may also change during the same season from one year to the next. You could say that Rattlesnake is worth fishing whether you like to do your trout fishing in little ponds or full-sized lakes; it might be either from one trip to the next.

But whatever the water conditions, the lake is stocked by the Department of Fish and Wildlife. Along with a mix of legal-sized rainbows and foot-long cutthroats planted every spring, Rattlesnake receives several thousand fingerling rainbows that grow to keeper size in the lake. The season here opens in late April and runs through October.

Location: South of North Bend; see map A3, grid j0.

Species: Rainbow and cutthroat trout.

Facilities: The east side of the lake has a rough boat ramp (leave the trailer boat home) with pit toilets and plenty of room for bank fishing. Food, gas, lodging, tackle, and other facilities are available in North Bend.

Directions: Take I-90 to North Bend, turn south on Cedar Falls Road SE, and follow it three miles to the lake.

Contact: Sky Valley Traders, 360/794-8818.

61 Keechelus Lake

Located at an elevation of more than 2,500 feet and covering some 2,560 acres at full pool, Keechelus certainly qualifies as one of Washington's biggest alpine lakes, although it's actually an impoundment on the headwaters of the Yakima River. Fluctuating water levels throughout the year and a lack of good facilities along its shores keep Keechelus from becoming a major destination of Washington anglers.

The lake does offer fairly good kokanee fishing in the spring and summer, but as the water level drops in late summer, anglers have a tougher and tougher time getting boats in the water to get at the fish. Find the kokes, though, and get set to enjoy some excellent fishing, since populations have been up in recent years. A 16-fish bonus limit has been in effect on Keechelus kokanee lately. Both stillfishing and trolling will work once you locate a school of fish.

Although it's an opportunity that is almost universally overlooked, Keechelus offers perhaps the best chance for western Washington anglers to catch burbot, those long, skinny, slithering bottom-feeders commonly referred to as freshwater lings. Keechelus has a large burbot population, and a few anglers—most of them from the eastern slope of the Cascades—put out set lines for them throughout much of the year. Such set line tactics are legal for burbot, and the results can be surprisingly good. Night crawlers, strips of sucker meat, and smelt are among the baits used by set-line anglers here. The same baits will also work at the ends of rod-and-reel rigs, and you certainly don't have to go the set-line route to catch these fine-eating fish.

Location: Alongside I-90 at Hyak; see map A3, grid j2.

Species: Kokanee, burbot, rainbow trout.

Facilities: The rough boat ramp near the northwest corner of the lake also has restrooms and a picnic area. The U.S. Forest Service campground at Crystal Springs has about two dozen campsites, some of which are large enough for RVs. Restaurants, motels, gas, and groceries are available at Snoqualmie Summit. Tackle can be found in Cle Elum and North Bend.

Directions: Take I-90 to Snoqualmie Pass and exit to the south at Hyak onto Forest Service Road 9070, following it to the northwest corner of the lake and the boat ramp. To reach the southwest corner of the lake, turn south off I-90 at Crystal Springs (Exit 62). Turn west on Forest Service Road 5480 and follow it two miles to the lake. If you want to fish the east side of Keechelus, stay on I-90 to where the freeway parallels the shoreline and look for wide highway shoulders where there's ample room to pull over and park.

Contact: Mount Baker–Snoqualmie National Forest, North Bend Ranger District, 206/888-1421; Wenatchee National Forest, Cle Elum Ranger District, 509/674-4411.

CHAPTER A4:
OKANOGAN

MID-LAKE ACCESS, BANKS LAKE

Map A4

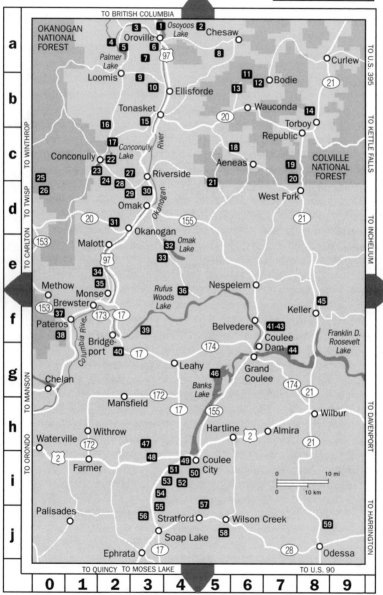

Chapter A4: Okanogan

Rolling hills and pine forests dominate this part of central Washington. It's primarily timber and cattle country, but irrigation water from the Columbia River has changed much of the region's southern half from arid scabland to rich agricultural lands. The damming and diverting of the Columbia also helped create some of the region's best fishing holes. Lake Roosevelt and Banks Lake came into existence when Grand Coulee Dam was built, and now they provide excellent fishing for walleyes, smallmouth bass, kokanee, and hefty rainbow trout. Chief Joseph Dam, the next one below Grand Coulee, backed up the Columbia to form Rufus Woods Lake, where anglers in recent years have caught dozens of triploid rainbow trout of 15 pounds and larger, including the state-record 25.5-pounder. The state-record Lahontan cutthroat, a whopping 18-pounder, was caught only a few miles away, in Omak Lake. Trophy Lahontan cutts are also found in the region's Lake Lenore and Grimes Lake. Jameson, Park, and Blue Lakes, for decades among eastern Washington's best and most popular rainbow trout producers, are also in the Okanogan region. One of the region's most overlooked fishing spots is the Okanogan River, where anglers find good fishing for smallmouth bass, rainbow trout, summer steelhead, and, in recent years, a growing walleye fishery.

❶ Osoyoos Lake

Good catches of smallmouth bass and an occasional lunker largemouth have helped to put Osoyoos on the fishing map in recent years. This lake with a year-round season offers excellent smallmouth action, and anglers seem to have good luck with everything from crankbaits and spinnerbaits to jig-and-grub combinations or even skirted spinners. May, June, and July are the top bass months.

That same time frame is also good for trolling or stillfishing for Osoyoos kokanee, most of which range in size from 10 to 14 inches. Wedding Ring spinners with a kernel of white corn on the hooks will take them as well as anything, assuming you locate a good school and get your lure down to the right depth.

Spring fishing is also fair to good for rainbow trout, most of which are the result of hatchery plants. Spring and fall can produce good catches of crappies for anglers casting small leadheads, usually suspended two to four feet beneath a bobber. The same jig-and-bobber combination will also take perch during the warm months. In winter, fishing a perch eye or small strip of perch meat near bottom may produce a bucket of plump perch in short order.

Location: North of Oroville; see map A4, grid a3.

Species: Largemouth and smallmouth bass, kokanee, rainbow trout, black crappie, brown bullhead catfish, yellow perch.

Facilities: There's a wide, two-lane ramp with two loading floats at Osoyoos Lake State Park, at the south end of the lake. The paved parking lot at the park has room for dozens of cars and trailers. Launch fee at the park is $4 round-trip, with an annual permit available for $40. Nearby is the City of Oroville's Deep Bay Park, which has a single-lane ramp with parking for about 20 cars and trailers. The state park has a large swim beach, 80 tent sites, restrooms with showers, and picnic tables. The city park also has a swim beach, picnic shelter, picnic tables, and restrooms. Food, gas, lodging, and other amenities are readily available in Oroville.

Directions: Take U.S. 97 to Oroville and continue through town along the west side of the lake.

Contact: Osoyoos Lake State Park, 509/476-3321; Washington State Parks and Recreation Commission, 360/902-8844 (information) or 800/452-5687 (reservations).

2 Sidley and Molson Lakes

The fishing is a whole lot better than it used to be here, thanks to the installation of an aerator that cuts down on winter trout loss at Sidley Lake, the more productive of the two lakes. Foot-long rainbows provide much of the action in this shallow, 120-acre lake, and don't be surprised if your spring or fall angling efforts turn up a trout in the 16- to 18-inch range.

Try casting or trolling a small, silver-and-red Super Duper if all else fails. It might not be a bad idea to take along your favorite fly rod, especially if you plan to be on the lake early or late in the day. Sidley is a favorite of bait dunkers, hardware trollers, and dry-fly purists alike, and all three groups seem to hook their share of fat rainbows.

At Molson Lake, spring plants of hatchery rainbow fingerlings provide most of the action. The catch consists primarily of pan-sized trout, which are caught on salmon eggs, Power Bait, bobber-and-worm rigs, and all the usual spoons, spinners, and small wobbling plugs.

Location: Northeast of Oroville, just south of the Canadian border; see map A4, grid a5.

Species: Rainbow trout.

Facilities: The north side of Sidley Lake has a public access area with a boat ramp and toilets. Limited services are available in Molson, but everything you'll need can be found in Oroville. The high point at Molson is the pioneer museum.

Directions: Take U.S. 97 to Oroville and turn east on Tonasket Creek Road. About eight miles east of Oroville, turn north (left) on County Road 9485, which leads to the town of Molson. Drive about a mile northeast from town, first to Molson Lake, then to Sidley, both of which are on the left.

Contact: Osoyoos Lake State Park, 509/476-3321; Washington State Parks and Recreation Commission, 360/902-8844 (information) or 800/452-5687 (reservations).

3 Similkameen River

Like many upper Columbia River tributaries, steelhead fishing is now prohibited on the Similkameen, and to help protect the dwindling steelhead runs, all other fishing is closed on the lower portion of this river, downstream from Enloe Dam, during the normal summer season. Trout fishing is a possibility above the dam, and it's a good place to enjoy some decent kokanee fishing.

Whitefish provide some excellent wintertime angling opportunity on the Similkameen, both above and below the dam. General regulations are in effect on whitefish above the dam, but downstream you're allowed to use hooks only if they're size 14 or smaller, which is somewhat small, even for whitefish. The small-hook rules are intended to protect against people landing any steelhead while they fish for whitefish.

Location: West of Oroville; see map A4, grid a3.

Species: Rainbow trout, mountain whitefish, kokanee, summer-run steelhead.

Facilities: Food, gas, lodging, tackle, and other amenities are available in Oroville.

Directions: Take U.S. 97 to Oroville and turn west on County Road 9425, which parallels the river upstream for miles.

Contact: Osoyoos Lake State Park, 509/476-3321; Washington State Parks and Recreation Commission, 360/902-8844 (information) or 800/452-5687 (reservations).

4 Chopaka Lake

About the time you think you're at one of the most desolate, out-of-the-way trout lakes in Washington, you'll arrive at the Chopaka Lake access area and wonder where all the float tubes and fly rods came from. This fly-fishing-only lake with a one-fish limit is extremely popular during the late spring and summer, and there's little chance you'll ever have it to yourself during that time of year. Weekends, in fact, are downright busy. Once you get through the bottleneck on shore and make it to the water in your car-topper or float tube, you'll realize why Chopaka is so popular—it's simply a quality fishery for quality trout.

Though anglers are allowed to keep one trout per day, most of the Chopaka regulars release everything, and that includes the beautiful 18- to 20-inch trophies that are hooked more often than you might suspect. Bring along a selection of leech and fresh-water shrimp patterns, and maybe some mosquitoes if you want to work the surface, but be prepared for the Mayfly hatch, because when it happens, it provides some of Washington's best fly-fishing action. Newcomers to Chopaka should note that most of the fishing pressure is concentrated on the shallower southern half of the lake, but you can catch trout virtually everywhere except in the 60- to 70-foot depths in the middle of the north end, where fly-fishing is just a little tough.

Location: Southwest of Oroville; see map A4, grid a2.

Species: Rainbow and a few cutthroat trout.

Facilities: The west side of the lake has a fairly well-used camping area, boat ramp, and toilets. Chopaka Lodge offers motel-type accommodations. The nearest food, gas, tackle, and lodging are in Tonasket and Oroville. Lake Osoyoos State Park is a half-hour drive to the northeast.

Directions: Take U.S. 97 to Ellisforde and turn west over the Okanogan River to County Road 9437, which parallels the west side of the river. Turn south (left), drive just over a mile to Loomis-Oroville Road (County Road 9425), and turn west (right). Drive past Whitestone and Spectacle Lakes to the town of Loomis and bear right on Stehekin Road. A little over two miles north of Loomis, turn west (left) on Loomis Lake Road, marked by a clearly visible sign. The road gets steep and ugly at this point and stays that way for about five miles, so drive slowly and take it easy. When you come to a Y intersection five miles farther up the road, go to the right and you'll wind your way down to the edge of the lake, which is on the right.

Contact: Chopaka Lodge, 509/223-3131; Osoyoos Lake State Park, 509/476-3321; Washington State Parks and Recreation Commission, 360/902-8844 (information) or 800/452-5687 (reservations).

5 Palmer Lake

Covering more than 2,000 acres, Palmer is one of Okanogan County's biggest lakes, but trout-fishing purists don't consider it one of the best. That's because the trout-fishing possibilities are limited to a few pan-sized brookies that take a distant backseat to a variety of other angling opportunities.

The hottest action these days is dished up by spunky smallmouth bass that were stocked in the lake a few years ago. Bronzebacks have reproduced well and grown quickly, and the only thing that keeps Palmer from being ranked among Washington's best smallmouth lakes is the fact that it's so darned far away from where most people happen to live. Those who live in the population centers of the Puget Sound region have to give themselves the better part of a day just to get to Palmer, and the trip home isn't any shorter. But if you have the time, bring along a selection of your favorite crawfish crankbaits, lots of leadheads and two- to three-inch grubs, or whatever happens to be your favorite smallmouth medicine, and plan on spending at least two or three days to make the trip worthwhile. You'll like what you find. You might even hook a smallmouth like the one young Ron Hobbs Jr. caught in 1996. The teenager was fishing with maggots (for what I'm not sure) when he hooked and eventually landed a smallmouth bass that tipped the scales at an impressive eight pounds, 10 ounces. That's not only the lake record for Palmer, but it's only two ounces shy of the state-record bronzeback caught from the Columbia way back in 1966.

As for the other fish Palmer has to offer, largemouth bass fishing is fair during the late spring and summer, with fish of three and four pounds a likely possibility. The lake has a set limit on both largemouth and smallmouth bass, which allows anglers to keep bass only under 12 inches and over 17 inches, a common slot limit for Washington bass lakes.

Crappie fishing is also good around the edge of the lake, and there are some keeper-sized perch. For a change of pace bring along some night crawlers, or cut strips from a couple of small perch and soak them in the depths for burbot. Or if you're serious about catching a few of these good-eating but homely "freshwater lings," use a multihook set line that might enable you to catch several at a time. Check the Palmer Lake regulations in the fishing pamphlet for details on what you can and can't do when set-line fishing.

Although abundant, the brown bullheads in the lake are often overlooked. Catch them at night on bobber-and-night-crawler rigs.

Location: Southwest of Oroville; see map A4, grid a2.

Species: Largemouth and smallmouth bass, burbot, crappie, yellow perch, brown bullhead catfish, brook trout.

Facilities: Lodging is available at Chopaka Lodge, within easy driving range of the lake. Additional amenities are abundant in Oroville.

Directions: Take U.S. 97 to Ellisforde and turn west over the Okanogan River to County Road 9437, which parallels the west side of the river. Turn south (left), drive just over a mile to Loomis-Oroville Road (County Road 9425), and turn west (right). Drive past Whitestone and Spectacle Lakes to the town of Loomis and turn right on Stehekin Road. From there it's about five miles to the lake.

Contact: Chopaka Lodge, 509/223-3131; Osoyoos Lake State Park, 509/476-3321; Washington State Parks and Recreation Commission, 360/902-8844 (information) or 800/452-5687 (reservations).

⑥ Blue Lake

Okanogan County alone has at least three Blue Lakes, and I don't know how many there are in all of Washington, but I think this is the only Blue Lake that offers anglers a crack at Lahontan cutthroats. Fall is a good time to cast a wet fly or a brightly colored wobbling spoon for husky cutthroats. Regulations require the use of artificial flies and lures only, with barbless, single hooks, and the daily bag limit is one fish. Although you can get a small boat into the water, it's also possible to hook trout by casting from the wide-open shores of the lake.

Location: Southwest of Oroville near Wannacut Lake; see map A4, grid a3.

Species: Lahontan cutthroat trout.

Facilities: There's nothing here but a wide spot along the road and a dirt road that leads off along the east side of the lake, but you can get a car-top boat or float tube in the water. Food, gas, lodging, tackle, and other amenities are available in Oroville. Sun Cove Resort on nearby Wannacut Lake has lots of tent and RV sites, plus restrooms, showers, and a small store.

Directions: Take U.S. 97 to Ellisforde, turn west onto the bridge that crosses the Okanogan River (you can't miss it), and turn north (right) on County Road 9437, which parallels the west side of the river. Drive north about eight miles to Blue Lake Road (County Road 4510) and turn west (left). Drive about two miles to the lake, which is on the right.

Contact: Sun Cove Resort, 509/476-2223; Osoyoos Lake State Park, 509/476-3321; Washington State Parks and Recreation Commission, 360/902-8844 (information) or 800/452-5687 (reservations).

7 Wannacut Lake

One look at the steep hillside bordering the east side of Wannacut might provide a hint about the character of this popular trout lake near the Canadian border. Spots near the lake's north end are well over 150 feet deep, and although you're not likely to be looking for rainbows 150 feet below the surface, the deep, cool waters provide good summertime trout survival and are part of the reason that Wannacut is one of the best. Not only does it produce a lot of trout, but a high percentage of the catch is composed of big, strong carryovers that have spent at least a year in the lake.

Both trolling and stillfishing produce good catches of Wannacut rainbows from spring to early fall. Berkley Power Bait is a favorite among anglers who stillfish, while trollers often favor Super Dupers. Much of the activity is focused on the many points that jut out from the east and west sides of the lake, but be sure to ask around when you arrive. The hot spots seem to change regularly, so you might be wasting your time if you go directly to the place that produced fish for you on the last trip to Wannacut.

If fly-fishing is your sport of choice, you might want first to investigate the shallow north and south ends of the lake. Nymphs and other wet patterns work well here throughout the day, but take along a floating line and a selection of dry patterns to cover the bases. Evening dry fly-fishing can be exceptional around the shallow weed patches at both ends of the lake. The season here runs from late April through October.

Location: Southwest of Oroville; see map A4, grid a3.

Species: Rainbow trout.

Facilities: Sun Cove Resort has a boat ramp and moorage, tent and RV sites, cabins, a store with tackle, restrooms with showers, and other facilities. The lake also has a public access area with a boat ramp and toilets. Additional amenities, including gas, are available in Oroville.

Directions: Take U.S. 97 to Ellisforde, turn west across the Okanogan River, and then turn north (right) on County Road 9437, which parallels the west side of the river. Drive north about eight miles to Blue Lake Road (County Road 4510) and turn west (left). Drive about four miles (past Blue Lake) to the T intersection, turn left, and drive about a mile to the lake, on the left.

Contact: Sun Cove Resort, 509/476-2223.

8 Muskrat Lake

There's nothing particularly notable about the fishing here, but anglers do take fair numbers of pan-sized brookies and an occasional rainbow by casting small spoons and spinners, salmon eggs, worms, and even artificial flies. Fall fishing can be especially attractive, since the angling crowds are gone and the brookies are at their brightly colored best. The season opens in late April and runs through October. I wouldn't consider driving any serious distance to fish here, but if you're really bored, knock yourself out.

Location: Southeast of Oroville; see map A4, grid a5.

Species: Brook and a few rainbow trout.

Facilities: The lake has no facilities. The nearest food, gas, tackle, and lodging are at Bonaparte Lake, to the southeast, and in

Tonasket and Oroville, to the west.

Directions: Take U.S. 97 north from Tonasket toward Oroville. About four miles north of Ellisforde, turn east (right) on Mount Hull Road, following it east to Havillah, where it becomes Havillah-Tonasket Road. Drive northeast on Havillah-Tonasket Road and turn north (left) on Kipling Road. Drive about 1.5 miles to the lake, which is on the right.

Contact: Cascade Outfitters, 509/826-4148.

9 Spectacle Lake

After becoming infested with various fish species that anglers didn't particularly want to catch, Spectacle was given the rotenone treatment in 1994, so it's once again all rainbows. At least that's the case until some barroom biologist once again takes it upon himself to dump something into the lake that doesn't belong. A slight variation on the all-rainbow theme was the addition of triploid rainbows to the lake in 2001. Yeah, they're still rainbows, but their plump size and fast growth puts them in a class by themselves, and they're a welcome addition to this big lake with a short fishing season.

Spectacle opens to fishing earlier than most Okanogan County lakes, kicking off the season on March 1 and staying open through the end of July. During that time, anglers who stillfish, trollers, and fly casters all enjoy productive trout action. Most prefer the deeper waters along the south side of the lake, where they take plump rainbows on everything from night crawlers, marshmallows, and Power Bait to Super Dupers, black Rooster Tails, and frog-pattern Flatfish. Artificial flies are also popular here, and many anglers simply troll them at the end of a monofilament line. Favorite patterns include green or black Woolly Worms and green Carey Specials.

Location: Northwest of Tonasket; see map A4, grid b3.

Species: Rainbow trout.

Facilities: The lake has not one, not two, but three private resorts on it, and among them they have everything you'll need for a weekend (or monthlong) visit. There's also a public access area with a boat ramp and toilets.

Directions: Take U.S. 97 to Ellisforde and turn west over the Okanogan River to County Road 9437, which parallels the west side of the river. Turn south (left) here, drive just over a mile to Loomis-Oroville Road (County Road 9425), and turn west (right). Drive past Whitestone Lake and continue on to Spectacle, which is on the left side of the road.

Contact: Spectacle Lake Resort, 509/223-3433 (April through October), website: www.spectaclelakeresort.com; Spectacle Falls Resort, 509/223-4141 (April through July); Rainbow Resort, 509/223-3700.

10 Whitestone Lake

Known to most Northwest anglers as a place to catch rainbow trout, Okanogan County also has some very good largemouth fishing, and Whitestone stands as one of the best examples, with bass to five pounds and over. It's an excellent place to practice your technique with plastic worm, jig-and-pig, crankbait, spinnerbait, or buzzbait. The afternoon wind sometimes causes problems for anglers on this long, narrow lake, so think about fishing it early in the day rather than late in the evening. Be sure to check the fishing pamphlet for details on the bass slot limit in effect here.

Whitestone used to be one of north-central Washington's better crappie lakes, but the (illegal) introduction of perch and sunfish has made things tough for the crappies. You're much more likely to find stunted five-inch panfish than you are a half dozen of the fat, 11-inch crappies for which the lake was once famous.

Location: Northwest of Tonasket; see map A4, grid b3.

Species: Largemouth bass, crappie, yellow perch, brown bullhead catfish.

Facilities: The public access area on the lake has a good boat ramp and toilets. Three resorts with virtually everything an angler might need are located at Spectacle Lake, a few miles to the west.

Directions: Take U.S. 97 to Ellisforde and turn west over the Okanogan River to County Road 9437, which parallels the west side of the river. Turn south (left) here, drive just over a mile to Loomis-Oroville Road (County Road 9425), and turn west (right). Drive about three miles to the lake, which is alongside the road on the left.

Contact: Spectacle Lake Resort, 509/223-3433 (April through October), website: www.spectaclelakeresort.com; Spectacle Falls Resort, 509/223-4141 (April through July); Rainbow Resort, 509/223-3700; Cascade Outfitters, 509/826-4148.

11 Lost Lake

Located in the high country of Okanogan National Forest near Strawberry Mountain, this 47-acre lake is a haven for brightly colored brook trout, hence brook trout anglers. Although it opens in late April, the fishing gets good here around Memorial Day and stays productive into early fall, with five- to 10-inch brookies providing most of the fun. But there are enough larger carryovers around to keep you guessing whether the next cast will produce trout of 13 inches or larger.

Many anglers fish worms, salmon eggs, or Power Bait for their trout, but brookies are active feeders that don't mind chasing down a shiny spinner or small wobbling spoon. Casting dry flies early in the morning or during the last hour of daylight can pay off, or you can try small wet patterns during the day to entice trout.

Location: Northwest of Wauconda in Okanogan County; see map A4, grid b6.

Species: Brook trout.

Facilities: The U.S. Forest Service's Lost Lake Campground has about 20 tent and trailer sites. Bonaparte Lake Resort a few miles to the south has tent and RV sites, cabins, and other amenities. The nearest food, gas, tackle, and lodging are in Tonasket.

Directions: Take U.S. 97 to Tonasket and turn east on Highway 20. Drive east to County Road 4953 and turn north (left), going about six miles to Bonaparte Lake and continuing another 10 miles to the short spur road leading to the north end of Lost Lake.

Contact: Cascade Outfitters, 509/826-4148, website: www.warecreations.com; Okanogan National Forest, Tonasket Ranger District, 509/486-2186; Bonaparte Lake Resort, 509/486-2828 (April through October).

12 Beth, Beaver, and Little Beaver Lakes

The pan-sized brookies stocked here every spring provide most of the angling action in all three lakes, at least as far as numbers are concerned. But the real excitement is generated by the occasional rainbow that's winched from these small lakes nestled in the pine-covered hills of the Okanogan National Forest. Some of them weigh in at three, four, even five pounds. Like the brook trout, the big 'bows can be caught on all the usual baits, lures, and artificial flies.

Since the lakes are small and shallow, they warm rather quickly in summer, which slows the trout fishing. Plan to visit in June, September, or October for the greatest success.

Location: West of Bodie in Okanogan National Forest; see map A4, grid b6.

Species: Rainbow and brook trout.

Facilities: The U.S. Forest Service maintains two campgrounds in the area. Beaver Lake Campground has five tent/trailer spaces, while Beth Lake Campground has eight sites. Both campgrounds have drinking water and vault toilets. Small boats can be launched on all three lakes. Bonaparte Lake Resort has cabins, RV and tent sites, groceries, tackle, and other amenities.

Directions: Take U.S. 97 to Tonasket and turn east on Highway 20, following it about 18 miles to Bonaparte Lake Road (County Road 4953). Continue about six miles past Bonaparte Lake to Beaver Lake. Little Beaver Lake is immediately to the east, and Beth Lake is about 1.5 miles to the northwest.

Contact: Okanogan National Forest, Tonasket Ranger District, 509/486-2186; Bonaparte Lake Resort, 509/486-2828 (April through October), website: www.bonaparte-lake-resort.com.

13 Bonaparte Lake

We're talking cold, clear, and deep, the ideal ingredients for trout and trout fishing. That certainly helps to explain why this 160-acre lake in the Okanogan highlands offers so much trout-fishing variety. Open year-round, you can find some kind of salmonid to catch here virtually 12 months out of the year. But the biggest of the bunch is the lake trout, or Mackinaw, which occasionally grow to more than 20 pounds in Bonaparte's chilly waters. Although Washington's official state-record Mackinaw is a fish of just under 31 pounds, folks around Bonaparte Lake like to tell the story of the monster 38-pounder that was caught here but not submitted for record consideration. If the scales were accurate and the story hasn't been embellished over the years, that's the largest trout or char ever caught from a Washington lake.

The best time of year for a trophy lake trout is shortly after the ice cover disappears from the lake, usually sometime in April. Vertical jigging with Buzz Bombs and other metal jigs is one productive technique, but trolling with large Rapalas, Flatfish, Kwikfish, and other big plugs is also effective. Get on the water around first light and/or last light to improve your chances of catching one of these trophies.

If you find the Mackinaws in a cooperative mood, remember that the limit here allows only one trout over 20 inches per day.

As for Bonaparte's smaller trout, the rainbows here sometimes grow to five pounds or more, which is substantially larger than the average lake rainbow. Trollers pull Pop Geer-and-worm rigs for them, while anglers who stillfish prefer orange Berkley Power Bait and salmon eggs. The same offerings also turn up an occasional brook trout. Kokanee can also be caught by trolling or stillfishing, but practitioners of either method should be willing to experiment a little until finding the right combination. Wedding Ring spinners and Triple Teazers are a couple of the old stand-by offerings for trolling, but trolling blades with worms also take kokanee. Some anglers score good catches by substituting a Berkley Power Wiggler or two for the worm. Again, experiment until you find the right combination of bait, lure, and color. Use your depthsounder to locate schools of these sweet-eating fish, and you may need a downrigger to get your bait or lure down to the strike zone.

Salmonids rule the roost here, but the lake does have a fairly good population of smallmouth bass, too, and now and then someone catches a decent one. Take a few small crankbaits and a selection of small plastic grubs and tube baits, just in case.

Location: Northwest of Wauconda in Okanogan County; see map A4, grid b6.

Species: Rainbow, brook, and lake trout; kokanee; smallmouth bass.

Facilities: Bonaparte Lake Resort has a boat ramp, tent and RV sites, cabins, tackle, and groceries. There's also a boat ramp and about two dozen campsites at the U.S. Forest Service's Bonaparte Lake Campground.

Directions: Take U.S. 97 to Tonasket and turn east on Highway 20, following it about 18 miles to County Road 4953 (Bonaparte Lake Road) and signs pointing to Bonaparte Lake. Turn north (left) and drive about six miles to the lake.

Contact: Bonaparte Lake Resort, 509/486-2828 (April through October only), website: www.bonaparte-lake-resort.com; Okanogan National Forest, Tonasket Ranger District, 509/486-2186.

14 Curlew Lake

The term "fish factory" probably applies here as well as anywhere in the Pacific Northwest. Curlew has long been a favorite of Washington trout anglers, and the addition of largemouth bass in the 1980s (compliments of the midnight biologist corps, not the old Department of Game) has added a new dimension to the fishery without causing any noticeable problems for the trout population.

But rainbow trout still rule the roost in this 870-acre lake bordered by pine-covered hills around much of its perimeter. Between Department of Fish and Wildlife plants and net-pen facilities on the lake, Curlew is stocked with something like 300,000 rainbows a year, and they grow quickly in its food-rich waters. Ten- to 14-inch trout provide much of the angling action, but potbellied lunkers of 18 to 22 inches are common enough to be a realistic possibility for anyone fishing here. Slow-trolling with various gang trolls is standard operating procedure, and anglers typically hang Rooster Tails, Wedding Rings, Flatfish, or Triple Teazers off the back end of those blade strings. Another productive trolling technique involves leaded line, a long monofilament leader, and a green Carey Special or other streamer fly of some kind pulled very slowly through the depths. Stillfishing also accounts for some good catches, and the fishing docks at the various resorts are some of the most productive spots on the lake. Night fishing can be especially productive from these structures, primarily because the dock lights are left on and attract freshwater shrimp and other aquatic organisms, which in turn draw the trout.

Casting flies, small spinners, or wobbling spoons, or fishing a plain ol' bobber-and-worm rig around the edge of the lake are all good ways to catch brook trout from Curlew. Like brookies everywhere, they're generally small but brightly colored, full of fight, and quite tasty if you keep 'em cool and cook 'em the same day you catch 'em.

Although Curlew is open to year-round fishing and provides at least fair trout fishing during every season, the bass fishery is pretty much a late spring and summer affair. The limited number of docks and other man-made structures usually have trout anglers on them, so bass anglers have to confine most of their efforts to natural cover around the edges of the lake. Luckily such cover is abundant, taking the form of submerged logs and trees, overhanging and submerged brush, and some fairly thick patches of grass and scattered weeds. There are lots of smaller bass (under half a pound) but enough big fish to make it worth your while.

After a great deal of environmental hoop jumping, the Department of Fish and Wildlife finally stocked tiger muskies in Curlew in 1998 in an effort to cut down a large population of squawfish and provide a trophy fishery. The muskies won't be big enough to catch and keep for another few years, but smaller fish might be encountered by anglers in search of bass and trout. Unless it's 36 inches long or bigger, release any tiger muskie you catch from Curlew.

Location: Northeast of Republic in Ferry County; see map A4, grid b8.

Species: Rainbow and brook trout, largemouth bass, tiger muskies.

Facilities: Four private resorts and a state park provide a wealth of facilities for visiting anglers, including boat ramps, moorage, boat rentals, fishing docks, cabins, RV and tent sites, restrooms with showers, and small stores with tackle and groceries. Some of the resorts allow nonguests to use their ramp facilities, others don't. There's a $4 launch fee at the state park unless you're camping there. Other services are available in Republic.

Directions: Take Highway 20 or Highway 21 to Republic and continue north on Highway 21, which parallels the east side of the lake. To reach the west side of the lake, turn west (left) on West Curlew Lake Road about six miles north of Republic.

Contact: Curlew Lake State Park, 509/775-3592 (April through October); Washington State Parks and Recreation Commission, 360/902-8844 (information) or 800/452-5687 (reservations); Pine Point Resort, 509/775-3643 (April through October), website: www.pinepointresort.com; Tiffany's Resort, 509/775-3152 (April through October), website: www.tiffanysresort.com; Black's Beach Resort, 509/775-3989, website: www.blacksbeachresort.com; Fisherman's Cove, 509/775-3641, website: www.fishermanscove.net.

15 Aeneas Lake

This is one of relatively few Washington lakes that's reserved for fly casters only, and it's long been a favorite of fly fishermen from all over the Pacific Northwest. Since I'm well down any list of accomplished fly casters, my success here has been limited, and I'm always out-fished by the ospreys that work the lake daily. But anglers who know what they're doing with a fly rod catch some beautiful rainbows from Aeneas, including the occasional trout to 20 inches or better. The average rainbows here run 12 to 16 inches.

Although this 60-acre lake isn't large, it's quite deep, with spots in the middle plunging more than 60 feet. Needless to say, fly anglers don't spend much time trying to ply these depths with their feathery offerings. Most regulars fish the relatively shallow waters near the north end, using various leech patterns or a local favorite known as the Stick, which is little more than olive or black chenille wrapped around a size 10 hook. It may look like a stick to us, but it looks like food to a hungry trout.

The season here runs late April through October, with May and June providing the best trout action. Late September and the entire month of October are also productive fishing times.

Location: Southwest of Tonasket; see map A4, grid b3.

Species: Rainbow trout.

Facilities: The lake has a few primitive campsites, a boat ramp, and toilets. Food, gas, lodging, and other amenities are available a few miles away in Tonasket.

Directions: Take U.S. 97 to Tonasket and turn west on Pine Creek Road (Forest Service Road 9400). Be sure to take the hard left about three miles west of town to stay on Pine Creek Road. The lake is on the right, just under a mile from that 90-degree turn.

Contact: Cascade Outfitters, 509/826-4148, website: www.warecreations.com.

16 Blue Lake (Sinlahekin Valley)

If you like to do your trout fishing with artificial lures and flies, this 160-acre lake in the Sinlahekin Valley is worth visiting anytime during the spring, early summer, or fall. Selective fishery regulations keep it from being hammered too heavily, and it seems as if a few foot-long rainbows are always in a biting mood. Patient anglers are sometimes rewarded with trout of 17 to 20 inches. The daily limit is one trout, but don't feel that you have to kill one; the fishing stays good because most anglers release everything they catch. If you're planning to toss feathers and fur for your trout, be sure to take along a selection of Muddlers and various leech patterns. The strike zone here is often quite deep, so include a fast-sink fly line in your arsenal.

Location: Southwest of Tonasket; see map A4, grid b2.

Species: Rainbow trout.

Facilities: The lake has an access area and boat ramp. Although there's not an official campground, lots of people camp at primitive sites around the lake. The nearest campgrounds and other amenities are in and around Conconully, 10.5 miles to the south.

Directions: Take U.S. 97 to Riverside and continue north about 5.5 miles to Pine Creek Road (County Road 9410). Turn west (left) here and drive about 10 miles to Fish Lake. Turn north (right) just past Fish Lake onto Sinlahekin Road. Continue about four miles north to Blue Lake.

Contact: Liar's Cove Resort, 509/826-1288 (April through October), website: www. omakchronicle.com/liarscove; Shady Pines Resort, 509/826-2287 or 800/830-1288 (April through October), website: www. shadypinesresort.com; Conconully Lake Resort, 509/826-0813 or 800/850-0813, website: www.conconullylakeresort.com; Okanogan National Forest Headquarters, 509/422-2704; Conconully State Park, 509/826-7408.

⓱ Fish Lake

Unlike many Okanogan County waters, this long, narrow lake produces trout pretty well for about the first month of the season and then tapers off quickly. Yearling rainbows from plants made the previous spring run about 10 inches long on opening day, but anglers do catch fair numbers of two-year carryovers that range 15 to 19 inches. Try trolling a small Flatfish or Kwikfish, preferably one in some shade of green, or stillfishing with the tried-and-true gang-troll-and-worms combination.

Although bass fishing isn't a big deal for most Okanogan County anglers, a few do

visit Fish Lake after the trout action tapers off in May or June to try for largemouths. Most work Rapalas on the surface for their fish, but don't hesitate to work a white or chartreuse spinnerbait along the shoreline if the fish aren't hitting on top.

Location: Northeast of Conconully; see map A4, grid c2.

Species: Rainbow trout, a few largemouth bass.

Facilities: The lake has two public access areas with a boat ramp and toilets. The U.S. Forest Service's Sugar Loaf Campground, with five campsites that have room for small trailers and RVs, is two miles south of the lake on Sinlahekin Road. Other amenities can be found in Conconully about seven miles to the south.

Directions: Take U.S. 97 to Riverside and continue north about 5.5 miles to Pine Creek Road (County Road 9410). Turn west (left) here and continue just under 10 miles to the lake.

Contact: Liar's Cove Resort, 509/826-1288 or 800/830-1288, website: www.omakchronicle. com/liarscove; Shady Pines Resort, 509/826-2287 or 800/552-2287, website: www .shadypinesresort.com; Conconully Lake Resort, 509/826-0813 or 800/850-0813, website: www. conconullylakeresort.com; Okanogan National Forest Headquarters, 509/422-2704; Conconully State Park, 509/826-7408; Washington State Parks and Recreation Commission, 360/902-8844 (information) or 800/452-5687 (reservations).

⓲ Long, Round, and Ell Lakes

All three of these lakes offer anglers a good shot at pan-sized yearling rainbows with a few husky carryovers mixed in for good measure. But Ell Lake now has different regulations and even a different open season from the other two, so anglers headed for these three neighboring lakes in the Aeneas

Valley need to remember which lake they're fishing and act accordingly.

Ell Lake is the only one of the three that remains open to fishing past the end of September, closing October 31. But angling regulations on Ell Lake are also more restrictive, with selective fishery rules now in effect. That means you can't use bait, and all lures must have single, barbless hooks. Ell also has a one-fish daily limit, while the other two have standard, five-fish limits.

Location: Southeast of Tonasket; see map A4, grid c6.

Species: Rainbow trout.

Facilities: All three lakes have access areas and launch sites for smaller boats. The nearest food, gas, lodging, and other amenities are in Tonasket.

Directions: Drive east from Tonasket on Highway 20 and turn south (right) on Aeneas Valley Road. Drive about five miles to Long Lake, then Round Lake and Ell Lake, all on the east (left) side of the road.

Contact: Cascade Outfitters, 509/826-4148, website: www.warecreations.com.

19 Ferry Lake

At just under 20 acres, this lake in the high country of western Ferry County often suffers fish losses due to winter-kill, so the fishery depends on annual plants of hatchery rainbows. Ferry Lake is a popular destination of hikers, off-road-vehicle enthusiasts, partiers, and other campers during the summer, so perhaps it's not the best choice for serious summertime anglers. But in spring and fall, when the crowds are light, it's worth a couple days of your time. The proximity of Swan Lake (see number 20) makes it easy to fish two different spots in the same day.

Location: Southwest of Republic; see map A4, grid c7.

Species: Rainbow trout.

Facilities: The U.S. Forest Service's Ferry Lake Campground has tent and RV sites, restrooms, drinking water, and picnic areas, as well as a boat ramp. The nearest food, gas, lodging, and other amenities are in Republic.

Directions: Take Highway 21 north from Wilbur or south from Republic and turn west on Swan Lake Road (Forest Service Road 53) about eight miles south of Republic. Drive about 6.5 miles and turn west (right) on Forest Service Road 500; then take the next right to Ferry Lake.

Contact: Colville National Forest, Republic Ranger District, 509/775-3305.

20 Swan Lake

Regular plants of hatchery brookies and rainbows offer some pretty good trout fishing in this 50-acre lake located at the 3,600-foot mark near Swan Butte. Early summer and early fall provide some of the best fishing, and when the bite is on, it doesn't seem to matter much what you throw at 'em. A big trout here is a fish of maybe 13 inches, but now and then someone takes a lunker brook trout of two pounds or better. The cool, clear water helps to make them excellent table fare.

A downside here, according to the Department of Fish and Wildlife, is that some mental midget has dumped largemouth bass in the lake. Besides growing slowly and seldom getting big enough to provide much angling action, the bass are dining on the small brook trout.

Location: Southwest of Republic; see map A4, grid c7.

Species: Rainbow and brook trout, largemouth bass.

Facilities: Swan Lake Campground (U.S. Forest Service) has tent and RV camp sites, drinking water, a boat ramp, restrooms, and picnic tables. Other amenities are available in Republic.

Directions: Take Highway 21 north from Wilbur or south from Republic to Swan Lake

Road (Forest Service Road 53), about eight miles south of Republic. Turn west and drive about 6.5 miles to Forest Service Road 500; then turn west (right) and continue about two miles to the lake.

Contact: Colville National Forest, Republic Ranger District, 509/775-3305.

21 Crawfish Lake

Since both rainbows and brookies do well here, this 80-acre lake straddling the border between the Colville Indian Reservation and Colville National Forest is stocked with both species on a regular basis. Pulling worms behind a string of gang trolls is an effective way to get the rainbows. Move into shallower shoreline areas and cast or troll a Super Duper and you'll be fishing for brookies the way most of the locals do.

As you might have guessed from its name, the lake is home to a fairly healthy crawfish population—at least it's becoming more healthy after a die-off a few years ago that nearly wiped them all out. If you want to try something a little different, drop a crawfish trap and catch a few of the little crustaceans while you fish. Boil the larger ones just like crab for the dinner table, peeling and eating only the tail section. Save a few of the smaller ones to use for trout bait. Don't boil them, but break them in half, peel the tail section, and use the little gray morsel of meat on a size six or eight worm hook. It's an excellent bait. What's more, the crawfish is one of the few critters you're still allowed to harvest without any kind of license or permit.

Location: Northeast of Omak; see map A4, grid c5.

Species: Rainbow and brook trout.

Facilities: Crawfish Lake Campground (U.S. Forest Service) has 22 tent and trailer sites and a boat ramp. Omak has food, gas, tackle, and lodging.

Directions: Take Highway 155 east from Omak and turn north (left) on Lyman Lake Road. Continue another seven miles to Crawfish Lake Road and turn north (left). When you cross the Okanogan National Forest border, the road becomes Forest Service Road 100, and it leads right to the shore.

Contact: Okanogan National Forest, Tonasket Ranger District, 509/486-2186; Cascade Outfitters, 509/826-4148, website: www.warecretions.com.

22 Conconully Lake

Like the reservoir immediately to the southwest (see Conconully Reservoir, number 23), this long, narrow lake provides excellent rainbow trout fishing from the time it opens in late April until about the middle of June. After slowing somewhat in the summer, it comes on strong with hefty strings of trout again in the fall.

Trolling with Wedding Rings, Triple Teazers, Double Whammys, Needle Fish, and other small spoons and spinners will take both trout and kokanee. Many anglers come to the Conconully area year after year because they know that even if the trout go on a hunger strike in the lake, they can drop down to the reservoir and pick up where they left off, and vice versa. There's real security in knowing that you have two of Washington's top trout lakes within a few hundred feet of each other.

Although most anglers come here for trout, a growing population of both largemouth and smallmouth bass is starting to interest some anglers. The bass are mostly small, but they will hit leadhead jigs adorned with three- or four-inch plastic grubs, small crankbaits, or spinnerbaits. Fish weedy cover for largemouths and rocky spots for smallmouths.

Location: Immediately east of the town of Conconully; see map A4, grid c2.

Species: Rainbow trout, some largemouth and smallmouth bass.

Facilities: Conconully Lake Resort has RV and tent sites, restrooms and showers, a boat ramp and moorage, boat rentals, and a small grocery store with fishing tackle. Nearby Conconully State Park has more than 80 tent sites, plus restrooms and showers.

Directions: From the south, drive north on U.S. 97 to Okanogan and turn north (right) on Highway 215 (Conconully Road), which continues north to the town of Conconully. You'll first pass Conconully Reservoir. The lake is just northeast of the reservoir. From the north, drive south on U.S. 97 to Riverside and turn west (right) on Riverside Cutoff Road, which joins Conconully Road six miles west of U.S. 97. Turn right on Conconully Road and continue north to the town of Conconully and the lake.

Contact: Conconully Lake Resort, 509/826-0813 or 800/850-0813, website: www.conconullylakeresort.com; Conconully State Park, 509/826-7408; Washington State Parks and Recreation Commission, 360/902-8844 (information) or 800/452-5687 (reservations).

23 Conconully Reservoir

When you call a particular body of water one of the best trout fisheries in Okanogan County, you're saying quite a lot, but that description can be used here without fear of exaggeration. This impoundment on Salmon Creek has long been a great place to catch rainbow trout, and over the decades few anglers have been disappointed. Both stillfishing and trolling are effective, and along with the yearlings from spring plants of fingerling rainbows, you'll hook a surprising number of husky carryovers measuring 16 inches and over. All the usual baits and lures have been known to take Conconully trout, but the hot number may change from week to week or even day to day, so be sure to ask around when you arrive.

Besides rainbows, the reservoir also has decent kokanee populations, which come on strong about the time the trout fishery begins to slow a little in early summer.

Location: Immediately south of the town of Conconully; see map A4, grid c2.

Species: Rainbow trout, kokanee.

Facilities: Liar's Cove Resort and Shady Pines Resort offer a wide range of facilities, including RV sites with hookups, restrooms and showers, boat ramps, boat rentals, and tackle. Conconully State Park has more than 80 tent sites, plus restrooms with showers, picnic areas, and a boat ramp.

Directions: From the south take U.S. 97 to Okanogan and turn north (right) on Highway 215, also called Conconully Road, which eventually runs along the east side of the reservoir. From the north take U.S. 97 south to Riverside and turn west (right) on Riverside Cutoff Road, which joins Conconully Road about six miles west of U.S. 97. Turn right on Conconully Road and follow it to the reservoir.

Contact: Liar's Cove Resort, 509/826-1288 or 800/830-1288 (April through October), website: www.omakchronicle.com/liarscove; Shady Pines Resort, 509/826-2287 or 800/552-2287 (April through October), website: www.shadypinesresort.com; Conconully State Park, 509/826-7408 (April through October); Washington State Parks and Recreation Commission, 360/902-8844 (information) or 800/452-5687 (reservations).

24 Salmon Creek

This little stream that heads into the heart of Okanogan National Forest, eventually merging with the Okanogan River at the town of Okanogan is important to thousands of Washington anglers, many of whom don't even realize it. That's because the North Fork and West Fork of Salmon Creek provide most of the water for Conconully Reservoir, one of north-central Washington's most productive and popular trout waters. Fishing in the creek itself is overshadowed by the action available in the reservoir and nearby Conconully Lake, but the North Fork, West Fork, and main Salmon Creek below the reservoir are productive trout fisheries in their own right and certainly worth some of your time if you happen to be in this steep, pine-covered part of the Pacific Northwest.

The lower 15 miles of the creek, much of which runs through private property where it's a must to get permission to fish, holds some nice rainbows and a few trophy-class browns. Those brown trout, by the way, are just myths as far as I'm concerned, but a few local anglers insist they exist. When and if you get permission from the local landowners to fish on the lower creek, it's OK to use your favorite baits, and night crawlers account for some of the big trout to come from this part of the creek.

On the North and South Forks selective regulations are in effect, so it's artificial lures and flies with single, barbless hooks only. These waters produce mostly pan-sized brookies and rainbows, and many of the brook trout don't make the eight-inch minimum size limit that's in effect here. Still, they're eager biters and lots of fun to catch and release. Both forks are popular with fly casters, and productive fly patterns here include small gnats, ant imitations, and grasshopper imitations. Grasshopper patterns are also popular with fly casters who work the lower end of the creek for browns and rainbows, since the long-legged insects become a staple of the trout diet throughout the summer.

Location: Northwest of Okanogan; see map A4, grid c2.

Species: Rainbow, brook, and some brown trout.

Facilities: Conconully State Park and the several private resorts in the Conconully area are good centers of operation for a Salmon Creek angling assault. The U.S. Forest Service's Cottonwood, Oreille, Kerr, and Salmon

Meadows Campgrounds also have tent sites for anglers who may want to camp along the North Fork Salmon Creek. Food, gas, tackle, and lodging all are available in and around Conconully.

Directions: Take U.S. 97 to Okanogan and turn west on Salmon Creek Road, which follows the stream northwest for several miles. At the tiny town of Ruby, turn east (right) to Conconully Road and turn north (left) to the town of Conconully. Continue north out of town on Salmon Creek Road (Conconully Road turns into Salmon Creek Road) to fish the North Fork Salmon Creek, or turn south along the west side of Conconully Reservoir to reach the West Fork Salmon Creek.

Contact: Liar's Cove Resort, 509/826-1288 or 800/830-1288 (April through October), website: www.omakchronicle.com/liarscove; Shady Pines Resort, 509/826-2287 or 800/552-2287 (April through October), website: www.shadypinesresort.com; Conconully Lake Resort, 509/826-7408 or 800/850-0813, website: www.conconullylakeresort.com; Okanogan National Forest Headquarters, 509/422-2704; Conconully State Park, 509/826-7408 (April through October); Washington State Parks and Recreation Commission, 360/902-8844 (information) or 800/452-5687 (reservations).

25 Cougar Lake

Like Campbell and Davis Lakes to the south (see number 26 in this chapter and number 24 in Chapter A3), Cougar Lake has had a reverse season for many years, opening to fishing in September and closing at the end of March. Fall fishing can be good for anglers who stillfish and troll, and decent catches are made off and on through the winter and spring as well. Spring plants of six- to seven-inch rainbows grow to worthwhile size during the summer and greet anglers as eager 10-inchers in the fall. Mixed in with those pan-sized fish are fair numbers of carryover trout measuring 14 to 18 inches. There's nothing fancy about the things folks use or the way they use 'em here, so bring along your favorite trout goodies and give them a try.

Location: East of Winthrop; see map A4, grid c0.

Species: Rainbow trout.

Facilities: The lake has a rough boat ramp. All other amenities are available in Winthrop.

Directions: Take Highway 20 to Winthrop and drive north out of town on County Road 9137. Go 1.5 miles and turn east (right) on County Road 9137 (Bear Creek Road). You'll come to a T about four miles up this road, and you'll want to go left. From there it's about 1.5 miles to the lake, which is on the right side of the road.

Contact: Okanogan National Forest, Winthrop Ranger District, 509/996-2266; Pine-Near Trailer Park, 509/996-2391; Methow Valley KOA Campground, 509/996-2255; Chewuch Inn, 509/996-3107.

26 Campbell Lake

Fishing for rainbows can be fairly good at Campbell Lake for the first couple of months after the September 1 opener. Trolling with Pop Geer and worms is popular, but stillfishing with salmon eggs, cheese, corn, marshmallows, and Power Bait also accounts for good numbers of fish. Most of the trout run 10 to 11 inches, but there's a chance you'll find an occasional carryover to 18 inches. Wintertime fishing can be off and on, depending on whether and when the lake freezes over with a good coat of ice. Spring plants of about 4,000 hatchery rainbows each year help to keep the fishing worthwhile. The lake closes to catch-and-keep fishing at the end of March, but an April through August catch-and-release season gives anglers a chance to exercise their casting arms even if they can't put anything in their creels.

Location: East of Winthrop; see map A4, grid d0.

Species: Rainbow trout.

Facilities: The lake has a rough boat launch and plenty of bank-fishing space. Other amenities are available in Winthrop and Twisp.

Directions: Take Highway 20 to Winthrop and drive out of town southeast on County Road 1631 (Bear Creek Road) past the golf course. Turn east (right) on Lester Road and follow it about three winding miles to the lake.

Contact: Methow Wildlife Area, 509/996-2559; Pine-Near Trailer Park, 509/996-2391; Methow Valley KOA Campground, 509/996-2255; Chewuch Inn, 509/996-3107.

27 Lime Belt Lakes

Of the dozen and a half lakes scattered around the hills between U.S. 97 and Conconully Lake, only one is stocked regularly with hatchery trout. That one is Blue Lake, the most readily accessible of the lot. But accessibility can be relative, and even the main road to Blue Lake can give you trouble early in the season or whenever a pouring rain hits the area to turn the road into a slimy mess. Assuming you can reach it, Blue Lake will provide fair spring and early summer action on brook trout of 8 to 10 inches. They'll hit flies, hardware, or bait, but most of the locals fish for 'em with good ol' worms.

Some of the other lakes in the group are fishless, some have remnant populations of brookies or rainbows from plants in years gone by, and a few have populations of various panfish courtesy of the midnight planting truck. High alkalinity is a problem in some of these lakes, and they may not ever provide much of a fishery unless the Department of Fish and Wildlife should decide to try stocking Lahontan cutthroats. If you want to try your luck anyway, the largest lakes in the group are Alkali (46 acres), Medicine (38 acres), Horseshoe (29 acres), Evans (27 acres), and Booher (25 acres). Castor, Price, Frye, Shellberg, and Sutton Lakes might be a waste of time, but you can always investigate them if you feel like exploring. All of these lakes are best fished in May or late September.

Location: Northeast of Omak; see map A4, grid c3.

Species: Brook trout, maybe a few rainbow trout.

Facilities: Blue Lake has a fairly good boat ramp, but the other lakes offer little or nothing in the way of amenities. Food, gas, tackle, and lodging are available to the south in Omak and Okanogan.

Directions: Take U.S. 97 to Okanogan and turn north on Highway 215 (Conconully Road). After passing the Riverside Cutoff Road, watch for Lime Belt Road and turn north (right). Lime Belt Road goes directly to Blue Lake and Sutton Lake, with side roads leading to other lakes in the area.

Contact: Cascade Outfitters, 509/826-4148, website: www.warecreations.com.

28 Brown Lake

Don't bother unless you have lots of spare time on your hands. This little lake doesn't offer much except a few small fish. Driving a half hour to Conconully (see number 22) would be a better use of your time.

Location: Northwest of Omak; see map A4, grid d2.

Species: Some bass and panfish, an occasional rainbow trout.

Facilities: There's nothing at the lake but some bank access for fishing or boat launching. The nearest food, gas, tackle, and lodging are available in Omak.

Directions: Take Highway 20 or U.S. 97 to Okanogan and drive northwest from town on Salmon Creek Road. Turn right on Green Lake Road and drive about a mile past Green Lake to Brown Lake, on the left.

Contact: Cascade Outfitters, 509/826-4148, website: www.warecreations.com.

29 Green Lakes

If you show up on the shores of Upper or Lower Green Lake on a sunny May morning and wonder why you have both lakes all to yourself, stop in your tracks and consult the current fishing pamphlet. What you'll notice when you run down the alphabetical listing in the "Eastside Lakes" section is that these lakes aren't open for catch-and-kill fishing during the regular spring-to-fall season, nor are they open to year-round fishing, as are more and more Washington lakes. Like a few other waters scattered around various parts of eastern Washington, Upper and Lower Green are open only during the winter, December 1 through March 31. Don't feel stupid if you've made this mistake, because it's happened to others before you and will no doubt happen to others after you. It's even happened to someone who's very close to me, but I won't mention any names. Perhaps in an effort to save some of us further embarrassment, the Department of Fish and Wildlife has added a catch-and-release season here April through November. That way, even though we can't keep any trout, at least it looks like we know what we're doing if we're the only ones fishing the Green Lakes on a nice May morning. Selective fishing regulations requiring artificial lures and barbless hooks are in effect during this catch-and-release season.

Anyway, winter fishing can be quite good here, especially on the 45-acre Upper Green. At nine or 10 inches, most of the rainbows aren't big, but they do well in the chilly Okanogan County winters and have a reputation for being among the hardest-fighting trout around. What's more, not all of the rainbows know they're only supposed to grow to about 10 inches, so a few of them grow to 15 or 16 inches. Those fish *really* fight well. Occasionally you'll reel in a pan-sized brook trout along with your catch of rainbows. Wintertime trout don't have big appetites, so whatever you use, make it small. Tiny flies work well, as do the small Berkley Power Nuggets, single salmon eggs, and marshmallows.

Location: Northwest of Omak; see map A4, grid d2.

Species: Rainbow and brook trout, a few largemouth bass.

Facilities: A public access area with a boat ramp and toilets is located on the upper lake, and there are other spots where it's easy to get a boat in the water. Food, gas, lodging, and other amenities are available in nearby Okanogan and Omak.

Directions: Take U.S. 97 or Highway 20 to Okanogan and drive northwest from town on Salmon Creek Road. Turn right on Green Lake Road and drive about 1.5 miles to the lake.

Contact: Cascade Outfitters, 509/826-4148, website: www.warecreations.com.

30 Duck Lake

If there's such a thing as a favorite local warm-water fish lake around the Okanogan-Omak area, this is it. Anglers like to cast Rapalas and similar minnow-type lures for their bass, and they're sometimes rewarded with fish to three pounds. Most of the bass, however, are on the small side. If you want to work at it and try a jig-and-pig, plastic worm in the weeds, or perhaps a spinnerbait, you might find enough worthwhile largemouths to make for a good day. If prospecting for bass doesn't pay off, try BeetleSpins for bluegills or small leadheads suspended beneath a bobber for crappies, both of which grow to respectable size here.

Location: North of Omak; see map A4, grid d3.

Species: Largemouth and a few smallmouth bass, black crappie, bluegill.

Facilities: The lake has a rough boat ramp. Other amenities are available in Omak and Okanogan.

Directions: Take U.S. 97 or Highway 155 to Omak and drive north from town on U.S. 97. About 2.5 miles north of town, turn west

(left) on Cherokee Road, drive two miles to Airport Road, and turn north (right). Drive half a mile to Bide-A-Wee Road and turn left; then continue a mile to the lake, which is on the right.

Contact: Cascade Outfitters, 509/826-4148, website: www.warecreations.com.

31 Leader Lake

Anglers who stillfish, troll, and fly-cast all do fairly well at Leader Lake during a normal year. But some years aren't normal, or at least aren't conducive to good trout survival. This 160-acre lake is actually an impoundment built to help provide irrigation for local farms and ranches, and things get tight when the lake is drawn down too far during a dry summer. The effects are felt the next spring and summer, when poor trout survival and carryover result in lackluster fishing.

Rainbows that do make it through the low-water period are fat 12- to 14-inchers the following spring. Stillfishing with Power Bait, salmon eggs, marshmallows, and combinations of the three is popular here. Most trollers go with the tried-and-true combination of a fat worm behind a string of trolling blades, especially for the first few weeks of the Apri through October season.

Location: West of Okanogan; see map A4, grid d2.

Species: Rainbow trout.

Facilities: A boat ramp and camping area are at the west end of the lake with lots of good bank-fishing access around most of its shoreline. The nearest food, gas, lodging, and other amenities are in Okanogan and Omak.

Directions: Drive east from Twisp or west from Okanogan on Highway 20. About nine miles west of Okanogan, turn north on Leader Lake Road and follow it about half a mile to the lake.

Contact: Cascade Outfitters, 509/826-4148, website: www.warecreations.com.

Avoid Being Ripped Off

Here are some tips to avoid having your fishing boat and equipment stolen:
- Engrave your name and driver's license number on everything.
- Keep records of all your valuables.
- Lock smaller, portable items out of sight, or remove them from the boat completely when the boat isn't in use.
- Moor your boat and park your trailer out in the open.
- Always use a hitch lock.
- Use wheel locks or remove a wheel from a trailer that isn't being used.
- Use alarms and warning decals.
- Report theft quickly and accurately.

32 Omak Lake

The Lahontan cutts were first stocked in Omak Lake in the mid-1970s, but it wasn't until the summer of 1993 that anglers began to take notice of the cutthroat fishery here. That's when Omak Lake regular Dan Beardslee smashed the lake and state record for Lahontans with a whopping 18-pound trout. Beardslee used a Ross Swimmer Tail spoon to fool his record-breaker, and that's a good choice for anyone whose sights may be set on a monster cutthroat. Other large spoons and wobbling plugs—the kind of stuff commonly associated with saltwater salmon fishing—will also work. You can't use bait at Omak, only artificial flies and lures with barbless hooks. Although the lake is open to year-round fishing, the best catches of big fish come during the summer and early fall, when it's legal to keep trout following a catch-and-release-only period in March through June. This is a huge lake, covering well over 3,000 acres, and you could waste a lot of valuable time trolling and casting to areas that don't hold fish. A sensitive depth-sounder that will mark fish is a valuable tool.

Most anglers coming to Omak Lake are already well aware that the lake is on the Colville Indian Reservation, where tribal regulations are in effect and where tribal angling permits are required. In case you didn't know, a three-day permit is available for $15, a seven-day permit for $20, and a season-long (calendar year) permit for $30. Kids under 16 years of age can fish without a license if they're with a licensed adult. Tribal permits are available in all towns on and around the Colville Reservation.
Location: Southeast of Okanogan; see map A4, grid e4.
Species: Lahontan cutthroat trout.
Facilities: A three-lane boat ramp, maintained by the Colville Tribe, is located near the north end of the lake. Food, gas, lodging, and other amenities are available in Omak and Okanogan.
Directions: Take U.S. 97 to Omak and turn east on Highway 155, then south (right) on Omak Lake Road through Antoine Pass to the lake.
Contact: Cascade Outfitters, 509/826-4148, website: www.warecreations.com; Colville Confederated Tribes, Fish and Wildlife Department, 509/634-8845.

33 Cook and Little Goose Lakes

These two Colville Indian Reservation lakes don't have much in common except that they're both under 15 acres and are located within about a mile and a half of each other on the same road. Cook Lake is known for its warm-water fishery, especially for crappies, while Little Goose Lake is a trout lake with good populations of rainbows and brookies.

If you want Cook Lake crappies, simply suspend a small, plastic-skirted jig from a bobber and fish around any cover you can find. If you can't locate cover, try working the bobber-and-jig rig in 6 to 10 feet of water wherever you feel like it until you locate a school of these cooperative panfish. For Little Goose rainbows and brookies, troll or cast any of your favorite trout goodies or fish a marshmallow-and-salmon-egg combination near bottom.

Location: Northeast of Brewster; see map A4, grid e3.

Species: Rainbow and brook trout, crappie.

Facilities: It's possible to launch a small boat or canoe at both lakes. The nearest food, gas, lodging, and tackle are available in Okanogan and Omak.

Directions: Take U.S. 97 to Okanogan and then Wakefield–Cameron Lake Road east from town. Drive about nine miles to Cook Lake and another 1.5 miles to Little Goose Lake.

Contact: Colville Confederated Tribes, Fish and Wildlife Department, 509/634-8845; Cascade Outfitters, 509/826-4148, website: www.warecreations.com.

34 Okanogan River

With the possible exception of the much-larger Snake River (see number 16 in Chapter B4 and number 5 in chapter B5), the Okanogan offers the best stream smallmouth fishing in Washington. (With all its dams, it's not very accurate to call the Snake a river, at least not in Washington.) Anyway, the Okanogan has been a favorite destination of smallmouth enthusiasts since the 1970s, and it's just as good now as it was then, perhaps better. The river has bronzebacks of five pounds and over, although they're not something you'll hook every day, and while you're looking for them, you'll hook and release a number of smaller fish. What's more, U.S. 97 and side roads off it provide miles of good river access for bank anglers. The season on the lower 14 miles of the river (from Malot downstream) is open year-round, but the best bass action occurs as the water begins to warm substantially, usually around the end of June, and holds up well into September. Leadhead-and-grub combinations, small crankbaits, size 1 or size 0 bucktail spinners, even wet flies and streamers will take them. If you don't have any smallmouth tackle, invest in a few one-eighth- to three-eighths-ounce leadheads and a dozen three-inch Berkley Power Grubs in the pumpkinseed color. If that doesn't take smallmouths, you're probably fishing where there aren't any fish.

Steelheading on the Okanogan is no longer an option, at least not for now. Like other upper Columbia River tributaries, steelhead fishing is now closed here, and anglers who hook a steelhead (or any trout) while trout or bass fishing must release it unharmed. The fishing regulations pamphlet now lists the river as closed to "all trout fishing."

Although not making up for the lost trout and steelhead fishing, the lower Okanogan in recent years has started providing some fairly good walleye catches. The fish no doubt have made their way up into the river from the Columbia, and a few locals have pretty well figured out how to catch them. Actually, it's no secret; just work a spinner-and-night crawler rig along the bottom or bounce a leadhead jig adorned with a three-inch pumpkinseed grub and you'll probably do as well as any of those local boys.

Location: Joins the Columbia River east of Brewster; see map A4, grid e2.

Species: Smallmouth bass, rainbow trout, steelhead.

Facilities: Plenty of motels and RV parks can be found in the major towns along the river, including Okanogan, Omak, Tonasket, and Oroville. Restaurants, grocery stores, gas stations, tackle shops, and other amenities also are available in all four. Osoyoos Lake State Park is in Oroville at the upper end of the Okanogan. As for boat ramps, there are lots of them:

- **Highway 97 Bridge:** The uppermost ramp, located along Highway 97 a mile south of Oroville, is a good Department of Fish and Wildlife gravel ramp with plenty of parking.
- **Tonasket Lagoons Park:** The next one is about 15 highway miles south (18 or 19 river miles) at Tonasket Lagoons Park just south of Tonasket. Maintained by the City of Tonasket, it's a concrete ramp with plenty of room to park about 20 cars and trailers.
- **Bonaparte Ramp:** About a mile south is another Department of Fish and Wildlife ramp, marked by a Public Fishing sign along Highway 97. A steep bank, moderate current, and some buildup of sand makes this more of a hand-carry ramp than a trailer ramp, and parking is limited.
- **Riverside-Crowfoot Ramp:** There's another Washington Department of Fish and Wildlife ramp in Riverside at the end of Cooper Street. This natural ramp (no surface materials) also gets some deep accumulations of silt at times. It has lots of parking and is marked by a Public Fishing sign at the intersection of Highway 97 and Kendall Street (which leads to Cooper).
- **East-Side Park:** Next is East-Side Park in Omak, with a gravel ramp and room for several dozen cars and trailers. It's located at the east end of the Highway 155 bridge and is maintained by the City of Omak.
- **Okanogan City Ramp:** The City of Okanogan also maintains a park with a boat ramp, located on Tyee Street. The ramp is concrete and is protected from the river current here by several upstream boulders. The gravel parking area is a little rough but has room for about a dozen cars and trailers.
- **Monse Bridge:** One of two ramps a short distance apart near Brewster is just down-

stream of the Monse Bridge. Both are on the Douglas County (west) side of the river and maintained by Douglas County PUD. This ramp is a gravel ramp with limited parking. Turn left after crossing the bridge (from Highway 97) and take the first left on an unmarked gravel road.

- **Monse River Road Ramp:** About three-quarters of a mile upstream from the bridge is a ramp that's easier to find. This upper ramp is also a gravel ramp, but with parking for at least a dozen cars and trailers. From Brewster go east on U.S. 97 about three miles and turn left on Monse River Road. Follow the road three-quarters of a mile and look for the ramp on the right.

Several of the Okanogan River ramps are maintained by the Washington Department of Fish and Wildlife, so remember that a $10 WDFW access decal is required to use those public launch areas.

Directions: Take U.S. 97 east or Highway 17 north to the confluence of the Okanogan and Columbia Rivers and continue north on U.S. 97 to follow the Okanogan upstream.

Contact: Cascade Outfitters, 509/826-4148, website: www.warecreations.com; Osoyoos Lake State Park, 509/476-3321; Washington State Parks and Recreation Commission, 360/902-8844 (information) or 800/452-5687 (reservations).

35 Rat Lake

This lake with the unusual name has an unusual fishing season, opening December 1 and staying open through March. When the water is open—as in no ice—anglers like to troll over the big flat along the western shore. Interestingly, fly casters also do well here. As you might guess, this cold-weather fishing calls for various wet patterns, and the Carey Special and the Stick are both popular at Rat Lake. Rainbows account for most of the catch, but the lake has a few trophy-sized browns.

As for the history of the lake's name, it has nothing at all to do with rodents, but with reptiles. This is serious rattlesnake country, and the "rat" is short for "rattler." Are we learning some neat stuff here or what?

Location: North of Brewster; see map A4, grid e2.

Species: Rainbow and (a few) brown trout.

Facilities: The south end of the lake has a boat ramp. Food, gas, lodging, RV sites, and other amenities are available in Brewster.

Directions: Take U.S. 97 to Brewster and turn north on Paradise Mill Road. Take Rat Lake Road to the right about 3.5 miles north of town and continue another two miles to the lake.

Contact: Columbia Cove Recreation Center, 509/689-2994; Brewster Chamber of Commerce, 509/689-2517.

36 Big Goose Lake

If you're looking for a place to catch lots of little bass and get plenty of hook-setting practice, Big Goose Lake could be the place for you. Some years—1995 was a good example—this large, shallow lake is over-populated with smallish largemouths. Would you believe a daily bag limit of 25 fish was in effect in 1995? But check the Colville tribal regulations pamphlet before killing two dozen small bass, since a hard winter can knock down the population considerably and prompt a change in the limits and fishing rules. A tribal fishing permit is required. It costs $15 for three days, $20 for seven days, and $30 for the calendar year. Permits are available in Nespelem, Inchelium, Republic, Colville, Kettle Falls, Elmer City, and Brewster.

Location: South of Omak Lake on the Colville Indian Reservation; see map A4, grid f4.

Species: Largemouth bass.

Facilities: It's possible to launch a boat from the road along the east side of the lake, but there are no facilities of any kind. The nearest food, gas, lodging, and other amenities are to the north in Okanogan and Omak, to the southwest in Brewster and Bridgeport, and to the southeast in the Coulee Dam area.

Directions: Drive northwest from Nespelem on Highway 155. About nine miles from town, turn south (left) on Omak Lake Road. Drive 11 miles and turn south (left) at Kartar Creek (there are no road signs). Continue southwesterly about six miles to the lake.

Contact: Colville Confederated Tribes, Fish and Wildlife Department, 509/634-8845, website: www.colvilletribes.com.

37 Methow River

It was once one of the Northwest's best summer steelhead streams, but things changed a lot on the Methow during the 1990s. First came wild-steelhead-release regulations; then in 1998 steelheading was closed on the river altogether. The Methow certainly wasn't the only upper Columbia River tributary where steelhead were put off-limits to anglers, but it was perhaps the best, so this fishery is missed by lots of people.

The summertime catch-and-release trout season from Gold Creek up to the Weeman Bridge doesn't go very far in removing the sting from the loss of steelheading, nor does the winter whitefish season, but it's all that's left of fishing opportunity on this beautiful little river. Let's hope things get better.

Location: Enters the Columbia River at Pateros; see map A4, grid f0.

Species: Mountain whitefish, summer steelhead, some rainbow trout.

Facilities: Alta Lake State Park, near the mouth of the river west of Pateros, has tent and RV sites, restrooms, showers, and picnic areas. Food, gas, lodging, and other amenities are available in Pateros, Twisp, and Winthrop.

Directions: Take Highway 20 east to Mazama and drive downstream along the river.

Near Twisp, turn south on Highway 153 to stay near the Methow. From the south take U.S. 97 to Pateros and turn north on Highway 153.

Contact: Methow Wildlife Area, 509/996-2559; Pine-Near Trailer Park, 509/996-2391; Methow Valley KOA Campground, 509/996-2258; Chewuch Inn, 509/996-3107; Alta Lake State Park, 509/923-2473; Washington State Parks and Recreation Commission, 360/902-8844 (information) or 800/452-5687 (reservations).

38 Alta Lake

The easy access off U.S. 97, full array of facilities, large size, and productive trout fishing make Alta one of Okanogan County's more popular lakes. Heavily stocked with hatchery rainbows, it provides good fishing into the early summer and again in the fall. One drawback is that Alta closes earlier than most lakes, with the season ending on the last day of September. Another problem is that shortly after the first warm weather hits, the water-skiers and personal watercraft terrorists show up, and they pretty much take over the lake from late morning to early evening. If you're a summertime angler, get up early or stay late to do your fishing.

Most of the trout are pan-size at 8 to 13 inches, but Alta always produces a few husky carryovers in the spring, some of them ranging to a brawny 20 inches. Try trolling a Wedding Ring spinner behind a string of larger trolling blades and you'll probably be happy with the results. If there's such a thing as a local favorite for Alta Lake rainbows, that's it. If you don't have something matching that description, go with a Flatfish or Kwikfish in green or your favorite small spoon and see what happens. For many years, anglers who stillfished here favored a single red salmon egg or a marshmallow-and-egg combination, but Berkley's various Power Baits have be-

come very popular among Alta Lake anglers the past few years.

Location: Southwest of Pateros; see map A4, grid f0.

Species: Rainbow trout.

Facilities: Alta Lake State Park has 15 tent sites and more than 30 RV sites with full hookups, restrooms with showers, picnic tables, and a boat ramp. Whistlin' Pines Resort also has a boat ramp, as well as 75 tent and RV sites, restrooms with showers, and a small store with groceries and fishing tackle.

Directions: Take U.S. 97 to Pateros and turn north on Highway 153. Drive two miles to Alta Lake Road, turn west (left), and drive two miles to the lake.

Contact: Alta Lake State Park, 509/923-2473; Washington State Parks and Recreation Commission, 360/902-8844 (information) or 800/452-5687 (reservations); Whistlin' Pines Resort, 509/923-2548, website: www .altalake.com.

39 Columbia River (Lake Pateros and Rufus Woods Lake)

Compared to most of the Columbia River system, the many miles of largely still water between Wells and Grand Coulee Dams are rather lightly fished by Washington anglers. Road access to much of this stretch—especially Rufus Woods Lake—is limited, and boat ramps are relatively few and far between. It's accurate to say that much of this portion of the Columbia holds angling secrets that few ever discover.

As most Washington anglers have heard by now, Rufus Woods Lake is the Evergreen State's newest trophy trout producer, having laid claim in February 1998 to the state-record rainbow trout. Robert Halverson of Republic boated a whopping 24.45-pound rainbow that fell for a trolled Rapala, so you can guess what most Rufus Woods trout enthusiasts have been fishing with ever since. The monster trout eclipsed the former rainbow record by nearly three pounds and measured 31.5 inches in length and 25 inches around its ample midsection. The long impoundment behind Chief Joseph Dam has long been a favorite of north-central Washington anglers looking for a trout of three pounds or better, but the newest addition to the state record book has made it a more popular destination than ever.

As is the case throughout much of the Columbia, walleyes can be found here, too. The walleye fishery in Rufus Woods Lake and Lake Pateros continues to provide new surprises as to where and how the fish may be caught. Because of the vast area available to walleye anglers, those who cover the most water often make the best catches. Try trolling along rocky points with diving Rapalas or Power Dive Minnows or with the standard Columbia River walleye trolling rig, which includes a half-ounce to two-ounce sinker, a spinner, and a night crawler stretched out straight on a two-hook rig.

Diving plugs similar to those used for walleyes are also effective for steelhead on some of this stretch of river. Lake Pateros is a popular destination for fall steelhead anglers, many of whom troll driving plugs for their fish. The waters around the mouth of the Methow River are some of the most popular, but trolling for steelhead can also be good in other places, including off the mouth of the Okanogan River. September and October are usually the best months, but steelhead may be caught until ice becomes a problem in December or January.

Kokanee fishing in Rufus Woods Lake can be quite good, but relatively few anglers outside the immediate area know much about it. Trolling with strings of blades and Wedding Rings or similar offerings will usually draw the attention of these fine-eating little salmon.

Location: From Chelan upstream to Grand Coulee Dam; see map A4, grid f3.

Species: Rainbow trout, steelhead, kokanee, walleye, smallmouth and largemouth bass.

Facilities: Let's take a look at the boat ramps along this stretch of the Columbia first:

• **Beebe Bridge Park:** Located just downstream from where Highway 97 crosses over the Columbia (and slightly west of where this map section begins) is Beebe Bridge Park, where you'll find one of the best launch ramps on the Columbia. The two-lane concrete ramp is big enough and offers good enough traction to launch boats of almost any size with almost any vehicle, and it has loading floats. It has parking for dozens of cars/trailers, and launching is free. It's maintained by Chelan County PUD.

• **Marina Park:** The next ramp on the Douglas County side of the river is at Marina Park, just west of Bridgeport off Seventh Street. It's a two-lane ramp with loading floats and is another good one, but parking is much more limited than at Beebe Bridge.

• **Upstream Ramp:** A few miles east is another ramp, this one at the bottom end of Rufus Woods Lake. Managed by the U.S. Army Corps of Engineers, it's a one-lane concrete ramp with a loading float and has room to park about 10 cars and trailers.

• **Chelan Falls Park:** On the Chelan/ Okanogan County side of the river, the first ramp you encounter upstream on Highway 97 is the ramp at Chelan Falls Park. It's a two-lane concrete-plank ramp with loading floats and parking for at least two dozen cars and trailers. Launching is free at this Chelan County PUD facility.

• **Carpenter Island Ramp:** Although it's maintained by Douglas County, the next ramp upstream is on the Chelan County side of the river just below Wells Dam. Launching is free at this single-lane ramp, but when the dam is spilling lots of water, the waves and current sometimes make for tricky launching.

- **Starr Ramp:** Now in Okanogan County, the next ramp is on the right side of Highway 97 about two miles south of Starr (look closely for that one on a map). The single-lane concrete ramp is on an unmarked gravel road about a mile after you cross into Okanogan County from Chelan County.
- **Northeast Pateros Ramp:** The next two ramps are at the town of Pateros. This one is maintained by the Douglas County PUD. Both are single-lane concrete ramps in pretty good shape and adequate for boats of any size. A donation is requested from boaters who launch at either of these ramps.
- **Pateros Boat Landing:** This ramp is maintained by the Pateros Parks and Recreation Department. For more information, see previous listing.
- **Brewster Park:** The next ramp along Highway 97 is at Brewster, off Seventh Street. Located right next to Columbia Cove Park, it's a good, single-lane ramp with loading floats and parking for maybe 20 cars and trailers.
- **Bridgeport State Park:** There's a very good two-lane concrete ramp with loading floats at Bridgeport State Park about two miles above Chief Joseph Dam on Rufus Woods Lake. Launching here costs $4, unless you're a registered guest at the park. An annual $40 launch permit is valid at all state parks.
- **Elmer City Boat Ramp:** The next ramp on Rufus Woods is clear up at the other end near the town of Elmer City. It has two lanes, one gravel and one concrete, and room for about 30 cars with trailers. Launching is free at this ramp, which is maintained by the Corps of Engineers.

Food, gas, RV parks, and lodging are available in Chelan, Pateros, Brewster, Bridgeport, Coulee Dam, and Grand Coulee. Lake Pateros Motor Inn is right on the river at Pateros and has moorage for guests who arrive by boat. Marina Park, near Bridgeport, has tent and RV sites, a large swim beach, picnic shelters, and other amenities. Columbia Cove Park in Brewster has RV hookups, picnic shelters, restrooms with showers, a swim beach, and other amenities. Bridgeport State Park, at the lower end of Rufus Woods Lake, offers about three dozen tent and RV sites. Beebe Bridge Park has tent and RV sites ($15 per night), a large swim beach, restrooms with showers, and tennis and basketball courts. The day-use park at Chelan Falls has a large, roped swim beach with plenty of sun and green lawn, picnic tables, a covered cooking area, baseball, tennis, volleyball, and basketball facilities.

Directions: Take Highway 155 north from Coulee City or Highway 174 north from Wilbur to Grand Coulee to fish the part of the river directly downstream from Grand Coulee Dam. To reach the upper end of this section of the Columbia, drive east from Pateros on U.S. 97 and turn south on Highway 17 near Fort Okanogan. Highway 17 parallels several miles of the river's northern shoreline. Highway 151 parallels the Columbia in the downstream portion of this section around the town of Chelan.

Contact: Big Wally's, 509/632-5504; Lake Pateros Motor Inn, 509/923-2203; Coulee Playland Resort, 509/633-2671; Bridgeport State Park, 509/686-7231; Washington State Parks and Recreation Commission, 360/902-8844 (information) or 800/452-5687 (reservations); Columbia Cove RV Park, 509/689-2994; Brewster Chamber of Commerce, 509/689-2517.

40 Foster Creek

You won't find great fishing and you aren't likely to find any trophy-sized trout, but this rather expansive stream system offers miles of worthwhile trout water where you can stretch your casting arm a little. Small spinners work well, or simply roll a salmon egg or garden worm along the bottom. Fly-fishing with small nymph patterns can also be effective. Be on your toes for rattlesnakes.

Location: Flows into the Columbia River near Bridgeport; see map A4, grid g2.

Species: Rainbow and brook trout.

Facilities: Food, gas, lodging, and other amenities are available in Bridgeport, and Bridgeport State Park, with both tent and RV sites, is eight miles to the north.

Directions: Drive south from Bridgeport on Highway 17 and turn west (right) on Bridgeport Hill Road to reach the Middle Fork and West Fork of the creek. Continue south (the road signs say you're going south, but at this point you're driving east) on Highway 17 to fish the East Fork.

Contact: Bridgeport State Park, 509/686-7231; Washington State Parks and Recreation Commission, 360/902-8844 (information) or 800/452-5687 (reservations).

41 Buffalo Lake

This is a big, deep lake with a lot of fishing variety. Since more than half of the water in the 500-acre lake is more than 100 feet deep, it warms rather slowly and continues to provide decent fishing well into the summer. Stillfishing with Berkley Power Bait, salmon eggs, or worms accounts for most of the rainbows and brookies, some of which are large, thick-bodied fish. Most of the kokanee action comes to trollers who use Wedding Rings, Double Whammys, Dick Nites, Triple Teazers, and other small spoons and spinners behind larger dodgers or flashers to attract fish. Tipping the hooks with Berkley Power Wigglers or maggots usually helps draw more kokanee strikes. The lake produces some fairly husky largemouth bass, most of them coming from the shallower north end of the lake. While all the usual bass offerings will work, many of the locals stick with bass bait that's readily available in the lake—crawdads. And if you want to enjoy some sweet eating yourself, take along a crawdad trap and catch a mess of them for yourself.

Besides the regular summertime season, Buffalo is one of few lakes on the Colville Reservation that offers a winter season, and anglers catch some trophy-sized trout here January through March. Stillfishing with the baits mentioned above is the way to go during the cold months.

Buffalo Lake is within the boundaries of the Colville Indian Reservation, where a tribal angling permit is required. The cost is $15 for a three-day permit, $20 for a seven-day permit, and $30 for a season permit valid January 1 through December 31. A winter-fishing permit costing $5 is also required for fishing during the lake's special winter season, which runs January 1 through March 15. The permits, as well as tribal angling regulations, are available from some resorts and businesses in Nespelem, Inchelium, Republic, Colville, Kettle Falls, Elmer City, Brewster, Omak, and other towns in and around the Colville Indian Reservation.

Location: Northeast of Coulee Dam on the Colville Indian Reservation; see map A4, grid f7.

Species: Rainbow and brook trout, kokanee, largemouth bass.

Facilities: The lake has two launch facilities, one at Reynolds' Resort and one at Buffalo Lake Access Campground. The resort has a single-lane gravel ramp with two loading floats and a gravel parking area with room for about 10 cars and trailers. There's a launch fee of $3 to $5, depending on the size of the boat. Launching is free at the campground, on a one-lane gravel ramp. It's managed by the Colville Confederated Tribes. Reynolds' Resort has fuel, boat rentals, cabins, and RV/tent sites. There are RV/tent sites and picnic tables at the campground. Food, gas, tackle, and lodging are available to the south in Grand Coulee and Coulee Dam.

Directions: Take Highway 155 north from Coulee Dam or south from Nespelem and turn east on Rebecca Lake Road. Drive about 3.5 miles, past Rebecca Lake, to Buffalo Lake Road and follow it two miles to the lake.

Contact: Reynolds' Resort, 509/633-1092; Colville Confederated Tribes, Fish and Wildlife Department, 509/634-8845, website: www.colvilletribes.com.

42 Rebecca Lake

Small Rebecca Lake has a fairly healthy bass population and provides fair fishing even for bank anglers. But the best fishing is available to boat anglers who can get away from the road and work the southern and eastern shoreline. Arrive early or stay late and you'll find decent surface action on largemouths to two or three pounds. Now and then someone pulls a lunker out of here, but such catches are rare.

The lake is within the boundaries of the Colville Indian Reservation, so don't forget the fishing permits available in towns throughout the area. The cost is $15 for a three-day permit, $20 for a seven-day permit, and $30 for a season permit that's valid from January 1 through December 31.

Location: Northeast of Coulee Dam on the Colville Indian Reservation; see map A4, grid f7.

Species: Largemouth bass.

Facilities: Small boats can be launched along the north side of the lake, but there isn't much else in the way of facilities. Reynolds' Resort on nearby Buffalo Lake is your best bet for overnight accommodations and other needs. Motels, restaurants, gas, food, and tackle are available to the south in the Coulee Dam area.

Directions: Take Highway 155 north from Coulee Dam or south from Nespelem and turn east on Rebecca Lake Road, following it about 2.5 miles to the lake.

Contact: Reynolds' Resort, 509/633-1092; Colville Confederated Tribes, Fish and Wildlife Department, 509/634-8845, website: www.colvilletribes.com.

43 McGinnis Lake

Good numbers of brook trout make McGinnis Lake a worthwhile possibility early and late in the season, when the water is cool enough for the brookies to be active. Try it from mid-April to about the first of June or from the middle of September until the lake closes at the end of October. Casting small spinners and wobblers around the edge of the lake will produce pan-sized brookies, as will wet flies throughout the day and dry flies in the morning and evening. As in many Colville Reservation lakes, the daily trout limit here is six pounds plus one fish, not to exceed eight fish.

This is another lake where a Colville tribal fishing permit is required. They're available for three days, seven days, or the entire season, with prices of $15, $20, and $30, respectively, and can be purchased in resorts and businesses throughout the area.

Location: Northeast of Coulee Dam on the Colville Indian Reservation; see map A4, grid f7.

Species: Brook trout.

Facilities: The north side of the lake has a small boat ramp, and camping facilities are available to the north at Buffalo Lake. Motels, restaurants, and other services can be found in and around Coulee Dam.

Directions: Take Highway 155 north from Coulee Dam or south from Nespelem and turn east on Rebecca Lake Road. About a mile past Rebecca Lake, turn south (right) on Buffalo Lake Road and drive about 2.5 miles to the sign pointing left to McGinnis Lake.

Contact: Reynolds' Resort, 509/633-1092;

Colville Confederated Tribes, Fish and Wildlife Department, 509/634-8845, website: www.colvilletribes.com.

44 Lower Lake Roosevelt

Except for the whitefish and perch, every species available in this huge Columbia River reservoir has stolen the angling limelight for some period of time during the past three decades. Throughout the late 1970s and early 1980s, it was the walleye that drew most anglers to Roosevelt, and walleye fishing is still popular and productive here. Troll diving plugs or spinner-and-worm rigs along the bottom or cast leadheads adorned with plastic grubs around the many rock slides and rocky coves that border the lake.

When the walleye action tapered off somewhat in the mid- to late 1980s, many anglers started focusing their attention on the lake's rainbow trout, which grow to impressive size. Casting from the bank around the lower end of the lake or trolling various spoons, spinners, or wobbling plugs farther up the lake all were found to take trout, and those same techniques continue to be effective today. Don't be too surprised if your efforts pay off with a rainbow or two in the 18-inch, 2.5-pound range. I like fall for trout, but anglers catch them here year-round.

The late 1980s also saw smallmouth bass populations blossom in the lake, and by the early 1990s anglers were coming from all over the Northwest to fish Roosevelt for fat and sassy smallies ranging from a few ounces to several pounds. The rocky structure throughout the lower lake is near-perfect smallmouth habitat, and the fish continue to do very well. Try casting crawfish-finish crankbaits around rocky points or bounce leadheads with two- or three-inch plastic grubs or tube skirts down the face of submerged rock piles or cliffs. Berkley's three-inch Power Grub in pumpkinseed has produced my best smallmouth catches here, but such colors as camo (camouflage) and smoke also can be effective. This 150-mile-long impoundment has more than 600 miles of public shoreline to explore, so if you can't find enough good bass water to explore for the entire summer, you're not looking very hard.

The last several years have seen interest in kokanee increase dramatically, thanks in great part to the fact that Roosevelt produced a couple of new state-record kokanee during the spring and summer of 1993. The year's second record breaker—a fish of 5.47 pounds—still stands as the state's best-ever kokanee. Many kokanee of four pounds and over have been caught since, and some of the Lake Roosevelt regulars feel that it's only a matter of time before the record is topped again. Besides running large, these fish are strong and lively, sometimes stripping reels before an angler can react to save his or her tackle. Perhaps the best part is that it isn't al-

© TERRY RUDNICK

LOWER LAKE ROOSEVELT

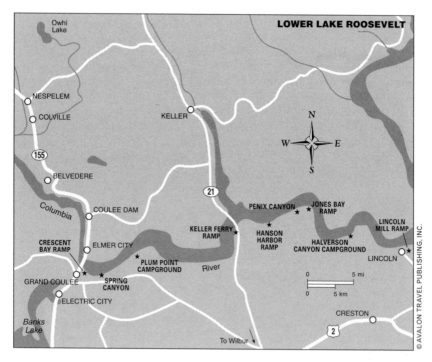

ways necessary to troll deep to find these lunker landlocked sockeyes. During the mid-1990s, anglers were catching lots of them only a few feet beneath the surface without the need for downriggers or any other deep-trolling equipment. Small spoons and spinners, such as Luhr Jensen's Super Duper and Needlefish and Yakima Bait's Rooster Tail, are among the favorite kokanee getters, and they're usually fished with white corn and/or maggots on the hooks.

With walleyes, rainbows, smallmouths, and kokanee available, it's easy to understand why lake whitefish are almost totally overlooked by Lake Roosevelt anglers. The fish provide good angling opportunities when they move into the shallows early in the spring, and some of them range to three or four pounds, but they hardly draw a second thought from anglers with other fish on their minds.

Location: From Grand Coulee Dam up to Lincoln; see map A4, grid g7.

Species: Rainbow, cutthroat, and brook trout; kokanee; smallmouth and largemouth bass; walleye; lake whitefish; yellow perch; crappie; brown bullhead catfish.

Facilities: There are launch ramps at six locations along this end of Roosevelt, plus three more within a few miles uplake (see chapter A5):

- **National Park Service Ramp:** Just above Grand Coulee Dam on the south side of the lake is the National Park Service ramp at Crescent Bay. There's a $6 launch fee at this single-lane ramp, which has a loading float and parking spaces for several dozen cars and trailers.

- **Spring Canyon Ramp:** The well-maintained ramp at Spring Canyon three miles east of Grand Coulee has two lanes and three loading floats, with plenty of paved parking. It's managed by the National Park Service as part of the Coulee Dam National Recreation Area, and a $6 launch fee was imposed here and at other Park Service ramps in 1998.

- **Keller Ferry Ramp:** The same fee is charged at Keller Ferry, where there's a three-lane paved ramp and large loading float, along with paved parking for dozens of boats and trailers.
- **Hanson Harbor Ramp:** This launch site several miles east of Keller Ferry on Hanson Harbor Road has a one-lane ramp with a large paved parking area. A $6 launch fee is charged here as well.
- **Jones Bay Campground:** The next ramp uplake is at Jones Bay Campground, also reached via Hanson Harbor Road. It has a one-lane paved ramp and loading float, and a $6 fee is also charged here.
- **Lincoln Mill Ramp:** About 14 miles farther up the lake is the Lincoln Mill ramp, a large, paved, four-laner with a loading float and lots of paved parking. Managed by Lincoln County, this excellent ramp has no launch fee.

There are campgrounds at Crescent Bay, Spring Canyon, Plum Point, Keller Ferry, Pennix Canyon, Jones Bay, Halverson Canyon, and Hawk Creek, all of which are on the south side of the lake. Keller Park Campground is along Highway 21 near the upper end of the lake's San Poil Arm. Houseboat rentals are available in Keller Ferry and uplake at Seven Bays Marina (reservations required). Skiffs, larger powerboats, and jet boats are also available for rent. On-the-water fuel docks are available at Crescent Bay and Keller Ferry. Boat-sewage pump-outs are available at Spring Canyon and Keller Ferry. There are roped swim beaches at Spring Canyon and Keller Ferry, and Hanson Harbor has a large, sandy beach that's adequate for swimming. Other services are available at Grand Coulee and Coulee Dam.

Directions: Take Highway 155 north from Coulee City, Highways 174 or 21 north from Wilbur, or Highway 25 north from Davenport to reach major access areas on the lower lake.

Contact: Grand Coulee Dam Chamber of Commerce, 800/268-5332, website: www.grand couleedam.org; Keller Ferry Marina, 509/647-5755; Roosevelt Recreational Enterprises, 800/648-LAKE (648-5253).

45 San Poil River

Although a state highway runs right along its banks for easy access, this pretty little river provides surprisingly good trout catches. Pan-sized rainbows constitute most of the action on the lower portion of the river, with a few brookies mixed in along the upper part of the main river and the West Fork. But don't be surprised if you turn up an occasional rainbow of two or three pounds. This food-rich stream with lots of good trout cover does produce more than its share of what most Northwesterners would consider trophy-class trout. The section of the San Poil from Nineteen Mile Bridge north to the reservation boundary is open to catch-and-release fishing only, with artificial lures and barbless hooks required.

Besides trout, the creek has a fair population of whitefish, but since it's closed in the winter, the fishery isn't what it might be. Walleyes have made their way up into the lower reaches of the river from Lake Roosevelt, and a night crawler rolled along the bottom of a deep pool might just turn up one of these hungry predators.

Most of the San Poil is within the boundaries of the Colville Indian Reservation, where a tribal angling permit is required. The cost is $15 for a three-day permit, $20 for a seven-day permit, and $30 for a season permit valid January 1 through December 31. The permits, as well as tribal angling regulations, are available in Nespelem, Inchelium, Republic, Colville, Kettle Falls, Elmer City, Brewster, and other nearby towns.

Location: Flows into Lake Roosevelt near Keller; see map A4, grid f8.

Species: Rainbow and brook trout, mountain whitefish, walleye.

Facilities: Tent and RV sites are available at Keller Ferry, on the south side of Lake Roosevelt and a ferry ride away from the mouth of the river. Beyond that, the nearest amenities are in Republic to the north and Wilbur to the south.

Directions: Drive north from Wilbur or south from Republic on Highway 21. The road parallels the river for well over 30 miles.

Contact: Colville Confederated Tribes, Fish and Wildlife Department, 509/634-8845, website: www.colvilletribes.com.

46 Banks Lake

It's not always easy to find a place where both the anglers and nonanglers in a family can be totally content for a weeklong vacation, but Banks Lake is one such place. The fishing variety and quality are enough to keep any angler busy and happy, while those who aren't so dedicated to the piscatorial pursuits can swim, water-ski, hike, bike, golf, play tennis, or simply lounge around the beach reading a good book and working on that tan.

Walleye fishing isn't as good here as it was a few years ago, but it's still pretty decent. Most anglers troll spinner-and-night-crawler rigs along the bottom for their fish, but when the walleyes are feeding along the broken rock and boulders so common along the lake's shoreline, pitching a small grub into the rocks and bouncing it across the bottom will also take fish. In spring and early summer, before most of the lake warms, the shallow flat on the east side of Steamboat Rock—known as the Devil's Punchbowl—is usually a good place to troll for walleyes.

The Punchbowl can also be a good bet for bass, especially largemouths that move into its shallow, weedy bays to spawn in late spring. Farther north is Osborne Bay, another big, shallow flat that draws lots of bass, especially largemouths. Smallmouths, which were stocked in Banks by the then–Department of Game back in 1980, are found throughout much of the lake, from the rocky islands down by the lower dam at the south end of the lake to the broken rock that makes up the upper dam at the north end. Wherever you find rocks or gravel—which means about 98 percent of the Banks Lake shoreline—you may find smallmouths large enough and abundant enough to make you a very happy angler.

The trout grow large in Banks but get relatively little attention from anglers. Many are caught accidentally by bass and walleye anglers, but you can catch them on any of the usual trolling gadgets or by stillfishing worms, salmon eggs, Power Bait, or marshmallows. When you catch one, it's likely to be a dandy 15 to 18 inches, red-meated, and in prime shape for the dinner table.

All the shallow bays and coves have panfish of some kind. Crappies are much sought after but not as abundant as perch. Prowl around a little and you should be able to find a few of one or the other large enough for a fish fry.

Night fishing in the shallows will produce brown bullheads, but hardly anyone bothers. Winter fishing for burbot is similarly overlooked, but an ever-growing number of anglers are taking to the lake—especially the upper end around the feeder canal from Lake Roosevelt—to fish for whitefish during the winter. Lake whitefish of two to three pounds are common here, and the key is to locate a concentration of fish and vertical jig for them.

Location: Between Grand Coulee at the north and Coulee City at the south; see map A4, grid g5.

Species: Largemouth and smallmouth bass, walleye, crappie, yellow perch, rainbow trout,

BANKS LAKE

© AVALON TRAVEL PUBLISHING, INC.

lake whitefish, brown bullhead catfish, burbot.
Facilities: Anglers at the south end of the lake will find a boat ramp, camping, food, gas, and lodging in and around Coulee City. The best source for fishing tackle and information at this end of the lake is Big Wally's, which is right along the highway, just north of town. A guide service is also available there. Steamboat Rock State Park, at the north end of the lake, has tent and RV sites (reservations required), boat ramps and floats, restrooms with showers, and a small store with ice, snacks, and groceries. A little farther north in Electric City are Coulee Playland and the Skydeck Motel, both right on the water. Groceries, restaurants, watering holes, gas stations, and motels are also available in Electric City. As for boat ramps, would you believe there are nearly a dozen of them on the lake? Here's a rundown:

- **Coulee City Park:** Working your way up the lake from the dam, you won't have to travel far before you find the ramp at Coulee City's Community Park. Maintained by the city's parks and recreation department, the ramp has four paved lanes and three loading floats. Launching is free.

- **Fordair Ramp:** Less than two miles out of town to the north is the Department of Fish and Wildlife's Fordair access area and ramp. It's a one-laner with room to park about a half dozen cars and trailers.

- **Million Dollar Mile South Access Area:** Another Washington Department of Fish and Wildlife ramp is located along Highway 155 about six miles north of Coulee City. It's a one-lane gravel ramp with room for about a dozen cars and trailers, marked by a Public Fishing sign along the highway.

- **Million Dollar Mile North Access Area (Midlake Ramp):** Another sign marks the Washington Department of Fish and Wildlife ramp about three miles farther up the lake, known by locals as the midlake ramp.

Located on a narrow little canal off the main lake, it can be a tricky place to load and unload a boat in low water, but it has plenty of parking.

- **The Poplars Ramp:** Another Department of Fish and Wildlife ramp is at the junction of Highway 155 and the entrance road into Steamboat Rock State Park. It's actually an old roadbed that drops into the lake at the south end of the shallow bay known as Devil's Punchbowl.

- **Steamboat Rock State Park:** There's an excellent four-lane ramp just north of the camping areas at Steamboat Rock State Park. It has a loading float and parking for more than 100 cars and trailers.

- **Steamboat Rock Satellite Ramp:** To the northeast, on the north side of the peninsula that juts off the eastern shore to form the upper boundary of Devil's Punchbowl, is another State Parks ramp. This one is not as good as the previous one. In fact, it's breaking up badly and may not be usable for long unless it gets some radical TLC pretty soon. There's a $4 fee to use the main park ramp and a $3 fee on the satellite ramp. Washington State Parks also issues a $40 annual launch permit, good at any park ramp.

- **Barker Canyon Ramp:** The only ramp on the west side of Banks is in Barker Canyon, in what would have to be called the lake's northwest corner. You reach this Department of Fish and Wildlife ramp by driving west from Grand Coulee on Highway 174, going about 10 miles to Barker Canyon Road, turning south (left), and driving six miles to the end of the road.

- **Sunbanks Resort:** There's another ramp at Sunbanks Resort, near the south entrance to Osborne Bay. This single-lane concrete-plank ramp has a loading float and room for about a dozen cars and trailers to park.

- **Osborne Bay:** This large bay near the north end of Banks also has a Department of Fish and Wildlife ramp near its east end. It's a natural ramp with no surfacing materials, and I wouldn't recommend launching large trailer boats here.

- **Coulee Playland Resort:** This longtime resort near the north end of the lake has a two-lane concrete ramp with three loading floats and nearby moorage.

A $10 WDFW access decal is required to use the public launch areas maintained by the Washington Department of Fish and Wildlife.
Directions: Take Highway 17 or U.S. 2 to Coulee City and turn north on Highway 155 to parallel the east side of the lake all the way to Electric City.
Contact: Big Wally's, 509/632-5504; Steamboat Rock State Park, 509/633-1304; Washington State Parks and Recreation Commission, 360/902-8844 (information) or 800/452-5687 (reservations); Coulee Playland Resort, 509/633-2671; Skydeck Motel, 509/633-0290 or 800/708-3014, website: www.grandcouleedam.com/skydeck.

47 Grimes Lake

On a calm morning, chances are you can see the husky cutthroats cruising just beneath the surface, and it's enough to get any angler worked up. As you row or paddle through the narrow canal connecting the lower pool to the main body of the lake, the locals recommend you have a Woolly Bugger fly soaked and ready for that first cast. The water is only three or four feet deep, and you'll see the trout tailing before you. If you're careful and if your cast is true, you could be in business right off the bat. If you don't hit fish right away, drift with the breeze and let your little offering of fur and feathers slip along a couple of feet off the bottom. Mend the line often to keep the slack out, and be on your toes for light strikes.

Grimes Lake has large Lahontan cutthroats,

special regulations, and a very short season. It all starts June 1 and ends August 31, so you have to fish hard for only a few weeks during the heat of the Douglas County summer. Is it worth the trouble? You bet. Ed Kearney, the big one behind Big One Guide Service, has brought cutthroats to 14 pounds to the side of the boat but is quick to add that an eight-pounder is a good fish these days. While fishing with Ed one warm June morning in the late 1990s, I coaxed a trout of about seven pounds in for a couple of photos, and I know I couldn't take the excitement that a fish twice that size might generate.

Lots of artificials will take Lahontans from Grimes—I even managed to fool one with a Berkley Power Teaser bounced along the bottom one time—but if you take along a selection of wet flies that includes brown Woolly Buggers and brown Carey Specials (especially with peacock bodies), you'll probably do just fine.

Remember that selective fishery regulations here mean no gas-powered motors; single, barbless hooks; no bait; and a one-fish daily bag limit.
Location: Southeast of Mansfield; see map A4, grid h3.
Species: Lahontan cutthroat trout.
Facilities: As of 1996, there's a portable toilet at the rough boat ramp near the south end of the lake, so you no longer have to share a spot behind a clump of sage with the neighborhood rattlesnakes. The nearest food, gas, tackle, and lodging are in Waterville and Mansfield.
Directions: Take Highway 172 to Mansfield and turn south out of town on Mansfield Road. Just over three miles from town, the road makes a 90-degree left. A mile farther along, it merges with Wittier Road, and you make a 90-degree right. You'll reach the bottom of Moses Coulee three miles farther down the road, and the road turns left. From there it's a dirt road for 1.5 miles, which used

to be one of the nastiest stretches of road in central Washington, but a local fly-fishing club has worked hard to improve it, so you can get in with most vehicles these days. **Contact:** Big One Guide Service, 509/682-4647.

48 Jameson Lake

Perhaps eastern Washington's most famous and most popular trout lake, Jameson has been pumping out plump rainbows for as long as I can remember, and I've been around a while. The lake gets quite warm and has an expansive algae bloom during the middle of the summer, so it has a split season that's open during the spring and fall. Both the early and late segments of the season provide some excellent trout-fishing opportunities.

Although a majority of Jameson Lake's trout anglers are using what you might call conventional trolling and stillfishing techniques with all the standard salmon eggs, worms, Power Bait, marshmallows, Triple Teazers, Flatfish, and Rooster Tails to catch their fish, this is an exceptional fly-fishing lake. Favorite patterns include Carey Specials, Peacock Specials, Woolly Buggers, leech patterns, and a local favorite called a Jameson Shrimp. Whether you stillfish bait, troll hardware, or cast flies, expect the trout you catch to be thick-bodied, red-meated, and hard-fighting specimens, the kind of fish for which this 330-acre Douglas County jewel has long been famous. A typical spring rainbow here measures about 11 inches, but one-year carryovers will measure 16 to 18 inches, and older fish may top 20 inches and weigh in at three pounds.

Location: Southeast of Mansfield; see map A4, grid i3.

Species: Rainbow trout.

Facilities: Besides the public access area and boat ramp, there are resorts at both ends of the lake that have tent and RV sites, boat ramps, small stores with groceries and tackle, restrooms, and other amenities.

Directions: Take Highway 2 west from Waterville or east from Coulee City and turn north on Jameson Lake Road, following it a little over six miles to the lake. A road leading around the east side of the lake to the north isn't always passable, so a different route may be in order if you want to reach the north end of Jameson by road. Take Highway 172 to Mansfield and turn south (right) from town on Mansfield Road. Just over three miles from town, where Berg Road begins, turn left and follow Wittig Road toward the north end of Jameson Lake.

Contact: Jack's Resort, 509/683-1095 (April through July and the month of October only).

49 Dry Falls Lake

This must have been an incredible place back when the flood waters and icebergs of Lake Missoula were crashing over the basalt cliffs and gouging out the bowl where Dry Falls Lake now lies. Had any of us been around, we likely could have heard the thundering falls from miles away, and we would have been awestruck by the amount of water coursing through the Grand Coulee. Actually, we're probably better off being around now, because the trout fishing at what we now call Dry Falls Lake is a whole lot better than what was available back when the ice-diverted Columbia River surged through this huge canyon.

Plenty of anglers think the fishing opportunities at Dry Falls are awesome. This 99-acre lake at the head of the so-called Sun Lakes Chain is shallow and filled with aquatic vegetation, perfect conditions for huge populations of aquatic insects that provide rapid growth and high energy to the rainbows and browns that gorge on them. Fly casters flock to Dry Falls throughout its April through November season, and they return with broad smiles and happy stories of trout topping 20 inches and weighing three, four, even five pounds. Fish of that size aren't the average Dry Falls trout, but they're common enough to keep it interesting. This isn't a fly-fishing-only lake, but it is a no-bait lake, where flies and lures must have only a single, barbless hook, and where the daily bag limit—should you choose to kill any trout at all—is one fish.

And while you're casting, it's okay to let your mind wander back to what it must have been like when the lake was being formed and to take a minute to thank Ma Nature for a job well done.

Location: Southwest of Coulee City; see map A4, grid i4.

Species: Rainbow and brown trout.

Facilities: There is no boat ramp on the lake, but it's fairly easy to carry a car-topper, canoe, or float tube to the edge of the water. Nearby Sun Lakes State Park has 18 RV sites and 175 tent sites for campers, as well as restrooms, showers, and picnic areas. Food and gas are available in Coulee City, and plenty of lodging is available to the south in Soap Lake.

Directions: Take Highway 17 south from Dry Falls Junction or north from Soap Lake to the Sun Lakes State Park entrance and turn east into the park. About 1.2 miles off the highway, turn left at the sign pointing to Dry Falls Lake. Continue following signs to the lake for about three miles, passing Rainbow and Perch Lakes on the left. The last mile to Dry Falls is over a rough dirt road, where pickups or four-wheel-drive vehicles are recommended.

Contact: Sun Lakes State Park, 509/632-5583.

50 Deep Lake

At just over 100 acres, Deep is one of the largest but perhaps least-famous lakes in the Sun Lakes Chain. The reason for its low profile is its location farthest from the highway and the condition of the road that leads to its banks. Unlike some of the nearby waters that draw anglers from all over the state, Deep is fished mostly by locals.

The lake is stocked with about 20,000 rainbow fingerlings every spring, and by the following season, they're running a chunky 10 to 12 inches. Casting from the bank or from a small boat with a bobber-and-worm combination or a slip-sinker rig baited with a marshmallow-and-salmon-egg combo or Berkley Power Bait is an effective weapon here. Trollers go with the standard trolling blades-and-worm offering, small Flatfish and Kwikfish, Triple Teazers, Dick Nites, Rooster Tails, and Canadian Wonders. Deep Lake also has kokanee and a few husky lake trout, and in 2001 it was stocked with thick-bodied triploid rainbows that should grow to impressive size here in a hurry. Spring fishing is best on this lake with an April through September 30 season.

Location: Southwest of Coulee City; see map A4, grid i4.

Species: Rainbow trout, kokanee, lake trout, triploid rainbow trout.

Facilities: Although there's no boat ramp on the lake, you can get a car-topper or canoe to the water quite easily, and there are a few campsites near the water's edge. Nearby Sun Lakes State Park has 18 RV sites and 175 tent sites for campers, as well as restrooms, showers, and picnic areas. Food, tackle, and gas are available in Coulee City, and there's plenty of lodging to the south in Soap Lake.

Directions: Take Highway 17 north from Soap Lake or south from Dry Falls Junction to the Sun Lakes State Park entrance and turn east into the park. After dropping down the hill into the bottom of the Grand Coulee, follow the signs and the paved road eastward to Deep Lake.

Contact: Sun Lakes State Park, 509/632-5583; Washington State Parks and Recreation Commission, 360/902-8844 (information) or 800/452-5687 (reservations); Big Wally's, 509/632-5504.

51 Perch Lake

This little lake often provides some of the hottest opening-day trout action in Grant County, but its annual plant of about 10,000 rainbows is usually removed within a few days, after which Perch Lake resembles a 16-acre biological desert. Fish it early in the season if you want trout, or fish it later in the spring if you want to simply get out on the water to enjoy the beauty of the Columbia Basin.

Location: Southwest of Coulee City; see map A4, grid i4.

Species: Rainbow trout (and you thought I was going to say perch).

Facilities: There's no boat ramp on the lake, but you can get a car-topper or canoe to the water easily. Nearby Sun Lakes State Park has 18 RV sites and 175 tent sites for campers, as well as restrooms, showers, and picnic areas. Food, gas, and tackle are available in Coulee City, and there's plenty of lodging available to the south in Soap Lake.

Directions: Take Highway 17 north from Soap Lake or south from Dry Falls Junction to the Sun Lakes State Park entrance and turn east into the park. After dropping down the hill into the bottom of the Grand Coulee, turn left at the sign pointing to Perch, Rainbow, and Dry Falls Lakes. Perch is the second lake on the left.

Contact: Sun Lakes State Park, 509/632-5583; Washington State Parks and Recreation Commission, 360/902-8844 (information) or 800/452-5687 (reservations); Big Wally's, 509/632-5504.

52 Vic Meyers (Rainbow) Lake

Since this lake is even smaller than Perch Lake (see number 51), when the crowds flock here on opening day, they make even quicker work of the 5,000 or so yearling rainbows stocked as fingerlings the year before. If you're going to fish for Vic Meyers' 11-inch rainbows, arrive early on opening weekend (or even before to get a good spot near the water) and be prepared for some elbow-to-elbow combat fishing.

Location: Southwest of Coulee City; see map A4, grid i4.

Species: Rainbow trout.

Facilities: There's no boat ramp on the lake, but you can get a car-topper or canoe to the water quite easily. Nearby Sun Lakes State Park has 18 RV sites and 175 tent sites for campers, as well as restrooms, showers, and picnic areas. Food and gas are available in Coulee City, and there's plenty of lodging available to the south in Soap Lake.

Directions: Take Highway 17 north from Soap Lake or south from Dry Falls Junction to the Sun Lakes State Park entrance and turn east into the park. After dropping down the hill into the bottom of the Grand Coulee, turn left at the sign pointing to Perch, Rainbow, and Dry Falls Lakes. Vic Meyers is the first lake on the left.

Contact: Sun Lakes State Park, 509/632-5583; Big Wally's, 509/632-5504.

53 Park Lake

Every time I think of Park Lake, I remember the June morning many years ago when as a boy of about 10 I set out in a rental boat with my dad at the oars to try for eastern Washington trout for the very first time. It was quite a lesson. About the only thing I ever trolled with back then was a string of Ford Fender trolling blades and a juicy garden worm, so that's what I was using.

My dad decided to take a more sophisticated approach, tying some kind of artificial fly to the monofilament on his spinning outfit. Half an hour into the trip, Dad's rod lurched toward the boat's stern and he was into a good fish, one that put a terrific bend in his spinning rod and would have no doubt peeled several yards of line off the reel if the drag had been adjusted downward even the slightest bit from the Power Winch setting. When the tight line snubbed its efforts to swim, the fish launched itself skyward, and we got a good look at what was then the largest rainbow trout I had ever seen. The sight of the huge trout made Dad turn the reel handle even faster than before, and certain laws of physics began to seep into my young brain for the first time. But before I could utter anything about unstoppable forces and immovable objects, the monofilament snapped and the fun ended.

Dad and I agreed that the 18-inch trout must have weighed at least six pounds, since it had broken his six-pound line, and he tied on another fly. Minutes later the entire episode was repeated, right up to and including the dull "ping" that rang through the still morning air as the line snapped. Without even considering backing his reel's drag off a little to the Dredge or Pull Stumps setting, Dad cussed his lousy line and tied on a third fly. Perhaps 15 minutes later it met the same fate as its two predecessors, and Dad was starting to think he had a starring role in "Rainbows from Hell: The Series." Luckily, the trout quit biting before my dad ran out of flies, and we eventually returned to the dock fishless. Although I hadn't hooked a single fish, I had learned a lot about fishing Park Lake, not the least of which was that its husky, hard-fighting rainbows demand respect.

Generous plants of hatchery rainbow and brown trout fingerlings make Park and nearby Blue Lake (see number 54) a couple of the best trout lakes in the Columbia Basin. Crowds of anglers show up here days before the opener to get a good spot, and limit catches are as common among bank anglers crowding the edges of Highway 17 as they are among boaters who troll Flatfish, Triple Teazers, or Ford Fenders—and—worm rigs. The fishing holds up well into June, slows a little during the heat of summer, and picks up again in September. Like other lakes in this popular chain, Park closes to fishing at the end of September.

Location: Southwest of Coulee City; see map A4, grid i4.

Species: Rainbow and brown trout.

Directions: Drive south from Dry Falls Junction or north from Soap Lake on Highway 17, which parallels the lake's southwestern shoreline. Turn east at the Sun Lakes State Park entrance to reach the resort, boat ramp, and state park at the northeast end of the lake.

Facilities:

Sun Lakes State Park: This state park has a two-lane, asphalt ramp with a loading float and parking for about 20 cars and trailers. There's a $4 launch fee, or a $40 annual permit is available, good at state parks throughout Washington. The park also has a large number of tent sites and a few RV sites with hookups.

Laurent's Sun Village Resort: This resort has two ramps, one concrete and one gravel, with several loading floats. These gently sloping ramps are in fairly shallow water, so people with larger boats usually go elsewhere. The resort charges a $2 launch fee. Sun Village also has over 100 RV sites, a big swim beach, store, rental boats, moorage, restrooms with showers, picnic shelters and tables, a large play field, and other facilities.

Department of Fish and Wildlife Ramp: This ramp, off Park Lake Road, is marked by a Public Fishing sign. It's a bit of a stretch calling this a boat ramp, since you can't really get a trailer into it, but it's good for launching cartoppers and paddle craft. But the fee's the same as on other Washington Department of Fish and Wildlife sites; you still need that access decal, which costs $10 per year unless you have a fishing and/or hunting license.

Contact: Sun Lakes State Park, 509/632-5583; Washington State Parks and Recreation Commission, 360/902-8844 (information) or 800/452-5687 (reservations); Sun Lakes Park Resort, 509/632-5291.

54 Blue Lake

Like Park Lake to the immediate north (see number 53), Blue is a real trout factory, giving up limit catches of chunky rainbows and browns from the opening bell until early summer, when the hot-rod traffic starts to make for tougher fishing. The speed-boaters all go home after Labor Day, and trout fishing comes on strong again until the season closes at the end of September.

Bank fishing is excellent along the west side of the lake, where Highway 17 provides hundreds of yards of access and a wide, gravel parking area. Berkley Power Bait has become one of the favorite enticements among bank anglers, and the hottest colors are chartreuse and pink. The usual worms, salmon eggs, marshmallows, cheese, and combinations of these are also effective.

Troll a dry fly along the surface early in the morning or in the evening if the wind isn't a problem. During the day, gang-troll-and-worm combos account for good catches, as do Triple Teazers and Needle Fish in silver/redhead finishes or various shades of green. Green is also a good choice in Flatfish and Kwikfish, both of which are popular here.

Location: Southwest of Coulee City; see map A4, grid i3.

Species: Rainbow and brown trout.

Facilities: Coulee Lodge Resort has a concrete ramp with loading float and room for several dozen cars and trailers. The resort charges a $3 launch fee. Blue Lake Resort has a one-lane gravel ramp with parking for about a dozen cars and trailers and charges a $2 launch fee. The lake also has a Department of Fish and Wildlife access area, with one concrete ramp and one gravel ramp located side-by-side with a rock barrier between them. There's room for about 30 cars and trailers at the Washington Department of Fish and Wildlife access area. A $10 WDFW access decal is required to use the public launch areas maintained by the Washington Department of Fish and Wildlife. Coulee Lodge, at the north end of the lake, has RV sites, a small store, restrooms and showers, a swim area, moorage dock, boat rentals, and other accommodations. Blue Lake Resort has boat moorage, a swim area, rental cabins, tent/RV sites, a play area, and convenience/tackle store.

Directions: Take Highway 17 north from Soap Lake or south from Dry Falls Junction. The road runs right along the west side of the lake, with side roads at the north and south end leading to resort facilities on the lake.

Contact: Coulee Lodge, 509/632-5565; Blue Lake Resort, 509/632-5364; Laurent's Sun Village Resort, 509/632-5664; Sun Lakes State Park, 509/632-5583; Washington State Parks and Recreation Commission, 360/902-8844 (information) or 800/452-5687 (reservations).

55 Alkali Lake

With trout everywhere around it, Alkali may seem out of place in this part of the Columbia Basin, but anglers need warm-water fish, too, and this lake certainly provides variety along those lines. Until recently, about the only thing Alkali lacked for a spiny-ray grand slam was walleyes, and now it has them, too. The Department of Fish and Wildlife stocked about 1,400 baby walleyes in the lake in June 1994, with more added in 1995, and with a little luck, it shouldn't be long before anglers can enjoy year-round, all-day and all-night warm-water fishing action.

Location: North of Soap Lake; see map A4, grid i3.

Species: Walleye, largemouth bass, crappie, bluegill, yellow perch, brown bullhead catfish.

Facilities: A boat ramp is located near the southeast corner of the lake. The nearest food, gas, and lodging are in Soap Lake, famous for its cabins and motels with "healing waters" mineral tubs. Resorts to the north, along with Sun Lakes State Park, offer tent and RV sites, showers, limited groceries, and tackle.

Directions: Drive south from Dry Falls Junction or north from Soap Lake on Highway 17, which crosses the lower end of the lake. A gravel road to the east runs a short distance up the eastern shoreline.

Contact: Blue Lake Resort, 509/632-5364; Coulee Lodge, 509/632-5565; Sun Lakes State Park, 509/632-5583; Washington State Parks and Recreation Commission, 360/902-8844 (information) or 800/452-5687 (reservations).

56 Lake Lenore

This highly alkaline lake in the long chain of waters near the south end of the Grand Coulee was once thought to be a lost cause as far as angling opportunities were concerned, but then along came the Lahontan cutthroat, which is known to thrive in some of the alkaline lakes of Nevada and other western states. Lahontans introduced into Lenore in the late 1970s and early 1980s not only survived but thrived, and it wasn't long before anglers were catching two-, three-, even five-pounders and larger, creating one of central Washington's most successful trout fisheries. The stocking of Lahontan cutts continues today, and so does the productive trout fishing, although an apparent die-off of some magnitude has dampened fishing success recently.

This isn't a place where anglers are encouraged to catch and kill a limit of fish. In fact, catch-and-release regulations apply during the early part of the season, from March 1 through the end of May. Beginning June 1 and through the end of the season in November, there's a one-fish daily bag limit. This is a selective fishery lake where bait is prohibited and single, barbless hooks are required on all lures and flies. Fishing is excellent in the spring and fall but drops off to only good during the summer. Most people don't seem to mind.

Location: North of Soap Lake; see map A4, grid j3.

Species: Lahontan cutthroat trout.

Facilities: There are several public access areas on the east side of the lake where launching a small car-topper or float tube is an easy chore. Resorts and the state park to the north provide RV and tent sites, showers, groceries, tackle, and other necessities. Food, gas, and lodging are available in Soap Lake, a few miles to the south.

Directions: Drive south from Dry Falls Junction or north from Soap Lake on Highway 17, which parallels the east side of the lake.

Contact: Blue Lake Resort, 509/632-5364; Coulee Lodge, 509/632-5565; Sun Lakes State Park, 509/632-5583; Washington State Parks and Recreation Commission, 360/902-8844 (information) or 800/452-5687 (reservations).

57 Billy Clapp Lake

If you haven't heard much about the fishing variety available in Billy Clapp, maybe it's because you aren't one of the locals. All you need to know is that the lake produces good numbers of walleyes, a mixed bag of largemouth and smallmouth bass, regular limits of rainbow trout, and some decent catches of kokanee to anglers who take a little time to learn its secrets. The walleye fishing here is one of eastern Washington's best-kept angling secrets, which should bode well for anglers these days, and enough net-pen rainbows from the south end of Banks Lake make their way through the Bacon Canal and into Billy Clapp to provide consistent trouting throughout much of the year.

Some anglers fish the lake specifically for bass, catching fair numbers of decent-sized largemouths and/or smallmouths, depending on where and how they fish. If you want faster action, a bobber-and-jig combination will take some large crappies, or tip the jig with half a worm to tip the balance more toward perch.

Location: Northeast of Soap Lake; see map A4, grid i5.

Species: Walleye, largemouth and small-mouth bass, rainbow trout, kokanee, crappie, yellow perch.

Facilities: The southwest corner of the lake has a good gravel boat ramp. Food, gas, tackle, and lodging are available in Soap Lake.

Directions: Take Highway 28 east from Soap Lake to Stratford and turn north on J Road NE. Turn right on the second gravel and dirt road to the south end of the lake.

Contact: Big Wally's, 509/632-5504.

58 Middle Crab Creek

A few years ago I stumbled across a tidbit of information that I found rather fascinating. According to whatever source it was, Washington's Crab Creek is the longest creek in the country or in all of North America, or maybe it was the entire northern hemisphere. As you can tell, I don't recall the details, but the revelation did send me scrambling for a map, and I found that Crab Creek is certainly the longest creek in Washington. Beginning south of U.S. 2 near the town of Reardan and eventually finding its way into the Columbia a few miles south of Vantage, the creek's course is roughly equivalent to 40 percent of the distance across Washington at its widest point. That makes it a mighty long creek.

The section of Crab Creek upstream from Moses Lake is stocked with trout every year, providing decent fishing for pan-sized rainbows and browns through the summer. But in places where you can get away from the road some distance, you stand to catch some large carryover fish, especially browns that have lived long enough to figure things out and not strike at just any old bait or lure that passes by within range. Browns of 16 or 18 inches are available from this part of the creek, but you have to be sneaky, stealthy,

and sophisticated to catch them consistently (or even occasionally).

Location: From Moses Lake upstream to Odessa; see map A4, grid j5.

Species: Rainbow and brown trout.

Facilities: Food, gas, tackle, and lodging are available in Moses Lake and Soap Lake, with limited services available in Wilson Creek and Odessa.

Directions: Take I-90 to Moses Lake and turn north on Highway 17, following it three miles to J Road NE. Turn right on J Road NE and drive six miles to reach parts of the creek near Moses Lake. Areas a little farther upstream are accessible by taking Highway 28 to Soap Lake, turning east on Road 20 NE to Adrian, and turning south toward the Willow Lakes. To reach areas farther upstream, take Highway 28 to Wilson Creek or Odessa and explore various side roads that cross and parallel the creek.

Contact: Big Wally's, 509/632-5504.

59 Lake Creek Chain

Coffeepot Lake at the north end of the chain is the biggest and best known of the dozen lakes in this chain, but Deer, Browns, Tavares, Neves, Wederspahn, Pacific, Walter, Waukesha, Bob's, and the smaller lakes in this long chain offer similar angling opportunities. All of them contain a mixed bag, so take along gear for bass, panfish, and trout. The only one that's stocked regularly with rainbows is Deer Lake, also known as Deer Springs Lake.

Some of these lakes are located on private property, where permission from the nearest landowner is required before you can legally gain access to fish. No two of the lakes are exactly alike, so you can spend a couple of days exploring and learning each one as you cast. All are open to year-round fishing, but April, May, and June offer the best angling opportunities.

Location: North of Odessa in Lincoln County; see map A4, grid j8.

Species: Largemouth bass, yellow perch, crappie, brown bullhead catfish, some rainbow trout.

Facilities: Food, gas, lodging, and RV facilities are available in and around Odessa, but the lakes have nothing except limited bank access.

Directions: Take Highway 28 or Highway 21 to Odessa and drive north on Highway 21. Lakeview Road, Trejabel Road, and several unmarked dirt and gravel roads about five miles north of Odessa, leading east and west, provide access to the various lakes in the chain. Coffeepot Lake, at the north end of the chain, is accessible from the north by driving east off Highway 21 on Coffeepot Road about 20 miles south of Wilbur.

Contact: Odessa Chamber of Commerce, 509/982-0049.

CHAPTER A5:
NORTHEAST WASHINGTON

Map A5

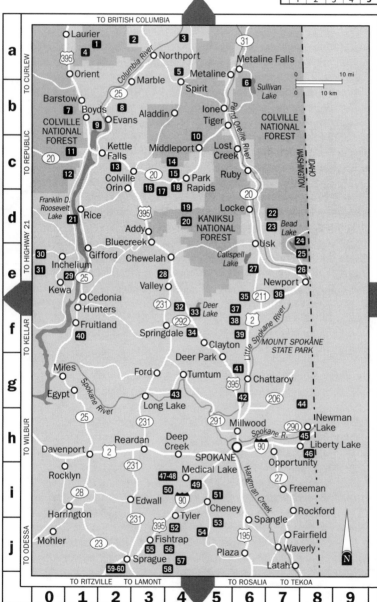

TO BRITISH COLUMBIA

a
TO CURLEW
Laurier **1**
2
3
31
4
Northport
Metaline Falls
395
Orient
Marble
Metaline **5**
Spirit
6
Sullivan Lake
0   10 mi
0   10 km

b
TO REPUBLIC
Barstow **7**
Boyds
8
Aladdin
Ione
Tiger
COLVILLE NATIONAL FOREST
25
9
Evans
COLVILLE NATIONAL FOREST

c
20
11
Kettle Falls
Middleport
10
Lost Creek
IDAHO
WASHINGTON
12
13
Colville
Orin
14
15
Park Rapids
Ruby
20
16 **17** **18**

d
TO HIGHWAY 21
Franklin D. Roosevelt Lake
21 Rice
395
19
20
KANIKSU NATIONAL FOREST
Locke
22
23 Bead Lake
Usk
24
Addy
Bluecreek
25

e
30
Inchelium
Gifford
Chewelah
Calispell Lake
27
26
31
29 25
Kewa
28
Valley
Newport
TO KELLAR
Cedonia
Hunters
231
32
33
Deer Lake
35 211 **36**
37

f
Fruitland
40
Springdale **34**
292
38
39
2
Clayton
Little Spokane River
MOUNT SPOKANE STATE PARK
Deer Park

g
Miles
Egypt
Spokane River
Ford
Tumtum
41
395
Chattaroy
43
42
206
44
Long Lake

h
TO WILBUR
25
231
291
Millwood
Spokane R.
290
Newman Lake
45
Davenport
Reardan
Deep Creek
SPOKANE
90
Liberty Lake
46
2
Medical Lake
Opportunity

i
Rocklyn
47-48
50 **49**
51
Hangman Creek
27
Freeman
28
Edwall
90
Cheney
53
Rockford
Tyler

j
TO ODESSA
Harrington
231
Fishtrap
52
54
Spangle
195
Fairfield
Mohler
23
55 **56**
Plaza
Waverly
59-60
Sprague
57
Latah
58
N

TO RITZVILLE   TO LAMONT   TO ROSALIA   TO TEKOA

0 1 2 3 4 5 6 7 8 9

© AVALON TRAVEL PUBLISHING, INC.

Chapter A5:
Northeast Washington

Spokane is the only major city in this corner of Washington, and the only place you may ever find yourself in a traffic jam. The rest of the towns here are small, friendly, and full of people who like to fish, hunt, camp, and spend as much time as possible outdoors. Much of the region is farmland and forestland, but there are also big rivers and small lakes to provide angling opportunities in any direction you may want to travel. The biggest river of all is actually a lake throughout most of this region, thanks to Grand Coulee Dam. The dam formed Lake Roosevelt, which extends over 100 miles near the region's western boundary. To the east is the Pend Oreille River, which also provides dozens of miles of fair to good fishing for everything from rainbow trout and whitefish to largemouth bass and walleyes. The Spokane River runs east to west across the lower one-third of the region to join Lake Roosevelt, providing some good trout fishing along much of its distance. A dam on the Spokane's lower reaches forms Long Lake, home to Washington's only known northern pike population. Scattered throughout the region are some of the Northwest's top trout lakes, including Medical, West Medical, Badger, Amber, the Little Pend Oreille Chain, Hatch, and Jumpoff Joe. The region also boasts more lake trout (Mackinaw) waters than any other part of the state, including Bead, Loon, and Deer Lakes.

©TERRY RUDNICK

LAKE ROOSEVELT HOUSEBOAT

◻1 Summit Lake

Although covering only seven acres, Summit is stocked every year with hatchery brookies and rainbows. They provide decent action through the summer for boat and bank anglers alike.

Fishing pressure becomes virtually nonexistent after Labor Day, but fishing can be productive here in late September and October. That's also the time of year when brook trout are at their prettiest, all decked out in fall spawning colors. Cast small spoons, spinners, or artificial flies around the edge of the lake. The season runs from late April through October.

Location: Southeast of Laurier in Stevens County; see map A5, grid a1.

Species: Brook trout, rainbow trout.

Facilities: The lake has a boat ramp, and there's a U.S. Forest Service campground about five miles south at Pierre Lake. The nearest food, gas, tackle, and lodging are in Kettle Falls.

Directions: Take U.S. 395 north from Kettle Falls and drive about four miles past Orient. Turn east (right) on Sand Creek Road, drive four more miles to Box Canyon Road, and turn north (left). Drive three miles to the lake, which is on the left side of the road.

Contact: Colville National Forest, Kettle Falls Ranger District, 509/738-6111.

◻2 Big Sheep Creek

The upper stretches of the river offer some beautiful pools that just beg you to stop and spend some time fishing for the pan-sized brookies and cutthroats in them. Farther downstream you're likely to find more rainbows than brook trout and cutts, and some of them will be respectable-sized fish. As summer progresses, the creek gets a little harder to fish because of the abundant foliage that chokes off access to some areas. That doesn't stop die-hard anglers, many of

whom are fly casters who use a variety of small, dark patterns to catch good numbers of trout here.

Fishing is best right after the season opens on June 1.

Location: Flows into the Columbia River near Northport; see map A5, grid a2.

Species: Rainbow, brook, and cutthroat trout.

Facilities: Food, gas, tackle, and lodging are available in Northport.

Directions: Take Highway 25 to Northport, cross the Columbia River, and turn west (left) on Sheep Creek Road, which parallels the creek for several miles.

Contact: Colville Chamber of Commerce, 509/684-5973, website: www.colville.com; The Sport Spot, 509/738-6711 (spring to fall only).

◻3 Cedar Lake   51 Acres

Because this is another one of those northeast Washington lakes that you aren't likely to pass on your way to somewhere else, anglers who fish Cedar Lake are there to fish Cedar Lake. Not only is this a pretty lake in a pretty part of the state, but Cedar also produces some pretty nice rainbows. Fry plants grow to about a foot long by the following spring, but two-year carryovers of 17 to 19 inches are fairly common. The lake's planted trout, however, seem to have good years and bad years, so you can't be sure how good the fishing might be from season to season. It's a fairly long trip from most places in Washington to Cedar Lake, so you might want to call ahead if hooking lots of fish is one of your priorities. Try trolling a green Carey Special fly very slowly during the day. Night fishing is also popular here, and most anglers use Glo Hooks with Berkley Power Bait for their nighttime trouting. Spring and fall are the best times to fish, but the season runs from late April through early October.

Location: Northwest of Northport in Stevens County; see map A5, grid a4.

Species: Rainbow trout.

Facilities: The lake has a public access area and boat ramp but no other facilities. The nearest food, gas, tackle, and lodging are in Northport.

Directions: Take U.S. 395 to Colville and turn east on Highway 20. Just east of town, turn north (left) at the sign pointing toward North-port (Colville-Aladdin-Northport Road) and follow it to the small town of Spirit. Go east (right) on Deep Lake–Boundary Road and follow it north, past Deep Lake, to the east side of Cedar Lake.

Contact: Homeland RV Park & Campground, 509/732-4367.

4 Pierre Lake

Stocked with fingerling rainbows, this 106-acre lake is also home to such a wide variety of fish species that it has something for virtually every angler. The lake used to produce some hefty cutthroats, but cutts over 12 inches or so are now rare. Casting or trolling for rainbows might also turn up an occasional brook trout, and there's a little bit of summertime opportunity for kokanee.

As the water warms in May, many anglers fish Pierre in the evening for trout and then stick around into the night to catch catfish (brown bullheads). They aren't big, but they are abundant, and it's possible to fill a five-gallon bucket with them on a good night. Some anglers use night crawlers, others prefer chicken livers, but the catfish don't seem to care one way or the other. While bass and crappies are available here, too, there are better places to fish for both.

Location: Northeast of Orient; see map A5, grid a1.

Species: Rainbow, brook, and cutthroat trout; kokanee; crappie; largemouth bass; brown bullhead catfish.

Facilities: The west side of the lake has a U.S. Forest Service campground and a boat ramp. The nearest food, gas, tackle, and lodging are in Kettle Falls.

Directions: Take U.S. 395 to Barstow and turn east onto Barstow–Pierre Lake Road, which soon turns north and leads about 10 miles to the west side of the lake.

Contact: Colville National Forest, Kettle Falls Ranger District, 509/738-6111; Colville Chamber of Commerce, 509/684-5973, website: www.colville.com.

5 Deep Lake

Since it covers nearly 200 acres but is only about 45 feet deep in its deepest spot, maybe it should be called Big Lake rather than Deep Lake. Who comes up with these names? Anyway, Deep is a steady trout producer and a popular spring and summer destination of anglers from all over northeastern Washington. It's a long drive from most places, but worth it.

The best angling advice from the folks at Wilderness West Resort is to think green. A green Carey Special fly with a red tail is so popular here that it's referred to as a "Deep Lake Special." Troll it fairly deep behind five or six colors of leaded line, and you'll probably do just fine. Flatfish and Kwikfish in various shades of green are also effective. As a general rule, fish around the north end of the lake—near the mouth of Cedar Creek—if you want brookies. Cutthroats, on the other hand, are more abundant at the lake's south end, especially in the fall before they head up into the lower reaches of Deep Creek to spawn.

Location: Southeast of Northport in Stevens County; see map A5, grid a4.

Species: Rainbow, brook, and cutthroat trout.

Facilities: The east side of the lake has a private resort with boats, campsites, restrooms, a small store, and other amenities. The lake also has a public access area with a boat ramp and toilets. The nearest food, gas, tackle, and lodging are in Northport.

Directions: Take U.S. 395 to Colville and turn east on Highway 20. Just east of town, turn north (left) at the sign pointing toward Northport (Colville-Aladdin-Northport Road) and follow it to the small town of Spirit. Go east (right) on Deep Lake–Boundary Road and follow it for four miles to the east side of the lake.

Contact: Homeland RV Park & Campground, 509/732-4367.

6 Sullivan Lake

Over three decades ago, an angler named R. L. Henry coaxed a whopping 22-pound brown trout from the deep, clear waters of this 1,300-acre lake near the northeastern corner of the state, and Sullivan has been somewhat of a mythical, mystical place ever since. Henry's trophy trout still stands as Washington's best-ever brown, and it's a record that may never be broken. It probably isn't very likely that you'll catch a 22-pounder, or even a 10-pounder here, but the lake still does hold some trophy-class brown trout, and there's always a chance of hooking a real lunker.

Besides big browns, the lake also offers the possibility of taking a bragging-sized cutthroat or even a rainbow over five pounds. The brook trout and kokanee don't grow nearly as large and may, in fact, serve as menu items for the bigger trout, along with providing opportunities for anglers to catch pansizers for the table.

Standard trolling and stillfishing techniques work for the kokanee and smaller trout, but for a fish worthy of a trip to the taxidermist, try trolling plugs and wobbling spoons large enough to impersonate the kokanee on which the bigger trout often feed.

Sullivan is open to year-round fishing, and in recent years a fairly popular winter icefishing season has developed for burbot, or freshwater lings. Jigging along the bottom produces most of these long, lean, sweet-eating fish, and this technique may even turn up a large trout or two.

Location: Southeast of Metaline Falls in Pend Oreille County; see map A5, grid b6.

Species: Brown, rainbow, cutthroat, and brook trout; kokanee; burbot.

Facilities: Boat ramps and U.S. Forest Service campgrounds are at the north and south ends of the lake. Food, gas, tackle, motels, trailer parks, and bed-and-breakfast inns are available in Ione.

Directions: Take Highway 20 to the small town of Tiger and turn north on Highway 31. Just south of Ione, turn east (right) on Sullivan Lake Road and follow it to the lake.

Contact: Colville National Forest, Newport Ranger District, 509/447-3129.

7 Davis Lake

This 17-acre lake seems to have been custombuilt for cutthroat trout. Hatchery cutthroats stocked by the Department of Fish and Wildlife flourish here, providing good fishing from late spring until the dog days of summer. After the summertime lull, they come on strong again for the final few weeks of the season in October. Davis is a good place to troll small wobbling spoons, Flatfish, Kwikfish, or other small plugs, but anglers casting bobber-and-worm rigs also make some good catches of 8- to 12-inch cutts. A few hatchery rainbows have been stocked in the lake from time to time, so there's a chance you'll find an occasional rainbow in your catch of pan-size cutts.

Location: Southwest of Barstow in Ferry County; see map A5, grid b1.

Species: Cutthroat and rainbow trout.

Facilities: The west side of the lake has a U.S. Forest Service campground and a boat ramp for small boats.

Directions: Take Highway 20 north from Kettle Falls and turn west (left) on Deadman Creek Road (County Road 460). Turn north (right) on County Road 465, east (left) on County Road 480, and north (right) on Forest Service Road 080 to the lake.

Contact: Colville National Forest, Kettle Falls Ranger District, 509/738-6111.

8 Williams Lake

Though this 38-acre lake east of Lake Roosevelt (see number 21) may look mighty inviting on a calm Saturday morning in mid-May, try to resist the temptation. Unlike most Washington lakes and reservoirs, Williams is closed to fishing in the spring. The season opens December 1 and runs through the end of March. But before you feel cheated, you should know that wintertime fishing here can be excellent.

Williams was treated with rotenone to eliminate various unwanted fish species in 1996, and the trout fishing now is as good as it's been in many years. Depending on the winter conditions, you may get a chance to fish "open water" early in the season, but by the first of the year, you can usually plan on fishing through the ice. That ice cover may be nearly a foot thick some years, so don't forget your ice auger or a good ax for chopping holes.

Your chances of catching a fat rainbow on top of the ice are about as close to zilch as you can get. Red salmon eggs account for a high percentage of the catch here, but if the bite is off and red eggs don't work, don't be afraid to experiment with Power Bait, marshmallows, yellow corn, or other baits.

Location: Northeast of Evans in Stevens County; see map A5, grid b2.

Species: Rainbow trout.

Facilities: The lake has a public access area with a boat ramp, but that's about it. The nearest food, gas, tackle, and lodging are in Colville and Kettle Falls.

Directions: Take Highway 25 north from Kettle Falls and turn east (right) on Williams Lake Road, following it about four miles to the lake.

Contact: Colville Chamber of Commerce, 509/684-5973, website: www.colville.com.

9 Kettle River

Once the scene of some pretty good spring and fall trout fishing, the Kettle now has some special regulations in place to give native rainbows added protection, especially at spawning time. While most of the river is open to year-round fishing, it's catch-and-release only for trout November through May. Selective fishery regulations are in effect above the Barstow Bridge throughout the year.

Those no-bait and barbless hook regulations now also apply to anglers fishing specifically for whitefish during the winter.

The Kettle offers some of Washington's best whitefish action in February and March. If you fish the lower end of the river, where it flows into Lake Roosevelt, don't be very surprised if you catch a walleye or two for your efforts. Trolling a spinner-and-worm combination or a diving plug near bottom is most likely to take these sweet-eating members of the perch family.

If you're looking for a little catch-and-release action on really big game, the Kettle even offers sturgeon fishing. All sturgeon must be released, but who cares? An afternoon wrestling with and releasing a four- or five-foot sturgeon is an afternoon well spent.

Location: Enters the north end of Lake Roosevelt north of Kettle Falls; see map A5, grid b1.

Species: Rainbow trout, mountain whitefish, walleye, sturgeon.

Facilities: The highway provides a great deal of access to the river. Food, gas, tackle, and lodging are available in Kettle Falls, with limited facilities in the several small towns along the river.

Directions: Take U.S. 395 north from Kettle Falls to parallel the west side of the river all the way to the Canadian border.

Contact: Colville Chamber of Commerce, 509/684-5973, website: www.colville.com.

10 Little Pend Oreille Chain of Lakes

These beautiful little lakes in the pine forests along the Stevens–Pend Oreille county line would be worth visiting even if they were fishless. This is gorgeous country, far away from the hustle and bustle of the rest of the world, where lots of folks come just to get away. Luckily the lakes of the upper Little Pend Oreille chain also offer some excellent trout fishing. Cutthroats of 9 to 13 inches provide the bulk of the angling opportunity, but some of the lakes also have rainbows, some have brookies, and some have all three species. Heritage, Thomas, Gillette, and Sherry Lakes are all connected by narrow channels, while Leo, Frater, and Nile Lakes are just to the northeast. Coffin Lake, located about three miles south of Sherry, is the southernmost lake in the chain and also the smallest.

While the lakes are open to hardware and bait, fly-fishing is a worthwhile possibility on every lake in the chain. It's especially effective for cutthroat during the late spring and summer. If you aren't too good at casting a fly, try trolling a red or green Carey Special tipped with a grub, moving along fast enough to keep the fly just under the surface. Rooster Tails, Super Dupers, and Wedding Rings all are popular here. Anglers who still-fish prefer corn, salmon eggs, marshmallows, and Berkley Power Bait, not necessarily in that order. These lakes all open in late April and close at the end of October.

Location: Northeast of Colville; see map A5, grid c4.

Species: Cutthroat, brook, and rainbow trout.

Facilities: A private resort on Gillette Lake offers tent and RV sites, boat rentals, fishing docks, and a grocery store. The public access area and boat ramp for several of the lakes is located on Gillette Lake. U.S. Forest Service campgrounds can also be found on Gillette, Thomas, and Leo Lakes. The nearest food, gas, tackle, and lodging are in Ione and Colville.

Directions: Drive west from Tiger or east from Colville on Highway 20, which runs right along the north or west shores of most of the Little Pend Oreille lakes.

Contact: Beaver Lodge, 509/684-5657; Colville Chamber of Commerce, 509/684-5973, website: www.colville.com.

11 Trout Lake

Spring plants of hatchery trout provide most of the action at Trout Lake, but a few rainbows carry over through the winter to give anglers a crack at 14- to 16-inchers. Casting spoons, spinners, and flies from the bank works, but trollers usually have better luck.

Location: West of Kettle Falls in Ferry County; see map A5, grid c1.

Species: Rainbow trout.

Facilities: The south end of the lake has a U.S. Forest Service campground and a boat ramp. The nearest food, gas, tackle, and lodging are in Kettle Falls.

Directions: Take Highway 20 east from Kettle Falls and turn north (right) on Trout Lake Road, which runs for five miles right to the south end of the lake.

Contact: Colville Chamber of Commerce, 509/684-5973, website: www.colville.com; Colville National Forest, Kettle Falls Ranger District, 509/738-6111.

12 Ellen Lake

If you fished this 80-acre lake just north of the Colville Indian Reservation up to and including 1994, you may have caught largemouth bass, but they've been eliminated, and the lake (at least for now) is back to a trout-only fishery. Rainbows are stocked every year and provide good to excellent fishing throughout the spring and early summer. During the early season when the water is still cool, focus your attention on the southern half of the lake where water depths range from 5 to 25 feet, but as the water temperature rises, work your way toward the deep end, where you'll find 30 to 40 feet of water in places. By midsummer this lake gets pretty busy, so if you want to avoid the crowds, visit Ellen before Memorial Day or after Labor Day.

Location: North of Inchelium in Ferry County; see map A5, grid c1.

Species: Rainbow trout.

Facilities: The lake has a U.S. Forest Service campground with tent and trailer sites, drinking water, restrooms, a boat ramp, and shore access. The nearest food, gas, tackle, and lodging are to the north in Kettle Falls.

Directions: Take Highway 20 east from Republic or west from Kettle Falls and turn south at Sherman Creek onto Kettle Falls Road. Drive four miles to Lake Ellen Road (County Road 412) and turn west (right). Follow Lake Ellen Road for four miles to the lake.

Contact: Colville Chamber of Commerce, 509/684-5973, website: www.colville.com; Colville National Forest, Kettle Falls Ranger District, 509/738-6111.

13 Colville River

The Colville has long had a reputation for producing some hefty brown trout, and they're still here, though catching them isn't always easy. The trout seem to be getting wiser all the time, and to complicate matters a little more, much of this river runs through private property, limiting angler access. But if you're willing to work at your fishing and to cultivate cordial relations with a few property owners, you might be rewarded with a trout of five pounds or more. Special regu-

lations during the fall allow anglers to keep no more than two browns per day.

If you're fly-fishing, try a grasshopper pattern of some kind. Hardware anglers might try a spinner painted in a grasshopper finish, such as Luhr Jensen's grasshopper BangTail. If you're not a fly or hardware angler, try a real grasshopper.

Among the river's many species of game fish, walleyes are gaining popularity, and the river also has some special walleye regulations that anglers should understand before fishing the Colville. Most of the usual walleye-fishing methods will work here, but a slot limit allows only fish under 16 inches and over 20 inches to be kept.

Like other Columbia River tributaries, the Colville also has a few sturgeon patrolling its depths, and there's a catch-and-release sturgeon fishery available to anglers looking for a chance to do battle with something of truly impressive proportions.

Location: Flows into Lake Roosevelt south of Kettle Falls; see map A5, grid c2.

Species: Rainbow and brown trout throughout the river; some sturgeon, walleye, largemouth and smallmouth bass, and yellow perch in the lower river.

Facilities: Food, gas, tackle, and lodging are available in Kettle Falls and Chewelah.

Directions: Take U.S. 395 north from Chewelah or south from Kettle Falls to parallel most of the river. The upstream portions of the river are accessible via Highway 231, which turns west off U.S. 395 about five miles south of Chewelah.

Contact: Colville Chamber of Commerce, 509/684-5973, website: www.colville.com.

14 Little Twin Lakes

The Department of Fish and Wildlife stocks cutthroat fry here every spring after the late-April opener, and by the following spring, these fish range from 10 to 14 inches long.

Cast small spinners or bobber-and-worm combinations from the bank and you'll do OK, but troll a small Triple Teazer, Dick Nite, or Flatfish from a boat and you'll probably do even better. Like most other cutthroats, these will readily take an artificial fly, so work the shoreline with your favorite fly pattern during the morning and evening hours.

Twin Lakes is a great destination for summertime family camping/fishing vacations. These twins, however, are actually one lake with a narrow channel connecting the larger eastern and much smaller western portions.

Location: Northeast of Colville; see map A5, grid c4.

Species: Cutthroat trout.

Facilities: The lake has a U.S. Forest Service campground with tent and trailer sites, restrooms, and drinking water, and it's possible to launch a small boat from the bank. The nearest food, gas, tackle, and lodging are in Colville.

Directions: Take U.S. 395 to Colville and turn east on Highway 20. About 11 miles out of town, turn north (left) on Black Lake–Squaw Creek Road. Turn right on Forest Service Road 150 after four miles and follow it for one mile to the lake.

Contact: Colville Chamber of Commerce, 509/684-5973, website: www.colville.com; Colville National Forest, Colville Ranger District, 509/684-7000.

⓯ Black Lake

Rainbows and brookies are stocked here every year, and such variety is one reason anglers keep coming to Black Lake. But the sheer beauty of the place is every bit as good a reason to visit. This 70-acre lake in the high country east of Colville is one of the Northwest's prettiest, and the pan-sized trout you might catch are merely a bonus. Fishing sometimes gets off to a slow start in this cold, clear, subalpine lake, but by June things

are usually hopping, and the good fishing holds up well into the summer.

Location: East of Colville; see map A5, grid c4.

Species: Rainbow and brook trout.

Facilities: There's a boat ramp on the lake, and a U.S. Forest Service campground with tent and trailer sites, water, and restrooms is a couple of miles away at Little Twin Lakes. Other amenities are available in Colville.

Directions: Take U.S. 395 to Colville and turn east on Highway 20. About two miles east of Park Rapids, turn north (left) on Black Lake–Squaw Creek Road and follow it for two miles to the east side of the lake.

Contact: Colville Chamber of Commerce, 509/684-5973, website: www.colville.com.

⓰ Rocky Lake

Stocked with hatchery fry every spring, this 20-acre lake gives up pan-sized rainbows at a pretty good clip through May and early June. Don't expect anything spectacular here, just decent trout fishing early in the season. After school gets out in June, you might have trouble finding a campsite. Rocky Lake regulars like to stillfish with Berkley Power Bait and red salmon eggs, but all the usual baits and hardware will take trout.

Location: Southeast of Colville; see map A5, grid c3.

Species: Rainbow trout.

Facilities: Thanks to the all-night partiers, vandals, and thieves, the Department of Natural Resources campground at the south end of the lake has been closed, so there's nothing in the way of facilities here now except for the boat ramp. Food, gas, tackle, and lodging are available in Colville.

Directions: Take U.S. 395 to Colville and go southeast on Graham Road for three miles to Rocky Lake Road, which leads to the lake.

Contact: Colville Chamber of Commerce, 509/684-5973, website: www.colville.com.

17 Hatch Lake

This lake with a winter-only fishing season was treated with rotenone in fall 1999 and not restocked with trout for the 1999–2000 season. But the rainbows are back once again and providing good cold-weather angling action. Since wintertime trout tend to have subdued appetites, anglers prefer small baits, such as a single salmon eggs, a kernel of corn, one or two maggots on a hook, or a couple of golden grubs, the small larvae found inside the goldenrod stalk.

Location: Southeast of Colville; see map A5, grid c3.

Species: Rainbow trout, yellow perch.

Facilities: The north end of the lake has a public access area and boat ramp. Food, gas, tackle, and lodging are available in Colville.

Directions: Take U.S. 395 to Colville and turn east on Highway 20. About six miles from town, turn south (right) on Artman-Gibson Road, which leads about 1.5 miles to the lake.

Contact: Colville Chamber of Commerce, 509/684-5973, website: www.colville.com.

18 Starvation Lake

The name may not sound promising, especially if you're hankering for a dinner of freshly caught trout fried over an open fire, but it's nowhere near as bad as it sounds. Yes, the trout population does sometimes take a pounding from low water levels and the winter ice cover, not to mention some oxygen-depletion problems during the summer, but the Department of Fish and Wildlife is usually standing by to plant more rainbows when that happens. During the years that Mother Nature is kind, trout fishing in this 30-acre lake can be excellent. That's how it has been in recent years, and anglers have had some very good seasons at Starvation lately.

Read the angling regulations pamphlet before fishing the lake, especially if you plan to visit after the end of May. Catch-and-keep

rules change to catch-and-release at that time, so don't kill any trout unless you know it's okay to do so. The regulations after June 1 also call for no bait and barbless hooks, so that's when many fly casters prefer to start fishing here. Starvation is considered by some to be one of eastern Washington's top fly-fishing lakes, and it's not unusual to see half a dozen float-tubers casting dry flies along the shoreline lily pads on a summer weekend.

Location: Southeast of Colville; see map A5, grid c4.

Species: Rainbow trout.

Facilities: The lake has a public access area and a boat ramp suitable for small boats. Colville has food, gas, tackle, and lodging.

Directions: Take U.S. 395 to Colville and turn east on Highway 20. After eight miles, turn south (right) on Narcisse Creek Road, marked by a sign announcing the Little Pend Oreille Wildlife Area, and follow it two miles to Starvation Lake Road.

Contact: Colville Chamber of Commerce, 509/684-5973, website: www.colville.com.

19 McDowell Lake

Don't even think about bringing the worms and salmon eggs to this one, because McDowell has fly-fishing-only regulations. What's more, it's all catch-and-release, which makes it easier to understand why the trout fishing can be so good here at times, especially early in the season. Rainbows provide most of the action, but the lake has long had a fair population of brookies, and browns were introduced a few years ago.

Since the lake is accessible only by a trail and has a no-motors regulation, it stays peaceful and quiet most of the time. The fact that there are no homes or any kind of development around the lake makes it even better. One word of warning: you'll have to share the lake with several Canada geese, numerous species of ducks, and other wildlife. Hope you can handle that.

On the down side, tench have found their way into the lake, and they compete with the trout population. Although they haven't resorted to dousing the lake with rotenone, the Department of Fish and Wildlife has been making an effort to trap the pesky rough fish from the lake to keep them from getting out of hand.

Location: East of Arden in Stevens County; see map A5, grid d4.

Species: Rainbow, brown, and brook trout.

Facilities: The lake has no facilities. Food, gas, tackle, and lodging are available in Colville.

Directions: Take U.S. 395 to Colville and turn east on Highway 20. After eight miles, turn south (right) on Narcisse Creek Road (marked by a Little Pend Oreille Wildlife Area sign) and follow it to the bridge crossing the Little Pend Oreille River. Just past the bridge, turn right and park at the gate. From there it's an easy quarter-mile hike to the lake.

Contact: Colville Chamber of Commerce, 509/684-5973, website: www.colville.com.

20 Bayley Lake

Bayley is another of several lakes in the immediate area where any angling method is OK as long as it's fly-fishing. No worms, no salmon eggs, no weighted spinners, and no wobbling spoons, period. Since the lake is small, covering only about 17 acres, the regulations no doubt help to get the most out of a trout population that would quickly be caught if standard rules were in effect. You can keep one trout per day early in the season, but in early July the lake goes to catch-and-release regulations.

No-motor rules and the size of the lake make this a great place to kick around in a float tube. If you arrive here for the first time and can't decide what to tie on the end of

your leader, the locals suggest a green Woolly Bugger. That should get you by at least until some kind of hatch occurs. You're on your own from there.

Location: North of Chewelah; see map A5, grid d4.

Species: Rainbow and brook trout.

Facilities: The lake has a public access area and a boat ramp. The nearest food, lodging, and other amenities are in Colville.

Directions: Take U.S. 395 to Colville and turn east on Highway 20. Drive eight miles to Narcisse Creek Road (marked with a Little Pend Oreille Wildlife Area sign) and turn south (right). Follow the road for two miles to a T intersection and turn left on Bear Creek Road, going just over 4.5 miles to a dirt road leading right. Take that dirt road and drive another mile to the north end of the lake.

Contact: Colville Chamber of Commerce, 509/684-5973, website: www.colville.com.

21 Upper Lake Roosevelt

The waters of Lake Roosevelt around the entrance to the Spokane Arm were the birthplace of the Northwest walleye fishery. If you don't remember that, you're either a kid or a relative newcomer to this part of the world. The lake still has walleyes, but it's safe to say that the fishing isn't as good as it was 15 or 20 years ago. Oh, there are still some husky walleyes to be caught from the upper end of the big lake, but they aren't all concentrated in one spot just waiting around with their mouths open as they used to be. If you want to catch walleyes now, you may have to do some trolling with diving plugs or spinner-and-night-crawler rigs to locate cooperative fish, then work them with a leadhead-and-grub combination or continue trolling the area.

Trolling for rainbows or kokanee might be more productive, especially during the spring and early summer months. Two- to five-pound

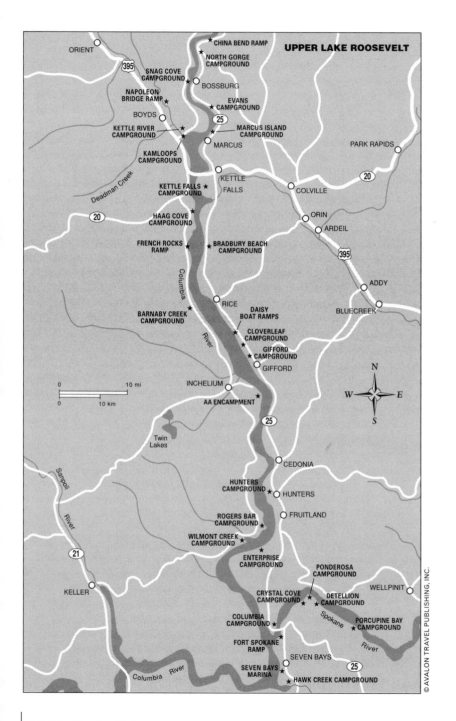

UPPER LAKE ROOSEVELT

ORIENT

CHINA BEND RAMP

NORTH GORGE
CAMPGROUND

SNAG COVE
CAMPGROUND

BOSSBURG

NAPOLEON
BRIDGE RAMP

EVANS
CAMPGROUND

BOYDS

KETTLE RIVER
CAMPGROUND

MARCUS ISLAND
CAMPGROUND

MARCUS

PARK RAPIDS

KAMLOOPS
CAMPGROUND

Deadman Creek

KETTLE
FALLS

KETTLE FALLS
CAMPGROUND

COLVILLE

HAAG COVE
CAMPGROUND

ORIN

ARDEIL

FRENCH ROCKS
RAMP

BRADBURY BEACH
CAMPGROUND

Columbia

ADDY

RICE

BLUECREEK

BARNABY CREEK
CAMPGROUND

DAISY
BOAT RAMPS

River

CLOVERLEAF
CAMPGROUND

GIFFORD
CAMPGROUND

GIFFORD

0   10 mi
0   10 km

INCHELIUM

AA ENCAMPMENT

N
W   E
S

Twin
Lakes

CEDONIA

Sanpoil

HUNTERS
CAMPGROUND

HUNTERS

River

ROGERS BAR
CAMPGROUND

FRUITLAND

WILMONT CREEK
CAMPGROUND

ENTERPRISE
CAMPGROUND

PONDEROSA
CAMPGROUND

WELLPINIT

CRYSTAL COVE
CAMPGROUND

DETELLION
CAMPGROUND

KELLER

COLUMBIA
CAMPGROUND

Spokane

PORCUPINE BAY
CAMPGROUND

FORT SPOKANE
RAMP

River

SEVEN BAYS

SEVEN BAYS
MARINA

HAWK CREEK CAMPGROUND

Columbia   River

© AVALON TRAVEL PUBLISHING, INC.

rainbows can be found throughout the lake, including this more lightly fished northern half. The lake's excellent trout fishing is due in large part to cooperative net-pen projects, from which thousands of healthy rainbows are released into the reservoir every year.

Lake Roosevelt's kokanee fishery has taken a downturn in recent years, and regulations are now in effect to protect naturally spawning kokanee. Anglers may keep only hatchery kokes, which have been fin-clipped to identify them.

Smallmouth bass are also abundant throughout the big lake, but the smallies in the northern half don't get all that much attention from anglers. Working a three-inch Berkley Power Grub along the rocky shoreline and submerged gravel piles will coax them to life, as will a small crankbait of some kind, especially if it happens to be painted in the general color scheme of a crayfish. The fishing season here runs year-round.

Although sturgeon are listed among the lake's possibilities, anglers should note that the sturgeon fishery, if any, is a catch-and-release proposition.

Location: From Kettle Falls south to the mouth of the Spokane River; see map A5, grid d1.

Species: Rainbow trout, kokanee, walleye, smallmouth bass, yellow perch, crappie, lake whitefish, sturgeon.

Facilities: There are 16 boat ramps available to anglers on the upper portion of Lake Roosevelt (from Hawk Creek north):

- **Hawk Creek Campground:** Starting at the south end, Hawk Creek Campground has a single-lane ramp with a loading float and a small, gravel parking area.
- **Seven Bays Marina:** Three miles north of Hawk Creek is Seven Bays Marina, where there's a good concrete ramp four lanes wide, with lots of room to park cars and boat trailers.

- **Fort Spokane Ramp:** The next ramp to the north is at Fort Spokane Campground, where the Spokane River enters Lake Roosevelt from the east. Fort Spokane has a three-lane concrete ramp with several loading floats.
- **Porcupine Bay Campground:** Up the Spokane Arm about 10 miles east of the main lake is the two-lane ramp at Porcupine Bay Campground. It has loading floats, lots of parking.
- **Hunters Campground:** Next is the three-lane National Park Service ramp at Hunters Campground, another good one, located in a protected bay about a mile off Highway 25.
- **Gifford Campground:** The Park Service ramp at Gifford Campground is next, a three-lane, concrete ramp with several loading floats and room for about two dozen cars and trailers on a paved parking area.
- **Daisy Boat Ramps:** There are two more single-lane Park Service ramps near Daisy, about a mile apart along the highway.
- **Bradbury Beach Campground:** Another National Park Service ramp is at Bradbury Beach Campground, about 12 miles north of the Daisy ramps.
- **French Rocks Ramp:** Across the lake from Bradbury Beach is the NPS ramp at French Rocks, a one-lane concrete ramp with a loading float.
- **Kettle Falls Campground:** Up the lake farther is Kettle Falls Campground, with an excellent four-lane concrete ramp with loading floats.
- **Marcus Island Campground:** The Park Service's Marcus Island Campground is next, with a single-lane, concrete-plank ramp and loading floats.
- **Evans Campground:** A short distance north is Evans Campground, another National Park Service site with a single-lane ramp and floats.
- **Snag Cove Campground:** The name may give you cause to wonder, but there's a good

ramp at Snag Cove Campground. It's a single-lane concrete ramp and loading float, with the usual $6 launch fee.

- **Napoleon Bridge Ramp:** Uplake another three miles is Napoleon Bridge, with another single-lane ramp.
- **North Gorge Campground:** This campgroung has a good concrete ramp, two lanes wide, with loading floats.
- **China Bend Ramp:** And finally, China Bend, another National Park Service ramp, is one lane wide, with loading floats.

All National Park Service ramps have a $6 launch fee, which covers the round-trip, in and out of the water.

Besides the campgrounds with boat ramps listed above, there are other road-accessible National Park Service campgrounds at (working uplake from Hawk Creek) Columbia, Pierre, Wilmont Creek, Rogers Bar, AA Encampment (east side of the lake), Cloverleaf, Barnaby Creek (east side), Haag Cove (east side), Kamloops, and Kettle River (east side). Boat-in campsites include Ponderosa, Crystal Cove, Detellion (all on the Spokane Arm), Enterprise, and Barnaby Island (east side).

Seven Bays Marina has campsites, a restaurant, convenience store, propane, and moorage. Facilities at Kettle Falls include RV/tent sites, moorage and boat rentals, a large swim area, picnic area, RV dump station, showers, and a convenience store. Houseboats are available for rent at Seven Bays and Kettle Falls (as well as Keller Ferry, down the lake).

Directions: Take Highway 25 north from Davenport for 20 miles to parallel much of the east side of the lake.

Contact: National Park Service, Kettle Falls District, 509/738-6831; Seven Bays Marina, 509/725-1676; Roosevelt Recreational Enterprises, 800/648-LAKE (648-5253); Dakota Columbia Houseboat Adventures, 800/816-2431.

22 Browns Lake

If you want to capture the true essence of what fly-fishing is supposed to be all about, you owe it to yourself to visit Browns Lake. Located between two steep, timbered hillsides and with no development except the Forest Service campground on its south shore, this 88-acre lake is a haven for anglers who think that sport fishing should be peaceful, quiet, and relaxing. If you take your fly-fishing seriously, you might even be happy that you won't run into any bait soakers or spinner casters here, since the lake is open to fly-fishing only.

Cutthroats provide most of the angling action at Browns, and most of them are pan-sized fish in the 8- to 12-inch class. But don't be too surprised if you stumble onto a much bigger fish, something in the 16- or 18-inch class.

Don't be surprised, either, if you catch an occasional rainbow from Browns Lake. It seems there was a shortage of hatchery cutthroat stocks in the mid-1990s, and for at least one year rainbows were planted here. Any 'bow you catch now should be a whopper.

Because the lake's shoreline is so steep, bank fishing is tough, so you should consider using a boat or float tube to fish Browns Lake effectively (and safely).

Location: Northeast of Usk in Pend Oreille County; see map A5, grid d7.

Species: Cutthroat and rainbow trout.

Facilities: The south side of the lake has a U.S. Forest Service campground with tent and trailer sites, water, restrooms, and a boat ramp. The nearest lodging and other amenities are back on Highway 20.

Directions: Take Highway 20 along the Pend Oreille River to Kings Lake Road and the sign pointing east to Usk. Drive through town and stay on Kings Lake Road across the river and north past the Skookum Lakes. Turn left on Forest Service Road 5030 and follow it to the

campground on the shores of Browns Lake.
Contact: Colville National Forest, Newport Ranger District, 509/447-3129.

23 Skookum Lakes

Take your pick when it comes to fishing North Skookum and its twin to the south, where the trout fishing quality is about the same. Both lakes are open year-round and are stocked with hatchery rainbows that provide decent fishing in the spring, early summer, and again in the fall. Whether you like to troll, cast hardware, or simply sit and wait for a trout to come along and take a liking to whatever bait you happen to be soaking, you'll probably do OK at either lake.

While you're fishing, be sure to take in the scenery. The pine-covered hills and clean, high-country (3,500 feet) air make fishing a pleasure even when the trout aren't biting. The season here runs late April through October.

Location: Northeast of Usk in Pend Oreille County; see map A5, grid d7.

Species: Rainbow trout, some brook trout.

Facilities: Both lakes have boat ramps and U.S. Forest Service campgrounds on or near their shores. Those campgrounds have tent and trailer sites, drinking water, picnic tables, and restrooms. The nearest food, gas, tackle, and lodging are back on Highway 20.

Directions: Take Highway 20 along the Pend Oreille River to Kings Lake Road and the sign pointing east to Usk. Drive through town and stay on Kings Lake Road across the river and north six miles to the Skookum Lakes.

Contact: Colville National Forest, Newport Ranger District, 509/447-3129.

24 Bead Lake

Although open to year-round fishing, much of the angling action at Bead takes place during the winter when the lake freezes over and anglers converge here to fish for burbot.

These long, skinny, freshwater bottom fish are abundant in the big (over 700 acres) lake, and they're easiest to catch during the winter months. Jigging with various metal jigs or heavy spoons accounts for most of the fish, and a majority of anglers tip their jigs with night crawlers, strips of sucker meat, smelt, or some other natural bait. Working the jig-and-bait combination just off the bottom is often the key to success.

Variety comes when a big lake trout decides it likes the looks of one of the bait fish–imitating jigs and decides to inhale it. A 10-pound lake trout (Mackinaw) may not be a common catch, but it's certainly within the realm of possibility. These big Mackinaws can also be caught in early spring after the ice lid has melted away. Like lake trout everywhere in Washington, they're best fished with large plugs and spoons that imitate the smaller fish on which lake trout feed. Fish them near the surface soon after the ice melts, but as the water warms, you'll have to work deeper and deeper, using downriggers or leaded line to take your lure down where the fish are living. Trolling is also the way most anglers fish for kokanee here, and they make fair catches through the late spring and summer.

After three or four years without a boat ramp, there is now a launch facility at the lake's south end, in Mineral Bay. It's nothing fancy, and parking is limited, but it's a whole lot better than what was available after the old ramp at the north end of the lake was closed.

Location: East of Usk in Pend Oreille County; see map A5, grid d8.

Species: Burbot, lake trout (Mackinaw), kokanee.

Facilities: The lake now has a boat ramp at its south end, but there isn't much else in the way of facilities anywhere in the vicinity. The nearest food, gas, tackle, and lodging are on Highway 20 near Usk.

Directions: Take U.S. 2 to Newport and across the Pend Oreille River. Then take the first left onto LeClerc Creek Road and continue north up the east side of the river. A little over three miles from the bridge, go right on Bead Lake Road and follow it for six miles to the lake.

Contact: Colville National Forest, Newport Ranger District, 509/447-3129; Washington Department of Fish and Wildlife, Spokane Regional Office, 509/456-4082.

25 Marshall Lake

This deep, clear, cold lake about eight miles north of Newport with an April through October season was treated to remove rough fish in 1999 and once again offers excellent rainbow and cutthroat trout fishing, especially in the spring and fall. Although it has standard regulations that allow the use of bait and hardware, many anglers prefer to pursue Marshall's 'bows and cutthroats with artificial flies. Dry fly-fishing can be very good here in the spring, but in fall, when the trout are gorging in preparation for the long, cold Pend Oreille County winter, wet flies and nymph patterns get heavy play. Dragonfly nymphs, Renegades, Black Leeches, and Black Ant patterns are among the favorites. Some anglers use flies whose hooks are tipped with a mealworm, just for a little real protein to sweeten the pot.

Although Marshall's cool, clear waters are far from ideal for warm-water species, someone dumped bass and perch in them a few years back, so the Department of Fish and Wildlife treated the lake with rotenone in the fall of 1999. Marshall is once again a trout-only lake, at least until the next bozo decides to play neighborhood fish manager.

Location: North of Newport in Pend Oreille County; see map A5, grid e8.

Species: Cutthroat trout, rainbow trout.

Facilities: A public access area with a boat ramp and a private fishing resort with tackle, campsites, showers, and moorage are at the south end of the lake. Food, gas, tackle, and lodging are available in Newport.

Directions: Take U.S. 2 to Newport and cross the Pend Oreille River on the east side of town. Take the first left onto LeClerc Creek Road after crossing the bridge and drive about three miles to Bead Lake Road. Turn right on Bead Lake Road, drive three miles, and turn right on Marshall Lake Road, which leads one mile to the lake.

Contact: Marshall Lake Resort, 509/447-4158, email: grimes1@povn.com.

26 Pend Oreille River

One of eastern Washington's largest rivers—more than 100 yards wide in spots—the Pend Oreille is in many ways an untapped angling resource. Although popular with many local anglers, it doesn't get the publicity and attention it deserves.

The river itself is big and wide, and when you add the many sloughs and side channels, it becomes a virtual potpourri of warm- and cold-water fishing possibilities. Pen-raised rainbows are abundant, and if you're willing to put in the time and effort, you might be rewarded with a hefty brown trout. The bass fishing is some of eastern Washington's best, especially in the warmer sloughs where largemouths congregate to spawn in the late spring and early summer. These same sloughs offer large numbers of crappies, and there are places where a few hours casting a bobber and a worm will produce all the yellow perch you need for a neighborhood fish fry. The Pend Oreille is best fished by boat, but don't get careless and forget that it's a moving, ever-changing river.

The season here runs year-round, but trout fishing is best in May and June. Bass and panfish action is tops June through August.

Location: Flows south from British Columbia

through Pend Oreille County and into Idaho at Newport; see map A5, grid e8.

Species: Rainbow and some brown trout, largemouth bass, crappie, yellow perch.

Facilities: Boat ramps are located at several points along the river, including near Newport, Dalkena, Usk, Ruby, Blueside, Ione, and Metaline. Food, gas, tackle, and lodging are available in Newport, Usk, Metaline, Ione, and at other points along the highway.

Directions: Take Highway 20 north from Newport and drive about 40 miles to the town of Tiger. From Tiger upstream, Highway 31 parallels several miles of the river.

Contact: Newport Chamber of Commerce, 509/447-5812, website: www.pendoreille.org; Keo's Korner, 509/445-1294; Blueside Resort, 509/445-1327, website: www.bluesideresort .com; Circle Motel (in Metaline), 509/446-4343; Box Canyon Resort, 509/442-3728; Boundary Dam, 509/446-3083; Colville National Forest, Newport Ranger District, 509/447-3129.

27 Davis Lake

Though not very well known to most Washington anglers, this 150-acre lake is easily accessible and offers a wide variety of angling opportunities. The lake is a long drive away for western Washington anglers, and those living in the Spokane area have plenty of other productive trout and bass lakes from which to choose for their weekend activities. As a result, Davis usually offers plenty of elbowroom, especially if you fish it during the week. Spring and fall provide the best fishing, but the season is open year-round.

Fish your favorite baits and lures during April and May for trout. For kokanee, pull trolling blades with Wedding Ring spinners behind or stillfish with maggots on Glo Hooks in July and August. Early morning and evening fishing for bass are also best in July and August.

Location: South of Usk; see map A5, grid e6.

Species: Rainbow and brook trout, kokanee, largemouth bass.

Facilities: A public access area with a boat ramp is located on the lake. The nearest lodging and RV facilities are in Usk, to the north. Food, gas, lodging, and tackle are available in Newport.

Directions: Drive north from Spokane on U.S. 2 for about 25 miles and turn left (north) on Highway 211, following it about 10 miles to the lake, which is on the left.

Contact: Hotel Usk, 509/445-1526; Keo's Korner, 509/445-1294.

28 Waitts Lake

If asked to name the lake that produced the state-record rainbow trout that stood atop the record list for more than 30 years, most Evergreen State anglers would fail the quiz. The fact that I'm mentioning it here should be a good clue. Bill Dittner caught a whopping 22.5-pounder at Waitts Lake back in 1957. Waitts continues to give up some big trout even to this day, although nothing approaching 22 pounds has been recorded lately.

The 450-acre lake is stocked with both rainbows and browns, and they put on weight and inches quickly. Carryovers are common, and many of them range to 17 inches and larger. If you don't have trophies on your mind, go with a string of trolling blades and a Wedding Ring spinner tipped with worms. But if you want a crack at a lunker, try trolling a Rapala or similar plug in a perch pattern, gold, or some shade of brown. The most popular trolling area is around the Winona Beach outlet. If stillfishing is your bag, stay well into the evening and soak green or pink Power Bait on a Glo Hook. Like to cast flies for your browns and 'bows? The locals recommend a green Muddler Minnow tied on a fairly large hook. Those angling efforts may also turn up a hefty brown trout.

While Waitts is known to most as a trout

lake, it also produces its share of husky large-mouth bass, some of them topping five pounds. The docks and floats produce most of the big ones, and anglers like to coax them out from hiding with spinnerbaits, crankbaits, or various plastic worms. There's also some decent fishing for good-sized yellow perch.

The lake has an April through October season, but trout fishing is best in May. Largemouths hit best May through July.

Location: West of Valley in Stevens County; see map A5, grid e3.

Species: Rainbow and brown trout, largemouth bass, yellow perch.

Facilities: The lake has a public access area and public boat ramp, as well as two privately owned resorts that offer RV and tent sites, cabins, boat rentals, groceries, tackle, and other facilities. Gas is available on U.S. 395.

Directions: Take U.S. 395 north from Spokane and after 23 miles turn west (left) at Loon Lake on Highway 292, following it seven miles to Springdale. Proceed north from Springdale on Highway 231 to the town of Valley and turn west (left) on Waitts Lake Road, following it about four miles to the lake.

Contact: Silver Beach Resort, 509/937-2811; Waitts Lake Resort, 509/937-2400; Winona Beach Resort, 509/937-2231, website: www.gocampingamerica.com/winona.

29 Borgeau Lake

This little, 12-acre lake doesn't get nearly as much angling attention as some of the bigger, more famous lakes on the Colville Reservation, but it does offer decent trout and bass fishing. The season usually opens in mid-May and runs through October, with trout fishing best through June and bass hitting June–August. Tribal fishing permits are required and can be obtained from businesses in the area. The cost is $15 for three days, $20 for seven days, and $30 for the calendar year.

Location: On the Colville Indian Reservation, south of Inchelium in Ferry County; see map A5, grid e1.

Species: Rainbow trout, largemouth bass.

Facilities: There isn't much at the lake, but limited facilities are available in Inchelium. Food, gas, and lodging are available in Kettle Falls.

Directions: Take Highway 20 east from Republic or west from Kettle Falls, turn south at Sherman Creek onto Inchelium–Kettle Falls Road, and follow it 22 miles to Inchelium. From there turn right on Twin Lakes Road and drive about two miles west, then turn south (left) on Silver Creek Road. Drive another three miles and turn west (right) on Apex Road, following it two miles to the lake, which is on the right.

Contact: Colville Confederated Tribes, Fish and Wildlife Department, 509/634-8845, website: www.colvilletribes.com.

30 North Twin Lake

Sprawling over more than 700 acres, North Twin is a big lake with some big trout. The thick-bodied rainbows grow to impressive size, and even some of the usually sleek brook trout are on the chunky side. Trollers typically go with strings of trolling blades, followed by Wedding Ring spinners or any of the usual trout offerings in some shade of green. Common wisdom around the lake also dictates using any lure with a red spot on it, so take along that bright red fingernail polish or fluorescent paint and be ready to do some customizing if the rainbows and brookies aren't showing enough interest in what you happen to be using. If you aren't into painting your trout spoons and spinners, try stillfishing with such proven trout getters as night crawlers and Berkley Power Bait.

If bass fishing is your bag—or if you catch your eight-fish trout limit early and are looking for something else to do—give North Twin largemouths a try. Like other lakes on the Colville Indian Reservation, this one has a liberal, 25-bass daily limit, only two of which may be over 14 inches long. The idea is that there are lots of small, stunted bass in the lake, and the Colville fish managers would like to see them thinned out. The lily pads and weed beds along the north side of the lake provide some of the fastest bass fishing.

Colville fishing permits are required. They're available at Rainbow Beach Resort (see below) or from businesses throughout the area and cost $15 for three days, $20 for seven days, and $30 for the calendar year.

Location: West of Inchelium on the Colville Indian Reservation; see map A5, grid e0.

Species: Rainbow and brook trout, largemouth bass, some kokanee.

Facilities: A privately owned fishing resort on the north side of the lake offers all the necessities.

Directions: Take Highway 20 east from Republic or west from Kettle Falls, turn south at Sherman Creek onto Inchelium–Kettle Falls Road, and follow it for about 22 miles to Inchelium. From there go west (right) on Twin Lakes Road, following it a little over eight miles to the lake.

Contact: Rainbow Beach Resort, 509/722-5901, email: rainbowbeach@theofficenet.com.

31 South Twin Lake

At more than 900 acres, South Twin is one heck of a big lake, and you could spend the better part of a month getting to know all of its secrets. Add North Twin Lake (number 30) to the menu and you can plan on staying busy all summer. Both trolling and stillfishing produce good catches of husky rainbows and some larger-than-average brook trout. Bass fishing is also good, especially if you don't mind catching a lot of small fish for every lunker you manage to hook. The daily bass limit is a liberal 25 fish, established in hopes of encouraging anglers to harvest a lot of the smaller fish. Only two of those 25 fish you

keep may be over 14 inches long. Tribal fishing permits—not state licenses—are required and are available from businesses throughout the area. The cost is $15 for three days, $20 for seven days, and $30 for the year.

Location: Southwest of Inchelium in the Colville Indian Reservation; see map A5, grid e0.

Species: Rainbow and brook trout, largemouth bass.

Facilities: A private resort with campsites, showers, bait, tackle, boat rentals, and moorage is located near the north end of the lake. The nearest food, gas, tackle, and lodging are in Kettle Falls and Chewelah.

Directions: Take Highway 20 east from Republic or west from Kettle Falls, turn south at Sherman Creek onto Inchelium–Kettle Falls Road, and follow it about 22 miles to Inchelium. From there go west on Twin Lakes Road and follow it about eight miles to the road turning south (right) to the lake.

Contact: Hartman's Log Cabin Resort, 509/722-3543 (April through October).

32 Jumpoff Joe Lake

Rainbow and brook trout do well at Jumpoff Joe, and anglers do well fishing for them. Both species carry over well through the winter, giving anglers a chance to catch some large trout in the 14- to 17-inch range. Brown trout have also been stocked here in recent years, providing some two- to five-pound browns to sweeten the angling pot. Favorite stillfishing baits include white or yellow corn, Pautzke salmon eggs, night crawlers, marshmallows, and Berkley Power Bait. Trollers favor Rooster Tails in shades of green, brown, yellow, and orange; Dardevles; and Kastmasters of one-eighth- to one-quarter-ounce size. Carey Specials and other fly patterns are also popular with some trollers. As for bass, they seem to prefer plastic worms fished around the docks, piers, and floats, especially if those worms are black or another dark color.

Location: Southeast of Valley in Stevens County; see map A5, grid f4.

Species: Rainbow and brook trout, largemouth bass, yellow perch, bluegill.

Facilities: Jumpoff Joe Resort has tent and RV sites, cabins, boat rentals, moorage, and fishing docks. The lake also has a public access area and boat ramp. Food, gas, tackle, and lodging are available in Chewelah.

Directions: Take U.S. 395 north from Spokane for 32 miles to Beitey Road and turn east (left). Turn left again on Jumpoff Joe Road and follow it one mile to the east side of the lake.

Contact: Jumpoff Joe Resort, 509/937-2133.

33 Deer Lake

Whether trout and kokanee ring your chimes or bass and panfish are your idea of worthy opponents, you'll find worthwhile angling action at Deer Lake, where there's something to fish for from the opening bell in April until the season comes to a close at the end of October.

Lake trout, or Mackinaw, are a big draw when the season opens, especially if the spring has been cool and the water temperatures are down far enough to keep the big lakers near the surface. Trolling with big plugs and spoons, like those used for saltwater salmon, will do the job if the big Macks are on the bite. If April weather is warm and the fish have gone deeper, you'll have to use leaded line or downriggers to take your plugs and spoons down to the action. Using your depthsounder to locate the fish is a big plus in giving you some idea at what depth you should be trolling.

Kokanee fishing has also been a big draw at Deer Lake for many years. The lake, in fact, gave up several record-class kokanee during the 1970s, and it still offers the chance for a koke in the three-pound class or larger.

Trolling Kokanee Killers, Triple Teazers, Wedding Rings, and all the other popular kokanee spoons and spinners works; just remember to lace those hooks with a kernel of shoepeg corn or a couple of maggots. Corn and maggots are also popular for stillfishing, which becomes the method of choice for summertime kokanee fishing. Many anglers concentrate their efforts during the night, when Glo Hooks (a brand of hook painted with luminescent paint) are an important part of the arsenal.

Brook trout can be found throughout much of the lake, especially around the edges where they're easy to get at with fly rods, spinning outfits, or trolling gear. You can even catch brookies from the bank at the resorts and public access area.

Rainbow trout are stocked in Deer every year, and they're caught on a variety of trolled and stillfished offerings. The Triple Teazers and Wedding Rings that work for kokanee will certainly take rainbows, as will Flatfish and Kwikfish in metallic finishes, Rooster Tail and BangTail spinners, or plain ol' gang-troll-and-worm combinations. Salmon eggs, marshmallows, Berkley Power Bait, and yellow corn will also do the job.

Largemouth and smallmouth bass are fairly abundant, especially around the narrow arm at the north end of the lake and in the relatively shallow flats near the southeast corner.

Location: Northeast of Loon Lake; see map A5, grid f4.

Species: Rainbow, brook, and lake trout; kokanee; smallmouth and largemouth bass; brown bullhead catfish; yellow perch; crappie.

Facilities: The lake has a public access area with a boat ramp, as well as two private resorts.

Directions: Drive north from Spokane on U.S. 395 for 26 miles and turn east (right) on Deer Lake Loop Road. Follow it about two miles to the lake.

Contact: Deer Lake Resort, 509/233-2081, website: www.deerlakeresort.com; Sunrise Point Resort, 509/233-2342.

34 Loon Lake

Like Deer Lake a few miles away (see number 33), Loon has something to offer every angler. The biggest fish in the lake are Mackinaws, or lake trout, and they sometimes top 20 pounds. (Loon gave up a whopper Mackinaw in the mid-1960s that weighed in at more than 30 pounds and stood as the state record until 1999.) Trolling large plugs accounts for most of them. Sutton spoons, blue Flatfish, and Kwikfish are popular, but other offerings in various shades of blue or pink are also effective. You can troll near the surface the first week or two of the season, but as the water warms, break out the downrigger and take that plug into the cool depths. If you're not a troller, use your depthsounder to locate fish, position your boat over them, and work a metal jig up and down until you coax them into striking.

Rainbows, browns, and brookies are all stocked with varying regularity, so you shouldn't have much trouble finding productive trout fishing throughout the spring. Troll the open water for rainbows and browns, the shallow shoreline areas for brookies. Rooster Tail spinners in brown or black shades seem to work best, or at least they're the favorite of local trout anglers.

Both trolling and stillfishing are top methods for taking Loon Lake kokanee, perhaps the most popular fish in the lake. As a general rule, trolling works better in the spring and early summer, with stillfishing gaining popularity about midsummer. Some anglers fish at night and report better catches than many of the daytime anglers. Favorite trolling rigs include leaded line, Kokanee Killers, or Luhr Jensen Cherry Bombs and hooks tipped with maggots or white corn.

Largemouth bass are found along much of the lake's west side, while smallmouths are often found hanging close to the rocky shoreline near the southwest corner of the lake. Fishing the docks and floats around the lake may take either or both.

Location: At the town of Loon Lake; see map A5, grid f4.

Species: Rainbow, brook, brown, and lake trout; kokanee; largemouth and smallmouth bass; yellow perch; crappie; brown bullhead catfish.

Facilities: While the west side of the lake has a public access area and boat ramp, both sides of the lake have privately owned resorts with boat rentals, moorage, RV and tent sites, cabins, and groceries.

Directions: Drive north from Spokane on U.S. 395 for 25 miles until you see the lake on the left. Turn at the Granite Point Park sign along the highway or turn left on Highway 292 to get to the north and west sides of the lake.

Contact: Granite Point Park, 509/233-2100, website: www.granitepointpark.com; Shore Acres Resort, 509/233-2474 or 800/900-2474.

35 Sacheen Lake

This cool, clear lake provides very good fishing for both rainbow and brook trout throughout the spring and early summer, with the brookies coming on strong again in the fall. All the usual stillfishing and trolling techniques work, and fly-fishing is also popular on warm spring and summer evenings.

The lake is unusual in that it offers steep banks where the water drops right off from shore to 30 or 40 feet in many areas, the kind of shoreline many anglers—especially trollers—like to explore. Adding to the intrigue are the many bays and shallow reefs, especially around the south end of the lake. Perhaps the lake's most interesting feature, though, is the deep hole at its extreme south end, where the shoreline drops away quickly into an abyss more than 70 feet deep. It might be a good place to look for trout in July or August.

Location: Near Highway 211 west of Newport; see map A5, grid f6.

Species: Rainbow and brook trout.

Facilities: The lake has a public access area and boat ramp. Diamond Lake Resort is a few miles away, to the southeast, off U.S. 2. Food, gas, tackle, and lodging are available in Newport.

Directions: Take U.S. 2 north from Spokane for about 25 miles and turn north (left) on Highway 211. The lake is on the left, about four miles off U.S. 2.

Contact: Diamond Lake Resort, 509/447-4474 (spring to fall only); Washington Department of Fish and Wildlife, Spokane Office, 509/456-4082.

36 Diamond Lake

Diamond was once primarily a trout lake offering lunker-class cutthroats and rainbows, but the Department of Fish and Wildlife says that illegally stocked bass and panfish have added variety but had a negative impact on the trout fishery. The fishing is still pretty good for 10- to 14-inch rainbows, and an occasional trophy-class cutthroat may still be found. In 2001 the lake received a healthy dose of fat triploid rainbows, which should provide anglers a good chance at a trophy trout now and then for the next few years.

The rule of thumb for trout anglers is "think deep, think green," especially as the water warms in the summer. A deep-trolled Carey Special fly in green or fluorescent green is a local favorite for rainbows and cutts. If you prefer stillfishing, go with a night crawler or green Berkley Power Bait, and fish it deeper and deeper as the season progresses. If you can locate one of the many underground

springs that feed the lake, so much the better for summertime fishing.

Location: Southwest of Newport; see map A5, grid e7.

Species: Rainbow and cutthroat trout, largemouth and smallmouth bass, yellow perch, brown bullhead catfish.

Facilities: The lake has a public access area and boat ramp, as well as a privately owned resort with tackle, RV and tent sites, boat moorage, fuel, and some groceries. Food, gas, tackle, and lodging are available in Newport.

Directions: Take U.S. 2 north from Spokane for 32 miles until you pass within casting distance of the lake's south side. Diamond Lake Road runs almost completely around the lake.

Contact: Diamond Lake Resort, 509/447-4474 (spring to fall only); Washington Department of Fish and Wildlife, Spokane Office, 509/456-4082.

37 Horseshoe Lake

If you like a little bit of everything when you visit a lake, and pretty scenery to boot, this spot off the beaten path is worth a few days of your time. Planted rainbows draw much of the attention from anglers, but trolling for kokanee with Wedding Ring spinners tipped with maggots is also productive. Limited numbers of lake trout don't get a lot of publicity, but hooking a 10-pounder is a possibility. When the weather warms in summer, work the shoreline shallows for bass, crappies, and other warmwater fish. The lake has a late April through October season.

Location: North of Eloika Lake in southwestern Pend Oreille County; see map A5, grid f6.

Species: Rainbow and a few lake trout, kokanee, largemouth bass, yellow perch, crappie.

Facilities: The lake has a public access area, a boat ramp, and toilets, as well as resort facilities that include cabins, RV hookups, tent sites, boat rentals, and a small store with groceries and tackle.

Directions: Take U.S. 2 north from Spokane for 20 miles and turn west (left) on Eloika Lake Road, following it three miles to Division Road. Turn north (right) on Division Road, which becomes Horseshoe Lake Road somewhere along the line, and follow it 7.5 miles to the lake.

Contact: Westbrook Resort, 509/276-9221.

38 Fan Lake

Liberal plants of hatchery trout make Fan Lake a good bet for anglers who want to get away from most of the crowds to do their trout fishing. Although not overlooked by local anglers, Fan certainly doesn't get the fishing pressure of the bigger and better-known trout lakes in the Stevens/Spokane/Pend Oreille Counties area. The ban on gas-powered boats may be part of the reason, or maybe it's the fact that Fan Lake closes to fishing at the end of September, a month earlier than most other lakes in the area. Whatever the reason, you'll find less competition and decent trout fishing. I think it's just about perfect for evening fly-fishing, but feel free to take along your hardware or bait; it all works here.

Location: Northeast of Deer Park; see map A5, grid f6.

Species: Rainbow and cutthroat trout.

Facilities: The lake has a public access area and a boat ramp. The nearest food, gas, tackle, and lodging are in Deer Park.

Directions: Take U.S. 2 north from Spokane for 20 miles and turn east (left) on Eloika Lake Road. After about three miles, the road makes a 90-degree left, then a 90-degree right, and another 90-degree left. At that second left, bear right onto the gravel side road that leads about 1.5 miles to Fan Lake.

Contact: Jerry's Landing, 509/292-2337; Washington Department of Fish and Wildlife, Spokane Office, 509/456-4082.

39 Eloika Lake

This has been one of my favorite lakes since I caught my first decent-sized Eloika bass back in the late 1970s, and I'm sure lots of other anglers feel the same way. Eloika is a bass and panfish angler's paradise, with very little shoreline development and lots of cattails, weed beds, and overhanging brush to explore. The largemouths can run well in excess of five pounds, but it takes them a long time to get that big. That's part of the reason most anglers release their bass here. The other reason is that they like to catch them over and over again. Among the effective bass-getting techniques are pitching plastic worms and plastic lizards into the shoreline cover and working spinnerbaits along the edges of the weeds and around the brush piles.

Both the perch and crappies are big enough to interest anglers, which you can't say about the panfish populations in all Washington lakes. Suspending a small leadhead with a plastic skirt or tube body will take the crappies, and you can add a piece of worm to the same rig and draw lots of interest from the perch. Stick around until darkness sets in and pitch a night crawler or chicken liver around until you find a few cooperative catfish.

This is one of the few eastern Washington lakes where trout fishing takes a back seat to warm-water species. Some respectable brookies and planted brown trout are available; the best fishing for them is in the spring and fall.

Oh yes, Eloika is open year-round, so you can fish it whenever you feel the urge. But most people don't feel the urge very much during cold Spokane County winters.

Location: Northeast of Deer Park; see map A5, grid f6.

Species: Largemouth bass; yellow perch; crappie; brown bullhead catfish; brown, rainbow, and brook trout.

Facilities: There's a public access area and boat ramp near the southeast corner of the lake and a resort about halfway up the east side that offers tent and trailer sites, fuel, moorage, tackle, and some groceries. Food, gas, tackle, and lodging are also available to the south in Deer Park.

Directions: Take U.S. 2 north from Spokane for 22 miles and turn west (left) on Bridges Road or Oregon Road to reach the east side of the lake.

Contact: Jerry's Landing, 509/292-2337; Washington Department of Fish and Wildlife, Spokane Office, 509/456-4082.

40 Mudgett Lake

The lake is stocked quite generously with hatchery rainbows, and they provide good fishing for a few weeks after the late-April opener. From then on things get pretty tough, although thanks to easy access and light traffic, this is a pleasant place to take the kids for an afternoon of laid-back fishing any time during the season. That season, by the way, runs through October.

Mudgett was treated with rotenone to remove largemouth bass in 1988 and is once again the home of rainbow trout only.

Location: South of Fruitland in Stevens County; see map A5, grid f1.

Species: Rainbow trout.

Facilities: The lake has a public access area where it's possible to launch a small boat. The nearest food, gas, tackle, and lodging are to the south in Davenport and to the north in Kettle Falls.

Directions: Drive north from Davenport on Highway 25, across the Spokane River Arm of Lake Roosevelt for about 20 miles. Turn east (right) on the Old Highway 22 Cutoff Road, drive a mile, and turn north on Old Highway 22. Drive 2.5 miles to the lake, which is on the left.

Contact: Washington Department of Fish and Wildlife, Spokane Office, 509/456-4082.

41 Bear Lake

This little 34-acre lake is so handy that everyone passing by on the highway should stop in and make a few casts. If you want trout, try casting a one-eighth-ounce Panther Martin spinner in black or brown or a Rooster Tail in silver or red, a couple of the favorites here. If you're into fly-fishing, break out the long rod and tie on a mosquito or leech pattern and work it around the shoreline.

Although anglers don't seem to catch many big bass at Bear Lake, there are enough smaller largemouths to make spending a few hours pitching plastic worms or spinnerbaits around the shoreline cover worthwhile. And if it's panfish you want, suspend a worm about four feet beneath a bobber and cast for perch. A few crappies call the lake home, too; replace that worm with a red-and-white Mini Jig below the bobber to catch them.

Location: North of Chattaroy in Spokane County; see map A5, grid g6.

Species: Rainbow trout, largemouth bass, yellow perch, crappie.

Facilities: There's bank access and a fishing dock near the north end of the lake, and it's easy to carry a small boat to the water for launching.

Directions: Drive north from Spokane on U.S. 2. The lake is 2.8 miles north of Chattaroy on the west (left) side of the highway.

Contact: Big 5 Sporting Goods, 509/533-9811; Washington Department of Fish and Wildlife, Spokane Office, 509/456-4082.

42 Little Spokane River

Although it doesn't receive large plants of hatchery trout, the Little Spokane does offer the possibility of decent catches, and some of the trout are surprisingly large. Try your hand with a fly rod and you'll have a good time even if you don't catch any fish. But plenty of 10- to 12-inch rainbows and eager 7- to 10-inch brookies are available to practi-

cally guarantee you'll find something in a biting mood. And, just to keep you on your toes,
the Little Spokane does have a few 20- to 24-
inch brown trout, making for the possibility of
a fantastic day if one of them comes to life on
your visit. Trout season here runs from late
April through October.

If you get the fishing bug during the dead
of winter, the Little Spokane has a winter
whitefish season that provides some good
fishing opportunity December 1 through
March 31.

A lot of private property borders this pretty
little stream, and many of the landowners are
unwilling to allow angling access, so you
won't be able to fish wherever you want along
the Little Spokane. Ask permission and don't
foul it up for the rest of us by trespassing.

Location: Joins the Spokane River at Nine
Mile Falls; see map A5, grid g6.

Species: Rainbow, brook, and brown trout;
mountain whitefish.

Facilities: Riverside State Park, located near
the mouth of the Little Spokane, has a limited number of tent and RV sites. Resorts on
Eloika and Diamond Lakes are good possibilities for the upper reaches of the river. In
between are lots of motels in and around
Spokane, as well as restaurants and other
amenities.

Directions: To reach the lower portion of the
river, take U.S. 395 north from Spokane about
three miles and turn west (left) on Hawthorne
Road, following it two miles and turning
south (left) to Waikiki Road, which crosses
and parallels parts of the river. To reach areas
farther upstream, drive north from Spokane
on U.S. 2, turning west (left) on various county roads to reach the river downstream from
Chattaroy. Roads to the east reach the river
above Chattaroy, where the highway crosses
over the river. Bridges, Oregon, and Scotia
Roads are among the possibilities on this
upper stretch of the Little Spokane.

Contact: Riverside State Park, 509/456-3964;
Washington State Parks and Recreation
Commission, 360/902-8844 (information) or
800/452-5687 (reservations); Big 5 Sporting
Goods, 509/533-9811(reservations); Wash-
ington Department of Fish and Wildlife,
Spokane Office, 509/456-4082.

43 Long Lake

Some people come to Long Lake to troll gang-
troll-and-worm rigs or spoons and spinners
for trout, while others come to work spinnerbaits, plastic worms, crankbaits, and other
offerings along the shoreline for bass. Both
groups consider this lower Spokane River
impoundment a pretty good fishery. Now and
then an angler hooks something unusual,
such as a big, nasty northern pike, though
that's probably not something you'd come
here specifically to do. But then again, if
you're the patient type who doesn't mind
casting all weekend for the possibility of a
single strike, you might want to gear up and
try your luck on northerns.

Long Lake is a big impoundment with miles
and miles of shoreline, so at least you'll get to
see a lot of scenery as you work your way
along the shore in search of that toothy trophy. The best time to fish Long Lake is during
the spring and early summer, from about
April through June.

Location: Spokane River impoundment west
of Spokane; see map A5, grid g4.

Species: Largemouth and smallmouth bass,
crappie, rainbow and brown trout, walleye,
northern pike.

Facilities: The lake has a public access area
with a boat ramp and a resort, both of them
on the north side, off Highway 291. The resort has moorage, tackle, RV sites, and
showers. Riverside State Park is also within
fairly easy driving range of about 18 miles.
Food, gas, tackle, and lodging are available in
Davenport.

Directions: Take I-90 to Sprague and turn north on Highway 231, following it for 26 miles to U.S. 2. Turn east on U.S. 2 and drive about three miles to Reardan; then continue north on Highway 231 for 12 miles, all the way to the Spokane River below Long Lake Dam. Cross the river and immediately turn east (right) on Corkscrew Canyon Road. Drive five miles and turn right on the gravel road that drops down the hill and leads to the boat ramp.

Contact: Riverside State Park, 509/456-3964; Washington State Parks and Recreation Commission, 360/902-8844 (information) or 800/452-5687 (reservations); Nine Mile Falls Resort, 509/468-8422 (Memorial Day through Labor Day); Washington Department of Fish and Wildlife, Spokane Office, 509/456-4082.

44 Newman Lake

Talk about 1,200 acres of fishing variety and you can only mean Newman Lake, perhaps one of Spokane County's best-kept fishing secrets. Not only is the lake huge, but it's one of those places where you never know what you're going to pull out of the water next. Both rainbows and browns are stocked in the lake for trout anglers, while bass anglers come in search of trophy-class largemouths and are often rewarded handsomely for their efforts. Fish during the day and you'll find good numbers of crappies, bluegills, and perch; fish at night and you'll find bullhead catfish in a biting mood.

The pot has become even sweeter with the addition of tiger muskies to the Newman Lake angling menu. The fast-growing, mean-spirited tigers were stocked to help eliminate a pesky sucker population, but they'll also provide some wonderful trophy fishing in the coming years, just as they've done in western Washington's Mayfield Lake (see number 65 in chapter B2). They'll hit large bucktail spinners and plugs similar to those used for bass, only a little bigger. With all

this angling variety, you can expect to have just one serious problem if you're heading for Newman Lake for the first time: You may not have enough room in your car for all the tackle you might need.

Location: Northeast of Spokane near the Idaho border; see map A5, grid g8.

Species: Rainbow and brown trout, large-mouth bass, tiger muskies, crappie, yellow perch, bluegill, yellow bullhead catfish.

Facilities: The lake has a public access area and boat ramp, as well as private resort facilities with all the amenities.

Directions: Drive east from Spokane on Highway 290 for about 12 miles and turn north (left) on Newman Lake Road.

Contact: Cherokee Landing Resort, 509/226-3843; Sutton Bay Resort, 509/226-3660.

45 Spokane River

Special regulations, including wild fish–release rules and restrictions on the use of bait, have helped to make the Spokane a respectable trophy-trout fishery in recent years. The stretch of river east of Spokane, which offers some beautiful trout water, is where I would recommend going if you really want to sample what this pretty river has to offer. The problem may be getting to the water, since brush crowds the bank in many areas. There are man-made trails through it in some places, but in other spots you avoid the brush by staying in the river.

Take along a good selection of Muddler Minnows and other streamer patterns if you plan on fly-fishing in search of a bragging-sized fish. If you prefer casting hardware for your trout, try a quarter-ounce BangTail or Rooster Tail spinner or a three-eighths-ounce Krocodile spoon. And remember that the lure must have a single, barbless hook, so replace that treble or clip off two of the points. A limited number of hatchery rainbows are planted here every year to provide some put-and-take harvest. The river is open to year-round fishing, but some of the best trout action is in the very early spring (March and April) and late fall (October and early November). Various parts of the Spokane have various regulations for trout and other species, so be sure to study the fishing pamphlet carefully for details on the stretch of river you plan to fish.

Location: Flows westerly through Spokane and into the east side of Lake Roosevelt at Fort Spokane; see map A5, grid h8.

Species: Rainbow and some brown trout.

Facilities: The best-known and most popular put-in/take-out spot on the river is at Plantes Ferry Park, managed by the Spokane County Parks and Recreation Department. Located on Upstream Drive (Wellesley Road), it's a natural-surface ramp where boats can be trailered or hand carried to the river. Upstream is a hand-carry launching spot at the north end of the Harvard Road bridge, and downstream it's possible to hand carry a boat from the water at Upriver Dam. Downstream from Spokane Falls, some paddlers hand carry their boats to the water at the base of the Maple Street bridge, and there's a popular put-in/take-out spot just downstream from the Fort Wright Drive bridge over the river, near Fort Spokane Community College. The ramps at Nine Mile Resort and Riverside State Park are on slow-water sections of the Spokane, near the upper end of Long Lake. Both are concrete ramps with loading floats. If you should decide to float the river in any kind of boat, you should be aware of the county regulation requiring all river boaters to wear a U.S. Coast Guard–approved life jacket. Food, gas, lodging, and tackle are available throughout the area. Riverside State Park, about seven miles west of Spokane on the north side of the river, has a limited number of tent and RV sites, showers, and other facilities.

Directions: Drive north out of Spokane on U.S. 395, then turn east (left) to reach portions of the river from downtown Spokane to the upper end of Long Lake. Drive east from town on I-90 and take roads to the north to reach the section of river between Spokane and the Idaho state line.

Contact: Silver Bow Fly Shop, 509/483-1772; Riverside State Park, 509/456-3964; Washington State Parks and Recreation Commission, 360/902-8844 (information) or 800/452-5687 (reservations).

46 Liberty Lake

Liberty used to be one of the Spokane area's top trout producers, but now warm-water species provide a mixed-bag fishery, and trout fishing is only a small part of the picture. The lake produces some big bass, many of them caught from the numerous docks and floats that dot much of the lake's shoreline. Perch, crappies, and bluegills are abundant around many of the same docks and floats, but don't be surprised if you locate a school of them just about anywhere around the edges of the lake. The put-and-take trout fishery provides fish for anglers using any and all of the usual trout baits and lures, so practice your favorite technique, and you'll be satisfied with the results. The trout plants here include both rainbows and browns.

Walleyes were stocked in the lake to provide additional fishing and help reduce the numbers of small warm-water fish after local residents resisted Department of Fish and Wildlife attempts to treat the lake with rotenone. The result is a new walleye fishery that was just starting to get noticed during the 1999 season. Look for better things to come on that front.

If you're into night fishing, you'll find good numbers of brown bullheads available in the spring and summer. The Liberty Lake season runs from late April through September.

Location: East of Spokane; see map A5, grid h8.

Species: Rainbow and brown trout, largemouth bass, walleye, yellow perch, crappie, bluegill, brown bullhead catfish.

Facilities: The lake has a public access area and boat ramp, with RV parks, food, gas, tackle, and lodging available in Liberty Lake and Spokane.

Directions: Take I-90 east from Spokane for 12 miles and turn south (right) at the signs pointing the way to Liberty Lake. The lake is about 1.5 miles off the freeway, on the left side of the road.

Contact: Sportsmen's Surplus, 509/467-5970; Washington Department of Fish and Wildlife, Spokane Office, 509/456-4082.

47 West Medical Lake

Food-rich West Medical Lake has many times been described as one of Washington's top trout producers, and I've been among those praising it. The lake bottom is alive with freshwater shrimp, dobsonfly larvae, and other creepy crawlers too numerous to mention, and the rainbows gorge on them, growing as fast as an inch a month during certain times of the year. It had some problems with non-trout species until 2000, when it was treated with rotenone and restocked with both rainbows and brown trout. Hefty triploid rainbows were added to the angling menu in 2001.

West Medical has so much food in it that the trout don't even have to work at it, and that's why some regulars say trolling isn't all that productive. "Why should the trout go out of their way to chase down a moving lure when there's all this stuff just sitting around for the taking?" they reason. Makes sense. Whatever the reason, stillfishing produces some of the best catches of rainbows, and the bait of choice is a live dobsonfly larva, fished by itself or in conjunction with a salmon egg, worm, or marshmallow.

If you simply can't sit still for stillfishing, some trolling lures seem to work better than others here. They include Luhr Jensen Needlefish in red and rainbow finishes, redhead Triple Teazers, Wedding Ring spinners, red Rooster Tails, and nickel/redhead or fire Super Dupers.

Lots of West Medical anglers do their fishing with flies, either the dry kind that float on the surface or the nymphs that sink toward the bottom and imitate the dobsonflies and other natural inhabitants of the lake upon which the rainbows feed. Speaking from personal experience, I can tell you that you don't have to be very good at fly-fishing to catch trout here on artificials.

One more important word of advice: The undeveloped west side of the lake always seems to provide better fishing than the east side. You may want to prospect around a little, but chances are you'll end up along the lake's eastern shoreline, like most everybody else.

Location: West of the town of Medical Lake; see map A5, grid i4.

Species: Rainbow trout, brown trout, triploid rainbows.

Facilities: A public access area with a boat ramp is located on the west side of the lake, while the south end has a privately owned resort with rental boats, a fishing dock, tackle, a café, showers, RV hookups, and snacks. The nearest gas is in the town of Medical Lake.

Directions: Take I-90 east from Sprague for 16 miles or west from Spokane for 14 miles. Turn north on Salnave Road (Highway 902) and go about six miles. Before getting to the town of Medical Lake, turn west (left) on Fancher Road and drive 0.4 miles to the south end of the lake.

Contact: West Medical Lake Resort, 509/299-3921 (spring to fall only); Washington Department of Fish and Wildlife, Spokane Office, 509/456-4082.

48 Medical Lake

Rarely are two of the best trout lakes in the state within a few hundred yards of each other, but that's the case with Medical Lake and West Medical Lake (number 47), both of which offer quality trout fishing. The main differences are that Medical Lake has browns instead of rainbows and fishery regulations that require the use of artificial lures and flies with single, barbless hooks for all fishing. Medical also discourages taking home a creel full of fish, with a two-fish limit and a 14-inch minimum size limit. Many anglers come here to catch and release, not to kill a meal of fresh trout.

A haven for fly-fishing, Medical is a place where you can bide your time catching foot-long browns on nymphs and wet patterns until some kind of hatch occurs, and then you might be able to get your fill of dry fly-fishing for a few minutes or a few hours. My advice is to plan a trip to West Medical, give yourself an extra day to fish its neighbor, and vice versa. The season here opens in late April and closes at the end of September.

Location: West of the town of Medical Lake; see map A5, grid i4.

Species: Brown trout.

Facilities: The south end of the lake has a public access area and boat ramp. Food, gas, tackle, and lodging are available in the town of Medical Lake.

Directions: Take I-90 east from Sprague for 16 miles or west from Spokane for 14 miles and turn north on Salnave Road (Highway 902). Drive about six miles, and before getting to the town of Medical Lake, turn west (left) on Fancher Road and take an immediate right into the public access area of Medical Lake.

Contact: West Medical Lake Resort, 509/299-3921 (spring to fall only); Washington Department of Fish and Wildlife, Spokane Office, 509/456-4082.

49 Silver Lake

This fishery is somewhat in limbo as we go into the new millennium. The Washington Department of Fish and Wildlife planned to treat both Silver and neighboring North Silver in the fall of 1999, but local residents feared that the treatment could taint residential water supplies, many of which come directly from the lake. The Department of Fish and Wildlife postponed its plans, so at last word the lake still had lots of small panfish, largemouth bass, and other nonsalmonid species competing with the trout population and affecting the trout fishing.

In the not-too-distant past, stocked with both legal-sized fish and hatchery fry, Silver Lake produced large numbers of trout throughout much of the season, which runs from late April through October. Resort fishing docks provided some of the best catches of all, especially early in the season when stillfishing is the most productive angling method.

Low water sometimes causes problems for anglers trying to get their boats in and out of the water. If you have a small car-topper craft or even a canoe, that might be the rig to consider using when the water levels are low.

Location: Southeast of Medical Lake; see map A5, grid i4.

Species: Rainbow and brook trout.

Facilities: The lake has a public access area and a boat ramp, as well as several private resorts and campgrounds that have rental boats, fishing docks, bait and tackle, some groceries, RV sites, and moorage. Food, gas, tackle, and lodging are available in nearby Medical Lake.

Directions: Take I-90 west from Sprague for 21 miles or east from Spokane for nine miles and turn north onto Four Lakes Road, following the signs for three miles toward the town of Medical Lake. Silver Lake is on the left, about three miles off the freeway.

Contact: Picnic Pines Resort, 509/299-3223;

Washington Department of Fish and Wildlife, Spokane Office, 509/456-4082.

50 Clear Lake

If you're looking for a place with easy access off the freeway and a good mixed bag of angling possibilities, Clear Lake may be the answer. It's planted with liberal doses of hatchery rainbow and brown trout, which means plenty of trout trolling and stillfishing opportunities. Stillfish with grubs and yellow corn, like many of the locals do from their boats or from the resort docks. If you like to troll, try a Jake's Spinalure, a Wedding-Ring-and-worm combination, a green or brown Carey Special, or a Woolly Bugger fly for rainbows. The browns seem to prefer green or brown Flatfish or Kwikfish, Rooster Tails in the same colors, or Mepps spinners.

If your timing is good—as in sometime during the second half of May—you may even be around when the mayflies begin to hatch, providing some of the best fly-fishing you'll ever find. The north end of the lake is usually the scene of the best action during one of these hatches.

If you should get tired of trout, stick around into the evening and work your way around the edge of the lake with a spinnerbait, plastic worm, or crankbait and see what's happening with the bass. Chances are you'll come up with a few nice largemouths for your efforts. The best bassing is May through July. Clear Lake's fishing season runs from late April through October.

The biggest unknown affecting Clear Lake's various fisheries is the water draw-down that sometimes lowers its level several feet. Depending on what you're fishing for and when, this changing water level can have negative or positive influences on fishing success.

Location: South of Medical Lake; see map A5, grid i4.

Species: Rainbow and brown trout, largemouth bass.

Facilities: Besides a public access area and boat ramp, the lake has resorts with boat rentals, moorage, bait and tackle, and other facilities. The nearest gas, food, and lodging are in the town of Medical Lake.

Directions: Drive west from Sprague for 16 miles or east from Spokane for 14 miles on I-90 and turn north on Salnave Road, also known as Highway 902. Less than a quarter of a mile from the freeway, turn right on Clear Lake Road and follow it for two miles to the east side of the lake.

Contact: Rainbow Cove Resort, 509/299-3717; Mallard Bay Resort, 509/299-3830.

51 Fish Lake

This has been Spokane County's best-known brook trout producer for decades, and the fishing can be as good now as it was 30 years ago. While most of us think of brookies as skinny little seven-inchers, Fish Lake brook trout are the exception. Sure, they all originate in Department of Fish and Wildlife hatcheries, and many are caught shortly after release while they're still skinny little seven-inchers. But lots of fish carry over here through the winter, providing a high percentage of fat 11- to 14-inch fish well worth anyone's time and effort.

Stillfishing with garden worms or night crawlers rates as the number one brook trout getter, but trolling one of the slick little wigglers behind a string of trolling blades will also pay off. If you do fish the lake in a boat, remember that the lake has a prohibition on gas-powered motors, so use your electric or your oars.

The best brook trout fishing is in May and June, but the newest addition to the Fish Lake lineup continues to bite through much of the summer and comes on even stronger in September. That new addition is the brown trout, and it has added an exciting dimension to the fishery here. Browns of three pounds and bigger were common here by the start of the 1997 season, and much larger fish can be found in the lake now. If you want a big one, troll a Rapala or similar wobbling minnow imitator.

Location: Northeast of Cheney; see map A5, grid i5.

Species: Brook trout.

Facilities: The north side of the lake has a county park with a boat ramp and beach access, as well as a privately owned resort with bait, tackle, snacks, campsites, and a fishing dock.

Directions: Take I-90 east from Sprague for 21 miles or west from Spokane for six miles and exit onto Highway 904 to Cheney. Drive northeast out of Cheney on Cheney-Spokane Road, which is the main drag out of town to the east. The lake is on the right, about 2.5 miles from Cheney.

Contact: Spokane County Parks and Recreation Department, 509/625-6200; Klink's Williams Lake Resort, 509/235-2391; Washington Department of Fish and Wildlife, Spokane Office, 509/456-4082.

52 Hog Canyon Lake

This winter-season lake with the unusual name offers some good trout fishing from the time it opens on December 1 until it closes at the end of March. Open-water fishing is usually possible early in the season, but the lake might freeze over any time after Christmas. Though the fishing can be just as good through the ice, the angling strategy obviously changes. Trolling is good in open water, but when the ice forms, nobody seems willing to cut large enough holes to keep the trolling paths open. That's when it's time to dangle a red salmon egg, a couple of kernels of yellow corn, or a small wad of Berkley Power Bait near the bottom. Be on your toes for

light, subtle strikes, even from the 16-inch rainbows that are quite common. And on those chilly days when the fishing is good, remember that the regulations require that no more than two trout in your five-fish limit may exceed 14 inches.

Location: Northeast of Sprague; see map A5, grid j4.

Species: Rainbow trout.

Facilities: The lake has a rough boat ramp at its south end. The nearest food, gas, tackle, and lodging are in Sprague.

Directions: Drive east from Sprague for nine miles or west from Spokane for 20 miles on I-90 and exit south at Fishtrap. Drive south just over half a mile to the first gravel road and turn east (left). Go another half a mile to the stop sign and railroad track, continuing straight ahead from the stop sign and following the rough dirt road about 1.5 miles to the south end of the lake. People take their cars to the lake on this road, but as far as I'm concerned, this is a four-wheel-drive-only road, especially right after it rains or snows.

Contact: Four Seasons Campground and Resort, 509/257-2332, website: www.fourseasonscampground.com; Purple Sage Motel, 509/257-2507, website: www.purplesage motel.com.

53 Chapman Lake

Chapman has long been one of Spokane County's top bass lakes, featuring both largemouths and smallmouths in good numbers. Arrive early in the morning or stay late into the evening and you may get in some good top-water action. But if the bass aren't on top, you'll still get in some quality fishing time, whether you work plastics around shoreline cover, snake spinnerbaits or crankbaits over and around underwater structure, or do whatever it is you like to do for bass.

Kokanee are in good enough supply here to warrant a sort of revised bonus limit on them. You can keep up to 10 "trout" per day, but at least five of those must be kokanee. Trolling Wedding Ring spinners whose hooks are tipped with maggots or white corn is the favored kokanee-catching technique, and it also accounts for many of the rainbow trout caught here. Stillfishing with worms, Berkley Power Bait, marshmallows, and yellow corn is also popular with trout anglers.

Perch and crappies are abundant here, and both will hit small leadheads adorned with plastic skirt bodies. Perch hit throughout the April through October season; crappies bite best in May and October.

Location: South of Cheney; see map A5, grid j5.

Species: Largemouth and smallmouth bass, rainbow trout, kokanee, yellow perch, crappie, brown bullhead catfish.

Facilities: A boat ramp with an access area is located on the east side of the lake, near the south end, and the lake also has a fishing resort with cabins and RV hookups. Food, gas, tackle, and lodging are available in Cheney.

Directions: Drive south from Cheney on Cheney-Spangle Road for seven miles and turn west (right) on Pine Grove Road. Drive a little over three miles to Cheney-Plaza Road and turn right. Continue 1.5 miles and turn right again down the gravel road leading half a mile to the south end of the lake.

Contact: Chapman Lake Resort, 509/523-2221.

54 Badger Lake

This 244-acre Spokane County lake has had its angling ups and downs over the years. Once the home of a two-pronged trout fishery that provided consistent action with rainbows and cutthroats, it was illegally stocked with bass sometime in the 1980s, and they eventually became well established in the lake. A heavy dose of rotenone put an end to all the bass fun, and the lake was restocked with rainbows in the spring of 1996, so trout fishing is once again very good at Badger. Besides your normal rainbows and cutthroats, triploid rainbows are also now available to Badger Lake anglers.

Trolling with small wobbling spoons produces some good trout catches early in the spring, but when the May sun warms the lake, a huge mayfly hatch brings both surface-feeding trout and eager fly-fishing enthusiasts out of the woodwork. If you're anywhere in this part of the state when you get word of the hatch, make it a point to visit Badger for some of the best dry-fly trouting you can hope to find.

Location: South of Cheney; see map A5, grid j5.

Species: Rainbow and cutthroat trout.

Facilities: The lake has a public access area with a very steep boat ramp where launching is sometimes a struggle, especially during times of low water. Resort facilities on the west side of the lake include rental boats, RV hookups, moorage, tackle, and food. The nearest gas stations and motels are in Cheney.

Directions: Drive south from Cheney on Mullinex Road for five miles and turn east (left) on Dover Road, following it to the west side of the lake.

Contact: Klink's Williams Lake Resort, 509/235-2391; Washington Department of Fish and Wildlife, Spokane Office, 509/456-4082.

55 Fishtrap Lake

Fishtrap offers some of the best early-season fishing in eastern Washington, at least in terms of catch-per-angler. Anglers catch limits of plump rainbows with uncanny consistency during the first few weeks of the season from late April through May. Stillfish with worms and/or marshmallows, or troll one-quarter-ounce and one-sixth-ounce Panther Martins in black, Rooster Tails spinners in frog or rainbow patterns, or small Flatfish or Kwikfish in a frog finish. Although not heavily fished, the lake now also has brown bullhead catfish for anglers looking for something to keep them busy at night.

Location: Northeast of Sprague; see map A5, grid j3.

Species: Rainbow trout, brown bullhead catfish.

Facilities: The north end of the lake has a public access area with a boat ramp and a privately owned resort offering food, fuel, tackle, rental boats, showers, and restrooms. Additional facilities are in Sprague.

Directions: Take I-90 east from Sprague for nine miles or west from Spokane for 20 miles and take the Fishtrap exit to the south. Drive three miles to Scroggie Road and turn east (left), continuing for one mile to the north end of the lake.

Contact: Fishtrap Lake Resort, 509/235-2284.

56 Amber Lake

If you want peace, quiet, and a laid-back atmosphere while trout fishing, you'll probably like Amber Lake. Selective fishery regulations prohibiting bait and barbed hooks are now in effect throughout most of the season, which lead many anglers hungry for fresh trout to go elsewhere. A two-fish daily limit also helps reduce the size of the crowds, and an electric-motors-only rule helps in the peace and quiet category. Only fin-clipped, hatchery trout may be killed during this limited catch-and-keep season. Anglers thin out even more after the end of September, when Amber's regulations switch to catch-and-release fishing only until the end of the season on November 30.

The catch consists of both rainbows and cutthroats, and both grow to pretty good size under Amber's restrictive regulations.

Trolling various spoons and spinners is effective, and fly-fishing is also productive beginning with the mayfly hatch in late May. Chunky and fast-growing triploid rainbows now sweeten the pot at Amber.

Location: Southwest of Cheney; see map A5, grid j4.

Species: Rainbow and cutthroat trout.

Facilities: A public access area with a boat ramp is located on the north side of the lake. The nearest food, gas, tackle, and lodging are in Sprague and Cheney.

Directions: From the west, exit I-90 at Sprague and drive east out of town on Old State Highway. After two miles, turn south (right) on Martin Road and follow it about 11 miles to Mullinex Road. Turn north (left) on Mullinex and follow it about six miles to Pine Spring Road. Turn west (left) on Pine Spring and follow it to the lake. From the east, exit I-90 at Tyler and drive south on Pine Spring Road, staying on it all the way for eight miles to the lake.

Contact: Four Seasons Campground, 509/257-2332, website: www.fourseasonscampground.com; Purple Sage Motel, 509/257-2507, website: www.purplesagemotel.com.

57 Williams Lake

Since it was treated with rotenone and restocked with trout in 1996, Williams is once again one of eastern Washington's best rainbow trout lakes.

Like other lakes in this part of the state, the mayfly hatch causes lots of excitement among trout and trout anglers alike around the end of May, providing a couple of weeks of the best fly-fishing you could want. If you're not into fly-fishing, try stillfishing near the bottom with orange or red Power Bait, red Pautzke salmon eggs, or a combination of the two. Trolling is also effective, especially for anglers who use frog-finish Flatfish, Kwikfish, or Hot Shots. Another trolling tactic is to trail a Muddler Minnow, Carey Special, or some other streamer or wet fly pattern behind a leaded line and a 30-foot leader.

Location: Southwest of Cheney; see map A5, grid j4.

Species: Rainbow trout.

Facilities: The lake has a public access area and boat ramp, along with two resorts that offer tent and RV sites, restaurants, boat rentals, moorage, fishing docks, groceries, and tackle. Gas, food, and lodging are available in Sprague and Cheney.

Directions: Take Martin Road east from Sprague for 10 miles, turn north (left) on Mullinex Road, and then east (right) on Williams Lake Road to the lake. From Cheney, follow Mullinex Road south for 10 miles to Williams Lake Road and turn east (left) to the lake.

Contact: Klink's Williams Lake Resort, 509/235-2391; Bunker's Resort, 509/235-5212 (April through November).

58 Downs Lake

This big, shallow lake warms quickly in the spring sun, providing some of its best trout fishing during the first few weeks of the season. Most anglers troll here, using the full range of standard goodies. But don't troll too slowly or use something too heavy, since much of the lake is only a few feet deep; you don't want to spend all your time dredging the bottom or trying to unhook your bottom-snagged lure. Downs is also well suited to fly-fishing, and you can easily spend a weekend working around the weeds and reeds in search of rainbows without casting to the same place twice.

Bass fishing can also be very good here as soon as the water warms in spring, and some years that means good bassing as soon as the lake opens in late April. Largemouths provide the action, and Downs produces its share of bigmouths of five pounds

and over.

You can almost always catch a few perch here—even when you're trying to catch something else—and catfish action is good at night May through August.

Location: Southeast of Sprague; see map A5, grid j4.

Species: Rainbow trout, largemouth bass, yellow perch, brown bullhead catfish.

Facilities: The north side of the lake has a private resort with camping sites, bait and tackle, a boat ramp, and other facilities. The nearest food, gas, and lodging are in Sprague and Cheney.

Directions: Take I-90 to Sprague, exit the freeway onto the Old State Highway east (left), and drive 2.5 miles to Martin Road, following it about six miles to the gravel road turning south (right) to the lake.

Contact: Downs Lake Resort, 509/235-2314.

59 Sprague Lake

Sprague is another one of those eastern Washington lakes that has almost everything an angler could want. But unlike most of the others, the mixed bag here was created by design, not by accident. In 1985, Sprague was a big mud hole, filled with tens of thousands of carp and little else. An energetic program to treat the lake with rotenone and restock it with trout, bass, and panfish was undertaken that year, and Sprague has been a piscatorial highlight film ever since. Rainbow and Lahontan cutthroat trout were stocked early in the process and within months were providing year-round trout fishing that was above and beyond everyone's expectations. A year and a half after the rotenone treatment, beautiful rainbows of 20 inches were coming from the lake with amazing regularity, and the cutthroats were measuring a good 14 inches each. Even though the lake is shallow, it's fed by numerous underground springs that keep water temperatures surprisingly cool, even in summer, so anglers were catching limits of big trout when all the other lakes in the area were dead for trout fishing.

But the trout were only a stopgap to provide angling action while various warm-water species were established, and as the trouting tapered off in the late 1980s, it wasn't long before good catches of smallmouth and largemouth bass were coming from Sprague—and they continue to provide excellent fishing from early spring to late fall. The lake is full of crawdads, so the bass grow fast, fat, and strong. There's no end to the weedy largemouth cover and the rocky hideaways that smallmouths like, so you can fish your brains out and never cover it all in a single trip.

Walleyes have responded pretty much the same as all the other species, and so have the bluegills and channel cats. Sprague at times in recent years has been the best bluegill lake in Washington, which was part of the plan back when the lake was poisoned and the lake-rehabilitation program started. Perch, crappies, and bullhead catfish tend to be overlooked in the excitement.

Be sure to check the regulations pamphlet before fishing Sprague, especially in the spring. Although the season runs year-round, special spring closures are in effect on part of the lake, and you'll want to know the details before fishing rather than finding out the hard way.

Location: Southwest of Sprague on the south side of I-90; see map A5, grid j2.

Species: Rainbow and cutthroat trout, largemouth and smallmouth bass, walleye, bluegill, channel catfish, crappie, yellow perch, brown bullhead catfish.

Facilities: There are four boat ramps on the lake, two of them at resorts and two along the undeveloped east side of the lake.

- **Sprague Lake Resort:** This resort at the lake's north end has a one-lane, blacktop ramp with a loading float and charges a launch fee. There are also RV/tent sites, moorage, a fishing dock, tackle and a few other supplies, restrooms with showers, and a picnic area.

- **Four Seasons Campground:** On the west end of the lake, Four Seasons Campground has a good hard-surface ramp with a loading dock and charges a launch fee. The Four Seasons also has RV/tent sites, cabins, moorage, rental boats, picnic areas, and a store.

- **Self-Serve Ramps:** The two concrete ramps with gravel parking areas on the east side of the lake are self-serve ramps, with a can to put money in for their use. Both have rough gravel access and parking areas with no facilities around them.

Restaurants, gas, and lodging are available in Sprague.

Directions: Take I-90 to the town of Sprague, hit main street, and follow it out of town to the southwest for about four miles. The road parallels the lake for several miles.

Contact: Sprague Lake Resort, 509/257-2864; Four Seasons Campground, 509/257-2332, website: www.fourseasonscampground.com; Purple Sage Motel, 509/257-2507, website: www.purplesagemotel.com.

60 Fourth of July Lake

Fourth of July is another winter-only lake that's open to fishing only from the first of December through the end of March. Although this is an extremely cold time of year in the Inland Empire, the winter fishing here can be as hot as a firecracker. You may still be able to fish by boat early in the season, but it doesn't take long for a thick ice cover to form on the lake, and from that time on it's strictly a through-the-ice proposition.

The rainbows here run 10 to 16 inches, with a few two-year carryovers of 18 inches or more. Pautzke's red salmon eggs have long been the favorite bait among Fourth of July ice anglers, but Berkley's Power Bait gets more popular every season. To be sure, take both along and see which works best for you. Just to cover all the bases, throw in some whole kernel corn and maybe a few miniature marshmallows. With all those supplies, if the trout aren't biting, at least you won't starve.

Location: South of Sprague; see map A5, grid j2.

Species: Rainbow trout.

Facilities: The north end of the lake has a rough boat ramp. Food, gas, tackle, lodging, and RV facilities are available in and around Sprague.

Directions: Take I-90 to Sprague and turn south onto Highway 23. Drive a mile and turn west (right) on the gravel and dirt road that begins at the one-mile marker. Head straight for about one mile to the lake.

Contact: Four Seasons Campground, 509/257-2332, website: www.fourseasonscampground.com; Purple Sage Motel, 509/257-2507, website: www.purplesagemotel.com; Sprague Lake Resort, 509/257-2864.

CHAPTER B1:
SOUTHERN COAST

©TERRY RUDNICK

WESTPORT COHO LIMITS

Map B1

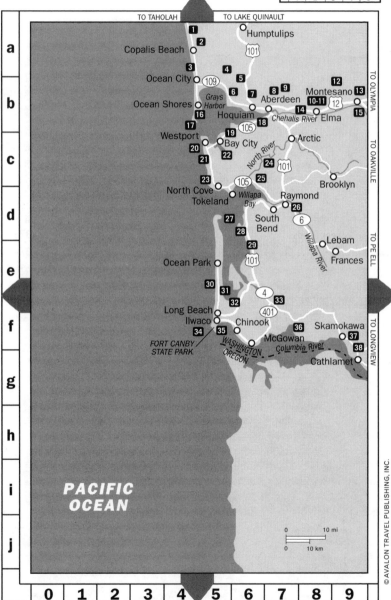

Chapter B1: Southern Coast

Water dominates the scene and to a large extent defines the way of life in this corner of the Evergreen State. The majority of families here make their living in the woods or on the water, and for most it's been that way for generations. The logger's world and the mariner's way of life merge in Grays Harbor, as huge ships snake their way up the Chehalis River channel to Cosmopolis, where they're loaded with Douglas fir, spruce, and western red cedar logs, on their way to mills in Asia. So much for the locally despised spotted owl causing the closure of all those saw mills over the past 30 years! There are also those who manage to make some or all of their living from the seal although their numbers have declined steadily since the heyday of the 1970s. Crabbers, oystermen, salmon trollers, and charter boat skippers can make a decent living for part of the year, but more restrictive seasons, changes in the character and health of the ocean, and other factors have had a great impact on their way of life. In Willapa Bay, for example, the natural habitat has been damaged forever by the accidental introduction of spartina, a cord-like aquatic plant that has choked out much the natural vegetation and left a large portion of the bay devoid of virtually all native species. But it's certainly not all bad news in this part of Washington. Huge returns of hatchery salmon have brought relief to all aspects of the fishing industry lately, and anglers around here are grinning from ear to ear. The lower Columbia has once again become a mob scene of fishing activitiy, as charters and private boats alike jockey for position to get their share of Buoy 10 coho and chinook. Westport's recreational salmon fishing has once again become a summerlong activity, where two-fish limits by lunchtime are the rule, not the exception. But salmon fishing along the coast and at the mouth of the Columbia aren't the only options for anglers in this corner of Washington. The Pacific also offers halibut, lingcod, rockfish, and other popular bottom fish species, and there's a wealth of fishing variety for salmon, steelhead, and sea-run trout in such rivers as the Humptulips, Wynochee, Satsop, Chehalis, Willapa, Grays, and Elochoman. And then there's the prehistoric sturgeon, a favorite among a growing number of Northwest anglers, available in both the Columbia and Chehalis Rivers.

©TERRY RUDNICK

LOWER COLUMBIA CHINOOK

◾ Moclips River

Although this coastal stream is open during the winter to allow for a steelhead season, the winter fishery doesn't amount to anything at all. Department of Fish and Wildlife records show that most winters it doesn't give up a single steelhead, at least not any that get recorded on any steelhead report cards. For most folks the Moclips is too far away and the steelheading too poor to be worth a wintertime trip.

Fall fishing for sea-run cutts, on the other hand, can be a worthwhile endeavor. Like many other streams around the Grays Harbor area, the best cutthroating occurs within about 24 hours of the end of a heavy rain that causes a good rise in water levels. Roll a night crawler or small clusters of salmon eggs along the bottom to catch them. It has the two-fish-per-day trout limit common on Washington streams.

Location: Flows into the Pacific Ocean at Moclips; see map B1, grid a4.

Species: Sea-run cutthroat trout, a few winter steelhead.

Facilities: Moclips has lodging, RV parks, groceries, gas, and tackle.

Directions: Take Highway 109 west out of Hoquiam and follow it up the coast 30 miles to Moclips and the mouth of the river. The only road leading east out of town parallels the south side of the river.

Contact: Hi-Tide Beach Motel, 800/662-5477; Moonstone Beach Motel, 888/888-9063; Ocean Crest Resort, 800/684-8439, website: www .oceanshores.com/lodging/oceancrest; All Seasons Sports, 360/538-7033.

◾ Copalis River

If there's such a thing as a big-draw fishery on the Copalis, it has to be the flurry of activity generated by the fall coho run. It starts in September and ends in October, and for the rest of the year there isn't a heck of a lot to do around here. The locals catch a few sea-run cutts, but for folks living around the population centers of Puget Sound, this stream is a long way from home for a shot at cutthroats. There are a few winter steelhead to be caught, but so few that it's probably not worth mentioning.

You can catch flounder, sole, and perch by casting pieces of shrimp, clam, or small crabs at the river mouth at the start of an incoming tide.

Location: Enters the Pacific Ocean near Copalis Beach; see map B1, grid a5.

Species: Coho salmon, sea-run cutthroat trout, seaperch, flounder and sole, winter and summer steelhead (maybe).

Facilities: Supplies are available in Ocean Shores, seven miles south.

Directions: Take Highway 109 west from Hoquiam and follow it up the coast for 20 miles to Copalis Beach and the mouth of the river. To reach the upper river, drive east out of Copalis on Copalis Beach Road for about five miles, turn north (left) on Ocean Beach Road, and drive just under four miles to the Copalis River bridge. An unimproved road leads a short distance downstream and several miles upstream from the bridge.

Contact: Copalis Beach Surf & Sand RV Park, 360/289-2707 or 800/867-2707; Riverside RV Resort, 360/289-2111; Iron Springs Resort, 360/276-4230; All Seasons Sports, 360/538-7033; Washington Department of Fish and Wildlife, Montesano Office, 360/249-4628.

◾ North Beach Surf

This stretch of beach, especially the northern portion, gets lighter fishing pressure than beaches to the south, and the perch fishing can be very good. Spring and early summer often produce best, but perch are available virtually all year. Fish the incoming tide, concentrating on spots with lagoons, channels, and other noticeable bottom structure. Perch like to forage in these deeper spots where tiny food items collect.

Location: From Copalis Beach south to Ocean Shores; see map B1, grid a4.

Species: Redtail surfperch.

Facilities: Food and gas are available at Copalis Beach, and all other amenities can be found at Ocean Shores. Ocean City State Park has tent sites, RV spaces, and restrooms with showers.

Directions: Take Highway 109 west from Hoquiam and turn west (left) on any of the public roads leading to the beach. Access roads at Ocean City, Copalis Beach, Pacific Beach, Moclips, and other areas are well marked.

Contact: Ocean City State Park, 360/289-3553; Washington State Parks and Recreation Commission, 360/902-8844 (information) or 800/452-5687 (reservations); Washington Coast Chamber of Commerce Visitor Information Center, 800/286-4552; Ocean Shores Chamber of Commerce, 800/762-3224; Washington Department of Fish and Wildlife, Montesano Office, 360/249-4628.

◢ Humptulips River

If you like catching fish fresh from the ocean, this may be the place for you. Many freshwater salmon and steelhead anglers count the Hump as their favorite, and the cutthroat fishing can be every bit as good. The best cutthroat fishing is in October, while the sea-run trout are available August through November.

Winter steelheading is best in December and January, when good numbers of hatchery fish return to the river, and again in March and April, when the catch includes a high percentage of big and tough wild fish. If a 20-pound steelhead is your heart's desire, fish the Humptulips in March from now until the time you die and you just might achieve your goal. Boat fishing offers definite advantages, but there are plenty of good places to fish

from the bank as well, including right under the U.S. 101 bridge (where I hooked my first Humptulips winter-run many years ago) and near the fish hatchery about two miles downstream from the highway bridge.

Although summer steelhead smolts are planted in the Humptulips, summer steelheading here is nothing to write home about. Persistent anglers catch a few dozen steelhead a month from June through September.

Salmon fishing is another matter, since the Humptulips ranks up among the Northwest's best fall salmon streams. Things start hopping in September, when good numbers of chinooks take over the river. Some of them are brutes, topping 40 pounds, and they're strong enough to knock you down and stomp all over you if you give them half a chance. This chinook run lasts longer than any other on the Washington coast, as anglers continue to catch big kings well into November. Long before they disappear, both coho and chum salmon show in the river, and there are days when you may hook all three species. The coho and chum fishing usually tapers off by Thanksgiving, but don't be too surprised to find stragglers of both species in the river as late as January.

There's a fall salmon season on the "Hump," but it's certainly not as worthwhile as it used to be. Big fall chinook provided excellent fishing here a few years ago, but recently the rules have called for the release of any adult chinook you catch on the river. Unclipped, wild adult coho must also be released, and you have to release chum salmon, too. That leaves nothing but jack chinook and hatchery coho from a river that only a few years ago was one of the coast's top salmon producers.

Location: Flows into Grays Harbor's North Bay northwest of Hoquiam; see map B1, grid a5.

Species: Winter and summer steelhead; fall

chinook, coho, and chum salmon; sea-run cutthroat trout.

Facilities: Boat ramps of various quality are located off East Humptulips and McNutt Roads, both of which are upstream from the U.S. 101 bridge. Donkey Creek Road, which heads east off of U.S. 101 a few miles north of the highway bridge, winds along and crosses the West Fork Humptulips, offering several places to launch small boats. There are also several launching spots off Copalis Crossing Road, which runs along the west side of the river between U.S. 101 and Copalis Crossing. There's also a good paved ramp at the Highway 109 bridge, a mile or so above the mouth of the river. A $10 WDFW access decal is required to use the public launch areas maintained by the Washington Department of Fish and Wildlife.

Food and gas are available at Humptulips. Tackle, lodging, and other facilities can be found in Hoquiam.

Directions: Take U.S. 101 north from Hoquiam, driving about 22 miles to the middle portion of the river. To reach the lower Humptulips, turn west (left) off U.S. 101 onto Ocean Beach Road about three miles north of Hoquiam and follow it for 10 miles to the river.

Contact: Blaine's Tackle, 360/532-1297; The Backcast, 360/532-6867; Washington Department of Fish and Wildlife, Montesano Office, 360/249-4628.

5 Failor Lake

At 65 acres, Failor Lake isn't very big, but it's a favorite of Grays Harbor County anglers. Stocked with both rainbow and cutthroat trout to the tune of about 6,000 fish annually, there are plenty of 8- to 10-inchers to go around. The carryover of fish from the previous year is fair, so there's always a chance you'll find a 14- to 16-incher early in the season. Fishing is good throughout May and June, slows during July and August, and

picks up again in September and October.

Stillfishing with all the standard baits works pretty well for Failor Lake rainbows, but worms are your best bet if you want a chance of catching a cutthroat or two along with the 'bows. As for trolling, gang trolls with worms trailing behind account for many of the fish, but you might try a silver/redhead Triple Teazer or a small Flatfish or Kwikfish in any light or metallic finish. The season here opens in late April and runs through October.

Location: North of Hoquiam and west of U.S. 101; see map B1, grid b6.

Species: Rainbow and cutthroat trout.

Facilities: The public access area has a boat ramp. All other amenities are in Hoquiam and Aberdeen.

Directions: Drive north about nine miles from Hoquiam on U.S. 101 and turn west (left) on Failor Lake Road. The lake is about 2.5 miles off the highway.

Contact: Blaine's Tackle, 360/532-1297; The Backcast, 360/532-6867; Washington Department of Fish and Wildlife, Montesano Office, 360/249-4628.

6 Chenois Creek

Local anglers, many of them Copenhagen-chewing loggers and mill workers, call this Snoose Creek, perhaps because the word "Chenois" sort of looks like "Snoose," or it may be that they spit in the creek and the water actually does contain a high percentage of snoose. Whatever the reason for the nickname, Chenois Creek is a fair sea-run cutthroat stream. Fish it anytime between September 1 and the end of October, but if you can get there at the tail end of a good rain, you'll at least double your chances of hooking fish. The season opens on June 1 and runs through October.

Location: Enters Grays Harbor's North Bay northwest of Hoquiam; see map B1, grid b5.

Species: Sea-run cutthroat trout.

Facilities: There isn't much here except a small grocery store along the highway at the mouth of the creek. Food, gas, tackle, and lodging are available in Aberdeen and Hoquiam.

Directions: Take Highway 109 west from Hoquiam about eight miles to the bridge that crosses over Chenois Creek.

Contact: Blaine's Tackle, 360/532-1297; The Backcast, 360/532-6867; Washington Department of Fish and Wildlife, Montesano Office, 360/249-4628.

7 Hoquiam River

Although it's stocked with a few hatchery steelhead smolts and is open for fall salmon fishing, the Hoquiam doesn't fit anyone's definition of a hot spot for either species. Winter steelheaders—mostly locals who know their way around and who can drop what they're doing to fish when conditions are right—catch a couple dozen fish a year, and the fall coho fishery is even less productive. The fall salmon season provides a decent opportunity for adult coho and chinook some years. The waters around the mouth of the Hoquiam were pretty hot for a few weeks in August 2001.

Sea-run cutthroats offer more action, and it's OK to keep two of them per day as long as they're at least 14 inches long.

The piers, bridge abutments, and old pilings at the mouth of the Hoquiam offer decent perch fishing on an incoming tide, but few anglers fish for them. Both pile perch and striped seaperch are available.

Location: Enters the east end of Grays Harbor at Hoquiam; see map B1, grid b6.

Species: Winter steelhead, coho and chinook salmon, sea-run and resident cutthroat trout, seaperch, pile perch.

Facilities: A boat ramp is near the mouth of the Hoquiam off 28th Street in Aberdeen, about a quarter mile above the river mouth. A good launch site on the West Fork Hoquiam

is found along U.S. 101 on the east side of the highway about a mile and a half north of where the Ocean Beach Highway takes off to the west. A good place to launch on the East Fork Hoquiam is off East Hoquiam Road about five miles upstream from the confluence with the West Fork.

Directions: Take U.S. 101 north from Hoquiam for about five miles to parallel the west side of the river. East Hoquiam Road out of Hoquiam parallels the East Fork of the Hoquiam and provides good access.

Contact: Blaine's Tackle, 360/532-1297; The Backcast, 360/532-6867; Washington Department of Fish and Wildlife, Montesano Office, 360/249-4628.

8 Wishkah River

Though only one valley away from the Hoquiam (see number 7), the Wishkah is a much better salmon and steelhead stream, thanks to its better fish habitat and access to the water. Although you'll have to release any adult chinook you might hook, work your way up Wishkah Road to the mouth of the West Fork Wishkah during October or early November and you just might locate a cooperative coho or two.

The winter steelheading is up and down from year to year, but some seasons the Wishkah gives up 150 to 200 fish. The best part is that the steelheading usually remains fairly consistent from December until the end of the season in March (the season opens on June 1). Sea-run cutthroat fishing is fair here in October. The regulations call for the release of all wild (not fin-clipped) cutthroats.

Location: Flows into the east end of Grays Harbor at Aberdeen; see map B1, grid b7.

Species: Winter steelhead; coho, chinook, and chum salmon; resident and sea-run cutthroat trout; seaperch.

Facilities: Food, lodging, gas, tackle, and

plenty of watering holes are available in Aberdeen.

Directions: Take U.S. 12 to Aberdeen and turn north (right) on Wishkah Road, which parallels the river.

Contact: Blaine's Tackle, 360/532-1297; The Backcast, 360/532-6867; Washington Department of Fish and Wildlife, Montesano Office, 360/249-4628.

9 Lake Aberdeen

Spring plants of legal-sized rainbows from the Aberdeen Hatchery only a few hundred feet away, along with some resident cutthroats that have been around ever since the lake was created, provide the excitement here. Fishing is fair as long as the rainbows hold out, but the action is slow after that, so plan your visit for some time before the first of June for best results. Standard gang-troll-and-worm rigs will take both rainbows and cutthroats, and that's what most of the regulars at Aberdeen like to use.

Location: Northeast of Aberdeen; see map B1, grid b7.

Species: Rainbow and cutthroat trout.

Facilities: The east side of the lake has a city park boat ramp, with all other amenities in Aberdeen.

Directions: Driving west on U.S. 12 toward Aberdeen, turn north (right) at the Fish Hatchery–Aberdeen Lake sign, which is about a mile west of the Central Park drive-in theater.

Contact: Blaine's Tackle, 360/532-1297; The Backcast, 360/532-6867; Washington Department of Fish and Wildlife, Montesano Office, 360/249-4628.

10 Wynoochee River

Although it doesn't get the praise or publicity accorded many other western Washington steelhead streams, this lower Chehalis tributary produces steelhead 10 months out of

the year. Not bad, since it's closed to fishing in April and May. The annual sport catch of about 3,000 steelies is pretty equally divided between winter and summer fish. If you don't have the luxury of being able to fish the Wynoochee throughout the year, concentrate your efforts during March and June, the months anglers always seem to score the best catches, according to statistics compiled by the Department of Fish and Wildlife.

Fall fishing for salmon is fair in the Wynoochee. The river is now closed to fishing for chinooks, so they have to go back, but decent numbers of coho are caught on spinners and wobbling spoons in November and December.

Sea-run cutthroat fishing gets under way on the Wynoochee as early as mid-July and runs well into the fall. The best fishing is in September and October, especially right after a drenching rain that raises the river level a few inches. This is one of many Olympic Peninsula streams where anglers can keep only hatchery cutthroat marked with a fin-clip.

Location: Joins the Chehalis River at Montesano; see map B1, grid b8.

Species: Winter and summer steelhead; chinook, coho, and chum salmon; sea-run cutthroat trout.

Facilities: There are two Department of Fish and Wildlife access areas with boat ramps on the river, both off Wynoochee Valley Road. The lower one is three miles off Highway 8 near the mouth of Black Creek, the second another six miles up the road where the turn is marked by a Public Fishing sign. There's a take-out spot on the Chehalis River just upstream from the mouth of the Wynoochee, and at a couple of places well upriver on the Wynoochee it's possible to drag a small raft or kayak over the bank or off the end of logging roads that come close to the river. One such spot is half a mile above the mouth of

Schafer Creek. A $10 WDFW access decal is required to use the public launch areas maintained by the Washington Department of Fish and Wildlife. Montesano has food, gas, lodging, and tackle.

Directions: Take Highway 8/U.S. 12 west from Olympia for 31 miles and turn north (right) on Devonshire Road about 1.5 miles past Montesano.

Contact: Blaine's Tackle, 360/532-1297; The Backcast, 360/532-6867; Washington Department of Fish and Wildlife, Montesano Office, 360/249-4628.

11 Lake Sylvia

Liberal doses of hatchery rainbows make this a popular and often downright crowded fishing spot. At 32 acres, Sylvia is big enough for using a boat, but you can cast from the beach at the state park and catch your share of rainbows. The state park ramp will handle boats of most any size, but note that the lake has a prohibition on the use of gas motors.

Sylvia produces some decent-sized cutthroats, especially in the fall, and summertime sees some bass to two pounds and better coming from shoreline areas. Bass anglers will find plenty of overhanging brush, submerged logs, stumps, and other debris to prospect for bucketmouths, but there isn't much in the way of pads or other aquatic vegetation.

Location: North of Montesano; see map B1, grid b8.

Species: Rainbow and cutthroat trout, largemouth bass.

Facilities: Lake Sylvia State Park has a boat ramp, restrooms, and 35 tent sites. Food, gas, lodging, and tackle are available in Montesano.

Directions: Drive west on U.S. 12 from Olympia to Montesano. Take the Montesano exit, which has a sign denoting Lake Sylvia State Park. Follow the signs through town to the park.

Contact: Blaine's Tackle, 360/532-1297; The Backcast, 360/532-6867; Washington Department of Fish and Wildlife, Montesano Office, 360/249-4628.

12 Satsop River

Fall salmon fishing is now a big draw at the Satsop, but this once-productive steelhead area is hardly worth fishing during the steelhead season these days. Skimming the steelhead catch figures compiled every year by the Washington Department of Fish and Wildlife and seeing that the Satsop produces only a handful of winter-run steelies every year is enough to bring a tear to the eye of those who were on hand to fish it in the 1950s, '60s, and early '70s. I had that opportunity only once, but it was a day of steelheading I'll never forget, as fishing partner Dave Borden and I floated the lightly fished West Fork Satsop on a rainy January day. We hooked three fish, all of them over 10 pounds, and landed a pair that weighed in at 14 and 18 pounds. We only saw one other angler, and he was fishing within sight of where we took the boat out of the water at the end of that special day. Standard stream regulations requiring that all wild steelhead be released are in effect here.

As I said, few people bother coming to the Satsop for steelhead now, but hundreds of them come for the salmon fishing. October can be good for coho, many of them quite large. There's also a fairly good chance you'll get a crack at a hefty adult chinook. The big chums that once drew anglers by the thousands during October and November have dwindled to the point that chums must now be released, as of the 2001 season. Smarter anglers fish the lower Satsop from boats to see a little scenery and get away from the mobs.

Sea-run cutthroat trout also are a possibility, but this is another of those Olympic Peninsula rivers where anglers must release all wild (non-fin-clipped) cutthroats they catch.

Location: Joins the Chehalis River west of Elma; see map B1, grid b9.

Species: Winter and summer steelhead; coho, chinook, and chum salmon; sea-run cutthroat trout.

Facilities: Schafer State Park, located on the East Fork Satsop, has tent sites and a few spaces with RV hookups, plus restrooms. Gas, food, lodging, and tackle are available in Elma.

Directions: Take Highway 8/U.S. 12 west from Olympia to Satsop, which is about four miles west of Elma. Turn north (right) onto East Satsop Road and follow it upriver.

Contact: Schafer State Park, 360/482-3852; Washington State Parks and Recreation Commission, 360/902-8844 (information) or 800/452-5687 (reservations); Blaine's Tackle, 360/532-1297; Washington Department of Fish and Wildlife, Montesano Office, 360/249-4628.

13 Cloquallum Creek

Timing is everything here, as it is on many small Northwest streams where water levels are the key to the presence or absence of fish. A couple of days of rain that raises the water level a foot or two will bring a run of winter steelhead or sea-run cutts surging out of the Chehalis and into Cloquallum Creek, but they soon scatter through the system and are hard to find. That explains why a few local anglers who can get to the creek on short notice when conditions are right catch most of the fish here. February and March are the best months for steelheading, while November is tops for cutthroat fishing.

Location: Flows into the Chehalis River near Elma; see map B1, grid b9.

Species: Winter steelhead, sea-run cutthroat trout.

Facilities: Food, gas, tackle, and lodging are available in Elma.

Directions: Take Highway 8 west from Olympia for 21 miles and either turn right at the Grays Harbor County Fairgrounds sign just east of Elma or take the Elma exit and go south (left) to the bridge that crosses the creek just south of town.

Contact: Blaine's Tackle, 360/532-1297; Washington Department of Fish and Wildlife, Montesano Office, 360/249-4628.

14 Lower Chehalis River

This is a place that can provide excellent salmon fishing opportunities, but you have to pay close attention to the fishing regulations pamphlet to know what you can fish for and when. It changes from one year to the next, depending on the strength of various runs that enter the river from spring to early winter. In 2001, for example, anglers were allowed to catch up to six salmon per day, no more than two of them adult fish. Of those, no more than one could be a wild adult coho and no more than one could be a chinook. All chum salmon had to be released. And so it goes. Read before you fish!

When the runs are booming, boat anglers flock to the popular boat ramp beneath the Highway 107 bridge just south of Montesano and work both upstream and downstream. Trolling with Wiggle Warts, Hot 'N Tots, Hot Shots, Flatfish, Kwikfish, and other diving plugs often works best for the kings, which sometimes top 35 pounds. Trolling Flash Glos, Metrics, Mepps, and other spinners does a good job of drawing strikes from the silvers. Most of this action takes place in September and October.

Both bank and boat anglers take winter steelhead from the Lower Chehalis, with the best fishing usually occurring January through March. As with the river's salmon, many of the steelhead caught here are bound for the river's two major tributaries, the Wynoochee and Satsop Rivers. Trolling plugs or diver-and-bait rigs accounts for many of the winter-runs, but plunkers fishing shrimp,

Coastal Jetties: Trails to Hot Saltwater Fishing

Washington's coast offers virtually limitless fishing opportunities, but you need a boat to get at all of the Pacific's piscatorial bounty, right? Not necessarily. If you know the wheres, whens, and hows of Washington's coastal jetties, you can reach good saltwater fishing by foot. The four major rock jetties and six smaller "finger" jetties along our coast provide a wealth of marine angling action to anyone willing to get out there and do some horizontal rock-climbing. Jetty-fishing provides anglers with good opportunities to catch lingcod, greenling, rockfish, flounder, saltwater perch, Dungeness crab, and even salmon. Here's where they are, from north to south:

- **Neah Bay Jetty** — Connects Waadah Island to the mainland just north of the town of Neah Bay.
- **Grays Harbor North Jetty** — At Point Brown, south of Ocean Shores via Ocean Shores Boulevard.
- **Westport Finger Jetties** — Six separate jetties just northwest of the Westport Boat Basin.
- **Grays Harbor South Jetty** — Juts west into the Pacific a short distance north of Westhaven State Park.
- **Columbia River North Jetty** — South end of Cape Disappointment via Fort Canby State Park.

roe, or Spin-N-Glos from the bank also take a few fish.

While catch statistics compiled by the Department of Fish and Wildlife show that the river produces a few summer-run steelhead, many of these fish are taken incidentally by early fall salmon anglers, and there isn't much of a targeted sport fishery on summer steelies. Any wild (unclipped) steelhead must be released, whatever the time of year you catch it.

The Chehalis is also the scene of a popular sport fishery on sturgeon. The stretch of river from Montesano downstream to Cosmopolis is the main focus of sturgeon-fishing activity. The chance of catching a monster eight- or nine-footer probably isn't as great here as it might be on the Columbia, but there are enough legal-sized 42- to 66-inchers to make this a worthwhile sturgeon fishery that extends pretty much throughout the year. Boat fishing certainly has advantages, and most

boaters launch at the Highway 107 launch or at Cosmopolis. Smelt are the most commonly used baits, but ghost shrimp, herring, and other offerings might work. Some Chehalis River sturgeon anglers do their fishing during the day, while others prefer night fishing. In either case the best action may occur immediately before or immediately after a tide change. As with salmon, check the fishing pamphlet to be sure of size restrictions and other regulation details before sturgeon fishing here for the first time.

The Chehalis has been stocked with as many as 14,000 sea-run cutthroat smolts a year, but such plants aren't something anglers can necessarily depend on. Regulations have changed in recent years, so it's now OK to keep a couple of cutts a day whether they're fin-clipped or not. The Lower Chehalis has the look of a natural sea-run cutthroat trout stream, with lots of slow water, undercut banks, and submerged trees to provide near-perfect cutthroat cover. If you can't find them down around Elma and Montesano, or if the salmon-fishing crowd on the extreme lower end of the river makes it impossible to fish in solitude, try going up to Cedarville or Porter to try your luck. These areas are usually lightly fished during the fall. Remember, though, that single, barbless hooks are required for all fall fishing on the Chehalis.

Although often overlooked because of the many other possibilities, the Lower Chehalis offers some fairly good bass fishing, especially in some of the slow-moving sloughs downstream from Montesano. Largemouths are the main target of anglers' efforts, but local rumor has it that some spots hold smallmouths as well.

Location: Enters the east end of Grays Harbor at Aberdeen; see map B1, grid b7.

Species: Winter and summer steelhead; chinook, coho, and chum salmon; sea-run cutthroat trout; white and green sturgeon; largemouth bass.

Facilities: Boat ramps are located at Cosmopolis, as well as off Highway 107 just south of Montesano, just upstream from the mouth of the Satsop River, at Porter, and at Cedarville.

Directions: Take I-5 to Grand Mound and turn west onto U.S. 12, following the river downstream. Or take Highway 8 west from Olympia and either turn south to follow the Chehalis upstream toward Oakville or continue west to parallel the river downstream to Aberdeen.

Contact: Blaine's Tackle, 360/532-1297; Washington Department of Fish and Wildlife, Montesano Office, 360/249-4628.

15 Vance Creek Ponds

Most of the trout fishing here takes place during the first few weeks after the late-April season opener. You can use a boat here, but it's not a necessity, since much of the water is within casting range of bank anglers. Once in a while someone lands a really big largemouth from these ponds. In the spring of 1999, a local youngster hauled a largemouth weighing over seven pounds from the bigger pond. That larger pond, by the way, known to some as Vance Creek Pond Number 1, is now open only to juvenile anglers under the age of 15, seniors (age 70 and over), and anglers with WDFW disability angling permits. Both ponds have decent populations of bass, but about the time they come to life and start cooperating well for anglers, the swimmers show up in large numbers. You might want to confine your bass fishing efforts to early or late in the day during the summer months.

Location: South of Elma; see map B1, grid b9.

Species: Rainbow trout, largemouth bass.

Facilities: A boat ramp is at the larger of the two ponds, and car-toppers may be carried to the bank of the smaller pond. Food, gas, lodging, and tackle are available in Elma.

Directions: Drive west from Olympia on U.S. 12 to the Elma exit. Turn south, go over the freeway, and drive half a mile to Wenzel Road. Turn right on Wenzel Road and right again into Vance Creek County Park.

Contact: Blaine's Tackle, 360/532-1297; Washington Department of Fish and Wildlife, Montesano Office, 360/249-4628.

16 Duck Lake

This long, shallow lake with coffee-colored water offers an interesting mix to any angler who takes the time to learn a few of its secrets. Both the bass and the trout sometimes grow to lunker proportions in the rich waters.

For rainbows, try trolling with small Kwikfish or Flatfish or stillfishing with Power Bait on the bottom or a bobber-and-worm rig near the surface. The few anglers who come to fly-fish also do fairly well with various nymph patterns during the day or with dry flies in the evening. Spinnerbaits and various plastics work well for bass, and during the summer it's easy to coax them to the surface for a plug, popper, or buzz bait.

If you want bluegills, try casting a Beetle Spin or Berkley Power Spin to shoreline brush piles and overhanging willows, especially when they congregate for spawning in the spring and early summer. Some of the bluegills grow to good size.

Location: South of Ocean Shores; see map B1, grid b5.

Species: Rainbow and cutthroat trout, largemouth bass, bluegill, crappie.

Facilities: There are two good boat ramps on the lake, at North Bay Park and Chinook Park, both of them along the east side. Food, gas, tackle, and lodging are available in Ocean Shores, and Ocean City State Park is only about 10 minutes away to the north.

Directions: Take Highway 109 west from Hoquiam for 14 miles to Highway 115. Turn south (left) and drive through Ocean Shores. Either turn left on Chance A La Mer and drive three blocks to the boat ramp near the north end of the lake, or continue south for one mile to Ocean Lake Way, turn left, and drive a quarter mile to Duck Lake Drive. Turn right and follow Duck Lake Drive one mile to the southern boat ramp.

Contact: Ocean City State Park, 360/289-3553; Washington State Parks and Recreation Commission, 360/902-8844 (information) or 800/452-5687 (reservations); Blaine's Tackle, 360/532-1297; Ocean Shores Chamber of Commerce, 800/762-3224.

🟦 Grays Harbor North Jetty and Point Brown

The jetty and the sandy beach to the northeast receive moderate fishing pressure during the summer and fall, but they go virtually unfished the rest of the year, which means many Washington anglers are missing out on about nine months of fishing opportunity each year. There's always something to catch here, since every high tide brings in a fresh supply of hungry customers.

Spring fishing can be especially good for lingcod, cabezon, and perch, and if you fish here in March or April, you'll probably have them all to yourself. Try leadhead jigs, herring, or live perch for lingcod, and small beach crabs or live shrimp for cabezon. Small baits such as limpets or pieces of clam, marine worms, or shrimp work best for perch. The early stages of the incoming tide are best for perch, while lings and cabezon may bite best just before and during the high slack.

The perch, lings, and cabezon continue biting through the summer, but other species also become important to anglers here, including black rockfish. They like leadhead jigs with small, plastic grub bodies, fished on an incoming and high tide.

Greenling, sole, and flounder are available around the North Jetty throughout most of the year, so you can fish for them whenever the mood strikes you and the weather isn't too rough. The same small baits that work for perch will also take these cooperative bottom fish.

Most anglers around here turn their attention to salmon fishing in the fall. A net-pen project started in the late 1980s has produced varying returns of adult cohos that make their way into the Ocean Shores boat harbor from September to November. These fish will sometimes hit herring baits that are either cast and retrieved or suspended beneath a large bobber, but more active artificial lures tend to be more productive for these fast-maturing silvers. Buzz Bombs and Blue Fox spinners are good bets.

Location: South of Ocean Shores; see map B1, grid b4.

Species: Black rockfish, redtail surfperch,

pile perch, cabezon, lingcod, greenling, various sole and flounder, coho salmon.

Facilities: Everything you need is in Ocean Shores.

Directions: Take Highway 109 west from Hoquiam to Highway 115, turn south, and drive through Ocean Shores. Bear west on any of the major cross streets to get on Sand Dune Drive and take it to Ocean Shores Boulevard, which ends at the North Jetty.

Contact: Blaine's Tackle, 360/532-1297; Ocean City State Park, 360/289-3553; Washington State Parks and Recreation Commission, 360/902-8844 (information) or 800/452-5687 (reservations); Ocean Shores Chamber of Commerce, 800/762-3224.

18 South Grays Harbor Streams

Resident cutthroat trout seem capable of living in the darnedest little ponds and ditches, so it should come as no surprise to find them in the many streams that flow out of the hills south of Grays Harbor. The names include Charley, Newskah, Chapin, Indian, Stafford, and O'Leary Creeks. All of these creeks have fishable populations of trout, but don't expect any lunkers; a mature fish may measure only nine or 10 inches. Be sure to read the regulations pamphlet before fishing, since stream-fishing rules and limits are very conservative in Washington, and many of the resident trout you hook will be too small to keep.

The trout will readily inhale a squirming garden worm, but where there's room to cast and fish them, why not try a small Metric, Mepps, or Panther Martin spinner? If you hunger to use your fly rod, try a small wet pattern or nymph, and you'll find the cutthroat will oblige.

The fish get bigger in the fall, when the sea-run member of the cutthroat clan invades these streams. That's when you have a real chance of catching a two-fish limit of keepers. Night crawlers and small clusters of salmon roe will entice them.

Location: Flow into the southeast side of Grays Harbor between South Aberdeen and Markham; see map B1, grid b6.

Species: Resident and sea-run cutthroat trout.

Facilities: Everything you need is available in Aberdeen.

Directions: Drive southwest from Aberdeen on Highway 105 and either stop at roadside turnouts near the bridges or turn south (left) on the various side roads that lead up the creeks.

Contact: Blaine's Tackle, 360/532-1297; Washington Department of Fish and Wildlife, Montesano Office, 360/249-4628.

19 Johns River

Hefty returns of hatchery chinook salmon have put this little Grays Harbor tributary on the salmon-fishing map in recent years, although anglers catch more of them from boats while the fish are still in the estuary than they catch in the river proper. Fall coho also return in decent numbers to provide good fishing for several weeks in the fall. The river also has chum salmon, but the season on them is currently closed. Fishing for winter steelhead is only fair, even though the river is planted with hatchery smolts. If you do decide to try it during the winter, you're better off fishing in December or January and looking for greener pastures later in the season.

Hatchery plants of sea-run cutts make the Johns a pretty good bet in the fall, and there are some fairly good walk-in spots on the middle and upper river that should produce trout in October. The boat ramp at the mouth of the river makes trolling for cutthroats a good possibility as well. Use your favorite small wobbling plugs or trout spoons, especially a size 960 Triple Teazer. If that fails, catch a couple of small sculpins, cut strips off their sides, and then fish the sculpin strips on a short leader behind a single or double-blade spinner. Cutthroats are located throughout the Johns River estuary. Remember that regulations allow you to keep only two cutts, and they must be at least 14 inches long. The river also has fall tackle restrictions, so read the fishing pamphlet carefully.

Location: Flows into the south side of Grays Harbor at Markham; see map B1, grid c6.

Species: Winter steelhead; sea-run cutthroat trout; coho, chum, and chinook salmon.

Facilities: A good boat ramp is located near the mouth of the river. Food, lodging, and other amenities are available in Westport and Aberdeen.

Directions: Drive southwest out of Aberdeen on Highway 105 for 10 miles and turn east (left) on Johns River Road.

Contact: Washington Department of Fish and Wildlife, Montesano Office, 360/249-4628.

20 Westport Inshore

The vast South Jetty and the half dozen shorter finger jetties that protect the Westport boat harbor offer a wealth of angling opportunities for the more adventurous rock-hopper. But there's also good fishing available to more restrained anglers on the long fishing pier near the north end of the boat harbor. Black rockfish provide excellent angling at all of these locations during the spring and early summer. With a small boat you can fish these spots even more effectively and get to other piers and bulkheads that shore-bound anglers can't reach. Fish quarter-ounce to three-quarter-ounce leadheads with two- or three-inch plastic curl-tail grubs for best results on rockfish; they shy away from the bigger lures some anglers use.

Early spring provides a good chance to do battle with big, toothy lingcod on the South Jetty and finger jetties. Fish leadheads with large, dark-colored plastic grubs for lings, or offer them a living snack in the form of a lip-hooked greenling, sole, or shiner perch. Lings to 20 pounds have been caught off the rocks here, and much larger ones have broken off to fight again.

The jetties and fishing pier also offer lots of smaller species that are just as good to eat as the big guys. Kelp greenling are abundant and will take almost any small bait or lure you might offer them. Cabezon will take shrimp or small crabs, and you might catch starry flounder and other flatfish species on just about any bait you offer.

Pile perch and redtail surfperch are popular with coastal anglers, and both are available in good numbers here. The pile perch population could use a little more fishing pressure, since many of the docks and piers around the boat harbor are inaccessible by land and can be reached only by boat anglers. Surfperch fishing is best in Half Moon Bay, the sandy beach on the northwest side of the peninsula on which Westport rests. The west side of the peninsula, on the ocean beach, is also a good place to fish for redtails.

Jetty fishing for salmon can be productive and is a specialized sport worth mentioning. Most commonly practiced near the end of the South Jetty, it involves the use of a whole or plug-cut herring on a standard, two-hook mooching leader with a spin sinker four to six feet above the bait. A large float made of wood or foam slides up and down the line above the sinker, with a bobber stop on the line wherever it needs to be to allow the angler to fish the proper depth. Some years (when salmon season is open along the coast) this rig accounts for good catches of both chinook and coho salmon.

A more dependable salmon fishery in recent years has taken place inside the Westport boat harbor. A successful net-pen project has resulted in large numbers of coho returning to the Westport docks, where anglers cast Buzz Bombs, spinners, and wobbling plugs for them. The fishing can be hot at times during September and October, but some so-called anglers have turned this fishery into somewhat of a snagfest.

Catch Dungeness crab with a rod and reel by casting a small tangle of line with a piece of fish tied into it. The crabs take the bait, become entangled, and you have 'em.

Location: South entrance to Grays Harbor; see map B1, grid c5.

Species: Lingcod, rockfish, cabezon, redtail surfperch, pile perch, greenling, sole, flounder, chinook and coho salmon, Dungeness crab.

Facilities: A three-lane boat ramp with a dock, public restrooms, food, lodging, gas, bait, and tackle all are available in and around Westport. There's also a single-lane ramp on the north side of Grays Harbor, at Ocean Shores. The Ocean Shores ramp is open 7 A.M. to 7 P.M. during the summer and 7 A.M. to 5 P.M. in the winter. It has a $5.50 launch fee.

Directions: Take Highway 105 west from Aberdeen for 18 miles and turn north (right) at the Y as you approach the coast. If you're trailering your own boat, turn right on Wilson Avenue and drive two blocks to the public boat ramp.

Contact: The Hungry Whale, 360/268-0136; Westport/Grayland Chamber of Commerce, 800/345-6223. For nautical charts of this area, contact Captain's Nautical Supply, 206/283-7242.

21 Westport Offshore

About the time many of us were about to write off the salmon fishing that made Westport famous back in the 1960s and 1970s, along came the 2001 salmon season. It was just like the good old days, only better, with charter boats and private craft alike returning to the docks before noon with limits of chinook and coho. The charter boats were full, the anglers were happy, the season was long, and the salmon took a beating, just the way it's sup-

posed to be. If there was a down side, it was the many unclipped, wild coho that were released with serious injuries, many of them to die at the bottom of the Pacific. The good side of that story is that many wild coho were released unharmed, and they provided added fishing action while anglers worked on catching their two-fish limit of chinook and hatchery coho. It was, all things considered, the best Westport salmon fishing in well over a decade, and let's hope there will be many more like it over the next several years.

The good salmon fishing had a limiting effect on charter trips for tuna, lingcod, rockfish, and halibut, but no one seemed to mind. Those fish will be around in coming years to provide consistent angling action, just as they have in the past.

Some charter offices run bottom-fish trips virtually year-round, concentrating mostly on black rockfish and lingcod during the winter and spring. Weather sometimes causes trip cancellations, but if the water is relatively flat, even in January or February, anglers stand to catch some husky lingcod this time of year. Halibut seasons have been getting more liberal in recent years, and when they're open, the Westport fleet has little trouble getting its charter anglers into fish, most of them caught from halibut grounds to the north.

There isn't much to say about the Westport salmon fishery that hasn't been said hundreds of times before, except to note that when the season is open and the kings and silvers are biting, no better fishing can be found anywhere. It might be the excitement generated when four or five people on the same boat are playing fish at once, multiplying the thrill not only for those involved but for all the others onboard, each knowing that he or she is going to be the next to hook up.

Albacore tuna pass by the Northwest coast every summer, but not always within range of the Westport charter fleet. Those years when they do get close enough, they provide from a few days to several weeks of red-hot angling action. August is the most likely month for this long-fin tuna madness, but it could start as early as July and some years lasts well into September. These 15- to 30-pound fish are as fast and tough as they come, and excellent table fare as well. Just as in bottom-fish and salmon trips, all tackle is included in the price of an albacore trip.

With the exception of albacore and those trips north for halibut, anglers with their own boats can get in on much of Westport's off-shore angling action. Larger, seaworthy boats equipped with all the necessary electronic and safety equipment are recommended, not only because this is open-water fishing in every regard, but because the bar at the entrance to Grays Harbor can become as rough and unpredictable as any water you'd ever want to run. Westport has a roomy boat ramp with plenty of parking space for those boat owners who know what they're doing.

Most folks have by now heard about some of the exotic catches made around Westport during the 1997 season, when the warm El Niño currents played havoc with coastal water conditions throughout the Northwest. At least two marlin and one California yellowtail were boated by albacore anglers during those strange days, and other species from southern waters also showed up off the Washington coast. Although such catches were interesting, they indicated that our coastal waters were much warmer than usual, too warm for our resident species. Water that holds marlin isn't good for salmon, lingcod, and other Northwest species. The good news is that the ocean was cooler in 1998 and 1999, even more like it should be in 2000 and 2001, so things have generally returned to normal, at least as far as what anglers are catching is concerned.

Location: South entrance to Grays Harbor; see map B1, grid c5.
Species: Chinook and coho salmon, albacore tuna, lingcod, halibut, black rockfish and several other varieties of rockfish.
Facilities: Charters, restaurants, motels, RV parks, watering holes, and anything else you might need are available within walking distance of the boat harbor. The three-lane boat ramp at the end of Wilson Avenue has a moorage dock for boaters trailering in and out, as well as a large parking lot with room for dozens of cars and trailers.
Directions: Take Highway 105 west from Aberdeen for 18 miles and turn north (right) at the Y as you approach the coast. If you're trailering your own boat, turn right on Wilson Avenue and drive two blocks to the public boat ramp.
Contact: Westport/Grayland Chamber of Commerce, 800/345-6223. For nautical charts of this area, contact Captain's Nautical Supply, 206/283-7242.

22 Elk River

This is another stream where an open salmon season provides virtually no angling action. Annual steelhead plants produce a few fish in December and January, but certainly not enough to generate much excitement. Sea-run cutthroat smolts are also stocked, and fishing for them is fair September through November. Check the fishing regulations pamphlet for details on single, barbless hook requirements in effect during the fall.

In spring and summer, fish around the highway bridge at the mouth of the river for striped seaperch and pile perch, which may be abundant on an incoming tide. Starry flounder and various species of sole are also possibilities if you let your bait sink to the bottom.

Location: Flows into Grays Harbor's South Bay near Bay City; see map B1, grid c6.

Species: Winter steelhead, sea-run cut-throat, coho and chinook salmon, seaperch, various sole and flounder.

Facilities: The nearest food, gas, motels, tackle, and other amenities are in Westport and Aberdeen.

Directions: Drive southwest out of Aberdeen on Highway 105 and turn east (left) on Johns River Road. After two miles, there will be a Y in the road. Turn right (west) and drive about one mile to the Elk River.

Contact: Washington Department of Fish and Wildlife, Montesano Office, 360/249-2648; Blaine's Tackle, 360/532-1297.

23 South Beach Surf

Several roads lead off the highway toward the beach, and any of them may lead to productive perch fishing. Although the best fishing usually occurs on the incoming tide, arriving early to check out the beach is a good idea. Look for deep ruts, humps, and lagoons that will draw fish as they move in with the tide. Pieces of razor clam neck make good bait, and if the clam season isn't open, you may be able to buy bait at local grocery and bait shops. If a particular spot doesn't produce right away, be patient. Take a coffee break and keep casting until the perch find you.

Location: Coastal beach from Westport south to Cape Shoalwater and the northern entrance to Willapa Bay; see map B1, grid c5.

Species: Redtail surfperch.

Facilities: Twin Harbors State Park to the north and Grayland Beach State Park to the south have tent spaces, RV hookups, and restrooms with showers; other facilities are available in Westport and Tokeland.

Directions: Take Highway 105 southwest from Aberdeen for 25 miles or northwest from Raymond for 17 miles and turn west at any of the well-marked beach access roads.

Contact: Twin Harbors State Park, 360/268-9717; Grayland Beach State Park, 360/268-9717; Washington State Parks and Recreation Commission, 360/902-8844 (information) or 800/452-5687 (reservations); Blaine's Tackle, 360/532-1297.

24 North River

This small river in the heart of Washington's timber country gets little publicity and is fished mostly by locals who would just as soon keep the river a secret. It's not so much that the river offers red-hot salmon, trout, or steelhead fishing; folks around here just aren't all that wild about outsiders stomping up and down their favorite rivers.

The North has been known to give up 200 to 300 steelhead a winter, the bulk of them in January. December and February offer fair steelheading as well. Lots of logs and streamside brush make this a challenging place to play and land an angry winter steelhead.

As for trout and salmon fishing, the North River has a heck of a lot of picky little regulations for such a small stream. The trout fishery is now a catch-and-release affair, and salmon fishing rules are complicated enough to warrant at least two readings of the latest fishing pamphlet, just to be sure you have it right.

Location: Enters Willapa Bay east of Tokeland; see map B1, grid c7.

Species: Winter steelhead, coho salmon, sea-run cutthroat trout.

Facilities: A good boat ramp is located at the mouth of the river, right off Highway 105. Arctic has a store and a tavern, and other facilities are available in Raymond and Aberdeen.

Directions: Take U.S. 101 south from Aberdeen or north from Raymond and turn east at Arctic on North River Road to reach the upper river. Turn west off U.S. 101 onto Lund Road and follow it downriver to American Mill Road to explore lower portions of the river. To fish the two miles of river at the mouth, take Highway 105 west from Raymond and turn north (left) near the west end of the highway bridge to the access area and boat ramp.

Contact: Blaine's Tackle, 360/532-1297; Washington Department of Fish and Wildlife, Montesano Office, 360/249-4628.

25 Smith Creek

For its size, this little Willapa Bay tributary receives a generous helping of hatchery steelhead smolts, helping to provide a fair fishery December through February. Department of Fish and Wildlife records show that anglers catch 60 or 70 winter steelhead here every year. Anglers willing to get off the back roads and do some exploring on foot along the middle and lower sections of the creek are often rewarded for their efforts.

Salmon fishing is fair for adult and jack coho on the lower portion of the creek in October, and there are also fair numbers of sea-run cutthroats in the creek at that time. All cuts in Smith Creek are wild, and the regulations now allow catch-and-release fishing only on them.

Location: Flows into the north end of Willapa Bay northwest of Raymond; see map B1, grid c6.

Species: Winter steelhead, coho salmon, sea-run cutthroat trout.

Facilities: A good boat ramp is located at the mouth of the creek. Other amenities are available in Raymond.

Directions: Take U.S. 101 north from Raymond for five miles or south from Aberdeen for 18 miles and turn east on Smith Creek Road to reach about 12 miles of the creek between the highway and the small town of Brooklyn. Turn west off U.S. 101 on Dixon Road to reach part of the lower section of the creek. To fish the waters near the creek mouth, drive west from Raymond on Highway 105 for eight miles and turn right into the boat ramp and access area just across the Smith Creek bridge.

Contact: Washington Department of Fish and Wildlife, Montesano Office, 360/249-4628; Blaine's Tackle, 360/532-1297.

26 Willapa River

This is arguably the best steelhead river among all Willapa Bay tributaries, and it's no slouch as a salmon river, either. The river is stocked with about 50,000 winter steelhead smolts every year, and anglers catch anywhere from 500 to 1,000 adult Willapa steelhead each winter. Hatchery fish, as most steelheaders know, return earlier in the winter, and the rule holds true here. December and January are the top months, but don't give up completely in February and March. Leave your drift boat home when you visit the Willapa during the winter, since you can't fish from the boat on most of the best steelhead water November through March.

The lower few miles of the Willapa produce good numbers of chinook salmon in September and October, especially for boat anglers who launch at the Old Willapa launch area near the mouth of Ward Creek. Many of them try to time their trips so they launch at high tide and fish as the tide ebbs. Flash Glo spinners are favorites of many of these anglers, but back-bouncing with roe clusters or back-trolling with Kwikfish or diver-and-roe combinations also work. The catch often includes a large percentage of jack chinooks weighing two to five pounds, but 25- to 35-pounders are also possibilities. Coho salmon are scattered through the Willapa September through December, filling the gap between the height of the chinook fishery and the start of winter steelhead action. There are also good numbers of chums in the Willapa to provide fishing action from about the middle of October into early December.

If you read the Willapa River listing in either of the first two editions of this book, you may remember that I recommended the sea-run cutthroat trout fishing possibilities along two or three stretches of the Willapa, but things have changed. You can still catch cutthroats from the river, but you can't keep any of them. Go elsewhere if you're looking for a trout for the frying pan.

Location: Enters the northeast corner of Willapa Bay near South Bend; see map B1, grid d7.

Species: Winter steelhead, chinook and coho salmon, sea-run cutthroat trout.

Facilities: There's a boat ramp near the river mouth, at the west end of South Bend, and another at Old Willapa on Willapa Road about 3.5 miles upstream from the U.S. 101 bridge. A fair selection of restaurants and some lodging, along with tackle, gas, and grocery stores, are available in Raymond and South Bend.

Directions: Take U.S. 101 to Raymond and turn east on Willapa Road at the north end of the highway bridge just north of town to reach some of the boat-fishing areas at the lower end of the river. To reach upstream sections of the Willapa, take Highway 6 east from Raymond for six miles or west from Chehalis for 22 miles.

Contact: Blaine's Tackle, 360/532-1297; Washington Department of Fish and Wildlife, Montesano Office, 360/249-4628.

27 Willapa Bay

Salmon bound for the Willapa, Naselle, and other river systems all have to pass through Willapa Bay to get home, but anglers have to compete for them with commercial netters. Depending on the length and timing of the commercial seasons, sport fishing for chinooks can be good here from the time the season opens around the middle of August until late September. Long before the chinooks taper off, the coho move in to take up the slack. Most of the salmon fishing is confined to the waters near the bay entrance, just west of Tokeland. Drift mooching with whole or plug-cut herring right up near the beach produces most of the kings, some of which top 30 pounds. Most of the silvers are caught farther from shore, usually by trollers.

Sea-run cutthroats are available here and can be caught by trolling near the shoreline or around any of the islands. The mouths of all rivers and creeks are especially good places to look for them. If Triple Teazers, Dick Nites, Canadian Wonders, and similar spoons don't work, try a strip of sculpin meat behind a spinner, worked just off bottom at a slow troll.

Willapa Bay in general and the mouths of such major tributaries as the Willapa and Naselle Rivers in particular also provide fairly good sturgeon fishing from late winter through the summer months. The sturgeon fishery is primarily a boat fishery.

Location: West of Raymond; see map B1, grid d5.

Species: Chinook and coho salmon, sturgeon, sea-run cutthroat trout, seaperch and surfperch.

Facilities: There are several possibilities for launching a boat on Willapa Bay:

- **Tokeland Marina:** Starting at the north end of the bay, there's a one-lane concrete ramp with a loading float at the Port of Willapa Harbor's Tokeland Marina.

- **North River Resort:** This resort along Highway 105 maintains a ramp at the mouth of the North River. This one-lane gravel ramp is a good one, and the resort charges a fee for its use.

- **Smith Creek Ramp:** A short distance to the east is the Department of Fish and Wildlife's ramp at the mouth of Smith Creek. This is a single-lane concrete ramp with a fairly large parking area, but boaters have to go under the nearby Highway 101 bridge to reach the bay, and this can be a tight squeeze, even impossible, for larger boats on a fairly high tide. A $10 WDFW access decal is required to use the public launch areas maintained by the Washington Department of Fish and Wildlife.

- **Helen Davis Park:** The Washington Department of Fish and Wildlife's ramp at Helen Davis Park, on the mouth of the Willapa River, also provides access to the bay. It's a single-wide concrete ramp that has seen better days. A $10 WDFW access decal is required to use the public launch areas maintained by the Department of Fish and Wildlife.

- **Palix River Ramp:** The Department of Fish and Wildlife ramp at the mouth of the Palix River near Bay Center also provides access to Willapa Bay. It's a two-lane ramp of concrete planks, with a fairly large, gravel parking area. The $10 WDFW access decal is required here, too.

- **Willapa National Wildlife Refuge:** Several miles south is the one-lane gravel ramp at the Willapa National Wildlife Refuge. It has a small loading float. A $5 launch fee is now charged at this ramp.

- **Nahcotta Boat Basin:** Around on the west side of the bay is Nahcotta Boat Basin, the only place on this side of Willapa Bay where a trailer boat can be launched. It's a fixed hoist managed by the Port of Peninsula, and a fee is charged for launching. Call ahead (360/665-4547) to check on weekend closures during the winter.

The little town of Tokeland has a couple of places to stay, including the historic Tokeland Hotel, which has some of the best home cookin' in Pacific County. Bush Pioneer County Park, about two miles north of Bay Center, has picnic tables and shelters, as well as RV and tent sites. There are also motels, cabins, and RV parks in Raymond and South Bend, which are at the northeast corner of the bay, and along much of the Long Beach Peninsula, which borders most of the bay's west side.

Directions: The north side of the bay is accessible by Highway 105 from Aberdeen or Raymond, the south end and east side via U.S. 101.

Contact: Tokeland Hotel & Restaurant, 360/267-7006; Bay Center Marina, 360/942-3422; Port of Willapa Bay/Raymond, 360/942-3422; Long Beach Peninsula Visitor's Bureau, 800/451-2542, website: www.funbeach.com; Raymond Chamber of Commerce Visitor Information Center, 360/942-5419. For nautical charts of this area, contact Captain's Nautical Supply, 206/283-7242.

28 Palix River

This has become pretty much a catch-and-release stream for all anglers in recent years, except that it's OK to keep one nonhatchery coho during the fall salmon season. Selective regulations (artificial lures only, single barbless hooks) have been eliminated, but all trout and steelhead must now be released. Still, it's a pretty little stream, at least some of it, and there are worse places to be catching and releasing fish.

Location: Enters the east side of Willapa Bay southwest of South Bend; see map B1, grid d6.

Species: Sea-run cutthroat trout, winter steelhead, coho salmon.

Facilities: There's a boat ramp near the river mouth just south of the U.S. 101 bridge. The nearest major facilities are in South Bend and Raymond, both within 12 to 14 miles.

Directions: Drive south from South Bend on U.S. 101 for 12 miles and take the left just before you cross the Palix River bridge or turn left on South Palix Road about a mile south of the bridge.

Contact: Dave's Shell Bait and Tackle, 360/642-2320; Washington Department of Fish and Wildlife, Montesano Office, 360/249-4628.

29 Nemah River

The busiest time of the year for Nemah River anglers is in October, when larger runs of coho and scrappy chum salmon invade from Willapa Bay. This fishery is hot but short-lived, providing several hundred fish in a few weeks. The three forks of the Nemah also give up a few chinook and coho salmon, most of them also caught in October. Check the regulations pamphlet, though, since restrictions are in place that change the legalities from year to year.

As for trout and salmon fishing, they've become catch-and-release only, with selective tackle regulations in place.

Location: Flows into the east side of Willapa Bay at Nemah; see map B1, grid e6.

Species: Winter steelhead; sea-run cutthroat trout; chum, coho, and chinook salmon.

Facilities: You'll find some necessities at Bay Center, but most facilities are to the north in South Bend and Raymond.

Directions: Drive south from South Bend on U.S. 101 for 18 miles and turn east on North Nemah Road or any of the next three gravel roads to the east, all of which reach upper portions of the Nemah. You can also fish some parts of the river by parking near the highway bridges and walking upstream or downstream.

Contact: Dave's Shell Bait and Tackle, 360/642-2320; Washington Department of Fish and Wildlife, Montesano Office, 360/249-4628.

30 Long Beach Peninsula Surf

Perch are as readily available here as they are in beach areas to the north, but fishing pressure is quite light. Fish pieces of clam neck or ghost or sand shrimp on an incoming tide, and remember to fish just beyond the first line of breakers.

If you have time during the low tide before or after you fish, venture across to the east side of the Long Beach Peninsula and the port town of Nahcotta, where you'll find Nahcotta Tidelands Interpretive Center and several acres of public tidelands on Willapa Bay

where you can gather oysters and dig clams. That way, even if the fishing is slow, you can still return home with enough fresh seafood for a delicious meal.

Location: Leadbetter Point south to Cape Disappointment; see map B1, grid e5.

Species: Redtail surfperch.

Facilities: Campgrounds, RV parks, motels, tackle, gas, and restaurants are located in Long Beach and Ocean Park.

Directions: Take U.S. 101 west to the small town of Seaview and go north on Highway 103. Several roads to the west lead to the beach.

Contact: Dave's Shell Bait and Tackle, 360/642-2320; Long Beach Peninsula Visitor's Bureau, 800/451-2542, website: www.funbeach.com; Washington State Parks and Recreation Commission, 360/902-8844 (information) or 800/452-5687 (reservations).

31 Long Beach Peninsula Lakes

Loomis Lake, at about 170 acres, is the largest and best known of the Long Beach lakes, and probably the most productive for anglers. It's stocked with about 7,000 legal-sized rainbows before the April opener and provides good fishing into early summer, even though it's only about 10 feet deep in its deepest spot. Loomis is a good fly-fishing lake, but most anglers troll hardware or stillfish with bait. Though trout fishing is the big draw, the lake also offers some decent-sized perch.

Immediately east of Loomis Lake is Lost Lake, which covers only a couple of acres and produces more perch than anything else. Then comes Island Lake, within walking distance to the south of Lost. Island has a rough boat ramp on its east side, where anglers launch car-topper boats and canoes to go after largemouth bass and yellow perch. Like other lakes in the area, it's very shallow, but it produces some largemouths of three pounds and larger. Next come Tape, Cranberry, and Litschke Lakes, all under 20 acres and all containing both largemouths and perch. A little farther south are Clam and Gile Lakes, at 10 and 18 acres respectively, both containing bass and perch. Gile now and then produces a trophy-class bass. Briscoe, Breaker, Clear, and Tinker Lakes, all connected by a small stream, run north to south along the west side of the peninsula, and all offer largemouths and perch.

About three miles south of the rest of the pack, between Seaview and Ilwaco, lies Black Lake, a 30-acre lake that has rainbow trout and black bullheads along with its population of bass and perch. Black is stocked with several hundred legal-sized rainbows every spring. An excellent fishing dock alongside the road offers a convenient place to park and fish. If you're lucky, maybe you'll get a chance to set the hook into a whopper rainbow trout like the one hauled from the lake on opening day a few years back, a lunker that tipped the scales at over 5.5 pounds.

Most of these lakes have some kind of public access, but be sure to ask around if you aren't sure. Even the lakes that offer public access, though, don't necessarily have a good place to launch a boat. While few anglers use them, float tubes would be the perfect way to fish virtually all of these lakes, so if you have one, bring it along the next time you head out on a fishing trip to the Long Beach Peninsula.

Location: Long Beach Peninsula from Ocean Park south to Ilwaco; see map B1, grid e5.

Species: Rainbow trout, yellow perch, largemouth bass.

Facilities: Loomis Lake has a boat ramp, but most of the other lakes don't. Food, gas, RV and tent sites, tackle, and lodging are readily available on the Long Beach Peninsula. Fort Canby State Park, one of the biggest and best in the state parks system, is nearby

to the south. If you're around at dinnertime, make reservations at the 42nd Street Cafe in Seaview (great home-cooked meals and fantastic service) or at the Ark Restaurant in Nahcotta (excellent food and a wonderful view of Willapa Bay).

Directions: Take U.S. 101 to the extreme southwest corner of Washington and turn north at Seaview at Highway 103.

Contact: Dave's Shell Bait and Tackle, 360/642-2320; Washington State Parks and Recreation Commission, 360/902-8844 (information) or 800/452-5687 (reservations); Long Beach Peninsula Visitor's Bureau, 800/451-2542, website: www.funbeach.com.

32 Bear River

A good run of brawling chum salmon disrupts the serenity of this otherwise placid little river at the south end of Willapa Bay. The wildest chum fishing usually occurs in October, but good fishing is a possibility during the first two weeks of November. You might find an occasional coho mixed in with all the chums, but remember that you can keep only one wild coho per day here. The salmon season here actually opens in early September, so there's a chance you could hook a chinook or two. If you do, you have to release any adult kings you bring to the bank. Winter steelheading here is a matter of fishing for wild fish, and there aren't many of them around, so catch-and-release is all that's allowed. Catch-and-release also is the rule for sea-run cutthroat trout.

Location: Enters the south end of Willapa Bay; see map B1, grid f6.

Species: Chum salmon, sea-run cutthroat trout, a few coho salmon and winter steelhead.

Facilities: Food, gas, lodging, tackle, and other amenities are available in Ilwaco.

Directions: Take U.S. 101 south from South Bend or follow Highway 4 west from Longview to its junction with U.S. 101 and follow it south.

The highway crosses over Bear River about six miles northeast of Ilwaco.

Contact: Dave's Shell Bait and Tackle, 360/642-2320.

33 Naselle River

It's not a big river, but the Naselle is a consistent producer of good winter steelhead and fall salmon catches. Hatchery-stock steelhead pour into the river throughout the winter, providing the possibility for good fishing from early December until the end of March. Roads upstream and downstream from Highway 4 offer lots of bank-fishing access throughout the winter.

Chinook salmon fishing can be good for both boat and bank anglers on the lower Naselle in September and early October, and an even bigger run of cohos moves into the river as the chinook fishery wanes. Some large chums join in for added variety and excitement about the same time the silvers arrive. Be sure to check the latest edition of the sport fishing regulations pamphlet for how many of each salmon species you can keep and other details.

Once a place where you could find pretty good fall fishing for sea-run cutthroat trout, that fishery has become catch-and-release in recent years.

Location: Enters the southeast corner of Willapa Bay; see map B1, grid f7.

Species: Winter steelhead; chinook, coho, and chum salmon; sea-run and resident cutthroat trout.

Facilities: You'll find food and gas in Naselle, and there's a campground on Highway 4 about three miles east of town. Long Beach has tackle, lodging, and restaurants.

Directions: Take Highway 4 west from Longview to Naselle or drive south from South Bend on U.S. 101, turn southeast on Highway 4, and drive about six miles to Naselle.

Contact: Dave's Shell Bait and Tackle, 360/642-2320; Washington Department of Fish and Wildlife, Montesano Office, 360/249-4628.

34 Ilwaco Offshore

Like Westport (see number 21), Ilwaco has a long-standing reputation for its excellent salmon fishing. That reputation was revived during the summer of 2001, when limits once again became the rule for both charter and private boat anglers around the mouth of the Columbia. There were times when the charters were pulling back into port before 9 A.M. with limits all around, even better fishing than Ilwaco provided during the heydays of the 1970s. You can call it "offshore" fishing, but some of those boats had only to clear the Columbia River bar before dropping baited hooks and instantly hauling in eager hatchery coho. Ilwaco salmon fishing once again became a "sure thing," as it was during the good old days of nearly 30 years ago.

Bottom-fish trips fill a big void for Ilwaco-area anglers before the salmon seasons open—and those openers have been very unpredictable lately. Spring trips for lingcod and rockfish produce well, and the catch often includes a few of those big, brightly colored yelloweye rockfish that are as impressive to the veteran saltwater angler as they are to the novice who has never seen one before. Much of the bottom-fish activity for the Ilwaco fleet takes place to the south over several rock pinnacles that lie off the Oregon coast.

As in Westport, the halibut fishing for Ilwaco anglers could be a whole lot better if the season were longer and more liberal, but that's not the way it is. Charters don't have much trouble finding halibut for their customers, but they don't get much opportunity to do it during a season that may last only a few days in July.

If and when the albacore show up within range of the Ilwaco charter fleet, trips are available from mid- to late summer. Most are overnight affairs, and the rewards can be impressive. The problem with albacore is that they're not dependable enough to allow much planning, so trips are scheduled on short notice and everyone has to scurry to get in on the action.

Even though salmon seasons have been restrictive in recent years, at least anglers know in advance that they're going to occur, and when the seasons are open, anglers know they can usually catch kings and silvers off the mouth of the Columbia. The only question may be whether the boat will make a 20-minute run or a two-hour run to where the fish are located. That's not a big problem where most anglers are concerned.

I consider charter fishing the safest and easiest way to fish off the mouth of the Columbia, but many anglers fish here in their own boats. If you're thinking about doing so for the first time, do your homework first. Crossing the bar here can be about as tricky and as potentially dangerous as anywhere on the West Coast. Monstrous energy is released when coastal winds and the mighty Columbia collide, and since the river is shallow, there's no place for the water to go but up. Some very good boaters have lost it all here, so don't take chances.

Location: Outside the mouth of the Columbia River southwest of Ilwaco; see map B1, grid f5.

Species: Chinook and coho salmon, lingcod, rockfish, halibut, albacore tuna.

Facilities: Charters, boat ramps, gas, restaurants, groceries, lodging, and other accommodations are available in Ilwaco. Fort Canby State Park, one of the state's largest campgrounds, is just south of town.

Directions: Take U.S. 101 south about 41 miles from Raymond or take Highway 4 west from Kelso to Highway 401 at Naselle, turn south (left), and follow Highway 14 about 21 miles to Ilwaco.

Contact: Pacific Salmon Charters, 360/642-3466 or 800/831-2695, website: www.pacific salmoncharters.com; Fort Canby State Park, 360/642-3078; Washington State Parks and Recreation Commission, 360/902-8844 (information) or 800/452-5687 (reservations); Long Beach Peninsula Visitor's Bureau, 800/451-2542; Dave's Shell Bait and Tackle, 360/642-2320. For nautical charts of this area, contact Captain's Nautical Supply, 206/283-7242.

35 Columbia River Estuary

The angling variety available in and around the mouth of the Columbia River is similar to that of Grays Harbor and the Westport area (see number 20), except that sturgeon fishing is a much bigger deal here. Not only do dozens of private boats and hundreds of bank anglers stake out their claims to what they hope will be productive sturgeon water every morning, but a number of charters out of Ilwaco also explore the Columbia estuary for "Ol' Diamond Sides," as the sturgeon is sometimes known. White sturgeon are more numerous and grow substantially larger than green sturgeon, but anglers catch both species. Now and then someone catches a monster white of 10 feet, 12 feet, or even larger, but all of these huge females must be released unharmed. The high point of any sturgeon trip is to see one of these prehistoric behemoths jump completely out of the water, looking and sounding every bit like a Douglas fir log when it crashes back into the river. Some of the best spots to anchor and wait out a big sturgeon are places where the bottom breaks away quickly from shallow to deep water, and it may take some exploring with a depthsounder to find such spots. An easier way for the newcomer is to watch where other boats anchor and pull in nearby (but not too near) to investigate. Smelt, ghost shrimp, and shad (when they're running through the lower river) are among the top sturgeon baits here.

As for salmon, the world-famous Buoy 10 fishery takes place here—at least it takes place most years. When the season is open and the fishing is good, the waters near the mouth of the Columbia become one of the world's biggest aquatic traffic jams, as boats of all sizes and styles jockey for a crack at incoming kings and silvers. Slow trolling with herring at the start of an outgoing tide is often the most productive combination, but be willing to do some experimenting. You didn't even have to bother experimenting around Buoy 10 during the red-hot 2001 salmon season, when more than a million hatchery coho and something like 400,000 chinook flooded into the Columbia during August and September. The good thing about this fishery when the fishing is really good is that you don't have to battle the mob at the buoy line to get your fish. If you want to avoid the crowds, just move upriver toward the Megler-Astoria Bridge and catch fish while enjoying a little more elbowroom.

Anglers also catch their share of salmon right off the North Jetty, a spot that has been known to give up a few kings of 40 pounds and larger. Subduing an angry chinook on those slick, barnacle-encrusted boulders, with the waves crashing at your feet, is no easy chore, but veteran jetty-jumpers can do it. Fishing a whole anchovy or plug-cut herring below a big slip-bobber accounts for most of the salmon.

The North Jetty is also a good place to fish for lingcod, rockfish, greenling, cabezon, and crab, not to mention smaller perch, sole, and flounder. Herring, anchovies, leadhead jigs with plastic grub bodies, even small metal jigs work well here. If you want perch, sole, or flounder, cast pieces of clam, bloodworm, or shrimp with a light sinker and fairly small hook.

Location: Mouth of the Columbia River near Ilwaco; see map B1, grid f5.

Species: Chinook and coho salmon, white sturgeon, green sturgeon, lingcod, rockfish, cabezon, greenling, Dungeness crab.

Facilities: Fort Canby State Park has RV and tent sites, restrooms with showers, and other amenities. The park also has a large boat ramp and a store with food, beverages, bait, and tackle. Restaurants, motels, gas stations, and watering holes are easy to find in Ilwaco and to the north in Long Beach. Several charter companies work out of Ilwaco.

Directions: Take U.S. 101 south from Raymond for 41 miles or drive west on Highway 4 from Kelso about 56 miles and turn south (left) on Highway 401 to the river.

Contact: Fort Canby State Park, 360/642-3078; Washington State Parks and Recreation Commission, 360/902-8844 (information) or 800/452-5687 (reservations); Long Beach Peninsula Visitor's Bureau, 800/451-2542; website: www.funbeach.com; Dave's Shell Bait and Tackle, 360/642-2320; Chinook Country Store, 360/777-BAIT (777-2248). For nautical charts of this area, contact Captain's Nautical Supply, 206/283-7242.

36 Grays River

Once a well-respected winter steelhead stream, the Grays has slipped a few notches over the past 10 years or so. Although the river is stocked with 40,000 to 50,000 steelhead smolts a year, the steelhead catch bounces up and down between only 150 and 400 fish a winter. That's probably enough to provide a ray of hope for any visiting angler, but you have to wonder what happened to those other 49,600 smolts, don't you? When the few adult steelhead that survive their oceanic adventure finally make it back to the Grays, most of them show up in December and January, so those are the months to fish here if you entertain any hope of catching steelhead. Fall salmon fishing is a whole lot worse and only open on parts of the river system for certain species of certain size, so be sure to read the latest copy of the regulations pamphlet before even considering it.

Unless you hit it right for fishing, the high point of a trip to the Grays might be getting an opportunity to gawk at Washington's only remaining covered bridge. Though there weren't many of them to begin with, now there's only one. Maybe that's why no one ever bought the movie rights to *The Bridges of Wahkiakum County.*

Location: Enters the Lower Columbia River west of Skamokawa; see map B1, grid f8.

Species: Winter steelhead; sea-run and resident cutthroat trout; chinook, coho, and chum salmon.

Facilities: Ilwaco, the nearest town of any size, is about 20 miles southeast and offers food, gas, tackle, and lodging. About 30 miles to the west is Fort Canby State Park, which has tent and RV sites, restrooms with showers, and a small store.

Directions: Take Highway 4 west from Cathlamet or east from Naselle. To reach much of the middle portion of the river, take Loop Road south off the highway (midway between the little town of Grays River and the highway bridge over the river), or turn south on Highway 403 near Rosburg to reach the lower river.

Contact: Chinook Country Store, 360/777-BAIT (777-2248); Dave's Shell Bait and Tackle, 360/642-2320.

37 Skamokawa Creek

Here's another stream where several thousand winter steelhead smolts are planted every year but nobody knows what happens to them. Very few have made it back to provide any decent winter steelheading during the past few years. You might get lucky and hook a fish in December or January, but the odds are against it.

Location: Enters the Columbia River at Skamokawa; see map B1, grid f9.

Species: Winter steelhead.

Facilities: There are limited visitor facilities in Skamokawa and Cathlamet.

Directions: Take Highway 4 to Skamakawa and turn north on Maki Road to follow the creek upstream.

Contact: Chinook Country Store, 360/777-BAIT (777-2248).

38 Elochoman River

After three hours of driving, fishing partner Dave Borden and I unfolded slowly from the cab of the pickup and strolled to the edge of the muddy parking area for a closer look at the river.

"It's not much, is it?" Dave observed. Going largely by the river's reputation as a steelhead producer, we both expected a bigger stream than the one that purred by so gently a few yards below. But we had driven more than 150 miles, there were no other anglers in sight, and the small pocket of potential steelhead-holding water just upstream looked pretty good, so we walked back to the camper for hip boots, rods, and bait boxes.

Dave's a lot smaller and a little quicker than I am, so he was rigged, ready, and standing at the edge of the river several minutes ahead of me. As I made my way down the steep bank toward the water, he reared back on the rod and let out a holler.

"There's one," he said, quite unnecessarily, as a silver-sided buck steelhead of about six pounds rolled violently on the surface for a couple of seconds and then blasted downstream, through a short riffle and into a long stretch of flat water below. Dave followed, I went along for moral support, and a couple minutes later our first steelhead of the day was on the bank.

But it wouldn't be our last. My partner hooked and lost another steelhead on his next cast into that little pocket of slick water before turning it over to me for a few casts. I pulled out a mint-bright nine-pounder, told Dave to take another shot, and darned if he didn't hook and land another fish that was a near dead ringer to his first. Seven hours later, after exploring a few miles of river upstream and returning to finish the day where we had started, our tally was 10 hatchery steelhead hooked, seven landed, and four killed for the table. I felt I had found the place I had been looking for all my life.

As it turned out, we had simply timed our first visit to the Elochoman perfectly. A couple of hours of rain the evening before had raised the river a few inches, attracting a fresh run of bright steelhead in from the Columbia, and since it was the middle of the week and most normal people were working, Dave and I had several stretches of the small stream to ourselves. By the next day the river had dropped back down to normal flow and below, and a full day of fishing produced only two fish.

But we had seen enough to know that southwest Washington's Elochoman can be red hot when conditions are right, and that very first trip to this little river with the big name was enough to convert me and my long-time fishing partner into confirmed Elochoman addicts. We're not alone in that regard. During the peak of the winter steelhead season, finding elbowroom along the banks of this small steelie producer is a tough proposition, especially on a weekend. Word has gotten out, and some of the more productive and popular stretches of river draw plenty of angler interest.

Despite its small size, the Elochoman regularly ranks among the state's top winter steelhead producers. During the 1993–94 season, it gave up just over 1,600 winter steelies, pretty much an average year, but some years it has been known to produce more than 6,000 steelhead in a single winter. The vast majority of those thousands of winter-run steelhead caught by Elochoman River anglers have been hatchery fish. The Beaver Creek Hatchery, operated by the Washington Department of Fish and Wildlife about six miles upstream from the river mouth, releases about 100,000 winter steelhead smolts a year into the river, and it's the adult fish returning to the hatchery a couple of years after their release that provide a bulk of the Elochoman's winter steelhead action. Because hatchery steelhead tend to return early in the winter season, December and January are the best months to fish the Elochoman.

This tiny river also provides worthwhile summer steelheading, producing 200 to 300 fish each year during the warm months from June to September. June, when the river is still running fairly high, is the top month for summer-runs, but July also can be worthwhile. By August and September the river is so low and clear that outsmarting one of these spooky, ocean-run rainbows becomes a real challenge.

As on many western Washington streams, fall means salmon and sea-run cutthroat fishing on the Elochoman. Anglers should check the regulations, especially where chum salmon are concerned, but October and November coho fishing can be quite productive. The regulations have become especially liberal for chinook salmon in recent years, and this is a river that has produced some monster kings, including the freshwater state record back in 1992.

The Department of Fish and Wildlife stocks 30,000 to 40,000 sea-run cutthroat smolts in the Elochoman every year, helping to provide excellent fall trout fishing. This is one of those streams where anglers may keep only hatchery (fin-clipped) cutthroat.

Location: Joins the Columbia River near Cathlamet; see map B1, grid f9.

Species: Winter and summer steelhead, chinook and coho salmon, sea-run cutthroat trout.

Facilities: Food and gas are available in Cathlamet.

Directions: Take Highway 4 to about a mile west of Cathlamet and turn north on Highway 407.

Contact: Chinook Country Store, 360/777-BAIT; Washington Department of Fish and Wildlife, Montesano Office, 360/249-4628.

CHAPTER B2:
SOUTHWEST WASHINGTON

© TERRY RUDNICK

WINTER STEELHEADING ON THE COWLITZ RIVER

Map B2

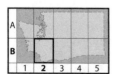

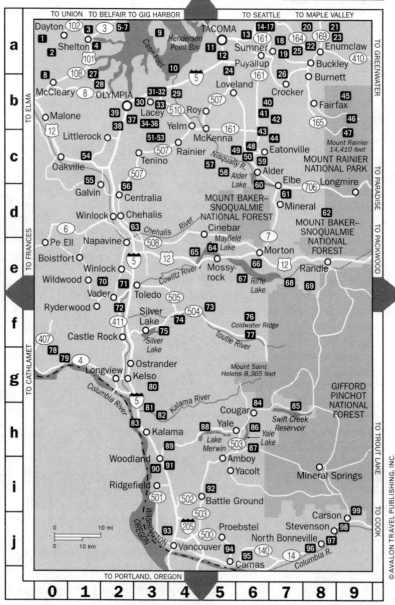

TO UNION   TO BELFAIR   TO GIG HARBOR   TO SEATTLE   TO MAPLE VALLEY

a
Dayton 102 **3** 3 **5-7**   **14-17** 20 **21**
1   9   Henderson   TACOMA **13** 161 **18** 164 169 **23**
2 Shelton **4**   Point Bay **11** Sumner 19 25 22 Enumclaw 410
101   **12** Puyallup 26   Buckley
8   **10**   161   Burnett
108 **27**   Loveland   Crocker
McCleary 8 OLYMPIA **31-32** 29   507   40   Fairfax **45**
28   **41** **42**
b Malone **39** **33** Roy 510   165 **46**
38 **37** 34-36   **47**
Littlerock 12   Yelm 161   Mount Rainier
51-53   McKenna   14,410 feet
c Oakville **54** 507 Rainier **49** **48** MOUNT RAINIER
Tenino   Nisqually R. **50** **59** NATIONAL PARK
55 507 **57** **58** Alder Eatonville
Galvin **56** Centralia   Alder **60** Elbe Longmire
Lake   **61** 706
d Winlock Chehalis **63** MOUNT BAKER– Mineral
Chehalis River SNOQUALMIE **62**
6 Cinebar NATIONAL FOREST MOUNT BAKER–
Pe Ell Napavine 508 Mayfield 7 SNOQUALMIE
e Boistfort 12 Lake **64** Morton NATIONAL
Wildwood **70** **65** Mossy- 12 FOREST
5 Cowlitz River rock **66** Randle
Vader **71** **67** Riffe **68** **69**
f Ryderwood **72** Toledo 505 Lake
411 Silver **73**
Lake 504 **76**
Castle Rock **74** Coldwater Ridge
75 **77**
Silver Toutle River
407 Lake
g **78** Mount Saint GIFFORD
79 4 Ostrander Helens 8,365 feet PINCHOT
Longview Kelso NATIONAL
Columbia River **80** FOREST
5 **81** **84** **85**
h **82** Cougar Swift Creek
83 Kalama River **88** Yale **86** Reservoir
Kalama Lake 503 **87**
89 Merwin Yale
Woodland Lake
90 91 Amboy
Ridgefield Yacolt Mineral Springs
i 501 502 **92**
Battle Ground Carson **99**
503 Stevenson **98**
j 205 500 Proebstel North Bonneville **97**
93 Vancouver 140 **96**
WASHINGTON **94** 14 Columbia R.
OREGON **95** Camas

TO ELMA   TO FRANCES   TO CATHLAMET

TO GREENWATER   TO PARADISE   TO PACKWOOD   TO TROUT LAKE   TO COOK

0   1   2   3   4   5   6   7   8   9

TO PORTLAND, OREGON

© AVALON TRAVEL PUBLISHING, INC.

0   10 mi
0   10 km

Chapter B2:
Southwest Washington

(CONTINUED ON NEXT PAGE)

S tretching from the south end of Puget Sound to the Columbia River and from the eastern flank of the Willapa Hills to the foothills of the Cascades, this is one of the most diverse regions of the entire Pacific Northwest. It extends from sea level at Olympia to over 14,400 feet at the Mount Rainier summit, from the heavily populated I-5 corridor to the sparsely inhabited countryside at the western edge of the Gifford Pinchot National Forest. The fishing possibilities are every bit as diverse as the geographic and demographic extremes. An angler here can jig for saltwater salmon during the first few hours of daylight, hook a trophy tiger muskie from a weedy freshwater bay early in the afternoon, and get in an hour of fly-fishing for pan-sized trout on a high-country lake before dark. To accomplish this feat, though, you might have to pass up some good river steelhead fishing, drive past lakes full of hungry rainbow trout, and pass on a chance to catch spring chinook salmon or eight-foot-long sturgeon from the Columbia River. Oh, the tough decisions we have to make! This region has western Washington's best largemouth bass lake (Silver Lake in Cowlitz County), top shad fishing (below Bonneville Dam), best opportunity for a trophy rainbow trout (Castle Lake), and some excellent sea-run cutthroat trout fishing to boot (the inlets of southern Puget Sound). It's truly an angler's paradise, and there never seems to be enough time to do it all.

❶ Lake Nahwatzel

This large, 270-acre lake provides good trout fishing from spring to fall and worthwhile opportunities for bass in the summer. It doesn't hurt that the lake is stocked with hatchery rainbows three times during the season. The rainbows, mostly 9- and 10-inchers from spring plants, are caught by both trolling and stillfishing in April and May, but by June stillfishing may be the better bet, especially around the 25-foot hole near the northwest side of the lake. Bass are found pretty much all around the lake's shoreline.

Location: Northwest of Shelton; see map B2, grid a0.

Species: Rainbow trout, largemouth bass.

Facilities: Lake Nahwatzel Resort has two cabins and a trailer for rent, plus RV sites, a restaurant (with very good food), a bar, and bait. A Department of Fish and Wildlife boat ramp (single lane gravel) with an access area is located near the resort. A $10 WDFW access decal is required to use the public launch areas maintained by the Washington Department of Fish and Wildlife. Other facilities are in Shelton.

Directions: Take U.S. 101 to Shelton and turn west on Shelton-Matlock Road, following it about 11 miles to the lake, which is on the north (right) side of the road.

Contact: Lake Nahwatzel Resort, 360/426-8323; Verle's Sport Center, 360/426-0933.

❷ Lost Lake

A liberal dose of hatchery rainbows helps to keep fishing interesting on this 120-acre Mason County lake. The Department of Fish and Wildlife stocks about 5,000 legal-sized trout here each spring, and they provide decent action into the summer months.

Lost is much like two lakes in one, connected by a narrow neck in the middle. The north end is quite deep—much of it over 50 feet—while the southern half is only 10 to 20 feet deep and features a large island. The entire lake offers fair to good trout fishing in April and May, but by midsummer you're better off fishing the cooler waters of the north half. Conversely, if you want to try your hand at nighttime catfishing, you should concentrate most of your efforts at the lower end of the lake.

Location: Southwest of Shelton; see map B2, grid a0.

Species: Rainbow trout, brown bullhead catfish.

Facilities: A boat ramp and restrooms can be found at the access area. A $10 WDFW access decal is required to use the public launch areas maintained by the Washington Department of Fish and Wildlife. Food, gas, tackle, and lodging are available in Shelton.

Directions: Take U.S. 101 to Shelton and exit onto Highway 3, following it two miles into town. Turn left onto Lost Lake Road and drive 10 miles to the sign pointing to the lake. Turn north (right) and drive about a mile to the lake.

Contact: Verle's Sport Center, 360/426-0933.

❸ Island Lake

Legal-sized rainbows are stocked in this lake every spring, providing good action until about mid-June, when trout fishing gives way to some very good warm-water fishing. Although I've caught trout here by stillfishing a bobber-and-worm rig around the south end of the small island near the center of the lake, trollers seem to score more consistently. Many of them use worms behind a string of trolling blades, but those fishing lighter with Dick Nites, Triple Teazers, Flatfish, Kwikfish, and Rooster Tails also make some good catches. The single trolling lure that has worked best for me here has been a K6 Kwikfish in a blue "pirate" finish. There have been times when it has caught more Island Lake rainbows in a day than three other lures combined, including other Kwik-fish finishes.

Perhaps Island Lake's biggest claim to fame is that it's one of very few western Washington lakes with a fishable population of smallmouth bass. Some are caught from the rocky areas around the island, but the shallow flats along the lake's northeastern shoreline may be the best places to fish for them. If you keep your eyes open, you may spot them feeding in the clear, shallow water, but seeing them is one thing, catching them quite another. The water's clarity makes for wary bass, so cast well ahead as you work your way along the shoreline and move as quietly and carefully as possible. Just to get you enthusiastic, I'll warn you that I have seen smallmouth bass of perhaps five pounds in this lake.

Because Island Lake is so clear and its bass so wary, many anglers prefer to fish it at night. The docks and floats along the northern shoreline produce both largemouths and smallmouths for nighttime anglers, and the brushy areas at the extreme south end of the lake and along the western side may also produce bass at night.

If you're looking for perch or brown bullheads, concentrate your efforts around the south end of the lake.

Location: North of Shelton; see map B2, grid a1.

Species: Rainbow trout, largemouth and smallmouth bass, yellow perch, brown bullhead catfish, pumpkinseed sunfish.

Facilities: A Department of Fish and Wildlife boat ramp is located on the west end of the lake. A $10 WDFW access decal is required to use the public launch areas maintained by the Washington Department of Fish and Wildlife. Groceries and gasoline are available at the intersection of U.S. 101 and Shelton Springs Road. All other amenities are available in Shelton.

Directions: Follow U.S. 101 north about two miles past Shelton and turn east (right) onto Shelton Springs Road, also known as the Dayton Cutoff. Drive one mile to Island Lake Road and turn left. The road circles Island Lake.

Contact: Verle's Sport Center, 360/426-0933.

◪ Lake Isabella

Open year-round, Isabella is a decent bet for 10- to 12-inch rainbows almost any time. Don't depend on it for hot opening-day fishing in late April; because of its year-round season, the lake isn't always stocked with legal-sized catchables during the spring. Troll with all the standard trout getters, or if you're the patient type, anchor somewhere around the edge of the lake and stillfish with a marshmallow or Power Bait on a slip-sinker rig. In the summer when this relatively shallow lake warms up, concentrate your stillfishing efforts in the 22- to 25-foot hole located about two-thirds of the way up toward the north end of the lake.

Summer is bass-fishing time here, and the many docks that line the shore offer good chances for a decent largemouth. Pitching plastic worms, lizards, or tube baits around and under the docks will eventually pay off.

Location: South of Shelton; see map B2, grid a1.

Species: Rainbow trout, largemouth bass, black bullhead catfish.

Facilities: The south side of the lake has a public access area with a boat ramp. A $10 WDFW access decal is required to use the public launch areas maintained by the Washington Department of Fish and Wildlife. Other amenities are available in Shelton and Olympia.

Directions: Turn west off U.S. 101 onto Delight Park Road just south of Shelton (the Golden Pheasant Tavern is the landmark to look for), drive a mile, and watch for the

"Public Fishing" sign on the right.

Contact: Verle's Sport Center, 360/426-0933.

5 Lake Limerick

The fishing season here runs year-round, but if you're looking for trout, you'd be wise to do much of your angling in April and May, after the hatchery planting truck makes its annual visit to this 100-acre lake on the hill above Shelton. You might also find a foot-long rainbow or two in the fall after the water cools. You don't need to know any special tricks to catch trout here; just troll or stillfish with your favorite stuff, and you'll catch your share.

One of the best things about Limerick—which is highly developed around much of its shoreline—is that it has an 8 mph speed limit. This keeps the powerboaters off the lake and allows bass and panfish anglers to do their thing without much interference. The lake has some large perch and decent-sized largemouths, and you probably won't have to compete with personal watercraft folks and water-skiers to catch them.

Location: Northeast of Shelton; see map B2, grid a2.

Species: Rainbow trout, largemouth bass, yellow perch, brown bullhead catfish.

Facilities: There's a concrete-slab boat ramp and restrooms at the lake's large access area. Food, gas, lodging, and tackle are available in Shelton.

Directions: Drive north from Shelton on Highway 3 just over four miles to Mason Lake Road. Turn left and drive up the hill 2.2 miles to the Lake Limerick sign; turn left and drive half a mile to the public access area on the right.

Contact: Verle's Sport Center, 360/426-0933.

6 Spencer Lake

With a long tradition of being one of Mason County's top opening-day trout producers, this 230-acre lake north of Shelton contin-ues to provide excellent catches of rainbows now that it's open year-round. Stocked with legal-sized trout in the spring, some of them weighing more than a pound apiece, Spencer is a worthwhile bet right on through much of the summer. Its deep water—with spots more than 35 feet deep near the southeast corner of the lake—remains cool and keeps the trout active. This deep area is a good spot for summertime stillfishing with a slip-sinker rig and a marshmallow or Power Bait combination of some kind.

As for bass, the lake is gaining a reputation for producing some husky ones. Largemouths weighing five pounds and better are possible, and there are also good numbers of smaller fish to keep you busy as you cast for something in the trophy range. The large, shallow bays at the east end and the north side of the lake are good places to start casting.

Location: Northeast of Shelton; see map B2, grid a2.

Species: Rainbow trout, largemouth bass.

Facilities: The west side of the lake has a public access area and boat ramp. A Department of Fish and Wildlife access decal is required to use it. There's a little restaurant right alongside the road on the north side of the lake. Other amenities can be found in Shelton.

Directions: Take Highway 3 northeast from Shelton about 10 miles and turn east (right) on Pickering Road, then right on Spencer Lake Road.

Contact: Verle's Sport Center, 360/426-0933.

7 Phillips Lake

This is another of several Mason County lakes where a year-round fishing season is a fairly new change in the regulations. Spring-planted rainbows average about nine inches in May but grow quickly to 12 inches or so by fall. There's a pretty good carryover of trout through the winter, which means early spring fishing might also produce a 14- to 16-inch rainbow for you. Planted cutthroats are larger, weighing about a pound each when they're stocked.

Both rainbows and cutts are caught on all the standard trolling rigs and on worms fished a few feet below a bobber. Salmon eggs, cheese baits, Power Bait, and marshmallows will take rainbows but few, if any, cutthroats.

Location: Northeast of Shelton; see map B2, grid a2.

Species: Rainbow and cutthroat trout.

Facilities: The lake has a Department of Fish and Wildlife boat ramp and access area. You'll need that $10 WDFW access decal here. Food, gas, tackle, and lodging are available in Shelton.

Directions: Take Highway 3 northeast from Shelton for about 10 miles and turn east (right) on Pickering Road. Drive about two miles (past Spencer Lake), turn south (right) on Phillips Lake Loop, and follow it about a mile to the lake.

Contact: Verle's Sport Center, 360/426-0933.

8 Stump Lake

Once the haunt of a few hard-core hermit-type anglers who came here as much for the peace and quiet as for the trout, bass, and catfish, this 23-acre pond hidden away in the foothills north of McCleary has been discovered. Now it's even touted by the Department of Fish and Wildlife whenever it gives up a good catch of husky rainbows. It is a decent place to find larger-than-average trout, and it also holds some bragging-sized bass. Fish it at night with crawlers and you could make a good catch of catfish.

Location: Northwest of McCleary; see map B2, grid a0.

Species: Rainbow trout, largemouth bass, brown bullhead catfish.

Facilities: You can launch a small boat at the lake, but there are no amenities. The nearest food, gas, lodging, and tackle are in Elma.

Directions: Take Hicklin Road east out of Elma and drive three miles to Lost Lake/Cloquallum Road. Turn north (left) on Lost Lake/Cloquallum Road and drive seven miles to the dirt/gravel road turning south (right). Follow this side road a mile and a half to the lake.

Contact: Verle's Sport Center, 360/426-0933.

9 Bay Lake

Spring plants of hatchery rainbows provide pretty good fishing for the first few weeks of the season, but by midsummer things are just about done for at Bay Lake. Although, at 115 acres, it's a fairly large lake, it's also extremely shallow, so the 6,000 or so rainbows planted annually get caught in a hurry. The shallow waters also heat up quickly with the summer sun, becoming too warm for good trout fishing by mid-June most years. The moral here, of course, is to fish Bay Lake soon after it opens to fishing in late April. Although long known as a trout producer, it's somewhat of a secret that Bay gives up its share of bragging-size bass, including the occasional five-pounder.

Location: On the Longbranch Peninsula; see map B2, grid a3.

Species: Rainbow trout, largemouth bass.

Facilities: The large, gravel access area has a boat ramp and restrooms. Penrose Point State Park has tent sites for camping. Food, gas, tackle, and lodging can be found in and around Lakebay.

Directions: Take Highway 302 southwest from Purdy to Lakebay. Cross the bridge, drive up the hill about 100 yards, and turn left at the sign pointing to Penrose Point State Park. Wind up and over the hill and turn right at the T intersection. The lake's public access area is on the right, about half a mile from the T.

Contact: Washington Department of Fish and Wildlife, Montesano Office, 360/249-4628; Washington State Parks and Recreation Commission, 360/902-8844 (information) or 800/452-5687 (reservations).

10 South Puget Sound

The south end of Puget Sound has been a real roller coaster for salmon anglers in recent years, providing good fishing for a time and then going dead for months, even years. The good news is that salmon action has been on a sharp upswing since 1993, especially for chinooks.

The most popular salmon fishing spot in south Puget Sound during much of the year is Lyle Point at the south end of Anderson Island. Located about two miles northeast of the Luhr's Beach boat ramp, it's an especially good spot for resident chinooks, known to many of us as blackmouth. On an ebb tide, try starting your drift in about 10 fathoms of water off Thompson Cove, drifting southeast out to about 30 fathoms, always checking the depthsounder for signs of bait fish. On the flood tide, start in 25 or 30 fathoms of water just east of the buoy and drift in toward Thompson Cove. While these are good general guidelines, the productive fishing pattern can change quickly, so be on your toes and watch where and how other anglers are fishing. The shoreline to the immediate east of Lyle Point can be good for coho as well. Try trolling or drifting small plug-cut herring, or casting wobbling spoons or small bait fish–imitating plugs toward the shoreline and retrieving it at a fast clip.

Johnson Point is another popular south Puget Sound salmon spot, especially for blackmouth. It's best fished on an ebb tide, and most chinook are caught at 8 to 15 fathoms. South Puget Sound blackmouth anglers also favor Point Gibson, at the south tip of Fox Island. It's good on the ebb tide

and is an excellent mooching spot. Fish in 15 to 30 fathoms of water here.

Other traditionally productive spots worth investigating by South Sound salmon anglers include Dugall Point (at the north end of Hartstene Island), the northeast corner of McMicken Island, Cooper Point (where Eld and Budd Inlets converge), the South Bay Light (southwest of Johnson Point near the entrance to Henderson Inlet), Devil's Head (the south end of the Key Peninsula), Eagle Island (between Anderson and McNeil Islands), Nearns Point (at the north end of Fox Island), the entrance to Wollochet Bay, and Point Evans (just north of the Narrows Bridge on the west side of the Narrows). During the summer of 1995, the waters around the Green Buoy near the mouth of the Nisqually turned into a real hot spot for summertime kings, and that action has been repeated virtually every summer since. Fall chinook headed into the Nisqually River tend to congregate around the buoy for several weeks before charging upriver.

I won't make any friends with this disclosure, but there's at least one productive bank-fishing spot for salmon in southern Puget Sound. Well, it's not really bank fishing—a more accurate description would be bridge fishing. The Steamboat Island Bridge, which connects Steamboat Island with the tip of the mainland at the confluence of Totten Inlet with Squaxin Passage, can be a productive fishing spot for chinook salmon in the spring and summer and for adult coho and chum salmon September through November. Most anglers fish Blue Fox spinners or Buzz Bombs here, casting off the west side of the bridge as the tide begins to ebb.

While we're mentioning chum salmon, they've become a more and more important part of the South Sound salmon-fishing scene in recent years. Much of the chum fishing occurs around the mouths of streams they're entering in record numbers these days. Those streams include McClane, Schneider, and Kennedy Creeks, where hundreds of anglers line up to catch their share of these hard-fighting fish that peak during the month of November.

The opportunities for catching bottom fish aren't as great in southern Puget Sound as they are in other marine areas of the Northwest. Much of the bottom is sand, mud, and gravel, so lingcod, rockfish, and other rock-dwelling species are hard to find. Exceptions include the waters immediately below the Narrows Bridge, where the skeletal remains of its predecessor lie in a tangled heap, providing good habitat for lingcod and rockfish. Fish it only on a slack tide or you'll be snagged on the bottom constantly, and remember that the lingcod season in this area is open only for about six weeks in May and early June. Remember, too, that the rockfish limit in Puget Sound these days is a mere one per day, so don't get carried away if you find a little concentration of them. Other spots worth fishing for springtime lings and rockfish throughout the year are the artificial reefs at Toliva Shoal and Itsami Ledge. The Toliva Shoal Reef is south of Point Gibson, 1,300 feet northwest of the Toliva Shoal navigational buoy and 2.4 miles from the Steilacoom boat ramp. The Itsami Ledge Reef, near Olympia, is southwest of Johnson Point, 1,100 feet northwest of the South Bay Light. The nearest boat ramp is at Zittel's Marina, 2.4 miles away.

If you want sole and flounder, you'll have little trouble finding them in south Puget Sound. Virtually every sandy-bottom bay has lots of them, and all you need to catch them is a supply of garden worms and a few small sinkers. The Nisqually River estuary is home to a fairly good summertime population of starry flounder, and you'll also find these large flatfish near the south end of Budd Inlet, where the Deschutes River empties into the south end of Puget Sound.

Pile perch and striped seaperch are an overlooked resource here. They're available around docks, piers, and pilings from Tacoma to Shelton and are best fished as the incoming tide first reaches these structures.

One of the mainstays of the south Puget Sound sport fishery has long been the sea-run cutthroat trout. Even though it's not as common as it once was and more restrictive regulations are now in effect, the sea-run is still a popular fish here. You can catch them from Point Evans to the mouth of Kennedy Creek, and the best fishing is right up next to the beach during an evening high tide.

Location: Marine waters from Tacoma's Commencement Bay south to Olympia and Shelton; see map B2, grid a4.

Species: Chinook, coho, and chum salmon; lingcod; rockfish; sole; flounder; seaperch.

Facilities: There are 29 boat ramps scattered along southern Puget Sound:

- **Ole & Charlie's Marina:** The northernmost launch site in this section is the hoist at Ole & Charlie's Marina in Tacoma, near the northeast corner of Commencement Bay off Marine View Drive. Round-trip launch fees here range from $15 up. Ole & Charlie's Marina has covered moorage with electricity and water, a small grocery store, fishing tackle, and restrooms.

- **Totem Marina:** Located on the south side of Commencement Bay, this facility has a pair of hoists and two loading floats. One-way use of the slings begins at $7 for boats 19 feet and under. Totem Marina has open and covered moorage, electricity and water to the docks, a small grocery store, a boat lift, laundry facilities, restrooms and showers, boat-sewage pump-out facilities, and restaurants right alongside it. The facilities are located off Schuster Parkway at Fourth Street.

- **Asarco Boat Ramp:** There's a one-lane

gravel ramp at the old Asarco plant, off the end of Ruston Way. A good ramp for smaller boats, it has parking for about 100 cars and trailers.

- **Point Defiance Waterfront Ramp:** Located next to the Vashon Island ferry terminal, off the end of Pearl Street, it's one of the Puget Sound area's busiest launch facilities. This site has a three-lane concrete ramp with loading floats and parking in three nearby locations for over 100 cars and trailers.
- **Narrows Marina:** Around the corner to the south of Point Defiance, just south of the Narrows Bridge, is Narrows Marina, where there's a one-lane concrete ramp with parking for about a dozen cars on a nearby gravel lot. This is a steep ramp that sometimes gets a little tough for two-wheel drive vehicles to use, but it's well protected from the weather by moorage floats and buildings surrounding it. It has a $6 launch fee during the week, $10 on weekends. Narrows Marina has fuel docks, fishing tackle, boat hardware, and boat-sewage pump-outs.
- **Gig Harbor Ramp:** Across Puget Sound from Point Defiance is Gig Harbor, where there's a single-lane concrete ramp across the harbor from the city's main business district.
- **Wollochet Bay Ramp:** South of Gig Harbor, through the Narrows and Hale Passage, is Wollochet Bay, where there are a couple of ramps, each with limited parking nearby. The first one, at the end of 10th Street via Point Fosdick Drive, is a pretty good concrete ramp with room to park half a dozen cars and trailers.
- **Wollochet No. 2 Ramp:** The second ramp has even more limited parking, and the nearby landowners aren't crazy about folks who park in their way. This ramp is at the end of 37th Street, off Wollochet Drive. Both Wollochet ramps are maintained by Pierce County.

- **Fox Island:** There's another Pierce County ramp on Fox Island, just north of the bridge. It's a single-lane concrete ramp that's seen better days, and the small parking area is also showing signs of slipping into Hale Passage.
- **Horsehead Bay Ramp:** Around Green Point from the north end of Fox Island is Horsehead Bay, where there's a one-lane asphalt ramp maintained by Pierce County. The No Trespassing signs could make you feel just a little unwanted here, but it's OK as long as you don't tie up to the private floats near the ramp.
- **Steilacoom Boat Ramp:** On the east side of Puget Sound is Steilacoom, where there's a boat launch maintained by Steilacoom Parks. It's one of a kind, and not the ramp to use if you're looking to practice backing a boat trailer into the water for the very first time. The ramp runs under railroad tracks, so you have to back a boat between the pilings of the rail overpass. It's kind of a tight squeeze, anyway, but it also has a little turn in it to keep you on your toes. As if all this weren't enough, you have to pay a small fee to launch here. Steilacoom Marina has open moorage, power and water to the docks, a grocery store, and a boat-sewage dump station.
- **Swantown Ramp:** The ramp closest to downtown Olympia is the two-lane concrete ramp at Swantown Marina, formerly East Bay Marina, operated by the Port of Olympia. The ramp has a long loading float and a parking area for 50 cars and trailers that overflows every nice weekend during the summer. Swantown Marina has open moorage, restrooms with showers, pump-out facilities and dump station for boat sewage, and the newest haul-out facility in Puget Sound. It's located on Marina Drive, off East Bay Road. There's a $5 launch fee here.

- **Boston Harbor Ramp:** East Bay Road eventually becomes Boston Harbor Road, and if you follow it about seven miles out of town, you'll come to 73rd Avenue NE. Turn left there and drive two blocks to Boston Harbor Marina, where there's a one-lane concrete ramp with a gravel parking area for two dozen cars and trailers. Boston Harbor Marina has open moorage, fuel docks, groceries, rental boats, and restrooms. This is a free ramp maintained by Thurston County Parks, but if you try to use it in the fall and winter you may sometimes have to wait for Squaxin tribal fishermen to off-load their fish and shellfish onto trucks in the middle of the ramp.
- **Budinich Ramp:** Off Johnson Point Road to the northeast of Olympia is the Budinich ramp, a private ramp where the public may launch for a small fee. It's located at the end of 86th Avenue, which turns left off Johnson Point Road to Henderson Inlet.
- **Zittel's Marina:** Around Johnson Point is Zittel's Marina, also northeast of Olympia, where there's a newly renovated concrete ramp and a fixed hoist, with a loading float serving both. Zittel's Marina has open moorage, fuel docks, bait and tackle, boat rentals, power and water to the floats, and restrooms. Reach it by driving north on Johnson Point Road to 92nd Avenue NE and turning right.
- **Puget Marina:** Southeast of Zittel's is Puget Marina, where there's a one-lane concrete ramp and loading float. It's located off Marvin Road via Exit 111 from I-5.
- **Luhr's Beach Ramp:** Near the mouth of the Nisqually River northeast of Olympia is the Department of Fish and Wildlife's ramp at Luhr's Beach. This single-lane concrete ramp has nearby parking for about a dozen cars and trailers. Be careful to follow the creek channel north out of the ramp or you'll soon be aground on a moderate to low tide.

You'll need the $10 WDFW access decal to use this ramp.
- **Young's Cove Ramp:** Northwest of Olympia off Gravelly Beach Loop from Highway 101 is another private ramp where the public can launch for a small fee. It's a single-lane concrete ramp with a somewhat rickety loading float and limited parking alongside the private driveway. The ramp is in Young's Cove, which opens to the west side of Eld Inlet.
- **Arcadia Ramp:** Between the entrance to Totten Inlet and Hammersley Inlet is Arcadia Point, where there's a Squaxin Indian Tribe ramp. It's two lanes wide and concrete, with parking for about two dozen cars and trailers up the hill about 100 yards.
- **Port of Shelton Ramp:** Follow Hammersley Inlet west into Shelton to find the Port of Shelton ramp, on the north end of town, along Highway 3. It has a one-lane gravel ramp with parking for about 20 cars and trailers.
- **Shorecrest Park Ramp:** Go north from Shelton up Oakland Bay to find Shorecrest Park, a Mason County Parks and Recreation Department facility with a one-lane concrete ramp with limited parking. It's on Shorecrest Park Way, off Highway 3 about six miles north of Shelton.
- **Latimer's Landing:** Continue north on Highway 3 about eight miles and turn right on Pickering Road to reach the ramp at Latimer's Landing. Located at the west end of the Hartstene Island bridge, it's one-lane wide and has a loading float. Parking on a gravel lot is nearby. Wind and running tides can cause some problems for people launching and retrieving their boats here. Launching is free at the Mason County Parks and Recreation Department ramp.
- **Fair Harbor Boat Ramp:** Located near Grapeview off Highway 3, this site has a two-lane concrete ramp with a loading float

and parking for about 20 cars and trailers. Fair Harbor Marina has fuel docks, open moorage, power to the docks, boat repairs, boat haul-out, and a grocery store.

- **Allyn Waterfront Park:** Three miles farther north on Highway 3 is the little town of Allyn, where there's a good, two-lane launch ramp with a loading float and parking for about 20 cars and trailers. This free launch is managed by the Port of Allyn.
- **Vaughn Bay Ramp:** The Key Peninsula, between Case Inlet and Carr Inlet, has boat ramps on both its west and east shores. On the west (Case Inlet) side, the northernmost ramp is in Vaughn Bay, off Hall Road. This Pierce County ramp has a single lane with a concrete surface and parking for only a few cars and trailers.
- **Joemma Beach State Park:** Farther south and around the end of the Longbranch Peninsula on the east side of Case Inlet is the Washington State Parks ramp at Joemma Beach (formerly the Department of Natural Resources' Robert F. Kennedy Park). This one-lane concrete ramp has a loading float. There's a $3 launch fee. The state park also has 500 feet of moorage on its float and five nearby moorage buoys. The park has primitive campsites.
- **Longbranch Ramp:** Around the corner on the Carr Inlet side is the Longbranch ramp, also a Pierce County facility. It's one lane wide, concrete, and is located at the end of 72nd Street.
- **Lakebay Marina:** Three miles north is the ramp at Lakebay Marina, a one-lane concrete ramp with a gravel parking lot for about five cars and trailers. You can launch a trailer boat here for $5, a car-topper for $3. Lakebay Marina offers electricity to the docks, open moorage, restrooms, and fuel docks.
- **Home Boat Ramp:** A mile farther north

is the ramp at Home. It's a one-lane concrete ramp with a gravel parking area for about a dozen cars and trailers.

Other Facilities without Boat Ramps:

Gig Harbor: Arabella's Landing has open moorage, electricity and water to the docks, restrooms with showers, and boat-sewage pump-out facilities. Peninsula Yacht Basin has open moorage, power and water at the docks, and restrooms with showers. Jerisich Park has over 400 feet of dock space, a nearby park with restrooms, and a boat-sewage pump-out facility.

Tacoma: Chinook Landing Marina, on the north side of Commencement Bay, has open moorage, power and water to the docks, a small grocery store, restrooms with showers, and boat-sewage pump-out facilities. Crow's Nest Marina has open moorage, electricity and water to the docks, a boat lift, restrooms with showers, and sewage pump-out facilities. Pick's Cove Marine Center has open and covered moorage, electricity and water to the docks, a boat lift, restrooms with showers, sewage pump-out facilities, and laundry facilities. At Point Defiance Boathouse Marina you'll find open moorage, rental boats, groceries, fuel docks, restrooms, boat-sewage pump-out facilities, and a restaurant. Breakwater Marina has open and covered moorage, power and water to the docks, rental boats, sewage pump-out facilities, restrooms with showers, and fuel docks.

Olympia: West Bay Marina has boat repairs, haul-out facilities, boat sewage facilities, and a restaurant that has changed owners and names many times but keeps hanging in there. Percival Landing in downtown Olympia has lots of open moorage, power to the docks, pump-out facilities, and easy access to many restaurants and watering holes.

State Marine Parks: Besides Joemma

Beach there are several other state marine parks in southern Puget Sound. Kopachuck State Park on the east side of Carr Inlet has a couple of moorage buoys but no moorage floats. Like many marine parks, it's a part of the Cascadia Marine Trail system, where paddlers can find a place to pitch their tents as they prowl south Puget Sound. Kopachuck also has an underwater park (diving reef) just offshore. Tiny Cutts Island is just north of Kopachuck. It's accessible only by boat and has nine moorage buoys. Penrose Point State Park is located in Mayo Cove on the west side of Carr Inlet. It has over 300 feet of moorage floats, eight moorage buoys, and boat-sewage dump facilities. On the north side of Anderson Island is Eagle Island, another marine park with moorage buoys only. Farther up Case Inlet on the west side is McMicken Island, also a state marine park. It has five moorage buoys and no other facilities. At the north end of Hartstene Island is Jarrell Cove State Park, where there's nearly 800 feet of moorage space on its float, as well as 14 moorage buoys. On the hill overlooking the cove are several tent and RV sites.

Directions: Launch at Narrows Marina (off 19th Street in Tacoma, just south of the Narrows Bridge), Wollochet (off Point Fosdick Drive south of Gig Harbor), Steilacoom (off Commercial Street near the McNeil Island ferry landing), Luhr's Beach (off 46th Avenue on the west end of Nisqually Flats), Zittel's Marina (off 92nd Avenue NE north of Olympia), Boston Harbor (off 73rd Avenue NE north of Olympia), or Swantown Marina (formerly called East Bay Marina, off Marine Drive at the north end of Olympia).

Contact: Arabella's Landing, 253/851-1793; Jerisich Park, 253/851-8136; Chinook Landing Marina, 253/627-7676; Port of Tacoma, City Marina, 253/572-2524; Breakwater Marina, 253/752-6663, website: www.breakwa-termarina.com; Point Defiance Boathouse Marina, 253/591-5325; Foss Waterway Marina, 253/272-4404; Narrows Marina, 253/564-4222; Pick's Cove Marine Center, 253/572-3625; Steilacoom Marina, 253/582-2600; Lakebay Marina, 253/884-3350; Longbranch Marina, 253/884-5137 (VHF ch. 16); Zittel's Marina, 360/459-1950; Boston Harbor Marina, 360/357-5670; Swantown Marina, 360/786-1400; West Bay Marina, 360/943-2022; Percival Landing Park, 360/753-8382; Fair Harbor Marina, 360/426-4028. For nautical charts of this area, contact Captain's Nautical Supply, 206/283-7242.

🔟 Steilacoom Lake

This large, shallow lake is well suited to the needs of largemouth bass, and it grows some hefty ones. Steilacoom has more than 300 acres to explore, so you'll never run out of places to cast. If you fish small, with two- or three-inch plastic grubs, quarter-ounce crankbaits, or little spinnerbaits, you might catch an occasional rock bass as you cast around the edges of the lake. Good catfish action can be had by fishing night crawlers, chicken livers, or various stinkbaits at night. Steilacoom Lake is open year-round, but the hottest fishing is in the spring and early summer, with some good bass catches possible into the fall.

Location: In Lakewood, southwest of Tacoma; see map B2, grid a5.

Species: Largemouth bass, rock bass, brown bullhead catfish.

Facilities: The north end of the lake has a boat ramp. Food, gas, lodging, and tackle are available throughout the area.

Directions: Take Exit 127 off I-5, drive north of South Tacoma Way, and turn west on Steilacoom Boulevard, following it about three miles to the north end of the lake, on the left.

Contact: Washington Department of Fish and Wildlife, 425/775-6211.

12 American Lake

One of Pierce County's largest lakes at more than 1,100 acres, American also offers some of the area's finest angling variety. Read the list of species below and it's easy to understand why there's something to catch here throughout the entire year-round season.

This is a lake known for big trout. Genevieve Anderson, the long-time owner of Bill's Boat House, seemed to have a story about a recently caught lunker trout every time I talked to her. Many's the time she'd report a seven-pounder caught the day before or the five-pounder she just weighed that morning, most of them caught from the boathouse dock. Talk of those fish once prompted me to ask Mrs. Anderson about the largest trout she'd ever seen caught from the lake. She told a story about another dock angler who came in with a big fish wrapped in his coat one day in the early 1990s. That fish pulled the scale pointer to 11 pounds, 5 ounces, and upon closer examination Mrs. Anderson noticed that it had already been cleaned. It might well have weighed 13 pounds when it was first caught.

American Lake, of course, doesn't treat everyone to a shot at its trophy trout, but the odds of catching a big one here are better than in most Western Washington lakes. They're often found quite deep, and one of the most consistent ways of catching them is trolling with two- or three-ounce sinkers with 100 to 150 feet of line off the reel. Small Wedding Ring spinners with maggots on the hooks are among the offerings that will take them.

Those same Wedding Ring–and–maggot combinations are commonly used by kokanee anglers at American. One of the area's top kokanee lakes, it gives up fish to two pounds or more from midsummer until these landlocked kokanee move inshore to spawn in the fall.

Trolling is also a good way to catch cutthroats here, but don't waste your time out in deep water. As is typical with these shallow-water trout, they're most often caught around the edges of the lake. Some of the largest cutthroats are caught in the fall, often by fly anglers working leeches and other wet-fly patterns in the shoreline weed beds.

If you like fish with red eyes, American has two species that fall into that category. Both smallmouths and rock bass are available here, and some of the best fishing for both is found at the lake's north and south ends and in the wide bay at the northwest corner of the lake. Casting around the several islands in the lake also produces bass.

Location: Southwest of Tacoma; see map B2, grid a5.

Species: Rainbow and cutthroat trout, landlocked steelhead, kokanee, smallmouth bass, yellow perch, rock bass, brown bullhead catfish.

Facilities: The lake also has a Department of Fish and Wildlife boat ramp and access area. Gas and lodging are only a few blocks away, along I-5.

Directions: Take Exit 122 off I-5 just south of Tacoma and head west, across the tracks, on Berkley Street. Drive half a mile to the T and turn right on Portland Avenue SW, following it four blocks to the lake, which is on the left.

Contact: Washington Department of Fish and Wildlife, Montesano Office, 360/249-4628.

13 Puyallup River

Some of the best fishing on the Puyallup is found from Sumner upstream to the mouth of the Carbon River, a few miles north of Orting. This is true of both steelhead and salmon. Many anglers float this stretch of the river, but McCutcheon Road provides plenty of access at more than a half dozen points.

Chinook start showing up in the Puyallup in August, and by mid-September the salmon fishery is going full speed. The hottest action is in October, when coho fill the river, most of them bound for the state salmon hatchery on Voight Creek, a Carbon River tributary near Orting. Boat anglers score good coho catches by back-trolling Hot Shots, Wiggle Warts, and other plugs, while bank anglers do well with Blue Fox, Metric, and Flash Glo spinners.

A few steelhead still trickle into the upper reaches of the Puyallup above the mouth of the Carbon, but you're much better off concentrating your efforts from McMillan downstream. If you're a drift angler, you'll find plenty of good water between Sumner and McMillan, with no areas better than the others. If plunking is your bag, stay downstream of Puyallup. Plunkers do well along North Levee Road, where there's plenty of bank access and a good chance of catching fish right after a period of high water.

Location: Enters Commencement Bay at Tacoma; see map B2, grid a6.

Species: Winter steelhead, chinook and coho salmon, cutthroat trout, mountain whitefish.

Facilities: The towns of Puyallup and Sumner have all the amenities you need.

Directions: Take the Puyallup exit off I-5 near the north end of Tacoma to reach the Lower Puyallup, which is paralleled by River Road on the south and North Levee Road on the north. To reach upper portions of the river, take Pioneer Avenue east out of Puyallup to Highway 162 (the Sumner-Orting Highway). Side roads to the east off Highway 162 provide river access at Alderton, McMillan, and other places along the way toward Orting. McCutcheon Road runs along the east side of the river from Sumner to McMillan.

Contact: Creekside Angling Company, 425/392-3800.

14 Lake Killarney

This shallow 31-acre lake is best noted for its panfish and fair largemouth bass fishing, but it also offers decent possibilities for rainbow trout stocked in the lake every year. The marshy north end is a good place to fish spinnerbaits and various plastics for bass. Killarney also has yellow perch and bluegills, but you may have trouble finding any large ones. If you're into night fishing, try the south end of the lake for brown bullheads, some of which run 15 inches or so. As the water drops in late summer and fall, the northern and southern portions of this small lake may separate when a shoal in the middle becomes dry land.

Location: Southeast of Federal Way; see map B2, grid a6.

Species: Rainbow trout, largemouth bass, brown bullhead catfish, yellow perch, bluegill.

Facilities: The lake has a boat ramp for craft of limited size.

Directions: Take Military Road south from South 320th Street in Federal Way and drive three miles to 352nd Street; turn west (right), then north (right) on 34th Avenue. Drive two blocks to the lake, which is on the left. (The lake on the right is Lake Geneva; see number 15.) Food, gas, tackle, and lodging are in Federal Way.

Contact: Auburn Sports and Marine, 253/833-1440.

15 Lake Geneva

Stocked with hatchery trout just prior to the April season opener, Geneva usually offers good fishing for a few weeks and then slows considerably. It's only about 29 acres in size and very popular with South King County anglers, which explains why it succumbs to fishing pressure so quickly. Because the carryover of fish from season to season is low, the Department of Fish and Wildlife often includes a few large trout in its spring plant just to help provide excitement. In 2001 they upped the ante further by adding a few hundred fat triploid rainbows to the mix.

Some anglers, though, wait until the trout are pretty well gone before even visiting Geneva; we're talking, of course, about bass anglers. The lake contains some nice-sized largemouths, fish to maybe three pounds, so it's certainly worth a summertime visit. There's plenty of bass cover here, both man-made and natural, to explore on a warm summer evening.

Location: Southeast of Federal Way; see map B2, grid a6.

Species: Rainbow trout, largemouth bass.

Facilities: A narrow boat ramp provides access on the west side of the lake. Federal Way has food, gas, tackle, and lodging.

Directions: Take Military Road south from South 320th Street in Federal Way. Drive three miles and turn west (right) on 352nd Street and north (right) on 34th Avenue. Drive two blocks to the lake, which is on the right. (Lake Killarney, number 14, is on the left.)

Contact: Auburn Sports and Marine, 253/833-1440.

16 Five Mile Lake

This lake is now open to year-round fishing and produces fair catches from March to June and again in the fall. A large public fishing dock is popular and fairly productive, but trolling the north end and east side of the lake pays off better. Trout fishing gets tough in the summer, but a large 30-foot hole near the south end continues to produce some rainbows even in hot weather. Stillfishing on the bottom often works best in this spot.

The warm weather that knocks trouting in the head does wonders for Five Mile's other fisheries, including bass and panfish. Largemouths here run to about three pounds, and there are some crappies big enough to be worth anyone's while.

Location: Southeast of Federal Way; see map B2, grid a6.

Species: Rainbow trout, largemouth bass, crappie, yellow perch.

Facilities: A King County park and boat ramp are near the south end of the lake. Food, gas, tackle, and lodging can be found in Federal Way.

Directions: Take Military Road south from South 320th Street in Federal Way. The lake is on the west side of Military, about three miles south of 320th Street.

Contact: The Reel Thing, 253/941-0920; Auburn Sports and Marine, 253/833-1440.

17 Trout Lake

Trolling and stillfishing for trout are fairly good here in the spring. June, July, and August provide some fair catches of largemouth bass, including an occasional trophy-sized fish. The lake covers only 18 acres, but much of it is more than 20 feet deep, with several spots nearly 30 feet deep. Stay along the edges if you want bass, but troll or stillfish the middle for rainbows.

Like nearby Five Mile Lake, Trout Lake also has some large crappies and fairly good perch fishing for those who may have a taste for panfish. Both may be caught on small leadheads with plastic grubs or tube skirts, and you might add a piece of worm to the jig to improve your chances of catching perch.

Location: Southeast of Federal Way; see map B2, grid a6.

Species: Rainbow trout, largemouth bass, crappie, yellow perch.

Facilities: The lake has a public boat ramp. All other amenities are available in Federal Way.

Directions: Take Military Road south from South 320th Street in Federal Way. Drive about 4.5 miles and turn east (left) on South 366th Street, which is about a quarter of a mile south of the south end of Five Mile Lake.

Contact: Auburn Sports and Marine, 253/833-1440.

18 White River

This glacial stream, which starts as a trickle on the eastern flank of Mount Rainier, is a glaring example of man's infinite lack of wisdom. Somebody back in the good old days at the start of the 1900s determined that it would be more convenient if the White, once a tributary to the Green River, flowed into the Puyallup instead, so it was diverted. Imagine the impact that a little change like that would have on the stream's salmon and steelhead runs. The White, also referred to as the Stuck River along its lower reaches, hasn't been worth a darn for fishing since. Much of the river is closed to fishing during the summer months, and only rarely does someone catch anything worth keeping during the time it's open. Check the fishing pamphlet before fishing White River; it has some unusual season dates. The lower river from Buckley downstream, for example, isn't open to fishing during the summer. There is some fair winter whitefish activity during a November through January season, but few anglers seem to notice.

Location: Joins the Puyallup River near Sumner; see map B2, grid a7.

Species: Winter and summer steelhead, cutthroat trout, mountain whitefish.

Facilities: Food, gas, tackle, and lodging are available in Auburn and Sumner.

Directions: Take Highway 164 or the East Valley Highway south from Auburn about two miles to the river.

Contact: Al's Sporting Goods, 360/829-0174; Auburn Sports and Marine, 253/833-1440.

19 Lake Tapps

During much of 1999 many people wondered if there would even be a Lake Tapps for much longer, but at least for now we can assume that Puget Sound Energy isn't going to let the lake go dry year-round and leave us with a dirty little stream running through the middle of a muddy lake bed. The power company has decided not to remove its hydroelectric dam on the White River that formed the sprawling lake, even though it's not the money-maker they'd like it to be. We'll let you know if all that changes.

In the meantime, there's a lake—or at least a reservoir—here from May to September, and anglers using gang trolls with worms or small wobbling spoons behind them catch some rainbows at Lake Tapps. But this huge reservoir is not a particularly productive trout fishery. Patient or lucky anglers will occasionally take a real lunker, though it's not an everyday occurrence. A few big largemouth bass are also caught, but again this certainly isn't one of the area's hot bass lakes. The water level is drawn way down from winter to early spring, and by the time it comes back up, water-skiers, drag-boaters, and personal watercraft enthusiasts take over much of the lake.

Location: Northeast of Sumner; see map B2, grid a7.

Species: Rainbow trout, largemouth bass, yellow perch, Dolly Varden.

Facilities: Boat ramps are located near the northeast and northwest corners of the lake. Other amenities can be found in Sumner and Auburn.

Directions: Take Highway 410 east from Sumner and turn north on the Sumner-Tapps Highway, which parallels the northwest, north, and east shoreline of the lake.

Contact: Auburn Sports and Marine, 253/833-1440.

20 Fish Lake

A small plant of hatchery rainbows and cutthroats is enough to provide year-round fishing on little 16-acre Fish Lake, located just east of Nolte State Park. The lake gets quite low and hard to fish by midsummer, but it fills again with the fall rains. If you prefer bass to trout, you'll probably think this lake looks like a good bet for largemouths, and you'd be right. All the usual bass stuff works here, including top-water offerings on a warm summer evening. Float tubes work well here, since you can easily make your way around in a few hours of casting small spinners or flies. The lake has a boat ramp where car-toppers and inflatables can be launched. Private property surrounds the water, so confine your efforts to the access area or stay in your boat.

Location: Northeast of Enumclaw; see map B2, grid a8.

Species: Rainbow and cutthroat trout, largemouth bass.

Facilities: The lake has a public boat ramp and access area. The nearest food, gas, tackle, and lodging are in Enumclaw.

Directions: Take Veazie-Cumberland Road north from Enumclaw for six miles and turn west (left) onto 295th Avenue SE. Turn left again on 371st Street and drive half a mile to the lake.

Contact: Al's Sporting Goods, 360/829-0174.

21 Deep Lake

Although the lake is now open year-round, April and May are still the best months to fish this 40-acre lake for rainbows, most of which are legal-sized hatchery fish planted in March or April. A few cutthroat are also stocked, and they may provide some fall fishing action. During the summer, troll a Wedding Ring spinner with white corn on the hooks behind a string of larger trolling blades for the kokanee. Stillfishing with maggots, white corn, or small pieces of worm may also be effective. Perch can be caught here pretty much year-round on worms or jig-and-worm combinations, and summertime bass fishing can be fairly good, especially if you gear down and practice a little finesse to compensate for the lake's gin-clear water.

Location: Northeast of Enumclaw; see map B2, grid a8.

Species: Rainbow and cutthroat trout, kokanee, largemouth bass, crappie, yellow perch, brown bullhead catfish.

Facilities: The east end of the lake has a narrow boat ramp, but it's built for carry-in boats, not trailers. Nolte State Park, where the lake is located, has picnic tables but no overnight camping. The closest food, gas, tackle, and lodging are in Enumclaw.

Directions: Take Veazie-Cumberland Road north from Enumclaw for 6.5 miles and watch for the Nolte State Park sign on the left.

Contact: Nolte State Park, 360/825-4646; Washington State Parks and Recreation Commission, 360/902-8844 (information) or 800/452-5687 (reservations); Al's Sporting Goods, 360/829-0174.

22 Bass Lake

So, with a name like this, does it really have any bass fishing? Yes, it does. Truth is, it has been known to provide fairly good largemouth action, especially early in the spring, before some of the larger lakes come to life. It also has fair panfish action, but the weeds get pretty thick by the middle of summer, cutting down on the amount of fishing room you'll find on this 24-acre pond.

The boat ramp on the east side of the lake isn't suited to that big bass boat, but you can launch a car-topper or small inflatable here with little trouble. This is also a good lake for float-tubers to investigate, except that by midsummer the milfoil gets so thick you might not be able to get through it.

Location: North of Enumclaw; see map B2, grid a8.

Species: Largemouth bass, yellow perch, crappie.

Facilities: The lake has a public access area and boat ramp. The nearest food, gas, tackle, and lodging are in Enumclaw.

Directions: Take Highway 169 north from Enumclaw for 3.5 miles and turn west (left)

onto 264th Avenue SE, which runs right by the north side of the lake.

Contact: Al's Sporting Goods, 360/829-0174.

23 Walker Lake

At only 11 acres, this probably should be called Walker Pond, but it's stocked with about 1,200 trout a year and provides fairly good spring trout fishing. The small boat ramp is a good place to drop a car-topper into the water or to wade in with your float tube cinched firmly around your waist. Arrive early or stay late in the evening and fish the edge of the lake with your favorite fly rod. The access area offers the only public beach on the lake, so stay off the surrounding private property.

Location: Northeast of Enumclaw; see map B2, grid a8.

Species: Rainbow and cutthroat trout.

Facilities: The south side of the lake has a public access area and boat ramp. Food, gas, tackle, and lodging can be found in Enumclaw.

Directions: Drive north from Enumclaw on Veazie-Cumberland Road, turn east (right) a mile past Nolte State Park onto Walker Lake Road, and drive about two miles to the lake.

Contact: Al's Sporting Goods, 360/829-0174.

24 Spanaway Lake

Spring plants of about 15,000 rainbows annually provide fair to good fishing for 8- to 14-inch trout, with a few carryovers to about 18 inches. Stillfishing with Berkley Power Bait is popular here; in the spring good catches are made this way from the public fishing dock at the north end and for boaters around the south end. As the water warms in summer, move toward the 20- to 25-foot-deep waters in the middle one-third of the lake.

The shallow flats at the south end of the lake are best for bass, perch, and bullheads. Spanaway produces some big largemouths from time to time.

Location: In Spanaway in Pierce County; see map B2, grid a5.

Species: Rainbow trout, largemouth and smallmouth bass, rock bass, yellow perch, brown bullhead catfish.

Facilities: The county park has a boat ramp, free fishing pier, rowboat rentals, and cooking facilities for picnickers. Lodging and other amenities are available nearby in Spanaway.

Directions: Take I-5 to Highway 512 and turn east. Head south on Highway 7 and drive south about three miles to Military Road. Turn west (right), go one-quarter mile to Breezeman Boulevard, and turn south (left) into the park entrance.

Contact: Spanaway Park Boat House, 253/531-0555; Auburn Sports and Marine, 253/833-1440.

25 Bonney Lake

Once a fly-fishing-only lake with special limits and other restrictions, Bonney is now at the other end of the spectrum, open year-round and stocked lightly with hatchery rainbows. Like other year-round put-and-take lakes, it offers good trout fishing for a few weeks in the spring and perhaps again in the fall. In 2001 the lake was stocked with a load of triploid rainbows that should give anglers trophy-trout opportunities for a few years. During the summer, largemouth and rock bass fishing can be fairly good around the many private docks and submerged stumps and logs that are quite common around the lake. There are also brown bullhead catfish and some decent-sized yellow perch to be caught from Bonney Lake.

Location: Southeast of Sumner; see map B2, grid a7.

Species: Rainbow trout, largemouth and rock bass, yellow perch, brown bullhead catfish.

Facilities: The public access area has a gravel boat ramp and chemical toilet. Food, gas, lodging, and tackle are available in Sumner.

Directions: Drive east from Sumner on Highway 410 about two miles to Myers Road. Turn north on Myers Road and drive three-quarters of a mile to 74th Street, then turn right and watch for the public access area on the right.
Contact: Creekside Angling Company, 425/392-3800.

26 Carbon River

Fish bound for the Puyallup River Salmon Hatchery on Voight Creek often provide good coho fishing and a crack at a 30-pound chinook on the Carbon. The three-mile stretch of river from Orting down to the mouth can be productive, but the biggest crowds congregate from the mouth of Voight Creek downstream about half a mile. Although the Carbon is a relatively small stream, it often produces good chinook catches in September and good to excellent coho catches in October, especially after a decent rain draws fresh runs in from the Puyallup. The river also has chum and pink salmon, but in recent years they have been off-limits to anglers.

As for steelheading, the Carbon can be quite good in December and January, but many of the 100 or so fish it gives up each winter are caught by locals who can get to the river when conditions are right. As with salmon, the right time to fish the Carbon for steelhead is immediately after a good rain.

Although overlooked by all but a few locals, the Carbon's whitefish population is worth exploiting during the winter. A couple of deep pools immediately behind Orting produce some good catches.

Location: Joins the Puyallup River northwest of Orting in Pierce County; see map B2, grid a7.
Species: Winter steelhead, fall chinook and coho salmon, mountain whitefish.
Facilities: Food and gas are available in Orting, while tackle and lodging can be found in Sumner.

Directions: Take Highway 162 (Sumner-Orting Highway) south from Sumner toward Orting. Drive five miles from Sumner to the concrete bridge and continue another quarter of a mile to the gated gravel road to the left. Park at the gate and walk to the river. Another option is to continue two miles past the concrete bridge on Highway 162 to a second gated road on the left. Park at the gate and walk a quarter of a mile to the river. Continue on Highway 162 about 1.5 miles past this second access road and you'll come to the town of Orting, where you can turn left on Bridge Street and drive four blocks to the river. One more option is to drive through Orting and continue southeast about 1.5 miles to the junction of Orville Road. Park along the highway (you'll see the other cars) and hike left on the old railroad bed toward the confluence of the Carbon and Voight Creek.
Contact: Auburn Sports and Marine, 253/833-1440.

27 Kennedy Creek

One of western Washington's best-kept secret steelhead holes in the late 1970s, Kennedy Creek is now best known for its fall chum salmon fishery. November is the top month for chums, and when conditions are right, as many as 100 anglers may line the banks at the mouth of this small stream. They cast small offerings of green yarn, green steelhead bobbers, or combinations of the two and score their best catches as the water level drops following a high tide that has brought fresh fish into the creek. Salmon fishing is allowed only at the mouth downstream of the freeway bridge.

Winter steelhead can still be found in Kennedy Creek from December until the season closes at the end of February, but certainly not in the numbers available back in the good old days when employees of what was then the Washington Game Department used to release extra steelhead smolts into this tiny stream. Adult steelhead returning from those lightly publicized hatchery plants provided some wild and woolly steelheading for the few anglers who caught on. But these days your best chance of hooking an occasional steelie will occur if you fish the lower half mile of the creek immediately after a high tide or the day the water level begins dropping after a heavy rain puts it out of fishing condition.

Location: Flows into Oyster Bay south of Shelton; see map B2, grid a1.

Species: Chum salmon, winter steelhead, sea-run cutthroat trout.

Facilities: Food, gas, and cold beer are available at the intersection of U.S. 101 and Steamboat Island Road about two miles south of the creek. Lodging and tackle are available to the south in Olympia and to the north in Shelton.

Directions: Follow U.S. 101 north from Olympia to the Kennedy Creek bridge, about three-quarters of a mile past the Thurston-Mason County line. The creek is midway between Olympia and Shelton.

Contact: Verle's Sport Center, 360/426-0933, Tumwater Sports, 360/352-5161 or 800/200-5161.

28 Summit Lake

At more than 500 acres, Summit is one of Thurston County's largest lakes, and it once was home to some of western Washington's largest resident cutthroat trout. If any of the whopper cutthroat still inhabit the lake, no one seems to catch them anymore, but Summit is one of the south Puget Sound region's favorite fishing lakes just the same.

Liberal plants of hatchery rainbows are what keep most Summit Lake anglers interested during the first several weeks of the season, which opens in late April. Trolling is popular, and the tried-and-true gang troll with a worm trailer probably catches more rainbows here than anything else. But still-fishing is very effective, especially around the west end of the lake. In May and early June, it's very possible to catch a limit of plump rainbows by simply anchoring in 20 to 30 feet of water and suspending a garden worm about six feet beneath a small bobber. If the day is bright and sunny or the water unseasonably warm, try a slip-sinker rig with a marshmallow or glob of Berkley Power Bait floating up two feet off the bottom.

By the time the trout fishing begins to slow, some Summit Lake anglers are getting serious about catching kokanee. June and July are the most productive months for these landlocked sockeye salmon, which run about 8 to 11 inches here. Trolling Wedding Ring spinners and similar lures accounts for some of them, but many Summit Lake kokanee are caught by stillfishing at the lake's west end and northwest corner. In warm weather, get on and off the lake before the skiers, knee-boarders, and other thrill seekers become active.

Perch fishing can be quite good at Summit, but the fish are usually on the small side. You may have to put up with three or four small ones for every perch large enough to be worth filleting, but keep the small ones too if you want to increase your odds of getting bigger fish next time.

As in other Northwest lakes, the brown bullheads here draw relatively little interest from anglers. But if you want to give it a shot, the odds would be in your favor if you were to launch your boat about sunset and row or motor into the shallows at the extreme west end of the lake. Much of the water here is in the four- to eight-foot depth range, shallow enough to heat up several degrees on a warm summer day and stay that way well into the night. Suspend a juicy night crawler, gob of beef, chicken liver, or other tasty catfish treat beneath a bobber for an hour or two and you should be in business.

Location: West of Olympia; see map B2, grid b1.

Species: Rainbow and cutthroat trout, kokanee, yellow perch, brown bullhead catfish, largemouth bass.

Facilities: A large, paved boat ramp and access area are located near the southwest corner of the lake. All other amenities are in Olympia.

Directions: Take Highway 8 west from Olympia about 12 miles to Summit Lake Road, turn north (right), and follow it about 1.5 miles to the lake.

Contact: Tumwater Sports, 360/352-5161 or 800/200-5161.

29 Nisqually River

Illegal fishing by tribal gillnetters all but wiped out the wild winter steelhead here a few years ago, and sport fishing has been closed during the peak of the steelhead runs ever since. With luck, worthwhile March and April steelheading will return to the Nisqually someday, but it could take a while.

In the meantime, chinook and chum salmon are the biggest draw for anglers on the Nisqually these days. The late summer and fall chinook fishing came on like gangbusters in 1998 and 1999 and provided some of the hottest fishing action this river has seen since the good old days of late-winter steelheading back in the 1960s. The good king fishing continued in late August and September of 2000 and 2001. A bumper crop of hatchery kings provided the great fishing, and chances are good for repeat performances in the coming years. This fishery begins to warm in late July, and by Labor Day it's at its peak.

Chums come on strong with the first high waters of November and provide fishing action well into January most years. Favorite fishing spots are the long drift immediately above the Pacific Avenue bridge, and a few miles upstream near the mouth of Muck

Creek. Nisqually River chums are fond of green yarn, small, green steelhead bobbers, or bobber-and-yarn combinations.

Sea-run cutthroat trout are available in the Nisqually from about August through November, but they get relatively little attention from anglers. The best cutthroat fishing is on the lower river between Yelm and the river mouth.

Location: Enters Puget Sound between Tacoma and Olympia; see map B2, grid b4.

Species: Winter and summer steelhead, chinook and chum salmon, sea-run cutthroat trout.

Facilities: Groceries, gas, and tackle are available in Yelm, and lodging can be found nearby in Olympia.

Directions: Take I-5 to the Old Nisqually exit and follow Pacific Avenue south two miles to Reservation Road. Turn left on Reservation Road and left again on Highway 510 (Olympia-Yelm Highway), which roughly parallels the south side of the river before crossing over it at the small town of McKenna.

Contact: Tumwater Sports, 360/352-5161 or 800/200-5161.

30 Chambers and Little Chambers Lakes

This flat shallow lake on the outskirts of Lacey is another favorite of some Olympia area bass anglers. Much of the lake is 4 to 7 feet deep, offering a wealth of bass-fishing possibilities. It's a good place to fish surface lures early and late in the day, and plastics or spinnerbaits the rest of the time.

As if the 72-acre main lake didn't have enough to offer bass anglers, there's another smaller lake attached to its southeast corner. Little Chambers Lake covers some 50 acres and offers about the same kind of fishing as the main lake. You probably won't want to attempt getting your $20,000 bass boat from one lake to the other, but it's possible to drag a car-topper or other small craft back and forth between the two if you feel adventurous.

Location: Southwest side of Lacey; see map B2, grid b3.

Species: Largemouth bass, yellow perch.

Facilities: There's a newly refurbished boat ramp at the access area, and all other facilities are in Lacey.

Directions: Take the Sleater-Kinney Road South exit off I-5 at Lacey and drive south to 14th Avenue SE. Turn west (right) and drive about half a mile to the public access area, on the left.

Contact: Tumwater Sports, 360/352-5161 or 800/200-5161.

31 Hicks Lake

Fairly large and quite deep by Puget Sound standards, this 170-acre lake south of Lacey warms rather slowly, so the rainbow and brown trout fishing may be slow early in the season and get better in May and early June. Legal-sized rainbows stocked just prior to the opener provide most of the action, but brown and rainbow carryovers to about 17 inches are a possibility. Triploid rainbows of a pound and a half and larger were stocked in Hicks for the 2001 season. Some trout are caught by bank anglers at the access area, but the first warm weather of the spring brings out the local kids who think the gravel beach is their personal swimming area. Although anglers pay for this and other access areas throughout the state and have a legal priority here, it doesn't always work out that way. That's the good thing about the new $10 access decal required by the Washington Department of Fish and Wildlife.

Although lakeside development over the past several decades has eliminated much of the brushy shoreline and other suitable habitat for warm-water fish, Hicks produces some nice largemouth bass and fair numbers of panfish. The best fishing for these species is near the shallow south end where there's still some weedy and brushy cover.

Location: In Lacey; see map B2, grid b3.

Species: Rainbow trout, largemouth bass, rock bass, warmouth, yellow perch.

Facilities: The lake has a single-lane boat ramp with ample parking and about 100 feet of gravel beach, plus a chemical toilet. A $10 Department of Fish and Wildlife access decal is required to use the ramp and public access area. Other facilities can be found in nearby Lacey.

Directions: Take the Pacific Avenue exit off I-5 at Lacey and drive east to Carpenter Road, turn right, and follow Carpenter about two miles to Shady Lane. Turn right, drive to the T intersection at Lilac Street, turn left, go a block and a half, and turn left again on Hicks Lake Road. The boat ramp and access area are about one-quarter mile down Hicks Lake Road on the left.

Contact: Sports Warehouse, 360/491-1346; Tumwater Sports, 360/352-5161 or 800/200-5161.

32 Long Lake

Preseason plants of legal-sized rainbows at this 300-acre lake make for fair fishing from the late-April opener until about mid-June. The lake, which is really more like two lakes connected by a narrow channel, treats trollers quite well, but anglers living around the lake also do fine stillfishing from their docks and floats. Stillfishing for rainbows is also popular on the beach alongside the boat ramp.

Decent bass fishing can be found along much of the lake's east side and wherever there's shoreline brush and trees. The many docks and floats also produce bass early and late in the day. Perch and crappies can be found throughout the lake, and anglers fishing for both occasionally score a rock bass or warmouth.

Location: East side of Lacey; see map B2, grid b3.

Species: Rainbow trout, largemouth and rock bass, warmouth, crappie, yellow perch.

Facilities: The lake has a large Department of Fish and Wildlife access area with a boat ramp and outhouses. A $10 WDFW access decal is required to use the ramp and access area. Food, gas, lodging, and other amenities are available in Lacey.

Directions: Take the Pacific Avenue exit off I-5 at Lacey. Go east (right) on Pacific to Carpenter Road, turn right, and follow Carpenter about three miles to the south end of the Thurston County Fairgrounds. Go left on Boat Launch Road just past the fairgrounds and follow it 200 yards to the lake.

Contact: Tumwater Sports, 360/352-5161 or 800/200-5161.

33 Lake St. Clair

A year-round fishing season and wide variety of fish species make St. Clair an interesting lake to fish. It offers fair trout fishing after the Department of Fish and Wildlife stocks it with about 5,000 legal-sized rainbows each spring, but there are also some chunky, winter carryover rainbows in the lake from fall plants of large fingerlings.

The lake's self-sustaining kokanee population provides fairly good fishing June through August, mostly for trollers using Pop Geer and Wedding Ring spinners or similar small, flashy offerings. Largemouth bass fishing can be good in the spring and summer, and there are plenty of docks, floats, and brushy shoreline areas to prospect for bass.

The lake's two most unusual species are warmouth and white crappies, neither of which is found in more than a handful of Northwest lakes, and you'll also find rock bass, a fairly rare catch in its own right. Pretty good perch fishing is also available here, and even though nobody but the kids seems

to notice, the lake also has a lot of pumpkin-seed sunfish to round out the angling menu. Grab a fishing rod and take your pick.

There's something to be said for confining your angling efforts to the north end of the lake, north of the boat ramp, especially during the winter months. That part of the lake has a 5 mph speed limit, while virtually anything goes on the southern half of the lake as far as boat speed is concerned.

Location: Southeast of Lacey; see map B2, grid b3.

Species: Rainbow trout, kokanee, largemouth bass, rock bass, warmouth, yellow perch, crappie, pumpkinseed sunfish.

Facilities: There's a two-lane Washington Department of Fish and Wildlife boat ramp on the lake. A $10 WDFW access decal is required to use the public launch area. Food, gas, tackle, and lodging can be found in Lacey.

Directions: Take Highway 510 southeast from Lacey or northwest from Yelm and turn east on Yelm Highway. Several roads and streets going north of Yelm Highway, beginning 1.5 miles from Highway 510, lead to the lake.

Contact: Tumwater Sports, 360/352-5161 or 800/200-5161.

34 Pattison (Patterson) Lake

A wide variety of cold-water and warm-water fish makes this 250-acre lake just south of Lacey a treat to fish. Although huge plants of legal-sized rainbows stocked just prior to the fishing season in late April provide most of the spring sport for trout anglers, you have a decent chance of hooking a carryover rainbow in the 15- to 18-inch class or a couple of brown trout that may be almost any size. Most anglers troll the usual spoons, spinners, and small wobblers, but give stillfishing a try and you might improve your chances of hooking one of the big carryovers.

Largemouth bass and yellow perch are also worth fishing for here, with the lake usually giving up a few very large bass during the course of a summer. Although not rare, rock bass always provide an interesting twist, and they're usually caught near shore by anglers who are fishing for something else, including trout.

One of the best things about fishing Pattison is that it's peaceful and you don't have to contend with any hot-rodders. Thurston County's no-wake speed limit is in effect here, so powerboaters have to go elsewhere, leaving Pattison to those who enjoy the more serene boating pleasures.

Location: South of Lacey; see map B2, grid b3.

Species: Rainbow and brown trout, largemouth bass, rock bass, crappie, yellow perch, bluegill.

Facilities: The east side of the lake has a Department of Fish and Wildlife access area and boat ramp. You'll need that $10 WDFW access decal to use the ramp. Food, gas, tackle, and lodging are available in Lacey.

Directions: Drive south out of Lacey on Ruddell Road for about 1.5 miles and turn east (left) on Mullen Road. Drive another 1.5 miles and turn south (right) on Carpenter Road. Drive half a mile and watch for the brown sign pointing to the public access area at the lake.

Contact: Tumwater Sports, 360/352-5161 or 800/200-5161.

35 Ward Lake

At perhaps 65 acres, Ward is probably an average-sized lake for the Puget Sound area. But what sets it apart from most of the rest is that it's unusually deep. It's more than 50 feet down in several spots, and nearly 70 feet in one place near the west side. This depth and the clearness of the water help make Ward a worthwhile prospect for trout throughout the summer, a rare quality among lakes in this area. Troll it with your favorite spoons, spinners, wobblers, or even flies early in the season, but by June and July make your way into the deeper waters around the south end or west side to try your hand at stillfishing on or near the bottom. As summer turns to fall and the water begins to cool, the rainbows will move back up into the more shallow areas where trolling will again be productive until the season comes to a halt at the end of October.

The clear, cool waters also offer an opportunity to catch kokanee, although this fishery seems to vary somewhat from year to year. Your best shot at these little landlocked sockeye salmon is during the summer. Try either trolling with a small, beaded spinner behind a string of larger trolling blades or stillfishing with white corn or maggots on brightly colored hooks. As always when trying for kokanee, try to locate the fish with your depthsounder or vary your fishing depth until you catch a fish, and then concentrate your efforts on that depth to find others.

Ward Lake also has some good-sized largemouth bass, but they can be a little shy and hard to fool in the lake's clear waters. That's probably why they're as big as they are here.

Location: East of Tumwater; see map B2, grid b3.

Species: Rainbow trout, kokanee, largemouth bass.

Facilities: The east side of the lake has a boat ramp and access area. It's a Department of Fish and Wildlife site, so you'll need that $10 WDFW access decal. Other amenities can be found in Tumwater.

Directions: Take I-5 to Tumwater and exit at the Olympia Brewery onto Custer Way. Drive east on Custer Way to the four-way blinking light and turn south (right) on Cleveland Avenue, which becomes the Yelm Highway. Turn north (left) on Boulevard Road, drive seven blocks to 42nd Way SE, turn left, and drive about three blocks to the lake.

Contact: Tumwater Sports, 360/352-5161 or 800/200-5161.

36 Munn Lake

A spring plant of about 3,000 rainbows provides fair trout fishing here in May and early June. Most of the rainbows are seven- to nine-inchers. After trout fishing drops off in the summer, there's another flurry of activity in the fall, especially from about the middle of September to early October. By this time the rainbows have grown to about 11 inches and are well worth catching.

The main warm-weather fishery is for largemouth bass, and this 40-acre lake (including Susan Lake, which is actually an extension of Munn) is a favorite of many Olympia area bass anglers. Much of the lake is less than 15 feet deep, so there are plenty of places to look for largemouths. One good place to fish in the spring is the shallow channel that connects the main lake to Susan Lake. This channel begins just to the right (north) of the boat ramp.

Location: Southeast of Tumwater; see map B2, grid b3.

Species: Rainbow trout, largemouth bass, bluegill.

Facilities: The public access area has a boat ramp and restrooms, but there are no other facilities on the lake. Don't forget, you need the $10 WDFW access decal to use this Department of Fish and Wildlife ramp. The nearest restaurants, accommodations, tackle, and gas are in Tumwater.

Directions: Take the Airdustrial Avenue exit off I-5 just south of Tumwater and drive east to the second stoplight. Turn south (right) on Capitol Boulevard (which becomes Pacific Highway SE at about this point) and drive less than a mile to Henderson Boulevard. Turn left and drive about two miles on Henderson to 65th Avenue. Turn right and go about half a mile to the public access area, on the right.

Contact: Tumwater Sports, 360/352-5161 or 800/200-5161.

37 Deschutes River

Not to be confused with its larger and more famous Oregon counterpart, Washington's Deschutes flows through the town of Tumwater and into the south end of Puget Sound at Olympia. Just before reaching saltwater it flattens out and becomes Capitol Lake for its final few hundred yards. Although fishing on the Deschutes isn't all that well known, the river does have one important claim to fame: It runs right by the Olympia Brewery, and its impressive falls are part of Olympia Beer's longtime logo.

As for the fishing, it's only fair. Although stocked with about 20,000 winter steelhead smolts annually, this little river doesn't provide much of a steelhead catch. It has some beautiful pools and drifts that look as though they should be full of fish all winter, but the average sport catch is only about a dozen steelhead a season.

A fair number of chinook and coho salmon make their way through the fish ladder and around the lower-river falls to a trapping facility operated by the Department of Fish and Wildlife. Fish that are allowed to pass by the facility and continue upstream provide some fishing action, but the river is often low and clear when the salmon are present, and they aren't very interested in what anglers have to offer. The fishery has been for chinooks only in recent years, with coho-release regulations in place.

Sea-run cutthroats also make their way into the Deschutes during the fall, and fishing for these little anadromous trout can be fairly good at times. Again, the clear water keeps them shy and spooky, so you may have to use stealth and patience to take them.

Location: Flows into Capitol Lake at Olympia; see map B2, grid b3.

Species: Winter steelhead, chinook and coho salmon, sea-run and resident cutthroat trout.

Facilities: Food, gas, lodging, and tackle are available in Tumwater.

Directions: Exit I-5 at the Olympia Brewery in Tumwater and take Custer Avenue to Capitol Way. Turn south (right) on Capitol and then left at the first light, which is E Street, to fish a productive part of the lower river. Follow Capitol Way south to Henderson and turn left to reach another worthwhile section of the Deschutes. Continue south on Capitol Way (which becomes Pacific Highway SE) to Waldrick Road and turn east (left) to reach several miles of the Deschutes near Offut Lake. To reach some of the better water farther upstream, drive east from Tenino about three miles on Highway 507 and turn north (left) on Military Road. Drive two miles to the bridge over the river. Parking here is on the skimpy side, so pull off the road as best you can.

Contact: Tumwater Sports, 360/352-5161 or 800/200-5161; Streamside Anglers, 360/709-3337.

38 Black Lake

When it comes to angling variety, Black Lake is Thurston County's biggest and best—biggest because it covers about 570 surface acres and best because there's something to catch here virtually all year. The trout fishing is often best early and late in the year, when the water is quite cool. I've made good catches of rainbows by trolling a small Triple Teazer or Dick Nite in a chrome/redhead finish along the east side of the lake as early as mid-March. One chilly November afternoon, I stopped to visit a friend who lives on the lake and found him and his son happily reeling in husky 12- to 14-inch rainbows on his dock. They were using salmon egg/worm combinations right on the bottom.

Cutthroat are often caught along with the hatchery-stocked rainbows, and during the past few years, trout anglers have also been surprised to find what seems to be an ever-growing number of small chinook salmon in their catch. Although Black Lake is connected to Puget Sound and the open Pacific Ocean via Percival Creek at one end and the Black River at the other, exactly how the chinooks are getting into the lake remains a mystery.

Black Lake begins to serve up pretty good largemouth bass catches by the first few warm days in April and remains productive through the summer. The weedy south end of the lake is a favorite stomping ground of local bass anglers, but respectable largemouths are caught all around the lake. By midsummer, when swimmers, skiers, personal watercraft riders, and other hell-raisers are flocking to the lake in raging hordes, you'd best plan on doing your bass fishing very early in the morning, very late in the evening, or during the black of night.

And, while we're talking about the black of night, that's the best time to fish for Black Lake's abundant brown bullheads. The lake provides some good catfish catches mid-June through August. Start looking for them at the weedy south end of the lake. Most of them will weigh about a pound and measure 11 to 14 inches.

Although I've never caught or even seen one, my friend and fellow outdoor writer Bob Johansen says Black Lake has some whopper rock bass. They tend to be something you catch by surprise rather than by design, but small spinnerbaits and little wobbling plugs will improve your chances if you have your heart set on catching one of these little red-eyed panfish—in Black Lake or anywhere else.

Location: Southwest of Olympia; see map B2, grid b2.

Species: Rainbow and cutthroat trout, chinook salmon, largemouth bass, yellow perch, black crappie, rock bass, brown bullhead catfish.

Facilities: Columbus Park, on the west side of the lake off Black Lake Boulevard, has tent/RV sites, picnic areas, and a very good swim beach. A store with gas pumps is located at the intersection of Black Lake–Belmore and Dent Roads on the east side of the lake. Nearby Olympia has a full line of restaurants, motels, RV parks, marine supply stores, and other facilities.

Directions: Take the Black Lake Boulevard exit off U.S. 101 in west Olympia and drive about two miles to the lake. Turn left on Black Lake–Belmore Road near the north end of the lake and bear right at the fire station. Drive about two miles to 66th Avenue, turn right, and follow it to the public access area and boat ramp near the south end of the lake. You'll need a $10 WDFW access decal to use the boat ramp and access area.

Contact: Tumwater Sports, 360/352-5161 or 800/200-5161.

39 Capitol Lake

Throughout most of the year, this wide spot at the mouth of the Deschutes River has little to offer anglers. But in August and September it can be a fairly good bet for chinook salmon. The best fishing is at the upper end of the lake where it narrows down and starts turning into a river, directly beneath the I-5 bridge. Some people anchor small boats here; others fish from the public fishing dock at the southwest corner of the lake. The boat launch and fishing dock are accessible from the Tumwater Historical Park. Most anglers fish roe clusters or fresh ghost shrimp for their kings, either suspended below a bobber or anchored to the bottom.

While trout fishing is fair at best, you might think otherwise if you read the Capitol Lake listing in a fishing regulations pamphlet. The Department of Fish and Wildlife devotes quite a lot of space to some rather complicated trout-fishing seasons on the lake, as-signing certain size and catch limits to part of the summer and a different set of rules to another part. Those regulations probably are aimed at protecting sea-run cutthroat that enter the lake during the summer, but that information isn't provided in print. Anyway, there are a few trout to be caught, but not many, and most anglers don't bother to try for them.

Location: Southwest Olympia; see map B2, grid b2.

Species: Chinook salmon, cutthroat trout.

Facilities: The upper end of the lake has a boat ramp and public fishing dock. Food, lodging, and other amenities are available in Olympia and Tumwater. Falls Terrace Restaurant, with good food and one of the best views anywhere, is half a mile south of the lake overlooking Tumwater Falls.

Directions: Take Exit 103 off I-5 and follow Deschutes Parkway about three-quarters of a mile to Tumwater Historical Park, where the upper end of the lake is on the right. To reach the lower part of the lake, continue past the park and under the freeway on Deschutes Parkway, paralleling the lake's west shoreline.

Contact: Tumwater Sports, 360/352-5161 or 800/200-5161.

40 Kapowsin Lake

As someone who grew up fishing this stump-filled wonderland, I can tell you that it's one of those places that has something for virtually every angler. It's even been known to give up a few steelhead, although you probably wouldn't want to come here just for the steelheading. The trout fishing doesn't get the recognition it deserves, maybe because lots of newcomers come to Kapowsin, take off trolling across the lake, and don't have very good luck.

For whatever reason, trolling produces only so-so results. If you insist on trolling, try a small Kwikfish or Flatfish in silver, gray, green, or yellow, or pull a nice, lively worm behind a string of small trolling blades.

Stillfishing, though, usually pays off best at Kapowsin. The good ol' bobber-and-worm combination works as well as anything, both early in the spring and again in the fall. During the summer, when most trout anglers give up on Kapowsin completely, try fishing early morning and late evening with a sliding bait rig right on the bottom. Berkley Power Bait, marshmallows, salmon eggs, and yellow corn all work well for this kind of fishing.

Kapowsin is a haven for bass and bass anglers, with a limitless supply of submerged stumps and logs and lots of shoreline brush and weed patches. Although it seldom gives up much in the way of trophy-class largemouths, there are enough one- and two-pounders to make things worthwhile. The north end of the lake is especially good.

The brown bullheads often grow quite large here, sometimes topping 18 inches and two pounds. Casting night crawlers in the shallows at the north end of the lake—at night, of course—is the way to catch them.

Kapowsin is one of those dozen or so south Puget Sound lakes that has rock bass, so take along a few BeetleSpins and other small spinnerbaits or small wobbling plugs if you're interested in catching one. A place to start casting might be the shallow bay on the east side of the lake, where St. Regis Paper Company (now Champion International) used to dump its logs.

Location: South of Orting; see map B2, grid b6.

Species: Rainbow trout, largemouth and rock bass, crappie, perch, brown bullhead catfish.

Facilities: Following several years during which there were no public facilities on the lake, the Washington Department of Fish and Wildlife has acquired what used to be the boat ramp/access area near the northwest corner of the lake and begun developing it. Lodging can be found in Puyallup.

Directions: Take Highway 161 south from Puyallup for 14 miles and turn east (left) on Kapowsin Highway. Drive three miles, and at the intersection of Kapowsin Highway and Orville Road, turn right to reach the south end of the lake or left to reach the north end.

Contact: Auburn Sports and Marine, 253/ 833-1440.

41 Whitman Lake

Small plants of hatchery rainbows provide fair early season spring trout fishing on this 30-acre Pierce County lake, which is now open to year-round fishing. Trollers might try a trolling pattern that takes them around the island or along the western and northern shorelines, but stillfishing is often better around the shallow flats near the southeast corner of the lake.

The docks and floats dotting the shoreline of the lake provide some of Whitman's best bass cover, but fish the lake's limited weed beds and brush, too. Crappie and perch may lurk in almost any part of the lake, while some of the best brown bullhead action is found near the boat ramp at the south end.

Location: North of Eatonville; see map B2, grid b6.

Species: Rainbow trout, largemouth bass, crappie, perch, brown bullhead catfish.

Facilities: A public access area and boat ramp are on the south end of the lake. Food, gas, and tackle are available in Kapowsin, about two miles to the northwest. The nearest lodging is in Eatonville and Puyallup.

Directions: Take Highway 161 south from Puyallup and turn east (left) on Kapowsin Highway and follow it two miles to 144th Avenue. Turn right and follow 144th about 1.5 miles to the lake.

Contact: Auburn Sports and Marine, 253/ 833-1440.

42 Tanwax Lake

This popular Pierce County lake is a haven for trout anglers, thanks in part to a liberal plant of about 40,000 legal-sized rainbows every spring. Both trolling and stillfishing work well, with anglers who stillfish often catching the large, carryover trout for which this lake is well known.

The wide variety of warm-water fish available at Tanwax makes this as good a bet for bass and panfish anglers as for trout enthusiasts. The east side and north end of the lake provide some of the best bass fishing. It has a slot limit that requires anglers to release all bass 12 to 17 inches long.

At more than 170 acres, Tanwax has plenty of elbowroom for everybody, although things can get a little congested at the public boat ramp on a sunny weekend. The season here runs late April through October, but the best trout fishing is in May and June. Bass and panfish bite best June through August.

Location: North of Eatonville; see map B2, grid b7.

Species: Rainbow trout, largemouth bass, yellow perch, bluegill, brown bullhead catfish, pumpkinseed sunfish.

Facilities: Rainbow Resort has a fishing dock, groceries, tackle, and tent and RV sites. Lodging and other amenities are available in Eatonville, five miles to the south.

Directions: Take Highway 161 south from Puyallup for 17 miles and turn left on Tanwax Drive to reach the resort on the north side. Go a quarter mile past Tanwax Drive and take the next left to reach the public boat ramp near the south end of the lake.

Contact: Rainbow Resort, 360/879-5115.

43 Clear Lake

Liberal spring plants of legal-sized rainbow trout supplement a healthy, self-sustaining population of kokanee in this popular south Pierce County lake. Clear Lake is no longer open to year-round fishing but instead has a late-April through October season. It produces fair to good rainbow action April through June and again for several weeks after Labor Day. The center of the lake has a couple of spots over 85 feet deep, so trout fishing is also a possibility during the warm months, but by then most folks are turning their attention to kokanee. Trolling with leaded line or downriggers may be required to get down to the kokanee in the summer, especially during the middle of the day. If you're not a troller, find a concentration of these small sockeye salmon and drop a hook baited with a kernel of white corn or a maggot down to the appropriate depth. As always, a good depthsounder is a valuable tool in locating Clear Lake kokanee, but you can also look for concentrations of other kokanee anglers on the surface, which requires no special electronic equipment. This lake lives up to its name, so be willing to fish light lines and leaders.

Clear Lake has had brown bullheads in it since I fished it as a kid more than 30 years ago, and they'll always be there. Night fishing almost anywhere in the lake should provide enough of these 10- to 12-inch catfish for a meal. Use worms or chicken livers for bait.

Summertime fishing can be a little tough because of the lake's popularity with skiers and swimmers, so do your fishing early and late in the day to avoid some of the commotion. Summertime weekends can be particularly hazardous to your health.

Location: North of Eatonville; see map B2, grid c7.

Species: Rainbow trout, kokanee, brown bullhead catfish, a few largemouth bass.

Facilities: A private resort near the south end of the lake has a small store, and there's a public access area with boat ramp and restrooms at the northwest corner of the lake. Food, gas, lodging, and tackle can be found in Eatonville.

Directions: Drive south from Puyallup for 15 miles on Highway 161 and watch for the lake on your left.
Contact: Ohop Valley Grocery, 360/847-2141; Auburn Sports and Marine, 253/833-1440.

44 Ohop Lake

Although stocked with legal-sized rainbows every spring, this large, 235-acre lake offers only fair trout fishing. Trolling with Flatfish, Kwikfish, Triple Teazers, Dick Nites, and garden worms behind a string of trolling blades is most popular, but lakeside home owners often catch some nice fish while stillfishing from their docks and floats. Carryovers to about 18 inches are rare but possible.

Lots of largemouth bass have been caught from Ohop since I caught my first one there nearly four decades ago, many of them from the undeveloped southwest shoreline and the many docks, stumps, and brushy spots along the east side of the lake. A two-pounder is a pretty good-sized bass here.

The perch, crappie, and brown bullhead fishing gets better as summer progresses, thanks in part to the fact that this big lake warms rather slowly.
Location: North of Eatonville; see map B2, grid c6.
Species: Rainbow trout, largemouth bass, black crappie, yellow perch, brown bullhead catfish.
Facilities: A large public access area with restrooms and a boat ramp is located near the south end of the lake. The nearest food, gas, lodging, and tackle are in Eatonville, a mile south of the lake.
Directions: Take Highway 161 south from Puyallup for about 24 miles and turn left on Orville Road, or take Orville Road south from Kapowsin for eight miles to reach the lake.
Contact: Eatonville Valley Grocery, 360/847-2141; Auburn Sports and Marine, 253/833-1440.

45 Coplay Lake/Clearwater Wilderness Lakes

Coplay offers anglers a sort of user-friendly version of the alpine lake experience, since it's a high-country lake with a road running virtually right to its shores. Coplay and the hike-in lakes to the north are stocked intermittently by the Department of Fish and Wildlife, so they offer only fair, take-what-you-get trout fishing. You may have company when you fish Coplay, especially on weekends, but if you hit the trail, there's a good chance you'll be fishing in solitude. Of all the hike-in lakes, Summit is the largest and deepest and offers the best potential for a couple of decent-sized trout. Spring and fall provide the best fishing at these lakes.
Location: East of Fairfax in northern Pierce County; see map B2, grid b9.
Species: Brook, cutthroat, and rainbow trout.
Facilities: There are no facilities at Coplay or any of the nearby lakes, but food and gas are available in Carbonado. Lodging and tackle can be found in Buckley.
Directions: Drive east from Sumner on Highway 410 and turn south on Highway 165 near Buckley. About four miles south of Carbonado (and a mile after crossing over the impressive high bridge over the Carbon River), turn left on Forest Service Road 7810 (Cayada Creek Road), which leads to Coplay Lake. Proceed past the lake a mile and take the trail that leads a mile to Twin Lakes, another mile west to Summit Lake, a mile northeast to Lily Lake, and 1.5 miles northwest to Coundly Lake.
Contact: Al's Sporting Goods, 360/829-0174.

46 Carbon Glacier Lakes

Green Lake, about a mile and a half off the road by way of a good trail, gets the heaviest fishing pressure of all lakes in the area, but it isn't very generous with its trout. Some say the cutthroats and rainbows here have grown wary in the lake's extremely clear water, and it's hard to find anyone who will argue the point. But there are some large trout in Green Lake that should be susceptible to light leaders and a clever strategy.

The lakes past Ipsut Creek, which don't see as many offerings from anglers, hold trout apparently less sophisticated than those in Green Lake; decent catches of brook trout, with an occasional cutthroat mixed in, are fairly common. Pack your favorite light spinning rod and a selection of small spinners, spoons, and both dry- and wet-fly patterns. You can fish the flies behind a clear plastic float with the spinning rod in the morning and evening. The best fishing is in June and July, but September can also be good.

Location: North of Mount Rainier within Mount Rainier National Park; see map B2, grid b9.

Species: Brook, cutthroat, and rainbow trout.

Facilities: Ipsut Creek Campground has tent sites, water, and restrooms. The nearest food and gas are in Carbonado. Lodging and tackle are available in Buckley.

Directions: Drive east from Sumner on Highway 410 and turn south on Highway 165 near Buckley. A mile past the high bridge over the Carbon River south of Carbonado, bear left on the well-marked road to the Carbon River entrance to Mount Rainier National Park and follow it to Ipsut Creek Campground. The mile-and-a-half trail to Green Lake is on the right side of the road, about three miles past the entrance station. To reach lakes to the east, continue past the Green Lake trail to Ipsut Creek Campground, where the road ends. A seven- to eight-mile hike will take you to James, Ethel, Marjorie, Oliver, and Adelaide Lakes.

Contact: Mount Rainier National Park, 360/569-2211; Al's Sporting Goods, 360/829-0174.

47 Mowich Lake

The lake is as pretty as it ever was, but decades of drive-to access and the Park Service's no-fish-stocking policy have greatly diminished the fishing potential of this large alpine lake. I can remember drifting around Mowich in an inflatable raft as a kid and catching several of what seemed at the time like trophy-class trout, but that scene is seldom repeated these days. It's still a nice place to practice your fly-casting or to troll a small wobbling spoon around on a light line, but don't promise anyone that you'll be home with freshly caught trout for dinner.

Location: Northwest of Mount Rainier in Mount Rainier National Park; see map B2, grid c9.

Species: Rainbow and brook trout.

Facilities: The only facilities here are a parking area and a trail around the lake. Food and gas are available in Carbonado, lodging and tackle in Buckley.

Directions: Drive east from Sumner on Highway 410 and turn south on Highway 165 near Buckley. Stay on Highway 165 all the way to the lake, a distance of about 25 miles.

Contact: Mount Rainier National Park, 360/569-2211; Al's Sporting Goods, 360/829-0174.

48 Rapjohn Lake

The Department of Fish and Wildlife stocks about 4,000 pan-sized rainbows here before the April opener, and they provide most of the fishing action through May. After that, some serious trout anglers switch from bobber-and-worm rigs and small wobbling spoons to larger offerings in hopes of finding a cooperative brown trout. Browns were stocked at Rapjohn several years ago, and every now and then someone tangles with one in the five- to 10-pound range. Some of those encounters are by design, others quite by accident. If you're fishing with your favorite ultralight outfit and four-pound line, you lose. Bass anglers casting crankbaits on 15-pound monofilament tend to come out a little better during these encounters of the brown trout kind.

Speaking of bass, Rapjohn has long been a favorite of largemouth enthusiasts, since the lake has plenty of productive bass cover to investigate and produces some large bass. If you haven't fished it before, check the regulations pamphlet for information about the slot limit on bass that's in effect here.

Evening fishing for perch and crappies can be excellent from late spring to fall, and if you're still on the water at dusk, you might stick around a couple more hours to try your hand at catfish. Brown bullheads are abundant and will gladly accept your offering of a juicy night crawler suspended from a bobber. Explore the edges of the lake until you find action.

Location: Northwest of Eatonville; see map B2, grid c6.

Species: Rainbow and brown trout, largemouth bass, yellow perch, crappie, brown bullhead catfish.

Facilities: The west side of the lake has a Department of Fish and Wildlife public access area and boat ramp. Don't forget the $10 access decal to use the ramp. The nearest food, gas, tackle, and lodging are in Eatonville, five miles south.

Directions: Take Highway 7 south from Spanaway. Exactly two miles south of the Highway 702 (352nd Avenue East) intersection, turn east (left) at the brown Public Fishing sign onto the narrow road that leads to the lake.

Contact: Auburn Sports and Marine, 253/833-1440.

49 Silver Lake

If it's true that variety is the spice of life, Silver Lake is a mighty spicy place. From the time it opens to fishing in late April until the day it closes at the end of October, there's always something to fish for—and to catch—from this 138-acre south Pierce County gem.

Silver is one of few western Washington lakes that offers three species of trout, many of them raised and released by resort owner George Henley in the large net pen at the resort. Rainbow, brown, and brook trout inhabit the lake, and depending on how and where you fish, you might catch all three as part of the five-fish daily limit. Troll Flatfish, Kwikfish, Dick Nites, Triple Teazers, or Pop Geer–and–worm combinations throughout the lake for all three, or stillfish Berkley Power Bait, earthworms, or mealworms off the resort dock, which may be the longest such freshwater fishing dock in the Northwest. To target brook trout, troll or cast small spoons and spinners close to shore, or catch them by casting your favorite wet- or dry-fly patterns in the shallows. Anglers in search of larger brown trout—some of which have grown to trophy proportions during several years in the lake—should troll with large, minnow-imitating plugs or wobbling spoons.

Silver Lake is one of Pierce County's best largemouth bass lakes, producing more than its share of fish in the five- to seven-pound range. They'll take surface plugs, buzzbaits, and other top-water goodies at first and last light. During the day, you'll find places to fish all your favorite things, whether they be plastics, crankbaits, spinnerbaits, or something else. A slot limit protects bass between 12 and 17 inches long.

The panfish possibilities include black crappies, yellow perch, and bluegills, all of which grow to worthwhile size in the lake's rich environment. This is also a popular catfish lake, with brown bullheads running 10 to 14 inches, sometimes larger. Most catfish anglers fish from boats, but the resort dock can also be a good place. Garden worms and mealworms are favorite baits.

Location: Northwest of Eatonville; see map B2, grid c6.

Species: Rainbow, brown, and brook trout; largemouth bass; yellow perch; crappie; bluegill; brown bullhead catfish.

Facilities: Henley's Silver Lake Resort has rental boats, a 250-foot fishing dock, a boat ramp, tackle, and tent and RV spaces. Food, gas, tackle, and lodging can be found in Eatonville, five miles away.

Directions: Take Highway 7 south from Spanaway and watch for the Silver Lake Resort sign 3.5 miles south of the Highway 702 (352nd Avenue East) intersection. Turn west (right) to the lake.

Contact: Henley's Silver Lake Resort, 360/832-3580, website: www.washington lakes.com.

50 Harts Lake

The season at Harts Lake is now year-round, and hatchery rainbows stocked in the spring provide a decent shot at trout throughout most of that time. Those rainbows run 11 to 12 inches by fall, making this a good place to try fly-fishing after the Labor Day weekend.

Like nearby Silver Lake (number 49), Harts is a good one for bass, too, with seven-pound largemouths a possibility. As at other area lakes, a slot limit protects bass between 12 and 17 inches from harvest. Yellow perch and crappies are abundant in the lake as well, and summertime provides some excellent catches of brown bullheads.

Location: Southwest of McKenna; see map B2, grid c6.

Species: Rainbow trout, largemouth bass, yellow perch, crappie, brown bullhead catfish.

Facilities: There's a public access area and boat ramp on the lake, managed by the Department of Fish and Wildlife. It's a single-lane gravel ramp with a fairly large gravel parking area and pit toilets. A $10 WDFW access decal is required to use the public launch. The lake also has a resort with a small swim beach, picnic area, and store.

Directions: Drive east out of McKenna on Highway 702 for a mile, turn south on Harts Lake Road, and follow it about 4.5 miles to the lake, which is on the right.

Contact: Harts Lake Resort, 360/458-3477.

51 Offut Lake

This 192-acre lake has a reputation for producing some of the biggest trout anywhere in Thurston County, perhaps anywhere in Washington. Carryover rainbows of three to five pounds aren't caught by everyone who wets a line here, but they are hooked often enough to keep things interesting. Now and then someone catches a real monster, such as the lake-record 10-pounder caught in 1976. Many of the biggest fish are caught by anglers stillfishing from the resort's fishing dock. But trolling and stillfishing in other parts of the lake are also effective.

Offut also provides good largemouth bass fishing, and some of the bucketmouths range from five to seven pounds. The docks along the northeast corner of the lake and the weed beds at the east end are good places to look for bass. No one is sure where the small-mouths came from, but they're in the lake, according to folks at the resort, and you might catch smallies to over three pounds if you're persistent (or lucky). The east end of the lake is also a good place to look for both perch and brown bullheads.

If you quit fishing early, stop by Wolf Haven on your way out. This wildlife park is home to wolves from all over North America, and the small entrance fee is money well spent for what you'll see and learn about these fascinating animals.

Location: Southeast of Tumwater; see map B2, grid c3.

Species: Rainbow trout, largemouth and (maybe a few) smallmouth bass, yellow perch, black bullhead catfish.

Facilities: Offut Lake Resort has a fishing dock, boat rentals, bait and tackle, groceries, rental cabins, an RV park, and tent sites. There's a grocery store and gas station at the intersection of Pacific Highway SE and Offut Lake Road.

Directions: To reach the public access area and boat launch on the north side of the lake, take Pacific Highway SE south from Tumwater and turn east (left) onto Waldrick Road about four miles south of the airport. Watch for the brown Public Access sign about 1.5 miles down Waldrick Road and turn right. To reach the south side of the lake, continue south past Waldrick Road on Pacific Highway SE for about 1.5 miles and turn left (east) on Offut Lake Road. That's where Offut Lake Resort is located.

Contact: Offut Lake Resort, 360/264-2438.

52 Deep Lake

If you launch your boat here, turn on your depthsounder and go looking for the cool depths that give this Thurston County lake its name, you'll eventually conclude that either your depthsounder has gone berserk or the lake is woefully misnamed. The latter happens to be the case. You would have to look a long time to find a spot in Deep Lake that's more than about 18 feet deep. Whoever named it either had a dry sense of humor or had been sipping his hair tonic before visiting the lake.

But just because the lake isn't really deep doesn't mean anglers should overlook it. Deep Lake provides fair to good fishing for rainbows from the time it opens in late April until about the middle of June, when it becomes a haven more for swimmers than for trout anglers. The trout action picks up again after Labor Day and can be quite good in September and Oc-

tober. Casting from the bank, either with small spoons and spinners or with bobber-and-worm or bobber-and-salmon-egg combinations, can be effective. The small fishing dock near the boat ramp at the northwest corner of the lake is a good place to fish marshmallows, salmon eggs, Berkley Power Bait, and other offerings near the bottom. When the dock isn't crowded, fly anglers often cast to rising rainbows here in the morning and evening. The addition of triploid rainbows at the start of the 2001 season has added to the trophy-trout possibilities at this popular lake.

Although not noted for its bass fishing, Deep Lake produces some fair-sized largemouths. The brushy, weedy waters around the uninhabited west end of the lake offer the best bass-fishing opportunities.

The brush piles, weeds, and overhanging trees at the west end also provide the best shot at bluegills. Try a BeetleSpin or small leadhead laces with a piece of worm to catch them.

Location: South of Tumwater; see map B2, grid c3.

Species: Rainbow trout, largemouth bass, bluegill.

Facilities: Millersylvania State Park has a boat ramp and a short fishing dock, tent and RV spaces, and picnic shelters, plus beach access for fishing along the lake. There's a gas station with groceries back at the 93rd Avenue exit off I-5. Additional amenities are available in Tumwater.

Directions: Take I-5 to the 93rd Avenue exit south of Tumwater and drive east on 93rd about a mile and a quarter to Tilley Road. Turn south (right) on Tilley and drive about three miles to the lake, on the right.

Contact: Millersylvania State Park, 360/753-1519; Washington State Parks and Recreation Commission, 360/902-8844 (information) or 800/542-5687 (reservations); Tumwater Sports, 360/352-5161 or 800/200-5161.

53 McIntosh Lake

Hatchery plants do pretty well at McIntosh, and the lake is often one of the area's better producers throughout the spring. Although the trout planted here are often quite small, they grow quickly in the early spring and provide good fishing throughout May. But by June this shallow lake warms up considerably, and trout fishing falls off until September. Trolling, stillfishing, and evening fly-fishing all work well here. Fly anglers should pay special attention to the brushy shoreline along the south side and the large patch of snags and stumps near the middle of the lake. The lake also has a growing bass population, with a slot limit that requires all 12- to 17-inch largemouths be released.

McIntosh Lake is also popular with nesting ducks and Canada geese, so watch out for them and their young during the spring.

Location: Northeast of Tenino; see map B2, grid c3.

Species: Rainbow trout, largemouth bass.

Facilities: The north side of the lake has a public access area with a boat ramp and restrooms. Get food and gas in Tenino, four miles away. The drive north a few miles to eat dinner at Offut Lake Resort is worth the trip. Lodging and tackle can be found in Tumwater.

Directions: Take I-5 to Grand Mound and exit east onto Pacific Highway SE, following it about eight miles to Tenino and the junction of Highway 507. Continue east on Highway 507 for about four miles to Military Road and turn north (left). Follow Military Road about 1.5 miles to the boat ramp on the right. If you continue on Highway 507 past Military Road, you'll drive along the south side of the lake.

Contact: Tumwater Sports, 360/352-5161 or 800/200-5161.

54 Black River

This is one of the slowest, most gently moving streams in the Northwest, flowing nearly 30 miles from the south end of Black Lake to the Chehalis River with hardly a riffle along the way. It can be floated quite safely in a canoe or small inflatable, and that's how many anglers fish it. Most anglers fish for trout with spinning tackle or fly rods, but there are also bass in the river that probably made their way out of Black Lake.

Whether you fish for trout or bass, you can't use bait. This river has selective regulations, which means artificial lures and flies only, with single, barbless hooks. The same goes

---

Fishing State Parks

The fact that Washington State Parks offer access to more than 100 freshwater and saltwater fisheries may be one of the Evergreen State's best-kept angling secrets. Some 56 parks are on freshwater lakes and streams, another 48 provide saltwater angling access, and two parks offer both freshwater and saltwater fishing. State Parks provide a whopping 825 miles of freshwater shoreline for anglers to explore, ranging from tiny ponds and creeks to vast expanses along the shores of the Columbia River and some of its largest reservoirs.

Besides shoreline access, the Washington State Parks and Recreation Commission also maintains boat ramps at more than 50 of its parks. Thirteen of those boat ramps are on saltwater, the rest on freshwater lakes and rivers. Daily launch fees of $3 to $4 are collected at these sites, or an annual boat-launch permit costing $40 is also available.

for Mima Creek, Waddell Creek, Beaver Creek, Salmon Creek, Dempsey Creek, and Blooms Ditch, all of which are tributaries to the Black River. The season here runs June through October.

Location: Flows from Black Lake into the Chehalis River near Oakville; see map B2, grid c1.

Species: Cutthroat and rainbow trout, largemouth bass.

Facilities: Rough boat launches are located about 1.5 miles north of Little Rock (off 110th Avenue), two miles south of Little Rock (off Highway 121), two miles west of Rochester (off Moon Road), and a little over four miles west of Rochester (on the south side of the U.S. 12 bridge). Food, gas, tackle, and lodging are available in and around Rochester.

Directions: Take U.S. 12 west of I-5 at Grand Mound and turn north on Highway 12 (Little Rock Road) at Rochester to go upriver, or continue west on U.S. 12 through Rochester to where the highway crosses the lower river.

Contact: Tumwater Sports, 360/352-5161 or 800/200-5161.

55 Upper Chehalis River

Like a number of western Washington rivers, the Chehalis assumes many faces as it winds its way northward from its humble beginnings in the hills of northwestern Cowlitz County to the low farmlands of Lewis, Thurston, and Grays Harbor Counties, finally entering Grays Harbor and the Pacific Ocean near Aberdeen. While the Lower Chehalis (number 14 in chapter B1) is a favorite among a broad range of Northwest anglers, the upper two-thirds of the river draws relatively little angler interest or fishing pressure.

Access is part of the problem. Much of the river runs through farmland and other private property, and some of the greetings you'll get if you go knocking on farmhouse doors asking permission to fish will give you a sense of what Burt Reynolds, Jon Voight, and Ned Beatty must have felt like during their little canoe trip a few years back. And even where it's OK to fish, the river has a lot of high, steep banks and a serious shortage of gently sloping gravel bars where you can stroll casually up and down the river. Boating this stretch of the Chehalis might be the answer, but the river is too slow-moving for drift boats and rafts and there are no developed boat ramps where larger jet sleds or other power boats can be launched.

A rare exception to this generally dismal story is the short section of river around Rainbow Falls State Park, where deep pools and at least some gravel beach provide the opportunity to fish several hundred feet of beautiful stream. The fishing isn't all that productive, but at least it's pretty. And if you take the time to explore some of the areas downstream, you're sure to find other short sections of the river where you can wet a line. I haven't found many such places, but maybe you will.

Location: From Oakville upstream; see map B2, grid c1.

Species: Winter and (some) summer steelhead; coho, chinook, and chum salmon; sea-run and resident cutthroat trout; largemouth bass.

Facilities: Rainbow Falls State Park has tent sites and restrooms. Food, gas, lodging, tackle, and other amenities are available in Centralia and Chehalis.

Directions: Take I-5 to Grand Mound, drive west on U.S. 12, and turn south on Albany Street to Independence Road to reach some of the river between Grand Mound and Oakville. Roads off Old Highway 99 between Grand Mound and Chehalis, including Prather Road and Cooks Hill Road, provide some river access. Take Highway 6 west of I-5 at Chehalis to reach more than 20 miles of the river from Chehalis upstream to Pe Ell.

Contact: Sunbirds Shopping Center, 360/748-3337 (sporting goods department).

56 Skookumchuck River

Hatchery plants of one kind or another provide virtually all the action for anglers on the Lower Skookumchuck. At least 80,000 winter steelhead smolts a year are released from the hatchery facility at the base of the dam, and when adult fish from those plants return to the river, they provide a flurry of fishing opportunity. The best fishing is in March and April, and most of the steelhead are caught from a short stretch of river near the dam. Like the Blue Creek Hole on the Cowlitz or the Tokul Creek fishery on the Snoqualmie (number 72 in this chapter or number 124 in chapter A2), what happens here is something short of an aesthetic angling experience—especially on weekends—but the catching can be good. There are a half dozen wide turnouts and parking areas along the last mile of road before you reach the end of the line, and there are good-looking steelhead spots near all of them. It doesn't take long to see why this stretch of river is so popular.

Several thousand hatchery cutthroat are also stocked in the Lower Skookumchuck most years, providing a pretty good October and November fishery. The standard river regulation of allowing two trout (at least 14 inches long) per day is in effect here. Wild steelhead must be released whenever you fish the Lower Skookumchuck.

There is also now a salmon season on the lower reaches of this little river, although it's quite limited in terms of what you can keep. Adult chinook must be released during the first half of the fall salmon season, while both adult chinook and wild adult coho salmon must be released during the second part. Check the fishing pamphlet carefully for those season dates and other details.

Things are a little different on the Upper Skookumchuck above the reservoir. This stretch has selective fishery regulations, so you can't use bait or barbed hooks. It's also pretty tough to find a legal-sized trout here throughout most of the season. Access to this upper-river fishery is via logging roads running south from Vail.

Location: Flows into the Chehalis River at Centralia; see map B2, grid d2.

Species: Winter steelhead, sea-run and resident cutthroat trout, chinook and coho salmon.

Facilities: Groceries and gas are available in Bucoda and Tenino, with other amenities in Centralia.

Directions: Take Highway 507 north from Centralia or south from Tenino to 184th Avenue SE and turn east. It's a 7.7-mile drive from Highway 507 to Skookumchuck Dam and the end of the road. You'll cross the river twice along the way, once at the 2.2-mile mark and again at 5.7 miles.

Contact: Sunbirds Shopping Center, 360/748-3337 (sporting goods department); Tumwater Sports, 360/352-5161 or 800/200-5161.

57 Lawrence Lake

Even though Lawrence Lake covers 300 acres, it's fairly shallow, so it warms quickly in the summer—so quickly, in fact, that rainbow trout don't do particularly well here. The Department of Fish and Wildlife started stocking brown trout in the lake during the mid-1990s, and they help to provide fair fishing for trout anglers during the spring and fall. But even if they don't, anglers who are busy catching bass and other warm-water fish won't mind. Lawrence offers some good bass fishing, and largemouths of five pounds and bigger are caught here throughout the spring and summer. A special slot limit on bass is in effect, so check the fishing regulations pamphlet before fishing the lake for the first time.

In addition to trout and bass, perch fishing can be very good during the day. Brown bullheads bite equally well during the evening and at night. If you plan to fish Lawrence Lake, do it from April through October. The public access area and boat ramp are closed from early November until early April each year.

Location: Southeast of Yelm; see map B2, grid c5.

Species: Largemouth bass, yellow perch, brown bullhead catfish, brown trout.

Facilities: The lake has an access area with a boat ramp and restrooms. The town of Yelm offers the nearest food, gas, tackle, and lodging.

Directions: Take Bald Hills Road southeast off Highway 507 at a place called Five Corners, about a mile southeast of Yelm. Follow the road southward until you come to a three-way fork (about a mile after 138th Avenue SE), and go west (right). Drive half a mile to Lawrence Lake Road and turn south (left). Drive another mile and you'll see the lake on the right.

Contact: Tumwater Sports, 360/352-5161 or 800/200-5161.

58 Clear Lake

This is one of the most productive—and therefore one of the most popular—trout lakes in the south Puget Sound region. Long known for its husky rainbows, Clear Lake is generous with trout in the 9- to 11-inch range early in the season, and they just get bigger as time goes by. The rainbows carry over pretty well, too, meaning your catch might include a dandy of 18 to 20 inches. The addition of brown trout several years ago made things that much more interesting and prolonged the fishing action a little further into the summer. Things got even better in the spring of 2001, when the Department of Fish and Wildlife started planting hefty triploid rainbows in the lake. Both trolling and still-

fishing work well, and one local favorite is a small, green Triple Teazer.

The lake has a growing population of largemouth bass, and they provide some mid-summer angling action.

Location: West of La Grande in eastern Thurston County; see map B2, grid c5.

Species: Rainbow and brown trout, triploid rainbows, largemouth bass.

Facilities: There's a Department of Fish and Wildlife boat ramp on the north side of the lake. It's a two-lane ramp with concrete planks. The nearby parking lot has room for perhaps 100 cars with boat trailers. A $10 WDFW access decal is required to use the public launch area. Food, gas, and lodging are available in Yelm and Olympia.

Directions: Turn southeast on Black Hills Road from Highway 507 at Five Corners, a mile southeast of Yelm. Follow Black Hills Road just under 10 miles to the south end of the lake, on the left.

Contact: Washington Department of Fish and Wildlife, Montesano Office, 360/249-4628; Olympia/Thurston County Chamber of Commerce Visitor Information Center, 360/357-3362.

59 Mashel River

The Mashel provides a little trout-fishing activity after it opens to fishing in June, but finding a two-fish limit of a legal-sized cutthroat here can be a challenge. Local anglers fish it pretty thoroughly at the start of the season, and these trout grow to eight inches rather slowly. You might do well to wait and fish it in October, after the interest and fishing pressure have waned. The Mashel is open through October 31.

Location: Joins the Nisqually River southwest of Eatonville; see map B2, grid c6.

Species: Cutthroat trout.

Facilities: Food, gas, tackle, and lodging are available in and around Eatonville.

Directions: Take Highway 161 to Eatonville.

Logging roads leading east from town provide access to the upper river. Highway 161 itself parallels part of the river to the west of Eatonville.

Contact: Washington Department of Fish and Wildlife, Montesano Office, 360/249-4628.

60 Alder Lake

Are you looking for the largest fish in the entire Northwest? Well, Alder Lake has it. That's right, I said "it," not "them." The fish in question is one of a kind, and it resides near the northwest end of the lake, not far from the dam. Fly over the lake sometime and you'll see it. That's how I first spotted it, and I was so impressed that I shot several photos of it out the airplane window. Since then I've even seen the monster on a few good maps.

OK, before you start thinking that I've been sniffing too much Smelly Jelly, I should tell you that this "fish" is actually Bogucki Island, a fish-shaped high spot that managed to keep its head above water after the Nisqually River was dammed near the little community of Alder to form the reservoir we now call Alder Lake. It's the most fishy-looking landmark I know of around here.

There are also enough real fish in Alder Lake, which is open to fishing year-round, to draw anglers from all over western Washington. Kokanee are perhaps the biggest draw, providing plenty of excitement and fine eating for Alder Lake anglers. May, June, and July are the top months to fish for them, and most are caught by trollers. Wedding Rings and similar spinners fished behind strings of trolling blades are most popular for Alder Lake kokanee, which average about nine inches in May but sometimes top the 12-inch mark by midsummer. Most anglers use bait on the hooks of those Wedding Rings, with worms being the most popular bait.

The lake is also planted with legal-sized rainbows in the spring, some of which are caught by the folks fishing for kokanee. If you want rainbows instead of kokanee, try small Kwikfish, Dick Nite or Triple Teazer spoons, Rooster Tails, or Mepps spinners near the surface, either cast or trolled. You might also pick up an occasional cutthroat this way.

Alder doesn't get a lot of recognition as a bass lake, but it does have a fair population of largemouths, which can be caught from brushy shoreline areas, rocky points, and submerged stumps and other woody structure. There's a persistent rumor that Alder also contains smallmouth bass. If you find out for sure, let me know. The lake has a bass slot limit, so all bass under 12 inches and over 17 inches must be released.

Some people come here just for the excellent perch fishing, especially in the spring and summer. A bobber-and-worm rig or plastic-skirted Mini Jig with a piece of worm on its hook will take all you want, once you locate a school. Some of the perch grow impressively large. If you're into panfish, you might also be interested in brown bullhead catfish that are fished by relatively few Alder Lake visitors.

Location: Southeast of La Grande in the southeast corner of Thurston County; see map B2, grid c6.

Species: Rainbow and (a few) cutthroat trout, kokanee, largemouth bass, yellow perch, crappie, brown bullhead catfish.

Facilities: Alder Park, near the north end of the lake, has a two-lane boat ramp, tent and RV sites, picnic tables, showers, restrooms, a moorage float, covered cooking areas, and a nearby store with groceries, bait, and other necessities. There's a public boat ramp and access area on the northeast side of the lake just off the highway, and another on the south side off Pleasant Valley Road. There's a gas station in Elbe at the east end of the lake.

Directions: Take Highway 7 south from Spanaway about 25 miles or north from Morton about 18 miles. The lake is on the south side of the road.

Contact: Alder Park Store, 360/569-8824.

61 Mineral Lake

People in these parts still haven't gotten over the monster rainbows a few anglers caught from this lake in the spring of 1995, so that's what you may hear about whenever you ask about the fishing here. Mineral produced several rainbows of 8 to 14.5 pounds—that's right, pounds, not inches—during that spring of monsters, greatly increasing the popularity of this already-popular Lewis County lake.

Not everyone fishing Mineral is going to catch a trout of such impressive proportions, but it does tend to treat anglers very generously. Both rainbows and browns put on weight fast in this rich lake, so anglers complain neither about the quality nor the quantity of their catch. In fact, it's turned out that the record year of 1995 wasn't really that unusual a year after all, since hefty trout have continued to come from the lake regularly since then. If anything, the chances of catching a trophy-size trout from Mineral have improved, now that surplus brood-stock trout and fast-growing triploid rainbows are being stocked here. Stillfishing with Berkley Power Bait produces some of the larger rainbows, but trolling is also lucrative. Since brown trout were added to the Mineral Lake menu a few years ago, the good fishing tends to last much longer, usually well into summer.

If there's a downside to fishing Mineral Lake, it's the fact that lots of folks converge on its tiny boat ramp and access area at about the same time every morning, sometimes creating traffic jams and tattered nerves. The key is to arrive early and be patient. The fishing is worth the wait.

Location: At the town of Mineral in Lewis County; see map B2, grid d7.

Species: Brown and rainbow trout.

Facilities: The lake has a public boat ramp. Mineral Lake Resort offers boat rentals, cabins and RV sites (no tent sites), a large and productive fishing dock ($4 per day), bait, tackle, and snacks. A small market in town sells fishing licenses, and gas is available in Mineral.

Directions: Take U.S. 12 east from I-5 to Morton and turn north on Highway 7, following it about 13 miles to Mineral Road. From there it's a two-mile drive to the town of Mineral and Mineral Lake.

Contact: Mineral Lake Resort, 360/492-5367, website: www.minerallakeresort.com.

62 Skate Creek

This large backcountry stream is easily accessible from Forest Service Road 52, and the liberal plants of hatchery rainbows make it very popular with summertime anglers. Skate Creek opens to fishing June 1 (closing at the end of October), but stocking may occur at any time after the opener, depending on stream conditions. Because it gets hatchery plants, the creek has an eight-inch minimum size limit, and anglers are allowed to keep five trout a day. Any bait, lure, or fly you use will work after the trout have been stocked.

Location: Flows into the Upper Cowlitz River west of Packwood; see map B2, grid d8.

Species: Rainbow trout.

Facilities: Food, gas, tackle, and lodging are available in Packwood and Ashford.

Directions: Drive east from Ashford for two miles on Highway 706 and turn south (right) on Forest Service Road 52, or take U.S. 12 to Packwood and turn north on Forest Service Road 52, which parallels the creek for about seven miles.

Contact: Washington Department of Fish and Wildlife, Vancouver Office, 360/696-6211.

63 Newaukum River

Wild steelhead runs on this small Lewis County tributary to the Chehalis have been in tough shape for many years, but a small-scale steel-head fishery is provided by hatchery fish, stocked on a somewhat infrequent basis. A typical winter's catch from the entire Newaukum system is 40 to 50 winter steelies. Any wild steelhead (those without any clipped fins) must be released. The river is also open to summer trout fishing, but few fish over the 14-inch minimum size are caught. The season here runs from June 1 through March 31.

A fall salmon season on this Lewis County stream provides very limited opportunity for anglers to catch a hatchery coho or two. If you catch a chinook or chum salmon, you have to let it go.

Location: Joins the Chehalis River northwest of Chehalis; see map B2, grid d3.

Species: Winter steelhead; coho, chum, and chinook salmon.

Facilities: Food, gas, tackle, and lodging are available in Centralia and Chehalis.

Directions: Take Centralia-Alpha Road southeast from Centralia for about 11 miles and turn on North Fork Road (left to go upstream on the North Fork Newaukum, right to go downstream). To reach the South Fork Newaukum, take I-5 south from Chehalis for six miles and turn east (left) on Highway 508, which parallels much of the river. To reach the Lower Newaukum, turn south off I-5 on Rush Road, about 3.5 miles south of Chehalis, then west on Newaukum Valley Road.

Contact: Sunbirds Shopping Center, 360/748-3337 (sporting goods department).

64 Tilton River

Generous late-spring plants of hatchery rainbows provide most of the fishing action on this small tributary to the Cowlitz River system. While most of the planters are legal-sized 8- to 10-inchers, the Department of Fish and Wildlife also includes a number of so-called jumbo legals, which range up to 15 inches. Trout fishing is best in June and July. Liberal regulations on the main Tilton allow anglers to use bait and keep up to five trout of eight inches or longer per day (only one of which can top 12 inches). On the North, South, East, and West Forks of the river, selective fishery regulations are in effect, so you have to use artificial lures and flies with barbless hooks, and the limit is two trout per day.

Before the construction of Mayfield Dam in the 1960s, the Tilton flowed directly into the Cowlitz River, but now it enters the river system at the north end of Mayfield Lake. As dams tend to do, Mayfield cut off the once-healthy runs of salmon and steelhead into the Tilton. Fish are now trucked from the Cowlitz Trout Hatchery and Cowlitz Salmon Hatchery to provide some salmon and steelhead fishing. Unfortunately, only a small percentage of the fish hauled to the Tilton are caught by anglers. This little stream where anglers were accustomed to catching wild 10- to 20-pound winter steelhead with amazing frequency 40 years ago now produces only a few dozen transplanted hatchery steelies each season. The coho trucking operation is a little more successful, providing anglers with some decent salmon fishing from October to December.

If you can't find any other fishing spot to your liking along the Tilton, check out the public access at Tilton River State Park, one of the state's newest public angling acquisitions. Although the 110-acre site is as yet undeveloped, it does provide access to the famous Dodge Hole, one of the best-known steelhead-fishing spots.

Location: Flows into the north arm of Mayfield Lake; see map B2, grid e5.

Species: Rainbow trout, winter steelhead, coho salmon.

Facilities: Ike Kinswa State Park is located where the Tilton flows into Mayfield Lake and has tent and RV sites, restrooms with showers, and other amenities. Food, gas, lodging, and tackle are available in Morton.

Directions: Take U.S. 12 to Morton, turn north on Highway 7, drive half a mile, and turn west (left) on Highway 508 to follow the river downstream. Drive three miles and turn north (right) to reach the North Fork Tilton.

Contact: Ike Kinswa State Park, 360/983-3402; Washington State Parks and Recreation Commission, 360/902-8844 (information) or 800/542-5687 (reservations); Fish Country Sport Shop, 360/985-2090.

65 Mayfield Lake

Mayfield was the first lake in Washington to be stocked with the voracious and spectacular tiger muskie. The fish were stocked to provide a trophy fishery and to eradicate some of the lake's huge squawfish population, and the program has been successful on both counts. The most important thing you need to know about Mayfield Lake's tiger

muskies is that they spend virtually all their time within about six feet of the surface, so don't waste time fishing any deeper than that. Of course if the bottom is also within six feet of the surface, you're fishing the kind of shallows that tigers are most likely to occupy. Spinnerbaits and bucktail spinners in black, red, brown, and various combinations of these colors will take them, as will five- to seven-inch shallow-diving plugs and surface plugs of the same size. Be sure to watch for fish in the shallows, and if they won't hit your plug or spinner on the first couple of casts, mark their location, move on to fish other areas, and come back to try the fish you've found every now and then. Eventually the muskies you've located will decide it's time to eat, and you'll be in for some excitement.

In the first section of this book, you'll find the how-to information you'll need to effectively pursue this worthy adversary. If you

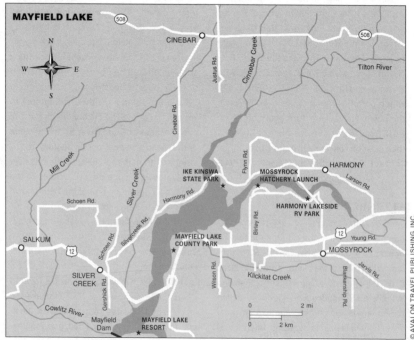

have the choice, fish the lake in the evening, and plan on staying right up until dark, since that's when tigers are most likely to go on the prowl. This is especially true if the day has been clear and warm. Among the places you'll want to spend some time looking and casting are the entrance to the Tilton Arm on the north side, the Winston Creek Arm at the south end, the big weed beds along the shoreline east of the county park, and the shallow bay south of the hatchery near the upper end of the lake. If you launch at the county park and still have a few minutes of daylight left when you return to the ramp, make a few casts just outside the east end of the swimming area. That's where I caught my one and only tiger muskie on a warm July evening in 1992, and I released it. If it's still there, it's a whopper by now.

Now that the tiger muskies have gotten a good start on reducing the once-abundant squawfish in Mayfield, Department of Fish and Wildlife biologists are once again planting rainbow trout in the lake. The trout fishery was in the dumps throughout the 1980s, but it's flourishing once again. Planted as fingerlings, trout soon grow to catchable size, and you might have the good fortune of hooking a fish or two in the 12- to 14-inch range. Most of the locals troll Pop Geer and worms for their trout, but Kwikfish, Triple Teazers, Rooster Tails, and all the other usual trolling fare will work. Don't be surprised if along with the rainbows you catch a small coho salmon or two. Coho from Riffe Lake and the Tilton River commonly make their way into Mayfield to mix with the trout population.

The smallmouths still remaining from a plant made several years ago are scattered all over the lake, but if you have your heart set on catching a couple of them, try fishing along the high bank on the north side of the lake, west of the state park. The submerged boulders found here and there around the entrance to the Cowlitz Arm also produce a few smallmouths.

Location: West of Mossyrock in Lewis County; see map B2, grid e4.

Species: Tiger muskies, rainbow trout, coho salmon, a few smallmouth bass, yellow perch.

Facilities: Kinswa State Park has RV and tent spaces, restrooms, and a boat ramp. Mayfield Lake County Park offers restrooms and a boat ramp. Snacks and beverages are available at the small store next to the turnoff to the county park, with everything else available four miles to the east in Mossyrock.

Directions: Take U.S. 12 east from I-5 about 17 miles to the lake. Turn north (left) at Silver Creek to reach Ike Kinswa State Park on the north side of the lake or cross over the lake on U.S. 12 and go just over a mile to Mayfield Lake County Park, on the left.

Contact: Fish Country Sport Shop, 360/985-2090; Ike Kinswa State Park, 360/983-3402; Washington State Parks and Recreation Commission, 360/902-8844 (information) or 800/542-5687 (reservations).

66 Riffe Lake

The coho fishery is the biggest angling attraction at Riffe Lake, and it draws both boat and bank anglers from all over western Washington. In the spring and early summer, cohos are near the surface, where they can be caught by trollers using strings of trolling blades and worms, white corn, cocktail shrimp, or combinations of these three baits. Bank anglers catch them by suspending the same baits three or four feet beneath a bobber. As the summer progresses and the thermocline establishes itself in this big, deep reservoir, the coho go deep, where both boat and bank anglers typically fish them 100 feet down with slip-bobber rigs. Most of this coho action takes place at the west end of the lake, within sight of the dam. As for size, two-year-olds make up most of the catch in the spring and early summer, and they average 12 to 14 inches. The one-year-old class begins to dominate the catch by July, and for the rest of the summer and fall the average Riffe Lake coho is an eight- to nine-incher.

Another coho fishery that's really taken off the past couple of years is at the other end of the reservoir, where the Cowlitz River flows into the east end of the impoundment. The so-called 108 Bridge on the Champion Haul Road near Taidnapam Park has become a mecca for anglers who stillfish using worms, salmon eggs, cocktail shrimp, and corn to catch coho to about 14 inches. Rainbow and cutthroat trout also are included in the catch here. Both spring and fall can be productive times to take part in this fishery, but leave your landing net at home; the bridge is about 40 feet above the water. Talk about flying fish!

Shortages of coho for planting in Riffe Lake have prompted Fish and Wildlife personnel at times to get creative and stock a few steelhead and even chinook salmon in the lake. Many anglers don't even notice the difference. Although rare, an occasional brown trout may grab one of the offerings meant for coho here. If you want to target specifically on these trophies, which may top 10 pounds, forget the worms and corn and offer them something like a slowly trolled Rapala or other large, bait fish–imitating plug or wobbling spoon.

Smallmouth bass are much more abundant than largemouths in this chilly reservoir, but you might catch both if you fish the upper end during May and June. As the creek channels fill with water that time of year, they draw hungry bass like a magnet, and the fishing with crankbaits or plastics can be very good. Another possibility for bass is Swofford Cove on the north side near the west end of the reservoir. Both largemouths and smallmouths tend to congregate in this shallow, warm bay in spring and summer.

Riffe has a healthy population of brown bullheads, and the best time and place to catch them is during the spring, in the shallow flats at the upper end of the lake. Most catfish anglers launch at the Kosmos boat ramp in the evening and fish the shallow water nearby with worms or night crawlers. Although not large at an average of 10 or 11 inches, they're abundant enough to provide plenty of fast action and good eating for a few hours' effort.

Location: East of Mossyrock in Lewis County; see map B2, grid e6.

Species: Coho and chinook salmon; rainbow, cutthroat, and brown trout; largemouth and smallmouth bass; brown bullhead catfish; crappie; perch.

Facilities: Mossyrock Park at the lower end of the lake has RV hookups, tent sites, boat ramps, and restrooms with showers, as does Taidnapam Park at the upper end. There's also a boat ramp at the northeast corner of the lake, about two miles off U.S. 12 via Glenoma Road. Groceries, restaurants, gas, tackle, and lodging are available in Mossyrock and Morton.

Directions: Take U.S. 12 east from I-5 about 23 miles to Mossyrock, turn south (right) into town and go east (left) on Aljune Road, which leads to Tacoma Public Utilities' Mossyrock Park Campground and boat ramps near the dam. To reach the upper lake, continue on U.S. 12 about five miles past Morton and turn south (right) on Kosmos Road. Bear right to reach the steep boat ramp at the northeast corner of the lake or turn left and drive about four miles to the entrance of the new Tacoma Public Utilities' Taidnapam Park near where the Cowlitz River enters the lake.

Contact: Fish Country Sport Shop, 360/985-2090; Mossyrock Park, 360/983-3900, website:

www.tacomapower.com; Taidnapam Park, 360/497-7707, website: www.tacomapower.com.

67 Swofford Pond

Few freshwater fishing spots in the Pacific Northwest can claim to have it all, but this 240-acre pond just south of Riffe Lake (number 66) comes pretty close. Whether your preferences lean toward pan-sized bluegills, sweet-eating channel catfish, or hook-nosed brown trout, you might find them here.

Thousands of legal-sized rainbow and brown trout are stocked here every spring, and anglers have little trouble catching a limit of them. Trollers use small spoons, spinners, wobbling plugs, or trolling blades with worms, while most bank anglers do just fine with that time-proven favorite, a garden worm suspended several feet below a bobber. Although anglers fishing for 8- to 10-inch planters seldom encounter them, the lake does have some huge brown trout. Biologists conducting tests with electroshock equipment—used to stun and count fish in a test area—have captured and released browns of 10 pounds.

Long a productive bass pond, Swofford is home to some husky largemouths. Unfortunately, it isn't home to many small bass, at least not lately, which could bode poorly for bass anglers in the future. But if you want a crack at a five-pounder, you have a realistic chance here. Hit it early in the morning or late in the evening with surface plugs or buzzbaits, or fish spinnerbaits or plastics during the day around the weedy shoreline. The lake has special size restrictions, so check the fishing pamphlet before trying for largemouths here.

Stocked long ago with bluegills, Swofford offers the possibility of excellent panfish action. Crappies are also abundant, and if you're willing to work at it with small leadheads or BeetleSpins, you'll catch enough for a family fish fry.

Brown bullheads are also plentiful, and the many bank-fishing spots along the road on the north shore of the pond are good places to fish for them. Anglers who fish night crawlers well into the night during the late spring and summer make some impressive catches. Along with the bullheads, don't be surprised if you catch a couple of large channel catfish. And when I say large, I'm not kidding. A 19.5-pound channel cat was caught from the lake in 1995, and even larger fish, topping 20 pounds, have been caught since.

Location: Southeast of Mossyrock; see map B2, grid e6.

Species: Rainbow and brown trout, largemouth bass, bluegill, crappie, brown bullhead and channel catfish.

Facilities: There's a boat ramp at the east end of the lake and plenty of bank-fishing access along the north side. The nearest food, gas, and tackle are in Mossyrock, and there's a Tacoma Public Utilities campground on nearby Riffe Lake.

Directions: Take Jarvis Road southeast from Mossyrock about 2.5 miles and turn south (right) on Swofford Road. Drive 1.5 miles, go left at the T, and drive to the pond, which will be on your right.

Contact: Fish Country Sport Shop, 360/985-2090.

68 Lake Scanewa

This is Washington's newest lake, having filled in 1994 with the completion of Cowlitz Falls Dam on the Cowlitz River. But even though it's just a youngster, Scanewa (pronounced Scan-EE-wah) draws enthusiastic reviews from trout anglers. Kamloops rainbows stocked in 1994 have done fairly well in the cool waters of this 600-acre impoundment, providing the opportunity for some bragging-sized fish. Subsequent plants of regular rainbows provide the bulk of the fishing action. When available, coho salmon from nearby hatcheries are planted here, too. This lake has a somewhat unusual season, designed to protect steelhead smolts migrating downstream in early spring, so be sure to check the regulations pamphlet for details before fishing this newest Cowlitz River reservoir. The fishing season runs from June 1 through February.

Location: Southeast of Glenoma in Lewis County; see map B2, grid e7.

Species: Rainbow trout, Kamloops-strain rainbow trout, coho salmon.

Facilities: The Lewis County Public Utility District operates a campground and a day-use park on the reservoir. The campground, which is closed in winter, offers tent and RV sites, restrooms, showers, and a boat ramp. Food, gas, tackle, and lodging are available in Randle and Morton.

Directions: Drive east from I-5 on U.S. 12 about 40 miles and turn south at Mile Marker 111 on Savio Road. Drive 1.5 miles and turn south again on Kiona Road, which eventually becomes Peters Road, and follow it about four miles to the campground and the reservoir on the right.

Contact: The Lake Scanewa Concessionaire, 360/497-7175; Lewis County Public Utility District, 360/497-5351; Taidnapam Park, 360/983-3900, website: www.tacomapower.com.

🖩 Cispus River

Wild cutthroat and planted rainbows provide some action on the Lower Cispus below the mouth of the Muddy Fork. Above the Muddy Fork, anglers will find a mix of small cutthroats and brook trout. The season here runs June 1 through October 31, and you'll find small trout available all season. Fishing pressure gets fairly heavy during the height of the midsummer camping season, but you'll have elbowroom before mid-June and after Labor Day. The lower portion of this Cowlitz

River tributary offers limited steelhead fishing. Even though it also offers a salmon season, the chances of catching salmon here certainly aren't great.

Location: Joins the Cowlitz River above Riffe Lake; see map B2, grid e8.

Species: Brook, cutthroat, and rainbow trout; winter and summer steelhead.

Facilities: There are a few Forest Service campgrounds along the river with campsites, restrooms, and water, but the nearest food, gas, tackle, and lodging are in Randle.

Directions: Take U.S. 12 to Randle and turn south on Forest Service Road 25 (Woods Creek Road). Drive just over a mile and turn east (left) on Cispus Road (Forest Service Road 23), which follows the river upstream for more than 20 miles.

Contact: Fish Country Sport Shop, 360/985-2090.

🖩 Olequa Creek

Steelheading is tough on this pretty little stream, since it has wild steelhead–release regulations and receives no hatchery plants. Still, anglers do manage to catch a few both winter and summer. Until the late 1990s, the best fishing here was for fall cutthroats, but the regulations now call for cutthroat release. So much for that. The creek opens to fishing on June 1, closing at the end of February.

Location: Flows into the Cowlitz River south of Vader; see map B2, grid e2.

Species: Winter and summer steelhead, sea-run cutthroat trout.

Facilities: Gas and food are available in Vader and Winlock. Lodging, tackle, and other amenities are in Chehalis.

Directions: Take Highway 506 west off I-5, drive four miles through the town of Vader, and turn north (right) on Winlock-Vader Road, which parallels the west side of the creek for more than six miles.

Contact: Sunbirds Shopping Center, 360/748-3337 (sporting goods department).

71 Lacamas Creek

Don't drive a long distance to fish this creek unless you have a lot of time on your hands. Winter steelhead fishing regulations require that all wild fish be released, but the creek isn't stocked with hatchery fish, so there just isn't a very good chance that you're going to catch one. There are cutthroat in the creek, but recent regulations changes have put them off-limits to anglers, so there isn't much opportunity left.

Location: Flows into the Cowlitz River near Vader; see map B2, grid e2.

Species: Winter steelhead, resident cutthroat trout.

Facilities: Gas and food are available in Toledo, Vader, and Winlock. Lodging and tackle can be found in Chehalis.

Directions: Take Highway 506 west off I-5, drive two miles, and turn north (right) on Telegraph Road, which parallels the river upstream for more than three miles.

Contact: Sunbirds Shopping Center, 360/748-3337 (sporting goods department).

72 Cowlitz River

Winter steelhead and spring chinook are the two biggest draws at this river, and for very good reason. The Cowlitz River has been one of Washington's top winter steelie streams consistently since 1971, giving up as many as 30,000 fish in a single season, although in recent years the catch has been more like 2,000 to 5,000 fish per year.

Boat ramps at the salmon hatchery, trout hatchery, and other points downstream make this one of the Northwest's most heavily boated rivers. During the winter season, a bulk of the boat traffic is concentrated on the two miles of river immediately downstream from the trout hatchery ramp. Some boaters back-troll plugs or diver-and-bait combinations for their steelhead, but a technique called free drifting has become very popular in recent years. It involves making long casts across and slightly upstream, using lighter sinkers than those commonly associated with drift fishing, and allowing the boat to drift downstream while the line drags behind.

Bank anglers also make good catches of winter steelhead from the Cowlitz, but if you want to fish the best spots, plan on getting shoulder to shoulder with your fellow anglers. The mouth of Blue Creek just downstream from the Cowlitz Trout Hatchery may produce several hundred fish in a single morning, with several hundred anglers on hand to catch them. If you don't like the idea of fishing with 200 to 300 fishing buddies on a 300-foot stretch of river bank, you won't like Blue Creek. But if catching steelhead takes precedence over anything remotely resembling an aesthetic angling experience, this spot is for you. Grab a selection of leadhead jigs and a couple of sliding bobbers (floats), take the quarter-mile trail leading from the back corner of the trout hatchery parking lot, and join the crowd at the mouth of Blue Creek. And when you reach the creek mouth, don't be shy; this isn't a place for the meek.

A lot more elbowroom can be found along the long stretch of public river bank upstream from Blue Creek, both above and below the boat ramp. Steelheading can be very good here, and the heavy boat traffic doesn't seem to bother the fish. There are those, in fact, who say the boats keep the steelhead stirred up and active, making them more likely to take a bait or lure. I'm not a fish psychologist, so I'm not sure about this theory.

Several miles upstream, below the salmon hatchery's barrier dam, is another spot where winter steelheaders like to congregate. You'll have a little more room to cast here than at Blue Creek, but on a winter weekend, it's still pretty busy.

The area below the barrier dam is also popular with spring chinook anglers, both those fishing from the bank and those who launch at the mouth of Mill Creek, where the gravel road ends in a two-lane boat ramp. Boaters can't fish between the ramp and the barrier dam, but they catch lots of chinooks from the half mile of river immediately downstream from the ramp. Back-trolling Kwikfish and Flatfish with a strip of sardine lashed to the belly of each lure is effective for boat anglers, as is back-bouncing with large clusters of salmon roe or shrimp-and-roe combinations. Bank anglers drift fish shrimp, roe, and the shrimp-roe combos known locally as Cowlitz Cocktails. Chinook fishing peaks in May.

Anglers fishing the lower section of the Cowlitz, around Kelso and Longview, get a crack at spring chinooks several days to a week before the gang at the barrier dam, as fresh runs enter the river. Some plunking with roe, spinners, plugs, and herring occurs on this lower part of the river, but boaters still have the advantage. They also back-troll plugs with that same sardine wrap used upstream, but large spinners and whole or plug-cut herring play bigger roles in the fishery on the Lower Cowlitz than they do up by the salmon hatchery.

As the spring chinook fishery tapers off, summer steelhead action picks up, and the Cowlitz often provides excellent summer steelheading from July through October. There are dozens of productive fishing spots between the trout hatchery and Toledo. Boat anglers probably account for 70 percent or more of those fish. Coho returns have improved considerably in recent years, and there is a chance of catching several good-sized hatchery coho in October or November. Liberal limits on hatchery fish can result in bumper-crop catches if your timing is right.

Hatchery production of sea-run cutthroat has been good enough on the Cowlitz over the past decade to allow anglers what amounts to a bonus trout limit. While the daily limit on most Washington streams is only two fish, it's five on the Cowlitz, and limits are well within the realm of possibility during the height of the fishery in September and October. The mouth of Blue Creek is the hottest cutthroat hole, and the crowds are much smaller in the fall than during the height of the steelhead fishery in December and January. If you don't want to hike to Blue Creek, try any deep, slow pool downstream, especially those containing downed trees, stumps, and other submerged wood cover. Rolling a night crawler along the bottom works best for Cowlitz sea-runs, some of which top 20 inches. You may keep only fin-clipped hatchery cutthroats, but that's what you're most likely to find anyway.

The worst news about the Cowlitz, at least for some people, is the absence of Columbia River smelt (eulachon) in recent years. Smelt dipping in the Cowlitz and other lower Columbia River tributaries has been put off-limits in recent years, for the first time ever.

Location: Flows into the Columbia River near Kelso; see map B2, grid f2.

Species: Spring and fall chinook salmon, coho salmon, winter and summer steelhead, sea-run cutthroat trout, Columbia River smelt.

Facilities: Boat ramps can be found at the trout and salmon hatcheries, with well-stocked tackle stores, gas stations, and grocery stores at the junction of U.S. 12 and Tucker Road and at Blue Creek Bait and Tackle. Barrier Dam Campground, a short distance north of the salmon hatchery, has RV spaces. A $10 WDFW access decal is required to use the public launch area maintained by the Washington Department of Fish and Wildlife.

Visitors to the upper river will find limited food, gas, and lodging in Packwood and Randle. On the lower Cowlitz, all amenities are available in Castle Rock, Longview, and Kelso. **Directions:** I-5 parallels the east side of the river from Kelso upstream to Toledo. But the most popular stretch of river is upstream, between Toledo and the Cowlitz Salmon Hatchery. To reach this area, take U.S. 12 east from I-5, turning south (right) on Tucker Road, left at the Y intersection onto Classe Road, left on Spencer Road, and right onto the road leading past the state trout hatchery and to the river. To reach the salmon hatchery farther upstream, continue about four miles farther on U.S. 12 to Salkum and turn right at the Salmon Hatchery sign. **Contact:** Barrier Dam Campground, 360/985-2495.

73 Green River

This little Toutle River tributary is stocked with hatchery steelhead smolts and provides pretty good fishing in June, July, and August. It's open only during the summer and fall, and only for hatchery steelhead and hatchery coho salmon; any chum or chinook salmon, wild coho salmon, trout, or wild steelhead you catch must be released. Be sure to check the current regulations pamphlet if you aren't sure about these somewhat complicated rules on what you can keep and what you can't.

Since the river is small and clear, fishing with a light touch helps, although you may find yourself hooked to an angry fish on tackle that seems woefully inadequate when the fish takes off downstream, through the brush, under the submerged trees, and around the boulders. Much of the river is small enough and shallow enough to wade, so all you can do is give chase. Good luck.

Location: Joins the Toutle River near Kid Valley; see map B2, grid f5.
Species: Summer steelhead, chinook and coho salmon.
Facilities: Food, gas, and tackle are available in Toutle and Kid Valley, both along Highway 504. Lodging can be found in Castle Rock.
Directions: Turn east off I-5 at Castle Rock onto Highway 504 and drive 26 miles to 19 Mile Camp. Turn north (left) onto Weyerhaeuser 1000 Road and follow it east to 2500 Road, which parallels much of the Upper Green.
Contact: Drew's Grocery, 360/274-8920; Toutle River Fly Shop, 360/274-6276.

74 Toutle River

After Mount St. Helens erupted in 1980, destroying the gorgeous North Fork of the Toutle and the main Toutle below the confluence of the North and South Forks, fish biologists estimated that it might take decades before the river again provided a steelhead fishery. Well, Mother Nature with some help from her human assistants shortened that timetable considerably, and the Toutle River system was providing fair to good steelheading before the end of the 1980s. It's still not like the glory days, but there are fish to be caught.

Roles have been reversed between the once-great North Fork and the South Fork that received relatively little angler attention or publicity before the eruption. Now it's the South Fork, which was only lightly damaged by the volcano, that provides most of the steelheading opportunity. Although both are stocked with 25,000 to 30,000 summer steelhead smolts annually, the catch by anglers ranges to more than 1,300 on the South Fork but only a couple hundred from the North Fork. Water clarity remains a problem on the North Fork, and anglers find relatively few days during the year when the river is in fishable condition. Wild steelhead, descendants from fish that started returning to the river shortly after the eruption and resulting mud-flows, must be released, whether you fish the North Fork, South Fork, or main river. June and July are the best months to fish for Toutle River steelhead, with anglers catching more steelhead from the South Fork in those two months alone than they catch during the rest of the year.

If you catch a trout anywhere in the Toutle, let it go; the river system has catch-and-release-only trout fishing these days.

There are now some opportunities to fish for salmon in the North Fork Toutle, where the fishing can be fair in September and early October for chinook and in October and early November for coho. The regulations in recent years have allowed anglers to keep hatchery coho, but wild coho and all chinook must be released. You also have to release any chum salmon you might hook. Check the pamphlet for details, because there are lots to know before you go.

Location: Flows into the Cowlitz River north of Castle Rock; see map B2, grid f4.

Species: Winter and summer steelhead, chinook and coho salmon.

Facilities: Seaquest State Park, located right on Highway 504 near Silver Lake, has a limited number of tent and RV sites, plus restrooms with showers and an RV sewage dump. There are also two private resorts on the lake, right alongside the highway. Other than those facilities, the nearest food, gas, tackle, and lodging are in Castle Rock.

Directions: Turn east off I-5 onto Highway 504, which parallels much of the North Fork Toutle. Weyerhaeuser 4100 Road from the town of Toutle 11 miles east of the freeway parallels the South Fork Toutle.

Contact: Drew's Grocery, 360/274-8920; Seaquest State Park, 360/274-8633; Washington State Parks and Recreation Commission, 360/902-8844 (information) or 800/542-5687 (reservations); Toutle River Fly Shop, 360/274-6276.

75 Silver Lake

A case could easily be made for calling Silver Lake Washington's best largemouth bass lake. Not only does it produce good numbers of bass for patient anglers, but it's also known for its big fish, giving up more than its share of eight-pounders. The lake is open year-round, and serious bass anglers never quit fishing it, although the bassing is mighty slow and you can find plenty of solitude in December and January. But the first few warm days of February may generate some real activity, and you can find largemouths being caught from that point until the first cold weather of November.

This 3,000-acre lake is only a few feet deep in most places and is very lightly developed, so bass are scattered throughout the water. If you tried to fish Silver's entire shoreline thoroughly, you would be at it for days, so many anglers concentrate their efforts on a few favorite spots that have produced before and are suited to their individual preferences. Whether you like to fish submerged rocks, docks, floats, submerged trees and logs, shoreline weeds and brush, pad fields, or any other kind of bass cover and structure, you'll probably find plenty of it at Silver Lake. As you might expect, the lake is a favorite with tournament anglers, so if you prefer a little solitude when you fish, especially during the spring and summer, either call ahead to inquire about weekend activities or fish it during the week.

Although bass get most of the publicity here, the fishing for other warm-water species can be every bit as impressive. Casting a tiny leadhead jig with a plastic skirt or marabou body can produce excellent catches of crappies, and perch fishing is also very good throughout the lake. Brown bullheads are abundant and provide good night-fishing opportunities from spring until early fall.

Until a few years ago Silver Lake was so overgrown with weeds that it was difficult to get around parts of it in a boat. But the Department of Fish and Wildlife stocked grass carp to help graze the vegetation down a bit, and the strategy worked. Now the lake has so much open water that in 1995 the WDFW planted rainbow trout in the lake for the first time in many years.

Location: East of Castle Rock; see map B2, grid f3.

Species: Largemouth bass, black and white crappie, yellow perch, warmouth, bluegill, brown and yellow bullhead catfish, rainbow trout.

Facilities: There's a Department of Fish and Wildlife boat ramp on the lake, and it's a new, paved one that's a heck of a lot better than the run-down mess that people were using until recently. A $10 WDFW access decal is required to use the public launch area. There's also a ramp at Streeter's Resort ($2.50 launch fee) and one at Silver Lake Resort ($4 launch fee for nonguests, $2 for those staying at the resort). All three launches have loading floats. There are three private resorts on or near the lake, two of them just off Highway 504. Streeter's Resort has RV sites, restrooms with showers, boat rentals, a café, and a store. Silver Lake Resort has moorage, boat rentals, a store, rental cabins, picnic area, play equipment, RV sites, and restrooms with showers. There's also a state park with limited tent and RV spaces right across the highway.

Directions: Take Highway 504 east off I-5 at Castle Rock and drive five miles to the lake on the south (right) side of the highway.

Contact: Silver Lake Resort, 360/274-6141, website: www.silverlake-resort.com; Streeter's Resort, 360/274-6112; Seaquest State Park, 360/274-8633; Washington State Parks and Recreation Commission, 360/902-8844 (information) or 800/452-5687 (reservations).

76 Upper Green River Lakes

Ranging in size from 8 to 30 acres, these five lakes on the Upper Green River drainage are somewhat typical of high-elevation lakes throughout the Northwest except that all are reached by various logging roads. At 30 acres, Elk is the largest of the bunch, but Hanaford and Fawn Lakes are just a little smaller. Forest Lake covers only eight acres, and Tradedollar Lake is only 12 acres. Fawn Lake is well known for its brook trout, while Tradedollar has a good population of westslope cutthroat.

Forest, Elk, and Hanaford are within easy walking distance of each other and offer brown trout as well as cutthroats and brookies. All three species will take small spoons and spinners or cast flies, either behind a bobber with your spinning rod or with your favorite fly rod. These lakes are open to fishing year-round, but May and June are the best months to fish them.

Location: North of Coldwater Lake near the Cowlitz-Skamania County line; see map B2, grid f6.

Species: Cutthroat, brook, and brown trout.

Facilities: Food, gas, and tackle can be found in Kid Valley and Toutle, both on Highway 504. The nearest lodging is in Castle Rock.

Directions: Turn east off of I-5 onto Highway 504 and drive 26 miles to 19 Mile Camp. Turn north (left) onto Weyerhaeuser 1000 Road and follow it east to 2500 Road. Take 2500 Road to Shultz Creek and turn right on 2800 Road; follow it to 3500 Road and take it uphill to the lakes.

Contact: Drew's Grocery, 360/274-8920; Toutle River Fly Shop, 360/274-6276.

77 Coldwater Lake

This lake northwest of Mount St. Helens didn't exist before the mountain's violent eruption on May 18, 1980. That's when millions of tons of mud and debris created a natural dam that blocked the flow of Coldwater Creek and created the 700-acre lake. Biologists thought the lake was void of fish and in 1989 stocked it with rainbows, which are now reproducing on their own and no longer supplemented with hatchery plants.

As it turns out, some resident trout apparently did survive the blast that buried the area in ash and mud, so Coldwater Lake also contains cutthroat trout. Most of the cutts are caught near the upper end of the lake, which is difficult to reach because gasoline engines are prohibited and float tubes are the most common form of aquatic transportation. It would take one heck of a pair of legs to kick all the way from the boat ramp to the north end of the lake and back.

Selective fishery regulations allowing anglers to use only artificial flies and lures with single, barbless hooks have been in effect since the lake opened to fishing in 1993. Most of the anglers fishing it are fly rodders, and they have their best luck with dark leech patterns and other wet flies, although summertime insect hatches often provide fairly good dry fly-fishing. If a dark leech works for fly casters, Jim Byrd of the Washington Department of Fish and Wildlife reasons that a black marabou jig might be just the ticket for spin anglers here.

Probably 90 percent of the fishing that occurs on Coldwater takes place at the south end, within sight of the U.S. Forest Service boat ramp. That makes sense if you recall that most of the fishing is done from float tubes. The wind that seems to blow here about 95 percent of the time would make the trip uplake a miserable one, too. A trail parallels much of the lake's northern shoreline,
but it's illegal to step off it to reach the water. Those who try are cited for their efforts.

Others who could be cited are those who fail to buy one of the new National Park Service passes to use the facilities at Coldwater Lake. Anglers raised a stink about the new fee when it went into effect in March 1997, but to no avail. The $8 pass is good for three days, or you can buy an annual pass for $24. The passes are available at the Coldwater Ridge Visitor Center on your way to the lake.

Leave enough time at the end of your fishing day to visit the Coldwater Ridge Visitor Center, at the edge of the hill overlooking the lake. And be sure to watch for the area's many elk herds as you drive along Spirit Lake Highway. The lake is open to year-round fishing.

Location: Northwest of Mount St. Helens; see map B2, grid f6.

Species: Rainbow and cutthroat trout.

Facilities: A boat ramp and restrooms are located at the southeast end of the lake, while the nearest stores are several miles west on Highway 504. Food, gas, and tackle are available in Toutle and Kid Valley, with lodging in Castle Rock. The U.S. Forest Service charges an access fee here.

Directions: Take I-5 to the town of Castle Rock and turn east on Highway 504, following it about 45 miles to the Coldwater Ridge Visitor Center and down the hill to the lake.

Contact: Mount St. Helens National Volcanic Monument Headquarters, U.S. Forest Service, 360/274-2131.

78 Abernathy Creek

Time it right—just after a soaking rain that raises the creek level a few inches during December or January—and you could find yourself right in the middle of some good small-stream winter steelheading on Abernathy Creek. The rest of the winter, though, the odds are against you. The fish come in with the rain, disperse, and are gone in a day or two.

It's pretty much the same with sea-run cutthroat, except that the months most likely to produce these little migratory trout are September, October, and November. Abernathy is stocked with about 7,500 steelhead and an equal number of cutthroat. It's okay to catch and keep hatchery fish of either species, but wild cutthroat must be released. Any steelhead caught June through August must be released.

Location: Enters the Columbia River west of Stella in southwestern Cowlitz County; see map B2, grid g0.

Species: Winter steelhead, sea-run cutthroat trout.

Facilities: Everything you need, including food, gas, tackle, and lodging, is available in Kelso and Longview.

Directions: Take Highway 4 west from Longview and turn north (right) on Abernathy Road about 2.5 miles west of Stella. Abernathy Road parallels the creek for about five miles.

Contact: Bob's Merchandise, 360/425-3870.

79 Germany Creek

Like nearby Abernathy Creek (number 78), this little Columbia River tributary provides winter steelhead and fall cutthroat action on the spur of the moment, usually in direct response to a slight rise in water levels that draws waiting fish in from the Columbia. Wild cutthroat release rules are in effect, but enough hatchery fish are stocked to provide fisheries for both. Cutthroat fishing can be quite good in October and November. You have to release any steelhead you catch here during the summer, but wild steelhead–release regulations have been eliminated during the winter season.

Location: Enters the Columbia River at Stella in southwestern Cowlitz County; see map B2, grid g1.

Species: Winter steelhead, sea-run cutthroat trout.

Facilities: Amenities are available in Longview and Kelso.

Directions: Take Highway 4 west from Longview and turn north (right) onto Germany Creek Road at the town of Stella. This road parallels the creek for 4.5 miles.

Contact: Bob's Merchandise, 360/425-3870.

80 Coweeman River

Although it receives generous plants of hatchery winter steelhead smolts, this little Cowlitz tributary either gives up only modest numbers of adult fish or lots of local anglers catch steelhead and don't bother to record them on their steelhead report cards. Department of Fish and Wildlife statistics show a steelhead catch of about 150 to 500 fish a year from the river. Most of those are caught above the confluence of Goble Creek, where Rose Valley Road parallels many miles of the Coweeman to afford lots of riverbank access.

Access to the lower river is very limited. As on many western Washington streams, wild steelhead caught from the Coweeman must be released. If you're into sea-run cutthroat trout, the Upper Coweeman is a good bet. Hatchery plants of Beaver Creek cutts provide good trout returns from September to November. Like sea-run cutthroating anywhere, the best fishing is with a lively night crawler right after a good rain. You can keep only hatchery (fin-clipped) cutthroat from the Coweeman.

Location: Enters the Cowlitz River south of Kelso; see map B2, grid g3.

Species: Winter steelhead, sea-run cutthroat trout.

Facilities: Food, gas, lodging, tackle, and other amenities are available in Longview and Kelso, near the mouth of the river.

Directions: Take Rose Valley Road off I-5 about four miles south of Kelso and follow it northeast about five miles to the river.

Contact: Bob's Merchandise, 360/425-3870.

81 Kress Lake

It's hard to believe how much angling opportunity is available from a lake that covers only 26 acres and has a maximum depth of about 17 feet. Of course, the fact that this is the only lake for miles has a lot to do with Kress Lake's popularity and productivity. Plants of hatchery trout totaling more than 20,000 fish a year don't hurt, either. Yes, that's 20,000 browns and rainbows a year, most of them stocked between the first of March and the end of April. As if those large numbers weren't enough, the plants include a few brood-stock trout of two to four pounds.

Not everyone is a trout angler, and when it comes to warm-water fishing, Kress doesn't disappoint either. Bass, crappies, and bluegills grow to impressive size here, and there's enough of a brown bullhead fishery to keep some anglers at the lake all night.

The long fishing season at Kress Lake, late April through February, offers anglers plenty of opportunity to try their luck.

Location: Just east of I-5 and north of the Lower Kalama River; see map B2, grid h3.

Species: Rainbow and brown trout, largemouth bass, crappie, bluegill, warmouth, brown bullhead catfish.

Facilities: The lake has a boat ramp suitable for small trailer boats and car-toppers. Food, gas, tackle, and lodging are available in Kalama, Kelso, and Longview.

Directions: Take Kalama River Road east off I-5 about 2.5 miles north of Kalama. Go left at the first turn (Kress Road) and drive about half a mile to the lake, which is on the right.

Contact: Bob's Merchandise, 360/425-3870.

82 Kalama River

Long a favorite of boat and bank anglers alike, the Kalama is a gem among southwest Washington streams. Easy access via I-5 and Kalama Road certainly doesn't diminish the popularity of this clear, green river. But popularity means fishing pressure, so there are times when solitude is difficult, if not impossible, to find.

Salmon and steelhead provide year-round angling opportunities. The river produces steelhead every month of the year, but summer-run fish dominate the catch. May, June, July, and August all offer excellent steelheading, with catches ranging from 250 to 900 fish during each of those four months. Anglers fishing from the mouth of Summers Creek downstream to the river mouth use ghost shrimp, roe clusters, crawfish tails, night crawlers, spinners, spoons, and all the usual steelhead bobbers to catch summer-runs. From Summers Creek up to the falls, the Kalama is open to fly-fishing only, and fly rodders do as well on this stretch as the bait and hardware folks do downstream.

Even though the Kalama was once considered a top-rate producer of both summer and winter steelies, and even though more winter-than summer-run steelhead smolts are stocked here, winter steelheading has dropped off in recent years. December sees a little flurry of activity, but wintertime steelheading on the Kalama is fair at best these days.

As for salmon, the Kalama offers decent spring chinook fishing from April through June. Fish of 10 to 25 pounds account for most of the catch, but now and then the river gives up a real bragging-sized springer of 30 pounds or more. Back-bouncing or drifting bait works here, as does back-trolling with plugs or diver-and-bait rigs. In the fall anglers catch both coho and chinook, but all wild coho must be released.

While decent trout fishing is available throughout much of the Kalama, it gets light fishing pressure from trout anglers. The wild cutthroat–release regulations that have been in place for several years are no doubt a factor.

Location: North of Kalama; see map B2, grid h3.

Species: Spring and fall chinook salmon, coho salmon, winter and summer steelhead, sea-run cutthroat trout.

Facilities: There are seven developed boat ramps on the Kalama, as well as several other commonly used rough launches where boats of various kinds may be launched, depending on how hard you want to work at it. A $10 WDFW access decal is required to use the public launch area maintained by the Washington Department of Fish and Wildlife. Tackle, snacks, and lots of fishing talk can be found at Pritchard's Western Angler on Kalama River Road, with other amenities in Kalama and Kelso.

Directions: Take I-5 to Kalama River Road, about 2.5 miles north of Kalama, and follow it east up the north side of the river.

Contact: Pritchard's Western Angler, 360/673-4690.

83 Lower Columbia River

This huge waterway and its many fish species and angling opportunities are worthy of an entire book in their own right, so I'm going to give you the short version here and send you off to find out more on your own. The highlight of the fishing scene around here in recent years has been the comeback of the spring chinook fishery, which was well into the dumps during the late 1990s. What anglers found here during the spring of 2001 was nothing short of phenomenal, and we can only hope for similar fishing over the next couple of years. Whole or plug-cut herring are productive strike-getters for these early-run kings, but in recent years more and more anglers have gone to large Flatfish and Kwikfish plugs with sardine or herring strips wrapped to the lures' bellies. Some anglers have had success by wrapping ghost shrimp to the lures instead of bait fish. The moral is obvious: be willing to experiment.

Except for a month or two in the spring, this section of the Columbia is open to steelheading, and it should come as no surprise that it's one of the region's top steelie producers. Steelhead bound for dozens of rivers in Washington, Oregon, and Idaho all have to pass through the Lower Columbia as they head for their upstream destinations, giving anglers lots of opportunity to practice their steelheading skills. Washington anglers alone caught 10,000 to 16,000 steelhead a year from the Lower Columbia during the first couple years of this decade, and Oregon anglers enjoyed similar success. Boat anglers throughout this stretch of the vast river enjoy obvious advantages, but bank anglers casting from the gravel bars and rock jetties along the river also take fish. This is plunking and trolling country when it comes to steelheading, so stock up on Bonneville Spinners, Spin N Glos, Hot Shots, and Wiggle Warts before hitting the river. You have to release all wild (not fin-clipped) steelhead here, but even hatchery fish might run 10 to 15 pounds, and most are beautiful, sleek, chrome-bright specimens.

This section of the Columbia produces more white sturgeon than all other Northwest waters combined. Even if you don't count the sturgeon that are too small or too large to keep, Washington sturgeon anglers boat more than 10,000 fish annually from the Lower Columbia. That's a lot of legal-sized sturgeon and a lot of fantastic eating. Legal-sized, by the way, means fish 42 to 66 inches long. Sorry, but the little three-footers have to go back. And those seven-footers, even though lots of fun to hook and play, also have to go back into the water unharmed. Sturgeon fishing is a waiting game, but one that's enjoyed by both boat and bank anglers throughout this stretch of river. Spring and early summer often provide the best chance at a catch-and-release monster, and the best bait that time of year is a whole shad. Smelt are good bait the rest of the year, and most sturgeon anglers rig backwards, with the tail pointing up the line and the head pointing down. Anchor to the bottom at the edge of a deep drop-off and settle in to wait. Perhaps more than any other kind of fishing, the Columbia River sturgeon fishery is one where it's a great idea to hire a guide for the first day, or hang around watching a gang of local anglers to pick up all the little tricks that can make the difference between successful fishing and just standing around waiting for days at a time between strikes.

The year's hottest fishing on the Lower Columbia occurs from the middle of May to the middle of June, when millions of American shad crowd into the river on their annual spawning migration. Boat anglers find good shad action in several locations along the lower river, including the waters around the mouth of Oregon's Sandy River and Washington's Washougal River, but the best bank fishing for shad is found within a mile or so downstream of Bonneville Dam. This fishery usually peaks in early June, when tens of thousands of shad pass over the Bonneville fish ladder every day.

Your favorite trout, bass, or light steelhead rod will work here, but be sure to take along lots of terminal tackle to fish this grabby part of the river. Small Mini Jigs or bare hooks with a couple of colored beads above them will do the trick. Although there's no limit on shad, most anglers prefer to catch-and-release these hard-fighting but bony members of the herring family.

Most of the bass fishing on the Lower Columbia is confined to the sloughs, bays, and side channels connected to the main river. The bay where the Beacon Rock boat launch is located, for example, provides some good smallmouth fishing during the spring and summer. The Camas Slough also offers decent bass fishing, and there are numerous side channels and sloughs between Vancouver and Woodland that are very popular with bass anglers. The stretch of river from Kalama downstream to Longview is also well known for its excellent largemouth fishing. You can fish bass here for two weeks and never cast to the same place twice, and you'd probably be surprised at the number of bass over four pounds caught from this river traditionally known for its salmon and steelhead.

Columbia River walleye fishing isn't much of a secret anymore, but it might come as news to you to learn that these transplants from the Midwest are now found as far downriver as the I-5 bridge. Trolling spinner-and-worm rigs and diving plugs accounts for some 10-pound-plus walleyes on the Lower Columbia, and if you can locate a good concentration of fish, you might also take them on leadheads/grubs bounced along the bottom.

Location: From Cathlamet upstream to Bonneville Dam; see map B2, grid h3.

Species: Summer and winter steelhead, chinook and coho salmon, sturgeon, shad, sea-run cutthroat trout, largemouth and smallmouth bass, walleye.

Facilities: There's no shortage of boat ramps along this stretch of the Columbia River:

- **Elochoman Slough Marina:** Working upstream from Cathlamet, the first ramp is at Elochoman Slough Marina, at the end of Second Street on the south side of town. This is a Port of Wahkiakum facility with a $3 launch fee for its two-lane concrete ramp with loading floats. It's a good ramp with a lot of paved parking nearby.

- **Abernathy Creek Ramp:** Next is the Department of Fish and Wildlife ramp about 400 feet up Abernathy Creek, 10 miles west of Longview on Highway 4. This single-lane concrete ramp is a pretty good one, but there's virtually no parking except along the entrance road, and there's no sign to tip off drivers along Highway 4. There is, however, a requirement that your vehicle sport a $10 WDFW access decal if you want to use this ramp.

- **Willow Grove Beach:** The park along the Columbia about four miles west of Highway 432 (Mount Solo Road), three miles west of Longview, has a natural-surface ramp sometimes plague by loose sand. It's best for smaller boats pulled by four-wheel-drive vehicles.

- **Coal Creek Ramp:** Coal Creek Slough is just west of Longview, off Highway 4 at milepost 55. There you'll find a Department of Fish and Wildlife ramp (don't forget the WDFW access decal) wide enough for launching one boat at a time, with parking for about a dozen cars and trailers.

- **Weyerhaeuser Ramp:** Located behind the Weyerhaeuser pulp mill in Longview, this two-lane concrete ramp has a loading float and lots of parking. It's the most popular ramp among local boaters.

- **Gerhart Gardens Ramp:** The next ramp upstream is actually on the lower Cowlitz River, but it provides access into the Columbia from Kelso. Located at Gerhart Gardens Park, just north of the Highway 432 bridge over the Cowlitz, it's a three-lane concrete ramp with parking for about three dozen cars and trailers.

- **Kalama River Ramps:** Next are a pair of Washington Department of Fish and Wildlife ramps on the lower Kalama River that also provide Columbia River access. Located just west of the I-5 bridge over the Kalama (via Exit 32), these ramps are both one-laners, one with a gravel surface and one with concrete planks. The gravel ramp has a small parking area; the second site has ample parking for a couple dozen cars and trailers.

- **Port of Kalama Ramp:** Next is the Port of Kalama ramp just upstream from the mouth of the Kalama and accessible off I-5 via Exit

30. This two-lane ramp has a hard surface and two loading floats, with room for lots of cars and trailers in the nearby gravel parking area. Boaters who use the ramp are asked to donate toward its upkeep.

- **Dike Road Ramp:** This ramp is at the mouth of the Lewis River. This is a natural-surface ramp where the bottom sometimes falls out. In other words, launch here with a four-wheel-drive vehicle.

- **Shillapoo Ramp:** The Department of Fish and Wildlife's Shillapoo Wildlife Area offers the next boat ramp upstream of Woodland. It's located northwest of Vancouver, off Highway 501, and has a single-lane concrete-plank ramp.

- **Marine Park Ramp:** The next ramp is at Marine County Park, just east of Vancouver on Marine Park Drive. This good, hard-surface, four-lane ramp with loading floats is managed by the Clark County Parks and Recreation Department.

- **Port of Camas/Washougal:** This ramp is at Camas-Washougal Marina. This four-lane asphalt ramp with several loading floats is perhaps the premier boat-launch facility on the lower Columbia. The launch fee is $4 round-trip. It's located at the Front Street stoplight on Highway 14 a mile and a half west of Washougal.

- **Beacon Rock State Park:** Thirty-five miles east of Vancouver is Beacon Rock State Park, where there's a tow-lane ramp and large float inside a protected side channel off the main river. The launch fee here is $4, which is included in the camping fee for anyone registered at the park.

- **Fort Cascades Ramp:** Launching is free at the Fort Cascades ramp just downstream from Bonneville Dam. This two-lane ramp has a loading float and is located in a back eddy that's out of the current except during spring high water.

- **Stevenson Ramp:** There's a single-lane

concrete ramp at the town of Stevenson, five miles upstream from Bonneville Dam. To find it, turn south off Highway 14 onto Russell Street and go two blocks to Cascade Avenue, turning left and following Cascade to the ramp.

- **Old Hatchery Ramp:** At the mouth of the Wind River is a good, two-lane concrete ramp on Old Hatchery Road, which is left off Highway 14 exactly 50 miles east of Vancouver. It has parking for about 20 cars and trailers, with additional parking along the road shoulder. Watch out for the submerged log in the water just out from the ramp; it has a marker on it that often gets torn off.

As for facilities of interest to anglers, Elochoman Marina has open moorage ($4 to $10 per boat, depending on size), electrical hookups, boat-sewage pump-out facilities, fuel dock, and restrooms with showers. Boat repair, grocery stores, and restaurants are nearby. Kalama Marina has both open and covered moorage at $5 to $7 per boat, electrical hookups and water at the docks, boat-sewage pump-out facilities, and fuel docks. Groceries and motels are available nearby.

Camas-Washougal Marina has open and covered moorage for $6 to $10, water and electricity to the docks, boat-sewage pump-out facilities, restrooms with showers, fuel docks, boat repair, and groceries. Beacon Rock State Park has about 30 standard tent sites (no hookups), picnic areas, cooking shelters, and restrooms with showers. Skamania Inn is the newest and biggest motel/conference center of its kind along the lower Columbia. It has a restaurant and also contains a U.S. Forest Service Interpretive Center with lots of information about the Columbia River Gorge. Home Valley County Park has campsites for $6.50 a night, $2 for each extra vehicle. There are several motels in Vancouver and others in Longview, Kelso,

Kalama, Camas, Washougal, and Stevenson. **Directions:** Take I-5 to Longview and drive west on Highway 4 to reach the 22-mile-long Cathlamet-to-Longview stretch of river. Continue south past Longview on I-5 to reach the 40-mile portion of the river between Longview and Vancouver. Drive east from Vancouver on Highway 44 as far as 43 miles to reach that part of the Columbia between Vancouver and Bonneville Dam.

Contact: Skamania County Chamber of Commerce, 800/989-9178, website: www.skamania.org; Skamania Lodge, 800/221-7117, website: www.skamania.com; Washington Department of Fish and Wildlife, Vancouver Office, 360/906-6702; Bob's Merchandise, Longview, 360/425-3870; Camas Sports Center, 360/834-4462; Dan's Specialty Guide Service, 360/225-5910 or 800/767-7326, website: www.dansspecialty.com.

84 Merrill Lake

The lake has a year-round season, but the road to it doesn't, so you can't drive to Merrill once the snow piles up. Brown trout have been added to the lake's menu in recent years, partly because the rainbows, brookies, and cutthroats have fallen victim to some aquatic parasite that catches more fish than anglers do. Merrill has fly-fishing-only regulations and a two-fish daily limit. To protect older, trophy-class trout, the lake also has a 12-inch maximum size limit.

Location: North of Cougar in Clark County; see map B2, grid h6.

Species: Brown, rainbow, cutthroat, and brook trout.

Facilities: The east side of the lake has a boat ramp and a Washington Department of Natural Resources campground. There's also a private campground in Cougar, about five miles to the south. Food, gas, and tackle are also available in Cougar. Motels can be found in Woodland.

Directions: Take I-5 to Woodland, turn east on Highway 503, and drive 30 miles to Forest Service Road 81. Turn north (left) and drive four miles to the lake.

Contact: Cougar Store, 360/238-5228; Yale Lake Country Store, 360/238-5246; Lone Fir Resort, 360/238-5210; Jack's, 360/231-4276.

85 Swift Creek Reservoir

This uppermost of the three big reservoirs on the North Fork Lewis River is stocked with rainbow fingerlings, but fluctuating water levels and varying water clarity keep things challenging for anglers. In the spring, when visibility may be down, fishing is often best around the mouths of creeks that bring clear water into the lake.

Trolling in and around the small bay at the mouth of Drift Creek, about a mile and a half west of the boat ramp, is popular in April and May. Most of the reservoir is clear by mid-summer, allowing anglers to catch fish pretty much throughout it. Although most anglers troll Triple Teazers, Needlefish, Dick Nites, and the like behind strings of trolling blades, stillfishing is also an option.

There are lots of places to park alongside the road and hike down the bank to fish along the north shore of the lake. Swift Creek Reservoir opens to fishing in late April and closes at the end of October.

Location: East of Cougar in western Skamania County; see map B2, grid h7.

Species: Rainbow trout.

Facilities: A public access area and boat ramp are near the upper (east) end of the reservoir at Swift Forest Camp. It's a good, two-lane concrete ramp, but because it's at the upper end of the reservoir, it collects deposits of silt and wood debris. There's a huge, gravel parking area nearby. Car-top boats and paddle craft may be launched at several locations along the highway on the north side of the lake.

Swift Forest Camp has RV and tent sites, picnic tables, a swim beach, restrooms, and playground equipment near the lake. Lone Fir, near Cougar, is the next-nearest campground, with both tent and RV sites.

Directions: Take I-5 to Woodland, turn east on Highway 503, and drive 35 miles to where the highway becomes Road 91013. Continue on this road several miles to parallel the north side of the lake.

Contact: Pacific Power and Light Company, 360/225-8191; Cougar Store, 360/238-5228; Lone Fir Resort, 360/238-5210; Jack's, 360/231-4276; Cougar RV Park & Campground, 360/238-5224. Call Pacific Power and Light Company, 800/547-1501, for information on water levels in the reservoir.

86 Yale Lake (Reservoir)

Even though it's not on the blast-devastated north side of Mount St. Helens, Yale was greatly affected by the 1980 eruption. Sediment from the volcano flowed into the reservoir and caused a severe drop in the kokanee population. If you fished for kokanee here in the mid-1980s, you may think Yale is the biggest biological desert in the Northwest, but things have changed. Kokanee populations have expanded to what they were in the good old days before the eruption, and the lake even has a bonus daily kokanee limit of 16 fish.

Most anglers troll for their fish, using three- or four-blade gang trolls with a Kokanee Killer, Jeweled Bead spinner, or Needlefish behind the trolling blades. Add a kernel of white corn to the lure, and you'll catch more fish. Yale Lake kokanee go on the bite around late May, and fishing is good June through September. Most of the cutthroat are caught along with the kokanee. You might also catch a bull trout here, but you must release it.

Location: Northeast of Woodland; see map B2, grid h6.

Species: Kokanee, cutthroat trout.

Facilities: The reservoir has four boat ramps, all managed by Pacific Power and Light Company and all with a $5 launch fee.

- **Saddle Dam Recreation Area:** Near the west end of the lake, this recreation area has a two-lane concrete ramp with loading floats. Reach it by driving 23 miles east from Woodland on Highway 503 and turning right at Jack's, where 503 splits (and remains 503 both ways). Follow Highway 503/Lewis River Road south for three miles, turning left on Frasier Road and following it a mile and a half to the park and boat ramp.
- **Yale Park Recreation Area:** This recreation area is 28 miles east of Woodland on Highway 503 and has a four-lane concrete ramp with three floats and a large gravel parking lot.
- **Cougar Camp:** Next is Cougar Camp, 31 miles east of Woodland on Highway 503, with a three-lane concrete ramp, loading float, and room for several dozen cars and trailers in its gravel parking lot.
- **Beaver Bay Recreation Area:** This recreation area is near the upper end of the reservoir, off Sherman Road some 33 miles east of Woodland via Highway 503. It has a one-lane concrete ramp and loading float. Although it's a good ramp, protected by concrete planks on the nearby banks, its location near the upper end of the reservoir makes it susceptible to collecting floating debris from the river. Watch for logs and limbs in the water around the ramp.

Saddle Dam Recreation Area, Yale Park Recreation Area, Cougar Camp, and Beaver Bay Recreation Area all have swim beaches, picnic tables, restrooms/changing areas, and grassy areas for sunning or sitting in the shade. Saddle Dam, Cougar Camp, and Beaver Bay also have tent and RV sites, showers, and other amenities for campers. Food, groceries, and tackle are available at Yale Lake Country Store and the Cougar Store, both near the lake. If you need a place to camp, Lone Fir in Cougar has tent and RV spaces.

Directions: Take I-5 to Woodland, turn east on Highway 503, and drive about 25 miles to the lake on the right.

Contact: Pacific Power and Light Company, 360/225-8191; Cougar Store, 360/238-5228; Lone Fir Resort, 360/238-5210; Jack's, 360/231-4276; Cougar RV Park & Campground, 360/238-5224. Call 800/547-1501 for information on water levels in the reservoir.

87 Canyon Creek

Spring plants of several thousand hatchery rainbows provide most of the angling action here. It's a popular spot with local anglers on the traditional June 1 stream opener and continues to provide fair fishing for campers and hikers into the early summer. Because it's stocked with legal-sized trout, this is one of few western Washington streams with a five-fish daily limit and an eight-inch minimum size limit.

Location: Flows into the North Lewis River a mile and a half downstream of Yale Dam on the Clark-Skamania County line; see map B2, grid h6.

Species: Rainbow trout.

Facilities: There's a primitive Forest Service campground off Forest Service Road 37, about 15 miles up Canyon Creek. The nearest food, gas, lodging, and tackle are in Woodland.

Directions: Take Cedar Creek Road NE or Highway 503 up the Lewis River from Woodland to Chelatche and turn east on Healy Road. At about the three-mile mark, Healy Road begins to parallel Canyon Creek, and continues to do so for several miles.

Contact: Jack's, 360/231-4276.

88 Lake Merwin

An annual plant of 200,000 cohos provides most of the fishing action on Merwin, the lowest of three large impoundments on the North Fork of the Lewis River. These cohos are about 10 to 11 inches long in the spring and early summer, when fishing is best here. Summertime trolling also produces some kokanee, which are escapees from Yale Reservoir, the impoundment immediately upstream of Merwin.

Following the success of stocking tiger muskies in Mayfield Lake (number 65) to reduce the squawfish population and provide a trophy fishery, the Department of Fish and Wildlife stocked Merwin with the big predators in late 1995. There are now decent numbers of legal-sized tiger muskies of 36 inches and longer to be caught, and you can bet on more to come.

Location: Northeast of Woodland; see map B2, grid h5.

Species: Coho salmon, kokanee, tiger muskies.

Facilities: There are three boat ramps on the reservoir, all of them managed by Pacific Power and Light Company:

- **Merwin Ramp:** The ramp at the west (lower) end of the lake is a rough and primitive one, consisting of a natural surface with a lot of large rocks that make trailering difficult. This ramp might best be used for launching paddle craft and other small boats rather than trailer boats. To reach it, drive nine miles east from Woodland on Highway 503, turn right on Merwin Village Road, then right again on Merwin Hatchery Drive to its end.

- **Speelyai Bay Park:** Marked by a sign on the right-hand side of Highway 503 about 21 miles east of Woodland, this park has a recently refurbished two-lane concrete ramp with two loading floats. It's in Speelyai Bay, which is well protected from

the wind and chop of speeding boats out on the main reservoir. Obey the no-wake signs here until you're well clear of the bay, and stay to the west side of the bay entrance to avoid the rocky reef on the east side.

- **Cresap Bay Recreation Area:** About two miles uplake from Speelyai, this is a new Pacific Power and Light facility with a good three-lane concrete ramp and two loading floats. This ramp sometimes has lots of floating wood around it from the river entering the reservoir nearby, especially in the spring and early summer. Reach it by driving 23 miles east from Woodland on Highway 503 and turning south at Jack's onto Highway 503/Lewis River Road (yes, it's Highway 503 in both directions now). Go three miles south on Highway 503/Lewis River Road and turn right at the sign pointing to the park. Like Speelyai, respect the no-wake rules until you're past the buoy line. Launching isn't cheap at either of these parks, thanks to an $8 entrance fee to the park and an additional $5 launch fee.

Speelyai Bay Park and Cresap Bay Recreation Area both have large sand-and-gravel swim beaches, restroom/changing facilities, picnic tables, fishing docks, and loading floats for boaters. Cresap Bay also has boat moorage and a large camping area with tent and RV spaces and an RV dump station. Gas and groceries are available from small stores along the highway.

Directions: Take I-5 to Woodland, turn east on Highway 503, and drive about 12 miles to the lake on the right.

Contact: Pacific Power and Light Company, 360/225-8191 or 800/547-1501; Jack's, 360/231-4276. Call Pacific Power and Light Company for information on water levels in the reservoir.

89 North Fork Lewis River

The Pacific Northwest has very few places where it's possible (and legal) to catch both salmon and steelhead 12 months out of the year. But the North Fork Lewis is one such place. Granted, the salmon numbers are mighty small in January, and the winter steelhead catch is unimpressive for a river of this size, but the fact that both adult salmon and steelhead inhabit this Columbia River tributary throughout the year says a lot for the river and its angling opportunities.

The North Lewis has a historic reputation as one of Washington's top spring chinook rivers, although the fishery has dropped off in recent years. April and May are the peak months, but springers are caught as early as February and as late as July. The most famous and most popular spring chinook spot on the entire river is the slow, deep pool at the Cedar Creek boat ramp, but be warned: You won't have the place to yourself. When the fish are in, it's gunwale-to-gunwale. Affectionately known as the Meat Hole, it often lives up to the nickname.

Fortunately for those who like a little more elbowroom, there are also productive springer holes upstream and downstream from Cedar Creek, including some excellent water near the salmon hatchery and the long, deep run a short distance downstream from the Haapa boat ramp. All the usual spring chinook goodies work, including roe clusters, live ghost shrimp, and combinations of the two. Many boaters back-troll sardine-wrapped Flatfish and Kwikfish plugs.

The North Fork Lewis also hosts fair runs of fall chinook, with September and October providing the best shot, but the coho run is what usually provides most of the fall fishing excitement here. These five- to 15-pound silvers begin hitting in September, peak in October, and continue to provide fair fishing through November.

Summer-run steelhead do a good job of keeping anglers from dozing off between the spring chinook fishery and the start of fall salmon action. They actually show in the river by April, and many are caught by spring salmon anglers during May and June, but July and August are by far the top steelheading months. As with salmon fishing, the best steelhead action is had by boat anglers, but all the public bank-fishing spots also produce summer-runs. Casting spoons, spinners, various steelhead bobbers, roe clusters, and fresh shrimp all work for bank anglers. The summer steelhead catch here over the past few years has ranged from 2,000 to 4,000 fish annually.

Winter steelheading on the North Lewis is a tougher proposition, despite liberal plants of hatchery smolts. Anglers may catch as many as 2,000 winter-runs a year, but in some recent winters the catch has been a piddling 400 winter steelhead. When you consider annual plants of as many as 200,000 winter-run smolts, this small catch is a puzzler. Keep in mind that you have to release any wild-stock steelhead you catch.

Cutthroat trout also are protected by wild fish–release regulations here, and fall cutthroating success may very well hinge on the size of recent hatchery cutthroat plants. Stocking efforts are impressive some years (more than 21,000 fish in 1993, for example), but too small to provide much action other years (only 2,500 fish in 1992).

Although overlooked by most serious anglers, the Upper North Fork above Swift Creek Reservoir provides some fairly good trout fishing, with rainbows making up a bulk of the catch. The river also offers some huge Dolly Varden, which must be released. Forest Service Road 90 above Swift Creek Reservoir provides bank access, and some anglers use inflatables or kayaks to float various sections of the river.

Location: Joins the Columbia River south of

Woodland; see map B2, grid h4.

Species: Winter and summer steelhead, spring and fall chinook salmon, coho salmon, sea-run cutthroat and rainbow trout.

Facilities: Boat ramps on the south side of the river include a rough one (four-wheel drive only) at the end of Haapa Road and the popular launch farther upstream at Cedar Creek. There are rough launches for paddlers above Swift Creek Reservoir off Forest Service Road 90. A $10 WDFW access decal is required to use the public launch area maintained by the Washington Department of Fish and Wildlife. On the north side of the river there's a launch near the mouth, off Dike Road, that gets a lot of use from anglers fishing the extreme lower river. Above Woodland on the north side of the river are the Island ramp (about three miles upstream from town) and the rough launch at the golf course, both of which are accessible off Highway 503. Restaurants, gas, tackle, and motel accommodations are in Woodland.

Directions: Take I-5 to Woodland and drive east on Highway 503 to parallel the north side of the river for more than 10 miles, or drive east on County Road 16 to parallel the south side.

Contact: Angler's Workshop, 360/352-5161; Jack's, 360/231-4276; Dan's Specialty Guide Service, 360/225-5910 or 800/767-7326, website: www.dansspecialty.com.

90 Horseshoe Lake

Trout fishing is very good at Horseshoe Lake the first few weeks of the late April through October season, thanks to spring plants of both rainbow and brown trout. Some years the Department of Fish and Wildlife includes a few lunker brood-stock trout in those plants, creating plenty of excitement when somebody hauls in one of these five- to 10-pound trophies.

Trout fishing gets tougher after those planters are gone, but summertime offers fair possibilities for largemouth bass to three pounds and some good catches of yellow perch and brown bullheads. Anglers occasionally catch yellow bullheads, too, but seldom notice the difference between them and the more common browns. To most folks who catch them, they're all just catfish.

Location: Immediately south of Woodland; see map B2, grid i3.

Species: Rainbow and brown trout, largemouth bass, yellow perch, brown and yellow bullhead catfish.

Facilities: A boat ramp and lots of beach access can be found at the city park on the north side of the lake. Tackle, food, gas, and lodging are available in Woodland.

Directions: Exit I-5 to the west at Woodland and take the frontage road on the west side of the freeway south about two blocks to the lake.

Contact: Angler's Workshop, 360/225-9445, website: www.anglersworkshop.com.

91 East Fork Lewis River

The East Lewis was perhaps once Washington's premier big-steelhead river, giving up a surprising number of fish over 20 pounds, a few over 25, and an occasional monster of 30 pounds or larger. Washington's state-record winter steelhead, in fact, came from the East Lewis back in the spring of 1980. That behemoth buck steelie weighed in at 32 pounds, 12 ounces. A few whopping wild steelhead still inhabit the river, but special regulations are now in effect to protect them from anglers.

Generous plants of both winter and summer hatchery steelhead smolts provide adequate angling opportunity these days, and if you work at it, you can hook steelhead every month of the year. June tends to be the best month for summer-runs, while December and January are the most productive winter-run months. The stretch of river between Lewisville Park and Daybreak Bridge is very popular among boat anglers, especially in winter, but there are lots of places along the East Lewis for bank anglers to try their luck.

The river has both resident and sea-run cutthroats, but read the fishing pamphlet carefully before going after them; the river has a regulation requiring release of all cutthroats.

Location: Meets the North Fork Lewis River three miles south of Woodland; see map B2, grid i4.

Species: Winter and summer steelhead, chinook and coho salmon, sea-run cutthroat trout.

Facilities: Boat ramps are located at Lewisville County Park, Daybreak Bridge County Park, and near the mouth of the river at Paradise Point State Park, which has about 80 campsites, restrooms with showers, an RV pump-out facility, and other amenities. Food, gas, tackle, and lodging are available in Battle Ground, La Center, and Woodland.

Directions: Take the La Center exit off I-5 south of Woodland and drive east on County Road 42 to County Road 48. Continue east on County Road 48 to N.E. 82nd Avenue and turn south (right). Drive about two miles to the Daybreak Bridge section of the river. To reach areas farther upstream, turn east off N.E. 82nd Avenue onto N.E. 299th Street, which intersects Highway 503. Turn south on Highway 503 and drive about two miles to reach Lewisville County Park. To reach areas upstream, turn north off N.E. 299th Street onto Highway 503 and east (right) on Lucia Falls Road.

Contact: Paradise Point State Park, 360/263-2350; Washington State Parks and Recreation Commission, 360/902-8844 (information) or 800/452-5687 (reservations); Angler's Workshop, 360/225-9445, website: www.anglers workshop.com.

92 Battle Ground Lake

This popular little lake, which opens to fishing in late April and closes at the end of October, is heavily planted throughout the spring with both rainbow and brook trout. The spring plants usually include a few lunker brook trout that may top five pounds. All the usual trolling lures and stillfished baits work as long as the trout last, usually into the middle of June. After that, bass fishing is the best bet, but this isn't a great bass lake.

Location: Northeast of the town of Battle Ground; see map B2, grid i5.

Species: Rainbow and brook trout, largemouth bass.

Facilities: Battle Ground Lake State Park has tent sites, restrooms, and a boat ramp (with a $3 launch fee). Food, tackle, and gas are available in the town of Battle Ground, and there's at least one bed-and-breakfast in town.

Directions: Drive east off I-5 on Highway 502 to Battle Ground, then north (left) on Heisson Road about three miles to the lake.

Contact: Battle Ground Lake State Park, 360/687-4621.

93 Vancouver Lake

Trout fishing takes a back seat to warm-water angling action on this big (over 2,800 acres) Columbia River backwater. Vancouver is open year-round but is at its best May through September. Night fishing for both brown bullheads and channel cats can be especially worthwhile, but don't overlook the perch and crappie during the daylight hours.

Location: Northwest of Vancouver; see map B2, grid j4.

Species: Rainbow trout, crappie, yellow perch, channel and brown bullhead catfish.

Facilities: A Department of Fish and Wildlife boat ramp is near the south end of the lake. A $10 WDFW access decal is required to use the public launch area. There's a county park and swim beach on the west side of the lake. Food, gas, lodging, and other amenities are available in Vancouver.

Directions: Take I-5 to Vancouver and take the Fourth Plain Boulevard exit. Drive west on Fourth Plain a mile and a half to Fruit Valley Road and turn north (right). Drive a half mile to La Frambois Road and turn west (left). Drive 1.7 miles on La Frambois Road to the lake's public access.

Contact: John's Tackle Rama & Reel Repair, 360/699-5046; Clark County Parks and Recreation Department, 360/696-8171; Washington Department of Fish and Wildlife, Vancouver Office, 360/906-6702.

94 Lacamas Lake

Hidden away in the heart of Clark County, Lacamas is quite a way off the beaten path for most Washington anglers, so it doesn't receive the publicity or the praise that it might deserve as a largemouth bass producer. The small, rough boat ramp and the jungle of aquatic weeds that sprouts throughout the lake don't do much to enhance its popularity, either. Maybe I'm prejudiced since I caught my largest bass from this shallow, 300-acre lake, but I think Lacamas is worth fishing if you're a serious bass angler. It produces far too many four- to six-pound largemouths for any of them to be flukes. Although my best-ever bass fell for a crankbait, you're better off fishing something a little more snag resistant in most of this vegetation-filled lake. Spinnerbaits, Texas-rigged plastics, and other offerings that are more or less snagless are your best bets. Lacamas is open year-round and provides bass-fishing opportunities from as early as February to as late as November.

This was the first western Washington lake to be stocked with brown trout, at least in modern times. Back in the early 1980s, biologists were looking for something that might work to provide a trout fishery in this lake that grows quite warm in the summer. The brown trout experiment proved successful, and browns have been providing most of the salmonid action here ever since. Although you might run into a carryover now and then, spring planters in the half-pound range provide most of the excitement. Small wobbling plugs, spinners, and spoons work well for them.

If you like catching crappies, perch, and catfish, Lacamas is a good bet during the spring and summer. Brown bullheads are especially abundant, and if you don't have a boat, you can catch them right off the bank at several points along the northeast side of the lake, where the road parallels the shoreline. Your catfish-catching efforts might even pay off with a channel cat or two; the lake does have a few.

Location: North of Camas; see map B2, grid j5.

Species: Brown trout, largemouth bass, yellow perch, brown bullhead and channel catfish.

Facilities: A public boat ramp is located on the northeast side of the lake. A $10 WDFW access decal is required to use the public launch area maintained by the Washington Department of Fish and Wildlife. Restaurants, tackle, gas, and other amenities are available in nearby Camas and Washougal.

Directions: Take I-205 to Highway 14 and drive east to Camas. Take Everett Road north out of Camas and turn west (left) on Leadbetter Road. It's about a mile to the lake on the left.

Contact: Camas Sports Center, 360/834-4462.

95 Washougal River

The Washougal has decent runs of winter and summer steelhead, thanks to generous annual plants totaling more than 100,000 of each. The summer run is by far the stronger of the two, and most years this relatively small Columbia tributary gives up at least 1,000 summer steelies. These are the famous Skamania Hatchery steelhead that were such a huge success and caused such a stir among anglers when they were transplanted to the Great Lakes system nearly two decades ago. May, June, and July produce the best catches, and the fishing often drops off considerably in August. Wild steelhead–release regulations are in effect during part of the year.

The highway provides fairly good bank-fishing access to the Lower Washougal, and there are three spots along the river where boat anglers launch to fish. This is a small river with plenty of boulders, so don't try boating it unless you know what you're doing and have a chance to check out the river before launching. The safest boating is when the river level is fairly high; during low flows boating is nearly impossible.

A state salmon hatchery on the Upper Washougal produces good numbers of coho and chinook salmon that return to the river throughout the fall. Check the fishing pamphlet for detailed regulations concerning salmon fishing on the Washougal, but as a general rule, you can catch and keep two adult salmon a day here, and that's exactly what many anglers do when conditions are right.

Take your favorite trout rod along if you visit the Washougal for fall salmon, and if they aren't biting, try your hand at sea-run cutthroat fishing. Some 30,000 to 40,000 cutthroat smolts are released here every year, and the returning adults provide excellent fishing possibilities. Only the Elochoman and Cowlitz Rivers (number 38 in chapter B1 and number 72 in this chapter) have been stocked with more cutthroat smolts than the Washougal over the past half dozen years or so.

Location: Joins the Columbia River at Camas; see map B2, grid j6.

Species: Summer and winter steelhead, coho and chinook salmon, sea-run cutthroat trout.

Facilities: There are several public access spots and a couple of places to launch boats along Highway 140. Food, gas, lodging, tackle, and other amenities are available in Camas and Washougal.

Directions: Take Highway 14 to Washougal and turn north on Highway 140, which parallels the main river for about 10 miles. Take Skye Road north off Highway 140 and turn east (right) on Washougal River Road to follow the main river upstream, or turn north on North Fork Road past the Skamania Hatchery to reach the West Fork Washougal.

Contact: Camas Sports Center, 360/834-4462.

96 Hamilton Creek

This little, steep-gradient creek that runs out of the hills north of Bonneville Dam has both wild and hatchery steelhead, but if you catch a wild one, you have to release it. Plants of about 5,000 hatchery steelhead a year, unfortunately, don't provide much of a return, and the biggest catch from the creek in recent years was about 50 fish. If there's such a thing as a best time to fish Hamilton, it's in December and January. The cutthroat picture is about the same, with hatchery plants accounting for most of the catch; anglers are required to release any wild cutthroats they hook.

Location: Joins the Columbia River at North Bonneville; see map B2, grid j8.

Species: Winter steelhead, sea-run cutthroat trout.

Facilities: Beacon Rock State Park has about 80 tent sites, plus restrooms and showers. The nearest town is Stevenson about eight miles to the east, and it has food, gas, lodging, and tackle.

Directions: Take Highway 14 east from Camas. The highway crosses Hamilton Creek about two miles east of Beacon Rock State Park. A gravel road leading north just west of the bridge goes upstream a short distance.

Contact: Camas Sports Center, 360/834-4462; Beacon Rock State Park, 509/427-8267; Washington State Parks and Recreation Commission, 360/902-8844 (information) or 800/452-5687 (reservations).

97 Little Ashes Lake

Liberal doses of hatchery rainbows make for good fishing here, not only during the spring and summer, but into the winter as late as the end of February. Like several other lakes connected to or near the Columbia River in Skamania and Klickitat Counties, this one is open late April through February and is stocked for winter fishing as well as spring angling action.

Don't be surprised if your efforts here pay off with a brood-stock rainbow of several pounds, since such trout are regularly stocked here along with the legal-sizers of 8 to 10 inches. Bass aren't stocked, but they are available, and early summer fishing might pay off to the tune of a two- or three-pound largemouth or a couple of one- to three-pound smallmouths. If you like the hard strikes you get from a bass hitting a crankbait, the clean, rocky bottom here will allow you to use them.

Location: Southwest of Stevenson; see map B2, grid j8.

Species: Rainbow trout, largemouth and smallmouth bass.

Facilities: Food and gas are available in Stevenson. Beacon Rock State Park, a few miles to the west, has a dozen tent/RV sites, and Skamania Lodge, also to the west, has lodging.

Directions: Drive west from Stevenson two miles on Highway 14 to the edge of the lake.

Contact: Beacon Rock State Park, 509/427-8267; Washington State Parks and Recreation Commission, 360/902-8844 (information) or 800/452-5687 (reservations); Camas Sports Center, 360/834-4462; Skamania Lodge, 800/221-7117, website: www.skamania.com.

98 Rock Creek

Don't hop in your car and drive a long distance to fish Rock Creek unless you have a lot of spare time on your hands. Anglers catch a few steelhead here in January and February, but the fishing is anything but hot. The catch is surprisingly small for a stream stocked with as many as 10,000 hatchery smolts a year. You might find decent cutthroat fishing in the fall, but all wild cutthroats must be released. Since the creek receives no hatchery cutthroat plants, you won't find many fish to keep.

Location: Enters the Columbia River just west of Stevenson; see map B2, grid j9.

Species: Winter steelhead, sea-run cutthroat trout.

Facilities: Food, gas, tackle, lodging, and camping are available in and around Stevenson. Beacon Rock State Park, about 10 miles to the west, has campsites and showers.

Directions: Drive east from Camas on Highway 14 toward Stevenson. As you approach town, turn left on Rock Creek Road just before crossing the Columbia River backwater known as Rock Cove. Stay to the left to continue upstream along the west side of the creek.

Contact: Beacon Rock State Park, 509/427-8267; Washington State Parks and Recreation Commission, 360/902-8844 (information) or 800/452-5687 (reservations); Camas Sports Center, 360/834-4462.

99 Wind River

Like so many other Northwest salmon and steelhead streams, the Wind has gone through its share of ups and downs in recent years. One of the ups was the good spring chinook salmon fishing of 1996 and 1997. Anglers fishing the extreme lower reaches of the river, mostly from boats, capitalized on excellent returns of these prime spring fish. One of the downs, on the other hand, has been the spring chinook fishing since 1997. In fact, there was no spring chinook fishing season at all in 1999, so anglers had to go elsewhere if they wanted a crack at river kings in the spring. Things got better again in 2000 and 2001, so an angler simply has to pay attention and head for the lower Wind when word gets out that the fishing has turned on.

Fall chinook fishing around the mouth of the Wind is another possibility, and it was good in the fall of 2001, as it was along much of the Columbia's length. Some of those fall kings move into the Wind itself, providing fairly good fishing in late September and much of October. If you catch coho, be sure to check for an adipose fin; only fin-clipped hatchery coho may be killed.

Planted with about 40,000 summer steelhead smolts annually, the river is closed to the taking of wild steelhead. June, July, August, and September all provide decent chances to hook a keeper summer-run. If you're planning to fish the Wind for the first time, be sure to check the fishing pamphlet for details about angling closures around Shipherd Falls and other spots.

Location: Enters the Columbia River at Carson; see map B2, grid i9.

Species: Summer steelhead, chinook salmon.

Facilities: A Department of Fish and Wildlife boat ramp is at the mouth of the river, and kayaks or small rafts can be launched off the road at the high bridge and upstream off Hemlock Road, near the hamlet of Stabler. A $10 WDFW access decal is required to use the public launch area maintained by the Washington Department of Fish and Wildlife. Carson Hot Springs is a funky old place with a hotel, a campground, a restaurant, and hot mineral springs. Restaurants, gas stations, and other accommodations can be found throughout the area, including huge Skamania Lodge a few miles west in Stevenson. The best bet for tackle is in Camas, to the west on Highway 14.

Directions: Take Highway 14 along the Columbia River to Carson and turn north on Wind River Road to reach the upper river. To fish lower portions of the Wind, drive east past Carson and turn left at the bridge crossing over the river mouth.

Contact: Camas Sports Center, 360/427-8267; Carson Hot Springs, 509/427-8292; Skamania Lodge, 800/221-7117, website: www.skamania.com.

CHAPTER B3:
SOUTH CASCADES/YAKIMA

©TERRY RUDNICK

SPRING CHINOOK CATCH ON THE WIND RIVER

Map B3

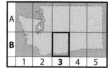

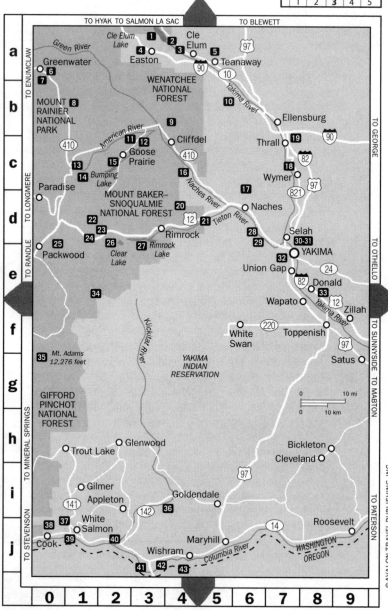

TO HYAK TO SALMON LA SAC

TO BLEWETT

TO ENUMCLAW

a

Green River

Cle Elum Lake

1

2 Cle Elum

3

4 Easton

5 Teanaway

97

90

10

Greenwater

6

7

Yakima River

b

MOUNT RAINIER NATIONAL PARK

8

WENATCHEE NATIONAL FOREST

9

10

Ellensburg

TO GEORGE

American River

11 **12**

Cliffdel

Thrall

19

90

c

410

Goose Prairie

410

82

13

15

16

Naches River

18

Wymer

97

14

Bumping Lake

17

821

TO LONGMERE

Paradise

MOUNT BAKER–SNOQUALMIE NATIONAL FOREST

20

Naches

d

22

23

12

21

Tieton River

28

Selah

30-31

24

Rimrock

29

32 YAKIMA

TO OTHELLO

TO RANDLE

25

26

27 Rimrock Lake

Union Gap

24

e

Packwood

Clear Lake

82

Donald

33

12

34

Wapato

Zillah

Yakima River

Wickiat River

White Swan

220

Toppenish

97

TO SUNNYSIDE

f

Satus

TO MABTON

35 Mt. Adams 12,276 feet

YAKIMA INDIAN RESERVATION

g

0   10 mi

0   10 km

GIFFORD PINCHOT NATIONAL FOREST

TO MINERAL SPRINGS

h

Trout Lake

Glenwood

Bickleton

Cleveland

i

Gilmer

Appleton

Goldendale

141

97

Roosevelt

38 **37**

142

36

TO STEVENSON

White Salmon

14

TO PATERSON

j

Cook

39

40

Wishram

Maryhill

Columbia River

WASHINGTON OREGON

41 **42** **43**

© AVALON TRAVEL PUBLISHING, INC.

0   1   2   3   4   5   6   7   8   9

Chapter B3:
South Cascades/Yakima

ts geographic boundaries can be defined easily enough, but this expansive piece of south-central Washington real estate is otherwise impossible to label or categorize. It has snow-capped peaks and alpine meadows, but it also has vast miles of shrub-steppe habitat that's green only during those few weeks that separate the icy winter from the blazing summer. Walk a few steps from its large, cold rivers and you're amazed at how quickly the ground turns dry and dusty. Those big rivers, though, have been controlled and diverted, and their water has been used to convert some of the dry, rocky ground to more people-friendly uses. Apple orchards and alfalfa fields dominate many of the valleys;

horse and cattle ranches spread across the rolling hills. The beef industry thrives in Ellensburg; Yakima's fruit and vegetable operations employ thousands. The fishing possibilities here aren't particularly varied, but they are numerous and in some cases top-notch. Trout fishing is big here, and nowhere is it bigger than along the upper reaches of the Yakima River, Washington's only consensus blue-ribbon trout stream. The Yakima also offers excellent winter whitefish action, and salmon are beginning to reappear in numbers large enough to allow for a sport fishery. The massive Columbia River, at the south end of the region, produces excellent walleye, steelhead, smallmouth bass, and sturgeon fishing. Clear Lake is a gem of a high-country rainbow trout producer, Rimrock and Bumping Lakes a couple of Washington's top kokanee waters, and Wenas Lake a place where trophy brown trout are almost commonplace. The region may be generally dry, but its wet places have plenty to offer.

RIMROCK LAKE

◻ Kachess Lake

The kokanee fishery is the big deal at Kachess, and it's been good enough in recent years to prompt a "bonus" kokanee limit of 16 fish per day. Since the lake covers more than 4,500 acres, you may have to do some prospecting to find the fish, or maybe you'll just want to tune in to where all the other boats are congregated and join the crowd. Take along your favorite gang trolls, a selection of Wedding Rings, Double Whammys, Needlefish, or other kokanee-getters, and go for it. Don't forget the white corn, maggots, or Power Wigglers to add to the hooks of whatever lure you use.

These same offerings will take rainbows and cutthroat trout now and then, but to increase your chances at these larger species, gear up a little and offer larger fish a bigger meal, something like a Kwikfish or Flatfish in a metallic finish or a Triple Teazer, silver with red head.

If you want lake trout, or Mackinaw, come to the lake early in the spring, when the water is still cold, and troll large plugs or wobbling spoons. These trophies can be caught later in the spring and even into early summer, but getting down to them in warmer weather makes trolling deep with a downrigger a virtual must.

The lake also has an abundance of burbot, or freshwater lings, and they'll take night crawlers or strips of sucker meat fished on the bottom. If you catch a big burbot, fillet it and either give it the deep-fryer treatment or let it bask in the warm glow of your barbecue. Delicious!

Whatever species you may want to catch, it might be a good idea to call ahead before your fishing trip to Kachess, to ask about the water level. When it's down, launching a boat can be difficult.

Location: North of Easton in Kittitas County; see map B3, grid a3.

Species: Kokanee; rainbow, cutthroat, and lake trout; burbot.

Facilities: There are two boat ramps at Kachess Campground, near the upper end of the lake. One is a two-lane, concrete ramp at the south end of the camping area, the other a single-lane, gravel ramp at the north end. Both are pretty good ramps, and there's a $2 launch fee to use them. These ramps may become high and dry by late summer, thanks to drawdown for irrigation. The U.S. Forest Service's Kachess Campground, located at the northwest corner of the lake, has nearly 200 tent and RV sites, restrooms, and a boat ramp. Crystal Springs Campground, three miles from the lake along I-90, has about two dozen tent and trailer sites. The nearest food, gas, tackle, and lodging can be found in Easton and Cle Elum.

Directions: Drive east from Snoqualmie Summit or west from Cle Elum on I-90. Turn north at Crystal Springs onto Forest Service Road 49 and go four miles to reach the upper end of the lake's west side. Forest Service Road 4828, which is accessible off Forest Service Road 49 or by turning north off the freeway near Lake Easton, provides access to six miles of the southern portion of the lake's west side. To reach the east side of the lake, turn north off I-90 near Lake Easton onto Forest Service Road 4818 and drive two miles to the lake.

Contact: Wenatchee National Forest, Cle Elum Ranger District, 509/674-4411.

◻ Lake Cle Elum

Kokanee fishing has come on strong here, and in recent years there has been a bonus limit of 16 kokanee per day in effect. Those bonus limits are a good indicator of worthwhile fishing for these little, landlocked sockeye salmon. Although Lake Cle Elum kokanee have a reputation for running small, anglers were catching decent numbers of plump 13- and 14-inchers in 1995, a good sign for kokanee anglers these days. Trolling with all the usual kokanee gear works, but be willing to travel some for your fish; this eight-mile-long reservoir covers nearly 5,000 acres. The best kokanee fishing is June through August, perfect timing for anglers looking to take a vacation in the high country of the central Cascades.

If you want lake trout, visit earlier in the season, when the water is still cold and the fish within easier reach. By May, you pretty much need a downrigger to have any chance of hooking a big laker. Like the other big reservoirs and lakes nearby, Cle Elum has a large population of burbot, which can be caught near the bottom with night crawlers, smelt, or strips of sucker meat. Regulations allow fishing with a set-line for burbot.

No visit to Lake Cle Elum would be complete without spending an hour or two in Roslyn, where the wacky but popular television show *Northern Exposure* was filmed. You won't find any moose, but all the familiar buildings are there. The town feels like it's from another era, except for all the tourists in their Nikes and baseball caps.

Location: Northeast of Easton in Kittitas County; see map B3, grid a4.

Species: Kokanee, rainbow and lake trout, burbot.

Facilities: Boat ramps are located at Wish Poosh, Morgan Creek, and Dry Creek. Wish Poosh Campground (U.S. Forest Service) has about 40 campsites. Food, gas, tackle, and lodging are available in and around Cle Elum.

Directions: Take I-90 to Cle Elum and turn north on Highway 903, following it for six miles through Roslyn and up the east side of the lake.

Contact: Wenatchee National Forest, Cle Elum Ranger District, 509/674-4411.

3 Lower Cle Elum River

This small stream, which flows out of Lake Cle Elum and into the Yakima River near the town of Cle Elum, remains pretty constant and predictable as eastern Washington streams go. The dam holding back the water to form Lake Cle Elum keeps spring runoff from getting out of hand, keeping the water fairly clear and the water level fairly constant. This pretty little river with lots of pools, medium-depth runs, and noisy riffles provides fair fishing during the summer and early fall. Deeper pools near the lower end of the Cle Elum offer good winter fishing for mountain whitefish. If you fish it at that time of year, regulations dictate that you release any trout you hook. Although it's legal to fish with bait during the winter whitefish season, selective-gear rules are in effect during the summer, requiring the use of artificial lures with single, barbless hooks.

Location: Joins the Yakima River southwest of Cle Elum; see map B3, grid a4.

Species: Rainbow trout, mountain whitefish.

Facilities: There are plenty of places to eat, sleep, buy gas and groceries, camp, and play tourist in and around Cle Elum. Lake Easton State Park is a few miles to the west.

Directions: Take I-90 to Cle Elum and turn north on Highway 903, then left over the next seven miles on any of several roads leading southeast (left) toward the river.

Contact: Lake Easton State Park, 509/656-2230.

4 Lake Easton

Since this 235-acre lake on the eastern flank of the Cascades is slow to warm in the spring, the trout fishing takes its time to heat up as well. It's stocked with about 8,000 legal-sized rainbows every year, and they come to life around the end of May, in time for Memorial Day anglers and the start of the June vacation season. The roomy, forested state park and abundance of trout make this a great place to take the kids on an early summer fishing vacation as soon as school is out. Troll a Flatfish, Triple Teazer, Dick Nite, Canadian Wonder, or a gang-troll-and-worm rig just about anywhere in the lake, and you should catch a few fish.

Location: Northwest of Easton in Kittitas County; see map B3, grid a3.

Species: Rainbow trout.

Facilities: Lake Easton State Park has nearly 100 tent sites and more than 40 RV sites with hookups, as well as restrooms, showers, and a roomy boat ramp. There's also a private RV park right next to the state park. Food, gas, tackle, and lodging are available in Easton and Cle Elum.

Directions: Take I-90 to Easton and follow the signs for a mile to Lake Easton State Park.

Contact: Lake Easton State Park, 509/656-2230; Washington State Parks and Recreation Commission, 360/902-8844 (information) or 800/452-5687 (reservations).

5 Teanaway River

Summertime plants of hatchery rainbows seem to be a thing of the past here, but there are a few pan-sized rainbows in the lower reaches of the Teanaway and small cutthroats in the upper reaches. Special regulations prohibit the use of bait. The river is high and off-colored in the spring, drops into excellent fishing condition around the end of June and throughout most of July, and continues to drop and clear through August. By September the fishing is often tough because of low water. Fly-fishing is a very good possibility during July. A lot of the river runs through private property, so be sure to get permission from the landowner before fishing.

Location: Joins the Yakima River southeast of Cle Elum; see map B3, grid a5.

Species: Rainbow and cutthroat trout.

Facilities: There are several primitive campsites and a couple of public camping areas on the upper reaches of the river. Food, gas, tackle, and lodging are available in Cle Elum.

Directions: Take I-90 about two miles east from Cle Elum and turn north on Highway 970, which parallels the Lower Teanaway and crosses it about three miles above the river mouth. Seven-tenths of a mile past the bridge crossing the river, turn north (left) on Teanaway Road, which parallels the river for several miles and has spurs running up the West, Middle, and East Forks of the Teanaway.

Contact: Washington Department of Fish and Wildlife, Yakima Office, 509/575-2740.

6 Greenwater River

Once stocked with hatchery trout to provide action for summertime anglers, the Greenwater is now managed as a wild-fish stream, with no-bait regulations, a two-fish daily limit, and 12-inch minimum size restriction on trout. That adds greatly to the challenge, but access is fairly easy and the stream has lots of inviting, fishy-looking pools. What's more, it's within fairly easy reach of anglers in the Seattle-Tacoma area. Cast small spinners or soak wet flies here during June or July for best results.

Location: East of Greenwater off Highway 410; see map B3, grid a0.

Species: Rainbow and cutthroat trout.

Facilities: Food and gas are available in Greenwater, and all other facilities can be found in Enumclaw.

Directions: Drive east from Enumclaw on Highway 410. About two miles east of the small town of Greenwater, turn north (left) off the highway on Forest Service Road 70, which soon crosses the Greenwater River and then crisscrosses it for several miles upstream.

Contact: Greenwater General Store, 360/663-2357; Mount Baker–Snoqualmie National Forest, White River Ranger District, 360/825-6585.

7 Upper White River

Get away from the road and down into some of the canyon areas of the White, and you'll find a few decent-sized trout. Living up to its name, the river is often off-color with snow runoff, so fishing with lures and artificial flies can be a tough proposition. Most anglers go with worms, salmon eggs, and other traditional trout offerings. You don't have to look too hard to find places where you can get away from the rest of the angling crowd.

The summer season here runs from June 1 through the end of October, with June and July often the most productive months. The three-month winter season is for whitefish only.

Location: Southeast of Enumclaw; see map B3, grid a0.

Species: Cutthroat trout, mountain whitefish.

Facilities: Enumclaw has food, gas, lodging, and tackle, and food and gas are available in the small town of Greenwater.

Directions: Drive east from Enumclaw on Highway 410 (Chinook Pass Highway) and after 19 miles take logging roads and Forest Service roads to the south (right) to reach various sections of the river. Take Forest Service Road 74 to reach the West Fork White River.

Contact: Greenwater General Store, 360/663-2357; Mount Baker–Snoqualmie National Forest, White River Ranger District, 360/825-6585.

8 Echo and Lost Lakes

It seems as if Echo Lakes and Lost Lakes are scattered all over Washington, but the names are perhaps most accurate when describing these two high-country jewels in the Norse Peak Wilderness. You really could get lost if you weren't paying attention getting to and from Lost Lake, and you can certainly hear an echo ringing off the nearby hillsides if you talk loudly along the shores of Echo Lake.

Echo Lake covers 67 acres and Lost Lake about 25, both large enough to harbor decent populations of trout for visiting anglers. Cutthroats provide most of the action at Echo, although now and then someone reports

catching a rainbow. Pan-sized brookies are the main targets at Lost Lake. Most folks visit these lakes in July and August, but you'll still enjoy good fishing and avoid most other anglers if you fish them after Labor Day weekend.

Location: Southeast of Greenwater in the extreme northeastern corner of Pierce County; see map B3, grid b1.

Species: Cutthroat and brook trout.

Facilities: The nearest food and gas are in Greenwater, with complete services in Enumclaw.

Directions: Take Highway 410 to about two miles east of Greenwater and turn north on Forest Service Road 70. Drive just over eight miles to Forest Service Road 7030 and turn right, following the road about one-third of a mile to the start of Forest Trail 1176. Put on your hiking boots and hit the trail; it's about a seven-mile hike to Echo Lake. To reach Lost Lake, hang a right off Trail 1176 onto Trail 1185, about three miles from the trailhead, and hike just over 3.5 miles.

Contact: Mount Baker–Snoqualmie National Forest, White River Ranger District, 360/825-6585.

9 Manastash Lake

It's a long, rough trip just to fish for pan-sized brook trout, but this 24-acre lake nestled among the pine-covered mountains of southwestern Kittitas County is a worthwhile reward for your effort. Casting Super Dupers, Panther Martin spinners, and other small lures from the bank will take fish, or wade out far enough to give yourself back-casting room and catch 'em with a fly rod. Either way, it's lots of fun. June is the best month to fish here, but anglers find decent success all summer.

Location: Northeast of Highway 410 near Cliffdel; see map B3, grid b4.

Species: Brook trout.

Facilities: U.S. Forest Service campgrounds are located at Little Naches, Halfway Flat, and Sawmill Flat, all just off Highway 410 near the turnoff to Forest Service Road 1708 and all offering campsites, restrooms, drinking water, and picnic tables. The nearest food, gas, tackle, and lodging are in Naches.

Directions: Take Highway 410 (Chinook Pass Highway) to Forest Service Road 1708 (about three miles north of Cliffdel) and turn east (right), following the road about 10 miles (it deteriorates more and more as you get closer to the lake). I wouldn't attempt the trip in anything but a four-wheel-drive rig.

Contact: Wenatchee National Forest, Cle Elum Ranger District, 509/674-4411; Wenatchee National Forest, Naches Ranger District, 509/653-2205.

10 Taneum Creek

The Taneum isn't a particularly big stream, but it can provide fair trout fishing in June and July. Most of the trout are pan-sized, with an occasional fish of 12 inches or so. Selective fishery regulations mean no bait and single, barbless hooks. Since the river runs almost totally through state or national forest land, you'll find plenty of access to good fishing water.

Location: Joins the Yakima River northwest of Ellensburg; see map B3, grid b5.

Species: Rainbow and cutthroat trout.

Facilities: There are 14 tent and trailer sites at the U.S. Forest Service's Taneum Campground, about seven miles east of the highway. The nearest food, gas, lodging, and tackle are to the east and west, near Cle Elum and Ellensburg.

Directions: Drive east from Cle Elum or west from Ellensburg on I-90 and turn south onto Taneum Road (Forest Service Road 33), which parallels the river upstream for about 10 miles.

Contact: Wenatchee National Forest, Cle Elum Ranger District, 509/674-4411; L.T. Murray Wildlife Area (Department of Fish and Wildlife), 509/925-6746.

11 American River

Once planted with lots of pan-sized rainbows from the Naches Trout Hatchery, this easy-to-reach river is now pretty much self-supporting as far as its trout population is concerned, so don't expect hot fishing. No-bait regulations are in effect, and the clear, cold waters of the American are perfect for stream anglers who like to entice their fish with small spinners or wet flies.

Easy access and the large numbers of summertime visitors using local campgrounds keep fishing pressure fairly high. If you want to escape other anglers, try parking along the highway just west of Lodge Pole and working your way upstream, away from the road. The season here opens in June, provides fair fishing all summer, and closes at the end of October.

Location: Joins the Bumping River northwest of Cliffdel; see map B3, grid c3.

Species: Rainbow, cutthroat, and brook trout; mountain whitefish.

Facilities: The U.S. Forest Service's Lodge Pole, Pleasant Valley, Hells Crossing, Pine Needle, American Forks, and Little Naches Campgrounds all have campsites, restrooms, and water, and they're all on or near the river. The nearest food, gas, tackle, and lodging are in Naches.

Directions: Take Highway 410 east from Greenwater or west from Cliffdel. The highway parallels the river most of the way from Lodge Pole Campground on the west to American Forks Campground and its confluence with the Bumping River on the east, a distance of 12 miles.

Contact: Wenatchee National Forest, Naches Ranger District, 509/653-2205.

12 Bumping River

The lower part of the river, downstream from the lake, gets fairly heavy fishing pressure through the summer and is no longer stocked with hatchery rainbows to bear the brunt of the onslaught. Fewer anglers put forth the effort to hike in and fish the upper river, so your odds are considerably better there. No-bait and barbless-hook regulations are in effect throughout the river during the summer season. Winter whitefish action can be good on the Lower Bumping, but snow, ice, and resulting highway closures keep most anglers from ever giving it a try.

Location: Joins the Naches River northwest of Cliffdel; see map B3, grid c3.

Species: Rainbow, cutthroat, and brook trout; mountain whitefish.

Facilities: U.S. Forest Service campgrounds at Little Naches, American Forks, Cedar Springs, Soda Springs, Cougar Flat, Bumping Crossing, and Bumping Dam all have campsites and other facilities. The closest food, gas, tackle, and lodging are in Naches.

Directions: Take Highway 410 (Chinook Pass Highway) to Bumping Lake Road (Forest Service Road 18) and turn south. The road runs alongside the river all the way from the highway to the east end of Bumping Lake. To reach the upper river, go south on Forest Service Road 174 along the east side of Bumping Lake, following it to the end, where a hiking trail continues upriver.

Contact: Wenatchee National Forest, Naches Ranger District, 509/653-2205.

13 Dewey Lake

You probably won't get lonely here in the northwest corner of the William O. Douglas Wilderness, since the nearby Pacific Crest Trail is often crowded with hikers, many of whom spend the night at Dewey Lake. The good news is that only about one out of 10 of them carries a fishing rod, and only about half of those know how to use it. If you're at least an average angler, you can out-fish the competition and catch your share of Dewey Lake's pan-sized brookies. Whether you cast flies, spoons, or spinners, two hours of casting should produce enough fish to fill the frying pan. The trout fishing is good enough to make the trip worthwhile; the scenery makes the trip memorable.

Location: Southeast of Chinook Pass; see map B3, grid c1.

Species: Brook trout.

Facilities: Several primitive campsites are located around the lake. The nearest food, gas, tackle, and lodging are in Greenwater (to the west) and Naches (to the east).

Directions: Take Highway 410 to the top of Chinook Pass and park in the Pacific Crest Trail parking lot. Hike south on the PCT about two miles to the Dewey Lake Trail, on the left. From there it's another mile to the lake.

Contact: Wenatchee National Forest, Naches Ranger District, 509/653-2205.

14 Swamp and Cougar Lakes

You might be able to find better fishing, but you'll have to look long and hard to find lakes in a prettier setting. Mount Rainier is only a few craggy ridges to the west, and there's usually snow on the nearby hillsides until August in this pristine corner of Yakima County. If you like to hike and catch pan-sized trout, you owe it to yourself to give these high-country gems a try.

At 82 acres, Big Cougar is the largest of the three lakes and offers perhaps the best fishing, but there are eager brookies in Little Cougar as well, and a mixed-bag catch of rainbows and brook trout is a possibility in Swamp Lake. All three lakes offer fly-fishing possibilities, but a spinning rod and selection of small spoons and spinners will also get you into fish. If you take a fly rod, be sure to include a few mosquito patterns in your fly box. Just as the mosquitoes here will feed on you, the trout feed heavily on the mosquitoes. The "season" at these lakes starts when the snow and ice melt, usually around the middle of June.

Location: West of Bumping Lake in the northwest portion of the William O. Douglas Wilderness near the Yakima-Pierce County line; see map B3, grid c1.

Species: Rainbow and brook trout.

Facilities: Primitive campsites can be found around the lakes. The nearest campgrounds are those at Bumping Lake and Bumping Dam (U.S. Forest Service). The closest gas, food, lodging, and tackle are in Greenwater and Naches.

Directions: Take Highway 410 to Bumping Lake Road (Forest Service Road 18) and turn south. When you get to Bumping Lake after driving 10 miles, bear left on Forest Service Road 174 and follow it for eight miles to its end at the confluence of Cougar Creek and the upper Bumping River. From there it's a 2.5-mile hike to Swamp Lake and another two miles to Big and Little Cougar Lakes.

Contact: Wenatchee National Forest, Naches Ranger District, 509/653-2205.

15 Bumping Lake (Reservoir)

Trolling for kokanee has long been a favorite pastime for Bumping Lake anglers, and most find the activity plenty rewarding. The fish aren't big, averaging maybe 10 inches, but all you have to do is locate a few of them, drop a gang troll rig equipped with a Wedding Ring or similar spinner over the side, and you're in business. Most anglers add a maggot or two to the hooks of the Wedding Ring, but white corn or Berkley's Power Wigglers should work just as well. Stillfishing with any of the same three baits, usually on a small, brightly painted hook, will also take Bumping Lake kokanee. Like other Washington lakes that have a good supply of small kokanee, Bumping has a 16-fish

bonus limit on the little, landlocked salmon.

While the kokanee are more or less self-sustaining, both rainbow and cutthroat trout come by way of the Department of Fish and Wildlife planting truck, usually in the form of fall fingerling plants that winter-over in the lake to provide angling action the next spring and summer. These yearling trout average about 10 inches and can be suckered into biting all the usual baits and lures. Bumping Lake has a year-round season, but June and July are best for kokanee, with June and September good for rainbows and cutts.

Location: Southwest of Goose Prairie in Yakima County; see map B3, grid c2.

Species: Rainbow and cutthroat trout, kokanee.

Facilities: The east side of the lake has a good boat ramp and a Forest Service campground with tent and trailer sites, restrooms, drinking water, and picnic tables. Several other campgrounds are within easy driving range along the Bumping River. For food, gas, tackle, and lodging, you'll have to go to Naches, about 30 miles away.

Directions: Take Highway 410 to Bumping Lake Road (Forest Service Road 18) and turn south. Follow Bumping Lake Road about 11 miles to the east end of the lake.

Contact: Wenatchee National Forest, Naches Ranger District, 509/653-2205.

16 Rattlesnake and Little Rattlesnake Creeks

No longer stocked with hatchery trout, the Rattlesnake depends on catch-and-release and selective fishery regulations to continue providing decent angling opportunities. Pan-sized cutthroats and rainbows up to about 12 inches provide most of the action. The best time to fish it is during late June and July, and again in September and October. The nearby Little Rattlesnake has standard regulations and provides fishing similar to the main creek.

Location: Joins the Naches River southeast of Cliffdel; see map B3, grid c4.

Species: Rainbow and cutthroat trout.

Facilities: Eagle Rock Resort, located just off Highway 410 about 1.5 miles from the turnoff, has tent and RV sites, restrooms, and a small store. The nearest food, gas, tackle, and lodging are in Naches.

Directions: Take Highway 410 to Forest Service Road 1500 (about nine miles northwest of the U.S. 12 junction) and turn east. The road follows the Rattlesnake Creek upstream for several miles. Access to Little Rattlesnake Creek is via Forest Service Road 1501, which turns south of the main road just over a mile east of Highway 410.

Contact: Wenatchee National Forest, Naches Ranger District, 509/653-2205; Eagle Rock Resort, 509/658-2905.

🔢 Wenas Lake

Being from the wet, green, west side of the state, I always think they should have built Wenas Lake in a better location, but I wasn't around when they decided to dam Wenas Creek and form this 61-acre reservoir, so I had no say in the matter. Luckily, most folks come here to fish rather than to check out the scenery, and they're usually happy with what they find. The truth is, Wenas has long been one of the best rainbow trout lakes on the east slope of the Cascades, and when the Department of Game—now the Department of Fish and Wildlife—decided to stock the lake with brown trout, they made it even better. Wenas is now home to some of the Evergreen State's biggest browns, a few of them reaching true trophy size of 10 pounds and over.

While trolling a little Triple Teazer or casting a bobber-and-worm rig might produce some nice rainbows, such simplistic techniques don't catch many of the big browns. That calls for trolling large, bait fish–imitating plugs

and wobbling spoons—and for the kind of patience it takes to troll for hours at a time between strikes. The lake is open to year-round fishing, and some of the best brown trout action occurs early in the spring and late in the fall, times when most of the less-serious anglers have forsaken the lake for more comfortable spots next to living room fireplaces.

To extend the summertime angling opportunities, the Department of Fish and Wildlife has stocked channel catfish in the lake, and it shouldn't be long before the lake starts to produce some hefty channel cats. Stay tuned.

Location: North of Naches; see map B3, grid c6.

Species: Rainbow and brown trout, channel catfish.

Facilities: The lake has a large public access area with a boat ramp and toilets. Wenas Lake Resort has tent and RV sites, a small store, restrooms, and other amenities. Food, gas, tackle, and lodging are available in Yakima.

Directions: From Ellensburg, drive south on Umtanum Road to Wenas Road, turn west (right), and follow it for 22 miles to the lake. From Yakima, take Highway 823 north through Selah to Wenas Road, turn left, and follow it northwest for 12 miles to the lake.

Contact: Wenas Lake Resort, 509/697-7670.

🔢 Upper Yakima River

The Yakima is Washington's best example of what can happen when a decision is made to manage a river for wild fish production and quality angling opportunity. The trend on the upper and middle portions of the Yakima since the early 1980s has been toward quality fishing, and it has paid off in a big way. Even though you can't kill a trout between Easton Dam and Roza Dam, you can certainly catch them, and some anglers experience days when they hook and release upwards of 50 wild rainbows or more. This part of the river is open year-round, and you may find excellent fishing during all but the coldest part of winter.

Although the majority of people who fish the Yakima do so with fly rods, spinning tackle and hardware are also used. In fact, small spinners such as the Luhr Jensen Metric or the Panther Martin are very effective. Just remember that the selective fishery regulations require that all lures be equipped with single, barbless hooks. Bait is prohibited for trout fishing on this stretch of the river.

Whether you fish flies or lures, casting precision is often a must on the Yakima. Much of the river is lined with grassy banks and overhanging brush or trees, and Yakima rainbows are notorious for hugging the river's edge and refusing to move more than a few inches into open water for a meal. That means, of course, that your spinner or fly has to touch down within an inch or two of the bank or it may be ignored. Sloppy casting under these conditions can quickly lead to frustration.

The Yakima is popular with both bank and boat anglers, and there are many places to reach the water along this stretch of the river. Several of those are along I-90 between Easton and Cle Elum, but some of the most popular are off Highway 10 from Cle Elum downstream to Ellensburg and along Highway 821—also known as the Yakima Canyon Road—from Ellensburg downstream to Yakima.

The only time of year you may use bait for fishing the Upper Yakima is during the winter, and then only for whitefish. Unlike many Northwest rivers, the Yakima is the scene of some fairly serious interest in whitefish among area anglers. Maggots, small grubs, and various aquatic larvae are the productive baits, but a few anglers stick with their fly rods and small nymph patterns to take whitefish throughout the winter. Any of the deeper, slower water upstream of Yakima is likely to produce good whitefish action.

Location: Easton downstream to Yakima; see map B3, grid c7.

Species: Rainbow trout, mountain whitefish.

Facilities: Several access sites and boat-launching spots are located along Highway 10 and Highway 821, most of them visible from the road:

- **East Nelson Ramp:** The uppermost possibility for launching a small raft is at the Department of Fish and Wildlife's access area off East Nelson Siding Road, about seven miles west of Cle Elum.

- **Three Bridges Access:** Another WDFW access spot, known locally as Three Bridges, offers another launching possibility above Cle Elum.

- **Highway 10 Access:** About five miles east of Cle Elum, on Highway 10 just east of its intersection with Highway 970, is a Department of Fish and Wildlife access area and boat ramp near the mouth of the Teanaway River. Remember that you need a $10 WDFW access decal to fish or launch a boat at any of these sites.

- **River Raft Rentals:** Some boaters take out at the Thorp Bridge, midway between Cle Elum and Ellensburg, but it's a steep climb. A more popular and less exhausting take-out is at the River Raft Rentals property, on the north side of the river on Highway 10. A small fee is charged to use the RRR ramp on the left side of the river. The next take-out is also on the left side of the river, at the diversion dam extending across the river a couple of miles east of Thorp.

- **Gladmar Park Access:** Some boat anglers launch at Gladmar Park, to the north of exit 101 off I-90 and float down to the Ellensburg KOA Campground. Check at the KOA office about parking and accessing the river here.

- **Ringer Loop Ramp:** Next is one of the most heavily used launch sites on the river, the Department of Fish and Wildlife's ramp off Ringer Loop, four miles south of Ellensburg on State Route 821, best known as the Yakima Canyon Road. This launch site has a paved ramp and large, gravel parking area, with a pit toilet. A $10 Washington Department of Fish and Wildlife access decal is required to use this launch.

- **Mile 22.5 Access:** Downstream about three miles is a rough launch/take-out with limited parking, just off the road between mile marker 21 and mile marker 22.
- **Umtanum Recreation Area:** This fee access spot is just north of mile 16 off Canyon Road.
- **Riverview Campground:** A mile farther downstream is Riverview Campground, where you can launch or take-out for a fee. The campground also provides a shuttle service.
- **Squaw Creek Access:** Between mile 12 and mile 13 along Canyon road is the Bureau of Land Management's Squaw Creek Recreation Site. This newly developed site has a paved boat ramp, picnic tables, tent sites, and pit toilets. There's a seven-day camping limit, and the camping fee is only $2 per night.
- **Mile 10 Access Site:** Near mile 10 is a rough ramp/take-out with a long stretch of bank access.
- **Roza Recreation Site:** The next launch/take-out spot is the BLM's Roza Recreation Site, marked with a large sign and easy to see from the road. It has a wide blacktop ramp, large paved parking area, pit toilets, and camping sites for $2 per night (seven-day limit).

As for food, gas, lodging, tackle, and other facilities, you'll find everything you need in Easton, Cle Elum, Ellensburg, and Yakima. A few guides run float trips down the river.

Directions: To reach the stretch of river between Cle Elum and Ellensburg from the west, take I-90 to Cle Elum and exit onto Highway 970 as though you were headed for Blewett Pass. But instead of going left at the Y intersection a few miles off the freeway, go right onto Highway 10, which parallels the river for several miles. Anglers headed west should follow I-90 to a few miles west of Ellensburg, exit north onto U.S. 97, and then turn west (left) onto Highway 10 to go downstream along the river. To reach the "Canyon" portion of the river, drive south from Ellensburg on Highway 821 or drive north from Yakima on I-82 and exit onto Highway 821 about five miles out of town.

Contact: Gary's Fly Shoppe, 509/972-3880, website: www.garysflyshoppe.com; Chinook Sporting Goods, 509/452-8205.

🔟 Fio Rito Lakes

These two lakes alongside I-82 between Ellensburg and Yakima provide some good, easy-access trout fishing throughout much of the year. Most folks fish from the bank, and most do quite well. Boat fishing is allowed, but you can't have a gas-powered motor on the boat. Most of the catch is rainbows, and every now and then the Department of Fish and Wildlife dumps some hog-size hatchery 'bows in one or both lakes. We're talking about trout that may top 10 pounds! The occasional hefty brown trout also comes along to keep things interesting. In 2001 the lakes received a liberal plant of big triploid rainbows. Stillfishing is the preferred technique of most Fio Rito regulars, but there's nothing to keep you from casting a weighted spinner or wobbling spoon. Although open year-round, the lakes produce best in spring, early summer, and mid- to late fall.

Location: Southeast of Ellensburg: Map B3, grid c7.

Species: Rainbow and some brown trout.

Facilities: There's good bank access around

both lakes, but no boat ramp for trailer boats. Hand-launching smaller craft from the beach is possible in several places. Motels, restaurants, gas, tackle, and other amenities are available nearby in Ellensburg.

Directions: Take I-90 to Ellensburg and turn south on I-82. Drive two miles to the lakes, on the east (left) side of the highway.

Contact: Washington Department of Fish and Wildlife, Yakima Office, 509/575-2740.

20 Oak Creek

Although it's still open to fishing from June 1 through the end of October, everything else has changed on this small Tieton River tributary. Once popular for its put-and-take fishery on smallish hatchery rainbows, Oak Creek is no longer stocked. The bad news in that, of course, is that there are fewer trout to catch, but the good news is that there still is a small population of resident trout in the creek, and the summertime angling crowds are much smaller now. If you're looking for a little solitude and a chance to dunk bait or soak flies for pan-size trout, Oak Creek is worth a look.

Location: Joins the Tieton River at Oak Creek Wildlife Area about two miles from the junction of U.S. 12 and Highway 410; see map B3, grid d4.

Species: Rainbow, cutthroat, and brook trout.

Facilities: Restrooms and drinking water are available at Oak Creek Wildlife Area. The nearest food, gas, lodging, and other amenities are to the east in Naches and Yakima.

Directions: Take U.S. 12 east from White Pass or west from Naches and turn north on Oak Creek Road, just east of the Oak Creek Wildlife Area. Oak Creek Road follows the creek upstream for more than 10 miles.

Contact: Oak Creek Wildlife Area, 509/653-2390; Washington Department of Fish and Wildlife, Yakima Office, 509/575-2740.

21 Tieton River

One look at the Tieton River makes it hard to believe that this little stream was the scene of what turned out to be a historic battle between an angler and a monster bull trout of over 20 pounds. Like a goldfish in a bowl, it doesn't seem likely that a trout could grow to trophy proportions in such a small stream system. But on an April day back in 1961, Louis Schott found out that the Tieton was capable of growing huge bull trout, and the 22-pound, eight-ouncer he wrestled to the beach that day still stands as the Washington state-record bull trout. Since most of the state's waters are closed to the taking of both bull trout and the closely related Dolly Varden, it's very possible that Schott's record will never be broken.

Rainbow trout provide most of the summertime angling opportunity on the Tieton these days. They're hatchery fish stocked by the Department of Fish and Wildlife, and the Tieton is one of relatively few streams that still receives such plants. The Tieton system also has some cutthroat trout in it, and anglers find most of them in the North Fork and the extreme upper reaches of the South Fork. The lower 12 miles or so of the South Fork Tieton are closed to fishing. Standard angling regulations apply on the Tieton, so anglers use everything from salmon eggs and worms to dry flies.

Grasshoppers are an important menu item to Tieton trout, and some anglers capture a handful of the long-legged insects to use for bait as they work their way from pool to pool. Grasshopper look-alikes are also effective, including Rooster Tail and Bang Tail spinners in various shades of brown, green, and yellow that imitate the insects. Fly-fishing with various grasshopper patterns also takes trout. Other popular fly patterns include the Hare's Ear, caddis, and other nymphs.

Besides trout, the Tieton produces good numbers of mountain whitefish. A winter whitefish-only season on the main river (below the dam) extends December through March, and 15-fish limits are fairly common for anglers who find schools of fish in some of the deeper pools and runs. Maggots, Berkley's Power Wigglers, and other small baits are most effective for these small-mouthed fish. Fly-fishing also accounts for good numbers of Tieton River whitefish, mostly on very sparsely tied, size 12 or 14 nymph patterns fished along the bottom on a sink-tip line or floating line with a long leader.

Location: Joins the Naches River northwest of Naches; see map B3, grid d5.

Species: Rainbow and cutthroat trout, mountain whitefish.

Facilities: Five U.S. Forest Service campgrounds are located along the river between the dam and the mouth of the river, all with tent and trailer sites, restrooms, and water, and all are easily accessible from U.S. 12. Forest Service campgrounds at Clear Lake are the primary facilities for anglers on the North Fork Tieton. Stores, restaurants, tackle, motels, and cabins can be found along U.S. 12 on the north shore of Rimrock Lake.

Directions: Take U.S. 12 east from White Pass or west from Naches to parallel the river between Rimrock Lake and the U.S. 12–Highway 410 junction. To reach the North Fork Tieton above Rimrock Lake, turn south off U.S. 12 near the west end of the lake onto Forest Service Road 12, then onto Forest Service Road 1207, which parallels the North Fork. To reach the South Fork Tieton, take Tieton Reservoir Road (Forest Service Road 12) off U.S. 12 about three miles east of the dam and follow it to the southeast corner of Rimrock Lake. Turn south (left) on Forest Service Road 100, which parallels the South Fork for several miles.

Contact: Wenatchee National Forest, Nach-es Ranger District, 509/653-2205; Getaway Sports, 509/672-2239.

22 William O. Douglas Wilderness Lakes

About three dozen lakes offer decent trout-fishing opportunities in this area, and there are lots of smaller ponds that might produce a fish if your timing is good. The catch depends on the lake you fish. Twin Sisters Lakes, the largest and among the easiest to reach, offer brook trout as a main course, although you might catch an occasional cutthroat or rainbow, especially in the bigger lake. The three Blankenship Lakes are primarily cutthroat lakes, while nearby Apple and Pear Lakes have both cutts and rainbows. Cramer, Dancing Lady, and Shellrock Lakes, all near the south end of the chain, are best known for their rainbows, with a few cutthroats mixed in. Other lakes well worth investigating and within reach of good hiking trails include Dumbbell, Otter, Long John, Beusch, Art, Hill, Pillar, Pipe, Jess, Penoyer, Bill, Henry, Snow, Jug, Fryingpan, Fish, and Lower and Upper Crag Lakes. Two lakes at the south end of the chain, Deep and Sand Lakes, are within easy reach of day hikers from White Pass, so they receive a lot of summertime fishing pressure and may not be very productive.

If you're planning to fish seriously for a couple of days, be sure to bring a tackle selection to cover all the bases. You'd be smart to include a few salmon eggs or even some worms in your arsenal, as well as an assortment of small spinners and wobbling spoons, a selection of dry and wet flies, and a couple of bobbers for casting both bait and flies.

Two things you can expect for sure if you fish these lakes and hike these trails during the summer are other people and lots of bugs. This may be the mosquito capital of the world, and deer flies often add to the excitement. Take along some good insect repellent or expect to donate at least two pints of blood. Depending on how long the snow and rain hold off, you can escape the insect plague—and most of the other hikers and anglers—by visiting after mid-September.

Location: North of White Pass along the Yakima-Lewis County line; see map B3, grid d1.

Species: Rainbow, cutthroat, and brook trout.

Facilities: There are a few campsites at White Pass Horse Camp and a few more at Dog Lake Campground, about two miles to the east. Motels, restaurants, gas, groceries, and other amenities are available in White Pass and Packwood, which are several miles to the west.

Directions: From the north, take Highway 410 to Bumping Lake Road (Forest Service Road 18) and turn south, following the road along the east side of Bumping Lake to Forest Service Road 395, which follows Deep Creek upstream to Deep Creek Campground and the trail to Twin Sisters Lakes and beyond. From the south, take U.S. 12 (White Pass Highway) to the top of White Pass and White Pass Horse Camp, on the north side of the road. The Pacific Crest Trail leads north from there, with the first lake about 1.5 miles up the trail.

Contact: Wenatchee National Forest, Naches Ranger District, 509/653-2205.

23 Dog Lake

It's not common to find a clear, cold, beautiful alpine lake right along a major highway, but Dog Lake is the exception to the rule. Except for the sound of the cars and RVs droning up and down the east slope of the White Pass summit, you might think you're a million miles from civilization as you cast small spinners along the big rock slide at the northeast corner of the lake. Then you remember you're casting from the comfort of a small boat or float tube and look around to see a dozen other anglers working the shoreline around the 61-acre lake. No, you're not alone in the world after all, but the brook trout continue to bite, so you don't really mind. Now and then you hook a nice rainbow for variety, and it occurs to you that you can have it both ways—wilderness setting and easy access. That's what Dog Lake has to offer.

Tip of the day: Fish the lake right after the ice melts off in June or wait until late September. The fishing pressure is lighter at both ends of the summer and the fishing is also better. Late season at Dog Lake is especially rewarding, since the mosquitoes are gone and the brook trout are at their brilliantly colored best.

Location: East of White Pass Summit; see map B3, grid d2.

Species: Rainbow and brook trout.

Facilities: Dog Lake Campground (U.S. Forest Service) has about 10 campsites, and there's a rough boat ramp near the campground. Food, gas, tackle, and lodging are available nearby at White Pass Summit.

Directions: Take U.S. 12 (White Pass Highway) to White Pass and turn north off the road just east of the summit. The lake is within sight of the highway, on the north side.

Contact: Wenatchee National Forest, Naches Ranger District, 509/653-2205.

24 Leech Lake

The name may not sound too attractive, but Leech provides pretty good fishing for a lake that's within casting distance of one of Washington's more popular mountain pass highways. The lake is open to year-round fishing, but few anglers come here to dig through the deep snow and chop a hole through the ice to try their luck in the dead of winter. Fly-fishing through the ice is next to impossible, and since Leech has fly-fishing-only regulations, wintertime angling is a nonevent.

Most anglers wait until about mid-June, by which time the ice usually has melted away and the brook trout are within reach of fly rodders. Both wet and dry flies are effective, and they produce some very respectable trout. By late summer the lake's shoreline becomes clogged with vegetation that makes bank fishing difficult; take a float tube or small boat to fish it effectively then. Don't overdo it if you get into the lunkers, since only two fish among the daily bag limit of five may exceed 12 inches. Better yet, release everything you catch except maybe a couple of pan-sizers for the dinner table.

Location: Near White Pass Summit; see map B3, grid d1.

Species: Brook trout.

Facilities: Forest Service campgrounds with tent sites, restrooms, and drinking water are located on and near the lake, with food, gas, tackle, and lodging available on the highway nearby. The lake has a boat ramp.

Directions: From Morton or Naches, take U.S. 12 (White Pass Highway) to the top of White Pass, where the lake is located just north of the highway.

Contact: Wenatchee National Forest, Naches Ranger District, 509/653-2205.

25 Packwood Lake

Although it's some distance away from the U.S. 12 traffic flow and even farther away from any of the state's population centers, this 450-acre lake in the mountains east of Packwood gets a surprising amount of foot traffic, mostly anglers who venture up here to try for the lake's foot-long rainbows. The trails and camping areas around the lake get pretty crowded on holiday weekends, but you can usually find plenty of elbowroom to test your skills with a fly rod or spinning outfit during the rest of the summer.

Leave the worms and salmon eggs at home, because Packwood is under selective fishery regulations; only artificial lures and flies with single, barbless hooks are legal. Fishing usually picks up around the end of May or first of June and stays good through July. The first cool nights of September also bring on a good trout bite, and by then the angling crowds have gone home for the winter.

Location: Southeast of Packwood; see map B3, grid e0.

Species: Rainbow trout.

Facilities: You can camp at any of several primitive sites around the lake. Food, gas, tackle, and lodging are available in Packwood.

Directions: Take U.S. 12 to Packwood and drive east on Forest Service Road 1260 for 3.5 miles. Park at the end of the road and hike about 2.5 miles to the lake.

Contact: Gifford Pinchot National Forest, Packwood Ranger District, 360/494-5515.

26 Clear Lake

The Department of Fish and Wildlife stocks hatchery rainbows in this 265-acre lake every spring to provide good fishing throughout most of the summer. Although these 8- to 10-inch planters provide most of the angling action, the catch also includes a fair number of carryover rainbows from previous years' plants, some of which top 18 inches.

This high-country lake gets pretty busy during the height of the summer camping season, so you may want to beat the crowds by fishing Clear Lake before school gets out. Trolling Rooster Tails is popular here, but all the other popular trout offerings will also work. Stillfishing around the edge of the lake with Power Bait, worms, or marshmallow–salmon egg combinations is also effective.

Location: East of White Pass Summit at the west end of Rimrock Lake; see map B3, grid d2.

Species: Rainbow trout.

Facilities: U.S. Forest Service campgrounds located on the north and south sides of the lake have more than 60 campsites between them. The south side of the lake also has a boat ramp with a $5 launch fee. Food, gas, tackle, and lodging can be found along U.S. 12, on the north side of Rimrock Lake.

Directions: Take U.S. 12 from Morton or Naches to the east end of Rimrock Lake and turn south on Forest Service Road 12 (Clear Lake Road). A Y intersection near the bottom of the hill will take you to the east or west side of the lake.

Contact: Wenatchee National Forest, Naches Ranger District, 509/653-2205.

27 Rimrock Lake (Reservoir)

Some years Rimrock is the most productive kokanee lake in Washington, giving up tens of thousands of the firm-fleshed little sockeye salmon in a single summer season. When it's prime, usually through July, anglers even catch kokanee from the bank, a rarity in most Northwest kokanee lakes.

Unfortunately, the reservoir's valuable kokanee population takes a backseat to agricultural irrigation, which is why Tieton Dam was built and the lake was formed in the first place. A few years ago the lake was drawn down to little more than a river running through a wide basin, but the Department of Fish and Wildlife had time to plan for the event and "saved" large numbers of kokanee for replanting after the reservoir refilled. As a result, kokanee fishing now is nearly as good as it was during its heyday in the mid-1980s. The fish aren't too big, averaging 8 to 11 inches, but there's a 16-fish daily bag limit and good anglers have little trouble reaching it in a few hours.

Strings of trolling blades, followed by Wedding Ring spinners, Needlefish, Double Whammys, and other flashy lures account for many of the kokanee. Tip the hooks with maggots or Berkley Power Wigglers to improve your chances.

The lake is also stocked with rainbow trout, which can be caught on all the usual spoons, spinners, wobbling plugs, and baits. Some of the trout caught here are taken on kokanee gear, but you can also stillfish for them with worms, salmon eggs, marshmallows, or Berkley Power Bait. Rimrock also has at least a small population of bull trout left, but if you catch one, you have to let it go.

Location: South side of White Pass Highway between White Pass Summit and Rimrock; see map B3, grid e3.

Species: Kokanee, rainbow trout.

Facilities: Forest Service campgrounds that offer tent and RV sites, drinking water, and restrooms, plus private lodges, boat ramps, stores, gas stations, and restaurants, are scattered along the highway on the north side of the lake. Boat ramps and campgrounds are also available on the south side of the lake, near the east end.

Directions: Take U.S. 12 east from White Pass or west from Naches. The highway parallels the north shore of the reservoir for several miles. Turn south on Forest Service Road 12 at either end of Rimrock to reach the south side of the lake.

Contact: Trout Lodge, 509/672-2211; Silver Beach Resort, 509/672-2500; The Cove Resort, 509/672-2470; Wenatchee National Forest, Naches Ranger District, 509/653-2205; Getaway Sports, 509/672-2239.

28 Naches River

The fishing may not be getting any easier on the Naches, but at least the rules are easier to understand than they used to be! It wasn't long ago that three different sets of regulations applied to various parts of this popular stream on the eastern flank of the Cascades, but things have changed. Selective fishery regulations now apply through the river during the summer season that runs from June through October. That means you can't use bait, and artificial lures and flies must be equipped with single, barbless hooks. You may not like that better, but you have to admit it's simpler. There's still an opportunity to catch a decent-size rainbow here, but don't catch anything too decent; trout over 20 inches are considered steelhead and must be released.

Like other rivers in the area, the Naches has a special winter whitefish season that provides good angling action during the cold months. If you absolutely, positively have to fish with bait, this is your chance. Winter regulations allow bait fishing with one single hook. Small flies, maggots, stonefly nymphs, and other tiny baits work best for whitefish. If you find one or two fish in a pool, stay with that spot for a while, because these are schooling fish.

Location: Joins the Yakima River at Yakima; see map B3, grid d6.

Species: Rainbow and cutthroat trout, mountain whitefish.

Facilities: Besides several U.S. Forest Service campgrounds with campsites, drinking water, and restrooms along the upper river, there are also private resorts and RV parks near the river on Highway 410. Other amenities can be found in Naches and Yakima.

Directions: Drive east on U.S. 12 from Yakima to parallel the Lower Naches. Turn north on Highway 410 to continue upriver. To reach the Little Naches, turn north off Highway 410 onto Forest Service Road 19, which follows the river upstream for miles.

Contact: Squaw Rock Resort and RV Park, 509/658-2926; Eagle Rock Campground, 509/658-2905; Whistlin' Jack Lodge, 509/658-2433; Wenatchee National Forest, Naches Ranger District, 509/653-2205.

29 Cowiche Creek

Though there are bigger and better stream fisheries around Yakima County, this stream

within an easy six-mile driving range of Yakima fills a niche for anglers in search of pan-sized trout. Selective fishery regulations were recently imposed on this little Naches River tributary, so leave the bait at home and do your fishing with spoons, spinners, flies, and other artificials with single, barbless hooks. The fishing is usually good by the end of June, and you'll find better fishing and fewer anglers if you work your way up the forks, away from town.

Location: Joins the Naches River northwest of Yakima; see map B3, grid d6.

Species: Rainbow, cutthroat, and brook trout.

Facilities: The best bet for food, gas, lodging, tackle, and other amenities is Yakima.

Directions: Take Summitview Avenue west out of Yakima for six miles and bear left on Cowiche Mill Road to reach the South Fork Cowiche Creek. Go right on North Cowiche Road to work your way up the North Fork Cowiche Creek.

Contact: Chinook Sporting Goods, 509/452-8205.

30 North Elton Pond

Gas-powered motors aren't allowed on this 15-acre pond right along the highway near Yakima, but during most of the fishing season you wouldn't need a motor anyway. That's because the season here is open only during the winter, December through March, and a coat of ice covers it much or all of that time. It's stocked with legal-size trout before the season opener and provides fair to good fishing all winter.

Location: East of Selah; see map B3, grid d7.

Species: Rainbow trout.

Facilities: There's plenty of bank access, and you'll find a couple of spots to hand-launch a small boat or canoe. Motels, food, tackle, and other amenities are nearby in Yakima.

Directions: Drive north from Yakima three miles on I-82/U.S 97 to the pond, on the east (right) side of the highway.

Contact: Chinook Sporting Goods, 509/452-8205; Washington Department of Fish and Wildlife, Yakima Office, 509/575-2740.

31 Rotary Lake

The only time I ever visited this 23-acre pond on Yakima's north side I stopped to chat with three college-age guys who were obviously having a great time. They had pretty much finished off the large supply of beer they had brought along, the sun had burned them all to a bright shade of red, and the trout were in a fairly cooperative mood. Only problem was that the fish weren't drinking alcohol, and with full control of their physical and mental capacities, they were all managing to escape before the inebriated trio could get them to the bank and up onto the beach. The young anglers laughed every time they lost a trout because of their own ineptitude, and it occurred to me that everyone was having a good time, including the fish.

Other anglers do fish Rotary Lake a little more seriously, and some come away with good catches of stocked browns and rainbows. Casting bobber-and-worm rigs, Berkley Power Bait, Rooster Tail spinners, and other offerings works well. The lake is open year-round, but trout fishing is best in April, May, and early June.

If you're not a trout angler, try working the shoreline with spinnerbaits, plastic worms, or various surface offerings to see if you can pick off one of the lake's many hefty largemouth bass. This small lake gives up a surprising number of bass over five pounds during the course of a typical summer.

Location: Near the confluence of the Yakima and Naches Rivers on the north side of Yakima; see map B3, grid d7.

Species: Rainbow and brown trout, largemouth bass.

Facilities: Good bank access and a fishing dock are available at the lake, and you can easily pack a float tube or small boat to its shores. Food, gas, lodging, and tackle are within a few blocks of the lake in Yakima.

Directions: Take First Avenue in Yakima about two miles from the center of town to the north end of the Greenway Trail and follow it a few hundred feet to the lake.

Contact: Chinook Sporting Goods, 509/452-8205.

32 Ahtanum Creek

Pan-sized trout provide most of the action for anglers at Ahtanum Creek. If you work your way up or down the entire length of the creek, you'll have a chance to fish everything from a high-country stream in the Cascade foothills to a slow-moving slough running through agricultural fields. There are some bigger trout in the lower portions of the creek, but you may have to get permission to fish, since much of it is bordered by private farmlands. Much of the land on the south side of the creek is on the Yakima Indian Reservation. The season here runs June 1 through October 31, with fishing best during the first two months and last month of the season. Selective regulations were imposed here in the late-1990s, so bait fishing is no longer allowed.

Location: Joins the Yakima River south of Yakima; see map B3, grid e7.

Species: Rainbow and cutthroat trout, mountain whitefish.

Facilities: Food, gas, tackle, lodging, and RV parks are easy to find in Yakima.

Directions: Take I-82/U.S. 12 to Union Gap and turn west on Ahtanum Road. Roads to the south every few miles cross the creek. The road splits at Tampico, and you can go south to fish the South Fork Ahtanum Creek or north to fish the North Fork.

Contact: Chinook Sporting Goods, 509/452-8205.

33 I-82 Ponds (Freeway Ponds)

Pond 1 may soon offer anglers a decent chance at walleyes right in Yakima's backyard, but for now those walleyes are there to eat their little cousins, the yellow perch. If they scarf down a few thousand pumpkinseed sunfish, that would also be okay with the Department of Fish and Wildlife biologists who planted the walleyes here. If things go as planned, some big walleyes will replace all the stunted panfish, eventually providing Yakima anglers with good fishing and great eating. For now, though, anglers have to release any walleyes they might catch from Pond 1.

In the meantime, largemouth bass are the best bet for Pond 1 anglers, and they can be caught on all the usual crankbaits, spinnerbaits, buzzbaits, and plastics that work for largemouths everywhere. You also have a chance of taking a trophy-class brown trout from Pond 1, as well as Pond 2, since both were stocked with hatchery browns a few years back.

Pond 2's main claim to fame is that it produced a state-record black bullhead catfish in 1994, and biologists suspect there may still be bigger black bullheads in the water. Like Pond 1, this one also has been stocked with walleyes, but it's not yet legal to catch and keep any of them.

Brown trout are stocked now and then in Pond 3, but if you don't catch one, you can busy yourself trying for some of the pond's husky largemouth bass. If the bass aren't biting either, try for yellow perch, since Pond 3 has some of the largest in the entire chain.

Ponds 4 and 5, which are connected by a culvert so that species may come and go from one to the other, offer a combined menu that includes rainbow and brown trout, largemouth bass, crappies, perch, bluegills, and channel catfish. Those channel cats were stocked in Pond 5 in 1994, but so far they haven't contributed much to the catch. While they offer a wide variety, Ponds 4 and 5 are most often visited by anglers in search of trout. Pond 4 is close enough to the road that some anglers carry or drag boats to it.

Pond 6, also called Buena Pond, is stocked with rainbows and is the most popular of the bunch among trout anglers. It surprised a lot of people in the fall of 1999 when it produced a new state-record channel catfish, a whopper that weighed in at over 36 pounds and shattered the previous record by nearly four pounds. It also has bass and perch. Since it's possible to drive to the edge of Pond 6, it gets the most boat traffic of the seven.

Pond 7, on the other hand, is nearly a mile from the nearest road, so it gets the lightest angling pressure. Anglers willing to make the hike find some very good crappie fishing and a few good-sized largemouth bass.

Location: Along I-82 on the east side of Yakima; see map B3, grid e8.

Species: Rainbow and brown trout, largemouth bass, crappie, bluegill, yellow perch, black bullhead catfish, walleye, channel catfish.

Facilities: The Yakima–Union Gap area has a full range of motels, RV parks, restaurants, grocery stores, tackle and fly shops, and other amenities.

Directions: Take I-82 east from Union Gap or west from Zillah. From the west end, Ponds 1 and 2 are between Mellis and Donald Roads, Pond 3 is east of Donald Road, Ponds 4 and 5 are near Finley Road, Pond 6 is off Buena Loop Road, and Pond 7 is east of Buena.

Contact: Chinook Sporting Goods, 509/452-8205.

34 Walupt Lake

You have to venture to the extreme southeastern corner of Lewis County to find Walupt, but it's worth the trip because of all the lake's unusual qualities, beginning with the fact that it's a high-country lake you can actually drive to. Less than a mile from the Pacific Crest Trail at one point, it has a well-used gravel road running right to its shores. Walupt's size and depth are also unusual, even unique among Washington's high lakes. It covers more than 380 acres, and its clear, cold waters are reported to be 200 feet deep in spots—huge for a lake located nearly 4,000 feet above sea level. Walupt's angling regulations set it apart, too. Though selective fishery regulations (no bait and single, barbless hooks only) are in effect, a standard, five-trout daily bag limit is allowed. Even the minimum size limit is an unusual 10 inches.

Whether anglers flock to Walupt despite all of these apparent contradictions or because of them, I don't know, but from about mid-June to Labor Day, this is one of western Washington's most popular camping/fishing/getaway destinations. Casting spinners, wobblers, or artificial flies from the banks takes fish, but a boat offers obvious advantages on a lake this big and deep. Unlike most lakes with selective fishery rules, it's okay to use a boat with a gas-powered motor, and many of the more successful anglers do.

Lots of anglers also put out crawdad traps. The lake is full of the little crustaceans, and they're large enough to make worthwhile hors d'oeuvres or a tasty addition to a green salad. Just boil 'em until they're red, break 'em in half, and peel the shell off the lower half. They taste and look just like lobster, only it takes a lot more of them to make a meal.

Location: Southeast of Packwood in the southeast corner of Lewis County; see map B3, grid e1.

Species: Rainbow and cutthroat trout.

Facilities: The north side of the lake has a U.S. Forest Service campground. Food, gas, lodging, and other amenities can be found in Packwood.

Directions: Take U.S. 12 to about three miles west of Packwood and turn east on Forest Service Road 21, staying on it about 15 miles to Forest Service Road 2160. Turn left there and follow that road about 3.5 miles to the north side of the lake.

Contact: Gifford Pinchot National Forest, Packwood Ranger District, 360/494-5515.

35 Horseshoe, Takhlakh, Council, Olallie, and Chain of Lakes

These lakes a few miles northwest of Mount Adams are a long distance from anywhere and yet accessible from almost everywhere. Located near the center of a maze of U.S. Forest Service roads that extends along the eastern flank of the Cascades from Mount Rainier to the Columbia River, these subalpine lakes are popular with anglers from Yakima to Vancouver, Goldendale to Tacoma. If the lakes weren't stocked regularly by the Department of Fish and Wildlife, they would most likely be depleted of trout in very little time.

Olallie Lake, the smallest of the bunch, is only 16 acres, and Council Lake, at 48 acres, is the largest. All receive steady angling pressure from the time they clear themselves of ice in the late spring until fall snows blanket the roads in October. The relative closeness of the lakes to each other and the network of roads connecting them makes it possible for an angler to fish all five lakes in a single day if desired. In case you have preferences about the type of trout you want to catch, Olallie has brown and brook trout, as does 30-acre Chain of Lakes; Council and 35-acre Takhlakh (pronounced Tak-a-lak) have brookies and cutthroats; and 24-acre Horseshoe Lake offers brook trout.

Location: Northwest of Mount Adams in northeastern Skamania County; see map B3, grid g0.

Species: Cutthroat, brown, and brook trout.

Facilities: U.S. Forest Service campgrounds with tent and trailer sites, drinking water, and restrooms are located on all but Chain of Lakes, and it's possible to get a boat into all of them. Bring everything else you need with you, since the nearest stores, motels, tackle, and gas stations are about 30 miles away.

Directions: These lakes are accessible via U.S. Forest Service roads from several directions. One route is to take U.S. 12 to about three miles west of Packwood and then turn south on Forest Service Road 21, following it to Forest Service Road 56. Turn south (left) on Forest Service Road 56, then right on Forest Service Road 5601, following it to Olallie and the rest of the lakes. Another option is to take U.S. 12 to Randle and turn south on Cispus Road, which is also called Forest Service Road 23. It runs directly to Takhlakh Lake. From the southwest, another way into these lakes is to take I-5 to Woodland and follow Highway 503 up the Lewis River until it becomes Forest Service Road 90. Stay on Forest Service Road 90 all the way to Forest Service Road 23, turn north (left), and the lakes are a couple of miles ahead. From the southeast, take Highway 14 to White Salmon and turn north on Highway 141, following it to Trout Lake. Continue north up the White Salmon River on Forest Service Road 23 all the way to the lakes. Once you're in the area, use Forest Service Road 2334 to reach Council Lake, Forest Service Road 2329 to reach Takhlakh and Horseshoe Lakes, Forest Service Road 5601 to reach Olallie Lake, and Forest Service Road 022 to reach Chain of Lakes. Whew!

Contact: Gifford Pinchot National Forest, Randle Ranger District, 360/497-7565.

36 Klickitat River

Take some of Washington's best summer steelhead fishing, put it in one of the state's prettiest rivers, then run that river through some of the region's most spectacular scenery, and what do you get? The Klickitat, a stream that I would rank right up there among the best the Northwest has to offer. In a part of the world where rivers seem to be running in every direction, that's quite a statement, but then the Klickitat is quite a river.

Summer steelheading is the biggest attraction, and even though the Klickitat doesn't often rank up there among the state's top 10 summertime steelie streams, it's a consistent producer that gives up 1,000 or more fish virtually every year. Summer steelhead are in the river when it opens to fishing on June 1, and the fishing gets better right on through July, then holds up pretty well into October. The action slows during the hottest periods of the summer, when snowmelt dirties the river and reduces visibility to an inch or two. But as soon as the weather cools, the river clears and fishing improves again.

All the usual steelhead baits and lures work, but for years Klickitat steelhead have had a reputation for favoring freshly caught grasshoppers for breakfast. Today's hatchery steelies may not have quite the same appetite for 'hoppers as the Klickitat's wild-run steelhead, but they're still worth a try if all else fails. And if you should happen to hook a wild steelhead with unclipped fins, it has to be released unharmed.

As for salmon, fall chinook runs in the Klickitat the past few years have been good enough to draw the attention of many anglers. September is the top chinook month, and most of the fish are caught around the mouth of the river and upstream several hundred yards into the slow water at the bottom end of the Klickitat Canyon. Trolling large Kwikfish and Flatfish plugs can be productive, but many anglers bounce large roe clusters or fresh ghost shrimp along the bottom for their fish.

There are some large resident rainbows throughout much of the Klickitat all season long, and many are caught accidentally by steelhead anglers. Hatchery rainbows are also stocked in the Little Klickitat, above the town of Goldendale. If you want to target them, work a small spoon or spinner through the tail-outs of the deeper pools or along the "edges" where fast and slow water meet. And, remember, if the hardware doesn't work, those rainbows will take grasshoppers, too.

The salmon fishing has seen its ups and downs in recent years, and the river's interesting regulations have kept salmon anglers on their toes. Would you believe the salmon fishery was open only on Wednesday and Saturday for a month in 1999? That regulation seemed to make at least some people happy, because it's continued with some modifications since then. In 2001, anglers could fish for salmon on Monday, Wednesday, and Saturday during the month of May. This is a great salmon-fishing stream, with both boat and bank-fishing possibilities that can pay off, but read the pamphlet carefully before dropping a bait or lure in the water.

Drift boats are popular modes of transportation on the Klickitat, but if you haven't floated it before, be sure to do some research before you launch. Tight spots and heavy rapids are scattered here and there along the entire length of the river, and sloppy boating or failure to scout ahead can get you in deep trouble in a hurry. As for the lower part of the river, where the Klickitat narrows and squeezes through a steep-walled canyon only a few feet wide, don't even think about boating it.

Location: Joins the Columbia at the town of Lyle; see map B3, grid i4.

Species: Summer steelhead, chinook and coho salmon, rainbow trout, mountain whitefish.

Facilities: Primitive camping areas are scattered along the river. There are several places along the highway where boats can be launched and where bank-fishing access is available. Groceries can be found in Klickitat, with more amenities to the east in Goldendale. A few fishing guides work various parts of the river.

Directions: Take Highway 14 to the town of Lyle and turn north on Highway 142, which follows the river upstream for nearly 20 miles. Continue up Highway 142 a few more miles and turn north at the sign pointing to Glenwood to follow the river several miles more.

Contact: Klickitat Wildlife Recreation Area, 509/773-4459; Peach Beach RV Park, 509/733-4698.

37 White Salmon River

As on the Little White Salmon to the west (see number 38), the White Salmon provides its best steelhead fishing in August and September. Anglers drift-fishing the moving water above town make some good catches, but boaters fishing in and around the river mouth account for a bulk of the steelhead. Some of the best catches are made at night, with anglers using a variety of baits and diving plugs. Access is sometimes a problem for boaters, since the lone boat ramp at the mouth of the river is on tribal property and the Indians who own it sometimes close it down. When that happens, it's a long run in rough water to reach the productive fishing spots at the mouth of the river.

Fall also provides some fair chinook salmon fishing, but the best shot at river-run kings is during the spring. Depending on run conditions, which can prompt closures of this fishery, April and May provide fair catches of spring chinooks in and around the mouth of the White Salmon. Trolling spinners or large plugs wrapped with sardine strips account for most of the spring kings. New regulations adopted in 1999 allowed anglers either one salmon or hatchery steelhead per day during the spring—*not* one of each.

Location: Joins the Columbia River just west of the town of White Salmon; see map B3, grid j1.

Species: Spring and fall chinook salmon, summer-run steelhead, rainbow trout.

Facilities: Food, gas, tackle, and lodging are readily available in White Salmon. For those who aren't on a diet, stay at the Inn of the White Salmon and enjoy a fantastic breakfast along with a comfortable bed in one of Washington's more interesting old hotel/B&B facilities.

Directions: Take Highway 14 to the town of White Salmon and turn north on Highway 141 to parallel the river upstream. Several side roads in and around White Salmon provide access to some good fishing water on the lower reaches of the river.

Contact: Miller's Sports, 509/493-2233; Inn of the White Salmon, 509/493-2335.

38 Little White Salmon River/Drano Lake

Much of the "river fishing" here occurs not in the river but in the big backwater at the river's mouth known as Drano Lake, and it has a long reputation for its outstanding steelhead and salmon fishing. One of the best fisheries here over the years has been the spring chinook action from April through June, when anglers have been known to catch hundreds of 10- to 30-pound springers per month. After several years of closures during the late-1990s, anglers again have an opportunity to troll big, sardine-wrapped Kwikfish and Flatfish, large spinners, and other offerings around the Highway 14 bridge to intercept large spring chinooks at the mouth of the Little White Salmon.

The fall chinook season remains open, and anglers trolling plugs or spinners or bouncing metal jigs or roe clusters along the bottom stand to pick off a few dozen fall salmon every year. The fishery starts in August, but September is by far the best month to try your luck.

August and September are also prime months to fish for steelhead in the Little White Salmon and Drano Lake. In fact, this is one of Washington's most productive summer steelie spots, giving up 2,000 to 3,000 fish a year. In 1992 anglers caught nearly 5,000 steelhead during the summer season. Fishing both day and night, anglers use everything from Hot Shots and other diving plugs to fresh ghost shrimp for their fish. The largest concentrations of anglers and the biggest catches come from the lake, but fishing the moving water of the river itself can also be productive.

If you're into smaller game, try the upper reaches of the Little White Salmon during the summer season. Hatchery brook trout provide much of the action, but a few rainbows are also scattered throughout the river. The presence of hatchery trout allows anglers to take as many as five trout per day, with a minimum size limit of eight inches.

Location: Joins the Columbia River east of Cook; see map B3, grid j0.

Species: Summer steelhead, chinook salmon, rainbow and brook trout.

Facilities: A boat ramp is located at Drano Lake, on the north side of Highway 14. Moss Creek and Oklahoma Campgrounds (U.S. Forest Service) have both tent and trailer sites. Big Cedar County Park has tent sites only. Food, gas, tackle, and lodging are available in Carson and White Salmon.

Directions: Take Highway 14 east from Carson or west from White Salmon to the tiny berg of Cook. Drano Lake and the mouth of the Little White Salmon are right along the highway about a mile east of Cook. To reach upriver areas, turn north at Cook and bear north on Cook-Underwood Road, then

Willard Road, and finally Oklahoma Road (Forest Service Road 18), which runs almost to the head of the river.

Contact: Gifford Pinchot National Forest, Mount Adams Ranger District, 509/395-2501; Miller's Sports, 509/493-2233.

39 Northwestern Lake (Reservoir)

Anglers fishing here should be ready for almost anything, because Northwestern has rainbows ranging from pan-sized to perhaps 10 pounds. All the usual baits and lures are used successfully on this 97-acre White Salmon River impoundment.

If you're looking for a lake at which to try your hand at trout fishing during the winter, when many of the state's lakes are closed to fishing, Northwestern is a good bet. After opening along with many of Washington's lakes at the end of April, it remains open to fishing through the end of February. You may, of course, freeze your butt off if you decide to go wet a line in this part of the state during the short days of January, but suit yourself. The fishing could be worth the misery.

Location: An impoundment on the White Salmon River northwest of White Salmon; see map B3, grid j1.

Species: Rainbow trout.

Facilities: There's a public access area with a paved boat ramp near the north end of the lake and a gravel boat ramp near the dam. Other amenities are available in the town of White Salmon.

Directions: Take Highway 14 to the town of White Salmon and turn north on Highway 141. About 3.5 miles north of town, turn west (left) onto Lakeview Road and follow it around the north end and down the west side of the lake.

Contact: Miller's Sports, 509/493-2233; Inn of the White Salmon, 509/493-2335.

40 Rowland Lake(s)

Most people cruise right over Rowland Lakes at about 60 mph without realizing the wide variety of angling potential available there. The highway runs right through the middle of this Columbia River backwater, dividing it into northern and southern halves and giving rise to the absolutely meaningless argument: Is it one lake or two? Both lakes (or both halves, if you're in that camp) are stocked with lots of hatchery rainbows each spring, including some whopper brood-stock trout weighing several pounds each. These fish provide fast fishing for the first few weeks of the general fishing season, making Rowland one (or two) of Washington's best April trout lakes.

As the lake warms and the trout fishing slows, bass anglers begin to make respectable catches of both largemouths and smallmouths, with bass fishing holding up pretty well through the summer. Panfish anglers casting bobber-and-jig rigs around the edges of the lake find perch, bluegills, and some hand-sized crappies. Night fishing can be fairly good for brown bullheads that run about a pound apiece. Like Northwestern Lake a few miles away (number 39), the Rowland Lakes remain open to fishing until the end of February, providing some fair winter trout-fishing opportunities.

Location: East of Bingen in Klickitat County; see map B3, grid j2.

Species: Rainbow and brook trout, largemouth and smallmouth bass, crappie, yellow perch, bluegill, brown bullhead catfish.

Facilities: There's a boat ramp on the lake and several spots where a small boat or canoe can be launched from the beach. Food, gas, lodging, and other amenities are available in White Salmon and Bingen.

Directions: Drive east from White Salmon and Bingen on Highway 14. The highway bisects the lake about four miles east of Bingen. Turn north (left) at the western edge of the lake to follow the gravel road around the north side.

Contact: Miller's Sports, 509/493-2233; Inn of the White Salmon, 509/493-2335.

41 Columbia River (Bonneville Pool to Lake Umatilla)

As you might expect, this long stretch of the Northwest's biggest river offers lots of angling opportunity. Depending on what you like to catch, you'll find good fishing all year long. Spring chinook angling may not be an option, but fall kings are still within the realm of possibility, especially around the major river mouths where cool water spilling into the big, warm Columbia acts like a magnet for upstream-bound salmon.

September is a prime month to troll or jig around the mouths of the Little White Salmon, White Salmon, Klickitat, and Deschutes Rivers. Those same spots are good bets for late-summer steelheading as well. Trolling with Hot Shots, Wiggle Warts, and other diving plugs is the most popular fishing method for these 8- to 20-pound sea-run trout, but in spots where the water is moving a little, it's possible to anchor in the current and work spinners along the bottom to catch steelhead.

The sturgeon fishery isn't quite as big a deal here as it is farther downstream, but there are some productive holes along this stretch that produce their share of bragging-sized white sturgeon. One such spot is between John Day Dam and Maryhill State Park, where a deep run along the north side of the river offers fairly good catches for both bank and boat anglers. Regulations in 1995 (and probably from now on) make this stretch of the Columbia a catch-and-release sturgeon fishery the second half of the year, July 1 through December 31, but there's nothing wrong with catching and releasing an eight-foot sturgeon on a warm summer's day.

Walleye fishing has been a popular pastime on this stretch of the Columbia since the early 1980s and remains a decent option today. These big cousins to the yellow perch are scattered throughout the river, with some of the best fishing still found within a mile or so downstream of the dams. Walleye fishing is a year-round possibility here, with some of the really big fish—trophies of 10 pounds and over—caught by deep trolling in the winter and early spring. Spinner-and-night-crawler combinations and deep-diving plugs are the favorite rigs among walleye trollers, but you can also catch fish by vertical jigging over the many gravel bars, rock piles, and boulder patches with leadheads or even small metal jigs.

Bass are abundant throughout this part of the Columbia, with smallmouths more common than largemouths in most areas. Although you may find them virtually anywhere in the river, some of the ponds, backwaters, and river mouths are especially productive. If you don't know where else to start, try the mouth of Oregon's John Day River or the mouth of Rock Creek on the Washington side. Casting or trolling small crankbaits or working leadhead-and-grub rigs along the rocky shoreline are good ways to find enough smallmouths to keep your wrists in shape.

Although the Northwest's American shad fishery centers on the stretch of the Columbia below Bonneville Dam, these big cousins of the herring make their way well up the Columbia, and anglers make some good catches below The Dalles and John Day Dams. Drifting small, brightly colored jigs or bare hooks adorned with a couple of small beads near the bottom will entice shad here just as anywhere else the fish are abundant. The best fishing is from early June through July, depending on what part of the river you're working. Check the newspapers for fish counts over the dams to get an idea of where the highest numbers of fish may be concentrated.

Location: From Bonneville Pool upstream to Lake Umatilla; see map B3, grid j3.

Species: Steelhead, chinook salmon, sturgeon, shad, walleye, largemouth and smallmouth bass.

Facilities: There are plenty of places to launch boats of various size along this stretch of the Columbia:

- **Home Valley Waterfront Park:** Managed by Skamania County, this park doesn't have a boat ramp, but it's a popular launch site with windsurfers, and anglers with small boats or canoes could use it as a launch for exploring the immediate shoreline. You'll have to carry or drag your boat about 50 yards from the parking lot to the river.
- **Drano Lake:** There's a Skamania County Parks and Recreation Department ramp on Drano Lake, at the mouth of the Little White Salmon River. It's a one-lane, concrete-plank launch with room for about three dozen cars and trailers on a gravel lot. That's usually plenty of parking room, unless there's a hot salmon fishery going on, when the place gets packed with anglers.
- **Bingen Marina:** This site has a one-lane, asphalt ramp and loading float, along with parking for about three dozen cars and trailers. Launching here is free for all craft, but if there's any wind at all, you'll have company in the form of windsurfers.
- **Lyle Ramp:** This ramp is located near the mouth of the Klickitat River and is a one-lane, hard-surface ramp with limited parking near the ramp entrance.
- **Dallesport Ramp:** Six miles east of Lyle is the natural-surface ramp at Dallesport. Use this one only for launching car-toppers or if you're really desperate to get your trailer boat in the water. It's rough, rocky, and requires backing a trailer about 100 yards to the ramp.

- **Dalles Dam:** Life gets easier farther up-river, at the ramp immediately above The Dalles Dam. This launch site has one hard-surface ramp and one gravel ramp, with a loading float between them and a large, gravel parking lot.
- **Horsethief Lake State Park:** The park has a two-lane ramp, one with concrete planks and the other gravel. There's a $3 launch fee here. This ramp is used by both boaters and windsurfers.
- **Avery Park:** Also popular with windsurfers as well as anglers and other boaters, this park lies about four miles upriver from Horsethief Lake. There's parking here for about 40 cars and trailers. It's a free ramp, operated by the U.S. Army Corps of Engineers.
- **Maryhill State Park:** Located near the junction of State Route 14 and U.S. 97 coming down the hill from Goldendale, the park gets a lot of use throughout much of the year. It has a two-lane, hard-surface ramp with loading floats. The launch fee here is $4 unless you're a registered park guest. An annual launch permit is available from the State Parks and Recreation Commission for $40.
- **Lake Umatilla:** Next is the Corps of Engineers ramp just above John Day Dam on Lake Umatilla. It's a one-lane, paved ramp with a loading float and room for about two dozen cars and trailers.
- **Rock Creek:** Another Corps of Engineers ramp is located at the mouth of Rock Creek, 12 miles upstream from John Day Dam. It's a one-lane, paved ramp with parking for about 25 cars and trailers, used mostly by bass and walleye anglers.
- **Sunday Cove:** About six miles west of Roosevelt, Sunday Cove has another poorly maintained Corps of Engineers ramp. This hard-surface ramp is one lane wide and has a small loading float.

- **Roosevelt Park:** This site has a good, two-lane, hard-surface ramp with two loading floats. Protected by a small cove off the main river, it's popular with boaters and windsurfers. Launching is free at this Army Corps of Engineers park.

The Port of Klickitat's Bingen Marina has open moorage (free), water and electricity to the docks, restrooms at the marina and showers nearby. Fuel docks, restaurants, and grocery stores are also nearby. Horsethief State Park has a dozen tent sites, restrooms, and showers. Maryhill State Park has over 50 tent/RV sites with water and electric and sewer hookups, as well as about 35 tent sites with no hookups. Skamania Lodge is just west of the mapped area (see section B2) and is the newest and biggest motel/conference center of its kind along the lower Columbia. It has a restaurant and also contains a U.S. Forest Service Interpretive Center with lots of information about the Columbia River Gorge.

Home Valley Marine Park has RV/tent sites for $6.50 a night, plus $2 for each additional vehicle. Also on the river at Home Valley is Home Valley RV Park. The Sojourner Motel at Home Valley is a handy stop for people on the river. Inn of the White Salmon in the town of White Salmon is a B&B that provides a real step back into the history of the Columbia Gorge.

Directions: From the west, take Highway 14 east from Camas to parallel the north side of the Columbia. From the east, take I-82 south from the Tri-Cities and turn west on Highway 14 to follow the Columbia downstream.

Contact: Miller's Sports, 509/493-2233; Bingen Marina, 509/493-1655, website: www .portofklickitat.com; Klickitat County Tourism, 800/785-1718; Skamania County Chamber of Commerce, 800/989-9178; Skamania Lodge, 800/221-7117, website: www.skamania.com;

Skamania County Parks, 509/427-9478; Inn of the White Salmon, 509/493-2335; Horsethief Lake State Park, 509/767-1159; Maryhill State Park, 509/773-5007; Washington State Parks and Recreation Commission, 360/902-8844 (information) or 800/452-5687 (reservations).

42 Spearfish Lake

This is another of those ponds along the Columbia River that has a long season. Opening in late April, it remains open to fishing through February, giving anglers a chance for some fairly good fall and winter trout fishing. Stocked with both legal-sized trout of 8 to 10 inches and brood-stock 'bows of several pounds, it offers angling variety with a chance for a trophy-sized trout. All the usual tricks work here during the spring and summer, but as the weather and water cool in the fall, you're better off fishing slow and easy with salmon eggs, Power Bait, night crawlers, and other baits.

Location: Just east of The Dalles Dam; see map B3, grid j3.

Species: Rainbow trout.

Facilities: There's a rather rough boat launch and access area on the lake. Food, gas, and lodging are available in The Dalles, across the nearby bridge over the Columbia.

Directions: Drive east from White Salmon on Highway 14 and turn south on U.S. 197. Go one mile and watch for the gravel road to the left, which winds down the hill about a mile and a half to the lake.

Contact: Miller's Sports, 509/493-2233; Washington Department of Fish and Wildlife, Yakima Office, 509/575-2740.

43 Horsethief Lake

Like many of the other "lakes" along this stretch of the Columbia River, Horsethief is really a Columbia backwater. Stocked with hatchery rainbows ranging from pan-sized to lunker-sized, it offers good trolling and stillfishing throughout the spring. By June the smallmouth fishery comes on and provides some good catches, including an occasional trophy-class smally of four pounds or bigger. Panfish also offer lots of action through the spring and summer months. Although there certainly are walleyes here, there aren't a lot of them, and most are caught by accident rather than by design.

Location: East of The Dalles Dam along the Columbia River; see map B3, grid j4.

Species: Rainbow trout, largemouth and smallmouth bass, crappie, brown bullhead catfish, a few walleyes.

Facilities: Horsethief Lake State Park offers a boat ramp and lots of shore access, as well as limited camping facilities. The nearest food, gas, tackle, and lodging are in The Dalles, about seven miles southwest.

Directions: Drive east from Lyle on Highway 14. The lake is on the south side of the highway, about three miles east of the intersection with U.S. 197.

Contact: Horsethief Lake State Park, 509/767-1159; Washington State Parks and Recreation Commission, 360/902-8844 (information) or 800/452-5687 (reservations).

CHAPTER B4:
SOUTH COLUMBIA BASIN

ICE FISHING FOR YELLOW PERCH IN LIND COULEE

Map B4

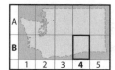

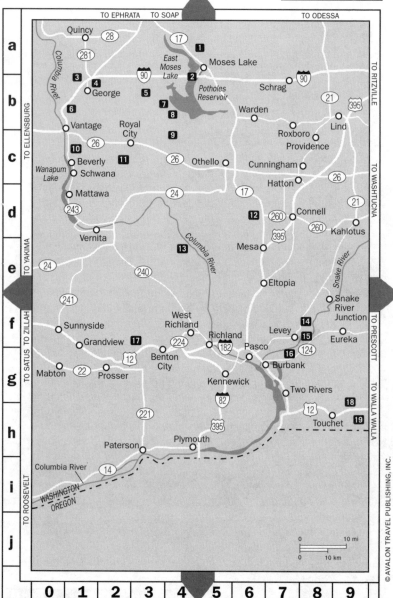

TO EPHRATA   TO SOAP   TO ODESSA

a Quincy ⟨28⟩   ⟨17⟩ ◼1

⟨281⟩   East   ◻ Moses Lake
                Moses
b ◼3   ◼4   ⟨90⟩ Lake ◼2   Schrag ○   ⟨90⟩
        ○ George ◼5   Potholes   ⟨21⟩ ⟨395⟩
                        ◼7   Reservoir
        ◼6   ◼8   Warden ○
                                        Roxboro ○ Lind ○
        ○ Vantage Royal   ◼9   Providence ○
c ◼10   City
        ○ Beverly ◼11   ⟨26⟩ Othello ○   Cunningham ○
Wanapum ○ Schwana   Hatton ○   ⟨26⟩
  Lake
        ○ Mattawa   ⟨24⟩   ⟨17⟩
d ⟨243⟩   ◼12 ⟨260⟩ Connell ○ ⟨21⟩
                                              ⟨395⟩   Kahlotus ○
        ○ Vernita   Columbia   ⟨260⟩
                          River   Mesa ○
e ⟨24⟩   ◼13
        ⟨241⟩   ⟨240⟩   Eltopia ○   Snake
                                                River
                                                Junction ○
f ○ Sunnyside West   ◼14
        ○ Grandview ◼17 Richland Richland Levey ○ ◼15 Eureka ○
                        ⟨224⟩   ⟨182⟩ Pasco ○ ⟨124⟩
                    Benton   ◼16
g ○ Mabton ⟨22⟩ ○ Prosser City   ○ Burbank
                    ⟨12⟩   Kennewick ○
                              ⟨82⟩   Two Rivers ○
                                                    ◼18
h ⟨221⟩   ⟨395⟩   ⟨12⟩ Touchet ○ ◼19
        ○ Paterson Plymouth ○
i Columbia River ⟨14⟩
        WASHINGTON
        OREGON
j   0   10 mi
                                  0   10 km

0   1   2   3   4   5   6   7   8   9

482 Washington Fishing

Chapter B4:
South Columbia Basin

The Columbia River and its water are key to everything here. This is dry country, where almost nothing grows without water from the big river and its major tributary, the Snake. Not only do these rivers provide the water that allows crops to grow, but they also serve as major highways for shipping the agricultural bounty to the marketplace. The Columbia Basin Reclamation Project gets credit for turning this once-harsh land into an agricultural capital, and in the process it created a wealth of recreational opportunities, including some great fishing. Potholes Reservoir and the seep lakes surrounding it provide some of the best rainbow trout, largemouth bass, walleye, and panfish action eastern Washington has to offer, and nearby Moses Lake is considered by some to be even better. Columbia and Snake River reservoirs have good fishing for largemouth and smallmouth bass, channel catfish, and various panfish. Harnessing the rivers to "reclaim" the land, however, has been accomplished at a great price. Wild salmon and steelhead runs that once numbered in the millions have been reduced to a trickle, and in some cases eliminated completely, replaced or diluted beyond recognition by hatchery clones raised to mitigate the losses of their wild ancestors. The last free-flowing stretch of the Columbia in Washington, known as the Hanford Reach, still offers excellent fall chinook salmon fishing, but it's only a shadow of what existed here 70 years ago.

❶ Rocky Ford Creek

This tiny stream that flows out of the ground east of Ephrata and into the upper end of Moses Lake (see number 2) offers anglers the very real possibility of hooking trout to 24 inches and larger. But besides being one of Washington's best quality trout waters, Rocky Ford is also one of its most challenging. The clear, cool waters are open to fly-fishing only, and you have to know what you're doing to fool one of its rainbows, most of which have to be described as sophisticated.

Rocky Ford is only about six miles long, and fishing is confined to the Department of Fish and Wildlife lands on the upper and lower ends. The middle three miles or so are on private property, and public access is prohibited. But three miles of prime stream fishing is enough for most anglers who visit Rocky Ford. You may go away fishless, but you go happy in the knowledge that you've spent a few hours in the company of some of the Northwest's largest rainbows.

Be sure to check the current fishing regulations pamphlet for details if you're thinking about fishing Rocky Ford for the first time. Besides its fly-fishing-only rules and catch-and-release regulations, this is the only stream in Washington where it's illegal to wade as you fish. The fragile aquatic vegetation is one of the keys to this stream's fantastic trout production, and it's protected by stay-on-the-bank regulations. Carp and suckers, however, don't live by those rules, and they've destroyed some of the prime trout habitat at the lower end of Rocky Ford in recent years. That means fishing isn't as good as it was half a dozen years ago, but quality is quality, and Rocky Ford has it.

Location: Flows into the north end of Moses Lake; see map B4, grid a5.

Species: Rainbow trout.

Facilities: There isn't much here except pit toilets at the upper end, room to park, and a trail along the creek. Food, gas, lodging, and other amenities are available to the south in Moses Lake and to the west in Ephrata.

Directions: Take I-90 to Moses Lake and turn north on Highway 17. The highway crosses Rocky Ford Creek about 15 miles after you leave the interstate, and trails leading upstream and downstream provide access to the west side of the creek. To reach upper portions of the creek, turn right off Highway 17 on C Road NE and follow Department of Fish and Wildlife signs to public land along the creek on the west (left) side of the road.

Contact: Tri-State Outfitters, 509/765-9338; Department of Fish and Wildlife, Ephrata Office, 509/754-4624.

❷ Moses Lake

The personality of 6,800-acre Moses Lake has changed a lot over the years. It has been a prime rainbow trout producer, one of the state's top panfish lakes, a place where hefty largemouth bass provided top-notch action,

MOSES LAKE WALLEYES

©TERRY RUDNICK

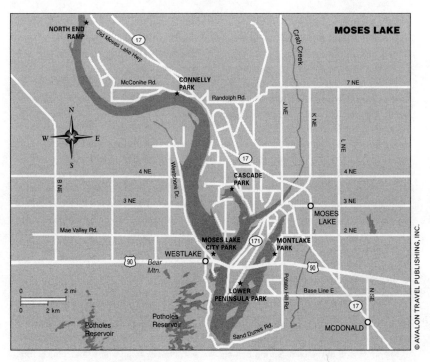

and a place anglers could go to have a crack at a bragging-sized smallmouth bass if they did things right. Now it's perhaps best known for its fine-eating walleyes, even though you still have a chance to catch all the previously mentioned species and more.

Walleye fishing has really come on here since the late 1980s, and many anglers agree that Moses is now a better walleye lake than either Potholes Reservoir (see number 7) to the south or Banks Lake (see chapter A4) to the north, both of which have long been recognized as eastern Washington's best walleye producers. Trolling with spinner-and-night-crawler rigs accounts for lots of fish at Moses, but don't hesitate to work small leadheads with tube skirts or three-inch grubs around the submerged rock piles and boulder patches. You shouldn't have to go too heavy with those sinkers or jigs since the lake has few spots where the water is much more

than 15 feet deep. Early spring provides some of the lake's best walleye action.

While walleyes reproduce on their own in Moses Lake, most of the rainbows come from Department of Fish and Wildlife hatcheries. The department typically stocks 150,000 to 180,000 small rainbows every year, and they provide good fishing in the spring and fall. Anglers who troll and stillfish share in the action, and they tend to spend more time around the south end of the lake than in the northern portion.

There was a time when anglers from all over the state came to Moses to catch panfish, especially crappies and bluegills. They enjoyed fantastic fishing, and some were pigs about it. Reports of anglers catching 150, 200, even 300 crappies or more in a weekend, then taking the catch home to Seattle and illegally selling them, prompted limit reductions here several years ago, but panfish populations continued to drop. Although there are still some big bluegills and panfish, five-fish daily limits are now in effect to help spread the catch around. Minimum size limits of eight inches for bluegills and 10 inches for crappies also apply here. The best way to catch bluegills is to work a small BeetleSpin lure, half a worm, a Berkley Power Wiggler, or other small bait in and around heavy brush cover. A small bobber with a red-and-white Mini Jig suspended three or four feet below it is good medicine for crappies. Panfish action warms up in April and continues right through summer and fall.

Bass fishing is now on the tough side at Moses, and you'll have to work for every fish you hook unless you fish the lake regularly enough to keep abreast of where the fish are located and what they're hitting. I like to work spinnerbaits around the rock piles and submerged reefs in the northern half of the lake, but decent numbers of bass are also caught around the islands and shoreline structure at the south end of the lake. Spring fishing here is the best for bass.

Like many lakes in the Columbia River Basin, Moses has large populations of lake whitefish, and just as on those other lakes, the fish are largely overlooked by anglers. They range from 1.5 to 4 pounds, fight reasonably well, and will readily take a small spoon or spinner when they move into the shallows to spawn in the early spring.

Location: Immediately west of the town of Moses Lake; see map B4, grid b4.

Species: Rainbow trout, largemouth and smallmouth bass, walleye, bluegill, yellow perch, brown bullhead catfish, lake whitefish.

Facilities: There are six boat ramps on the lake, most of them very good facilities:

- **Connelly Park:** Working downlake from the north end, Connelly Park is on the east side of the lake, off Highway 17 at McConihe Road. It's a two-lane concrete ramp with a loading float and large, paved parking area.

It's maintained by the Moses Lake Irrigation District, and launching is free.

- **Cascade Park:** Next is Cascade Park, near the north end of Lewis Horn, off Valley Road near the fairgrounds. Launching is also free at this Moses Lake Parks and Recreation Department ramp, a two-lane concrete site with loading floats.
- **Moses Lake State Park:** The two-lane concrete ramp at Moses Lake State Park is on the north side of I-90 at West Shore Road. There's a $3 launch fee at this ramp.
- **Montlake Park:** On the east side of Pelican Horn off Division Street and Linden Avenue, this two-lane concrete ramp with loading floats is another free ramp managed by the Moses Lake Parks and Recreation Department.
- **Lower Peninsula Park:** Farther south on Pelican Horn's west side (off Peninsula Drive) is Lower Peninsula Park, with two concrete launching lanes at its ramp. This is another city ramp where launching is free.
- **Sand Dune Road Ramp:** Farther south off Sand Dune Road is a Department of Fish and Wildlife ramp. This natural-surface ramp is lightly used, because it becomes high and dry by midsummer. A $10 WDFW access decal is required to use the public launch areas maintained by the Washington Department of Fish and Wildlife.

Rental boats and canoes are available from Cascade Water Rentals, located at Cascade Marina, near Cascade Park. Hallmark Inn & Resort is located right on the lake, with docks, kayak rentals, and other lake-oriented facilities. Moses Lake has a wide array of possibilities for lodging, food, and other amenities.

Directions: Take I-90 to Moses Lake. Exit on Wapato Drive or Broadway (between the two freeway bridges) to reach the south end of the lake or follow the signs to the state park just west of the first bridge. To reach upper portions of the lake, exit north on Highway 17 and follow it three miles up the east side of the lake.

Contact: Cascade Park Campground, 509/766-9240; Tri-State Outfitters, 509/765-9338; Sun Crest Resort, 509/765-0355, website: www .suncrestresort.com; Big Sun Resort, 509/765-8294; Lakeshore Resort, 509/765-9201; Hallmark Inn & Resort, 509/765-9211, website: www .hallmarkinns.com; Cascade Water Rentals, 509/766-7075 (March through October).

3 Quincy Wildlife Area Lakes

Some of these lakes are open to year-round fishing, and at least one is a popular ice-fishing lake, while the others are among the Columbia Basin's early-opening trout lakes where the spring season kicks off March 1 and runs through July. Burke, Quincy, and Dusty Lakes open in March, and all three offer excellent fishing for rainbows ranging from 10 to 16 inches. All three have also been treated with rotenone to remove trash fish and restocked with trout. Those fish will be mostly pan-sized for the next few seasons, but don't be surprised if you hook a trout or two that's even bigger. Fish eventually reach pretty good size here; these lakes have been known to give up rainbows over five pounds, and I know of a 10-pound, 13-ounce 'bow that was caught from Quincy Lake several years ago.

Easy access and roadside boat ramps at Burke and Quincy make them especially popular with early spring anglers, but the hike-in trout fishing at Dusty Lake is well worth the effort if you don't mind a little warm-up exercise before you start casting. Trout of 20 inches aren't at all uncommon at Dusty. Stillfishing with red salmon eggs is popular at all three lakes; you can either suspend an egg or two beneath a bobber or float it up from the bottom with a little help from a mini- marshmallow. After the lakes warm up a few degrees in April,

fly-fishing around the edges with a variety of wet fly and nymph patterns becomes popular. Burk and Quincy Lakes were treated with rotenone in the fall of 1999 to remove undesirable fish, and the trout fishing at both should be better in the new millennium than it was at the end of the old one.

If you can't wait until March to do your fishing, visit the area in January, when a firm layer of ice covers Ancient, Stan Coffin, and Evergreen Lakes. The best bet of the three is Evergreen, where some large strings of yellow perch are caught through the ice. A Swedish Pimple or just about any other small spoon or metal jig tipped with a perch eye on the hook for flavor is the ticket for wintertime perch here.

Location: Northwest of George; see map B4, grid b1.

Species: Rainbow trout, yellow perch, crappie, bluegill.

Facilities: Stan Coffin, Quincy, Burke, and Evergreen Lakes all have rough boat ramps. The nearest food, gas, tackle, and lodging are in George and to the north in Quincy.

Directions: Take I-90 to George and then Highway 281 north to Road 5 NW and turn west (left). Drive to White Trail Road and turn left again. Stan Coffin Lake is the first lake on the left, followed by Quincy, Burke, and then Evergreen. Closed roads (hike in only, about 1.5 miles) to the west lead to Ancient and Dusty Lakes.

Contact: Washington Department of Fish and Wildlife, Ephrata Office, 509/754-4624; Trinidad Trading Post, 509/787-3083; Villager Inn Motel and RV Park, 509/787-3515; Shady Tree RV Park, 509/785-2851.

4 George and Martha Lakes

Two more of the small Columbia Basin seep lakes that open to fishing March 1, George and Martha tend to provide fast fishing for a week or two and then taper off quickly for the rest of the season. Neither lake has a developed boat ramp, so bank anglers do most of the catching, but both George and Martha can be fished very thoroughly by anglers who pack their float tubes or small boats to the edges of the lakes.

Location: Northeast of George; see map B4, grid b2.

Species: Rainbow trout.

Facilities: Food, gas, tackle, and lodging are available in George.

Directions: Take I-90 to George, turn off the freeway, and follow frontage roads along the south side of the freeway to Martha Lake or along the north side to George Lake, each about a mile east out of town.

Contact: Washington Department of Fish and Wildlife, Ephrata Office, 509/754-4624; Shady Tree RV Park, 509/785-2851.

5 Winchester Wasteway

How can something called a "wasteway" provide decent fishing? The term is a little misleading, since the "waste" refers to water that has already been used for irrigation in the Columbia Basin fields and is flowing back into the vast irrigation system at Potholes Reservoir. High in nutrients, the water produces a lot of fish food, and both bass and panfish grow quickly in it.

The areas just above I-90 and around Potholes get fairly heavy fishing pressure at times during the spring and fall, but there are lots of places east of Dodson Road that other anglers seldom explore where you can find good fish cover. The mouth of the wasteway often provides good spring and summer walleye fishing, while the best fall action in the lower part of the wasteway is provided by schooling crappies.

Location: Flows into the west side of Potholes Reservoir; see map B4, grid b3.

Species: Largemouth bass, yellow perch, crappie, walleye, rainbow trout.

Facilities: It's possible to put a small boat in the water from places both north and south of the freeway. Food, gas, tackle, and lodging are available in George. Potholes State Park is a few miles to the southeast, as is MarDon Resort. Both are on the west side of Potholes Reservoir.

Directions: To reach the fishing area north of I-90, take I-90 to the Dodson Road exit and leave the freeway to the north. Immediately turn west on the northern frontage road and follow it three miles to the west side of the wasteway. To reach southern parts of Winchester Wasteway, turn south off I-90 on Dodson Road and follow it 3.5 miles to the water. The wasteway is also accessible by boat from the northwest corner of Potholes Reservoir (see number 7).

Contact: Washington Department of Fish and Wildlife, Ephrata Office, 509/754-4624; Potholes State Park, 509/346-2759; Washington State Parks and Recreation Commission, 360/902-8844 (information) or 800/452-5687 (reservations); MarDon Resort, 509/346-2651.

6 Caliche Lakes

These two little lakes along the south side of I-90 are loaded with more than 10,000 rainbow trout every spring, providing good fishing opportunity for several weeks after the start of the season on March 1. Most anglers cast bait from the bank, but you can catch trout on hardware or artificial flies if you want to use them. Just ignore the looks you'll get from all the egg-dunking, marshmallow-soaking locals.

Location: Southwest of George; see map B4, grid b1.

Species: Rainbow trout.

Facilities: The lakes have no facilities, but food, gas, tackle, and lodging are available in Vantage and George.

Directions: Take Exit 143 to the south off I-90 between Vantage and George, drive a quarter mile to the T intersection, and turn east (left). Drive about a mile to the lakes.

Contact: Vantage KOA, 509/856-2230, website: www.vantagewa.com; Shady Tree RV Park, 509/785-2851.

7 Potholes Reservoir

Part of the vast Columbia Basin Irrigation Project, Potholes was formed by the construction of O'Sullivan Dam across a canal known as Crab Creek. Ranging in size from 10,000 acres in the fall to 30,000 acres in the spring, this impoundment provides fishing opportunities virtually year-round.

The north end of the reservoir is a maze of sand islands separated by winding, narrow waterways and is commonly referred to as the Dunes. It's an exciting place to fish, but pay attention to where you are and remember the route you took in so you can get back out again. Besides offering excellent largemouth bass fishing, the Dunes also provide good spring fishing for walleyes, crappies, and perch. Many bass anglers cast plastic worms or grubs to shoreline cover for their fish. Spinnerbaits are also effective. A typical summertime largemouth from the Dunes is a fish of a half pound to two pounds, but the area also produces some dandies in the four- to six-pound range.

Potholes has a reputation for good catches of large crappies, many of them taken on small spinner-and-grub combinations or leadheads fished below a bobber. The hot color may change many times during the season, but take along a few lures in red and white, yellow, and black and yellow and you'll probably have what you need. Fall is often best for crappies, and good places to look for them include the lower portions of Winchester and Frenchman Hills Wasteways.

Perch fishing can be good any time of year at Potholes, including the hottest part of the summer. Find a school and you may catch dozens of plump 8- to 12-inchers. There are times, however, when all you can find are perch in the six-inch range, and if that happens don't hesitate to move on. Leadhead-and-worm combinations or just plain worms will take all the perch you want once you locate a school.

The shallow channels that wind throughout the Dunes warm quickly in the summer and are favorite haunts of swimmers and other nonanglers. Many families boat out to the Dunes, pick a small island that suits their fancy, pitch a tent, and call their little island home for several days. Just remember to bring plenty of drinking water.

The south end of Potholes, especially around Goose Island and along the rocky face of the dam, is another favorite spot of bass anglers, and they find good populations of both largemouth and smallmouth. Early in the summer, cast around the islands and submerged rocks with crawfish-colored crankbaits (diving plugs) or leadhead jigs fitted with curl-tail grubs in brown, gray, or green shades. By July some excellent topwater bassing can be had, especially during the first hour or two of daylight and again during the last few minutes of dusk.

Walleye fishing can be as good here as the bass action, and Potholes does produce some trophy-sized walleyes every year. Again, the south end of the reservoir, especially around Goose Island, is one of the favorite places to look for them, but walleyes are scattered throughout much of the reservoir, including the entrances to the wasteways that enter from the southwest, north, and southeast, and throughout the Dunes during the spring, where they move to feed after spawning. Fish a chartreuse, red-and-white, or yellow plastic grub on a leadhead jig, being careful to tip the hook with a live night crawler, and you could be in business with a walleye in the 10-pound range. Trolling diving plugs or spinner-and-worm combinations are also popular walleye-fishing methods at Potholes. Some of the best news about the Potholes walleye fishery is that the reservoir seems to be producing good numbers of young fish, which bodes well for the future.

Most anglers from other parts of the Northwest come to Potholes Reservoir for the bass, walleyes, and other warm-water fish, but a high percentage of the locals come here to catch trout, and some of the rainbows they haul out are trophy-class specimens. Twelve-inchers might be average, but 'bows of 5 to 10 pounds and larger are caught more commonly than you might suspect. Trolling Needlefish, Dick Nites, and other small wobbling spoons is effective, but many of the bigger trout fall to the Power Bait, marshmallows, salmon eggs, and other baits offered up by anglers still-fishing from the bank. The popular Medicare Beach area on the east side of the reservoir produces many big trout, as does the fishing dock at MarDon Resort near the southwest corner of Potholes.

Location: Southwest of Moses Lake; see map B4, grid b4.

Species: Largemouth and smallmouth bass, rainbow trout, kokanee, walleye, crappie, yellow perch, bluegill.

Facilities: Several boat ramps are located along the south side of Potholes Reservoir and adjoining Lind Coulee Wasteway:

- **Potholes State Park:** This paved ramp with loading floats is near the southwest corner of the reservoir. The launch fee here is $4, or you can buy an annual launch permit, good at all parks, for $40.
- **Glen Williams Ramp:** Just south of the park is the Department of Fish and Wildlife's Glen Williams launch site, with two concrete ramp lanes and lots of parking.
- **MarDon Resort:** Near the west end of the dam at the southwest corner of the reser-

voir is MarDon Resort's single-lane concrete ramp.
- **Highway 262/Road K5 SE Ramps:** Two Department of Fish and Wildlife ramps are near the mouth of Lind Coulee, one on the south side off Highway 262 and one on the north side off Road K5 SE. Both are one-lane gravel ramps. A $10 WDFW access decal is required to use the public launch areas maintained by the Washington Department of Fish and Wildlife.

MarDon Resort is a full-service facility with a café, bar, grocery and tackle store, a huge fishing dock, boat ramp, RV and tent sites, cabins, gas for cars and boats, and other amenities. Potholes State Park, two miles north of the resort, has about a dozen tent sites and over 60 RV sites with hookups, restrooms, showers, and a boat ramp. Food, gas, and lodging are also available to the south in Othello and to the north in Moses Lake. Fishing guides are available for Potholes and some of the surrounding lakes.

Directions: From the southwest, take Highway 26 east from Vantage and turn north on Highway 262, following it to the southwest corner of the reservoir. From the southeast, take Highway 26 to Othello, turn north on Highway 17, then west on Highway 262 to the reservoir. From the north, take I-90 to Moses Lake and turn south on Highway 17. Drive just two miles to M Road SE and turn south (right). Follow M Road to Highway 262 and turn west (right) to the south end of Potholes.

Contact: Potholes State Park, 509/364-2759; Washington State Parks and Recreation Commission, 360/902-8844 (information) or 800/452-5687 (reservations); Washington Department of Fish and Wildlife, Ephrata Office, 509/754-4624; MarDon Resort, 509/346-2651.

8 Lind Coulee Wasteway

It would have been easy to lump Lind Coulee in with Potholes Reservoir, since the two offer much of the same kind of fishing for many of the same species. Lind Coulee Wasteway, in fact, is really a long, narrow extension off the southeast corner of the reservoir. The wasteway is also different from Potholes in some ways, and the fishing is sometimes good enough to merit special recognition.

The difference is most obvious in winter, when Lind Coulee often freezes over with a thick lid of ice that supports a thriving ice fishery. While Potholes may freeze, its ice lid isn't as thick and usually isn't safe for fishing. Lind Coulee comes into its own during this season, providing some of the best perch fishing you'll find anywhere in the Columbia Basin. Exactly where the best action may take place varies from year to year, but you can almost always expect to find good perch action if you look around a little and go to where other anglers are congregated. The only question may be the size of the fish; they're big and fat some years, almost too small to mess with other years. Whatever their size, they'll take a small Triple Teazer, Crippled Herring, or Swedish Pimple with a perch eye or small strip of perch meat on the hook.

Winter also produces some fairly good through-the-ice catches of rainbow trout and sometimes large crappies. Again, the best fishing may be here today and somewhere else tomorrow, but a good place to start looking is around the end of the coulee along M Road. The overhanging willows at the upper end of the coulee attract crappies and bluegills at other times of the year, especially in spring and early summer.

Lind Coulee can also be a very good place to fish for bass, both largemouths and smallmouths. It offers a variety of rocky structures, shoreline cover, and warm, shallow bays that attract bass like magnets, providing productive fishing from spring until late fall.

Location: Enters the southeast corner of Potholes Reservoir; see map B4, grid b4.

Species: Largemouth and smallmouth bass, yellow perch, crappie, walleye, rainbow trout.

Facilities: Boat ramps are located at the west end of Lind Coulee and at the bridge where M Road crosses over the coulee. MarDon Resort is a full-service facility with a café, bar, grocery and tackle store, huge fishing dock, boat ramp, RV and tent sites, cabins, gasoline, and other amenities. Potholes State Park two miles north of the resort has about a dozen tent sites and more than 60 RV sites with hookups, restrooms, showers, and a boat ramp. Food, gas, and lodging are also available to the south in Othello and to the north in Moses Lake.

Directions: From the southwest, take Highway 26 east from Vantage and turn north on Highway 262, following it past the southwest corner of Potholes Reservoir to Lind Coulee. From the southeast take Highway 26 to Othello, turn north on Highway 17, and then head west on Highway 262. From the north take I-90 to Moses Lake and turn south on Highway 17. Drive two miles to M Road SE and turn south (right). Continue on M Road, which parallels the west side of Lind Coulee's upper end before intersecting Highway 262. Turn west (right) on Highway 262 until you reach the confluence of Lind Coulee with the southeast corner of Potholes Reservoir.

Contact: Potholes State Park, 509/346-2759; Washington State Parks and Recreation Commission, 360/902-8844 (information) or 800/452-5687 (reservations); MarDon Resort, 509/346-2651.

9 Potholes Area Seep Lakes

Yes, I know a good argument could be made for devoting a section to each of the more than four dozen lakes scattered around the scablands in and around the Columbia National Wildlife Refuge, but I lumped them all together for two reasons. First, by giving the driving directions and listing the facilities only once, I reduced the size of this book by enough pages to save two or three large trees. Nearly as important, I think anglers should visit this place with an open mind and no set ideas about where they want to fish or what they want to catch. If you arrive for a weekend of fishing the seeps and stubbornly spend all your time at one lake because you liked what you read about it here, you might miss out on some fantastic fishing just over the hill or just down the road. I couldn't sleep at night with that on my conscience. Some of these lakes offer excellent spring trout fishing, others are hot spots for walleyes, perch, crappies, bass, even whitefish, and you owe it to yourself to explore several of them every time you visit this fish-rich part of the state.

One of your first stops should be Soda Lake, the second largest of the bunch at more than 180 acres. It offers perhaps the best perch fishing of any lake in the chain and is also a good bet for walleyes. Open year-round, Soda gives up good numbers of both much of the time. If you hit the lake in March, cast small spoons, spinners, and plugs for lake whitefish, which go on a striking rampage for a couple of weeks every spring. Soda also has rainbow trout and largemouth and smallmouth bass.

Another big lake near the top end of the chain is Upper Goose, which covers more than 110 acres and which, like 50-acre Lower Goose immediately to the south, is open to year-round fishing. Both have boat ramps and provide good fishing for bass, perch, crappies, and other warm-water species.

Besides Soda and the Goose Lakes, another 30 or so of the seep lakes are open to year-round fishing. Some, like Blythe, Corral,

Canal, South Teal, and the Windmill Lakes, are heavily stocked with hatchery rainbows and provide good trout fishing throughout much of the year. Winter ice fishing for trout often pays big dividends on these lakes. Many of the other year-round lakes are also stocked with trout, but perhaps not as many as those I've mentioned. Of these, Quail Lake is particularly popular with one segment of the angling fraternity, the fly casters. Quail is the only one of the seep lakes that's only open to fly fishing and catch-and-release fishing throughout the year. South Teal was treated with rotenone in 1999 and restocked with trout, and it should provide excellent fishing the next several years.

About a dozen of the seep lakes below Potholes are among the Columbia Basin lakes that open March 1 and stay open to fishing through July 31. The list includes Warden Lake, which at 186 acres is the largest of the entire group. It's also the most heavily stocked with rainbow trout and almost always the best early-season bet in the chain when March 1 rolls around. Not only are the rainbows abundant here, but they carry over fairly well, so there's always the chance you'll hook a husky rainbow of 14, 16, even 18 inches or longer. Other seep lakes falling under the March 1 through July 31 season plan are Cascade, Deadman, Hutchinson, Shiner, Cattail, Pillar, Shoveler, Widgeon, Upper and Lower Hampton, Para (juvenile-only fishing for kids 14 and under), and South Warden Lakes.

Location: Southeast of Potholes Reservoir; see map B4, grid c4.

Species: Rainbow, brown, and Lahontan cutthroat trout; largemouth and smallmouth bass; walleye; yellow perch; crappie; bluegill; lake whitefish.

Facilities: Boat ramps are located on many of the seep lakes, and on others it's fairly easy to drag a boat to the edge of the lake for launching. MarDon Resort is a full-service facility with a café, bar, grocery and tackle store, huge fishing dock, boat ramp, RV and tent sites, cabins, gas, and other amenities. Potholes State Park, two miles north of the resort, has about a dozen tent sites and more than 60 RV sites with hookups, restrooms, showers, and a boat ramp. Food, gas, and lodging are also available to the south in Othello.

Directions: From the north, take Highway 26 from Vantage or Highway 17 from Moses Lake to Highway 262 and take any of several gravel or dirt roads to the south from the south end of Potholes Reservoir to reach various lakes in the chain. Or take Highway 26 from the south to Othello and turn north on McManaman Road. Stay on McManaman to reach a few of the lakes along the south end of the chain. To reach most of the others, turn right onto Lava Lake Road or Morgan Lake Road.

Contact: Potholes State Park, 509/346-2759; MarDon Resort, 509/346-2651; Columbia National Wildlife Refuge, 509/488-2668.

🔟 Lenice, Nunnally, and Merry Lakes

Some serious fly-fish anglers may want to have me burned at the stake for lumping these three exceptional trout lakes together under a single heading, but the fact is that if you learn how to fish one, you've figured it out for all three. A one-fish daily limit and selective fishery regulations (no bait, and barbless, single hooks only) keep the harvest small and allow the planted rainbows and browns to reach impressive size. What's more, they're some of the toughest, strongest, most stubborn fish you'll find anywhere. I'll never forget the first Lenice Lake rainbow I ever caught, more than 20 years ago, because it was the first rainbow trout that ever took me 20 or 30 feet into the backing line on my fly reel in its first powerful run. All the trout I had caught on flies before that were little dinks that couldn't take 20 feet of line if you

tied your leader around 50 of them and dropped them off a building.

Opening day on these three lakes was changed from late April to March 1 in 1997, but the prime time is in the early summer, when hatches of damselflies and other aquatic insects may spawn piscatorial pigouts like you've never seen. Spoon and spinner anglers may not hit it big during one of these gorge-a-thons, but fly casters equipped with the right patterns to match what's hatching will be in for an hour or two of fantastic fishing.

If you're looking for added incentive to visit these prime central Washington trout factories, be advised that all three were treated with rotenone in 2000 to eliminate sunfish that were competing for food with the trout. That translates into even bigger and stronger trout for the new millennium. Wow!

I've been known to pack, drag, push, roll, and carry small boats to these lakes, but smarter people carry float tubes to get around in once they reach the water. The trails to each of these lakes are all at least a quarter of a mile long—some longer—so smaller, lighter craft are certainly the best way to go.

And a word of caution is in order: This is one of those places where you may find yourself getting up close and personal with a rattlesnake that isn't all that happy to see you. Be on your toes, especially if you try to fish any of these lakes from the bank. Veteran anglers use a float tube not only to avoid the shoreline reeds that make for tough fishing but also to get that much farther away from the rattlers.

Location: Northeast of Beverly in Grant County; see map B4, grid c1.

Species: Rainbow and brown trout.

Facilities: Except for pit toilets, you're on your own here. There's a small café in Beverly and food, gas, tackle, and lodging in Vantage.

Directions: Take I-90 to the east side of the Columbia River (across from Vantage) and turn south onto Highway 26. When Highway 26 turns up the hill away from the river, continue south on Highway 243, following it about seven miles to Beverly/Crab Creek Road. Turn east (left) and watch for the gravel roads to the north (left) that lead to the parking areas of the three lakes. The road to the Nunnally Lake parking area is two miles up Beverly/Crab Creek Road; the road into Merry Lake is just over four miles; the Lenice Lake turn is at the five-mile mark. A trail leads from each parking area to the south side of the lake.

Contact: Washington Department of Fish and Wildlife, Ephrata Office, 509/754-4624; Vantage KOA, 509/856-2230, website: www.vantagewa.com.

11 Lower Crab Creek

The fishing isn't as good at the bottom end of this stream system as it is at the upper end, but a few rainbows make their way out of the lakes above and grow to worthwhile size in the lightly fished stretches of Crab Creek between Potholes Reservoir and the stream's final destination in the Columbia. I wouldn't drive halfway across the state just to fish lower Crab Creek, but if you have a few hours on your hands after a day of fishing at Lenice Lake or on your way home from the Potholes area, do some exploring here.

Location: Flows into the Columbia River south of Beverly in Grant County; see map B4, grid c2.

Species: Rainbow and brown trout.

Facilities: The nearest food, gas, tackle, and lodging are in Vantage.

Directions: Take I-90 to the east side of the Columbia River near Vantage and turn south onto Highway 26. Turn off Highway 26 as it cuts left, away from the river, bear right onto Highway 243, and continue down the Colum-

bia. Turn east (left) on Beverly/Crab Creek Road and take side roads to the north (left) for 10 miles to reach the creek.

Contact: Washington Department of Fish and Wildlife, Ephrata Office, 509/754-4624; Vantage KOA, 509/856-2230, website: www.vantagewa.com.

12 Scooteney Reservoir

Although the reservoir's open year-round, many anglers save Scooteney for their winter fishing adventures, since it offers very good ice fishing, especially for yellow perch. The perch are abundant and tend to run large, a perfect combination for anyone in search of the makings of a whole-hog fish fry. Ice anglers also catch some nice-sized crappies and an occasional walleye, usually by accident but sometimes by design. Standard fare for winter perch is a Swedish Pimple, Triple Teazer, or Crippled Herring with a single perch eye or small strip of perch skin on the hook.

In the spring and summer, anglers find fair numbers of bass around the edges of the reservoir, and areas with ample cover may turn up some good catches of bluegills and crappies. The perch fishing also remains good in spring and early summer.

Location: Southeast of Othello; see map B4, grid d6.

Species: Largemouth and smallmouth bass, walleye, yellow perch, black crappie, bluegill.

Facilities: Boat ramps are located on both sides of the reservoir, and a campground with RV sites, restrooms, and showers is on the west side. The closest food, gas, tackle, and lodging are in Othello, 12 miles north.

Directions: Take Highway 26 to Othello and turn south on Highway 17. Turn south (right) on Schoolaney Road and east (left) on Horseshoe Road to reach the west side of the reservoir. Continue past Schoolaney Road about three miles and take either of the next two right-hand turns off the highway to reach the reservoir's east side.

Contact: Washington Department of Fish and Wildlife, Ephrata Office, 509/754-4624; Paul's Desert Tackle, 509/269-4456.

13 Columbia River (Wenatchee to Crow Butte State Park)

Before planning any fishing trip to this long and varied portion of the Columbia, remember that it's every bit as much a series of reservoirs as it is a river. This stretch does include the last free-flowing section of the river, but it also includes dead-water impoundments behind Rock Island, Wanapum, Priest Rapids, McNary, and John Day Dams. There's so much water to fish—and so much angling variety and opportunity—that this portion of the Columbia is probably worthy of a book in its own right. On the other hand, you'll also find miles of water that are either not much worth fishing or that have been so lightly fished that little is known about the area. I'll try to hit the high points—the places and species that provide the most angling opportunity and are worth driving to from anywhere in the Evergreen State.

Steelheading is a big deal here, and some of the hottest steelhead fishing on the entire Columbia River system takes place between Priest Rapids Dam and McNary Dam. Thousands of these sea-run rainbow trout swarm into this middle stretch of the river in the fall, providing excellent fishing from September through December. Steelheaders on Lake Wallula, the impoundment behind McNary Dam, like to troll Hot Shots, Power Dive Minnows, Hot Lips Express, Wiggle Warts, and other diving plugs for their fish, not only during the daylight hours, but well into the autumn darkness. Luckily, you don't need great visibility to tell when a fish comes along, because they usually pound those plugs with all the subtlety of a runaway truck. If you'd

rather stand on the bank and drift fish for your fall steelies, you might want to visit the free-flowing stretch of river at Ringold several miles upstream from the Tri-Cities. A long gravel bar here provides room for plenty of anglers, and the fish often pass near enough to the east shore to be within easy casting range. Fresh roe clusters, Blue Fox, or Super Vibrax spinners are among the favorite strike getters. Boaters also fish this area for steelhead, and they hook fish both with drift tackle and by pulling the same kinds of plugs that work farther downriver.

The moving water above is the scene of some productive fall salmon fishing. This so-called Hanford Reach part of the river still has a good population of naturally spawning fall chinooks, some of them monster fish of 40 pounds and larger. Trolling large spinners and big diving plugs is one way to get them. Another is to position a boat over holding fish in some of the deeper pools and work a metal jig in front of their noses until they can't take it any more and pounce savagely on the dancing slab of shiny metal. If fishing the free-flowing stretch of this big river from a boat sounds like fun, please be advised that this is big, merciless water, and a boating mistake could cost you more than a cold dunking. Don't tackle the river unless you know what you're doing.

While the middle, free-flowing part of the Columbia is lightly explored by walleye anglers, the pools at the upper and lower ends of this stretch do have walleyes in catchable numbers. The portion immediately below McNary Dam is especially interesting, since it's here that both the Oregon and Washington state-record walleyes were caught. Both of these were monster fish of more than 18 pounds. Spring provides the best shot at a trophy-class walleye of 14 pounds or bigger, but this stretch of river provides good walleye fishing virtually throughout the year. Trolling

Power Dive Minnow plugs along the bottom is one of the more popular walleye-fishing techniques here, but anglers also catch them on trolled spinner-and-worm rigs or leadheads with plastic grubs bounced along the rocky bottom.

Lake Umatilla, the big impoundment behind John Day Dam, is a great place to explore for smallmouth bass. Besides having large numbers of these scrappy bronzebacks, this part of the river is home to some of the river's trophy smallmouths. Bass of four pounds and over, true lunkers of the smallmouth world, are caught with amazing regularity here. Some go for deep-diving crankbaits worked over and around submerged rock piles and underwater ledges, while others are taken on leadheads adorned with small plastic grubs. This is a good place to fish a one-eighth-ounce leadhead jig with a three-inch Berkley Power Grub in the productive pumpkinseed color. Columbia River smallmouths just can't seem to resist this little brown grub that looks an awful lot like a crawdad when twitched and hopped along the rocks and gravel.

The fishing can get tough along the Columbia when the cold eastern Washington winter sets in, but wintertime is prime if you happen to be a whitefish angler. If there's such a thing as an overlooked fishery on this big river, it has to be the vast whitefish population that congregates in preparation for spawning during the late fall and winter of every year. The upper end of the Hanford Reach is especially popular with whitefish anglers, and many of them catch quick 15-fish limits here throughout the winter. Small, sparsely tied flies tipped with maggots, goldenrod grubs, Power Wigglers, or stone fly larvae account for most of the fish.

White sturgeon are the monsters of the Columbia, and this stretch of the river has its share of them. The best sturgeon fishing is below McNary and John Day Dams, and both of these areas have good numbers of oversized fish that provide great angling memories between the time they're hooked and the time they're carefully released back into the river to fight again. One September morning a few years ago, I caught an impressive 8.5-footer below McNary. I bragged a little about my lunker-catching skills to my fishing companions and then stood by as they caught and released sturgeon of 10.5, 11, and 13 feet. There's no justice when an 8.5-foot fish turns out to be the smallest of the day. Anchoring smelt, shrimp, even shad baits to the bottom is the surest way of hooking a big sturgeon below the two dams. Boat fishing is productive below McNary, but don't try it unless you know what you're doing and understand the power and potential danger of anchoring in heavy river currents.

A productive bank-fishing spot is located about a mile downstream from John Day Dam, just above Maryhill State Park.

Location: From Wenatchee downstream to John Day Dam; see map B4, grid e4.

Species: Steelhead, chinook salmon, sturgeon, smallmouth bass, walleye, mountain whitefish.

Facilities: This stretch of the Columbia and its impoundments offers a wide selection of boat-ramp facilities:

- **Rock Island Hydro Park:** Working downstream from Rock Island Dam, the first ramp is at Rock Island Hydro Park, about two miles south of East Wenatchee on Highway 28. Managed by the Chelan County Public Utilities District, it's a one-lane ramp wide enough to allow two boats at a time if they were friends in a hurry to get on or off the water (and both knew how to back a trailer).
- **Crescent Bar Ramp:** Next is the Grant County PUD's ramp at Crescent Bar, off Highway 28 about six miles west of Quincy. This two-lane concrete ramp has loading floats and gets a lot of use during the sum-

mer months. There's a $7 daily fee for parking here, $15 for overnight parking, with a $50 annual permit available.

- **Sunland Estates:** Downstream a few miles is the Department of Fish and Wildlife's ramp at Sunland Estates. This is a one-lane concrete-plank ramp with nearby parking for about 35 cars and trailers. The $10 WDFW access decal is required here.
- **Ginko State Park:** The next ramp is on the Kittitas County (west) side of the river, at Ginko State Park. It's a one-lane hard-surface ramp with limited parking nearby. There's a $4 launch fee here.
- **Vantage Ramp:** About a mile farther downstream on the Kittitas County side of the river is the Wanapum/Vantage boat ramp, right alongside I-90 at the west end of the Vantage Bridge. This concrete ramp has a launch float and room for over 50 cars and trailers in the paved parking lot. It's a little strange in that it has a two-lane ramp by the float and a third one about 50 feet away from the others. Launching is free at this Kittitas County facility.
- **Wanapum State Park:** On the same side of the river about three miles downstream is the two-lane concrete-plank ramp at Wanapum State Park. It has a loading float and lots of parking, and the launch fee is $4 unless you're a registered park guest.
- **Getty's Cove:** Also on the west side of the river a short distance past the state park is Getty's Cove Resort, which has a one-lane paved boat ramp. A launch fee is charged here.
- **Upstream Wanapum Dam Ramp:** The next ramp is on the Grant County (east) side of the river just upstream from Wanapum Dam, off Highway 243. Managed by the Grant County Public Utility District, this single-lane concrete ramp has a loading float and parking for about a dozen cars and trailers.

- **Downstream Wanapum Dam Ramp:** Just downstream from Wanapum Dam on the Grant County side is another county PUD ramp, this one a one-lane concrete ramp with a large, gravel parking area.
- **Buckshot Ranch Boat Ramp:** The next ramp, about four miles north of Priest Rapids Dam, is another Grant County PUD launch. It's at the Buckshot Ranch site and has two lanes, both concrete-ramp construction, with a large, gravel parking area.
- **Desert Aire Ramp:** Two miles south, off Desert Aire Road, is yet another Grant County PUD ramp, this one with two concrete lanes and a loading float. There's a $3 launch fee here.
- **Vernita Bridge Ramp:** Nine miles downstream from Priest Rapids Dam is the Highway 24 bridge at Vernita, where the Department of Fish and Wildlife has a natural-surface ramp about four lanes wide and a gravel parking area with room for about 50 cars and trailers. Although it's rather rough and primitive, this ramp gets a lot of use during the fall chinook salmon fishing season. You need a $10 WDFW access decal to use this ramp.
- **White Bluffs Ramp:** The next ramp downstream is the Department of Fish and Wildlife ramp (don't forget that WDFW access decal) at White Bluffs, in Franklin County (east side of the river) about 18 miles downstream from Vernita. It's a very good two-lane concrete ramp at the site of the old White Bluffs Ferry Terminal.
- **Wahluke Ramp:** Also on the Franklin County side of the river is the one-lane gravel ramp at the Department of Wildlife's Wahluke Wildlife Area, 11 miles northwest of Pasco via Taylor Flats and Ringold Spring Roads. Steelhead and salmon anglers use this one extensively. You'll need to display that WDFW access decal here and at the next ramp downstream.

- **Ringold Springs Ramp:** Next is the Department of Fish and Wildlife ramp at Ringold Springs, another gravel one-laner used mostly by anglers.
- **Grove's Park:** It's about 14 miles downstream to the next ramp, this one on the Benton County (west) side of the river at Groves Park, off George Washington Way in Richland. This Richland Parks and Recreation Department launch is a good one, with a four-lane concrete ramp, loading float, and spaces for about 50 cars and trailers.
- **Howard Amon Park:** Three miles south, also off George Washington Way, is the Richland Parks and Recreation Department's Howard Amon Park, which has two sets of boat ramps, one at the north end of the park and one at the south. Between the two they provide five lanes of concrete-surface ramps, with loading floats available at the northern site. There's room to park perhaps 100 cars and trailers near the two ramps.
- **Columbia Point Ramp:** Another mile south on George Washington Way is Columbia Point, a Richland Parks and Recreation facility with a four-lane concrete ramp, three floats, and parking for about 150 cars and trailers.
- **Wye Park Ramp:** Richland's Wye Park is next, with a two-lane concrete ramp and loading float. It's on Columbia Drive, north of Highway 240. Across the river on the Franklin County side is Chiawana Park. Reached via Court Street and Road 88 west from Pasco, this park has a two-lane concrete ramp and loading float, with parking for about 30 cars and trailers.
- **Columbia Park West Ramp:** Back on the west side of the river, the next ramp is at Columbia Park West, a Richland Parks and Recreation facility with a two-lane concrete ramp, loading floats, and parking for about 100 cars and trailers.

- **Columbia Park Ramp:** This park, a Kennewick Parks and Recreation Department site, offers a huge boat-launching facility. Located just off Highway 240 at Edison Street, it has an eight-lane concrete ramp, loading floats, and a gravel parking area with room for over 100 cars and trailers.
- **Road 54 Ramp:** Across the river in Pasco is the U.S. Army Corps of Engineers ramp off Sylvester Street and Road 54. It's a two-lane concrete ramp with a gravel parking area that holds 30 cars and trailers. It's seen better days but is still very usable.
- **Pasco Boat Basin:** Off Fourth Avenue near the east end of Pasco is the Pasco Boat Basin and its four-lane concrete ramp. This is an Army Corps of Engineers site with a loading float and room to park about 20 cars and trailers.
- **Metz Marina:** Across the river is the Port of Kennewick's Metz Marina, where there's a four-lane concrete boat ramp with loading floats and room to park about three dozen cars and trailers. A hoist is also located nearby.
- **Sacajawea State Park:** On the north side of the Snake River mouth is Sacajawea State Park, with a two-lane concrete ramp and loading floats located in a protected cove. The launch fee here is $4, with a yearly permit available for $40.
- **Hood Park/Hood Park Boat Basin:** Two Corps of Engineers ramps on the south shore of the Snake River also provide access to Lake Wallula and the Columbia. Hood Park is equipped with three lanes of concrete ramps and two loading floats, and the nearby Hood Park Boat Basin offers a one-lane concrete ramp and one loading float.
- **Two Rivers Park:** Straight across the Columbia from the mouth of the Snake is the two-lane concrete ramp at Benton County's Two Rivers Park.

- **McNary Wildlife Refuge:** Near the southwest corner of McNary Island, on the east side of the Columbia is the U.S. Fish and Wildlife Service's boat ramp that serves the McNary National Wildlife Refuge. It's a one-lane concrete-plank ramp in a shallow cove where the water level sometimes drops below the end of the ramp. It's accessible via gravel roads leading west off U.S. 12 about eight miles south of Pasco.
- **Madame Dorian Park:** About 15 miles south of Pasco is Madame Dorian Park, in the large bay where the Walla Walla River enters the Columbia from the east. The Army Corps of Engineers ramp here is a one-lane gravel ramp with a gravel parking area that holds about two dozen cars and trailers.
- **North McNary Ramp:** It's more than 20 miles downstream to the next ramp on the Washington side of the river just east of McNary Dam. The Army Corps of Engineers' North McNary ramp has a single concrete lane and parking for about 80 cars and trailers.
- **Plymouth Park:** Just downstream from McNary Dam is another Corp of Engineers ramp at Plymouth Park. It's a wide, two-lane concrete ramp with loading floats and parking for about 20 cars and trailers.
- **Paterson Ramp:** About 12 miles west is the Paterson access on the Umatilla National Wildlife Refuge. The U.S. Fish and Wildlife Service ramp here is a natural-surface, gently sloping gravel bar with room to park along the beach nearby. There's nothing here in the way of facilities.
- **Crow Butte State Park:** Ten miles downstream (west) is Crow Butte State Park, where there's a three-lane hard-surface ramp with parking for about 50 cars and trailers. The launch fee here is $4 round-trip, with a $40 annual permit available from the State Parks and Recreation Commis-

sion. If you use any of the Washington Department of Fish and Wildlife ramps upriver, remember that a $10 WDFW access decal is required. (I keep reminding you.)

Directions: Highway 28 between Wenatchee and Quincy provides access to the east side of the river between Wenatchee and Crescent Bar. To reach the east side of the river downstream from Vantage, turn south off I-90 on Highway 243. Turn south on Highway 24 at Vernita to reach the popular stretch of river around the Vernita Bridge. Turn south off Highway 24 onto Seagull Road and then west on Road 170 to reach the popular steelhead-fishing stretch of river at Ringold. Roads out of Richland and Pasco provide access to the stretch of the Columbia between Ringold and the Tri-Cities. The best access here is via South Columbia River Road, which runs up the east side of the river from Pasco. Access on the east side of the Columbia from the Tri-Cities to Wallula is via U.S. 12. To reach the stretch of river between McNary Dam and John Day Dam, take Highway 14 east from Wishram or west from U.S. 395.

Contact: Crescent Bar Resort, 509/787-1511; Vantage KOA, 509/856-2230, website: www.vantagewa.com; Desert Aire Motel, 509/932-4300; Maryhill State Park, 509/773-5007; Columbia Park Campground, 509/783-7311; Sacajawea State Park (no overnight camping), 509/545-2361; Crow Butte State Park, 509/875-2644; Washington State Parks and Recreation Commission, 360/902-8844 (information) or 800/452-5687 (reservations).

14 Emma Lake

Open year-round, Emma provides good panfish action throughout much of the year. Spring and fall are excellent times to catch perch and crappies, and both can also be caught through the winter ice. Use small jigs in white combinations or all white for crappies, and whatever you like for perch. In summer some folks fish

Washington's Top Ice-Fishing Lakes

Did you know that Washington offers some decent ice-fishing oportunities? Many anglers, especially those living on the west side of the Cascades, have no idea that fishing on ice can be, well, hot for several weeks every winter. About 20 lakes and reservoirs scattered around the central and far-eastern parts of Washington offer the best chance for through-the-ice success. Here's the rundown on where they are and what they have to offer:

Sidley Lake: This 100-acre lake, located a mile from the town of Molson, near the Washington–British Columbia border, is a good winter trout producer. The rainbows range from 7 to 17 inches and are caught on salmon eggs and marshmallows. Sidley is open year-around and has a two-trout limit.

Palmer Lake: Burbot (also called freshwater ling) and yellow perch draw anglers to this 2,000-acre lake, four miles north of Loomis in Okanogan County. Set-lines are legal for burbot here, and most set-liners use gobs of night crawlers or pieces of flesh from suckers or other rough fish. For perch, a small leadhead jig with a perch eye on the hook works best.

Campbell, Cougar, and Davis Lakes: All three small lakes have winter seasons and provide fair to good fishing for rainbow trout of 10 to 14 inches. Salmon eggs, egg-and-marshmallow, and egg-and-corn combinations do most of the damage. The three are located a few miles east of Winthrop in Okanogan County.

Roses Lake: Anglers fish red eggs on the bottom here for rainbows up to 18 inches. Brown trout and panfish also are available. Roses is located about a mile north of Manson in Chelan County.

Fish Lake: This Chelan County lake, located about 15 miles north of Leavenworth, offers an interesting mix of warm-water species and trout for ice anglers. Big perch are common, but the lake also has rainbow and trophy brown trout in good supply.

Banks Lake: At 25,000 acres, Banks is one of the state's biggest ice-fishing waters. It extends for miles along the Grant-Douglas county border, and when its sheltered coves and bays begin to freeze, they offer some of the state's best ice fishing. Banks produces yellow perch by the thousands, as well as good catches of crappies and rainbows. Lake whitefish, walleyes, burbot, and even smallmouth bass are also caught through the ice.

Evergeen Reservoir: Yellow perch are big and abundant in Evergreen, which covers about 240 acres southwest of Quincy in Grant County. The standard wintertime perch-fishing method, bouncing bottom with a jig or other small lure with a perch eye on the hook, works best here.

Potholes Reservoir: This sprawling, 25,000-acre impoundment provides a variety of ice-fishing opportunities. Most of the catch is yellow perch, which sometimes reach 12 inches and weigh close to a pound. Catch them on Triple Teazers and other small, flashy lures, fished with a perch eye on the hook. Crappies are caught on plastic leadheads in yellow, purple, or red and white. Walleyes, rainbow trout, and lake whitefish are also caught through the ice at Potholes. The big reservoir is 10 miles south of Moses Lake in Grant County.

Soda Lake: This 150-acre lake, located just southeast of Potholes Reservoir, is best known for its crappie and walleye fishing. Soda also gives up some good catches of perch, rainbow trout, and husky lake whitefish.

Lind Coulee Wasteway: Lind Coulee is connected to the southeast corner of Potholes and offers much the same ice-fishing opportunity. You'll find excellent perch fishing around the islands between the O'Sullivan Road Bridge and the main reservoir, while crappies and pan-size trout are found near the end of the wasteway's north arm. Lind Coulee also gives up a few walleyes and bass during the winter.

Scooteney Reservoir: Scooteney is a 680-acre impoundment that provides fair to good fishing for yellow perch and other warm-water species. It has a year-round season and is located 12 miles southeast of Othello in Franklin County.

Fourth of July Lake: Located in northeastern Adams County about two miles south of Sprague, Fourth of July provides about 75 acres of productive rainbow trout fishing. Most of the rainbows are 8 to 11 inches, with a fair number to 15 inches.

Hog Canyon Lake: Hog Canyon is located about 10 miles east of Sprague, in southwest Spokane County. Traditionally one of eastern Washington's top wintertime trout lakes, it gives up lots of 10- to 12-inch rainbows.

Eloika Lake: Eloika has something for everyone, but perch, crappies, and a few largemouth bass make up most of the wintertime catch. This 660-acre lake in northern Spokane County has a huge population of perch and good-sized crappies, and both are caught on mini jigs and other small lures, fished near the bottom. Add a perch eye, maggot, or piece of worm to the hook for perch.

Bead Lake: At 720 acres, Bead is one of northeast Washington's biggest lakes. Burbot are the most popular targets of most ice anglers here, most are caught on night crawlers or strips of scrap-fish meat hung on the hooks of large spoons and bounced along bottom. Anglers also catch a few Mackinaw, or lake trout, through the ice at Bead, usually on the spoon-and-bait rigs fished for burbot. The lake is located eight miles north of Newport, in Pend Oreille County.

Hatch Lake: This 35-acre lake, located about five miles southeast of Colville in Stevens County, has produced a lot of rainbow trout over the years, all of them caught in winter. The season runs December through March.

Williams Lake: Rainbows to about 14 inches make up the catch at Williams, and most are caught on red salmon eggs, Power Bait, or egg-and-marshmallow combos. It's a 40-acre lake, located about 15 miles north of Colville in Stevens County.

Emma all night, catching fairly large catfish for their efforts. The lake also has largemouth and smallmouth bass, some of them growing to impressive size.

Location: Along the lower Snake River northeast of Pasco; see map B4, grid f8.

Species: Yellow perch, largemouth and smallmouth bass, crappie, channel and brown bullhead catfish.

Facilities: There's nothing here but the lake itself. Food, gas, tackle, and lodging are available in the Tri-Cities.

Directions: Take Pasco-Kahlotus Road northeast out of Pasco for 16 miles and turn east (right) on Murphy Road. Drive three miles and bear to the right at the Y intersection to reach the north end of the lake.

Contact: Motyka's Bait & Tackle, 509/375-6028; Hole in the Wall, 509/783-1111, email: scott@holewall.com.

▯5 Dalton Lake

Not very well known throughout the state, Dalton is a 30-acre lake that has a lot to offer. Although stocked with hatchery rainbows every year, it's the warm-water fish that really steal the show. Whether you like fat bluegills, feisty crappies, or tasty perch, you'll find lots of them here. Bass anglers working around the edge of the lake catch both largemouths and smallmouths in good numbers, and there are some big channel catfish for the benefit of anglers who like to fish at night. The lake is open year-round and is a good winter ice-fishing spot.

Location: Northeast of Pasco; see map B4, grid f8.

Species: Rainbow trout, largemouth and smallmouth bass, channel catfish, yellow perch, crappie.

Facilities: There's a boat ramp at the west end of the lake and enough room to park RVs, which some people do if staying the night. Food, gas, tackle, and lodging are available in the Tri-Cities.

Directions: Take Pasco-Kahlotus Road northeast from Pasco about 14 miles to Herman Road and turn east (right). The lake is at the end of Herman Road about a mile off the highway.

Contact: Motyka's Bait & Tackle, 509/375-6028; Hole in the Wall, 509/783-1111, email: scott@holewall.com.

▯6 Lower Snake River

The steelheading and the smallmouth fishing are the two main draws on this part of the Columbia River's biggest tributary, and one takes off just about the time that the other begins to slow. Smallmouths come to life here as the water warms in early spring, and by June the lower end of the Snake is just about as good a place as any to cast crankbaits or bounce leadheads along the bottom for smallies in the half-pound to five-pound class. As the water cools and the bassing drops off around the end of September, the steelhead start showing up in waves, and by October steelhead fever has made just about everyone forget about bass for a while. Steelhead catches on the Snake below Lower Monumental Dam have ranged about 1,300 to 2,000 fish a year, with the months of October, November, and December providing the bulk of the action. As in other big-water steelhead fisheries throughout the Columbia/Snake system, trolling various diving plugs is a popular and productive fishing method.

Location: Joins the Columbia River southeast of Pasco; see map B4, grid g7.

Species: Steelhead, smallmouth bass, largemouth bass, channel catfish, white sturgeon.

Facilities: There are plenty of places to launch a boat along the lower reaches of the Snake and its reservoirs:

• **Hood Park Boat Basin:** Working upstream from the river mouth on the Walla Walla County (south) side of the river, the first ramp is at the Hood Park Boat Basin, almost under the Highway 12 bridge, about a mile upstream from where the Snake joins the Columbia. This U.S. Army Corps of Engineers launch is a single-lane ramp with a loading float. Unless they've done some grading since the last two times I was there, the road to this ramp has about a million chuckholes and bumps; take it easy.

- **Hood Park:** Just upstream is the main boat ramp at Hood Park, a three-lane concrete-plank ramp with several loading floats and lots of parking. This is a very good ramp, suitable for boats of almost any size.
- **Charbonneau Park:** About nine miles upstream above Ice Harbor Dam is Charbonneau Park, where there's a four-lane concrete ramp with loading floats and lots of parking. It gets lots of use but is protected by a rock jetty and can be used in virtually all water and weather conditions.
- **Fishhook Park:** Seven miles upstream on Lake Sacajawea is Fishhook Park, with its two-lane concrete boat ramp. Ten years ago this was one of the best ramps on the Snake, but it has seen lots of use and is beginning to show its age. Still, you can launch most boats here, and there's plenty of room to park.
- **Matthew Ramp:** The next ramp on the south side of the river is some distance upstream at Matthew, just two miles below Lower Monumental Dam. Like the others mentioned so far, this is a Corps of Engineers facility, with a one-lane concrete ramp, loading float, and parking for about 30 cars and trailers. This steep ramp is protected from wind and rough water by a pair of rock jetties, one upstream and one downstream.
- **Sacajawea State Park:** Back to the mouth of the Snake, on the Franklin County (north) side, the first ramp is at Sacajawea State Park, located right at the point of land where the Snake meets the Columbia. This two-lane concrete ramp has loading floats and is located in a calm bay where river currents and wind have minimal influence. There's a $4 launch fee here, with a $40 annual permit available from State Parks and Recreation Commission headquarters.

- **Ice Harbor Dam Ramp:** Next is the Corps of Engineers ramp just above Ice Harbor Dam, a two-lane concrete ramp with a loading float and lots of room to park in a large gravel lot.
- **Levey Park:** Three miles upstream is Levey Park, a Corps of Engineers site with a single-lane concrete-plank ramp and loading float. This park and its boat ramp are closed in the winter.
- **Windust Park:** Three miles downstream from Lower Monumental Dam is Windust Park, with a less-than-inviting name but a decent two-lane boat ramp. One lane is gravel, the other concrete. There are no loading floats at this Corps of Engineers ramp.

Picnic areas and other amenities are available at Hood Park, Charbonneau Park, Fishhook Park, Sacajawea State Park, Levey Park, and Windust Park. RV and tent sites for campers are available at Charbonneau Park, Fishhook Park, Sacajawea State Park, and Windust Park. Food, gas, lodging, marinas, and other facilities are available in Kennewick, Pasco, and Richland.

Directions: Drive east from the Tri-Cities on Highway 124 to reach the lower end of the river. Upstream sections of the river are accessible from the town of Kahlotus by driving south for seven miles on Highway 260 or for 10 miles on Highway 261.

Contact: Sacajawea State Park, 509/545-2361; Washington State Parks and Recreation Commission, 360/902-8844 (information) or 800/452-5687 (reservations); Tri-Cities Visitor and Convention Bureau, 800/254-5824; Motyka's Bait & Tackle, 509/375-6028; Hole in the Wall, 509/783-1111, email: scott@holewall.com.

🔟 Lower Yakima River

Unlike the blue-ribbon trout waters upstream from Yakima, this lower stretch of the river meanders slowly through the flat river valley, warming fairly fast in the spring and summer and offering a haven for warm-water species. Clean rock and gravel make up much of the river bottom throughout this stretch, providing perfect habitat for smallmouth bass, and they thrive in these waters. Although the Yakima doesn't get much fishing pressure, those who do fish this part of the river tell lots of stories about the huge smallmouths that live here. The extreme lower end of the Yakima also has largemouths, but this river doesn't offer a whole lot of prime cover for largemouth bass.

It does, however, suit channel catfish very well, and anglers have made some good catfish catches here over the years. Casting from the bank with chicken livers, night crawlers, and foul-smelling stinkbaits produces some channel cats of 10 pounds and over, with the best fishing usually occurring in June and July.

On the cold-water species side of the coin, the Yakima has been closed to the taking of steelhead in recent years, and that situation probably won't change for the better in the near future.

Location: Flows into the Columbia south of Richland; see map B4, grid f3.

Species: Smallmouth and largemouth bass, channel catfish.

Facilities: Launch ramps on the lower Yakima include:

- **Harlan Landing:** Starting just north of Yakima, the first launch site on the river is the single-lane concrete ramp at Harlan Landing, on the east side of the river at the mouth of the Naches. Take Rest Haven Road off I-82 to reach it.
- **Sarg Hubbard Landing:** Small boats can be hand-carried to the west bank of the river at Sarg Hubbard Landing, just south of Terrace Heights Drive and east of I-82 in Yakima.
- **Robertson Landing:** Just north of Highway 24 near Yakima Meadows Race Track is Robertson Landing, where it's easy to get boats into the river from the east bank. Century Landing is also on the east side of the river near the I-82 bridge at Union Gap.
- **Century Landing:** This is a one-lane concrete ramp.
- **Mellis Road Ramp:** Another one-lane concrete ramp, this one maintained by the Department of Fish and Wildlife, lies just south of Union Gap, off Mellis Road. You must have a $10 WDFW access decal on your vehicle to use this ramp.
- **I-82/Parker Exit Ramp:** Next is the natural-surface Department of Fish and Wildlife ramp off I-82 at the Parker exit a few miles south of Union Gap.
- **Zillah Road Ramp:** A one-lane concrete ramp managed by the Department of Fish and Wildlife is located on Zillah Road at the south end of town in Zillah.
- **South Emerald Road Ramp:** The next ramp is about 14 (river) miles downstream, southwest of Sunnyside. This Department of Wildlife ramp, located off South Emerald Road, is a one-laner with a natural surface that sometimes gets muddy and difficult to use.
- **Midvale Road Ramp:** Five miles downstream is the Bureau of Reclamation's Sulfur Creek ramp, located at the end of Midvale Road, between Sunnyside and Mabton. This is a steep, rough launch that requires dragging or carrying boats over the bank to the river.
- **Gannon Launch Site:** Another mile and a half downstream is the Gannon launch site, a one-lane gravel ramp managed by Washington Department of Fish and Wildlife where trailer boats can be launched. Turn south on Midvale Road in Sunnyside, left

on Alexander Road, and right on Highway 241, following it about four miles to the river and the ramp.

- **Riverfront Park:** Prosser's two-lane concrete ramp is managed by the Prosser Parks and Recreation Department.

- **Benton City Ramp:** From Prosser it's more than 15 river miles down to the next ramp, the Department of Fish and Wildlife site at Benton City. This natural-surface ramp is in an area of fairly fast current and is best used for hand-launching smaller boats. A $10 WDFW access decal is required to use the public launch areas maintained by the Department of Fish and Wildlife.

- **Horn Rapids:** From Benton City the Yakima turns sharply to the north, running in that direction for about 10 miles before twisting back to the southeast, toward Richland. Near that bend in the river is Horn Rapids, site of a two-lane concrete-plank ramp managed by Benton County's Parks and Recreation Department. This is one of the best ramps on the river, and the last one on the Yakima itself.

- **Tri-Cities-area Boat Ramps:** The lower end of the river is best reached from Tri-Cities-area boat ramps on the Columbia. (See listing 13 in this chapter for Columbia River ramp locations.)

Perhaps the best-known facility along the river is the Yakima Greenway Trail in Yakima, one of eastern Washington's best riverside trails for hiking, running, biking, skating, and other recreation. Several parks and playgrounds are scattered along the 10-mile trail throughout Yakima. Picnic areas along the river include those at Harlan Landing, Sarg Hubbard Park, Sherman Park, Robertson Landing, Century Landing, Riverfront Park in Prosser, and Horn Rapids Park. The Yakima KOA campground and Yakima Sportsman State Park are both located near the river.

Food, gas, and lodging are available in Yakima, Granger, Sunnyside, Grandview, Prosser, and the Tri-Cities. Food, gas, tackle, and lodging are available in Yakima, Granger, Sunnyside, Grandview, Prosser, and the Tri-Cities.

Directions: Drive east from Yakima to Granger on I-82, paralleling the river most of the 24 miles. Take Granger-Emerald Road east from Granger to parallel several miles of the river downstream of Granger. Continuing downstream, the stretch of river between Sunnyside and Prosser can be reached by driving south off I-82 on Highway 241 about seven miles to the river or south from Grandview on Euclid Road. I-82 parallels the river again along the 14 miles between Prosser and Benton City. Drive north from Benton City on Highway 225 for 10 miles to fish some of the lowest stretches of the Yakima.

Contact: Motyka's Bait & Tackle, 509/375-6028; Hole in the Wall, 509/783-1111, email: scott@holewall.com; Chinook Sporting Goods, 509/452-8205; Sunnyside Wildlife Area, 509/837-7644.

18 Touchet River

The trout fishery downstream from Dayton is primarily a put-and-take effort for hatchery rainbows and browns, but it provides a lot of fun for spring and early summer anglers. Things change dramatically above Dayton, where selective fishery regulations and a two-fish limit protect a largely native rainbow trout population.

The Touchet also has a fall/winter steelhead season downstream from the Wolf Fork bridge near Dayton. Although they can keep only marked hatchery steelies, anglers here manage to catch anywhere from 200 to 400 fish a year during this winter fishery. Depending on weather and water conditions, the catch may be spread out well from December through March. But when winter conditions are nasty, the best fishing is later in

March and April, after the ice has melted and the water has warmed a little.

Location: Joins the Walla Walla River at the town of Touchet; see map B4, grid g9.

Species: Rainbow and brown trout, steelhead.

Facilities: Food, gas, tackle, and lodging are available in Waitsburg and Dayton. Lewis and Clark Trail State Park is right along the river between Waitsburg and Dayton, and it has a limited number of campsites, restrooms, and showers.

Directions: Take U.S. 12 to Touchet and turn north on Touchet Road to reach the lower 12 miles of the river. The middle stretch of the Touchet, between Harsha and Waitsburg, is paralleled by Highway 124. To reach the upper part of the main Touchet, take U.S. 12 east from Waitsburg or west from Dayton. To reach the river's north and south forks, drive southeast out of Dayton on North Fork Touchet Road or South Fork Touchet Road.

Contact: Lewis and Clark Trail State Park, 509/337-6457; Washington State Parks and Recreation Commission, 360/902-8844 (information) or 800/452-5687 (reservations).

19 Walla Walla River

The mouth and lower reaches of the Walla Walla produce some of Washington's biggest catfish every summer, with the best fishing usually occurring in June and July. This area, in fact, has produced some whopping channel cats over the years, including at least a couple of former state-record fish. Night fishing with chicken livers, night crawlers, stinkbait, and other nasty little snacks accounts for the biggest fish and the best catches.

West-siders who think they have a stranglehold on the state's best steelhead fishing might be surprised to learn that the Walla Walla is also a fine steelhead stream, giving up as many as 1,000 steelies a year. The runs come on strong in October and provide surprisingly consistent action through the winter and into March. Techniques that work for drift anglers in western Washington will also do the trick here.

Location: Joins the Columbia River south of Wallula; see map B4, grid h9.

Species: Steelhead, rainbow trout, channel catfish.

Facilities: Food, gas, motels, RV parks, and other amenities are available in Walla Walla.

Directions: Take U.S. 12 east from the Tri-Cities for 14 miles or west from Walla Walla for five miles to parallel much of the river's north side.

Contact: Motyka's Bait & Tackle, 509/375-6028; Hole in the Wall, 509/783-1111, email: scott@holewall.com.

CHAPTER B5:
SNAKE RIVER

A SMALLMOUTH CATCH ON THE **SNAKE** RIVER

Map B5

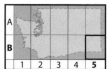

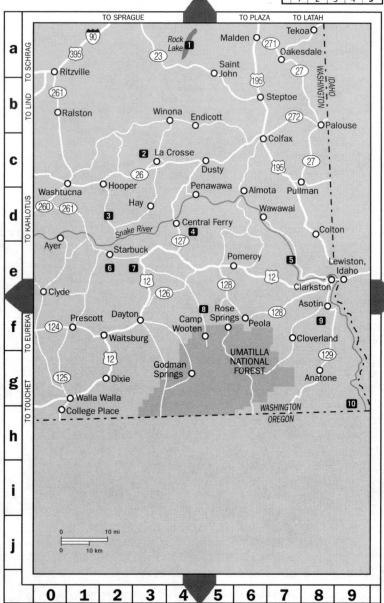

Chapter B5: Snake River

Like the Olympic Peninsula at the opposite corner of the state, Snake River country is considered by some Washingtonians to be a desolate outpost, with few people, a handful of small towns, and a good deal of land where there's little or no human activity for long periods of time. The setting is rural and its residents are conservative. It's a place where county inspectors, state biologists, and federal land managers are about as popular as venereal disease. But low population densities and conservative politics are the only parallels between the northwest and southeast corners of Washington; in many ways, they couldn't be more different. There's no ocean here to keep the air cool in summer and warm in winter, so moderate weather is something that occurs for only a few weeks in April and September. But if you like to hunt and fish, this is heaven, especially if your idea of a good day outdoors is one where you have things pretty much to yourself. Much of the fishing here is river fishing, unless you count the reservoirs, which are nothing more than slow spots on the rivers caused by dams. There are lots of smallmouth bass, channel catfish, rainbow trout, and other species you'd expect to find here, and some you might not expect. The steelhead fishing on the Snake and Grande Ronde, for example, can be very good, considering the fact that you're hundreds of miles from the Pacific Ocean. You may have to travel a few miles from one fishing hole to the next, but chances are good you won't find anyone else around when you get there.

◨ Rock Lake

This narrow, seven-mile-long lake is a long way from any of eastern Washington's major population centers, so it's a good place for getting away from the crowds. Unfortunately, you can also get away from the fish at Rock Lake, depending on your timing. The best fishing is when the lake is at its clearest early in the spring season and again in the fall. During the summer when irrigation runoff is heavy, much of the dirty water ends up in Rock Lake, lowering visibility and just plain taking some of the fun out of visiting this place.

The lake is stocked with rainbows and browns, some of which grow to impressive size, but better places can be found a few miles north if you want fast trout action. (Williams, Fishtrap, and Amber Lakes come to mind; see numbers 8, 55, and 56 in chapter A5). Anglers occasionally pick off a big brown or mature rainbow in the fall or early winter near the upper end of the lake. These trout are presumably moving up into Rock Creek to attempt spawning. At other times of year they can be caught by casting all the usual baits from the bank or by deep trolling with downriggers and leaded line. Gang trolls with bait are popular, as are Carey Special flies and some of the smaller Rapalas.

Bass fishing is a good bet, especially in the bays along the east side or on the shallow flats where largemouths congregate to gorge on crawdads. Anything in a crayfish finish should work well in these spots.

Although much of the lake is very deep, be careful about buzzing around parts of the lake with which you aren't familiar. There are some shallow spots where you might not expect them, and you can really do a job on the prop or the lower unit of your outboard motor if you don't pay attention.

For a lake that doesn't get all that much attention from anglers or anyone else, Rock seems to have a lot of myths and legends surrounding it. Depending on who's talking, you might hear that the lake is haunted by the ghosts of Indians who used to camp near its south end, or that a train once derailed and plunged to the bottom of the deep lake, and that sometimes you can still hear the sound of the moaning engine or the wail of its steam whistle rising from the depths. Still another story is that the lake has some kind of resident monster that occasionally picks off an unwitting swimmer or farm animal. I hope that last one's true, and that we might be able to communicate with the thing and train it to go for a few of the bozos on personal watercraft who like to give anglers a hard time.

Location: Northwest of St. John; see map B5, grid a4.

Species: Rainbow and brown trout, largemouth bass, crappie, yellow perch, brown bullhead catfish.

Facilities: A one-lane gravel ramp with a parking area large enough for about 30 cars and trailers is at the south end of the lake. It's managed by the State Department of Fish and Wildlife. A $10 WDFW access decal is required to use the public launch areas maintained by the Washington Department of Fish and Wildlife. Food and gas are available in St. John. For lodging you'll have to go to Cheney or Sprague.

Directions: Take Highway 23 south from Sprague or west from St. John to Ewan and turn north on Rock Lake Road, which leads about three miles to the lake.

Contact: Washington Department of Fish and Wildlife, Spokane regional office, 509/456-4082; Four Seasons Campground, 509/257-2332; Purple Sage Motel, 509/257-2507; Sprague Lake Resort, 509/257-2864.

◪ Union Flat Creek

Planted rainbows provide fair to good spring and early summer fishing on this long creek that enters Washington near the small town of Uniontown and flows into the Palouse River west of LaCrosse. It doesn't have any special regulations, so feel free to fish it with bait, hardware, or flies. You'll need landowner permission to fish some of the creek, but roads paralleling its banks make for easy access in most places.

Location: Joins the Palouse River west of LaCrosse in Whitman County; see map B5, grid c3.

Species: Rainbow trout.

Facilities: Food, gas, tackle, and lodging are available in Colfax and Pullman.

Directions: Drive west from Colfax on Highway 26 and turn north (right) on Union Flat Creek Road to parallel about 20 miles of the creek. Driving south out of Colfax on Almota Road and turning east (left) on Union Flat Creek Road will get you to several miles of the upper creek between Highway 26 and the town of Colton.

Contact: Tiffany's River Inn, 509/397-3208.

3 Palouse River

Although the main Palouse and its north and south forks wind through more than 125 miles of eastern Washington's rolling countryside, making it one of the state's longest rivers, much of that length has little to offer serious anglers. The river is downright beautiful in places, especially around Palouse Falls just a few miles upstream from the river's confluence with the Snake at Lyons Ferry. But even though the Palouse is open to year-round fishing, there isn't much angling activity. Night fishing around the mouth of the river produces a few channel catfish, some of them of fairly respectable size, and there are some smallmouth bass to be caught in the lower river, but it seems as if the other 122 miles of river are more for looking at than for fishing.

Location: Joins the Snake River at Lyons Ferry on the Columbia–Walla Walla county line; see map B5, grid d2.

Species: Channel catfish, smallmouth bass.

Facilities: There are places to fish or even carry a canoe or small raft to the river off Main Street in Palouse, off Brown Road near Elberton, off Highway 26 just west of Colfax, off Endicott–St. John Road north of Endicott, off Endicott West at Winona, and off Highway 26 and adjoining side roads both east and west of Hooper. There's a two-lane concrete ramp at Lyon's Ferry State Park, where the Palouse River joins the Snake. Launching at the park costs $4 round-trip, with a $40 annual permit available from State Parks and Recreation Commission. Lyons Ferry State Park and Palouse Falls State Park have tent sites, restrooms, showers, picnic areas, and other amenities. Food, gas, and lodging are available in Colfax.

Directions: Take Highway 260 east from Connell and turn south on Highway 261 to reach the lower Palouse and Palouse Falls. The best access to upper portions of the river is provided by the Endicott Road, which is reached by driving west from Colfax about four miles on Highway 26 and turning north on Endicott Road.

Contact: Lyons Ferry State Park, 509/646-3252; Washington State Parks and Recreation Commission, 360/902-8844 (information) or 800/452-5687 (reservations); Tiffany's River Inn, 509/397-3208.

4 Deadman Creek

Spring plants of hatchery rainbows provide most of the action here. Although the creek is open to year-round fishing, your best shot at catching trout is in May and June. Many local anglers use bait and hardware here, but it's a decent place to work a small wet fly or nymph pattern along the bottom.

Location: Flows into the Snake River near Central Ferry; see map B5, grid d4.

Species: Rainbow trout.

Facilities: Central Ferry State Park has tent sites, restrooms, showers, picnic tables, and

other facilities. The nearest food, gas, tackle, and lodging are in Pullman, more than 20 miles to the east.

Directions: Take Highway 127 to Central Ferry and turn east onto Lower Deadman Road, which parallels the creek for more than 10 miles.

Contact: Central Ferry State Park, 509/549-3551; Washington State Parks and Recreation Commission, 360/902-8844 (information) or 800/452-5687 (reservations); Washington State Department of Fish and Wildlife, Spokane Office, 509/456-4082.

5 Upper Snake River

You get a little bit of everything if you spend some time investigating this section of the Snake. A lot of the Upper Snake is more like one big, continuous lake than a river, thanks to Lower Monumental, Little Goose, and Lower Granite Dams, which back up much of the river between Clarkston and Kahlotus. South of Clarkston, however, the river gains speed as you move upstream toward world-famous Hells Canyon, and there's no doubt that you're on one of the Northwest's biggest and most inviting rivers.

Lake Herbert West, Lake Bryan, and Lower Granite Lake, the reservoirs behind the three dams on this stretch, offer very good lake smallmouth bass fishing. The fishing is best after the water warms to at least 60 degrees in the late spring, and from then on it's possible to enjoy fast action with small grubs, crawdad-finish crankbaits, and other standard smallmouth lures. Work them around the base of rock cliffs and over submerged rock piles, scattered boulders, and points of land jutting into the water.

Trolling for steelhead is also productive in the reservoirs, and the fishing is at least as good during the night as it is in daylight hours. October, November, and December provide the best catches, so be sure to bun-

dle up if you plan a night of steelheading in this part of the state. Land a 15-pound steelhead, of course, and it will probably keep you warm and charge your batteries for another several hours. Hot Shots, Wiggle Warts, Hot Lips Express, and Hog Boss plugs are among the consistent strike-getters.

Blue catfish aren't found just anywhere in Washington, but anglers get 'em here, and some of them are bragging-sized fish of 15 pounds or more. Like the (usually) smaller channel cats, they can be caught at night on chicken livers, strips cut from sucker bellies, night crawlers, Berkley's Catfish Power Bait, and various stinkbaits. The upper ends of the reservoirs, where there's some moving water, often produce some of the best catfish action.

Modified versions of the catfish technique also work for sturgeon, the real monsters of the Snake. Be sure to change the bait since sturgeon prefer herring, smelt, and pieces of eel. Some of the better sturgeon holes are located immediately downstream of Clarkston, but remember, this is catch-and-release only. If you want to keep sturgeon, you'll have to fish below Lower Granite Dam.

Panfish action in the Snake River reservoirs is outstanding. Find a school of active crappies and it's not unusual to go away with 50 of the mild-flavored little fish for a day's efforts. Small leadheads adorned with red-and-white plastic skirts or tube bodies are most effective, but other color combinations also work. If you know there are panfish around but you're not getting them to hit, do some experimenting with color until you find the right one.

Most of the same species that provide action for reservoir anglers can also be found in the moving water upstream from Clarkston. Back-trolling with diving plugs is still one of the best ways to catch fall steelhead in the river, and the same crankbaits or jigs you might use for smallmouths in the reservoirs

STEELHEAD ON THE SNAKE RIVER

will work in moving water. The same goes for catfish and sturgeon; a good bait anchored to the bottom is the best bet for both. One difference is that summertime trout fishing is better in the river than in the reservoirs downstream. There are some husky rainbows from Hells Canyon downstream to Clarkston, including fish of 17 inches and larger, and they'll hit small spinners and wobbling spoons with great enthusiasm.

Location: From Lower Granite Dam to the Oregon border; see map B5, grid e7.

Species: Steelhead, smallmouth bass, white sturgeon, channel and blue catfish, crappie, yellow perch.

Facilities: Although they're spread out over many miles of river, you'll find a number of boat ramps along this section of the Snake and its impoundments:

- **Devil's Bench Ramp:** Working upstream from Lower Monumental Dam, there's a U.S. Army Corps of Engineers launch site on the Franklin County (north) side of the river (Lake Herbert G. West) at Devil's Bench, just upstream from the dam. It's a two-lane concrete ramp with a loading float and parking for at least 100 cars and trailers.
- **Ayer Boat Basin:** About nine miles upstream on the south side of the river is Ayer Boat Basin and a two-lane Corps of Engineers ramp. It's a concrete ramp, good for launching any size boat, and has a loading float.
- **Lyons Ferry State Park:** Several miles upstream, where the Palouse River enters the Snake from the north, is Lyons Ferry State Park, with its two-lane concrete ramp and loading float. The launch fee is $4 here, with an annual permit available for $40 (good at all state parks). The park and its ramp, by the way, are closed November 1 through March 31 every year.
- **Lyons Ferry Marina:** The marina, operated by the Port of Columbia on the south side of the river, has a one-lane concrete-plank ramp with a loading dock and parking for several dozen cars and trailers. It has a $4 launch fee, round-trip.
- **Tucannon River Ramp:** Still on the south side of the Snake, at the mouth of the Tucannon River there's another Corps of Engineers ramp used mostly by paddlers and anglers. It's doubtful that a trailer boat can reach the water here, but it's useful for launching kayaks, canoes, and car-top fishing boats. This ramp is actually in the Tucannon, requiring a short trip downstream to reach the Snake.
- **Texas Rapids Recreation Area:** The next ramp is also on the south side of the Snake, about four miles downstream from Little Goose Dam, at a spot called Texas Rapids. This single-lane concrete Corps of Engineers ramp, with parking for about 30 cars and trailers, has a rock jetty near it to protect against wind and water action.

- **Riparia Ramp:** The next ramp, located at Riparia on the north side of the river, is a single-lane concrete ramp managed by the Corps of Engineers. As of spring 1999, large deposits of sand and gravel had clogged this ramp to the point that large trailer boats could no longer use it.
- **Little Goose Landing:** The next ramp is a short distance above Little Goose Dam on the south side of the river (Lake Bryan). It's another Corps of Engineers ramp, a one-laner with a loading float and parking for about two dozen cars and trailers.
- **Central Ferry State Park:** Next is the four-lane concrete ramp at Central Ferry State Park, on the north side of the river off Highway 127. This ramp has loading floats and lots of paved parking, but be careful when trailering a large boat down the ramps here; some of the concrete slabs are buckled and widely spaced. This ramp has a $4 launch fee and an additional fee for overnight parking of cars and trailers.
- **Port of Garfield Ramp:** Just upstream and across the river from Central Ferry, in a large bay on the west side of Highway 127, is a Port of Garfield ramp. This one-lane concrete ramp has a waterlogged loading float and parking for about 20 cars and trailers.
- **Willow Landing:** Next on the south side of the river is Willow Landing, a Corps of Engineers site with a one-lane concrete ramp and loading float, located in a small cove that offers protection from wind and water action. This is a good ramp, but it sometimes collects sand and gravel that hinders launching larger boats.
- **Lambi Creek Campground:** The next ramp is about 15 miles upstream on the south side at Lambi Creek Campground. It's a narrow, concrete ramp that has been falling apart for some time. I wouldn't launch a large boat here unless I considered it disposable.

- **Illia Landing:** The single-lane concrete ramp at Illia Landing, just upstream, is in somewhat better shape. This Corps of Engineers ramp has a loading float and is protected from the wind by a concrete breakwater.
- **Boyer Park:** Next is the Port of Whitman County's Boyer Park, on the north side of the river about two miles downstream from Lower Granite Dam. This is a very good, three-lane concrete ramp with loading floats and a fair amount of parking.
- **Offield Landing:** The next two ramps are a short distance upstream from Lower Granite Dam, one on either side of the river (Lower Granite Lake). Offield Landing, on the south (Garfield County) side of the river, has a one-lane concrete ramp with a float and parking for about a dozen cars and trailers.
- **Wawawai Landing:** On the other side of the river is Wawawai Landing, where the one-lane concrete ramp and loading float are well protected by a concrete breakwater. Both Offield and Wawawai are Corps of Engineers facilities.
- **Blyton Landing:** Next is the single-lane concrete-plank ramp at Blyton Landing on the north side of the river. This ramp has a float and is protected by rock breakwaters on both sides.
- **Nisqually John Landing:** Four miles upstream is the single-lane concrete ramp at Nisqually John Landing. Naturally protected from the elements by its location at the entrance to Nisqually John Canyon, this ramp tends to collect some debris that may sometimes hinder launching. It's a Corps of Engineers ramp.
- **Chief Timothy State Park:** Next is Chief Timothy State Park, located on a large island where U.S. 12 meets the river about 10 miles west of Clarkston. The park has a four-lane concrete ramp with a couple of loading floats and a parking lot for about 40 cars and trailers. Launching here costs

$4 round-trip, with a $40 annual permit available from State Parks.

- **Hells Canyon Marina:** This facility at the northwest edge of Clarkston has a good, two-lane concrete ramp and large loading float.
- **Greenbelt Ramp:** Next is the Greenbelt Trail ramp, managed by the Corps of Engineers. This two-lane concrete ramp has a loading float and lots of paved parking for cars and trailers. There's a $2 launch fee, round-trip.
- **Swallows Park:** At the south end of Clarkston is Swallows Park, with a very good, four-lane concrete ramp and several loading floats. Maintained by the Corps of Engineers, this is another site where a $2 launch fee is charged.
- **Chief Looking Glass Park:** Three miles upstream at the town of Asotin is Chief Looking Glass Park, managed by the Asotin Parks and Recreation Department. This is a good ramp, with two concrete lanes and a loading float, with lots of paved parking.
- **Asotin Slough Ramp:** About a mile upstream is the Corps of Engineers' Asotin Slough ramp, a one-laner that sometimes gets large accumulations of silt to foul things up for boaters.
- **Heller Bar:** It's about 20 miles upstream to the next ramp, the two-lane concrete-plank ramp at Heller Bar, near the mouth of the Grande Ronde River. There's parking for about 50 cars and trailers at this site, which is managed by the Bureau of Land Management.

The Port of Columbia's Lyons Ferry Marina has both open and covered moorage, electrical hookups, boat-sewage pump-out facilities, a fuel dock, showers, boat repair, groceries, and a restaurant. Lyons Ferry State Park, at the confluence of the Palouse and Snake Rivers, has 49 campsites, restrooms,

showers, and a good swimming beach. Central Ferry State Park, just off Highway 127, has 60 tent and RV sites with electrical and water hookups, showers, picnic areas, boat-sewage pump-out facilities, and a swimming beach. Boyer Park and Marina has open moorage ($5 minimum moorage fee), boat-sewage pump-out facilities, showers, a fuel dock, grocery store, restaurant, RV sites, picnic shelters and tables, motel rooms, and a large swimming beach. Chief Timothy State Park, off U.S. 12 west of Clarkston, has 33 tent sites and 31 RV sites with hookups, restrooms, showers, and boat-sewage pump-out facilities, along with a long expanse of swimming beach and river frontage. It even has some RV sites on the south side with their own moorage docks. Hells Canyon Marina has open moorage (121 slips, $5 daily minimum), bait and tackle, sewage pump-out facilities, electrical hookups, fuel dock, boat repair, a grocery store, and restaurant. There are large swimming beaches at Swallows Park in Clarkston and Chief Looking Glass Park in Asotin. It's OK to camp at Heller Bar for a maximum of two weeks; fuel and a restaurant are also available at Heller. Food, gas, lodging, river outfitters, and other facilities are available in Clarkston.

Directions: Parts of the river are accessible by taking Highway 127 south from the small town of Dusty or north from the even smaller town of Dodge. Highway 261 crosses the river near Lyons Ferry and the mouth of the Palouse River. Highway 263 runs south from Kahlotus to parallel the river beginning at Lower Monumental Dam. Drive west from Pullman on Highway 194 to Almota and that part of the river immediately downstream from Lower Granite Dam. The most accessible part of the Snake in Washington is that section from Clarkston downstream to Wawawai, where the Wawawai River Road parallels the east side of the river for more than 20 miles. Take the Snake River Road south out of Clarkston to drive along the Snake's west bank all the way to the mouth of the Grande Ronde.

Contact: Lyons Ferry Marina, 509/399-2001; Boyer Marina, 509/397-3208, website: www.portwhitman.com/rec/boyer.html; Hells Canyon Marina/Resort, 509/758-6963; Lyons Ferry State Park, 509/646-3252; Central Ferry State Park, 509/549-3551; Chief Timothy State Park, 509/758-9580; Washington State Parks and Recreation Commission, 360/902-8844 (information) or 800/452-5687 (reservations); Beamer's Hells Canyon Tours & Excursions, 800/522-6966, website: www.hellscanyon tours.com; U.S. Army Corps of Engineers, Walla Walla District, 509/527-7424, or Clarkston District, 509/751-0240.

6 Tucannon River

Steelheading is the big draw, and it takes off in September and runs through the winter until March. Anglers catch 300 to 400 steelies here during a good year, most of them on the same kinds of drift-fishing gear used on western Washington steelhead streams. The stretch of river from the mouth up to the Tucannon Hatchery remains open to fishing during the winter to provide anglers with a good shot at steelheading, and it's also OK to fish for whitefish during this period. Whitefish action can be quite good, although it's enjoyed by only a few local anglers. During the spring and early summer, parts of the Tucannon are stocked with hatchery rainbows, always providing a few weeks of decent trout fishing immediately after the fish are released. With those plants available, the Tucannon is one of few streams where it's still OK to keep five trout per day as long as they're eight inches or longer.

Location: Joins the Snake River northwest of Starbuck; see map B5, grid e2.

Species: Steelhead, rainbow trout, Dolly Varden, mountain whitefish.

Facilities: There's a U.S. Forest Service campground on the Upper Tucannon and a good deal of public access on state and federal land. Camp Wooten State Park, located near the Forest Service facility, is an environmental learning center and has no drop-in camping facilities. The nearest food, gas, tackle, and lodging are in Dayton.

Directions: Take Highway 26 to Washtucna and turn south on Highway 260, following it six miles to Highway 261. Turn east and follow Highway 261 to the mouth of the Tucannon and upstream to U.S. 12. Turn south on U.S. 12 and then east on Tucannon Road to reach upstream portions of the river.

Contact: Umatilla National Forest, 509/522-6290; W. T. Wooten Wildlife Area, 509/843-1530.

7 Pataha Creek

Stocked with hatchery trout, this little Tucannon River tributary provides fair fishing every spring and early summer. From its mouth to Pomeroy, Pataha Creek is open all year to all anglers, but inside the Pomeroy city limits, it's open only to juvenile anglers and only from late April through October. Upstream of Pomeroy the season runs from June 1 through October 31 for all anglers, but selective fishery regulations are in effect.

Location: Joins the Tucannon River near Delaney in Columbia County; see map B5, grid e3.

Species: Rainbow trout.

Facilities: Central Ferry State Park, with tent and RV sites, is on the Snake River, north of the creek. Food, gas, tackle, and lodging are available in Pomeroy.

Directions: Take U.S. 12 west from Pomeroy to parallel the south side of the creek for several miles.

Contact: Central Ferry State Park, 509/549-3551; Washington State Parks and Recreation Commission, 360/902-8844 (information) or 800/452-5687 (reservations).

8 Tucannon River Lakes

These little man-made lakes scattered along the banks of the Tucannon River from the W. T. Wooten Wildlife Area to the Tucannon Campground cover no more than 10 acres each, yet they're heavily stocked with hatchery rainbows to provide good fishing throughout the spring and summer. Spring, Rainbow, Deer, Watson, and Beaver Lakes have a March 1 through July 31 season, but they may not be stocked in time for the opener if the lakes are still covered with ice. Big Four Lake also opens March 1, but it has special fly-fishing-only regulations. Because Curl Lake is also used as a holding pond for chinook salmon smolts from the nearby Tucannon Hatchery, it doesn't open to fishing until the general, statewide lake opener in late April.

Boats and float tubes are prohibited on all these little lakes, so you have to do your fishing from the bank. That's not a problem, though, since you can nearly cast from one bank to the other on most of these lakes.

Except on the fly-fishing-only waters of Big Four Lake, standard trout getters are worms, salmon eggs, and a variety of small spoons and spinners. One favorite is the Rooster Tail spinner, and many anglers prefer various shades of green or fluorescent color schemes.

Location: East of Dayton in eastern Columbia County; see map B5, grid f5.
Species: Rainbow trout.
Facilities: There's a U.S. Forest Service Campground on the Upper Tucannon, and a good deal of public access on state and federal land. Camp Wooten State Park, located near the Forest Service facility, is an Environmental Learning Center and has no drop-in camping facilities. The nearest food, gas, tackle, and lodging are in Dayton.

Directions: Take Highway 26 to Washtucna and turn south on Highway 260, following it six miles to Highway 261. Turn east and follow Highway 261 to the mouth of the Tucannon River and upstream to U.S. 12. Turn south on U.S. 12 and then east on Tucannon Road to reach upstream portions of the river and the small lakes that border it.
Contact: Umatilla National Forest, 509/522-6290; W. T. Wooten Wildlife Area, 509/843-1530.

9 Asotin Creek

Once a fairly good little summer steelhead stream, Asotin Creek is now closed to steelheading in order to protect the wild steelies that spawn here. The season on Asotin Creek runs from June through October, and during that time it's planted with hatchery rainbows. Because of those plants, the creek has an eight-inch minimum size limit, but you can keep only two trout per day.

Location: Flows into the Snake River south of Clarkston; see map B5, grid f8.
Species: Rainbow trout.
Facilities: The Asotin Motel is located near the mouth of the creek in the town of Asotin. Food, gas, tackle, and lodging are also available in Clarkston.
Directions: Take Highway 128 to Clarkston, turn south on Highway 129, and drive six miles to the mouth of Asotin Creek. Turn west on Asotin Creek Road to follow the creek upstream.
Contact: Asotin Motel, 509/243-4888.

10 Grande Ronde River

While the lower end of the Grande Ronde offers some decent bass and catfish action, most anglers come here for one thing: steelheading. The steelhead action turns on around the end of September and goes strong through the winter to the end of the season in mid-April. During that time, anglers use spoons, spinners, diving plugs, and artificial flies to take as many as 400 to 500 fish a month from the deep pools and inviting runs along this beautiful river. Although roads provide access to the river mouth and to several miles of river upstream from the bridge on Highway 129, many anglers prefer to float the Grande Ronde. While floating or even hiking the various upriver stretches of the river provides both good fishing and outstanding scenery, many steelhead are caught by bank anglers casting from the not-quite-so-scenic beach where the Grande Ronde meets the Snake at Heller Bar. The lower end of the river, from the mouth upstream about two miles, is now catch-and-release only for steelhead. Upstream of that stretch, anglers can keep hatchery steelies but must release all wild fish (with unclipped fins).

Location: Joins the Snake River near the southeastern corner of the state; see map B5, grid g9.

Species: Steelhead, smallmouth bass, channel catfish.

Facilities: The only ramp for the lower end of the Grande Ronde is at Heller Bar, near where the river flows into the Snake. This two-lane concrete ramp managed by the Bureau of Land Management has a large parking area. There are two ramps near the south end of the Highway 129 bridge over the Grande Ronde. On the upstream (west) side is a single-lane gravel ramp managed by the Department of Fish and Wildlife. On the east side of the road is another gravel ramp, located at a State Department of Transportation gravel pit. Both ramps are rough and best suited to launching small trailer boats or car-toppers. A $10 WDFW access decal is required to use the public launch areas maintained by the Washington Department of Fish and Wildlife.

Fields Spring State Park, located a few miles north of the river on Highway 129, has a limited number of tent sites. There's a river-accessible restaurant at Heller Bar, near the mouth of the Grande Ronde. Camping is allowed for a maximum of 14 days at the BLM access area and boat ramp at Heller Bar.

Directions: Take Highway 129 south from Clarkston. The highway crosses the river about three miles from the Oregon border, and Grande Ronde Road parallels the north side of the river for several miles west of the bridge. To reach the lower few miles of the river, drive south out of Clarkston on Highway 129 to Asotin and then follow Snake River Road along the Snake to the mouth of the Grande Ronde.

Contact: Fields Spring State Park, 509/256-3332; Washington State Parks and Recreation Commission, 360/902-8844 (information) or 800/452-5687 (reservations); Washington Department of Fish and Wildlife, Spokane Office, 509/456-4082.

Fall cutthroat fishing near the mouth of Blue Creek on the Cowlitz River

©TERRY RUDNICK

Washington State Fishing Records

Freshwater

Type of Fish	Weight	Angler	Location	Year
American Shad	3.44	Pete Green	Columbia River	1999
Atlantic salmon, resident	8.96	Gregory Lepping	Goat Lake	1992
Atlantic salmon, sea-run	14.38	Ron Howard	Green River	1999
Black bullhead	1.75	John E. Moore	Mud Lake	1998
Black crappie	4.50	John Smart	Lake Washington	1956
Blue catfish	17.75	Rangle Hawthorne	Columbia River	1975
Bluegill sunfish	2.31	Ron Hinote	Tampico Park Pond	1984
Brook trout	9.00	George Weekes	Wobbly Lake	1988
Brown bullhead	3.90	Joe Ochota	Ludlow Lake	1997
Brown trout	22.00	R. L. Henry	Sullivan Lake	1965
Burbot	17.01	Patrick Bloomer	Palmer Lake	1993
Bull trout	22.50	Louis Schott	Tieton River	1961
Channel catfish	36.20	Ross Kincaid	I-82 Pond #6	1999
Chinook salmon	68.25	Mark Salmon	Elochoman River	1992
Chum salmon	25.97	Johnnie Wilson	Satsop River	1997
Coho salmon	23.50	David Bailey	Satsop River	1986
Cutthroat trout, Lahontan	18.04	Dan Beardslee	Omak Lake	1993
Cutthroat trout, resident	12.00	W. Welsh	Crescent Lake	1961
Cutthroat trout, sea-run	6.00	Bud Johnson	Carr Inlet	1943
Dolly Varden, sea-run	10.94	Leroy Thompson	White Chuck River	1999
Flathead catfish	22.50	C. L. McCary	Snake River	1981
Golden trout	3.81	Mark Morris	Okanogan County	1991
Kokanee	5.47	Don Growt	Lake Roosevelt	1993
Lake trout	35.44	John E. Hossack	Lake Chelan	2001
Lake whitefish	6.63	Jerry Hamilton	Lake Roosevelt	1997
Largemouth bass	11.56	Carl Pruitt	Banks Lake	1977
Mountain whitefish	5.12	Steven Becken	Columbia River	1983
Northern pike	32.20	Fred Ruetsch	Long Lake	1995
Pink Salmon	14.49	Avis Pearson	Skykomish River	2001
Northern squawfish	7.25	Louis A. Picard	Snake River	1996
Rainbow trout	25.71	Dick Hill	Rufus Woods Lake	2002
Rainbow trout, Beardslee	16.31	Richard Bates	Lake Crescent	1989
Rock bass	1.37	Dion Roueche	Snake River	1995
Smallmouth bass	8.75	Ray Wonacott	Columbia River	1966
Sockeye salmon	10.62	Gary Krasselt	Lake Washington	1982
Steelhead, summer-run	35.06	Gilbert Pierson	Snake River	1973
Steelhead, winter-run	32.75	Gene Maygra	East Lewis River	1980

Type of Fish	Weight	Angler	Location	Year
Tiger musky	28.25	Ronald Jutte	Mayfield Lake	1995
Walleye	18.76	Mike Jones	Columbia River	1990
White crappie	2.50	Don Benson	Columbia River	1988
Yellow bullhead	1.63	Mike Schlueter	Banks Lake	1994
Yellow perch	2.75	Larry Benthien	Snelson's Slough	1969

Saltwater

Type of Fish	Weight	Angler	Location	Year
Albacore	52.00	Kurt Strickland	Pacific Ocean	1997
Big skate	130.00	Dan Cartwright	Double Bluff	1986
Black rockfish	10.25	Joseph Eberling	Tacoma Narrows	1980
Blue rockfish	3.91	Erik M. Herbig	Westport	1996
Bocaccio	23.62	Carson Kendall	Swiftsure Bank	1987
Cabezon	23.00	Wesley Hunter	Dungeness Spit	1990
Canary rockfish	10.56	Ben Phillips	Neah Bay	1986
China rockfish	4.19	Steven Ripley	Duncan Rock	1989
Chinook salmon	70.50	Chet Gausta	Sekiu	1964
Chum salmon	25.26	Fred Dockendorf	Westport	2001
Coho salmon	22.50	James Vesselovec	Strait of Juan del Fuca	2001
Copper rockfish	10.00	David Northington	Point Roberts	1989
Great sculpin	4.59	Mark Reynolds	Port Angeles Harbor	1999
Greenstripe rockfish	1.62	David Wedeking	Possession Bar	1985
Kelp greenling	4.42	Danita Rixen	San Juan Islands	1999
Lingcod	61.00	Tom Nelson	San Juan Islands	1986
Pacific cod	19.625	Ralph Bay	Ediz Hook	1984
Pacific halibut	288.00	Vic Stevens	Swiftsure Bank	1989
Petrale sole	7.56	John Stone	Jefferson Head	1980
Pile perch	3.56	Steve Urban	Quartermaster Harbor	1981
Pink salmon	11.56	Jeff Bergman	Possession Point	2001
Quillback rockfish	7.19	Bror Hultgren	Middle Bank	1987
Ratfish	3.90	William Denning	Hein Bank	1996
Red Irish lord	3.19	Ryan Dicks	Mid-channel Bank	1985
Redtail surfperch	4.05	Chris Maynard	Kalaloch	1996
Rock sole	4.19	Alan Schram	Hein Bank	1989
Sablefish	30.00	Jeff Rudolph	Westport	1994
Sixgill shark	220.00	Jim Haines	Gedney Island	1991
Spiny dogfish	20.25	Roger Petersen	Middle Bank	1998
Starry flounder	8.57	Danny Patterson	Sekiu	1996
Striped seaperch	2.06	Chris Urban	Quartermaster Harbor	1980
Tiger rockfish	7.50	James Wenban	Middle Bank	1989
Yelloweye rockfish	27.75	Jan Tavis	Dallas Bank	1989
Yellowtail rockfish	7.37	Ken Culver	Westport	1992

Current IGFA All-Tackle World Records Set in Washington

Black Rockfish

| 10 lb. 0 oz. | William Harris, DDS | Puget Sound | July 20, 1986 |

Bocaccio

| 21 lb. 4 oz. | Terry Rudnick | Swiftsure Bank | July 29, 1986 |

Cabezon

| 23 lb. 0 oz. | Wesley Hunter | Strait of Juan de Fuca | August 4, 1990 |

Canary Rockfish

| 10 lb. 0 oz. | Terry Rudnick | Westport | May 17, 1986 |

China Rockfish

| 3 lb. 11 oz. | Edward Schultz | Neah Bay | August 24, 1992 |

Pacific Hake

| 2 lb. 2 oz. | Steven Garnett | Tatoosh Island | June 26, 1988 |

Yellowtail Rockfish

| 5 lb. 8 oz. | Steven Garnett | Cape Flattery | August 28, 1988 |

Current IGFA Line-Class Records Caught in Washington

Chum Salmon

| 19 lb. 14 oz. | 8-lb. line | William Harris, DDS | Satsop River | 1986 |
| 25 lb. 15 oz. | 16-lb. line | Johnnie Johnson | Satsop River | 1997 |

Mountain Whitefish

| 5 lb. 2 oz. | 8-lb. line | Steven Becken | Columbia River | 1983 |

Pink Salmon

| 10 lb. 2 oz. | 16-lb. line | F. John Erickson | Snohomish River | 1985 |

Current IGFA Fly Rod Records Set in Washington

American Shad

| 5 lb. 0 oz. | 16-lb. tippet | William Harris, DDS | Columbia River | 1986 |

Chum Salmon

| 23 lb. 14 oz. | 12-lb. tippet | Roger Nelson | Stillaguamish River | 1990 |
| 19 lb. 2 oz. | 20-lb. tippet | James Ames | Satsop River | 1991 |

Accommodations and Campgrounds

Species by Location

Brown Bullhead Catfish

state record: 68

Sculpin
Point No Point: 158–159
Possession Point: 159–160

Seaperch
Copalis River: 353
Elk River: 366–367
Hoquiam River: 356
Lower Hood Canal: 196–199
South Puget Sound: 387–392
Upper Hood Canal: 177–180
Willapa Bay: 369–370
Wishkah River: 356–357

Shad
Columbia River (Bonneville Pool to
    Lake Umatilla): 476–478
Lower Columbia River: 435–438

Smallmouth Bass
American Lake: 393
Banks Lake: 298–301
Billy Clapp Lake: 307–308
Bonaparte Lake: 275–276
Chapman Lake: 343–344
Columbia River (Bonneville Pool to
    Lake Umatilla): 476–478
Columbia River (Lake Pateros and
    Rufus Woods Lake): 290–292
Columbia River (North Cascades): 258
Columbia River (Wenatchee to Crow
    Butte State Park): 495–499
Colville River: 320
Conconully Lake: 280–281
Dalton Lake: 502
Deer Lake (Northeast Washington):
    332–333
Diamond Lake: 334
Duck Lake (Okanogan): 285
Emma Lake: 499, 502
Fish Lake (North Cascades): 254
general discussion: 34–37
Grand Ronde River: 517–518

Horsethief Lake: 478–479
Island Lake (Southwest Washington):
    383–384
Lake Chelan: 248–250
Lake Goodwin: 151–152
Lake McMurray: 142
Lake Meridian: 209
Lake Sammamish: 188–189
Lake Sawyer: 220–221
Lake Stevens: 157–158
Lake Washington: 186–188
Lake Whatcom: 125–126
Lind Coulee Wasteway: 491
Little Ashes Lake: 447
Long Lake (Northeast Washington):
    337–338
Loon Lake: 333
Lower Columbia River: 435–438
Lower Lake Roosevelt: 295–297
Lower Snake River: 502–503
Lower Yakima River: 504–505
Mayfield Lake: 422–423
Moses Lake: 484–487
Offut Lake: 413–414
Okanogan River: 287–288
Osoyoos Lake: 268–269
Palmer Lake: 270–271
Palouse River: 511
Potholes Area Seep Lakes: 491–493
Potholes Reservoir: 489–490
Riffe Lake: 423–425
Rowland Lake(s): 475–476
Scooteney Reservoir: 494–495
Shoecraft Lake: 152
Spanaway Lake: 398
Sprague Lake: 346–347
state record: 35
Upper Lake Roosevelt: 323–326
Upper Snake River: 512–516

Smelt
Cowlitz River: 427–429

Sockeye Salmon
Baker River: 230–231

Index

National Forests and Parks in Washington

State and Marine Parks in Washington

State and Marine Parks in Washington (cont'd)

About the Author

A lifelong Washingtonian, Terry Rudnick has fished the lakes, streams, and marine areas of the Evergreen State for as long as he can remember and has been writing about Northwest fishing since he sold his first magazine article in 1971. An award-winning freelance writer and photographer, Rudnick has written feature articles and columns for more than 30 newspapers and regional and national magazines. His angling seminars and slide shows are also in demand, and he has been a featured speaker at more than three dozen sports and boating trade shows throughout the West. His efforts on behalf of fish, fishing, and the aquatic environment earned him the 1990 National Conservationist of the Year communications award from Trout Unlimited.

Rudnick is also the author of *Foghorn Outdoors: Washington Boating and Water Sports* and co-author of *How to Catch Trophy Halibut.*

Maps

Washington Overview

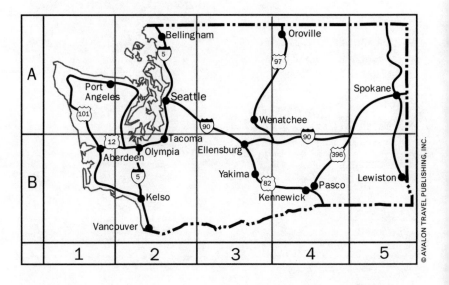

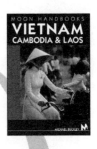

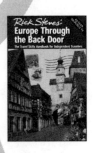

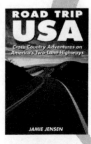

Beda Lake | Grant County

Brown's Lake   pg 326